NEPAL
HANDBOOK

NEPAL
HANDBOOK

KERRY MORAN

MOON
PUBLICATIONS INC.

NEPAL HANDBOOK

Please send all comments,
corrections, additions,
amendments, and critiques to:

KERRY MORAN
c/o MOON PUBLICATIONS
722 WALL STREET
CHICO, CA 95928, USA

Published by
Moon Publications, Inc.
722 Wall Street
Chico, California 95928, USA

Printed by
Colorcraft Ltd.

Printing History
1st edition—October 1991
reprinted May 1992

Library of Congress Cataloging in Publications Data

Moran, Kerry.
  Nepal Handbook / Kerry Moran. — 1st ed.
    p.   cm.
  Includes bibliographicalo references and index.
  ISBN 0-918373-64-6
  1. Nepal—Description and travel—Guide-books.   I. Title.
DS493.3.M67   1991
915.49604—dc20   91–19095
                                          CIP

ISBN 0-918373-64-4

Printed in Hong Kong

To Chris

❧

Like the desire for drink or drugs, the craving for mountains is not easily overcome, but a mountaineering debauch, such as six months in the Himalaya, is followed by no remorse. . . . Having once tasted the pleasure of living in high, solitary places with few spirits, European or Sherpa, I could not give it up. The prospect of what is euphemistically termed "settling down," like mud to the bottom of a pond, might perhaps be faced when it became inevitable, but not yet awhile.

—H.W. Tilman, WHEN MEN AND MOUNTAINS MEET

IS THIS BOOK OUT OF DATE?

Things change rapidly in a developing country like Nepal—hotels open and close, new trekking trails become popular, transportation hopefully improves, and prices inevitably rise. To keep up with it we plan a complete revision of this book every three years. We'd appreciate comments based on your own travels in Nepal. Did *Nepal Handbook* tell you what you needed to know? Opinions, insights, compliments and complaints are all welcome. Accounts of travels to new destinations would be particularly appreciated.

Please send your comments to:

Kerry Moran
c/o Moon Publications
722 Wall Street
Chico, CA 95928, U.S.A.

CONTENTS

INTRODUCTION 11
Land 13
Flora 19
Fauna 21
Environment 26
History 29
Government 39
Economy 41
People 46
Language 58
Religion 60
Festivals 70
Art 76
Crafts 88
Music and Dance 98
Conduct and Customs 102
Accommodations 108
Food 112
Passports and Visas 117
Money 120
Health 123
Services 131
What To Take 136
Getting There 140
Getting Around 145

THE KATHMANDU VALLEY 155
Introduction 155
KATHMANDU 163
Introduction 163
Durbar Square 168
The New Town 175
The Old City 179
Swayambhunath 187
Pashupatinath 191
Boudhanath 195
Practicalities 200

PATAN AND BHAKTAPUR 213
Patan 213
Bhaktapur 223
EXPLORING THE VALLEY 235
Introduction 235
North of Kathmandu 237
South of Kathmandu 241
East of Kathmandu 251
Over the Rim 258

BEYOND THE VALLEY 263
The Road to Tibet 264
Daman and the Rajpath 265
Gorkha 267
Pokhara 269
Tansen 284
Bhairawa and Sunauli 287
Lumbini 288
Chitwan National Park 293
Beyond Chitwan: More Safaris .. 303
Rafting 304
Janakpur 306

TREKKING 309
Introduction 309
The Annapurna Region 317
Solu-Khumbu: The Everest Region .. 328
Treks North of Kathmandu 339
Off the Beaten Track 344

**NEPALI PHRASES
AND VOCABULARY** 355

**GLOSSARY OF NEPALI
AND TIBETAN TERMS** 362

BOOKLIST 366

INDEX 371

MAPS

Annapurna Region 318
Around Pokhara 277
Bhairawa and Sunauli 287
Bhaktapur 224-225
Bhaktapur Durbar Square 228
Boudhanath 197
Central Nepal 350
Changu Narayan 254
Chitwan National Park 294
Dakshinkali Temple 249
Dhulikhel 260
East Valley 252
Eastern Nepal 352
Ethnic Distribution 47
Gorkha 267
Janakpur 307
Kathmandu 164-165
Kathmandu Backstreets 183
Kathmandu Durbar Square 169
Kathmandu Valley 156
Khumbu 333
Kirtipur 245
Lakeside and Pardi 279
Land Transportation 146
Langtang, Helambu, and Gosainkund 339
Lumbini 289
Major Natural Divisions 13
Nagarkot 256
Nepal 14-15
Nepal and Southeast Asia 12
New Kathmandu 176
North Valley, The 237
Old Bazaar, The 179
Pashupatinath 192
Patan 214
Patan Durbar Square 216
Pokhara 271
RNAC's Domestic Routes 150
Sauruha 301
Solu 331
South Valley, The 242
Swayambhunath 187
Tansen 284
To Dhulikhel 258
Tripureshwar 185
Western Nepal 346

MAP SYMBOLS

INTERNATIONAL BOUNDARY
ROADS, HIGHWAYS (NOT ALL ARE PAVED)
UNPAVED ROADS
FOOT PATHS
BRIDGE
RAILROAD
PASS
GLACIER
RIDGE LINE

WATERFALL
WATER
MOUNTAIN
GATES
STUPAS

o   TOWNS / VILLAGES
O   CITIES
●   ACCOMMODATIONS
■   POINT OF INTEREST
    TEMPLES (PAGODAS)

ALL MAPS ARE ORIENTED WITH NORTH AT TOP UNLESS NOTED

ACKNOWLEDGEMENTS

This book is the result of six years of meetings, travels, conversations, and experiences in Nepal. It would be impossible to list everyone who has contributed to it, but special thanks to the following: Mukunda Aryal, Beltronix for computer troubleshooting, Deepak Chaudhary, Bidur Dangol, Sallie Fischer, Wendy Brewer Fleming, John Frederick, Dr. Chandra Gurung, Shyam Hada, Frances Wall Higgins, Barbara Ierulli and Russell Johnson, Frances Klatzel, J.P. Lama, Buddha Limbu for advice on river-rafting, Denker and Suresh Manandhar, Charles Parish Jr., Patricia Roberts, Mingmar Sherpa, Bijay Shrestha of TAAN, Christa Skerry, Cyrus Stearns, Hugh Swift, and Alison Wright.

Most of all, thanks to my husband, Christopher Gamm, for getting me here in the first place and making our life in Nepal fun throughout. His sensible advice and constant support have contributed much to this book.

The staff at Moon Publications efficiently and gracefully transformed a handful of computer diskettes into an actual book. I'm especially grateful to my editor, Taran March, mapmaker and illustrator Bob Race, and art director Dave Hurst.

Finally, warm thanks to all the Nepalis who have welcomed, fed, and entertained me, made me feel at home, and helped me understand their beautiful and complex country.

CHARTS

Average Monthly Temperatures. 17
Bus Fares and Destinations 147
Foreign Embassies and Consulates. . . 119
One-way Air Fares from Kathmandu . . 151
Recommended Immunizations 124
Recommended Trekking Companies. . 315
Royal Nepalese Embassies 117
Trekker's Medical Kit 129
World's 8,000-meter Peaks 15

ABBREVIATIONS

a/c—air conditioning
ACAP— Annapurna Conservation Area Project
Am Ex—American Express
d—double occupancy
GI—gastrointestinal illness
GNP—gross national product
GPO—general post office

NP—national park
RNAC—Royal Nepal Airlines
s—single occupancy
STOL—short takeoff and landing
TAAN—Trekking Agents Association of Nepal
WR—wildlife refuge

BOB RACE

INTRODUCTION

The kingdom of Nepal packs more in its 147,181 square km than most countries 20 times its size. Crowned by eight of the world's 10 highest mountains, Nepal's landscape compresses lush tropics and arctic tundra into an amazingly small span. Altitude ranges from near sea level to 8,848 meters above it—the summit of Mt. Everest, the highest piece of the planet.

This wild variation fosters an incredible variety of ecosystems: steamy jungles and terraced valleys, forested hills, frozen peaks and high-altitude deserts. Tropical flowers frame views of not-so-distant snow peaks; tigers and rhinos roam lush jungles while less than 150 km north, snow leopards patrol barren mountain slopes. Whatever you say about Nepal is bound to be true—somewhere.

The natural diversity is only the beginning. Nepal's rugged terrain has preserved a variety of linguistic, ethnic, and cultural traditions rivaled by few nations. Dozens of different ethnic groups live among these rugged ranges, each with their own language, costumes, customs, and beliefs. The Valley of Kathmandu, a fertile green bowl set in the midst of Himalayan foothills, is an oasis of magnificent art, and the home of the ancient and sophisticated Newari culture.

Once isolated by suspicious rulers, Nepal only opened its borders to the outside world in 1951. At the time barely 200 Westerners had ever visited the country. Few had ventured far beyond the Kathmandu Valley. Today, 200,000 tourists come to Nepal every year to explore the rugged land, rich culture, and the harmony of a traditional way of life. In terms of statistics, Nepal is one of the least developed countries in the world but it's rich with humor, warmth, and natural beauty.

> *Nature alone makes it one of the most fascinating countries in Asia: a confusion of mountains and hills, almost as if the Himalayas, in an attempt to reach the heavens, had crumbled back down to earth.*
>
> —Giuseppe Tucci,
> *Journey to Mustang*

THE LAND

Dramatic, extreme, often outrageous, mountains shape Nepal's reality, molding its culture, history, economy, and politics. For 80% of the country, vertical is the main orientation, and up-and-down is the determining fact of life. The rugged topography is both a blessing and a curse. The spectacular landscape is world-famous, and the isolation enforced by the mountains has preserved age-old cultures and traditions. But for a nation attempting to modernize, those breathtaking mountain ranges are nothing but trouble. Nepal is less than 900 km long from east to west and only 150-200 km wide north to south. You could drive the length of the country in a day, if only there was a good level road. As it is, it takes several months to traverse central Nepal end to end on foot, a rugged journey few would care to make. The mountainous terrain makes the country far larger than its actual size in terms of transportation and development.

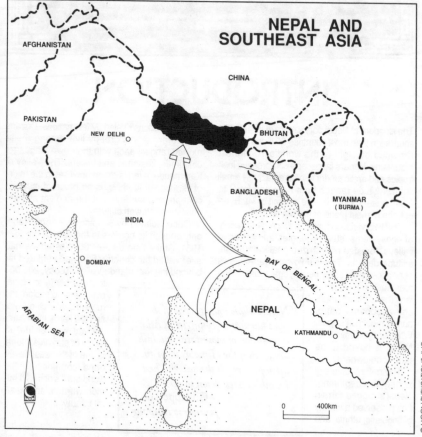

NEPAL AND SOUTHEAST ASIA

AFGHANISTAN

CHINA

PAKISTAN

NEW DELHI

BHUTAN

BANGLADESH

MYANMAR (BURMA)

INDIA

BAY OF BENGAL

BOMBAY

NEPAL

ARABIAN SEA

KATHMANDU

0   400km

© MOON PUBLICATIONS, INC.

Borders And Boundaries

The eastern section of Nepal's long northern border with Tibet runs along the crest of the Himalaya. West of Kathmandu the border is delineated by the Tibetan Marginal Range, a slightly lower series of mountains rising up about 30 km north of the Himalayan crest. This range also defines the region's watershed, between Tibet's great Tsangpo River to the north and India's sacred Ganges to the south. In the small high valleys between the Himalaya and the Marginal Range, tiny pockets of Tibetan culture have been preserved from the political turmoil which has devastated Tibet itself.

Nepal's remaining borders are shared with India: the protectorate of Sikkim in the east, the states of Bihar and Uttar Pradesh to the south and west. Sandwiched between China and India, Nepal is in a ticklish spot, geopolitically speaking. India is 22 times larger in area than Nepal, and China is over three times as big as India. An 18th-century Nepalese ruler succinctly described his kingdom's location: "like a yam between two rocks."

The Himalayan barrier mutes Chinese and Tibetan influence, but the unobstructed southern border has always been an open gateway to India. The country plays an important role in modern Nepali politics, economics, and culture, though sovereign Nepal remains sensitive about India's unofficial, though indisputable, influence.

THE THREE REGIONS

Nepal can be roughly divided into three geographic regions, each with its own distinctive

Nepali women planting rice

BOB RACE

environment, peoples, economy, customs, and culture. The varied landscapes have shaped different lifestyles. Flying over Nepal, you get a birds'-eye view of the dramatic extremes: the level lush fields and jungles of the Terai rise into the crumpled, corrugated landscape of the Hills, patchworked with fields and forests and ribboned by streams. These in turn rise up—and up, and up, into the highest of all mountains, the Himalaya, floating on the northern horizon like a dream. Only by walking can you appreciate the true immensity of this land. Trails ascend 2,500 vertical meters, plummet down to a river valley, and rise again, crossing what seems to be an endless ocean of land frozen into huge breakers.

The Terai

This narrow strip of land running along the southern border averages only 20 km in width and constitutes less than one-fifth of Nepal's total area. Yet the flat, fertile Terai contains virtually the only reasonable farmland in Nepal and supports nearly half of the population. Seventy percent of its arable land is in the Terai; over 60% of its grain is grown here.

The hot lowland Terai is a geographic extension of Northern India's Gangetic Plain, and In-

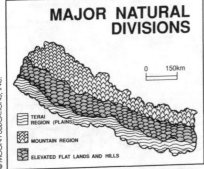

MAJOR NATURAL DIVISIONS

0   150km

☐ TERAI REGION (PLAINS)

▨ MOUNTAIN REGION

▧ ELEVATED FLAT LANDS AND HILLS

© MOON PUBLICATIONS, INC.

dian influences have shaped its cultures and societies as well. Terai dwellers (Madeshi) are Hindus speaking Sanskrit-based dialects. The open border with India allows people, influences, and goods to move across freely.

> *Upon what gigantic scale does Nature here operate!*
> —botanist/naturalist Joseph Hooker, speaking of the Himalaya

ing state of Bihar. Today the Terai is the major agricultural and industrial region of Nepal. Most of the country's roads and industry are found here, as well as the majority of urban centers outside the Kathmandu Valley.

Through the 1950s, much of the Terai was uninhabited jungle. Even a single night spent in the area could prove fatal during the fever season, April-Oct., when the malaria-carrying mosquito appeared. Except for a few indigenous tribes with a natural immunity, malaria kept out everyone—Nepalis, Indians, and foreigners alike. It was the perfect natural defense for Nepal's vulnerable southern flank. A British historian wrote: "Sundown in the Terai has brought an end to more attempted raids into Nepal and has buried more political hopes than will ever be known."

Beginning in the mid-'50s intensive DDT spraying opened the region for settlement. Hundreds of thousands of Nepali farmers poured down from the hills to settle on the new land, joined by landless Indians from the neighbor-

The Hills
Nepal's heartland is the Hills, a rugged region of deep valleys and terraced ridges covering about half its total area. The name is misleading. Nepal's "Hills" would rank as mountains anywhere else, and they would almost certainly be uninhabited. Few people would climb down 1,000 vertical meters to fetch water and then haul it back up, but for many Nepalis it's part of daily life. About 47% of the population lives in this up-and-down region, farming terraced fields patiently carved out of hillsides by generations of farmers.

The Mountains
The Himalaya extends over 3,800 km in a great arc welding the Indian subcontinent to Asia.

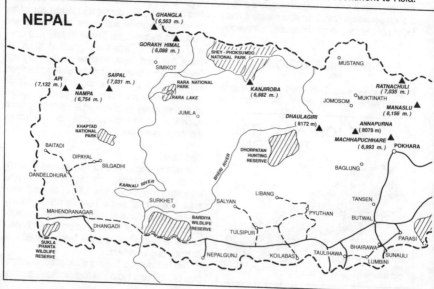

THE WORLD'S 8,000-METER PEAKS

1. Everest	8,848 meters	Nepal/Tibet
2. K-2	8,750 meters	India
3. Kangchenjunga	8,598 meters	Nepal/India
4. Lhotse I	8,501 meters	Nepal/Tibet
5. Makalu I	8,470 meters	Nepal/Tibet
6. Lhotse II	8,440 meters	Nepal/Tibet
7. Dhaulagiri I	8,172 meters	Nepal
8. Manaslu I	8,156 meters	Nepal
9. Cho Oyu	8,153 meters	Nepal
10. Nanga Parbat	8,126 meters	Pakistan
11. Annapurna I	8,078 meters	Nepal
12. Gasherbrum	8,068 meters	Pakistan
13. Broad Peak	8,046 meters	Pakistan
14. Gosainthan (Shishapangma)	8,011 meters	Tibet

meters—nobody's ever bothered to count them all.

Figures alone don't manage to convey the overwhelming presence of the 45-km-wide strip of mountains dominating the northern horizon. Ancient Hindus called the range "The Abode *(alaya)* of Snows *(him)*" and revered it as the abode of gods and saints, and a place of pilgrimage. Some peaks are worshipped as the embodiment of a region's protective spirits, an ancient belief predating even Hinduism and Buddhism.

It's easy to see why the Himalaya has made such a deep impression upon the people dwelling in its shadows. Its jagged ice-capped peaks crown the horizon; its snows

Twice the height of the Alps, it's the undisputed king of mountain ranges, containing the world's 86 highest peaks. The cream of the Central Himalaya, nearly one-third of the range's total length, falls in Nepal. Here rise eight of the world's 10 highest mountains, nine of its 14 8,000-meter-plus peaks, two dozen 7,000-meter-plus giants, and perhaps 240 peaks over 6,000

water the region's great rivers; its massive bulk is the weather-maker for much of Asia. The range serves as a great climactic divide between the lush southern slopes and the arid northern side, and the range of vegetation and wildlife covering its lower flanks is among the richest in the world.

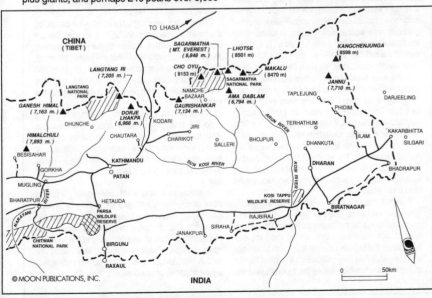

© MOON PUBLICATIONS, INC.

Only 8% of Nepal's population lives in this region, in permanent settlements which go up to 4,000 meters (summer herding settlements are found even higher). The region's culture and religion are closely linked to Tibet, and the traditional economy was (and sometimes still is) based on trans-border trade with its northern neighbors.

GEOLOGY

The birth of the Himalaya is an epic saga played out in slow motion over an inconceivably long period of time. Forty million years ago, Asia and India lay separated by the tropical Sea of Tethys, floating atop slowly moving tectonic plates. Gradually the two landmasses drifted together; the convulsive force of their collision crumpled the land lying between into mountain ranges. About 25 million years ago India began to overthrust against the main Asian continent, pushing up the main Himalayan chain at the point of impact. Sculpted by erosion and polished by the slow slide of glaciers, the Himalayan peaks emerged in their present spectacular form, more sharply defined than other, older mountains.

The tectonic plates continue to slowly shift, and the mountains keep growing at the rate of 10-12 cm a year. Nepal's regular earthquakes attest to the ongoing activity beneath the earth's crust (a great quake occurs roughly every century in the Valley), while frequent landslides and erosion signal the steepness of the Himalaya, the youngest of all mountain ranges.

Nepal's major rivers rise on the north side of the Himalaya and run southwards, eventually joining India's Ganges River and emptying into the Bay of Bengal. These rivers actually preceded the Himalaya; as the mountains emerged they were strong enough to simply cut through, creating tremendously deep transverse gorges. The rivers divide the main chain of the Himalaya

THE MONSOON

The annual summer rains sweep into eastern Nepal around the beginning of June, bringing welcome relief from the hot, dusty spring and water to nurture fields of sprouting rice. By mid-month the monsoon reaches the Kathmandu Valley, moving gradually northwest and diminishing in intensity. By the time it reaches the great barrier of Dhaulagiri west of the Kali Gandaki River, most of its force has been spent. As a result, western Nepal is far drier than the eastern portion of the country, reflected by the sparser vegetation and lower crop yields.

The seasonal rains are orchestrated as precisely as a symphony, climaxing slowly to a crescendo in July and early August, then tapering off. About 80% of the year's total precipitation falls between June and September. The amount of rainfall varies according to location. The village of Lumle just west of Pokhara got a torrential one meter of rain one July, while five days' walk north, Jomosom recorded a bare four centimeters.

The monsoon cycle begins in the spring as the blazing sun sucks up moisture from the Bay of Bengal, creating masses of heavy moist air. These low-lying clouds are drawn northeast by the temperature differential between the central Asian landmass and the sea. Soon they collide with the great barrier of the Himalaya, which forces the clouds upwards.

As they rise the air cools into water vapor and condenses into rain. Most falls on the Himalaya's lower southern slopes, watering the lush rainforests of Sikkim, Bhutan, and Nepal.

The clouds have dumped most of their moisture by the time they reach higher altitudes, and few make it across the Himalaya, explaining the rainshadow effect that's freeze-dried the Tibetan Plateau. In Nepal, north-south mountain ranges like the Langtang and Annapurna Himals have a similar effect, and their western flanks remain relatively dry throughout the summer.

The monsoon, at least in the Kathmandu Valley, is not the continual downpour most people visualize. Rain falls in predictable patterns, either a 30-45 minute shower during the morning and afternoon, or more typically a brief daytime downpour followed by a long, soaking night rain. Rarely will it pour all day.

A monsoon visit is worth considering if for no other reason than you'll have Nepal virtually to yourself: tourist arrivals are lowest May-Sept. and the country's trails, temples, and streets regain their tranquillity. The rainy season is one of the loveliest times in Nepal. Fields of sprouting rice carpet the land in vivid, electric green, and sunsets are spectacular displays of cloud-caught light. After the rice

into separate *himal* or sub-ranges. The passages they have carved through the maze of hills have been used for millennia as trade routes between Tibet and India.

CLIMATE

On the same date you can be sweltering in subtropical valleys, basking in the temperate Kathmandu Valley, or shivering atop a frozen summit. Visitors expecting Nepal to be nonstop snowy mountains are often surprised by the fierceness of the sun, but at 26°-30° north of the equator, Nepal's latitude is similar to central Florida or Cairo.

Seasons are typical of the Northern Hemisphere: hot from April-Aug., cold from Nov.-Jan. with two brief warm periods in Feb.-March and Sept.-Oct. Regional variations on this basic theme are distinct. The humid, tropical Terai re-

ceives the most monsoonal rain and records the country's highest temperatures (over 39°C in Nepalgunj in May). The lower Hills (900-2,700 meters), including the Kathmandu Valley, are subtropical, with hot summers and moderate winters with only occasional frost. The higher Hills (2,700-4,000 meters) are more temperate. Because clouds frequently rest at this level, they tend to get plenty of rain, fog, and frost. Above 4,000 meters, the Mountains have a cooler, drier alpine climate; daily temperatures here vary wildly depending on sunshine, wind, and altitude. Generally speaking, temperatures drop 6°C for every 1,100 meters ascended.

Seasons

At 1,371 meters the Kathmandu Valley has a near-ideal climate, reflected in its lush vegetation and beautiful gardens. Residents distinguish six distinct seasons:

Sheet: From mid-Dec.-Feb. a chilly mist rises

---

transplanting is finished, people celebrate with a flood of festivals beginning in August and leading into the great harvest celebrations of the fall. Himalayan peaks are usually hidden, but appear in breathtaking, unexpected glimpses framed by clouds.

There is a down side to the rainy season, especially for trekkers. Trails can be treacherously slippery, rivers dangerously high, high passes may be blocked by fresh snow. Leeches emerge (see pg. 24), disease is rampant, and there's always the chance of an endless week of solid rain. Preparation and patience can minimize these problems so that even a monsoon trek is possible. Many who have done it rave about monsoon trekking. Trails are uncrowded, and Nepalis have time to sit back from the hectic rush of the main season and relax. Many return to their villages for long visits, accompanied by celebrations, festivals, and weddings.

Rainy Season Survival

High-tech outdoor raingear can be useful, but a US$250 raincoat is not essential for survival. Asia's classic big black umbrella is the best monsoon protection, sheltering you from rain and sun alike and doubling as an emergency walking stick on slippery slopes. Rubberized plastic ponchos sold in trekking shops are useful for cyclists; heavy plastic bags or sheets available in the bazaar keep backpacks dry. If a downpour catches you unprepared don't be shy about ducking into the nearest shop or beneath the

nearest eaves. With a bit of patience, the inevitable delays become enjoyable. A downpour is a great excuse to sit and watch the world, and to meet people you otherwise never would.

Shoes inevitably become soaked and muddy: leather repels water longer than cloth sneakers, but takes longer to dry and will be ruined after a few good soakings. Plastic sandals, easy to slip off, wash, and dry, are the best solution for Kathmandu's muddy streets, but avoid flip-flop thongs that fling mud all the way up your backside. Look for plastic sandals with straps on both ankles and toes, or get a pair of Chinese-made rubber boots. Unless you're a woman with small feet, bring them with you—larger sizes are hard to come by in Kathmandu.

The monsoon season is definitely hazardous to your health. All the waste deposited over the winter is washed into rivers, contaminating the water supply. Hepatitis, typhoid, and intestinal parasites abound, and you should be scrupulous about food and water. Infection is also a problem; the smallest cut or scratched mosquito bite can take weeks to heal in this season if your resistance runs down. Keep breaks in the skin clean and protected.

When planning a monsoon trek choose a relatively dry area—the upper Kali Gandaki, Manang, Khumbu—and make allowances for high rivers, washed-out roads and frequently cancelled flights. It's best to skip July, the wettest month. Late Aug.-early Sept. is usually a reasonable bet.

from moist fields at dawn, swaddling the Valley in white until the midmorning sun burns through. Farmers call the fog "milk" because it nourishes their fields in the dry winter season. Winter afternoons are clear, crisp and pleasantly warm in the sun, but nights can be quite cold, especially in Kathmandu's unheated buildings. Snow falls in the Valley only once in a generation. Occasionally the surrounding hilltops are dusted with a light snowfall.

Basanta: The festival of Basant Panchami in late January celebrates the official first day of spring, but usually it takes a few more weeks for the weather to obey. When the morning fog stops, spring is on its way. Fruit trees and mustard crops blossom in February, the air stays clear but the bite of winter is gone, though nights can still be a bit chilly. This season is a very pleasant time to visit the Valley and explore the surrounding hills.

Grisma: From April-May heat and dust are on the rise and the sun is increasingly fierce. Winter wheat and mustard are harvested in April, and all across Nepal and India the remaining stubble is burned to fertilize the earth with the ashes. The smoke combines with dust to form a murky brown haze blurring distant views, though higher altitudes rise above it. Spring is the second most popular trekking season; nearly 25% of trekkers head out in March-April. By May, temperatures in the low river valleys and Terai are sweltering, flies and mosquitoes are everywhere, and disease is on the rise.

Barkha: (see "The Monsoon," p. 16)

Sharad: The monsoon departs with a final burst by mid-October. Skies are clear, the air crisp, the sun warm, and the Himalaya appears in the north beneath a fresh coat of snow. The second week of October is the unofficial start of the trekking season, and overnight Kathmandu fills with tourists. Autumn is popular for good reason. The dry, clear, sunny days offer the best chances of mountain views, exhilarating weather, and moderate temperatures.

Hemanta: Early winter continues the clear fresh air of autumn, edging slowly into colder temperatures by November. Late Nov.-early Dec. is a good time to avoid crowds while keeping clear views and good weather. The only drawback is that nights above 3,500 meters start to get cold.

AVERAGE MONTHLY TEMPERATURES

	Meghauli (Terai)		Kathmandu (Hills)		Namche (Mtns.)	
	Max.	Min.	Max.	Min.	Max.	Min.
Jan.	23	8	17	2	6	-6
Feb.	28	11	21	3	6	-4
March	33	17	25	9	8	-1
April	37	19	27	11	11	1
May	37	22	28	16	14	3
June	34	23	28	19	15	7
July	33	25	28	20	16	8
Aug.	32	24	27	20	16	8
Sept.	32	24	26	19	15	7
Oct.	31	19	25	12	11	1
Nov.	27	14	21	8	8	-3
Dec.	24	8	19	3	7	-4

FLORA

The Himalaya compresses a wider range of vegetation into a smaller area than possibly anywhere else in the world. Like nearly everything else in Nepal, flora is classified in vertical terms. Long bands of tropical, temperate, and alpine vegetation zones ribbon the country from east to west. The rapid increase in altitude compresses them into extraordinarily narrow areas. In North America, coniferous forests extend nearly 1,400 km north before giving way to tundra; in Nepal conifers appear in a narrow band extending only one vertical km (2,700-3,700 meters).

Forests

Through the '50s the Terai's tropical deciduous forests were among Nepal's greatest natural resources, protected by the malaria-carrying mosquitoes that kept the region nearly uninhabited. Over the last 40 years much has been cut, both for timber and to clear land for settlement. The straight-trunked sal trees (Shorea robusta) which grow up to 30 meters in height yield top-quality hardwood used to build temples, houses, railway sleepers and bridges. The exquisitely carved sal wood pillars and beams of the Valley's temples have endured for hundreds of years. Woodcarvers say that sal wood can be immersed in water for a thousand years, be exposed to air for another thousand, and still remain intact.

Intermixed with Terai forests are dense stands of grasses, over 50 different species, some of which grow up to six meters tall. Local people use it for thatching roofs and building walls. It's commonly called "elephant grass," whether because elephants eat it or because it can only be crossed on elephant-back, nobody knows.

Moving north, subtropical wet hill forests appear in the lower Hills, typified by the broadleaved chilaune, bamboo, and tree rhododendron. Upper Hill regions are covered by temperate moist montane forests, a mix of conifers, oaks, bamboo, and rhododendrons. Forests of this type once blanketed the entire southern side of the Himalaya until villagers and farmers

PIPAL TREES AND CHAUTAARA

Nepal's endless steep climbs are mercifully interrupted by stone platforms built beneath giant trees, cool resting places for weary travelers. These chautaara are built and maintained by individuals as a public service which earns them religious merit. Usually a chautaara is shaded by a pipal tree (Ficus religiosa), the same tree under which the Buddha gained enlightenment. Often a multi-trunked baar or banyan tree (Ficus bengalensis) stands alongside, its round leaves representing the female principle, the pointed-leaved pipal the male.

A village chautaara is the local meeting place, the rural Nepali equivalent of a Parisian sidewalk cafe or the American coffee shop. It rivals the water tap as a place for flirting and romance. Even Kathmandu has its pipal tree: the Pipal Bot on New Road, the place to buy newspapers and catch up on political gossip.

More than a social center, the pipal is the residence of the gods. Village deities live beneath some chautaara embodied in sacred stones. The goddess Lakshmi is said to visit the pipal on Sundays; others say her husband Vishnu comes every Saturday. Hindu women honor the tree by pouring water or milk on the roots and annointing the trunk with vermillion powder, rice, and flowers. Pipal worship is a remedy for infertility and a way to nullify the evil omen of widowhood appearing in a bride's horoscope. Astrologers may advise individuals mis-aspected by Saturn to girdle a pipal tree in a network of red thread.

The banyan tree is sacred to Shiva and is also revered. Both trees are considered supernatural and nearly immortal and are never cut—to do so would bring bad luck. The pipal especially is associated with naga, ghosts, and spirits. Nepalis say it's not the wind that rustles its leaves, but the movements of invisible beings like yaksha, kinnara, and the celestial musicians, gandharva.

cut down vast amounts to clear land. Clouds, rain, and mist are all common at this altitude, and in some pockets the moisture nurtures luxuriant cloud forests of moss-draped trees, orchids, and ferns.

Above 4,000 meters plantlife dwindles to tough grasses, alpine plants, and dwarf varieties of rhododendron, juniper, and birch. Beyond the alpine zone vegetation virtually disappears, leaving only the colorful, hardy lichen. Treeline is typically around 4,500-5,000 meters, lower in dry rainshadowed valleys. Permanent snowline begins at about 5,330 meters.

BOB RACE

Rhododendrons

Nepal's national flower, the tree rhododendron (*R. arboreum*), is the world's tallest species, with an average height of 7-14 meters. Some specimens in wet eastern Nepal may grow to 20 meters. Rhodies flourish all across the eastern Himalaya, with 50-60 species appearing in Nepal, Sikkim, and Bhutan—29 in Nepal alone. They grow right up to timberline, most commonly on exposed slopes and ridgelines between 1,800-4,000 meters. They thrive in harsh conditions and help to anchor soil to steep slopes, but their soft wood makes them a favorite target for woodcutters.

Between February and May, depending on altitude, clusters of trumpet-shaped blossoms appear in a spectacular display of scarlet, pink, and white, the paler colors appearing higher up. Nepalis love *laligurans,* especially the red ones. Women tuck the blossoms in their hair, woodcutters place them atop their loads, devotees offer them to the gods. Rhododendron flowers are kept on hand in homes as a folk remedy for a bone stuck in the throat.

Rhodies have their bad side too. Raw honey from their flowers may contain a potent neurotoxin which can cause nausea, vomiting, or loss of consciousness. Susceptible people may fall into a coma after consuming a small amount, while their companions are unaffected. There is no guarantee local honey is cooked. Beware of rhododendron honey on your breakfast pancake.

Plants And Flowers

At least 6,500 species of flowering plants appear in Nepal. Orchids are abundant in the moist hills, appearing in more than 18 different forms. Nearly every variety of garden flower flourishes in Kathamndu's beneficent climate. Many have been introduced from Europe, Africa or the Middle East, including the ubiquitous marigolds strung into garlands for the great autumn festivals. Many of the ornamental trees in the Kathmandu Valley, like the blue-blossomed jacaranda, the bottlebrush with its bristling red flowers, silver oaks, eucalyptus, and the silk oak, have also been introduced from abroad.

The gods have their favorite plants and flowers too. Tulasi (holy basil) is sacred to Vishnu because it incarnates his consort Lakshmi. It's worshipped in homes and temples. All the goddesses love the bright-red poinsettias which blossom in tropical winters. The lotus is an ancient sacred symbol of purity, representing the pure mind of Enlightenment rising untainted from the mud of earthly concerns. Deities are often depicted holding a lotus or seated atop one. The goddess Lakshmi is especially associated with it, praised as lotus-eyed, lotus-colored, and decked with lotus ornaments.

Ganja

Cannabis sativa grows like the weed it is all through the Hills and Terai. Before the arrival of foreigners who made a big fuss about it (and eventually caused it to be declared illegal), ganja was no more than a respected herb, said to have first appeared during the mythic Churning of the Ocean. Older men meet in the evening to relax with some *charas* (hashish) to fuel their singing and conversation. Traditional medicine prescribes charas for many ailments, including headaches, tetanus, malaria, even insanity. Ganja itself is said to cure insomnia; there is also *bhang,* a potent brew of marijuana sticks and stems which can leave you reeling for days. Ganja is sacred to Shiva, Lord of the Yogis, who is said to consume prodigious amounts as an aid to meditation. On the festival of Shiva Ratri hundreds of Hindu saddhus gather at the Pashupatinath Temple to pay homage to Shiva with prayer, singing, and austerities, all fueled by massive doses of ganja.

FAUNA

Nepal's animal life is a veritable Noah's Ark, embracing snow leopards and rhinoceroses, crocodiles and mountain goats, over 500 species of butterflies, and 800 species of birds. Located in the heart of Asia at the juncture of two great bio-geographical regions, Nepal harbors species from both. Distinct zones are determined by altitude; species also vary from east to west as the land becomes progressively drier and less forested.

Himalayan wildlife in general was a scientific mystery until the 19th century. Credit for exploring it goes to Brian Hodgson, a consumptive clerk for the British East India Company who had been given the rather grim choice of dying in England or in a hill post. He chose the unknown and was shipped off to Kathmandu in 1821 to serve as assistant to the British Resident. The Valley suited Hodgson: he thrived on the exotic culture, plunging into scholarly studies and producing stacks of research papers. He eventually succeeded the British Resident, stayed a total of 22 years in Nepal, and finally died in England at the age of 95.

In spite of the ban on travel outside the Kathmandu Valley Hodgson managed to assemble the world's first major collection of Himalayan species, over 900 mammals and 9,500 birds which he finally presented to the British Museum. Working entirely on his own, he published over a hundred papers on 563 Nepali species, 150 of them previously unknown. His work laid the foundations for the study of Himalayan natural history, till then a little explored field.

DOMESTIC ANIMALS

Domestic animals are extremely important in rural Nepal but the Western concept of pets is practically unknown. Cats are shunned as familiars of witches and most dogs are ownerless scavengers, yapping nuisances after dark. They bark a lot but are generally too cringing to bite. In a few city neighborhoods dog packs harass late-night cyclists and pedestrians. A couple of well-aimed stones will disperse them. The dog to watch out for is the Tibetan mastiff, bred to sink its teeth into unannounced visitors. It's a popular guard dog for homes; Bhotia villagers sometimes keep them as well. Beware.

Livestock
Just about every Hill family has at least a few goats and chickens. A cow or water buffalo, if they can afford it, supplies a small cash income from the sale of milk. Nepal's livestock population equals or exceeds its human population. The meat, milk, hides, and wool are essential for farming families, but these are bought at a major cost to the environment. Herds of sharp-hooved goats and sheep graze grassy slopes into dust, earning the nickname "hooved locusts." Good pasture is scarce, but a water buffalo needs two large loads of grass and leaves; the daily chore of cutting and hauling fodder falls to women. Altogether, Nepal's livestock is estimated to consume over 50 million tons of green fodder a year—a major cause of deforestation.

Yaks
Larger, stronger, and shaggier than domestic cattle, the yak is uniquely adapted to heights. It thrives above 3,000 meters but can't survive in the lowlands. A yak sent to the London Zoo soon died—of malaria, the Sherpas explained. Yaks are an essential part of Nepal's high-altitude economy, serving as pack and plough animals and providing milk, meat, and wool. In the Sherpa language a female yak is a *nak,* giving rise to the old joke "there's no such thing as yak milk." Yak or nak, the milk is wonderfully rich, and yak/nak yoghurt is deliciously creamy. To preserve it, highlanders turn it into butter and

the rock-hard dried cheese called *churpi*. Another yak-provided product is the yarn spun from the long hair and soft underwool, used in blanket-weaving. Before the advent of synthetics, fluffy white yak tails were the main source for Santa Claus beards in the U.S. They are still in demand as ceremonial fly whisks for Hindu temples.

SACRED COWS

Serene in their sanctity, cows rule Kathmandu streets, flopping down in the middle of rush-hour traffic to ruminatively chew their cud. They make hazardous driving conditions even worse, but for every motorist who silently curses a cow, ten passersby will reverently touch it, then lift their fingers to their foreheads in a blessing.

The cow is Nepal's national animal, the symbol of fertility and prosperity and the giver of the "five gifts": milk, yoghurt, ghee (clarified butter), dung and urine. Worship and protection of cows is an ancient Hindu tradition. Anthropologists speculate that the wise men of Vedic India realized the cow's milk, manure, and draft power were essential to agriculture. To protect this valuable beast from being turned into hamburger, they proclaimed a taboo on beef. When I told this pragmatic theory to a Nepali friend, he looked hurt. "Cows are sacred because they're such kind and gentle creatures," he protested.

As the giver of milk, the cow is revered as man's second mother. Cow manure is another precious gift. It fertilizes fields and in dried form is burned as fuel; a purifying mixture of cow dung and mud is smeared daily on the floors and walls of orthodox Hindu homes, and a cow dung poultice is the traditional remedy for cuts and wounds. Not surprisingly, orthodox Brahmans refuse to harness such a revered beast to the plow.

Cow worship is believed to have the power to nullify an unlucky horoscope, and one day a year, a cow leads the souls of the dead across the great river blocking entry into heaven. Cow worship reaches its peak on the third day of the festival of Tihar, when wandering cows are washed, fed and adorned with garlands.

Beef-eating is abhorrent to nearly all Nepalis, and *gai khaane maanche,* "cow-eater," is an impolite epithet for foreigners. (If you want a provocative conversation, try explaining what McDonald's serves). Water-buffalo meat, "buff" on local menus, is the rather tough, stringy substitute served in most tourist restaurants. But beef *is* available in Kathmandu: expensive restaurants serve chateaubriand flown in from India (where Moslems do the butchering) and the larger cold stores sell roasts to foreigners and a few daredevil Nepalis.

During the Malla era, killing a cow was one of the five great sins, ranked just behind murdering a Brahman, woman, child, or relative. A century ago cow slaughter was the legal equivalent of murder, punishable by death. Today the penalty is a Rs20,000 fine or two years' imprisonment: killing a cow is taken very seriously, and the street scene will not be pretty if you run into a cow while driving.

Mountain people eat yak and crossbreed cattle, a practice frowned upon by Hindus, but the yak's status has always been flexible. During a campaign against Tibet, when Nepali troops were starving in the snow, Prime Minister Jung Bahadur Rana "discovered" that yak were not cattle, but deer. He persuaded the Raj Guru, the ultimate Hindu authority, to go along with his find, and his soldiers got a supply of meat.

the "wish-fulfilling cow," Kamdhenu

Tibetan Yak

Sixteen different words in Nepali and Tibetan describe all possible crossbreeds of yaks and lowland cattle. A nak bred with a regular bull produces a *dzum* (female) or *dzopkio* (male). These crossbreeds combine the stamina of the yak with the tractability and higher milk production of the cow. Dzopkio make excellent pack animals, unlike purebred yak, which are temperamental beasts equipped with wicked upward-curving horns.

Monkeys *(Bandar)*
Halfway between domesticated and wild, bands of rhesus monkeys roam Kathmandu temple grounds, sliding down banisters, swinging from power lines, and begging or stealing food. The largest communities are in Swayambhu and Pashupatinath, where they are protected by religion and tradition. Believe it or not, several scientific studies have been done on Kathmandu's monkeys. They all conclude that these monkeys have lost their natural fear of man and can be exceptionally aggressive, especially when they're eating. Look out for monkey thieves snatching your lunch or your camera. Monkeys can carry rabies, so any bite that breaks the skin should be treated.

WILDLIFE

Terai Wildlife
The jungles and forests of the Terai were once rich in game, but widespread resettlement has drastically altered habitats and populations. Less than 50 wild Asiatic elephants *(hatti)* remain in small scattered groups along Nepal's southern border. A remnant population of fierce, strong wild buffalo *(arnaa)* are huddled in a wildlife refuge on the small island of Kosi Tappu Wildlife Preserve in southeast Nepal. The Terai is also home to the gaur *(gauri gai)*, the world's largest wild cattle, standing 1.8 meters at the shoulder and weighing over 900 kilos. The Narayani River, on the western boundary of Chitwan National Park, harbors a quarter of the world's remaining *gharial* population. This fish-eating crocodile is hunted for its hide and the reputed aphrodisiac power of its long, slender snout.

The one-horned rhinoceros *(gaida)* has a semi-magical aura about it. A rhino skin bracelet is said to protect against evil spirits; rhino dung acts as a laxative and rhino urine cures stomach pains and tuberculosis. Rhino horn is the most coveted of all, fetching up to US$17,000 per kilo in China, where it's used as a fever remedy. Poaching has reduced the world's population of *Rhinoceros unicornis* to 1,800. About 400 of these live in Chitwan National Park. With armour-plated skin and stubby legs, rhinos are shortsighted and must rely on hearing and smell to target a victim. Antisocial and unpredictable, they can charge without provocation, and contrary to popular belief they are quite agile. Every year during grass-cutting season, several villagers are trampled by rhinos.

Chitwan (and the adjoining Parsa Wildlife Reserve) is one of the world's best remaining tiger habitats, harboring about 70 royal Bengal tigers *(bagh)*. In 1972 it was set aside with Suklaphanta and Bardia wildlife preserves as part of the World Wildlife Fund's "Operation Tiger." Probably 200 tigers are left in all of Nepal.

Hill And Himalayan Wildlife
Because the Hills are so densely populated you're not likely to spot much wildlife on a trek. In some regions local people hunt wild pigs and game like the tahr, argali, blue sheep, and Himalayan ibex. The leopard, a bold and intelligent cat still common in midland Nepal, lives off game, livestock, and village dogs. A few still lurk in the forested hills surrounding the Kathmandu Valley.

The snow leopard lives in the remote mountains of central Asia; the creatures are so elusive nobody has managed to determine how many dwell in northwest Nepal, despite years of re-

BIRDWATCHING

With less than one percent of the world's land mass, tiny Nepal contains 10% of its birds, or 801 species. Some of the names are as entertaining as the birds themselves: plumbeous redstart, satyr tragopan, Himalayan tree pie, hoary barwing, coal tit. Over half are found in the Kathmandu Valley. The area around the **Royal Botanical Gardens** at Godavari is especially rich: on the three-hour walk from Godavari to the summit of Phulchowki (2,765 meters) it's possible to spot 100 different species. The wooded summit of Nagarjun and the area around Thankot on the Valley rim are other good sites.

Chitwan National Park, with its wide range of natural environments, also hosts over 400 bird species. Spring migration season, February-March, brings the most sightings. The marsh and reed beds of **Kosi Tappu Wildlife Reserve** in eastern Nepal are on the spring migration route of thousands of water birds.

Trekking greatly increases the variety of sightings. It's also the only way to spot the Impeyan pheasant *(danphe)*, the gorgeously colored national bird of Nepal which prefers high altitudes. One of the better birdwatching treks is the western side of the Annapurna Circuit. The trail leads from tropical Pokhara up the Kali Gandaki Valley (a migratory route for water birds) onto the dry highlands beyond Jomosom, where species typical of the Tibetan Plateau appear.

Serious birdwatchers should come in spring and summer, when the birds are in full breeding plumage. An excellent field guide is *Birds of Nepal* (see Booklist), compiled by a father-and-son team of missionary doctors from 25 years of field research. With color illustrations by Nepali artist Lain Bangdel, it's one of the world's classic bird books. Salim Ali's *Indian Hill Birds* or *Field Guide to the Eastern Himalayas* may be useful for cross-referencing.

Kathmandu's most memorable birdwatching experience involves mammals. From April through December, tourists heading to Thamel stop dead in their tracks to stare at the hundreds of giant fruit bats roosting upside down in the poplars in Kaiser Mahal. Hanging from the branches like so many ripe plums, the bats squabble and sleep during the day, then fly off at dusk in search of a dinner of fruit (they prefer mangoes) and flowers.

The Impeyan pheasant (danphe) *is Nepal's national bird.*

BOB RACE

search. Their numbers are dwindling due to trapping and hunting. Although the animal is supposed to be protected, it's easier to find a snow leopard-skin coat in the exclusive shops on Durbar Marg than a live snow leopard in the wild. The same goes for the skins of the clouded leopard, another endangered and supposedly protected species.

Langur monkeys, larger than rhesus and always wild, are handsome gray-furred creatures with distinctive white heads and black faces. Even their feet are equipped with "thumbs" for grasping at tree branches. They're regarded as sacred and never killed, even if they raid crops, because in the *Ramayana* an army of langur monkeys fought under the direction of the Monkey King Hanuman to rescue the kidnapped maiden Sita. They inhabit the sal forests of the Terai and the conifer forests of central Nepal, and can be spotted on some main trekking routes.

Leeches

The lowly terrestrial leech is possibly Nepal's most detested creature. For most of the year it hides in an underground burrow. During the rainy season it emerges in moist, shaded forests and meadows between 1,200-2,700 meters. Sensing the body heat of a warm-blooded victim, the leech uncurls from its hideout and extends to an amazing length to attach itself. The modus operandi of a leech is fascinating to everyone but its victim. Its mouth forms an ideal suction device. Inside are three moveable internal lips, each lined with a row of teeth. The leech first secretes a local anesthetic to numb its host, then drills a hole through the skin and injects an anticoagulant to assure a continuous flow of blood—the reason why bleeding continues even after the creature is removed. Left to feed their fill, leeches swell up to 10 times their size and can then live several months without eating.

The whole process is repulsive rather than painful. You might feel a twinge as the leech latches on, but probably won't notice a thing until you see blood. Leeches don't transmit diseases but a bite can easily get infected, especially during the monsoon, so treat leech bites as carefully as other small wounds.

Prevention is the first course of defense: move fast through damp, shady places. If you're traveling in single file with several companions, space yourselves out. Those at the end of a line gather the most leeches. Keep as much skin covered as possible; wear long pants tucked into socks. Soaking trouser cuffs and socks in salt water might be one way to repel them. If you spot a leech inching aboard, brush it off immediately; if it's attached itself to you, it can be pulled off with a bit of determination (unlike ticks, the head won't remain embedded). Or rest assured it will withdraw after sucking its fill (however, most victims are unwilling to play the good host). Touching the leech with a hot match tip or lit cigarette should precipitate a speedy withdrawal. So will coating it with salt, iodine, or alcohol. The Nepali method is to smear it with *kaini,* tobacco snuff available in small tins from any shop.

The Yeti

This shaggy man-ape is the most elusive of all Nepal's creatures, rumored but never proven to inhabit the remote eastern Himalaya. Reports of "hairy wild men who are believed to live among the eternal snows" date to 1832 and go back even further among Sherpas, Bhutanese, and Tibetans, who call him *Yeh Teh* ("Man of the Rocky Places"), *Kang Mi* ("Snowman") or *Dzu Teh* ("Cattle Lifter"). The sensational term "Abominable Snowman" was coined by a popular British columnist in 1921.

Since 1950, mountaineering expeditions have fueled speculation with reports of giant footprints found on uninhabited frozen slopes, bigger than those of humans but with prehensile toes. Skeptics point out that footprints normally enlarge with melting snow, and a bear or similar creature walking upright can replicate a man's stride. (What a bear would be doing at 7,000 meters they can't explain.) Other tantalizing scraps of evidence include a tuft of strange black fur, mysterious droppings, again unidentifiable; a piercing scream ringing out from a ledge, terrifying members of one expedition.

Over a dozen expeditions mounted in search of the yeti have found little beyond a few more footprints and some skins which turned out to be from other animals. Taken to the West for lab analysis, the famous yeti scalp of Pangboche Gompa was declared to be fashioned from the 200-year-old skin of a serow, a Himalayan goat-antelope.

Reports of actual sightings are equally inconclusive. The yeti viewer always turns out to be a "friend's cousin's wife's brother" who lives in a distant village and who wouldn't be there even if you did visit, because he's gone away for business. For now, at least, the yeti is shadowy symbol rather than solid fact, and will probably remain that way for a long time.

Tibetan charm used as a protection against dog bites

THE ENVIRONMENT

The Himalaya may seem eternal, but it is one of the most fragile ecosystems on earth. Steep slopes, poor soil, and heavy monsoon rains make its mountains vulnerable to erosion. Deforestation accelerates the process, as topsoil slides down into rivers and is washed away into the sea. What's happening in Nepal is occurring all across the Himalaya, and has been for centuries. The pace has accelerated in the last few decades because of intense population pressures. Much has been made of tourism's environmental impact, but 60,000 trekkers per year use far less wood than the eight million tons burned annually by 19 million Nepalis. Tourism's greatest threat is cultural rather than environmental erosion.

Nepal's population doubled between 1951 and 1983 and is due to double again in thirty years. The delicate ecological balance of the Himalaya can't support many more people; even now there are signs of strain. In the Hills every available scrap of land is already cultivated. Nepali hillmen are skilled and sensible farmers, but growing families and shrinking plots leave them with no choice but to extend their holdings onto land better left unplowed, to graze their animals on steep slopes, and to cut down forests.

The result is frequent landslides, silted rivers, and barren hills furrowed by deep gullies. For rural Nepalis it translates into lowered crop yields, dried-up water sources, and longer walks to cut firewood and fodder as nearby forests vanish. Trees are the weakest link in the ecological chain. Demands for fuel and fodder are simply too great to allow time for natural regeneration. The government sponsors reforestation under the slogan *hariyo ban, Nepalko dhan* —"Green forests are Nepal's wealth"—but so far the rate is not enough to make a dent in the damage.

Deforestation

Over half of Nepal's forests have been cut in the last 30 years, most cleared for new cropland or to fill rising demands for firewood, timber, and livestock fodder. Current estimates show forests are being destroyed at a rate of two to three percent yearly, far faster than the natural regeneration rate. At this pace, accessible forests could vanish in the next 10-20 years, spelling disaster for a country where nearly 90% of the energy comes from firewood.

This is the doomsday scenerio put forward by some experts; others admit that they don't know precisely how fast forests are disappearing, since rates vary widely from place to place. It does appear, however, that deforestation has become critical with the recent doubling of Nepal's population. Another culprit was the nationalization of forests in 1957 which wiped out many traditional community systems that had effectively limited local forest use. Since the trees didn't belong to the people anymore, they had no reason to preserve them, and woodcutting became a grab-all-you-can-get affair.

The need for firewood is frequently blamed for deforestation, but clearing land for farming and overgrazing by livestock are equally responsible, if not more. Too many goats or sheep can reduce rich pasture to barren stubble in just a few years, and grass is more important than trees in soaking up excess moisture and preventing erosion. Once grazed bare, high pastureland is unlikely to recover naturally. Livestock are an essential part of the rural economy, but the average animal eats two tons of fodder a year. Altogether the country's livestock consumes twice as much biomass per year as the annual demand for firewood. In fact, the farm animal population outnumbers the human population. An "animal family planning program" has been suggested, only half jokingly.

Erosion

Nepal has one of the world's most acute erosion problems. Fertile topsoil is disappearing at the rate of 35-70 metric tons per hectare per year, 20 times the weight of the rice crop from the same area. The soil is washed into south-flowing rivers which eventually dump it in the Bay of Bengal, where islands are being created from the siltation. Rueful references are made to this new "Nepali territory," growing with the addition of 240 million cubic meters of topsoil per year, Nepal's most precious and unpaid export.

Probably half the erosion is due to geological causes. A high rate is typical of steep, young mountains like the Himalaya. The remainder comes from human interference: deforestation, farming of marginal land, grazing, fodder-lopping, and road-building, all accelerated by a growing population. The impact is difficult to assess nationwide, but apparently in many Hill regions soil fertility is vanishing with the topsoil, rivers and springs are drying up, the earth is retaining less water, and the runoff cycle increases every year. In the Terai, silt-laden rivers alter their courses more frequently, causing increased flooding. Siltation also reduces the lifespan of hydropower dams by as much as 50%. The ultimate prospect some scientists are already warning of is desertification. Soil and nutrients can be lost to the point where even irrigation will not restore the land. Experts speculate that barren high-altitude tracts in Mustang and Dolpo went through this process long ago.

Pollution

The Valley's ancient towns are afflicted with that plague of modern life, smog. The bowl-shaped Valley is an ideal place for a thermal inversion à la Los Angeles and Mexico City. Dust particles and exhaust fumes combine with the winter mist to form murky haze. Thirty years ago the Himalayan peaks appeared crystal-clear behind the Valley rim to the north; nowadays they're frequently hidden behind a brown smudge. Public Enemy Number One for environmentalists is the coal-burning Himal Cement Factory at Chobhar, the Valley's major industrial employer. In most of Nepal the air outside is clear. Pollution is hidden indoors, in poorly ventilated houses that trap smoke from cooking fires, causing eye infections and respiratory illnesses.

Gravely polluted water is a major carrier of disease. The Valley's sewage treatment and water purification plants are rendered practically useless, as low water pressure and the close proximity of water and sewage pipes mean the water is dangerously fouled by the time it reaches home taps. Chemical pollution is a growing danger in the Valley, as industries pour untreated wastes directly into rivers, the traditional dumping ground for all kinds of garbage, despite their sacred status.

Litter

The most visible pollution appears on trails strewn with biscuit wrappers, noodle packages, and (the exclusive mark of tourists) used toilet paper. Foreign visitors are the biggest sinners in this category because they can afford expensive packaged products, but Nepalis litter too. Until recently everything was either natural or recycled. Feasts were served on leaf plates and clay cups, scrap paper was recycled into paper bags, old bits of metal were melted down into new cookpots. The advent of plastic has outpaced the realization that when you throw it away, it's there to stay.

A few neighborhoods in Kathmandu are organizing effective community clean-up efforts to keep trash off the streets, but out in the countryside there's no control, and everyone has someone else to blame. Group treks generate a tremendous amount of garbage from prepackaged and canned foods, half-heartedly buried at best or dumped in a river. Independent trekkers, who should know better, are often just as bad. The lack of local trash depots leaves no real solution to the problem, other than generating less. Carrying litter back to Kathmandu shifts the problem somewhere else (hopefully to a municipal garbage dump), but it doesn't go away. Mountaineering expeditions deserve special mention for bringing more garbage to higher heights in Nepal than anywhere else in the world. The South Col of Everest, which sees at least a dozen foreign expeditions a year, is renowned as the world's highest garbage dump. Periodically clean-up expeditions haul down used oxygen cylinders, tin cans, and plastic barrels, but the supply is endless. Still, though litter is a highly visible problem, much of it doesn't go beyond being an eyesore. Less visible threats like deforestation are far more serious.

NATIONAL PARKS AND PRESERVES

Over seven percent of Nepal's area, nearly 11,000 square km, is set aside as national parks and wildlife preserves. The movement began in the early '60s with the establishment of a rhinoceros sanctuary in Chitwan. The purpose is to conserve and manage at least a portion of Nepal's splendid natural heritage, protecting representative examples of threatened and unique ecosystems. Some of the National Parks, like Chitwan and Sagarmatha, have been proclaimed UNESCO World Heritage sites for their unique natural and cultural environments.

Organization

Parks and reserves are managed by the Department of National Parks. In 1982 a private nonprofit organization, the **King Mahendra Trust for Nature Conservation**, was founded with the purpose of protecting Nepal's wildlife wherever it may be.

The standard national park model inspired by the New World's vast tracts of virgin territory is ill-suited for Nepal, where thousands of people live in protected areas in an intimate relationship with the environment. In the beginning, park designers tried to follow the traditional model by evicting local residents and resettling them outside the boundaries. In the case of Chitwan NP this created widespread local resentment; at Rara NP it caused a small-scale tragedy when two mountain villages were evicted and resettled in the totally alien environment of the Terai. A similar eviction was suggested for the Sherpas of Sagarmatha NP but fortunately was shot down. Now parks try to encompass villages rather than eradicate them. Villagers are legally excluded from park jurisdiction, but conservation-oriented restrictions on woodcutting, hunting, and trapping affect their lives. The resurgence of wildlife in protected areas includes wild boars, pheasants, rhinos, and other beasts fond of uprooting farmers' crops. In the past, villagers would have been able to shoot or trap the offenders; now they must stand by and watch their crops being destroyed.

Achieving the right balance of ecological and human needs is a tricky matter. One potential model is offered by the Annapurna Conservation Area Project (see p. 326), an innovative scheme to protect the natural environment of the heavily trekked Annapurna Himal with minimal disruption to the lives of the region's 40,000 inhabitants.

Parks

For more information on parks and reserves, contact the Department of National Parks and Wildlife Conservation (tel. 220-912), P.O. Box 860, Babar Mahal, Kathmandu.

Chitwan National Park, Nepal's first, is among southeast Asia's finest wildlife preserves, protecting rhinos, tigers, and over 40 other species of mammals and 400 species of birds. **Sagarmatha National Park,** the most famous and most visited of all, encompasses Mt. Everest and a host of other great peaks, several famous monasteries, and villages housing about 2,500 Sherpas. (The proposed **Makalu-Barun National Park** would adjoin it to the east, protecting the headwaters of the upper Arun River.) **Langtang National Park,** directly north of Kathmandu, stretches from rich forests through alpine terrain up to Himalayan peaks.

Remote western Nepal holds less visited parks and preserves. **Lake Rara National Park,** 370 km northwest of Kathmandu, preserves Rara Lake, Nepal's largest, surrounded by magnificent conifer forests. Because it's several days' walk north from the remote Jumla Airfield, it receives few visitors. Tiny **Khaptad National Park** in the middle hills of far western Nepal en-

royal Bengal tiger

BOB RACE

compasses forests, grassland, and the ashram of Khaptad Baba, a revered Hindu saint. **Shey-Phoksumdo National Park** is Nepal's largest, 3,555 square km of trans-Himalayan territory including forests and the high-altitude desert typical of the Tibetan Plateau. Currently foreigners can only travel up to Phoksumdo Lake; the vast and fascinating region northward is restricted.

Wildlife Reserves
Parsa Wildlife Reserve was a famous Rana hunting ground; now it provides additional territory for the tigers of Chitwan NP. **Royal Suk-laphanta Wildlife Reserve** in extreme southwestern Nepal is a prime habitat for endangered swamp deer. Slightly east, **Royal Bardia Wildlife Reserve** preserves typical Terai wildlife. **Koshi Tappu Wildlife Reserve** in the eastern Terai shelters the country's last surviving population of wild water buffalo; its swamps and mud flats are excellent birding areas. **Dhorpatan Hunting Reserve** in the Dhaulagiri Range of west-central Nepal supports game like blue sheep, serow, goral, Himalayan thar, pheasants, and partridges—all available to hunters, for a price.

HISTORY

The history of Nepal centers on the Kathmandu Valley. Until the country assumed its present form in the 18th century the Valley *was* Nepal, in both name and fact. Even today, Hill people heading to Kathmandu will tell you *"Nepalma jaane"*—"We're going to Nepal." From the beginning the Valley has been the center of politics, intrigue, religion, trade, and urban civilization—in short, everything worth recording. Compared to it, life in the Hills was unremarkable, and it continued for centuries unnoted, much as it does today.

The Valley's traditional prosperity came from its fertile soil and its strategic location on the trans-Himalayan trade route between India and Tibet. Kathmandu was a pleasant place for caravans to wait out the malarial summers of the southern Terai or the winter snows blocking the northern passes into Tibet. Traders, scholars, monks, pilgrims, and envoys from many countries journeyed through the Valley and left a legacy of diverse ideas and influences.

Despite the constant stream of visitors, outside historical sources are scanty, limited to a few Chinese diplomats, Christian missionaries, and the British Residents who were forcibly settled in Kathmandu in the 19th century. Local history on the other hand appears everywhere in the Valley. Royal edicts were etched in copperplates, carved onto pillars, or engraved on stone slabs. Later came manuscripts of palm leaves or handmade paper, and the *Vamsavali,* historical chronicles blending myth and history, legend and fact. In a larger sense, history is en-coded in the Valley's traditional art and architecture and lives on in legends, festivals, and customs, some over 1,500 years old, that act as direct links to the past.

Prehistory
Neolithic artifacts discovered in the Valley indicate man has inhabited it since prehistoric times, but archaeologic exploration has been hampered by the dense urban population, religious restrictions, and a shortage of funds. There is no doubt that a treasure trove of history lies underground. Workmen digging foundations for buildings regularly find ancient sculptures, artifacts, and 1,300-year-old bricks from vanished palaces.

The transition from the mythic beginnings described in the Valley's creation legend to the historical era is blurred. In ancient histories the Valley seems to be floating somewhere between heaven and earth. Kings are divine and gods are remarkably human in the old chronicles, which say the gods themselves came on pilgrimage to the holy Valley to view the Swayambhu light. Many stayed and settled there, while kings brought in other deities from abroad and installed them in temples placed in the four directions to protect the land. Images were endowed with supernatural powers: they sometimes spoke, relating their desires to kings, who took care to please them with lavish offerings. The Valley's ancient role as a Buddhist and Hindu pilgrimage site is rooted in these vague legends.

LEGENDARY BEGINNINGS

The origin of the Kathmandu Valley is recorded in the **Swayambhu Purana,** an ancient chronicle:

Long, long ago, eons before our present epoch, the Kathmandu Valley was a holy lake fourteen miles in circumference, ringed by mountains and dense forests. In its clear blue depths dwelt magical snake-like creatures called naga; thus the lake was called Nagavasahrada, the Lake Kingdom of the Serpents, or because of its depth, Kalihrada, "Tank of Blue-black Waters."

In the Golden Age the first of all Buddhas, Vipaswi, came to the sacred lake on pilgrimage. From the summit of Nagarjun mountain he tossed a lotus seed into the lake and predicted it would one day become a holy site.

Eighty thousand years later the earth quaked as the seed split open. A thousand-petaled lotus with jeweled pollen and golden seeds, as large as a chariot wheel, rose above the waters. In the middle of the flower appeared the dazzling self-created light of Swayambhu, the "self-born." The Buddha Manjushri came from the north to see this marvel. Thinking to open this place to pilgrims, he circled the Valley rim until he found the lowest point. With a single stroke of his Sword of Wisdom he cleft the gorge of Kotwal and the lake waters rushed out, the naga floating along with them. Manjushri persuaded Karkotaka, king of the naga, to remain and entrusted him with guarding the Valley's wealth. Karkotaka was awarded a golden palace with diamond windows, set in the bottom of a deep black pond near Chobhar Gorge.

The miraculous Swayambhu light shone upon the newly revealed Valley for centuries. Finally a Buddhist priest, realizing the sinful present age of the Kali Yuga was approaching, hid the magic light in a hole and covered it with a precious stone. Atop it he built a stupa, topped by a gilded spire—the Swayambhunath Stupa, among the holiest Buddhist shrines in Nepal.

Strange as it seems, the legend is a poetic and uncannily accurate rendering of historical fact. Ages ago the Valley was indeed a lake; the rich black soil called ko that Newari farmers dig up and spread on their fields as fertilizer is leftover sediment from aquatic vegetation. "Manjushri's sword" has its natural equivalent in the earthquake which split asunder the rock cliffs of Chobhar, leaving fault marks visible on the sheer walls of the gorge.

The Kirati

Factual history begins with the Kirati, a Mongoloid people believed to be the ancestors of the modern Rai and Limbu hill tribes of eastern Nepal. Some historians think they were indigenous to the Valley; other accounts say they swept down from the east around 800-700 B.C. and ruled for a thousand years. Very little is known of them aside from the fact a Kirati king is mentioned as fighting in the epic battle described in the *Mahabharata.* During their rule Buddhism was brought from India to Nepal.

Legend says the Indian emperor Ashoka, a devout Buddhist who spread the young religion throughout his vast empire, visited the Valley in the 3rd century B.C. and built Patan's five ancient stupas. They're still called the "Ashoka stupas," but his visit is pure legend. By Ashoka's time the Valley was already a thriving commercial center. An Indian chronicler of the 4th century B.C. noted Nepal's woolen blankets and carpets, and later accounts mention caravans carrying musk, yak tails (used as ceremonial fly whisks in Indian temples), iron, and red copper from the Valley to India.

Licchavi Period (300-879 A.D.)

About 300 A.D. the Kirati kingdom was invaded from India by the Licchavi Dynasty, which introduced the Hindu caste system and a number of social and religious traditions that endure to the present day, including the *guthi* system and the sacred cow. Nepali art and architecture was already highly developed by this time, and included Buddhist *vihara* or monasteries, stupas and smaller *chaitya,* and exquisite stone sculptures. Recorded history begins in 467 A.D. with a lengthy inscription on a pillar erected at the temple of Changu Narayan.

Life in 7th-century Nepal is preserved in the accounts of Wang Hsuan Tse, a Chinese diplomat who journeyed several times between the Tang Court to India by way of Kathmandu. He marveled at the city's long-vanished royal palace, with a seven-story copper-roofed tower inset with gems, ornamented with dragon-headed fountains and "sculptures to make one marvel." The Nepalese king, Narendra Deva, rivalled his splendid palace with his ornaments of pearl, mother-of-pearl, rock crystal, coral, amber, jade, and gold. Some of Wang's observations remain true even today: the Valley people eat with their hands, live in carved and painted wooden houses, and build "multistory temples (so tall) one would take them for a crown of clouds."

The Chinese Buddhist Hsuan Tsang, a contemporary of Wang's, never set foot in Nepal, but during a lengthy pilgrimage in India he recorded what he had heard about the land of "Ni-Po-La": "The national character is stamped with falseness and perfidy, the inhabitants are all of a hard and savage nature; to them neither good faith nor justice nor literature appeal. . . . Their bodies are ugly and their faces are mean." But even his informants had to admit "they are gifted with considerable skill in the arts."

Transitional Period (879-1200)

Few records survive from the next four centuries, and little is known except that it was a time of turmoil. As the central rule of the Licchavi era crumbled the Valley fragmented into petty kingdoms ruled by a succession of dynasties. Power-hungry nobles feuded with their rulers, instituting a pattern of conflict between the aristocracy and the royalty that would endure for centuries.

Despite the instability, religion and art flourished. The Valley became a center for Buddhist pilgrims, monks, teachers, and translators, a major channel through which the Buddhist Dharma was transmitted from India to Tibet.

THE MALLA DYNASTY

By the 13th century the Valley was divided into the three small kingdoms of Kathmandu, Patan, and Bhaktapur, plus the realm of Banepa-Panauti over the eastern rim. Frequent skirmishes took place over which would control the lucrative trading routes with Tibet. The Valley took on the appearance of a medieval battlefield, with walled cities ringed by moats and fortifications crowning strategic hilltops. Out of this turmoil sprang a period of unprecedented creativity and unity that would endure for over five centuries. Historians call it the Malla Period, after an honorific title Valley kings adopted around this time. Different dynasties came and went, but the Malla epoch endured for 550 years in a continuous pattern, over twice as long as the better known Moghul and Gupta empires of India.

statue of King Bhupatindra Malla, Bhaktapur Durbar Square

The era shaped the Valley's rich cultural and artistic legacy, as well as many of its festivals and social traditions. Kings poured their wealth into tiered pagodas, superb woodcarvings, sculptures, jewelry, and paintings. The most intimate reminders are the gilded images of three great Malla rulers, kneeling atop pillars facing the palaces they inhabited centuries ago.

The Early Malla Period (1220-1482)

The stability of the Malla period began with Jayasthiti Malla, an orthodox Hindu outsider summoned to wed the princess of the ruling lineage of Bhaktapur. Swiftly and vigorously he consolidated his rule, until by 1382 he had won control of the entire Valley. *Sthiti* means "rule, regulation," and Jayasthiti lived up to his name by codifying existing caste restrictions, ordering the Newar population into a system of 64 occupational castes. The lowest castes were forbidden to wear sleeved garments, caps, or shoes, or to roof their houses with tiles. He, on the other hand, proclaimed himself an incarnation of the god Vishnu, a tradition borrowed from Indian rulers which has continued to Nepal's present king. Jayasthiti's reign marked the beginning of the Hinduization process which was to increasingly dominate religion and society.

His son Jyoti Malla and grandson Yaksha Malla followed in his footsteps. All were orthodox Hindus who worshipped Buddhist deities as well. To the Malla kings and their subjects the gods were living, active entities with the power to intervene in human affairs, and supplicants performed elaborate *puja* (ritual worship) when threatened with the disasters of the time: famine, smallpox, invasions by Mithili and Muslim raiders, and horrifying earthquakes. A great quake shook the Valley nearly every century, killing up to one-third of the population and destroying cities and temples.

Yaksha Malla (1428-82) is said to have expanded his rule up to the Tibetan border in the north, the Ganges in the south, the Kali Gandaki in the west, and Sikkim in the east, though his acquisitions did not endure. One of the greatest of the Valley's kings, he lavishly patronized gods and temples and developed the Tibet trade. On his deathbed he distributed his domain among his children, expecting them to rule jointly, but they soon carved up their territory, and the Valley that had been united only a century ago was again fragmented.

The Three Kingdoms (1482-1767)
For the next 200 years Yaksha Malla's descendents squabbled among themselves, ignoring their common ancestry. The three cities of Kathmandu, Patan, and Bhaktapur (or Kantipur, Lalitpur, and Bhatgaon, as they were known) became rival centers of power with territory extending far into the surrounding countryside.

Political disunity proved better for the arts than the century of harmony which preceded it. By the 15th century the Valley entered its golden age. Much of its superb architecture, carving, and sculpture date back to this time. Rival kings vied to produce the most magnificent palaces, the tallest pagodas, the most lavish offerings. Whatever one created the others were compelled to surpass. The main battlefields for this artistic warfare were the Durbar squares. These bricked plazas across from palaces sprouted a fantastic array of temples, shrines, and statues as the palaces themselves expanded into ever

finer quadrangles and temples.

Kings sponsored the artists who created these wonders, paying them with grain collected as taxes, and lavishing fantastic quantities of gold onto temple roofs and images. Much of the wealth came from the lucrative Tibet trade which flourished in the late Malla period. Rulers heavily taxed revenues passing through their domains, and in addition the Valley had a monopoly on Tibetan money. The Tibetan government sent the silver, and for a hefty cut, the Nepalese minted it into coins—a lucrative privilege that gave the Three Kingdoms something else to squabble over.

Cultured Kings
Kings took responsibility for public and private affairs, sponsoring gutters, water tanks and taps, resthouses, and temples, and providing endowments of land to fund their perpetual maintenance. They took care of entertainment too, with royal proclamations initiating or restarting many festivals, including Gai Jatra, Bisket Jatra, and the chariot ride of the Kumari, the young girl who serves as a living embodiment of the goddess Durga. Wealthy nobles performed extravagant sacrifices like the *kotyhoma,* the "ten million burnt oblations" of ghee, grain, and yoghurt carried on day and night for six weeks. Only the very wealthiest could perform the *tuladana* or "scale gift" in which a donor had himself publicly weighed against a heap of gold and gems and offered the entire mound to a deity, or more likely the proxy of the gods, the Brahmans.

Malla court life was a sophisticated affair. Nobles and kings divided their time between fighting, worship, and dabbling in dance, drama, poetry, and music. Patan's King Narendra proclaimed himself on coins as "one who has crossed the ocean of music"; King Pratapa Malla of Kathmandu chose the title *Kavindra,* "King of Poets." His ambition culminated with a prayer to Kali he composed one day in 1654 and had inscribed on stone in 15 different languages—all of which he had supposedly studied. The inscription, embedded in the wall of the Kathmandu palace, is a gobbledygook of fragments, including *l'Hiver* and *l'Otomn,* possibly contributed by a pair of Jesuit missionaries who briefly settled in the Valley during Pratapa Malla's reign. The first Westerners to set foot

Boudhanath Stupa (Kerry Moran)

(top) Everest (Kerry Moran);
(bottom) Annapurna peak near Ghandruk (Christopher Gamm)

in the Valley, they brought with them a telescope and several mathematical instruments which thrilled the king so much he extracted a promise from them to speedily return. By the time they could, though, the Malla reign had ended.

The Mallas' Downfall

The splendor of their kingdoms could not hide the fact the Mallas were quarrelsome and suspicious rulers who broke treaties as soon as it became convenient. The Three Kingdoms era is a series of shifting alliances: one week Kathmandu and Patan would unite against Bhaktapur, then Patan and Bhaktapur would be against Kathmandu. A few months later the three cities would be proclaimed friends, then the whole round would begin again. Quarrels often centered around the lucrative trade route to Tibet; ironically, the constant fighting eventually drove the caravans to other, more peaceful, routes.

UNIFICATION OF NEPAL

While the Mallas were busy alternately beautifying and fighting over the Valley, Hindu princes and local chiefs had carved western Nepal into a number of fiefdoms and petty states. One of the most important was the Shah Dynasty of Gorkha, a hilltop fortress-town midway between Pokhara and Kathmandu. The Shah kings were bold and powerful, none more so than Prithvi Narayan Shah (1723-1775). The first time he stood atop the Chandragiri Pass and viewed the cities of the Valley spread out below, he set his heart on their conquest. His wish took 26 years of planning, sieges, and battles to come true, but Prithvi Narayan had the tenacity, vision, and skill to do it.

He began by seizing the town of Nuwakot in 1744, thus gaining control of the profitable Tibetan trade route and the northern approach to the Valley. The Gorkhas slowly encircled the entire Valley, building forts on the mountaintops and winning disgruntled nobles and chieftans over to their side. By the time the Valley's kings realized the threat and dropped their quarrels to unite against their common enemy, it was too late.

Next the Gorkhas attacked Kirtipur, a hilltop city in the southeast of the Valley. The city was virtually impregnable, and its Newar defenders withstood two sieges before they succumbed to a third attempt in in 1766. In retaliation for the death of his brother who had been killed in an earlier siege, Prithvi Narayan ordered the nose of every Kirtipur male over the age of 12 be cut off—a humiliating punishment also used for adulterous women. The chronicles record that 865 men were thus mutilated, and that the cut noses filled several baskets and weighed about 80 pounds. Only the players of wind instruments were spared to serve as musicians for the conquering army.

With a firm foothold in the Valley it didn't take long for the Gorkhas to mop up the remainder. Opposition was weak in any case. The king of Kathmandu raided the treasury of Pashupatinath to pay his mercenary troops and begged the British East Indian Company for military assistance, but the poorly organized English expeditionary force was practically wiped out by the Gorkhas before they ever reached the Valley.

King Prithvi Narayan Shah

Gorkha troops entered Kathmandu in September 1768, in the midst of the boisterous celebration of Indra Jatra when most of the town was drunk. That night was the occasion for the king to receive ritual *tika* (an auspicious mark on the forehead) from the Kumari, validating his rule for the coming year. The Shah conqueror seated himself on the royal throne and accepted tika from the virgin goddess as Kathmandu's last Malla king fled to Patan. Patan fell without a struggle a few days later and the recently deposed rulers took refuge in Bhaktapur. The three Malla kings huddled together for over a year, united at last in their downfall. When Gorkha troops finally assaulted the city it fell easily into their hands, and thus the era of the Three Kingdoms ended.

The Anglo-Nepal War

Prithvi Narayan Shah died only seven years after his conquest. His successors continued to use the fine-tuned Gurkha war machine, relentlessly annexing new territory, but none equaled its ruthless brilliance. By 1814 Nepal had expanded to nearly twice its present size, stretching from Kumaon/Garwahl in the west to Sikkim in the east. Its bold incursions into Indian territory exasperated the British East India Company, and in 1814 war was declared, which Nepal lost after some hard fighting. The 1816 Treaty of Segouli forced Nepal to relinquish much of its newly acquired domain and fixed the country's eastern and western borders at their present location on the Mahakali and Mecchi rivers.

The most painful concession for Nepal was to admit a British Resident observer to Kathmandu. Other points the British were willing to negotiate, but they were adamant that Nepal "must take either the Resident or war." Forced to concede, the Nepalese government settled the unwanted Englishman in the worst piece of land in the Valley, a tract rumored to be ghost-infested and malarial. Then it steadfastly ignored him. Forbidden to venture beyond the Valley, bereft of duties save for a once-a-year meeting, the Residents were left to putter in their gardens and record observations on Nepalese life that today provide a window on the past.

The 1816 treaty also required that Nepal's contact with Western nations be made through Britain, making it in a sense a political dependent of the Raj. But Nepal was never colonized or directly ruled by outsiders, a fact still cited with pride.

After Segouli, Nepal withdrew into seclusion, closing its borders to all foreigners except Indians. The power amassed by Prithvi Narayan Shah was usurped by noblemen and regents who ruled in the stead of his descendents. From 1799-1951 the Shah kings were deliberately kept in the background as semi-revered but powerless figureheads. The intrigue and plotting of court life was brutal. From 1769-1846, not one of Nepal's prime ministers died a natural death; all were either assassinated or forced into suicide. Writing in the 1850s, Laurence Oliphant summarized the era's politics: "The power of the Prime Minister is absolute until he is shot, when it becomes unnecessary to question the expediency of his measures. . . . The ability to gain office is not talent so much as his ability in taking aim and his skill in seizing any opportunity offered by his rival of showing his dexterity in a manner more personal than pleasant."

THE RANA ERA

The Kot Massacre

In 1844 a new player appeared on the tumultous political scene, an ambitious young soldier named Jung Bahadur Kunwar. Ingratiating himself with an influential queen, he rose to power through a series of increasingly bloody intrigues. The final coup came on 15 September 1846. The queen's main supporter and rumored lover, the military commander-in-chief, was murdered late at night. Distraught, the Queen summoned an immediate assembly of ministers and state officials to the state assembly hall (Kot) to find the murderer. What happened next is uncertain, but during the course of the stormy discussion which ensued Jung's soldiers attacked the unarmed officials. Within a few minutes, dozens of Nepal's nobles and over a hundred lower-ranking officials were dead, and the gutters of the Kot ran red with blood.

The Kot Massacre left Jung Bahadur the most powerful man in Nepal. He rapidly consolidated his hold by exiling the queen, deposing the king, and keeping the young heir apparent powerless. Changing his family name to the more prestigious Rana and adopting the title of Ma-

JUNG BAHADUR IN ENGLAND

As soon as he had squelched all opposition and was confident his rule was secure, Jung Bahadur turned the government of Nepal over to a few of his more trusted brothers and in 1850 sailed off to visit England and Queen Victoria. It was a courageous act for a high-caste Hindu of the time. Anyone who dared to cross the great "Black Water" to Europe and take food and drink from the hands of foreigners was threatened with automatic loss of caste. But Jung Bahadur had an intense desire to see the powerful English in their own land, and he defied the warnings of the Brahman priests to become the first Hindu ruler to visit Europe.

The account of a member of his retinue, juxtaposed with British newspaper reports of his visit, makes interesting reading. The British were impressed by their foreign guest's "strange and gorgeous" attire; he was impressed with their coal mines, horse races, and ballerinas. Newspaper reports devoted columns to describing the "Nepaulese" prime minister's magnificent costumes of embroidered satin, gold, diamonds, and jewels—the epitome of an Oriental potentate. The Nepali men were overwhelmed by the beautiful, fair-skinned young women who mingled freely with them at gatherings, and the women in their turn took the young and dashing Jung Bahadur to heart, though they probably would not have been nearly so thrilled had they been aware of his bloody past. Jung Bahadur was all the rage of London for a season. He visited Paris as well before returning to Kathmandu a little over a year after his departure.

The journey abroad evidently made a profound impact on him. Upon his return he revised Nepal's punitive criminal code, restricted capital punishment, and tried to discourage the deep-rooted custom of *sati,* which demanded that a good high-caste wife lay herself on her husband's funeral pyre. Along with social changes came fashion fads. Nepali noblewomen stuffed their buxom figures into corsets, curled their hair into fat sausages, and draped their saris over bustles. The Ranas built columned, neoclassical palaces and furnished them with crystal chandeliers and mirrors to rival Versailles. Jung Bahadur started the trend with his now vanished palace at Thapathali, where four rooms held a permanent display of English bric-a-brac.

haraja ("King") as opposed to the Shah ruler, who was Maharajdhiraj, ("King of Kings"), he founded the Rana Dynasty, a succession of hereditary prime minsters who would rule Nepal for the next century.

The Shah kings remained on the throne as powerless rulers, pampered figureheads who were indulged (some said debauched), closely guarded, and kept from sight. "One may live for years in Nepal without either seeing or hearing of the king," noted a 19th-century Englishman. It was easy enough for the Ranas to explain that the king, an incarnation of the god Vishnu, was too holy to deal in affairs of state.

Jung Bahadur secured his power further by arranging marriages between members of his family and the upper classes—everyone from the king down to the lowest officials. With over 100 children by his five wives and numerous concubines, he had plenty of opportunities to develop connections. Intermarriage between the Shahs and the Ranas continued through each generation to the present day. The present queen of Nepal is a Rana and her two younger sisters are married to the King's two younger brothers.

"Ranocracy"

Succession within the Rana regime was passed onto the eldest living male of the family, be he cousin, nephew, brother, or son of the former prime minister. Just *who* qualified as next in succession became such a problem for the prolific Ranas that in the 1920s an "A-B-C" classification method was established to rank descendents according to the caste and status of their mothers. A-Class Ranas, born of primary wives, got the most perks, the highest military posts, and the right to rule the country. B-Class Ranas got the perks, but couldn't be king. C-Class Ranas were the numerous offspring of concubines and unofficial wives. Inevitably the inequity between them and A-Class Ranas led to dissent and contributed to the system's eventual demise.

The Rana regime was the ultimate autocracy—some call it "Ranocracy." The rulers did not oppress their subjects as much as ignore them. Nepal remained in a virtually medieval state well into the 1950s, with no public medical care, transportation, or education. The one Rana prime minister liberal enough to suggest public

Rana royal family

GANESH PHOTO LAB

schooling was booted out of office by his brothers. A few grudging changes were made in the status quo during the Rana years. Slavery, an institution involving one percent of the population, was finally abolished in 1926, and the custom of *sati* or widow-burning, discouraged by Jung Bahadur, was officially made illegal in 1920.

The country was in essence the Ranas' private estate. The entire national revenue of Nepal was at their personal disposal with no need to account for how they spent it. Appropriating vast plots of land from farms and temple endowments, they built huge European-inspired neoclassical palaces. The Rana prime minister-cum-maharaja dwelt in Singha Durbar, reportedly the largest private residence in Asia. Its grounds were fully half the area of the city of Kathmandu; its white stuccoed wings contained anywhere from 1,000 to 1,800 rooms, up to 500 of them occupied by concubines. A British visitor in the 1920s described a ground-floor salon:

The walls were almost entirely covered with bad but realistic frescoes, all of them depicting past rulers engaged, in various situations calling for personal bravery, in the sport of big-game hunting, for which the Terai is still world-famous. The floor was covered in tiger-skins, so that it was necessary to walk with circumspection lest one tripped over their gaping mouths.

Stuffed animals, rhinoceros, tigers, buck of every description, were ranged along the walls, giving the room the appearance of a natural history museum.

Another visitor noted: "You passed through hall after hall, every one of them as big as a parade ground, glittering with marble and crystal and showy furniture which made anyone with good taste feel quite seasick."

The palaces were overflowing with Victorian bric-a-brac: plush upholstery, bronze statues, crystal chandeliers, and Carrera marble pillars, all carried into the Valley by barefoot porters. Roads were another modernity sternly opposed by a government bent on isolating itself from the outside world. There were a few short, bumpy tracks within the Valley, used by the aristocracy for brief spins in their Rolls Royces. Even automobiles were carried over the hills by porters. The wheels were removed and the cars were lashed to bamboo racks, carried by relays of up to 60 men. Moving at about one km per hour, they took a month to haul their burden to Kathmandu.

Prithvi Narayan Shah's famous maxim, "First the Bible, then the trading stations, then the cannon," was taken to heart by the Ranas. The few foreign guests invited were restricted to hunting big game in the Terai. Rarely were they permitted to enter the Kathmandu Valley, much less venture beyond it. Even Nepalis needed a permit to leave the Valley. The result was as late as 1948, Nepal was the largest inhabited country unexplored by Europeans. Ancient traditions, beliefs, and customs, some over 1,000 years old, were preserved in a vital, living culture that endured nearly untouched into the '50s. The last 40 years have brought tremendous changes to Nepal, and in 40 more years only traces of the past will exist. Like buried artifacts which crumble when exposed to light and air, ancient cultural patterns are vanishing in the face of modern times.

REVOLUTION OR RESTORATION

The changes which swept the globe in the years following WW II came even to Nepal. After India won independence in 1947, Nepalese participants formed the Nepali National Congress Party. Joined by a group of young dissident Ranas and supported by the new Indian government, the opposition challenged Rana rule, uniting behind the long ignored king of Nepal as a symbol of promised freedom.

Heartened by the support, King Tribhuvan made a dramatic break for freedom in Nov. 1950. He and his family had set off on a routine leopard-hunting excursion to Nagarjun forest, but unknown to the guards, the picnic baskets were stuffed with the Shah family jewels. The king, driving the lead car, suddenly swerved into the grounds of the Indian Embassy. Before his guards caught up, he was granted asylum by a waiting Indian officer. In a prearranged plan the royal family was whisked to New Delhi as Nepali Congress forces attacked Nepal from India. The fighting ended in a stalemate by Jan. 1951,

when a compromise settlement installed a coalition government. Free elections, the country's first, were promised by 1952.

King Tribhuvan returned to a hero's welcome in Kathmandu on 16 Feb. 1951. The divided coalition government soon crumbled and the king called on the Nepali Congress to form an interim one. Those early years were chaotic, but the divisiveness worked in the king's favor. The crisis continued after Tribhuvan died in Switzerland in 1955 and his eldest son Mahendra was crowned king.

The opposite of his quiet, withdrawn father, Mahendra was a vigorous, powerful ruler who liked direct contact with the people and wanted direct control of the government. Elections held in 1957 swept the Congress Party into power, but the fledgling democracy ended abruptly on 15 Dec. 1959, as King Mahendra declared a state of emergency. Potitical turmoil had paralyzed the government, he announced, and indeed he had a point—since the 1951 revolution, Nepal had been through 10 different governments. The king dissolved the parliament, dismissed the government, and arrested leading politicans on charges of bribery and corruption. All political parties and activities were outlawed. In their place Mahendra announced a new constitution investing the king with extensive powers.

Mahendra died in 1972 and was succeeded by his son Birendra, the present King of Nepal, who inherited the political framework introduced by his father. The partyless panchayat system was a contradiction from the start, claiming to be both partyless and democratic. *Panchayat* means "Assembly of Five," and the concept was supposedly modeled on traditional village councils of elders, of minor significance in most areas. The system ran through indirect elections. Voters elected members to a local-level assembly, and these officials chose representatives for the village or town panchayat, who in turn selected district panchayat officials. Until a 1980 constitutional amendment established direct election of most members of the National Panchayat, national officials were also chosen indirectly.

Through the 1980s hundreds of dissident students, activists, and journalists were arrested under a vague Public Security Act permitting imprisonment for up to three years without charges or trial. The 1951 revolution with its

THE FIGHTING GURKHAS

Nepal's best-known export is the Gurkha soldier. In over 140 years of fighting these fierce hillmen have earned a reputation as the world's finest infantrymen. Contrary to popular belief, the Gurkhas are not a race or tribe. The term is derived from Prithvi Narayan Shah's old capital of Gorkha in central Nepal. The Gorkha army that conquered the Kathmandu Valley was composed of Magar and Gurung soldiers, and these two ethnic groups, plus Rai and Limbu from eastern Nepal and a few Chhetris, dominate the British and Indian Gurkhas today. All are hardy hillmen, instinctive survivors, and the determination, independence, and resourcefulness bred by the Hills are put to good use on the battlefield. The Gurkhas' good humor and loyalty are legendary; so is their bravery and their skill with the wickedly curved Nepali knife, the khukri. In the 1982 Falkland Islands encounter, Argentine forces supposedly fled at the news the Gurkhas were approaching, adding another chapter to the legend.

The British first encountered Nepali soldiers in the 1814-16 Anglo-Nepalese conflict. Though the British won the war, they were deeply impressed by the bravery of their opponents, and even built a memorial at the site of a famous battle as a tribute of respect to the commander of the fort, "our gallant adversary . . . and his brave Gurkhas." Officers lost no time in recommending Nepalis be drafted into British forces at the first opportunity.

The relationship between Britain and Nepal was cemented when Jung Bahadur Rana sent 12,000 of his soldiers to aid Queen Victoria during the Indian Mutiny of 1857. After Nepali forces helped put down the rebellion, a grateful Britain returned a large portion of the Terai lands taken by the 1816 Treaty of Segouli. The Gurkha soldiers paid the British troops the highest compliment when they said "The English fought almost as well as the Gurkha."

British military literature of the period is full of pithy comments about the Gurkhas. A British major-general described them in 1893: ". . . the Gurkhas of Nepal, a small diminutive race of men not unlike the Huns, but certainly as brave as any man can possibly be. A Gurkha thought himself equal to any four other men of the hills. . . .

The other men of the hills began to think that he really was so, and could not stand before him."

The Gurkhas were formally incorporated in the Indian army in 1850; formal British recruitment began in 1886. As Nepal was closed to outsiders, an enlistment camp was set up in Darjeeling; later, recruiting centers were established near Pokhara and in Dharan in eastern Nepal (the latter was recently closed). Positions have always been coveted, but Britain's recent plans to halve its Gurkha regiments has intensified competition even further. The job brings social status, the chance to see the world and prove one's bravery, plus a generous salary and pension. For decades until it was replaced by foreign aid and tourism, Nepal's largest source of foreign currency was Gurkha remittances from abroad.

Upon retirement, Gurkha soldiers usually return to their village and live on a comfortable pension. Some become schoolteachers or political leaders or open teashops and trekking lodges. The Hills are full of retired soldiers who like to reminisce, some in excellent English, about all they've seen and done. In the hills around Pokhara I met a Gurkha who was still laughing at the ironies of fate. "Thirty years ago in the jungles of Burma we were cutting off the heads of Japanese soldiers," he said. "Now here I am serving tea to Japanese tourists!"

Over 300,000 Gurkhas fought in World Wars I and II and were highly decorated for bravery. After Indian independence in 1947, Gurkha regiments were divided between the Indian Gurkha Rifles and British Brigade of Gurkhas. Their impressive list of battle honors covers most of the major sites of action in a century of fighting. Their courage, strength, and loyalty form the basis of many legends. There was the hardheaded Gurkha who deflected a bullet which then killed a British officer on the ricochet, and the Gurkha POW who found his way through a thousand kilometers of Burmese forest aided by a wrinkled, stained map—of the London subway. Then there was the Gurkha regiment that was asked for volunteers to jump from planes behind enemy lines. Half the regiment stepped forward on the first request; the other half joined after it was explained they would be jumping *with* parachutes.

Gurkha soldier with his symbol, a pair of crossed khukri

BOB RACE

hopes for democracy had seemingly ended in a restoration of autocratic rule, exchanging the Ranas for the Shahs.

DISSENT AND DEMOCRACY

In April 1979, popular dissatisfaction with corruption, inflation, and shortages of goods erupted into demonstrations across the kingdom. To defuse the situation King Birendra announced a national referendum would be held the following year on whether to keep the panchayat system or change to a multiparty government. The government mounted a vigorous pro-panchayat campaign, while the opposition fragmented into factions. The panchayat system won 54% of the May 1980 vote, a victory taken as confirmation of the status quo.

Even before the referendum, the king had amended the constitution to open most seats in the National Panchayat to direct election. Still, the National Panchayat remained an ineffective rubber-stamp assembly with little real power. One-fifth of its members were named directly by the king, and all representatives had to swear loyalty to the king, the royal family, and the principle of partyless politics. The real holder of power was clearly defined in the 1962 constitution, which stated: "The sovereignity of Nepal is vested in His Majesty. . . . All powers, executive, legislative, and judicial, emanate from him."

Latent dissatisfaction continued to grow in urban areas. The situation came to a head with a 1989 trade embargo India slapped on landlocked Nepal. In theory the dispute involved an expired trade and transit treaty between the two countries; in fact, a major aggravation was a weapons purchase Nepal had made from China. In retaliation, India closed 13 of the 15 routes crossing Nepal's southern border and halted shipment of fuel. Traffic in Kathmandu vanished, petrol and kerosene were rationed, and people waited in lines for hours for their supply of cooking fuel, or reverted to cooking over wood fires. The fuel blockade lasted nine months, until Rajiv Gandhi's government lost the Nov. 1989 elections and the new Indian government lifted the ban as a signal of goodwill.

On 18 Feb. 1990, the 40th anniversary of King Tribhuvan's declaration of a multiparty democracy, Nepal's outlawed political parties announced a campaign to restore the multiparty system. The Nepali Congress and a left-wing coalition of Nepal Communist Party factions joined in a movement led by respected Congress Party leader Ganesh Man Singh. Demonstrations and rallies spread across the country, swelling as people joined in to protest police shootings of demonstrators. By early April the movement reached a crescendo in the Valley, as normally apolitical professionals, peasants, even women and children joined the protests.

On 6 April a huge crowd of over 200,000 rallied at Kathmandu's central Tundikhel. Joined by processions from Bhaktapur, Patan and Kirtipur, demonstrators marched towards the Royal Palace in late afternoon, shouting "Death to the panchayat system," and "Long live democracy." Police stationed on Durbar Marg tried to stop them with tear gas; when that failed, they fired into the crowd. The official government death toll was ten; eyewitness accounts estimated 200 to 300 people were killed. The bloodiest violence recorded in modern Nepal shocked the country and provoked major changes. A few days later King Birendra bowed to demands for democracy and lifted the ban on political parties; the following month he dissolved the panchayat system. An interim government headed by Congress Party leader K.P. Bhatterai was formed to govern the country until free elections could be held, and an independent commission was formed to rewrite Nepal's constitution in a more democratic mold.

GOVERNMENT

The victory of the 1990 "Movement to Restore Democracy" threw Nepal into a state of flux from which it's still emerging. Thirty years of the partyless panchayat system, preceded by centuries of autocratic rule, doesn't provide much of a foundation for democracy, but democracy is what people want. Exactly what's meant by the term is unclear. Just as the panchayat system has become the scapegoat for every evil, "democracy" is the codeword for good. It can be used to advocate freedom of speech or a half-day off from school for protesting students.

Nepal's fledgling democracy faces serious challenges, among them a horrendously low standard of living, a feeble economy, governmental corruption, and a burgeoning population with growing expectations. Beset with its own problems, the government is not yet able to effectively address development. People (especially urbanites) look to the new government to increase their standard of living, and will be dissatisfied if improvements don't come soon. Such sentiments helped sweep the old system out of power and remain among the new government's biggest challenges.

The Constitution
One positive result of the *jana andolan* or "People's Movement" was the promulgation within the year of a new constitution, which, though it doesn't please everybody, does invest sovereignty in the Nepalese people. The document includes a carefully worded description of Nepal as "a multiethnic, multilingual, democratic, independent, indivisible, sovereign, Hindu, and Constitutional Monarchical Kingdom." (The "Hindu Kingdom" business was retained despite the protests of non-Hindus.) The king remains as a constitutional monarch and a symbol of Nepalese unity. He and a Council of Ministers form the executive branch; the legislative branch is composed of a 205-member House of Representatives (directly elected), and a smaller National Council. How this system will work out in practice still remains to be seen.

Political Parties
Twenty parties vied in the May 1991 general elections, most of them tiny communist splinter groups struggling to get a piece of the pie. Elections in a country with a 35% literacy rate take on a strange twist. Each party is assigned a symbol—fish, umbrella, glass, plough—easily recognized by illiterate voters. This leads to cryptic campaign slogans like "Vote for Fish" or "Be as Rocket, Vote For Bucket." spray-painted on every wall and building around election time.

The election results shook up the status quo. The old standby "Tree" (the Nepali Congress Party, which complacently predicted a repeat of its sweep of the 1958 democratic elections) was closely followed by "Sun," the Nepal Communist Party (United Marxist Leninist). Among other victories the NCP swept four of Kathmandu's five districts, unseating Congress leader and then-Prime Minister Krishna Prasad Bhatterai. Congress gained 106 seats, forming a simple majority in the House of Representatives, but the NCP and a half-dozen smaller parties, mostly communist factions, promise to create lively opposition.

The communists maintain they're the party of the oppressed and poor (a sizable portion of Nepal's population), and promise social justice and a decent standard of living for all. Meanwhile, Congress portrays itself as *the* democratic alternative, appealing to conservative and middle-of-the-road voters. Most of the small parties formed by old panchas to pull in the conservative votes were soundly trounced at the polls, though a few old politicos remain on the scene.

Sooner or later, all these diverse factions must overcome their mutual dislike to work together, but past history in this respect is not encouraging. Nepal's previous brief fling with democracy was marred by partisan politics, providing the perfect excuse for King Mahendra to step in and assume direct rule.

Government Issues
Inefficiency, widespread corruption, and general public distrust are among the biggest problems facing the new government; cleaning its own house will be a major task. The civil service is a sluggish bureaucratic mire, staffed by low-paid workers who find the best policy is to do as little as possible. Initiative isn't rewarded; in fact it's generally discouraged as a threat to higher-ups. What counts is *soras phoras* (higher-up connections) and obeisance to bosses and important people. Criticism is taboo and loyalty and nepotism are valued over energy and talent. Chronically low salaries and a long tradition of bribery have practically institutionalized corruption. One fundamental flaw is that politics is not regarded as social service, but a means of personal advancement. There are of course honest and intelligent government officials, but they

find themselves stymied at every turn. It's now fashionable to blame all these problems on the panchayat system. Whether this is true, or these problems are more deeply rooted, is perhaps the biggest question facing the new government.

The Royal Family

King Birendra is the 10th in the succession of Shah kings. His full title is "Shri Panch Maharajdiraj Birendra Bir Bikram Shah Dev." There is an intricate system regarding the honorific prefix *shri*. Ordinary respectable gentlemen have a single shri preceding their name, the equivalent of the English mister. Members of the royal family are *shri teen*, "three shri", while the king is *shri panch*, "five-times shri." This is as high as the scale goes for humans, though deities like Gorakanath may be honored by 108 shris.

Born in 1945, the king studied four years at Eton and a year at Harvard, though he didn't receive a degree at either. He ascended the throne in 1972 after the death of his father, and was officially coronated in 1975 (the delay was due to astrological reasons). The king's status as an emanation of Visnhu has waned in Kathmandu, but many rural people remain in awe of their ruler.

In 1970, then Crown Prince Birendra married Aishwarya Rajya Laxmi Devi Rana, the daughter of Lt. General Kendra Shamsher J.B. Rana, the man who would effectively have run Nepal had the Rana domination continued. In a simultaneous ceremony the bride's two sisters married the groom's younger brothers, continuing a long tradition of intermarriage between the Ranas and Shahs. The royal couple have three children; the eldest, Crown Prince Dipen-dra, was born in 1971. The queen, her relatives, and the king's relatives held a considerable amount of behind-the-scenes power before the 1990 uprising, though things seem to have toned down a bit since then. The royal family and the intrigues surrounding them generate an endless supply of wild rumors for the public mill; keep your ears open for the latest.

International Relations

Foreign policy is based on nonalignment, a prudent course for a tiny buffer state between India and China. On his coronation day, King Birendra made an official proposal that Nepal be declared an international "Zone of Peace." So far this has been accepted by 87 countries, but China and India are not among them, and probably never will be. Despite the Zone of Peace rhetoric, Nepal has a large and well-trained standing army. Relations with China are relatively formal, with Nepali government generally careful not to do anything (like allow the Dalai Lama to visit) which might ruffle Chinese feelings. Little Nepal is feistier in its relationship with India, which is frequently accused of trying to dominate Nepal or interfere with national politics. While India's "big brother" attitude is commonly resented, Nepal's deep economic dependence on the country remains undeniable.

Relations with other countries revolve around foreign aid. King Mahendra was particularly skilled at playing off one donor against another and reaping profits from both. This relationship cuts both ways now: as funding from foreign donors grows, their opinions and input becomes increasingly important to Nepal's new government.

ECONOMY

Stastistically Nepal ranks among the world's poorest countries. The average per-capita income is US$160 a year, and over 40% of the population earns less than that. But the calculation of cash income doesn't take into account the large non-monetized percentage of the national economy running on trade and barter. Most Nepalis are subsistence farmers. They manage to grow enough to feed their families and sell a small surplus, which buys a few necessities like salt, tea, and cloth.

Nepal's economy was not really born until it opened to the outside world in 1951. Rana rule had kept the country secluded from everything outside, including trade, industry, and roads. Economists called in to examine the situation labelled Nepal's Rana-era economy "pre-feudal."

*farmer ploughing field
for rice planting*

KERRY MORAN

Despite 40 years of effort and huge infusions of foreign aid, economic development has been slow and spotty, in part because of natural challenges. Geography has dealt Nepal a hard hand. Landlocked, with the nearest seaport Calcutta, 500 km away, it must rely on India for all imports and exports aside from what trickles down from China via Tibet. Nepal's economic vulnerability became painfully clear during the 1989 trade and transit treaty dispute, when India clamped an economic blockade on Nepal, halting passage of petroleum products for six months and bringing industry and transportation to a near standstill. Marketable natural resources are scanty. Mineral and metal deposits exist, but access and shipping difficulties make them too expensive to extract. Nepal's greatest asset is its tremendous hydropower potential, as yet largely untapped.

AGRICULTURE

Nepali life is based on farming. Agriculture supports over 90% of the population and contributes 55% of national production, one of the world's highest rates. The fact that a land which is roughly four-fifths nonarable still manages to support so many people is tribute to the skill and tenacity of its farmers. Massive hillsides are layered top to bottom with terraced fields, patiently carved out over the centuries with simple hand tools. Nepal has over 450,000 hectares of terraces, one of the highest densities in the

world. It has to be like this. In some overpopulated areas, each cultivatable hectare must support 12-18 people, a figure rivaling the fertile, lush delta regions of India and Bangladesh.

Crops

Rice *(dhan)* is the favorite lowland crop, grown in irrigated fields up to 2,000 metres. Maize *(makai),* introduced from the New World in the early 19th century, is planted in unirrigated fields up to 2,400 meters; wheat *(gau)* is popular in the dry winter season. Between 1,900-2,400 meters farmers plant millet *(kodo),* barley *(jau),* and potatoes *(alu).* Indian rapeseed *(tori)* is cultivated in lower regions for the oil pressed from its seeds, used for cooking and oil lamps.

The fertile, flat Terai contains 70% of Nepal's arable land and produces over half its grain, but lack of transportation means that much of the surplus is sold in India. Meanwhile, many families in the western mountains and the Hills are chronically short of food, producing enough for only six or seven months of the year. To survive the lean period, male members or entire families may migrate into the Terai and India in search of temporary labor. Shrinking farmland and growing families have forced many Nepalis to permanently emigrate in search of work. Most go to India, where they work as laborers or night watchmen and send back a portion of their salaries to support their families and farms.

Land Reform

Under the Rana regime portions of Nepal suffered under one of Southeast Asia's worst land tenure systems. Terai landlords commonly extracted rents of up to 80% of the annual crop from their tenants. Families found it impossible to survive on the remaining 20% of their harvest and were forced to borrow money from the landlord, who doubled as the local moneylender. A vicious cycle of debt began, for interest could be as high as 100%, compounded annually.

The Land Act of 1964 abolished the *zamindar* system of ownership, fixed rents at 50% of production, and restricted the amount of land a single family could control. But the reform failed due to lax enforcement and redistribution. Though tenancy rates have dropped and most of today's farmers are independent, their plots are tiny. By one estimate, the bottom 50% of the population owns only seven percent of the land, while the top nine percent of the population controls nearly half the total.

TRADE

Domestic Trade

Nepal's rural economy is dictated by season. The monsoon is the time for planting and herding, when high rivers and slippery trails make travel unpleasant or impossible. The dry season, Oct.-May, is the travel and trade season, when millions of Nepalis hit the trails. Bhotia head down to the Hills with Tibetan salt and wool to exchange for grain; in the summer they will cross over snow-free mountain passes into Tibet and begin the cycle again. Hillmen trek into India and the markets of the Terai on an annual shopping trip, perhaps carrying homemade ghee or bamboo matting to sell for a small profit.

Landlocked Nepal's need for salt spawned an ancient trans-Himalayan trading system. Hillmen would commonly walk two to four weeks north into the mountains to pick up their annual supply of salt, bartering grain for it in a set measure that fluctuated yearly. Strategically located Bhotia peoples like the Sherpas and Thakalis acted as middlemen in the lucrative trade, obtaining salt from Tibetans and grain from Nepalis and exchanging them at a profitable rate. Long caravans of yaks, mules, even goats and sheep carried bags of the precious salt down narrow trails, the type of pack animal changing with the region.

PORTERS

The backbone of Nepal's internal economy and transport system, porters haul whatever needs to be moved—rice and cigarettes for a shopkeeper, wooden beams and tin roofing for a new building, tables and chairs for a trekking group, tinned food for a mountaineering expedition, cases of Coca-Cola for a tourist lodge. Just about anything can be carried in a porter's doko or bamboo basket, including a sick relative who needs to visit a hospital.

Loads are carried with a *namlo,* a jute headband worn over the top of the head. This arrangement evenly distributes weight along the spine, using the weight of the head to support the load with minimal muscular strain and maximum leverage for legs—in terms of engineering principles, a far better arrangement than a backpack. A five-foot-tall hillman can carry well over twice his weight all day with hardly a pause, and loads up to 100 kilograms are common. A porter's only other equipment is the *teko,* a short, T-shaped wooden stick that provides balance on slippery slopes and serves as a load support when there's no resting place. Many porters don't even have shoes, just quarter-inch-thick calluses built up on their feet.

Subsistence farmers turn to portering in the slow winter season to earn extra money. Other porters are landless laborers, doing the only work they can find. Portering is a hard life. Most of the daily salary (current average Rs60) goes for food. No medical studies have been done on the physical effects of long-term portering, but the wear and tear of carrying 50-85 kilogram loads up and down steep hills must be incredible. A porter's movements are a study in strength, agility, and energy conservation. He climbs uphill with a steady stride, seldom pausing for breath. Resting briefly at the top and steadying his load on the wooden teko, he then heads downhill, the hardest part, with quick short steps. There is little breath left to spare for talking on the trail, and communication is mostly through long, breathy whistles. At mealtimes porters leave their loads by the trail to cook their dhiro or mix up their sattu and relax for an hour or two.

The 1959 closure of the Nepal-Tibet frontier halted this vital trade. Later the border was reopened, but by then people had shifted to using Indian salt, made widely available with the development of a southern road network. Today the old system lingers in a few remote areas, but many of the traders (notably the Sherpas) have turned their business acumen to modern jobs like guiding trekking.

Industry And Foreign Trade

Nepal's industry is minimal, employing less than one percent of the population and producing less than 14% of the GNP, one of the world's lowest rates. The Tibetan carpet industry brings in US$60 million a year, over half the total of national foreign exchange earnings. It's also possibly the largest industrial employer, with over 200,000 workers. Other establishments include oil and grain processing mills, jute processing factories, and factories for textiles, building materials, soap, matches, cigarettes and liquor. Industry is concentrated in the Kathmandu Valley and in Terai towns like Biratnagar and Birgunj, with ready access to Indian markets and supplies. About one-third of Nepal's exports (mainly livestock, jute, and food products) go to India and thus don't generate desperately needed hard currency.

The import list is long: Nepal needs petroleum products, machinery, construction and industrial materials, textiles, medicine, and nearly every kind of manufactured good. Through 1987, the value of imports was three times greater than that of exports, creating a huge trade deficit. The government attempts to control the outflow by placing heavy import duties on imported goods like TVs, computers, motorcycles, and cars.

Energy

Nepal has no known petroleum deposits, though some exploratory drilling is currently going on in the eastern Terai. Nearly 90% of the country's energy is supplied by wood, and the rising demand is rapidly depleting forests. The bright spot is Nepal's immense hydropower potential—an estimated 83 million megawatts, about a quarter of it economically feasible for development. Only a small fraction of it has been tapped so far.

Ironically, only four percent of the population has access to electricity, yet falling water is all around. A tremendous amount of water rushes down from the Himalayan heights, its power intensified by narrow gorges and monsoon rains which swell rivers up to 30 times in volume. Foreign aid has built several large dams, and even larger ones are being studied. The Karnali Project in the far western Hills, a US$4.7 billion monster currently under study, would be among the world's largest hydropower projects, producing enough electricity to equal the entire installed capacity of India. Nepal could potentially earn millions from selling electricity and irrigation water to India, but construction and environmental problems plus uncertainties with India make hydropower a less-than-perfect solution.

Development And Foreign Aid

For a tiny country Nepal draws an incredible amount of foreign aid. Up to 40% of the government's total budget is funded by outside assistance, the exact amount varying with the year. Generosity aside, political expediency plays a big part in this, and Nepal is well aware of the advantages of its precarious location between two giant countries. As a Nepali official described it: "We have struck political oil by our location between China and India; the result is a lasting flow of aid."

Foreign aid funds a portion of Nepal's regular budget, and up to 70% of the development budget (the amount varies yearly). Annual per capita foreign aid works out to nearly US$20 per Nepali, but little of it actually reaches the people it's meant to help. Part of the problem is with poorly designed programs developed by "experts" who fly in, spend a few weeks in the field (or more frequently, in Kathmandu), make their recommendations, and depart, without ever comprehending the situation. Much of the money is diverted into private bank accounts, or swallowed by the gigantic foreign-aid mechanisms themselves.

Nepal's development problems ("challenges" in the jargon of the trade) are daunting: a burgeoning population expected to double in 30 years; one of Asia's worst health situations; declining agricultural yields; a mortality rate of 20-50% for children up to age five; and a national literacy rate of only 35%. Attempts at developing a basically medieval and largely non-monetized economy began only in 1951, and have proceeded slowly due to Nepal's rugged geography and tremendous cultural diversity.

TOURISM

As late as 1948 Nepal remained the largest inhabited country still unexplored by Westerners. Only 224 had visited since a pair of Jesuits arrived in the Valley in 1664. The gates opened with 600 tourists in 1951, and things have rapidly changed since then. Now over 200,000 non-Indian tourists arrive yearly, and Indian tourists boost the figure by another 30 percent. The government has set a target of 500,000 foreign tourists for the year 2000.

Tourism is welcomed as an economic lifesaver for Nepal, an industry with an apparently sky-high potential for employment and foreign exchange. Currently it's the third largest source of foreign currency (after foreign aid and exports), providing at least 20% of its total foreign exchange receipts. But as in most Third World countries, at least half of the money received goes back out to pay for foreign goods and services demanded by tourists and unavailable in Nepal. The money that remains stays mainly in the Kathmandu Valley, and tourism jobs are restricted to service occupations like hotel and restaurant work, portering, and guiding.

Cultural Pollution

Rather than being a general economic panacea, tourism is proving to be a luxury export, contributing little to integrated national development. (It does, however, bring in the foreign currency.) Because tourism demands a relatively high ratio of capital to labor, it doesn't produce as many jobs as industrial development. Benefits are clustered in the Kathmandu Valley and along a few main trekking trails. Unfortunately (or fortunately, if you manage to get beyond these places) so are the damaging effects—the resulting inflation, environmental degradation, and above all, the "cultural pollution." About 200,000 temporarily unemployed pleasure-seeking consumers (a good working definition of tourists) pour into Kathmandu annually. With a roughly 2:1 ratio of Nepalis to tourists, disruptive effects are bound to occur.

Mass tourism involves the sale of a country, in which culture becomes an object and way of life an industry. Forty years of tourism, even on a relatively small scale, has already deeply affected Nepal. The negative results become more apparent every year. Behavior and values are rapidly changing, as traditional religious values are pushed aside by the new gods: VCRs, motorcycles, and Hong Kong/Bangkok fashions. Rambo and Madonna replace Rama and Sita as folk heroes; entertainment comes from violent/sexy videos instead of *bhajan* and festivals. The Valley's ancient traditional culture is still alive, but just barely. It's suffered a fatal blow in the last 30 years; in 30 more it will all be gone.

This is not just the fault of tourism, of course. Education, mass media, development, and urbanization all play a part in the drastic social upheaval. Modernization is an inescapable trend currently affecting nearly every traditional society on earth. Many of them have already sunk beneath the flood of seductive, powerful new influences. Tourism merely accelerates the rate of change, introducing clothing, behavior, and values quickly adopted as new (and therefore good) by the younger generation. Unfortunately the lifestyles it introduces are usually alien, unsuited to the place and time.

Ironically, tourists inevitably change the traditional life they've traveled so far to see. Their very presence advertises a world of unimaginable wealth, reinforced by their expensive clothes, cameras and outdoor gear. Their constant quest for pleasure and recreation is understandable—after all, they're on vacation—but it gives an unrealistic impression of the West as a place where everyone is rich and no one needs to work. Nearly every young Nepali you meet wants to go to the West (preferably America), but few can cite a reason beyond "it's a rich country." For 40 years now Nepal has been told it's a poor country, and this attitude is starting to erode strong national pride. It's only one step from it to a hands-out mentality, typified by begging children who line the trails in touristed areas and are rarely seen off the beaten track.

Tourists support indigenous arts and crafts, but because they're ignorant of traditional styles they unwittingly encourage shoddy imitations. Art loses its authenticity when it loses its connection with life, as is happening in Nepal.

Nepal's 20,000 junkies are an unpleasant fruit of tourism; marijuana and hashish were used moderately and widely, but heroin was unknown until foreigners started demanding it in the '60s.

Mutual Stereotypes

Tourism also hasn't solved the high unemployment rate among Nepali youth. Groups of denim-clad "punks" (that's what they're called in Nepali too) hang out waiting for Western girls who, even if they don't do everything they're shown doing in pornographic videos, are far more willing than their conservative Nepali sisters. In much of Asia the norm is Western men pursuing Asian women, but Nepal's strict sexual mores reverse the roles, and it's mainly Western women who end up pursuing or being pursued by Nepali men.

The saddest change is the slow erosion of the genuine hospitality and friendliness once found everywhere, replaced by a reserved welcome, stereotypes, or a "what-can-I-get-out-of-you" attitude. Nepalis have seen so many weird foreigners that their image of them is understandably skewed. Summed up, they see a unpredictable, temperamental, and very wealthy people, prone to irrational generosity, but just as frequently irrationally cheap. The fallout is apparent along the most popular trekking trails, especially among proprietors of tourist lodges—sometimes the only Nepalis independent trekkers ever contact. They're still polite and friendly, and really the professional veneer is to be expected. Someone who's catered to 8,000 tourists in the past 12 years is not going to be excited about the 8,001st.

The reassuring part is that tourism hasn't penetrated into the rugged majority of Nepal, and probably never will. Transportation difficulties and meager accomodations will concentrate it around Kathmandu, Pokhara and the main trekking trails for years to come. If you get out of the standard tourist ruts, the Durbar Square-Mount Everest-Annapurna circuit, and into the small villages (even those of the Kathmandu Valley), you will find traditional society flourishing, though perhaps on the brink of extinction.

THE PEOPLE

INTRODUCTION

The Gorkha king Prithvi Narayan Shah called Nepal "a garden for all types of people." Its steep mountains and isolated valleys preserve a complex mixture of ethnic groups, castes, and tribes —exactly how many depends on how closely you look. The national census lists 17 different groups, a very general summary. Ethnologists variously estimate 36, 45, or 100 different groups, many of the smaller ones unknown even to most Nepalis.

This splendid variety is the result of centuries of intermingling between two main groups: Indo-Aryans from the south and west and Mongoloid peoples from the north, or put another way, Hindu rice-growers and Buddhist herders and barley farmers. These two distinct types remain in their purest forms along Nepal's northern and southern borders. In the middle of the country they've met and mixed, blurring the clear distinctions, so that many Mongolian Hill tribes are now Hindu.

Hindu caste groups tend to dwell in lowland settlements (up to 1,800 meters), growing rice in irrigated paddies. Ethnic villages are located on higher ridges, surrounded by fields of millet, corn, barley, and wheat. Constant trade and contact between the two assures that ideas as well as goods are exchanged.

Each culture has its own typical houses, farming methods, diet and costume, all tailored to the natural environment. Each predominates in a certain region, but all move and mix, creating small pockets of different cultures throughout the country. Atop this basic strata waves of immigrants have overlaid their cultures, from the Rajput princes fleeing the Muslim conquest of India to the recent Tibetan exodus.

Nepal's bubbling ethnic stew reaches full boil in the Kathmandu Valley, which adds its own contribution, the Newars, to the blend. An astonishing variety of features and costumes appear on city streets. Picking out Tamang from Limbu, Chhetri from Newar is an endlessly fascinating game, and it reveals how much Nepal remains a mixing rather than a melting pot.

Several forces are having a homogenizing effect on this variety. Modern influences transmitted by tourists, development, and the inevitably changing times are replacing the old ethnic-oriented values of family and religion with an increasing emphasis on material wealth and independence. Equally strong is the process of "Sanskritization," in which ethnic peoples hoping to increase their status in Nepal's Hindu-dominated society adopt the values and practices of high-caste Hindus as they make their way up the social scale. Though in theory Hinduism allows no converts—a Hindu is born, not made —in practice it's simple enough for a Nepali to make the change, and after several generations nobody knows the difference.

National Identity

In many ways the Tharu hunter, Chhetri farmer, and Bhotiya yak-herder have less in common than the inhabitants of three different European countries. Only since Nepal's 18th-century political unification have they shared even a nominal nationality; a distinct cultural and political character didn't emerge until after 1950. The government now cultivates a sense of national unity through mass media and public education, but old customs die hard, and in most vil-

lages ethnic affiliations remain more important than the vague concept of national identity.

The keynote of Nepali identity is struck by the inhabitants of the middle Hills, the Brahman and Chhetri castes who dominate business and politics and are the original Nepali speakers. The Newars and Sherpas may rival them in wealth, but Hindu castes have always held political power in Nepal, and the "official" values of Nepal are high-caste Hindu values.

Characteristics

Describing a people as diverse as Nepal's is difficult, but a distinctly Nepali character becomes apparent when you compare Nepal with India. In religion, culture, and social practices the two nations share much in common, but Nepal is a world apart from India's brand of intensity. Crossing the border, you feel a palpable sense of relaxation in the air on the Nepal side, and immigration officials smile at you (as long as your visa is in order). Despite the growing pressures of modern life there's still plenty of time in Nepal—simultaneously a frustrating and a

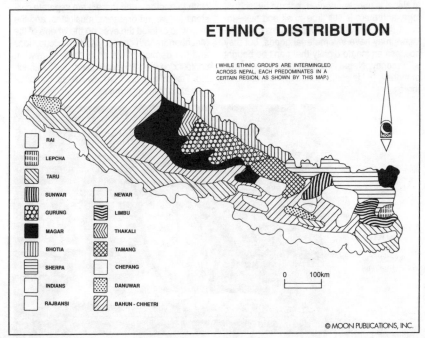

ETHNIC DISTRIBUTION

(WHILE ETHNIC GROUPS ARE INTERMINGLED ACROSS NEPAL, EACH PREDOMINATES IN A CERTAIN REGION, AS SHOWN BY THIS MAP.)

RAI
LEPCHA
TARU
SUNWAR
GURUNG
MAGAR
BHOTIA
SHERPA
INDIANS
RAJBANSI

NEWAR
LIMBU
THAKALI
TAMANG
CHEPANG
DANUWAR
BAHUN - CHHETRI

0   100km

© MOON PUBLICATIONS, INC.

charming trait. Things take longer to get done, but if you keep some patience and humor, you'll have a lot of fun in the process.

> *A whole country can never be reduced to a single concept and perhaps the name of Nepal evades concise definition more than any other.*
>
> —David Snellgrove,
> *Himalayan Pilgrimage*

The Nepali approach to caste restrictions and religious rules is more relaxed than that of orthodox Indian Hindus, an inevitable result of cultural intermingling. Nepalis are generally easygoing, willing to overlook a mistake or faux pas, but a deliberate insult may arouse a surprisingly fierce pride. British officers have long marveled at the bravery of the Gurkha soldiers recruited from Nepali Hill tribes, as well as their loyalty, stamina, and constant good humor. Life in Nepal is people-oriented, not run by technology, and there is still time to sit and talk—indeed, that's one of the main pleasures of life. Villagers may have few material goods, but they possess an innate dignity that can't be bought with money. Nepal is a poor country in terms of money, but in spirit it's one of the wealthiest there is.

CASTE

Nepali society is based on the Indian caste system, introduced and reinforced by successive waves of immigrants, but Nepal's ethnic diversity has molded it into a unique form. Popular belief has it the caste system was introduced in the Kathmandu Valley by King Jayasthiti Malla (1382-1422), who classified his Newar subjects into 64 different occupational categories. While he did codify many regulations, right down to details like forbidding outcaste sweepers to wear shoes, he was strengthening patterns already centuries old. Records from the Licchavi Period (A.D. 300-879) document the existence of a caste system based on the classic fourfold Indian division: the priestly Brahmans, the warrior/ruling class of Kshatriya (Nep. Chhetri), the trading and farming Vaishya, and the menial Sudra, servants and laborers.

The old occupational caste divisions were incredibly specific. Among the Newars, dyers of red cloth belonged to one caste, dyers of blue cloth to another, and there were separate divisions for wound-dressers, musicians, and the men who painted the eyes on the wheels of the Machhendranath chariot. Modern occupations and the demise of old ones have somewhat confounded the traditional system, but it's adapting. Taxi drivers are from low castes, computer operators from high ones.

three young Nepali boys sporting the official national dress

ALISON WRIGHT

smoke break for a hard-working porter

Legal punishment for violating the caste system were eliminated in the early '60s, but caste is still very much alive in Nepal. Caste is both social and religious, determining who can marry, eat, drink, and even smoke together. As these old taboos loosen, it now serves mainly to indicate political and economic status, uniting some people and dividing others.

Understandably, high-caste members take the matter most seriously. Brahmans and Chhetris look down upon lesser Hindus, who in turn can still feel superior to the yak-eating (i.e. cattle-eating) Bhotia, who rank just above outcastes in the scheme. These casteless Buddhists can ignore the system, but the outcastes can't—they are still an inseparable part of the society which discriminates against them.

A literal "waterline" runs through society, dividing the pure and impure castes, illustrated in the Nepali terms *pani chalne jaat*, "water-touching caste" and its negation, *pani nachalne jaat*. A high-caste man loses caste if he accepts food or water from an outcaste, or food from a member of any lower clean caste. The loss of caste can only be remedied by ritual purification. Well into this century, Nepali traders returning from non-Hindu lands had to undergo this ceremony and have it legally certified before being admitted back to "clean" society. Strict Brahmans cannot accept food or drink from anyone except another Brahman—a restriction which kept Kathmandu's potential restaurant customers near zero until the advent of tourists.

Hindu Caste Groups

These people are the mainstay of the middle Hills, particularly in western Nepal, where they constitute 80% of the population. Brahman and most Chhetri men wear the *janaai,* the sacred thread symbolizing their ritual purity and the "twice-born" state of the upper castes. Lower castes and ethnic groups sometimes disparage it with the slang term "buffalo's intestine."

Bahun or Brahmans sit at the top of the heap. Traditionally they serve as priests and moneylenders (earning a bad reputation for usury); nowadays they're found in government, education, and commerce. Rural Bahun may be no wealthier than other peasants, but they tend to cluster together in small villages. As a price for receiving the social privileges of the highest caste, orthodox Bahun are supposed to honor a number of ritual prohibitions—they shouldn't eat onions, garlic, and tomatoes, drink alcohol, or harness cattle to ploughs—but these are increasingly ignored.

Chhetri (Sanskrit *Kshtriya*) are the largest Hindu caste, specializing in military and political affairs. The Shah dynasty and the powerful Rana family are members of an aristocratic Chhetri subcaste called **Thakuri.** Many Chhetri are descendants from the union of Brahman immigrants and Nepali Hill women, awarded the honorary rank of Chhetri to strengthen the caste system. Thus their features may resemble ethnic groups rather than the "pure" Brahmans.

The traditional middle-caste slots are vacant in Nepal, filled instead by ethnic groups. At the bottom of the totem pole are the occupational castes: the **Kami** or blacksmiths, **Sarki** or cobblers and leatherworkers, and the **Damai,** tailors who moonlight as musicians in out-of-tune wedding bands. Outcaste sweepers, butchers, and executioners form the poorest strata of society.

ETHNIC GROUPS

Terai Ethnic Groups
About a quarter of Nepal's people belong to one of the Indo-Aryan groups of the Terai, but few visitors come in contact with them as the Terai is not a major destination except for Chitwan.

Tharu: One of Nepal's few indigenous tribal peoples, as opposed to ethnic groups descended from later waves of immigrants. The Tharu are based in the midwestern Terai in forested land along the southern base of the Silwalik Range. They were among the few people who could live here, having a limited natural immunity to malaria. They claim to be descendants of Rajputs, but are probably of Dravidian stock.

Maithili: Of Indo-Aryan stock, they take their name from Mithila, the capital of a rich and highly advanced culture which greatly influenced the Malla rulers of the Kathmandu Valley. According to the census they're Nepal's largest single ethnic group, with 11% of the population.

Hill Ethnic Groups
These peoples predominate in the higher hills (1,800-2,700 meters). Though nearly all speak Nepali, their mother languages are Tibeto-Burman dialects. Many share close linguistic and cultural links but have developed differently, according to their local environment and history.

Newar: The indigenous inhabitants of the Kathmandu Valley, the Newars now make up a little less than half the population. Shrewd traders, expert farmers, and superb craftsmen, their art ranks among Asia's finest and their old cities are masterpieces of urban planning. Originally Buddhist, the Newars are now predominately Hindu; more precisely, their beliefs are an impossibly tangled mixture of both. Their language, a Tibeto-Burman offshoot, has its own alphabet, now largely replaced by Devanagri script, and an ancient literary tradition. Newari society is divided into 64 occupational castes and hundreds of subcastes, with parallel systems for Buddhists and Hindus. Among the largest is the **Jyapu,** peasant farmers clustered in Bhaktapur and Patan, who ardently support the old traditions, festivals and gods.

Tamang: One of the largest Hill ethnic groups (five percent of the national population), the Tamangi homeland is eastern and central Nepal, especially the hills ringing the Kathmandu Valley. Their Tibeto-Burman language is vaguely related to Newari; more than the Newars they have retained their Buddhist beliefs, blended in their case with animistic folk religion. The Tamangs are relatively recent arrivals from the northeast; according to one account their ancestors were horse traders or cavalrymen from an invading Tibetan army who settled in Nepal, hence the name *Ta-mi,* "Horse People." Tamangs work as farmers, porters and craftsmen, manufacturing many of Kathmandu's "Tibetan" souvenirs; many serve in Nepal's army.

Gurung: The Gurung homeland is in the foothills of the Lamjung and Annapurna Himal, a region they've intensively farmed and covered with a network of trails paved with precisely cut and fitted stone blocks. Gurung villages of neat stone houses are some of the largest in Nepal, and their standard of living is relatively high. They speak an unwritten language, again Tibeto-Burman, which appears in at least three main dialects. In higher regions, Gurungs retain their Buddhist traditions; in lower ones they've converted to Hinduism. Many young Gurung men have become mercenary soldiers in the British or Indian armies to

MIKE WELLINS

support their families on their shrinking farms back home.

Magar: These people live in roughly the same area as Gurungs, but farm the lower slopes. Their homeland is around the southern slopes of the Dhaulagiri Himal. Again, they speak a Tibeto-Burman language appearing in several regional dialects. Originally practitioners of animistic folk religion with a Buddhist veneer, most have switched to Hinduism over the last few centuries. Along with Gurungs, Magar soldiers make up the bulk of the Gurkha and Nepalese forces. Their role as fighters goes back to their service in the army of Prithvi Narayan Shah, and even before that to the Palpa ruler Mukunda Sen's attempted invasion of the Kathmandu Valley in the sixteenth century. The Magar reputation as honest and hardworking (some unkindly call them "strong and stupid") make them the *sojho* or "straight" people of Nepal.

Thakali: Natives of the Thak Khola region near Annapurna in central Nepal, the Thakali are known as shrewd and aggressive traders. Formerly they profited from their role as middlemen in the salt trade between lowland Nepal and Tibet. Originally they were Tibetan Buddhists, influenced by shamanism, but many have become Hindus in recent years. The Thakali are quite prosperous and many have resettled in Kathmandu or the Terai for business reasons. Thakali women are famed for their spic-and-span lodges and tasty food. In the past, they had a reputation (perhaps unearned) for seducing their guests, then robbing them as they slept.

Kirati Rai and Limbu: The Kirati tribe, mentioned 2,300 years ago in the Hindu epic the *Mahabharata,* is said to have once ruled the Kathmandu Valley. Driven out by a succeeding dynasty they resettled in the eastern Hills. The name "Kirati" is kept by the Rai and Limbu as a reminder of these ancestors. They're easily identified by their striking, tilted almond eyes and flat Mongolian features. Rai and Limbu each have their own related language and share a mixture of animistic, Buddhist, and Hindu beliefs. Independent and proud, they make excellent soldiers and tend to hold themselves a little apart from other Nepalis.

Mountain Peoples

Bhotia or *Bhote* is a term used throughout the subcontinent to describe northern mountain peoples with close ties to Tibet. Bhotia dialects are all Tibetan-based and their religion is invariably Tibetan Buddhist, with a sprinkling of animistic Bönpo influences.

Life at these heights can't be supported by farming or herding alone, so these people practice both, and supplement their income with trade. In winter they travel south to trade and graze their flocks; in summer they move back up into the high pastures and cross the northern passes to trade in Tibet.

There are dozens of Bhotia subgroups, many named after their region suffixed by "-pa," Tibetan for "people" or "man": Dolpo-pa, Lo-pa (the inhabitants of the Kingdom of Lo or Mustang), Manang-pa (renowned traders and smugglers) and the famous **Sher-pa** of Solu-Khumbu, the best known of all Nepal's ethnic groups. In English "Sherpa" has become a synonym for porter or expedition worker, but properly speaking, Sherpa are a people who trace their origins to eastern Tibet, from where they emigrated about 400 years ago. Their traditional life combined yak-herding, barley and potato farming, and trading with nearby Tibet. After the Chinese invasion of Tibet in the 1950s they quickly adapted to a new role, serving as guides and expediters for the blossoming trekking and expedition business. Today the "Sherpa Mafia" runs the trekking trade. Sherpas own 90% of registered trekking companies and are among the most prosperous and successful of all Nepalis.

LIFE AND CUSTOMS

The sheer variety of ethnic groups makes it impossible to even mention most customs and rituals, which differ among peoples. The "standard" (or at least most common) norms are set by the Brahman/Chhetri Hindu castes.

Urban And Village Life

Nepal is still an overwhelmingly rural place, but the rate of urbanization is rapidly increasing. Currently about eight percent of its 18 million people live in the 33 cities and towns with a population over 9,000, most in the Kathmandu Valley or the Terai. The remainder are scattered among 80,000 or so tiny villages and hamlets, where life has changed little over the centuries. People still raise their own food, rely very little on cash, build their own houses from local materials, and seldom see much of the world beyond their own particular valley. This is the real heart of Nepal; nobody who visits only the capital can claim to have come to an understanding of the country. Trekking immerses you in village life, but all you need to do for a glimpse is get off the main roads and explore the villages of the Valley.

Population

Nepal's population in 1990 was 18.3 million and growing at 2.7% per year. At this rate, the population is due to double every 26 years. By 2020 it's expected to reach 34 million, an intolerable burden for the fragile Himalayan environment. Natural resources and arable land in the Hills are already stretched to the limit, and the "pressure valve" provided by new Terai land is disappearing as the Terai fills up.

Despite efforts to popularize birth control, population growth isn't likely to decrease soon. About half of all Nepalis are under the age of 20, just entering their childbearing years. Like all rural peoples, Nepalis value large families for the help children can give in farming and household chores, and also for their own sake. In a materially poor society with little entertainment children are one of the greatest joys in life. A high premium is placed on sons. Every Hindu man needs a son to perform *shraddha* rites for him after death, and with Nepal's high infant mortality rate, couples feel they need to have plenty of kids to ensure that some will reach adulthood. The average Nepali woman bears six children in her lifetime; one or two of them will die before the age of five.

Men's Clothing

The official national dress for men is the *daura suruwal:* tight-legged, baggy-seated drawstring trousers (the extra material makes squatting easy) topped by a long-sleeved tunic closed with cloth ties. Worn with a Western-style suit coat, it's the official uniform of high government officials. Among younger men and city dwellers, shirts and trousers have become the norm. The trendy punk boys of Kathmandu, arrayed entirely in denim, wouldn't be seen dead in the daura suruwal, nor in the accompanying *topi,* a brimless, lopsided cap that rests atop the head

like an inverted flowerpot.

Nepal's tremendous ethnic variety offers endless alternatives to this standard. Terai men wear Indian-style *lungi,* a long wraparound piece of printed cotton, or a *dhoti,* a length of white cloth wound between the legs and about the waist like a set of baggy culottes. Porters and laborers wear shorts, a loincloth or maybe just a towel wrapped about their hips, but bare-legged men are considered low class—which is why hairy-legged tourists seem out of place. Rai hillsmen wear a vest and loincloth or *langauti;* Gurung men wear homespun, undyed cotton *khadim* or *anti bhanro.* Tamangs may wear sleeveless woolen jackets similar in weave and pattern to radi carpets. Bhotia men wrap themselves in Tibetan-style wool *chuba,* a voluminous coat-like garment. Modernized Bhotia like the Sherpas save their chuba for weddings or New Year celebrations,and prefer jeans and down jackets.

Women's Dress

Always more conservative than men, Nepalese women are just beginning to adopt Western dress. Five years ago a Nepali woman in jeans was unimaginable, but fashionable young Nepali women now wear Lycra tights and miniskirts. It's a shame because few garments equal the grace of the Indian sari still favored by married Hindu women, a five-meter length of cloth draped over a tight blouse called a *choli.* Throughout Kathmandu, brightly colored saris hung up to dry flutter like banners from upper-story windows. Wrapping a sari is an intricate process, mastered by the inexperienced with the aid of a few strategically placed safety pins.

More practical is the *shalwar kurta* or Punjabi borrowed from northern India. Popular with younger women, it's a dress-like top slit up the sides to reveal matching trousers, tight about the calves but loose at the waist. A thin diaphanous scarf worn over the shoulders completes the ensemble. Comfortable, good-looking, and modest, Punjabis are excellent for women travelers. Dozens of shops in the bazaar sell ready-made outfits in bright colors, or you can buy your own material and have a tailor stitch it up.

Peasant women of the Valley and Hills find the flowing sari impractical for their endless round of work. They wear cotton lungi or the *fariya*, a length of flowered cotton wrapped into a skirt, often topped by a five-meter length of white cotton wound about their waist. This *patuka* keeps the back warm and supported, provides padding for loads, and makes a handy cache for snacks, keys, and money. Jyapu women wear a distinctive black sari bordered in red, arranged in multiple pleats in front to allow easy walking, and hiked high in back to reveal the blue tatooes adorning their calves. (After death, it's said the woman can sell her tatooes to obtain food in the afterworld.) Newar women also favor cotton blouses block-printed in red and black patterns. In cooler weather they wrap themselves in patterned shawls of the same material, the colors muted by an overlayer of transparent muslin.

Bhotia women dress in *chuba* (Tibetan) or *bhakkhu* (Nepali), long sleeveless wraparound dresses tied in the back and worn over a blouse. Married women top it with a striped woolen apron, which serves as a handy sit-upon, towel, and handkerchief.

Adornments

Nepali women delight in decoration, layering themselves with jewelry in carnival colors. They braid their long black hair with red cotton tassels, or twist it into a neat bun and set a flower in it. Red is considered the most auspicious and beautiful color, worn by brides on their wedding day as a symbol of marital happiness. A Nepali saying goes *raato raamro, guliyo mitho*, "red is beautiful, sweet is tasty."

The auspicious tika mark made on the forehead with red *sindhur* powder is part of daily puja. Special tika mixed with yoghurt and rice are distributed as a blessing on auspicious occasions like weddings and Dasain. In a mystic sense the tikka represents the third eye of spiritual insight; for women, it's become a cosmetic essential. Plastic stick-on tika kits are sold with a variety of colors and shapes.

Jewelry is more than an adornment; it's an investment and a status symbol. Nobody knows the value of your bank account (and interest is low anyway) but everyone understands the value of gold. For a married woman jewelry is one of the few possessions she can call her own. Whatever jewelry she brings into a marriage as dowry remains hers to keep.

a young married woman wearing the traditional tilhari

With the exception of Newars and Bhotias, many Nepali women have pierced noses, adorned with anything from a tiny jeweled stud to a collection of discs and rings. The larger pieces hanging from the septum of some Hill women make you wonder how the wearer can eat. (They manage by bending their heads far over their plate.) Earrings include a dozen or so tiny rings inserted along the outer rim and huge golden discs which must be put in and taken out by the goldsmith. Some women (Tharu, Tamang) wear heavy anklets of hollow silver or gold; Terai women may wear linked silver anklets. Some hill women wear necklaces of silver rupees. Most valuable are the old *kampani*, coins of the British East India Company, which contain a fair amount of real silver.

Married Hindu women display signs of their wedded state, as predictable as a wedding ring in the West. Red *sindhur* powder in the part of their hair is a sure sign; ideally the powder should be mixed with a portion of the sindhur the bride received on her wedding day. Another sign of marriage is the *tilhari,* a cylindrical golden bead hanging from strands of tiny multicolored glass beads. Married women also wear an armful of tinkling glass or plastic bangles; widows break theirs as a sign of mourning.

Bhotia women favor big chunks of turquoise, coral, and amber, strung into necklaces, set into rings, or woven into their hair. Men and women wear all sorts of religious artifacts: amulet boxes containing blessings or holy relics, colored knotted neckcords blessed by lamas, rosaries of prayer beads *(trengwa)* for reciting mantras. Another treasure is the black and white *dzi* stones said to be created by lightning bolts. The finest cost hundreds of thousands of rupees and are worn as protection against evil spirits.

Similar protection is provided to Hindus by rosaries of the furrowed brown *rudraksha* ("eye of Shiva") seeds worn by saddhus and pilgrims. From the *Elaeocarpus ganitrus* tree, rudraksha appear in different configurations with up to 21 divisions or "faces," each combination sacred to a different god. A single-faced *ek mukh rudraksha* is extremely rare and highly valued: it's said the mere sight of it erases sins, and the owner will be blessed by the goddess Lakshmi.

FAMILY LIFE

Society is based around the family, and loyalty to one's kin supercedes duties to caste, ethnic group, or nation. It's difficult for independently minded Westerners to understand how an individual's identity can be so submerged in family and social considerations. In smaller villages, virtually everyone is related some way or another. Children grow up in an extended family, surrounded by relatives. The Nepali language reflects this with its dozens of detailed kinship terms. Frequently people are called by a relationship word—"older brother's wife" or "little sister" rather than their personal name, which may be forgotten.

Children
Children are treasured in Nepalese society. They help with household and field chores, support their aged parents, and bring a great deal of joy to a life with little entertainment. Not surprisingly, they're the goal of virtually every married couple. Couples without children are nearly incomprehensible to Nepalis. Whatever your

explanation may be, they will secretly pity your presumed infertility (failure to bear children is always considered the fault of a woman). Infertility is a curse for a Nepali woman, who doesn't attain full social status until she bears a child, preferably a son. Though polygamy has been outlawed, a man whose wife doesn't produce a living child after ten years can legally take a second wife, and often does before that time. Boys are preferred for several reasons: male offspring continue the family lineage, only sons can perform the *shraddha* offerings for ancestors, and sons continue to economically support their parents after marriage, while daughters join their husbands' families.

Children are christened with a first name and clan/caste surname 11 days after birth. Hindu caste children are often named after deities: Shiva, Ganesh, Ram, Narayan, Lakshmi, Saraswati. Or they're given auspicious names like Kamala (Lotus), Sushil (Courteous), Bijay (Victory). Magar and Gurung men, proud of their fighting abilities, often have Bahadur (Brave) as a middle name. Bhotia children may be named after the day they were born—Nima, Dawa, Mingma, Lhakpa, Phurbu, Pasang and Pempa are Sunday through Saturday. The Sherpa prefix "Ang" (Ang Dawa, Ang Nima) is something like "junior" in English.

Given names are often replaced by a kinship term from the elaborate and extensive vocabulary. In order of birth, boys are Jetha (the eldest) Maila, Saila, Kaila, Raila, Taila, and Kancha ("junior"). Girls are Jethi, Maili, Saili, and so on. This system covers a total of 16 children; it's highly unlikely a woman would bear more than eight of each! As children grow up to assume roles in their own families, the names change: women become "bhauju" (brother's wife) or simply "so-and-so's mother."

Mothers go about their work with their infants tied to their backs and nurse the babies for several years, sometimes until the age of six or seven. Infants are given a daily sunbath and massaged with mustard oil, said to make their skin fair and their limbs straight and supple. Toddlers wear heavy silver anklets to make their legs grow straight. Small children are vulnerable to evil spirits and are protected in a variety of ways: their eyes are lined with black *gajal* to avert sickness and the evil eye; cords tied around their wrists and ankles protect against

boys in Kagbeni

spirits. Around six months of age a baby receives its first symbolic mouthful of rice off the edge of a coin in the *pasni* ceremony, symbolizing his or her transition into a separate individual.

As soon as they can walk children are given over to the care of an older sibling and begin a few years of intensive playing and running about. Adults keep an eye on them but rarely interfere with their games. As a result, Nepali children learn to be self-sufficient early on and never seem whiny or bored, despite their lack of conventional playthings. Every action becomes a game and every object is a toy—the rusty rim of a bicycle wheel serves as a hoop, a plastic bag is a mask, a leaf and stick are imaginary dolls, and a dead dog makes the ultimate pull toy.

As children grow they take on household tasks, especially girls, who help their mothers with the endless round of cutting fodder for animals, fetching water and wood, and tending younger children. Boys might be sent to graze the family's livestock. Nepali boys are about three times more likely to be sent to school than their sisters, at least for a few years. A girl's labor is too valuable to do without, and many parents see no point in educating a daughter who will never do more than field and housework and will soon leave them to work for her husband's family. The primary school enrollment rate is over 80% on paper, though attendance is far below that. After age 10 children start to drop out. Few make it to the 10th and final grade; fewer still pass the exam for the School Leaving Certificate (SLC), which is the equivalent of a high school education.

Rites Of Passage

Sometime between the age of eight and marriage, Brahman and Chhetri boys undergo the *bartaman* ceremony initiating them as a full-fledged member of their caste. Long ago it marked the boy's initiation as the disciple of a Hindu guru; nowadays it's purely symbolic. The boy dons the *janaai*, the triple-knotted sacred thread worn over the left shoulder as the exclusive prerogative of higher Hindu castes.

The *ihi*, a mock marriage for young Newari girls, is one of the most elaborate life-cycle ceremonies. Groups of girls decked out in sumptuous finery gather at a local temple, where a priest weds them to the god Narayan (Vishnu), represented by a decorated fruit of the *bel* tree. Ceremonies can last several days and involve several dozen girls; because of the great expense it's often performed in groups. The ritual is a precaution against the social ostracism of widowhood. Even if the girl's mortal husband dies, this first marriage to the god will guarantee her status as a married woman.

A girl reaching puberty undergoes a far less pleasant ceremony called *gupha basne*, "staying in the cave." At the onset of menstruation she's whisked away from her home and confined in a secluded dark room for 12 days—often an animal shed or a neighbor's house. The symbolic onset of female sexuality threatens her male relatives, who must avoid the sight of her. Even the sun, as the male principle, is supposed to be hidden from the girl. At the end of the allotted period she's blindfolded, ritually bathed, then brought outside for a ritual viewing of the sun.

Marriage

Marriage is often the greatest event in a Nepali's life, and it's celebrated with all due pomp and splendor. Poor families may go into a lifetime of debt to give their children the appropriate send-off. The marriage age is increasing: while the mothers of today's brides were usually wed at 13, their modern daughters wait until 17 or 18, though plenty of youthful marriages still occur. Child marriages were banned in 1963 but they still occasionally take place with children as young as six. According to orthodox Hindu beliefs, a father should arrange an early marriage; an eight-year-old girl is the ideal candidate for the "virgin gift" of a bride.

Arranged marriages remain the norm, though love matches are on the rise. The romantic ideas conveyed in movies, pop music, and magazines have a lot to do with this trend. Strangely (or perhaps predictably) many of these end unhappily in a few years. A traditional marriage is an economic and social partnership, rooted in the shared goals of earning a living and raising a family. Love isn't a consideration, and the bride and groom may only meet once before the wedding. What counts is social and financial standing and, to a lesser extent, character.

Weddings

Parents of a marriageable son or daughter search for a likely partner within their caste and social group. In this family-oriented society, marriage is as much a union between families as individuals. Arrangements may be made through a matchmaker hired by the bride's family. The next step is a visit to the astrologer, who determines the couple's compatability and sets an auspicious wedding date. The month of Magh (usually January) is the biggest wedding season, and on certain lucky dates the streets are filled with endless processions. Fronted by a blaring brass band, the couple moves slowly forward in a gaily decorated car. In the old days, the bride would have been carried on a shoulder litter or *khat,* as rural brides still are. A good bride shows

her chagrin at leaving her parents' home by weeping, the more violently, the better. Everyone crowds about to see her sobbing in her finery; the bride's departure is the dramatic peak of the whole event, and can be a real tearjerker.

A full-scale wedding involves several days of ceremonies, gift exchanging, feasting, and ritual games and entails a considerable expense for both families. The family of the bride must provide a dowry and feast the groom's relatives; the groom's family offers gold jewelry, the red wedding sari, and another feast.

Rural weddings are less elaborate. The bride is borne in a jolting palanquin ride to her husband's home, accompanied by a procession of family and friends. Weddings among Bhotia people are accompanied by dancing, drinking, and feasting. Among the Sherpas, matchmaking is a protracted affair. Frequently several years pass between betrothal and the actual wedding ceremony; in the interim, the couple lives together and often produces their first child.

Family Relations

Until polygamy was outlawed in the 1950s, largely under the influence of Western morals, men who could afford to often had two or three wives. The practice continues today, especially in rural areas where such laws are rarely enforced. Multiple wives are a sign of status and improve the odds of having sons, but bickering among co-wives can make family life miserable.

Another tense relationship is that between mother-in-law and daughter-in-law. The new bride is expected to serve her husband and his parents with unquestioning devotion, performing daily chores like plastering the kitchen with fresh mud, cutting grass and fetching water, and massaging her mother-in-law's and husband's feet. Her status improves over the years as she bears children, especially sons, in which case she can look forward to becoming a mother-in-law herself.

A high-caste Hindu wife is expected to treat her husband with the utmost respect. Before each meal, she should wash her husband's feet and splash a little of the water into her mouth. A wife may eat only after her husband has finished, and then consumes whatever food he's left on his plate. Since the feet (the lowest part of the body) and leftover food are both *jutho,* ritually impure, these actions are forceful symbols of the complete obedience expected from a wife towards the man who, as a famous Nepalese poet phrased it, is "the lord of her breath." Widowhood is a disaster for a high-caste woman, who loses all social definition when her husband dies. Until the custom of sati was banned in the 1920s, Hindu widows were encouraged to join their husbands on the funeral pyre, a tradition imported from India in Licchavi times. Death by sati was said to earn a widow a happy rebirth, and provided an honorable escape from the ostracism of widowhood. It was especially popular among the royal and noble Nepali families. King Yoganendra Malla was joined on his funeral pyre by 33 wives, and a few immolated themselves with Jung Bahadur Rana, even though he tried to ban the custom after his return from England.

Bhotia women occasionally marry more than one man, a custom which originated with long trading trips that keep men away from home for six months to a year at a time. To remedy this a woman might marry two or three brothers, who would share work, wife, and children, keeping out of one another's way with frequent travel. The custom reduces property divisions between sons as well.

Old Age

On paper a Nepali's life expectancy is among the lowest in the world: 53 years for men, 51 for women. In fact, though, if a child survives the most dangerous first five years, there's a good chance of he or she reaching a respectable old age, which is venerated in Nepal's tradition-based society. The Newars celebrate a reenactment of the infant's pashni when a man reaches the auspicious age of 77 years, seven months and seven days. The birthday boy is carried through the streets in a palanquin by his relatives during a day filled with ceremonies and offerings. From then on he is considered to have reached the first stage of divinity, and his blessing and curse take on special significance.

A second ceremony is held at the "thousand-full-moon" date of 83 years, four months and four days, and rarely, a third celebration called "going to heaven" at the attainment of 99 years, nine months and nine days, which earns a man the status of a semidivine being.

Death

Death from old age or sickness is viewed as inevitable, but an untimely death is often blamed on malignant spirits or witches. A dying person may be carried to a riverbank to die with his feet in the sacred water; if this isn't possible, a continuous stream of water is poured over the feet to prevent the soul from escaping into a lower rebirth. After death, the body is wrapped in white, the color of mourning, and carried to the riverside cremation ghat on a bamboo bier. While male relatives undergo ritual purification, the body is burned. The ashes are distributed among various pilgrimage sites in the Kathmandu Valley or are tossed into the Bagmati to eventually flow into the holy Ganges.

Close relatives undergo a general mourning period of 13 days, followed by a year of mourning for the immediate family. The chief mourner, the eldest son, is expected to wear only white clothes for the entire year. Periodically he must perform shraddha, offerings for the spirit of the deceased. At the end of the year the spirit officially arrives in the spirit realm, the *pitorlok,* where it relies on continued offerings for food, water, and comfort. This dependency contributes to the value placed on sons.

Coexisting with the belief in ancestor spirits is the conviction that a soul can be reborn in many realms, according to the karma earned by its previous actions. Meditation and asceticism can liberate it from the cycle of birth and death; meritorious acts and devotion can send the deceased to *swarga,* the blissful heaven of the gods, but evil actions bring the tortures of a hell realm or rebirth as an animal.

LANGUAGE

Nepali, the official language, is an Indo-Aryan tongue derived from classical Sanskrit. Like Sanskrit and Hindi, it's written in Devanagri script. It's related to Hindi about as closely as Italian is to Spanish. If you've picked up some Hindi in your travels through India, many of the nouns will be useful in Nepal (and vice versa). Nepali is widely spoken in Sikkim, Bhutan, and the Darjeeling region of west Bengal.

Nepali originated from the language of the Khas, a hill tribe that migrated east along the Himalaya and by the 14th century established an empire in northwest Nepal. Khas influence spread far beyond their small kingdom. Their language was officially used in the Newar courts of the Malla kings a century before the Nepali-speaking Gorkhas conquered the Kathmandu Valley.

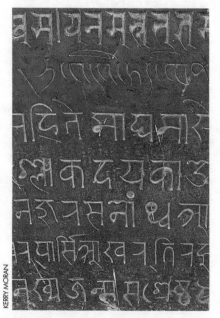

KERRY MORAN

Pratapa Malla's multi-lingual inscription, Hanuman Dhoka, Kathmandu

The Gorkhas' rise to power solidified Nepali's role as the primary language and spread it further. Today it's the mother tongue of 58% of the population; probably another 30% speak it fluently as a second language. As the official language of government, schools, and mass media it's become the national lingua franca for the many ethnic groups speaking diverse languages.

Somewhere between 24 to 100 different languages and dialects are spoken in Nepal, depending on how closely you look; some of the more obscure are spoken by a few thousand people at most. Many Nepalis may be illiterate, but they're fluent in two, three, or even four languages—proof that language learning is not some kind of miraculous talent, but a skill born from the need to communicate.

Nepal's languages fall into two groups. A quarter of the population speaks one of the Sanskrit-related languages of the Terai like Maithili, Bhojpuri, and Avadhi, or the aboriginal Taru. The majority of languages are spoken by the many Mongoloid Hill tribes and belong to the Tibeto-Burman branch of the Sino-Tibetan family of languages. Gurung, Tamang, Magar, Sherpa, Rai, and Limbu tribes all have their own languages, frequently subdivided into regional dialects. Most are unwritten, though Newari has its own alphabet and a tradition of classical literature.

The native tongue of nearly half the residents of the Kathmandu Valley, Newari is a special case. Structurally related to Tibeto-Burman, it's absorbed much Nepali vocabulary but remains linguistically unique. Newari script faintly resembles the Tibetan alphabet, but since the advent of the printing press it's been replaced by Devanagri. During Rana rule Newari literature was banned as subversive, and the literary tradition didn't resurface until 1946. Today the Newars proudly cling to their language as a symbol of cultural identity. In some parts of the Valley (the back streets of Bhaktapur, for instance) many Newars don't understand Nepali. Newari is a tonal language, not easy to learn, but even a few words will amaze and delight people in the Valley.

Studying Nepali

Though most visitors get by with little more than *namaste,* the ability to speak even very basic Nepali is *the* single best way to enhance your stay. Just about every Kathmanduite who deals with tourists knows some English (even if it's only the "You—how much!" of street hustlers). Hotel, shop, and restaurant workers are reasonably fluent, and some speak Japanese, German, or French as well. Taxi and bus drivers are more problematic, but you can usually find a bystander to help you out in a jam. Rudimentary English is taught in public schools—much to the exasperation of the traveler who finds himself endlessly greeted by gangs of children chanting "Hello-mister-how-are-you" and "Give-me-one-pen/rupee/chocolate."

Outside the Valley, lodge and teashop owners along the main trekking routes manage to communicate with their foreign clientele, some quite fluently. But the Nepali-less trekker is isolated from just about every other person he passes on the trail. On less-traveled trails you'll need either an English-speaking guide or porter, or a basic knowledge of the language. The latter is preferable no matter what. Even a rudimentary knowledge quickly opens doors and hearts, and distinguishes you from the crowd.

Nepali is a nontonal, reasonably phonetic language and it's relatively easy to learn the rudiments. The hard parts are: a) understanding the voluble answer, and b) perfecting the language once you've gotten the basics. Nepali is an exceptionally rich language with a tremendous variety of verb forms, nouns, and colorful expressions. Verbal commands change according to the social level of the person you address, ranging from the Royal Honorific Form used only for talking with, or about, members of the royal family, through high honorific (very respectful), medium honorific (for social equals), low-grade honorific, and a *ta* form used for animals and presumably inferior humans. For beginners the safest way to wade through all this is to use the medium-honorific *tapaai* form with adults and try to pick up the less formal usage for children. (Tapaai-ing a small child for some reason seems extremely funny to Nepalis.)

On the tongue of a native speaker with a flair for rhythm Nepali is a bouncing, musical language full of marvelous syncopations and rhymes. There's a whole collection of silly-sounding words like *rungi-chungi* (multi-coloured), *bango-tingo* (crooked, winding), *wari-pari* (here and there), and *ukkus-mukkus* (full to bursting, said of your stomach after two plates of daal bhaat). The pages of a Nepali-English dictionary reveal concerns peculiar to the country, like lists of special words for different types of jugs and baskets, and over four dozen precise kinship terms. But for things like radio, school, taxi and petrol, it's simply the English word with a slight alteration in pronunciation.

Like the Eskimos with their 40 words for snow, Nepali has terms uniquely suited to its mountainous terrain: *lari-bari,* defined as "the game of rolling down a slope," and *tigre,* literally "thigh-y" or "with big thighs," meaning "well-built." (This one you'll understand after seeing the physique of a bare-legged porter carrying a 100-kg load.)

Studying Tips

If your visit is limited, you need to focus on words and phrases that will get you the farthest. Start your basic vocabulary with greetings, farewells, and numbers, then add important nouns, verbs and a few simple adjectives and adverbs—"good," "fast," "difficult," "expensive," "crazy"—that express feelings about an infinite number of situations. There's a big difference between book learning and actually being able to speak a language. The only way to acquire a language is to use it, practicing on everyone you meet. Don't be embarrassed by mistakes; they're part of the process. It may be difficult to find someone to practice on in Kathmandu, since everyone seems to be bent on practicing their English. A few weeks of study followed by a few weeks trekking will drum the basics into you.

Spoken "village" Nepali treats grammar casually, while the more sophisticated written and scholarly language employs a number of stylistic niceties and a large vocabulary of Sanskrit words. The informal, colloquial language is easier and quicker to learn and will serve you better than the *Sanskriti khura* a well-meaning educated Nepali might teach, which, coming out of a foreign mouth at least, seems to be virtually incomprehensible to a villager. Choose your Nepali teachers carefully, even if your lessons are informal. A taxi driver, porter, or a six-year-old kid can be a far better instinctive teacher than someone who's hung up on "proper" speech. If you doubt the usefulness of a word,

emphasize you want to learn what people say—
chaltiko khura.

The Devanagri alphabet is easily learned, but you'll seldom need to read or write in Nepal, a country with a 35% literacy rate and virtually no street signs. Studying Romanized Nepali saves time in the beginning; later you can add Devanagri if you like.

Books And Courses
The **Experiment in International Living** in Naxal (tel. 414-516) periodically offers Nepali courses and can also arrange private teachers for Nepali and Tibetan. Private tutoring is best if you're a quick learner because you can move ahead rapidly and tailor lessons to your needs (like Nepali phrases relevant for trekking), and fees are reasonable: Rs120 per hour for an experienced teacher. A month of serious study should give you the basic framework; from there you can go off and learn on your own. There are a few excellent private teachers in town, and a lot of mediocre ones; shop around if you're in doubt. If you're really serious, Tribhuvan University's **School of International Languages** offers courses in Nepali, Newari, Sanskrit, and Tibetan starting in August every year.

There are dozens of small do-it-yourself Nepali phrasebooks on the market, but they're essentially useless unless you get some native-speaker help with pronunciation at first. If you're really intent on teaching yourself, pick up one of the lengthier books with a background in grammar. Chij Shrestha's *Basic Course in Spoken Nepali,* developed to train Peace Corps volunteers, is simple and very popular, though it requires some drilling. David Matthews's *A Course in Nepali,* published by the School of Oriental and African Studies, is excellent but later lessons are in Devanagiri. T.W. Clark's *Introduction to Nepali* is also good and uses Roman transliterations. Among dictionaries, Ralph Turner's *Nepali Dictionary* is the standard classic, but it weighs three pounds and is seldom available. The handy *Basic Gurkhali Dictionary* compiled by M. Meerendonk, with English-Nepali and Nepali-English, is small enough to carry around in your pocket.

RELIGION

Religion is the wellspring of traditional Nepali life, inspiring art, defining culture and regulating daily routine. The birth of a child and the symbolic "birth" of a house; the maintenance of a temple or a truck—all are influenced by religion. The term covers a net of magical, mystical, and spiritual beliefs. The multiple gods reflect the many facets of human nature. They dwell in temples, rocks, trees, rivers, homes, and most of all in the hearts and minds of their devotees, who worship them with a daily round of *puja* (ritual offerings) and prayer.

Nepali religion follows a complex and unique pattern, in which Hindu and Buddhist beliefs are interwoven with tantric influences upon a background of ancient animistic cults. The many strands overlap and blend until it's impossible to separate them. Nepalis don't even try. They simply live their beliefs, and their faith keeps the ancient gods alive.

Nationwide, religion falls into a general pattern of Hindu lowlanders and Buddhist highlanders, with the people of the Hills exhibiting a mixture of both. The greatest intermingling of the two appears in the Kathmandu Valley, where there is hardly a "pure" temple to be found. One site may serve three or four different cults. Wang Hsuan Tse noted wonderingly in the 7th century that "Buddhist convents and the temples of Hindu gods touch each other," and little has changed today. Shiva *linga* and Buddhist chaitya stand side by side in temple courtyards, and Hindus and Buddhists worship the same image under different names. Regardless of creed, everyone joins in the great festivals and worships the most popular deities—elephant-headed Ganesh, the bringer of luck; Nepal's patron god Pashupati (a form of Shiva), and the Valley's patron, Machhendranath.

This spirit of tolerance dates back to the Licchavi era, when the two faiths flourished side by side and kings sponsored both Hindu temples and Buddhist monasteries. With the advent of the Malla Dynasty in the 13th century Hinduism became the dominant religion, increasing its hold over the centuries until today the population is 90% Hindu, 5% Buddhist, and 3% Muslim. These figures are an indication of social realities.

The switch is not so drastic, for Buddhism developed out of the Hindu context of 6th century B.C. India, and the two share fundamental premises despite their differences. Both postulate multiple rebirths within *samsara,* the delusory aspect of earthly existence; both decree the soul's fortunes are determined by its previous actions, the law of karma; and both offer hope for escaping the endless wheel of samsara and achieving the ultimate release beyond ego—the Hindu's *Moksa,* the Buddhist's Nirvana. In the meantime, for the vast majority of followers not inclined to struggle, they offer multiple paths to please the gods and thus earn spiritual merit and its accompanying earthly rewards.

Buddhism and Hinduism are heavily influenced by animistic folk beliefs which preceded them, and both have incorporated practices and philosophies from the esoteric realm of tantra. Both religions are remarkably accommodating when it comes to indigenous native gods, recycling them into more acceptable forms. Nepalese beliefs are flexible and infinitely expandable, resulting in a profusion of cults, deities, and celebrations.

Pashupatinath crowded with worshippers at Shiva Ratri.

Hindus hold political and social power in Nepal's caste-dominated society, and many ethnic groups formerly practicing Buddhism or animistic faiths have converted to Hinduism in an effort to raise their social status.

WORSHIP

Deities are not a matter of faith but a matter of fact, living beings to be pleased or appeased by devotees. Westerners find it difficult to keep track of the bewildering pantheon. Some are

women waiting in line to perform puja at Kumbheswar Mahadev Mandir (Patan) during Jamai Purnima festival

KERRY MORAN

KERRY MORAN

repelled by the vast number of idols and the sometimes grotesque rituals like blood sacrifice. Others are seduced by the exoticism of it all. Perhaps the best approach is to view the gods as manifold expressions of the depth, reach, and range of the human mind. Seen thus, they are transformed from superstition into archetypes, creative expressions of universal psychic forces—precisely their role in the highest Hindu and Buddhist teachings.

Probably 95% of people, including monks and priests, are content to accept the gods literally, making offerings and supplications to ensure better circumstances in this life or the next. A small minority have a more esoteric vision, treating the gods as stepping-stones to an inner reality.

Like people, the gods have their own individual characters. They can be motherly or fierce, compassionate or wrathful, and they assume multiple forms to express their various moods. Nepal's huge pantheon encompasses all the possibilities of the human spirit and mirrors the Nepalese delight in abundance, whether it be in art, religion, or feasting. As A.W. MacDonald writes: "A one-spirit or a one-god religion is as unthinkable in Nepal as a storyteller without listeners, a healer without clients, a priest without faithful."

Offerings And Oblations

The gods live everywhere: in shrines and images, in sacred trees, rocks, rivers, and mountains, in the rafters, windows, and hearth of traditional Newar houses. There is even a god hidden in the household trash dump, uncovered and honored once a year. All these must be adored or propitiated according to their temperament: to ignore them risks misfortune, sickness, and death.

A Valley day begins with worship of household deities followed by a visit to neighborhood temples. Generally women take care of their family's religious obligation, making the rounds of temples with a tray of offerings and a small daughter in tow. The first stop is always the local Ganesh shrine, for this god intercedes with other deities to grant requests. On Saturdays, holy days, and festivals, entire families head to more distant shrines for outings which take on a holiday air.

The basic rite of worship is puja, offerings meant to please divine senses. Devotees scatter flower blossoms, uncooked rice, and red tika powder on images, light oil lamps and incense, and ring temple bells to alert the gods to their presence. In larger shrines priests act as intermediaries between worshippers and the gods, tending to the most sacred icons as carefully as if they were living beings. Images like Machhendranath and the sacred linga of Pashupati are dressed, bathed, "fed" and entertained with music and prayer according to a daily schedule.

This devotion is nothing compared to the Malla era, when rich noblemen sponsored the kotyhoma, the "ten million burnt oblations" of grain and ghee offered day and night for six weeks, and kings offered the tuladana or "scale gift" of their weight in gold and gems. The Chronicles record one king who ordered the Pashupati linga constantly bathed with a stream of "golden water" poured from two golden vessels, and another who nearly buried it with an offering of 125 million oranges.

On special full moons or astrologically auspicious days thousands of worshippers flock to a certain temple or sacred site to celebrate a mela in honor of the chosen deity. The sacred lake of Gosainkund, three days north of Kathmandu, is a well-known example, but nearly every region has its own particular holy place to be honored at an appropriate time. Part festival, part bazaar, part county fair, mela are scenes of great merriment. Vendors set up tea shops and snack stands, peddlers spread out their wares, and flirting and drinking are as common as worship—by late afternoon, even more so.

Pilgrimages are a more personal occasion than mela. Hindus and Buddhists alike journey hundreds of miles, often on foot, to worship at an especially revered place like Muktinath in the Annapurna region. The temple of Pashupatinath draws thousands of Hindus from India for the festival of Shiva Ratri, while the nearby Boudhanath stupa is a magnet for Tibetan Buddhist pilgrims who prostrate themselves full-length around it.

Other means of worship include circumambulation (walking clockwise about a holy shrine or object), repeating mantras, and ritual bathing in holy rivers or springs. Fasting is a common means of purification, especially for women, but even more popular is the feasting (bhoj) that

Kanphatta saddhu, Pashupatinath

accompanies most Newari ceremonies and celebrations and is the happy outcome of a family's blood sacrifice.

Sacrifices

Gentle puja of flowers and milk is not enough for terrifying deities like Bhairab and Durga who must be placated with offerings of blood and alcohol. Animal sacrifice is against Buddhist tenets but remains popular among Nepali Hindus even though it's disappearing in India. Only male animals are sacrificed. Killing female animals is not only a sin but a violation of Nepali law. A water buffalo is the greatest offering, but also the most expensive and infrequent. Next best is a black goat or sheep, then a duck or rooster. The various animals symbolize mental obscurations sacrificed by the donor: the buffalo stands for anger, sheep and goats for stupidity, roosters for desire.

Just before the sacrifice, water is sprinkled on the animal to make it shake its head, taken as a sign of its assent. Those who refuse get a lifetime reprieve, but usually a balky beast is so

thoroughly soaked it's forced to shake. A ritual butcher then severs the animal's jugular vein and sprays the blood over the image in offering. Traditionally the head goes to the butcher as his fee; the horns of a water buffalo might be nailed up beneath temple eaves in commemoration of the offering. The carcass is returned to the donor and provides a much appreciated meat feast for the entire family.

In the past certain bloodthirsty goddesses demanded human sacrifice, a tradition dating from Licchavi times which reportedly continued into this century in Kathmandu. The summer festival of the warrior god Kumar was marked with ritualistic rock-throwing battles between the inhabitants of upper and lower Kathmandu. The wounded were dragged off by the opposing sides and sacrificed at the shrines of two mother goddesses. An English writer in 1877 noted seeing the bodies of what he delicately termed "suicides" in front of Kathmandu's great Black Bhairav image, and references to "the supreme incense"—dried, powdered human flesh—and rumors of human sacrifices persist to this day. The most frequently mentioned site is the temple of Harasiddhi, a small Newar village a few miles south of Patan.

FOLK BELIEFS

Alongside the great religious traditions are a multitude of invisible natural forces more ancient even than the great gods, with the power to affect human lives for good or ill. These mysterious local spirits or *deuta* inhabit natural sites which instinct and tradition have labeled sacred. Regular offerings to them ensure good harvest, health, and fortune; if neglected they can cause disease and death. The Valley's ancient "curing god" shrines for toothache, paralysis, deafness, mental illness, and poxes are based on this belief. The *naga,* serpent guardians of water and underground wealth, can also cause sickness if their domain is trespassed upon by a misplaced building or well. And the ancient cult of the Mother Goddess lives on in the mother and grandmother goddesses, the often bloodthirsty *mai* and *ajima* of Newari beliefs.

Ghosts And Spirits

Hordes of minor malevolent spirits also have

the power to torment humankind and must be placated. *Preta,* the restless spirits of dead ancestors, will torment their descendants unless satisfied with offerings. Iron nails driven into thresholds or iron rings worn on the fingers protect against *pisach,* the malevolent spirits of suicides or violent deaths. To see the headless *mulkatta* with eyes on its chest is a certain omen of death. Cremation grounds are the abode of *bir masan,* dangerous evil spirits which can strike a man dead on sight; crossroads are haunted by *bhut,* a standard sort of ghost.

The belief in *boksi* or witches is widespread, and many villagers will accuse a disliked neighbor or relative of being a witch, though few are brave enough to say it to her face. Supposedly a boksi must sacrifice her husband or son to obtain her supernatural skills—the ability to transform into an animal, fly in the air, or bring illness or death upon a neighbor. Then there is the *kichkinni,* the spirit of a woman who died in childbirth and reappears as a beautiful and insatiable young woman intent on seduction. Her unlucky lover withers away as he saps his vital energies. If he can overcome his passion to notice his girlfriend has her feet turned backwards—the distinguishing mark of a kichkinni— he has a chance of escaping.

Jhankri

To deal with this assortment of powerful, unfriendly spirits Nepalis turn to traditional faith healers, *jhankri.* A jhankri is born, not made, selected by psychic abilities which usually manifest in adolescence. He can come from nearly any ethnic group, caste, or economic level, and regardless of his social standing, his strange powers earn respect from the community.

A jhankri mediates between the villager and the invisible spirit world by going into a controlled trance. In this state he can diagnose and sometimes cure illnesses, tell the future, or act as an oracle. His medical treatment may include herbal medicine, animal sacrifices, exorcism, or physical manipulation; quite often it's successful, due to the faith of the patient more than anything else. Jhankri are community psychotherapists rather than doctors, and are quite effective in the role. During festivals like Holi and Indra Jatra they appear in full ceremonial costume: pleated white skirt, rosaries of rudraksha seeds, strips of bells crisscrossed about

the chest, and a headdress of braided strips of colored cloth. They circumambulate holy sites and walk down streets doing their hopping, twirling dance, beating the double-headed drum *(dhyangro)* which symbolizes their ability to cross between the spirit and human worlds.

TANTRA

The intricate tangle of religions is further complicated by the addition of tantra, that strange strain of mysticism which first emerged in 6th-century India as a revolt against orthodox caste restraints. A technique or approach rather than a religion, tantra has influenced both Hindu and Buddhist art, meditation, and rituals. The term "tantra" refers to a vast compendium of esoteric texts. Literally it means "thread," referring to the belief that all things—man and the cosmos, the relative and the ultimate—are linked by the same vital energies. Tantra maps the psychic channels of the human body and teaches ritual and meditative techniques to effect a complete psychophysical transformation. Exceedingly powerful, it's a shortcut to enlightenment, a way to attain divinity in human form.

Tantra uses the senses rather than rejecting them and cultivates ecstasy instead of detachment. While orthodox religions shun worldly life, the tantric attitude is a qualified, intense "yes." Because the energies it tries to harness can easily degenerate into self-indulgence, careful preparation is emphasized and teachings are closely guarded. Old texts were recorded in a cryptic "twilight language" of veiled metaphors, and the most important teachings could only be obtained from a teacher capable of directly transmitting spiritual reality.

Despite an alluring reputation for "sex magic" nurtured by some risqué art, the sexual element in tantra is symbolic, representing the union of opposites. Ritual tantric worship includes an elaborate assortment of techniques: mystic diagrams (yantra), magical incantations (mantra), symbolic gestures (mudra), and physical postures (asana).

Mantras are Sanskrit syllables imbued with mystic power which concentrate energy in the form of symbolic sound. Recited to invoke deities, to obtain certain effects, or as a form of prayer, mantras create a meditative state and

(top) Women dressed in red crowd Pashupatinath at Teej. (Christopher Gamm)
(bottom) Bhairab's chariot smashes into a building during Bisket Jatra, Bhaktapur. (Kerry Moran)

(top left) metal statue of the Buddhist deity Vajrasattva (Kerry Moran);
(top right) seated Buddha at Swayambhunath (Kerry Moran);
(bottom) prayer wheels at Sitala Mandir, Swayambhunath (Kerry Moran)

earn spiritual merit. Best known are the Hindu *om,* said to be the fundamental sound of the universe, and the Tibetan *Om Mani Padme Hum,* carved, painted, and muttered all over the Buddhist Himalaya. Countless attempts have been made to explain the latter, but like all mantras it's inherently untranslatable. Literally rendered as "Hail, the Jewel in the Lotus," and metaphorically described as "the symbolic representation of divine coitus," its meaning goes beyond words.

Yantras are to sight what mantras are to sound, condensed patterns embodying the essence of reality in symbolic form. These concentrated diagrams of cosmic power are created for rituals in temporary form with colored powders; more permanent yantra are painted onto scrolls or encoded into the symbolic architecture of shrines and temples. Best known is the mandala, a particular type of yantra depicting the various realms and divinities of the multidimensional universe.

Mudras, ritual hand positions, encapsulate symbolic meaning in gesture and accompany mantras in rituals. Deities in sculptures and paintings can be identified by their characteristic mudra.

MUDRAS

BOB RACE

HINDUISM

Hinduism's roots go back over 2,000 years to the meeting of India's Indus Valley civilization with Aryan invaders from the north. The first contributed beliefs in natural forces, fertility, and mother goddesses; the second introduced the caste system and the sacred book of the Vedas which forms the foundation for Hindu beliefs. The result blended elemental symbols like the linga and mother-goddesses with a concern for ordering society through caste and regulations. Hinduism is a vast, all-encompassing set of beliefs, a social system as much as a religion, which explains its pervasive influence in Nepalese society.

Practices And Beliefs

The ultimate goal is to break the endless cycle of life, death, and rebirth. In the meantime, ritual worship and the fulfillment of duties can improve conditions in one's present life and earn a better rebirth. Life is structured by *samskara* or "threshold crossings." These rituals mark significant events like the naming of an infant, the first feeding of rice, the first head-shaving for boys at age seven, investiture with the sacred thread (for higher castes only), marriage, death, and shradda rites for ancestors. A *saddhu,* or itinerant Hindu holy man, renounces these rituals along with his caste and family to lead a wandering life of asceticism, prayer and sometimes just plain vagabonding. Ordinary people are guided through life by the proper samskara, plus devout daily worship. Within the restraints of society and caste, an individual is left to find his own way. Priests officiate at certain rites, but ordinary puja is personal and much more essential.

The Gods

Understanding Hinduism, the saying goes, is like shoveling mist. There are as many paths as there are believers, for a basic tenet is that reality is too vast to restrict within a single set of beliefs. The ultimate source of creation is the formless Supreme Brahma, which manifests in infinite forms. Three main gods emerged, each representing a different aspect of life: Brahma the creator, Vishnu the preserver, Shiva the transformer and destroyer. Brahma has a very minor role among Nepalis, who worship all deities but often choose one as a special patron *(ishtadevata)*.

Essentially there's no difference between the various forms. The Hindu trinity is likened to the sun at dawn, noon, and sunset, or a man as an infant, adult, or elder man—varying in appearance, but fundamentally the same. Just as a drop of water eventually reaches the ocean, every act of worship ultimately reaches the Supreme Brahma. The gods are unimaginably diverse in terms of their manifestations, however. Each has his own special symbols, consort, animal mount to transport him about the universe, mudras, and posture, all of which serve to identify him to worshippers.

Vishnu: Preserver of life, Vishnu or Narayan is the benevolent savior, adored in multiple forms. His ten main incarnations *(Das Avatara)* include tortoise, fish, boar, and dwarf, each associated with a different legend. Other forms have achieved a divinity of their own, like **Krishna,** the handsome flute-playing god of love, or **Rama,** the hero of the epic *The Ramayana.* Even **Buddha** is considered an incarnation of Vishnu (though not in a complimentary sense: Vishnu assumed this form in order to delude demons with the "corrupt" Buddhist doctrine). Since the 13th century, Nepal's kings have proclaimed themselves to be Vishnu *avatar.* Vishnu's mount is the winged man-bird **Garuda,** a minor divinity in its own right; his consort Lakshmi is goddess of wealth and fortune. His symbols are the conch, mace, lotus, and disc.

Shiva: The origins of Shiva, "The Auspicious," go back 5,000 years to pre-Aryan India. Unlike Vishnu, the gentle preserver of the status quo, Shiva is the upsetter of the apple cart, an embodiment of tremendous energy manifesting in a thousand forms: MahaDev, the Great God; Nataraja, the cosmic Lord of the Dance; Yogeshvara, an ash-smeared, matted-haired ascetic. As the Great Lord, Mahesvara, Shiva appears as a family man with his beautiful wife **Parvati** seated upon his knee; the couple's sons, Ganesh and Karttikeya, are gods in their own right. And as Pashupati, the benevolent

"Lord of the Beasts," Shiva is the guardian and protector of all Nepal and a patron of Nepal's kings since the 7th century.

Shiva's fierce energy bursts forth as the fanged and fearsome **Bhairab,** the destroyer of ignorance and evil whose cult permeates Nepal. There are 64 different Bhairabs, each with an equally terrifying female consort. They manifest in unworked stones, glaring masks, or gigantic reliefs. As the principle of locomotion, Bhairab's all-seeing eyes are painted on the wheels of festival chariots; his fierce visage painted on the fuselage of RNAC planes guards them from evil.

Shiva's cognizances are the trident, the double-headed shaman's drum, the rudraksha-seed rosary, and the water pot; his mount is the faithful bull, Nandi. His most ancient symbol is the cylindrical linga, a representation of many things, including masculine generative power. Calling the linga a phallic symbol is a common oversimplification.

Other Deities

Plump elephant-headed **Ganesh** is among Nepal's most popular gods, for as the creator and remover of obstacles and the bringer of luck, his worship must proceed any undertaking, including worship of another god. The unlucky days of Tuesday and Saturday are especially sacred to him, but each morning and evening his shrines are thronged with people bringing offerings. In his hands Ganesh holds a wreath, a hatchet, his broken tusk, and a dish of milky *laddu,* his favorite sweetmeat. His mount is the long-nosed, short-legged shrew, an unlikely choice for the portly elephant.

Minor gods include **Bhimsen,** a hero of the *Mahabharata* who has become the patron of traders, and ancient Vedic deities like **Surya, Agni** and **Indra,** lords of the sun, fire, and rain.

Beneficient Hindu goddesses are worshipped for good fortune and wealth: **Parvati,** the lovely wife of Shiva; lotus-eyed **Lakshmi,** the consort of Vishnu, and **Saraswati,** goddess of music and learning. More compelling to the Nepalis are the fierce goddesses associated with the fearsome **Durga** or **Bhagwati,** the slayer of demons and defender of good. The country's greatest festival, Dasain, honors her victory over a buffalo-demon with the sacrifice of thousands of water buffalo. As **Kali,** the "Dark One," she demands more sacrifical blood; as **Taleju,** the patron goddess of the Malla Dynasty, she played an important historical role in the Valley, inspiring impressive temples and art. The human virgin Kumari is another manifestation of Durga-

Taleju. The **Ashta Matrika** ("Eight Mothers") and the **Navadurga** ("Nine Durgas") are collective examples of Durga's multifaceted nature, each representing a single aspect of the Great Goddess.

THE KUMARI

Nepal's religious syncretism is epitomized in the tradition of the Kumari, a young Buddhist Newar girl worshipped as the incarnation of the Hindu goddess Durga. Even the King of Nepal bows before Kathmandu's Royal Kumari, for she has the power to confirm his rule for the coming year.

Kumari worship dates back at least to the 16th century. Malla kings worshipped her as an incarnation of the royal patron goddess Taleju, a manifestation of Durga. Legend says the goddess used to appear before Malla kings and pass the day playing dice, but she withdrew in anger after a lustful king insulted her. Repentent, the king begged forgiveness, and the goddess finally agreed to return in the body of a young Newari virgin.

There are at least 11 different Kumari worshipped by various villages and communities of the Valley. The most revered is Kathmandu's Royal or State Kumari, who resides in a richly decorated house on Durbar Square. Five high priests conduct the search for likely candidates among the young girls of the Shakya caste. Signs of a Kumari include the *battis lakshin,* or "32 perfections" which include "thighs like a deer, chest like a lion, neck like a conch shell, eyelashes like a cow, body like a banyan."

The final candidate is tested in a dark room filled with bloody buffalo heads, remnants of the Dasain ritual sacrifices. The girl who endures this ordeal with equanimity has proven she embodies the fierce goddess Durga. In a last step, her horoscope is compared with the king's to avoid conflict. She is then installed in a secret ritual held at the Taleju temple, as the spirit of Taleju slowly possesses her body.

The girl goddess is settled in the 18th-century Kumari Bahal, where she lives a sheltered life, cared for by two at-

tendants who every day bathe her, dress her in a red robe and ritual jewelry, and paint black collyrium about her eyes and the ritual third eye on her forehead. The high priest of the Taleju temple worships her daily, and she spends several hours receiving devotees who come to do Kumari puja, said to bring wealth and good fortune. The Kumari is also used to divine the future of Nepal. If she behaves restlessly or erratically during a puja, it's a bad omen for the country.

The rest of the time she leads a more normal life, playing with the children of her attendants, eating specially prepared meals, occasionally making a perfunctory appearance at a carved wooden window for tour groups. Being an omniscient goddess, the Kumari doesn't need to attend school. She is not allowed to play outside because her feet shouldn't touch the bare ground, and on the rare occasions she leaves her house (usually to make festival appearances) she is carried by attendents. She has her own special festival, Kumari Jatra, three days set within the longer festival of Indra Jatra, when men drag her chariot through the streets of the old city, and crowds gather to receive the blessing of the regal little girl enthroned on her wheeled shrine.

The Kathmandu Kumari leads this charmed life until she reaches puberty or sheds blood, when she automatically loses her divinity and another girl is appointed to take her place. The ex-Kumari is then free to lead a "normal" life—however normal human life can be for an ex-goddess. Former Kumaris get no extra respect or honors beyond a small stipend from the state. The belief that that the husband of an ex-Kumari will die young makes marriage difficult, and many find adult life anticlimactic after their deified childhood.

MIKE WELLINS

BUDDHISM

The Buddha was born Siddhartha Gautama, a prince of the Sakya clan, in 543 B.C. in the present-day Nepal Terai. Leaving his wealth and family he set out to find something of ultimate worth. Years of rigorous asceticism brought him no closer to his goal, until one day he sat beneath a pipal tree and vowed to remain there until he achieved ultimate understanding. He meditated throughout the night, and when he arose the next morning he was a Buddha, one of the "Awakened Ones" who have transcended dualistic knowledge. For the next 45 years, Sakyamuni (the name means "Sage of the Sakyas") taught the Buddhist path to liberation, the Middle Way between extremes.

In the centuries following his death Buddhism expanded to include a vast quantity of gods and philosophies. The main schools fell into into three *yana* or vehicles. The orthodox **Hinayana** of southern Asia is based on the spoken word of the Buddha and aims at individual enlightenment. Northern Asia follows the **Mahayana,** the "Great Vehicle" whose goal is the eventual enlightenment of all beings. It includes esoteric doctrines and rituals and emphasizes transforming, rather than renouncing, desires.

Buddhism's final development was **Vajrayana,** the "Diamond Vehicle" relying even more heavily on mysticism, symbolism and ritual. Vajrayana developed from the tantric schools of eastern India and spread through the Himalaya and beyond into Tibet. In the process it absorbed many other gods, both Hindu and indigenous native deities.

This tolerant expansiveness has been the saving grace of both Hinduism and Buddhism; both have been immensely strengthened by their ability to accommodate local beliefs and incorporate them into a vaster system. The Buddha himself didn't deny the existence of the gods or forbid their worship: he merely noted it wouldn't lead to enlightenment. For the majority of Buddhists, enlightenment remains a vague and distant goal. They're more interested in the present life and propitiate the gods for plentiful crops, children, and health.

Newari Buddhism

The Buddhism of the Kathmandu Valley is the

KERRY MORAN

Newari puja for Buddha Jayanti, Swayambhunath

last living remnant of medieval Indian Buddhism. Scholars speculate it was the original religion, until Indian kings introduced Hinduism in the fourth century. Since then Newari Buddhism has slowly waned, and today is in the process of vanishing altogether. Newari Buddhism began as Mahayana, with an emphasis on monkhood, scholarship, and meditation. Monastery-temple complexes *(bahal)* in Kathmandu and especially Patan housed thousands of monks and served as centers of study and devotion for Nepalis, Tibetans, and even visiting Chinese pilgrims. Vajrayana influences entered soon after their origin in India and by the 15th century had given Newari Buddhism its mystic, ritualistic character.

Celibate monks were gradually transformed into *bare,* married priests who inherited their caste position. Their clients were caste-based as well, organised around the formerly monastic bahal, now transformed into living quarters for families who shared common priests. The bare perform life-cycle rites for their flock just as Brahman priests do for their Hindu clients. This preoccupation with caste and ritual, so atypical to

Buddhism, helped to preserve the tradition, though it solidified it into a distinctly Hinduized form.

With the 14th-century destruction of the great Indian monasteries, Valley Buddhism was cut off from its main source of inspiration and guidance. Newar Buddhism entered a long and gentle decline, becoming more Hinduized with every century. Today it has become mainly ritual for ritual's sake. Few bare know the meaning of the prayers and mantras they intone, and worshippers, currently about one-third of all Newars, are decreasing as more convert to Hinduism every year.

Tibetan Buddhism

Bhotia people of northern Nepal are essentially Tibetan Buddhists. This school of Vajrayana Buddhism includes tantric influences, and traces of the ancient indigenous Himalayan religion, Bön. (The latter lingers in a very few remote mountain villages.) Tibetan Buddhism is a vast system of beliefs, ranging from simple superstition to a highly developed unerstanding of the human mind. Esoteric teachings include complex visualization practices and meditation techniques, and an understanding of the fundamental emptiness of all relative states of being. Most Buddhists live on a less exalted plane and perform rituals influenced by folk beliefs: burning juniper incense to drive away evil influences; spinning prayer wheels and circumambulating prayer walls carved with sacred mantras; sponsoring elaborate pujas to invoke deities or exorcise evil. Tibetan Buddhists are exceptionally devout, and much time is spent in prayer and the pursuit of religious merit through prostrations, mantras, circumambulation, pilgrimage, and offerings. Buddhists abhor blood sacrifices and offer ritual cakes (torma), incense, prayer flags and butter lamps instead.

Monasteries and monks play an important role in institutional Tibetan Buddhism, though a master may be a yogi, layman, or married householder. Tibetans differentiate be-

tween ordinary monks (trapa) and spiritual teachers (lama). A relationship with the latter is essential to spiritual progress. Most revered are tulku, high-level lamas believed to be embodiments or emanations of enlightened principles, incarnated in human form to help sentient beings. Of the four major sects of Tibetan Buddhism, Bhotia tend to follow the older "Red Hat" divisions, the Nyingma and Kargyö, with their emphasis on ritual and meditation.

Buddhas And Bodhisattvas

Mountain dwellers acknowledge legions of invisible forces inhabiting their land, but these are mere spirits, to be placated and soothed rather than worshipped. Devotion is directed to various divine beings who help humans achieve enlightenment. The historical Buddha is believed to be just one in a long succession of enlightened beings who appear in different aeons and realms. The five celestial Pancha Buddhas (Tathagata or Dhyani Buddha) are often painted as guardians over the doorway to Newar houses. Each is associated with a different direction, color, mudra and symbol, manifestations of a particular divine wisdom.

Bodhisattvas are compassionate semidivinities who have deferred entry into Nirvana in order to help suffering beings. Most beloved are the sword-wielding **Manjushri, Vajrapani,** and **Avalokitesvara** (Lokeswar).The merciful bodhisattva-goddess **Tara** appears in 21 forms, the best known being Green and White Tara. They are based on two actual historical figures, a Nepalese and a Chinese princess who married the king of Tibet in the eighth century and are said to have introduced Buddhism to that country.

The other side of reality is represented by the many terrific protective deities embodying the ferocious aspect of the peaceful bodhisattvas. They come into play when fierceness is required instead of compassion, but essentially they serve the same purpose of protecting and spreading Buddhist teachings.

MARK MORRIS

FESTIVALS

In Kathmandu "every other building is a temple, every other day a festival," an 18th-century Englishman observed. His intended exaggeration is close to the truth. Kathmandu's calendar includes more than 50 holidays totaling over 170 days, and that tally takes no account of lengthier celebrations which can last up to three months. There's probably one festival every day *somewhere* in Nepal, but the Valley's greatest season begins in August after the rice is transplanted and continues through early fall, climaxing with the harvest celebrations of Dasain and Tihar.

Festivals bring color and excitement to daily life, evoking magic out of thin air with their blend of worship, mythology, and jubilation. Until recently they were a main source of entertainment; now their power is waning as films, television, and videos infiltrate the culture. But the festival cycle remains a vital part of life for the Valley's farmers, rooted in the rhythms of planting and harvest and the changing seasons.

Festivals mark every aspect of Nepali life, telling people when to clean their wells, watch out for ghosts, visit a certain temple, or worship a certain deity. The shared celebrations regulate obligations to the gods, the earth, and fellow humans, reaffirming social ties and tradition. Some rowdy festivals are social pressure valves, providing a rare opportunity to break out of traditional roles. All of them celebrate not just religion, but life itself.

> *There are many, many religious festivals, something every week in honor of one god or another. There are very many gods, and they are all so easily offended that basically it is quite understandable that the Nepalese should be unwilling to insult any of them, and that they have festivals for them all.*
>
> —Giuseppe Tucci,
> *Journey to Mustang*

Calendars And Dates

The matter of New Year's Day is a typical example of the profusion (and confusion) created by Nepal's multicultural society. The official Nepali year begins in mid-April and is the most widely celebrated. But the Tibetan New Year is already celebrated earlier in February and the Newari New Year falls in November—plus, the Western date of January 1st is increasingly acknowledged in a rapidly modernizing society.

The standard Nepali calendar, based on ancient Indian astronomy, contains twelve lunar months of 28-32 days, every one immersed in religion. Each date is ruled by a particular deity or being: Ganesh is the lord of the fourth, the naga the ruler of the fifth, etc. Worship ebbs and flows with the phases of the moon. The 15 days following the full moon are the increasingly unlucky "dark half" *(badi)* of a month. The progressively more auspicious "bright half" of the waxing moon *(sudi)* begins the day after the new moon. Both new and full moon days are ritually important and are marked by big puja.

Festivals are according to the Nepali month, which bears little correspondence to the Western solar calendar. Dasain usually takes place in October, but sometimes it starts in September, and sometimes it runs into November. You need a Nepali calendar to determine festival dates.

Eras

There are also multiple systems of reckoning years. Bikram Sambat, abbreviated B.S., is said to have been founded by a semi-legendary king, Bikramditya, in 57 A.D. The Bikram era is the official reckoning used by the government and most Nepalis; B.S. 2048 began in April 1991. The Newaris still follow the Nepal Sambat era, which reckons year one as 879 A.D. This era is said to have commenced after a Newar Jyapu discovered a riverbank of golden sand and paid off all the debts of the Valley's people—a good enough reason to commemorate a new start. Finally there's the Tibetan system (similar to the Chinese), a 60-year cycle of 12 animals and five elements. Iron Sheep Year began in February 1991.

Finding Festivals

Since each calendar has its own set of festivals pegged to lunar dates, finding out what occurs when is not easy, especially for smaller but still very much worthwhile celebrations. Even the times of festival events may be set anew every year by astrologers searching the sky for auspicious conjunctions. To discover what coincides with your visit, ask hotel staff, shopkeepers, friends, whomever. Older, more traditional Nepalis are more likely to be in tune with the festival cycle than younger ones. Descriptions and dates of major festivals are published in *The Nepal Traveller.*

In addition to the great celebrations that periodically sweep the old cities, many lesser-known festivals *(mela)* are held at various temples and holy sites. Few tourists attend these but thousands of Nepalis do; it's well worthwhile to seek them out as genuine religious and social celebrations. Mary Anderson's *The Festivals of Nepal* (see Booklist) is a good resource for tracking down obscure festivals and appreciating major ones.

Festival Activities

Just about every festival honors some deity or another. Worshippers crowd around a shrine to perform puja, until the god is buried beneath flowers, rice, and red powder. Women come decked in their finest clothing and jewelry, the bright hues creating an ocean of color, while rural families down from the surrounding Hills add ethnic costumes to the scene.

Temple courtyards may be filled with long lines of seated people sharing a *bhoj* or ritual feast, served on sal-leaf plates. Less frequently, people, usually women, will fast for a period, a less joyful but more meritorious act. Ritual bathing in the sacred Bagmati is an important part of many festivals, even in the chilly winter months. The gods too are bathed, as in the annual shower for Seto Machhendranath.

Great processions or *yatra* wind through the streets of the old cities, sometimes accompanied by bands of Newar musicians or masked dancers. Images may be taken from their shrine and carried about on men's shoulders in a *khat* or palanquin. Some of the yatra routes are ancient, leading through little-known corners of the cities.

Sometimes the gods are paraded in the gigantic wooden chariot-shrines unique to Nepal. These *rath jatra* honor gods like Machhendranath or the virgin goddess Kumari. For most of the year the chariot is stored in pieces beside the temple. A week or so before the festival guthi members gather to assemble the parts and build the towering 15-meter bamboo spires decorating the Machhendranath chariots. For days or weeks the great carts are hauled down cobbled streets by devotees tugging on long ropes. Sometimes the chariot hits a downhill stretch and picks up speed, and everyone races out of the way. Usually an animal has been sacrificed in advance as appeasement, but occasionally a bystander is crushed under the great wooden wheels, a bad omen for the coming year.

Masked dancers appear at certain festivals, and ordinary people dance as well, though the role of women is always played by men, as it's improper for Hindu women to dance in public except for the festival of Teej. And there's music—bands of Newari musicians with drum, flute and cymbals, roving children at Tihar, or groups of older men gathered to sing *bhajan* (devotional songs) with great gusto, accompanied by harmonium and drum.

VALLEY FESTIVALS

The following lists the Valley's major festivals and the month in which they *usually* occur. Occasionally they may fall in the preceding or following month.

Bisket Jatra (April)

Nepalese New Year is celebrated most jubilantly in Bhaktapur, where it combines with the 10-day local festival called Bisket. Images of Bhairab and the goddess Bhadrakali are enshrined in chariots and hauled about city streets, and a 25-meter-high "victory pole" is hoisted upright in an open field, then sent crashing down, driving away evil spirits and officially marking the New Year.

The following day the nearby village of Thimi celebrates **Bal Kumari Jatra** with a procession of palanquins bearing neighborhood deities. Later in the day crowds gather in nearby Bode to see the bizarre tongue-piercing ritual, in which priests pierce the tongue of a volunteer with large steel needles, an act of penitence said to earn great merit and to leave the pure unharmed.

Raato Machhendranath Rath Jatra (April-June)

Machhendranath, "Lord of the Fishes," is the patron protector of the Valley, an amalgam of religious beliefs worshipped with equal fervor by Buddhists and Hindus. Patan's beloved Raato (Red) Machhendranath, the patron of the Valley's Newar farmers and the controller of rain, is feted every spring with a chariot procession lasting up to three months, as the deity is pulled about town to bless each neighborhood. Local people crowd into the chariot's nightly resting place with offerings, while bands of Newar musicians tootle out hymns of praise with horns, drums, and cymbals. The festival culminates with **Bhoto Jatra,** the showing of the sacred vest to a huge crowd assembled at Jawalakhel, an event said to be always followed by rain.

Buddha Jayanti (May)

The full moon of Baisakh is Buddha Jayanti, the triply auspicious anniversary of Buddha's birth, enlightenment, and death. Neighborhoods are decorated with paper flags, stupa are newly whitewashed, and temples get a thorough polishing and cleaning. From early morning on, Buddhists flock to the stupa of Swayambunath for puja. In the afternoon, crowds gather at Boudhanath to see an image of Buddha paraded atop an elephant.

The early monsoon period sees few festivals since farmers are busy in the fields transplanting rice. The monsoon month of Shravan (July-August), marked by minor propitiatory festivals to malignant ghosts, is a general time of sickness and trouble. It's said the gods have gone down to the underworld, leaving men temporarily defenseless. By mid-August the rains have slowed, the rice is up, and the great festival season begins.

Gunla (August)

This holy month is a time for even more prayer and puja than usual among Newar Buddhists.

Processions of worshippers make their way to Swayambunath every morning before dawn for special puja. A week before the full moon is Patan's **Pancha Dana,** when housewives make ritual gifts to Buddhist priests. A few days later, Buddhist bahal in Kathmandu and Patan display their normally hidden treasures of ancient images, paintings and manuscripts. Two days after full moon Patan holds its **Mata Ya,** a daylong procession visiting every one of the city's hundreds of Buddhist holy places.

Janai Purnima (August)

On the full moon of Shravan high-caste Hindu men change their *janai* or sacred thread; everyone else receives a protection cord from Brahmans—a sacred yellow thread tied about the wrist. Festivities center on Patan's Kumbeshwar Mahadev temple, where thousands gather to worship the sacred linga ceremonially placed in the middle of the temple's sacred pond the preceding evening. Boys splash and frolic in the water, said to be connected by subterranean channel to the sacred lake of Gosainkund in the mountains north of the Valley. Hardier pilgrims make the three-day trek here to join a mela in honor of Shiva. Janai Purnima is also a main festival for jhankri, who congregate at various holy sites to make sacrifices and puja.

Gai Jatra (August)

The "Cow Festival" is Nepal's equivalent of the Halloween masquerade, right down to the associations with death. Recently bereaved families honor the soul of their dead by sending a cow out on parade—either a real one, elaborately adorned, a cow effigy borne on a khat, or small boys dressed as a cow. Groups of these "cows" parade through the streets, accompanied by a wild array of costumed men dressed in drag, camping it up in rouge and saris. Bhaktapur celebrates Gai Jatra with the most abandon, with liberal doses of homemade alcohol and great processions following behind blaring brass bands. Political lampoons, mockery, and satire are permitted the entire week, appearing in skits and parades around Kathmandu's Durbar Squre.

Krishna Jayanti (August)

The birth of the seductive Lord Krishna, youthful god of love, is celebrated with processions and displays of pictures narrating the events of his life. At night women gather at Patan's exquisite Krishna Mandir to chant prayers, sing hymns, and light hundreds of flickering oil lamps, while at other places throughout the cities, men sing bhajan in praise of Krishna, worshipped as one of the many incarnations of Vishnu.

Teej/Rishi Panchami (September)

Exclusively women's celebrations, these two festivals are gay and colorful despite the solemn overtones of fasting and purification. Teej begins with a late-night communal feast as the women of a household gorge themselves in preparation for the next day's strict fast. The fast replicates the 3,600 years of austerities the goddess Parvati performed to attract her husband Shiva, and is intended to ensure their husbands' long life. In the morning, women gather at Pashupatinath temple for a ritual bath in the sacred Bagmati River. Then, adorned in their finest red wedding sari and gold jewelry, they dance and sing all afternoon in praise of Shiva—unthinkable for high-caste Hindu women any other day of the year. Two days later on **Rishi Panchami** they gather again at the river (this time the Shiva temple at Teku) for another ritual bath and puja, this one meant to purify them from the sin of accidentally touching a man while menstruating.

Indra Jatra (September)

The quintessential Nepali festival, Indra Jatra marks the end of the monsoon and the beginning of harvest. For eight days Kathmandu reconnects with its medieval past with nightly performances of masked dances, bhajan and costumed dramas. Ancient images of the god Bhairab, including the gigantic painted masks of Seto Bhairab at Hanuman Dhoka and Akash Bhairab in Indra Chowk, are displayed for this single week each year.

The third day marks the beginning of **Kumari Jatra,** a festival within a festival. Thousands of brightly dressed Hill women crowd onto on the steps of Durbar Square's pagodas to view the arrival of the king and the appearance of the virgin goddess Kumari, who is carried to her gilded chariot, attended by two young boys embodying the gods Bhairab and Ganesh. For the next three evenings the three chariots are pulled about the old city. Upon their return a rowdy

> *It is the loveliest sight to see the groups of women sitting on the steps in a blaze of colours and flashing ornaments which turn the Kathmandu square into a superb theatrical scene under the shadow of the temples which send their darts of gold into the sky.*
>
> —Giuseppe Tucci,
> *Journey to Mustang*

crowd gathers in front of the mask of Seto Bhairab at Hanuman Dhoka, and young men vie for a mouthful of the rice beer flowing from a pipe jammed between Bhairab's snarling teeth. On the final night, the King of Nepal recieves tika from the Kumari, reaffirming his right to rule for another year.

Dasain (October)

This 10-day celebration is the year's greatest festival, a time for gifts, feasting, and visits. Because Dasain's focus is on home and family, it presents fewer spectacles for the visitor. Symbolically, it's both a harvest festival of thanksgiving and a bloody sacrificial reenergizing of natural powers, symbolised by the victory of the great goddess Durga over the buffalo-headed demon Mahisasura.

Houses are scrubbed clean and replastered with mud in preparation; every family member gets a new set of clothes; special food and drink is prepared; and everyone tries to return to their family home for at least a few days. Business slows as employees take leave, and all offices are closed on the final three days.

Each of Dasain's **Navaratri,** ("Nine Nights") are dedicated to a different form of the mother-goddess. On the first day, altars are established in every home and grain seeds placed in a darkened vessel to sprout. Temples are crowded with worshippers, especially at dawn and dusk; in the evenings, masked dance troupes perform in the Valley's three cities. On the seventh day, fruit and flowers brought from the royal family's ancestral home of Gorkha is presented to the king with a procession through city streets.

The eighth evening is **Kalratri,** "Black Night," when the great blood sacrifices commence and continue into the following day. Every family who can afford it will offer an animal to Durga, preferably a black male goat. The offering is then transformed into a feast; for many families Dasain is one of the few occasions they get to eat meat. The sacrifices include hundreds of water buffalo slaughtered by priests in Taleju temples throughout the night, and continued by the army in the infamous Kot courtyard behind the Hanuman Dhoka police station the morning of the ninth day. (Tibetan Buddhists, who abhor animal sacrifices, meanwhile hold special puja for the sacrificial victims at Boudha and Swayambu.) Sacrifices on the ninth day

MASKED DANCERS

The half-dozen traditional dance troupes of the Valley preserve a once widespread tradition of sacred masked dance-drama. Malla kings sponsored ceremonial dances in the courtyards of their palaces, offerings to please the gods and edify their subjects. Ritual dances are still performed today during autumn festivals, blending mysticism, drama, dance and entertainment. Just as artists provide painted or sculpted forms for deities to manifest in, masked dancers offer their bodies and minds to the god, entering a trance the moment they don their heavy masks.

Most famous are the Nava Durga dancers of Bhaktapur, representing the nine sister goddesses who protect the city. Dancers are chosen every year from among the young men of the *gatha,* a Jyapu subcaste, and train for several months under the direction of caste priests. Later the high priest of the Taleju temple invests the dancers with mantras so they can control and bear the tremendous spiritual power of the massive painted masks, which have been consecrated with tantric rituals. Unlike most ritual dance masks, sacred only during the performance, these are worshipped year-round in their own temple.

Since Bhaktapur's Nava Durga tradition began two centuries ago the masks have been carefully modeled anew every year by members of the same family. A special black clay called "god-soil" is kneaded together with cotton and flour paste. The mixture is plastered over a low relief mold, dried and sanded, then painted with a white clay base. Then the features are painted on in brilliant colors, exactly the same as the year before. Each goddess has a symbolic third eye, an elaborate headress and

gigantic earrings; different facial features and colors distinguish skull-faced Kali, serene Maheshvari, bright-red Kumari. There are also attendent deities: Shiva, Ganesh, various Bhairabs, and the fanged and fierce lion and tiger goddesses Sima and Duma.

For performances the masks are topped with heavy gilded copper crowns; some have wild manes of yak tails attached. Dancers dress in full skirts and tight blouses, with gold bracelets, silver chain necklaces, and silver bells strapped on their calves. The story they tell through steps and gestures is of Durga's conquest of the buffalo-demon, commemorated by the festival of Dasain.

Compared to the controlled and refined movements of Patan and Kathmandu troupes, Bhaktapur's dancers use vigorous sweeping gestures and whirling steps. Instead of sophisticated study, they rely on devotion. Those with sufficient faith become a vehicle for the gods the moment they don the masks. Their role is somewhere in between that of a transformed shaman and a mere actor. Sometimes the presence of the god is felt within them as a "coolness in the heart," sometimes not. Then the dancer may resort to drink to stimulate the power.

When the Nava Durga cycle is completed in June, dancers bring the masks to the priest of Taleju, who divests them of power in a ritual known as "cutting their life." Now the dancers cannot dance even if they try. The masks are burned in a funeral ritual near the Hanumante River cremation ghat. The ashes are preserved in a sacred vessel in the river until September, when they're mixed with clay to make new masks and the cycle begins again.

MARK MORRIS

honor the tools of various trades. The god Bhairab, the locomotive principle, is placated with blood sacrifices to protect motorcycles, taxis, even RNAC jets from accidents in the coming year.

On the tenth "Day of Victory," **Vijaya Dasain**, Durga's household shrine, is opened and the sprouted grain distributed as a symbol of the goddess's blessings, along with thick, sticky tika made of yoghurt, uncooked rice and red powder. Families dressed in their best clothes visit older relatives to receive tika and blessings, and long lines queue at the royal palace to receive tika from the King and Queen of Nepal.

Tihar (November)

Falling two weeks after Dasain, Tihar, the Festival of Lights, is among the Valley's most beautiful celebrations, involving five days of rituals honoring Yama, the Lord of Death. The first two days honor Yama's messengers, the crow and the dog. On the third day, **Laskhmi Puja**, sacred cows are garlanded, tika-ed and fed, and houses are scrubbed from top to bottom. At dusk, hundreds of tiny oil lamps are placed in doors and windows to welcome Lakshmi, the goddess of wealth and good fortune who, drawn by the purity and light, is said to visit homes and bestow prosperity for the coming year. Groups of young girls go door to door singing and begging for coins and sweets. On the next day (which also happens to be Newari New Year), bands of young men visit houses with rowdier improvisations, ending each verse with a rousing chorus of *deushi rey!* The final day is **Bhaai Tika**, when sisters perform puja for their brothers' long lives. Even married women return to their parents' homes for this important ritual. Brothers reciprocate with tika and a gift of money, and the day ends with feasting, gambling (normally illegal, but permitted during the holiday season), and playing on great bamboo swings.

Losar (February)

Tibetan New Year is a time for prayer, feasting, and visits; like Dasain it's a family-oriented event. The preceding week is marked by intense rituals and puja in Buddhist monasteries. Public activities climax on the morning of the fourth day as hundreds of Tibetans dressed in their finest *chuba* arrive at Boudhanath Stupa to offer incense, string up prayer flags, and make prayers. At the right auspicious moment everyone grabs a handful of tsampa (barley flour), and on the count of three, tosses it into the air in a jubilant blessing. A tsampa-throwing free-for-all ensues, along with singing and long shuffling Tibetan line dances. Then everyone disperses to visit friends, relatives, and Boudha's chang shops for an afternoon of celebration and feasting.

Shiva Ratri (February)

"The Night of Shiva" draws thousands of Indian pilgrims to Pashupatinath, one of the subcontinent's four great Shiva shrines. Temple grounds are transformed into a fairground with vendors, tea stalls, beggars, and pilgrims huddled around campfires. A side attraction are the hundreds of Indian and Nepali saddhu, bearded, longhaired wandering Hindu ascetics. Some perform incredible physical austerities; others smoke quantities of ganja in imitation of Shiva, who is known to favor it. All during the day thousands visit to ritually bathe in the Bagmati and worship the temple's sacred linga; young men indulge in *bhang* and ganja and by late afternoon are stumbling home red-eyed.

Holi (March)

Spring is welcomed with Holi's riotous throwing of water and colored powder. In the last century Holi was reportedly a Bacchanalian orgy. The licentious displays were toned down after Prime Minister Jung Bahadur Rana returned from Victorian England, but a distinctly sexual atmosphere still infuses the holiday. On full moon day roving bands of young men and boys patrol the streets, dousing passersby and vehicles with water balloons and fistfuls of brightly colored powder. Women sheltered on rooftops retaliate by dumping buckets of water. Nobody is safe; women are favorite targets, especially young Western ones. Dress accordingly, and don't go out on Holi unless you're in the mood to "play colors," *rung khelne*.

Seto Machhendranath Rath Jatra (April)

The White Machhendranath of Kathmandu, an androgynous deity for some reason considered the "sister" of the Patan god, is honored with a chariot festival of its own, complete with adoring crowds, wildly careening chariot, and great excitement.

ART

Over the centuries the Newari artists of the Kathmandu Valley produced a wealth of sculptures, statues, paintings, and monuments dedicated to the glory of the gods. Their exquisite creations reveal a superbly developed aesthetic sense which even today makes the Valley a treasure house of art and culture.

Newari art is one of flowing lines, sensuous curves, and elaborate arabesques. The canvas of a painting, the brick facade of a house, the gilded robe of an image are all targets for the artist, who seems compelled to fill empty space. Intricate patterns spread over every available surface like the exuberant growth of jungle creepers.

Newari images are masterpieces of modeling and proportion. The finest figures are supremely graceful, with a natural elegance that captures the essence of divinity. Few artists have captured the combination of sensuality and spirituality as well as the Newars.

Art, architecture, religion, and life are hopelessly entangled in Newari culture, as they are throughout Nepal. It's impossible to mark off where one ends and another begins. The greatest example of this are the Valley's old Newar cities, where exquisite stone sculptures of deities preside over neighborhood water taps, and children fly kites from pagoda steps. Temples are the dwelling places of the gods, and the laundry drying on their steps, the goats tethered to their pillars, and the grain stored beneath their eaves don't diminish their sanctity in the least.

Nepali art is completely symbolic. Every element is imbued with significance, down to the tiniest leaf, the snake twined around a pillar, or the dragon's head carved on a water tap. Literacy was rare in the past, and the rich symbolism of religious art spoke far more powerfully than words, telling a story which reaffirmed tradition and religion yet managed to be new each time.

Above all Nepalese art is meant for worship. A painting or sculpture can edify, terrify, or enlighten—sometimes all at the same time. Images of the gods are physical supports for spiritual ideals. Icons are treated as living entities, intimately known and adored. It's the complete opposite of the Western concept of art as something to be admired, analyzed, and isolated in sterile museums. This difference makes Nepal's high rate of art theft doubly tragic. Torn from its setting and encased behind glass in a temperature-controlled gallery, Nepalese art is diminished, robbed of the meaning which gives it life. The marvelous technical skill remains, but without the support of adoring eyes, the faith that impelled the artist to create cannot shine through.

temple doors, Changu Narayan

KERRY MORAN

Cultural Influences

Living along a major Asian trade route, Newar artists drew from a wealth of cross-cultural influences to create a style they spread far beyond their Valley. They linked the great traditions of China and India, contributing their own unique touches in the process.

India was the major inspiration for their styles and subjects. Nepali artists adopted India's Buddhist and Hindu pantheons and rendered them in faithful imitation of Indian schools. Their meticulous preservation of long-vanished styles makes Nepal an art historian's dream. In the isolated Valley artistic elements from the 7th century have survived as part of a living tradition.

Having learned from India, Nepali artists went on to teach Tibet, making important contributions to Tibetan art and decorating Tibetan monasteries. In medieval times the Valley was a thriving center for Buddhist art, and Patan's small family-run ateliers produced a flood of gilded images and ritual implements. Their fame spread across Asia, and in 1250 the great Kublai Khan summoned the young Newar artist Arniko to Peking to supervise Chinese workers. Arniko remained in China the rest of his life, earning the title "General Director of Bronze Workers" and "Controller of Imperial Manufacturers."

The Artist's World

Painting and metalwork are caste occupations passed on from father to son. Most artists were born into the profession, though occasionally an outsider would join as an apprentice. Artists and craftsmen were among the lower-status castes. Usually their work would be commissioned by a wealthy patron, who then donated it to a temple or monastery in the hope of gaining spiritual merit. Sometimes a small image of the donor would be incorporated into a painting, or be placed near the shrine he helped to build. A piece of art might also be commissioned to commemorate a ceremony, decorate a householder's shrine, aid a meditator in visualization practice, or help speed a dead soul to a good rebirth.

Portraits of people are rare in Nepalese art; those of the gods are all-pervasive. Art was a way to transmit the invisible images of divinities to worshippers, a means of providing the god with form. The artist was only an intermediary in the process. For an artist to sign his name to his work would be an act of unprecedented egoism. Nearly all Nepal's masterpieces are by unknown craftsmen.

Working in a highly traditional and formalized world, artists strove to replicate past designs rather than create new ones. Iconographic canons dictated the pose, gesture, implements, dress, symbols, and shades of a deity, right down to the exact proportions, taken from the "finger-measure" (angul) of the artist or donor. Any deviation from this code—a green Ratnasambhava or a blue-robed Shakyamuni—would have seemed absurd. Scope for creativity remained in the general composition, and in rendering the fine details of a statue or painting, the faces, background designs, and intricate patterns of brocade robes.

SCULPTURE

Stone Sculpture

Sculptors have left the Valley strewn with images of deities, carved columns and pillars, delicately engraved chaitya, and sacred symbols like the Shiva linga. Most are only three or four centuries old—young in the Nepali context—and are uninspired compared with earlier masterpieces, but their abundance turns the Valley into an open-air museum. In few places in the world would a fifth-century sculpture be left unguarded in the middle of a road. Heavy and durable, sculptures have better survived the art theft which has depleted Nepal's store, but even they are not immune.

Stone was the first medium Nepali artists fully mastered. From about the 5th century Licchavi-era sculptors rendered classic Hindu and Buddhist themes in powerful yet graceful images influenced by the Indian Gupta school. Favorite subjects were the 10 incarnations of Vishnu, Shiva with his lovely wife Parvati perched on his knee, voluptuous goddesses, and serene Buddhas and bodhisattvas. These last were often incorporated into the delicate detail adorning the Licchavi chaitya scattered about the Valley.

Mythology blended with the mundane in the makara, fantastic water serpents transformed into stone spouts with water gushing from their open mouths. The spouts are set in a large square sunken dhara which serves as neigh-

KERRY MORAN

sculpture at Teku, Kathmandu

borhood bath, laundry place, water source, and social center. More stone sculptures are set into niches or stand alone, making some dhara the artistic rivals of temples.

From the 9th century on, artistic impulses were increasingly channeled into painting, metal, and wood, while stone sculpture drifted into an artistic backwater. Sculptors were still prolific but had somehow lost the mastery of an earlier era. With few exceptions, sculptures from the 14th century and later are pedestrian images, technically precise yet stocky and unexpressive.

Metalwork

Skilled metalworkers produced cast images in gilded copper and bronze, gold and silver ornaments for gods and humans, hammered repoussé reliefs for temple facades, and accessories like temple bells, lamps, and jars, segueing down the scale into household goods like hammered brass water pots and plates. Classic Nepali metalwork ranks among the world's finest. Patan metalworkers especially were renowned for the ease with which they manipulated their unyielding material into fluid images, using techniques passed on from father to son.

Most old images were made of bronze with a high proportion of copper giving a ruddy glow. Religious images were often made of the *ashtadhatu*, a symbolically significant alloy of eight metals including copper, tin, iron, gold, and silver. More recently sculptors have shifted to brass, a less expensive alloy of copper and zinc.

Metal sculpture peaked in the 14th and 15th centuries, when graceful images with sensitive, expressive features and rich ornamentation predominated. In the 16th century the introduction of tantric deities from Tibet's vast pantheon provided a new opportunity for Nepali artists to display their skills. Rendering multi-limbed and many-headed deities locked in embrace with their consorts offered an engineering challenge if nothing else.

Today a few superb metalworkers remain, but most workshops produce mundane pieces sold to tourists, with a limited demand still coming from temples and monasteries (especially Tibetan Buddhist *gompa*). Nepal is one of the few countries to preserve the ancient technique of *cire perdue*, the "lost wax" process of casting, once practiced across the subcontinent. The craftsman forms a detailed wax model and coats it with a mixture of clay and rice husks. This plaster-encased image is left to dry for several weeks, then baked to melt the wax. Molten brass or bronze is then poured into the empty clay mold and left to cool. Heating the metal to the proper temperature over a charcoal fire is a time-consuming, laborious process. Usually a core is inserted at casting time to produce a hollow image and reduce the amount of metal needed. What results is a one-of-a-kind piece, for the mold must be broken to reveal the metal image, still in a rough state.

The metal is filed, polished, and finished by engraving the fine details of face, garments, and ornaments. The quality of the finish and the precision of the engraving largely determines the quality of the piece. The statue, or perhaps only its face, may be plated with a thin coat of gold and inlaid with semiprecious stones like coral, agate, and turquoise. If the image is of Buddha Shakyamuni, it will probably be given a coiffure of tightly curled blue hair, a symbol of purity. Images fashioned for use by Tibetans often have mantras, relics, or blessed grains of barley inserted in the hollow middle during a consecration ceremony; the bottom is then sealed with a copper plate.

Another ancient and nearly forgotten technique preserved in the Valley is repoussé, the art of hammering metal sheets from the reverse side into embossed designs. This method is used to form the lavish temple ornaments, bells, and gilded sheathing for images and temple doorways. The "Golden Temple" of Patan and Bhaktapur's Golden Gate provide magnificent examples of this art. So do the dazzling inlaid and gilded crowns of Buddhist priests, now preserved in the collections of foreign museums. Some images, like the statues of the Malla kings in the Durbar squares, were made with a masterful combination of the two techniques, repoussé for the larger portions and *cire perdue* for the details.

Buying Sculptures

Stone sculpture is nearly a lost art in Nepal. A few stonecutters in Patan and Kathmandu chip away at commissioned works, but the only items commonly available are the heavy mortar-and-pestle sets used to pound spices. Metal sculptures, on the other hand, are sold in every souvenir shop of the Valley. Probably the best and certainly the most interesting place to look is Patan—not just the tourist shops around Durbar Square, although some are very fine, but the old metalworking quarters of Mahabuddha, Thaina, and Nag Bahal to the northeast, where craftsmen in tiny dark workshops hammer away surrounded by images in all stages of completion. Look for a satin-smooth and flawless finish, fine engraving, a balanced pose, and a pleasing facial expression. (This will rule out 95% of the pieces you see.) The hands and feet are a sure giveaway: they should be well proportioned and have separated fingers and toes, but in most they're a solid lump. Finally, the back of a good piece should be as carefully finished as the front.

PAINTING

Painting rivals metalwork as Nepal's finest art, but many of the best examples have been taken out of the country. If you want to revel in Nepali paintings, visit the superb collection at the Los Angeles County Museum of Art. They have illuminated manuscripts, artists' sketchbooks, thangka and paubha—everything but wall frescoes, which fortunately remain in Nepal.

Nepali painting reflects a potpourri of cultural influences: Indian and Tibetan elements, traces of Rajput and Moghul styles, even a hint of Chinese ideas. Figures are round-faced and supple-limbed, frontally portrayed in graceful postures. Color is used for its symbolic meaning rather than shading and depth, with rich red, the color of happiness, being a favorite.

One characteristic feature of Nepali paintings is that they're devoid of perspective, compressing everything onto one plane regardless of differences in time or space. Multiple scenes

putting in the finishing
details of a thangka

ALISON WRIGHT

may be clustered around a main image, each illustrating a different episode of the story. Paintings are stylized and symbolic rather than realistic, befitting their function of telling a religious story or embodying a deity.

Illuminated Manuscripts

Buddhist and Hindu texts copied onto palm leaves and illustrated with miniature paintings date back to the 11th century and were popular throughout medieval times. They were bound between ornately carved and painted wooden bookcovers, works of art in themselves. Many of the durable palm leaf manuscripts have remained intact to the present day. Paper was introduced in Nepal in the 15th century from India. The most precious volumes were hand-lettered in gold or silver ink on burnished dark-blue or black paper. Kathmandu's Itum Bahal and Tham Bahal have 500-year-old volumes in this style, displayed during the Newar holy month of Gunla.

Thangka

Most paintings were done on flat scrolls, easy to roll up and transport for use in teaching, worship, decoration, or meditation. These scroll paintings are called *thangka* in Tibetan, *paubha* in Newari. Though Newari artists produced both types, the two show distinct stylistic differences. Tibetan thangka have finer lines and brighter colors, and crowd multiple figures into a small space (modern thangka follow a pseudo-Tibetan style). Paubha used more flowing, natural lines to emphasize the sensuous grace of a single deity, usually Buddhist but sometimes Hindu. Richly detailed miniatures on the border reveal minor gods and scenes of worship or court life.

Thangka are intrinsically religious paintings, meant to manifest any of the hundreds of gods. A painting might show a wrathful Dharmapala ("Protector of the Dharma") surrounded by an aureole of flames, decked with a garland of skulls, wearing an apron of human bones and a tiger skin, trampling a corpse, and brandishing an array of choppers and skull cups filled with blood—all symbols of his intense power. Or it could depict a peaceful Buddha or bodhisattva, a serene being crowned, ornamented and dressed in royal garments, hands in the boon-bestowing mudra or holding a lotus. The same divinity may appear in fierce or peaceful form according to the situation. Or he might appear seated in the middle of a geometric mandala, a formalized design that serves as a meditative device and a visual guide to enlightenment. Other subjects include high lamas and lineage holders of the four main Tibetan Buddhist sects, assemblies of lineage deities, and various mystical beings.

Painting A Thangka

A thangka begins with a white cotton cloth stretched onto a wooden frame, treated with gesso, then sanded until smooth. The central figures are outlined first, then outer scenes fill in the composition. Before the 19th century colors were ground from minerals like azurite, malachite, lapis and cinnabar, or obtained from plants. The expense and trouble of obtaining natural colors means tempera colors are generally used nowadays, resulting in a glossy sheen rather than the traditional smooth matte finish. As a final step, powdered 24-karat gold is made into paint and used to highlight fine details of ornaments and robes. Some modern thangka painters substitute powdered brass, which will tarnish within a year. Check the difference by observing the direction light reflects off a gilded section. Gold diffuses light in all directions; brass shines only in one.

As a final step the finished painting may be consecrated with a ritual to bring it to life. The mantra *Om Ah Hum* might be painted behind the forehead, throat, and heart of each main figure to imbue them with the mystic essence of Body, Speech, and Mind. Thangka are traditionally bordered in Chinese brocade, two contrasting strips of red and yellow followed by a broad band of blue. The first two colors form the "rainbow" separating the sacred from the mundane. A "door" of a contrasting color is sometimes inserted in the middle of the lower section. A piece of light silk protects the painting from dust, sunlight, and smoke, and hides secret forms from uninitiated eyes.

Buying A Thangka

Kathmandu is flooded with new thangka, 90% of them low-quality travesties cranked out for the undiscerning tourist by amateurs in large workshops. Many are attempted imitations of old pieces, painted on old crumpled canvases or smoked over wood fires in an effort to reproduce the characteristic coating of soot from monastery butter lamps. Don't be fooled. If the soot is from butter lamps, the smell would impregnante the fabric; in any case the painting's style (or lack thereof) is a dead giveaway. Because unvarnished thangka rapidly degenerate with age, old ones are seldom in good condition; those that are sell for extremely high prices. It's highly unlikely you'll come across a genuine old thangka.

Thangka are a good example of a formerly religious art which has lost its essence by being transformed into a souvenir. Tourists now buy them for the colors that go with their living room decor, not for their inner meaning. The bottom line in any purchase is personal taste, but if you're interested in buying something beyond the run-of-the-mill painting, try to learn a little about quality beforehand. Visit many shops and ask to see their very best pieces; look at genuine old thangka in books, monasteries, and museums.

The differences are quickly apparent. Detail work on genuine thangka is fine, the figures graceful, and the background richly ornamented, not left blank. The quantity of gold paint and the type of colors are not important in themselves as long as the end result is pleasing. As in statues, look at facial expressions and hands to judge quality. Subjects of the best thangka seem to leap off the canvas, radiating outwards in a burst of intensity. They're alive and vibrant, multidimensional rather than flat, and the eyes of the main figure seem to follow you about the room. A handful of painters in Kathmandu know the inner meaning of their work and are capable of creating these, but their paintings must be specially commissioned.

Paubha

Paubha are the pure Newari version of the thangka, stylistically different than their Tibetan cousins. They may be the normal rectangular shape or horizontal scrolls up to 12 meters long, meant to be slowly unrolled to reveal different scenes of a story, rather like a comic book. Paubha were used for worship or recording events like festivals and temple consecrations. Surviving ones are rare; most are hidden away as temple treasures and displayed only on special occasions. The background scenes of familiar Valley settings, temples, and stupas make them seem timeless. A few modern paubha-derived paintings appear on the market and use a naive, folk-art style. They show Valley landmarks, worship, processions, and offerings, even contemporary events like the 1990 democracy demonstrations.

Mithila Paintings

Colorful and vigorous, these line and tempera paintings on rough native paper are created by the women of Mithila, a former ancient kingdom centered around Janakpur in what is now the Nepalese Terai. Originally women decorated their mud-walled homes and courtyard floors with these designs (they still do.) Later they transferred them to paper and began to use them in courtship rituals, sending their betrothed

a Mithila painting of Krishna and Radha

KERRY MORAN

paintings bursting with fertility symbols. The handsome Krishna, Shiva's terrifying consort Kali, and the legendary Maithili princess Sita, luckless heroine of the *Ramayana,* are favorite themes. Some villages produce only black-ink outline sketches of intricate detail; others add bright mineral colors: red, yellow, blue, purple. These folk-art creations aren't available in many shops, but occasionally exhibitions are held in Kathmandu galleries. Swami Dharmajyoti, the librarian at the Hotel Vajra, may have a supply for sale, or try **Hastakala** in Kopundol.

Contemporary Art

Within the last ten years, many small Kathmandu galleries have opened to display the work of a handful of contemporary Nepali artists. The best of these painters, like M.M. Poon and Kiran Man Manandhar, render traditional ethnic-toned scenes in evocative, nontraditional styles. The popular "neo-Tibetan" style originated with Pema and Gyaltsen Sherpa, brothers from the village of Khumjung who broke away from the old thankga mode to paint fantastic mountain landscapes of their homeland, all fluffy yaks and floating clouds set amid stylized peaks. Former thangka painter Binod Moktan paints similar watercolors of Valley landscapes.

Galleries And Workshops

The burgeoning gallery scene will give you some idea of what's available, but you can save 50-75% by contacting the artists directly. Given Kathmandu's lack of street names and shortage of telephones, this isn't always easy. Visiting the studio has several advantages besides price: you can review a number of paintings (many artists keep a photo portfolio of past works) and discuss ideas for a commission. If you have the time and are willing to pay for the extra work and top-quality materials, commissioning a painting can produce superb results. The best thangka are specifically ordered for temples or private shrines and never make it to the galleries.

The **October Gallery** at the Hotel Vajra in Bijeswari exhibits paintings by traditional and modern local artists. More are tucked away in the back room for sale, and there's a scrapbook of previous displays. Hours are 0630-1100 and 1630-1930 daily. **Sirjana Art Gallery,** near the American Express office, is one of the best of the

lot. **Indigo Gallery** in Thamel displays good thangka, mostly Newari style, painted in stone-ground colors—high prices and good quality. **Phunsok Art** on Durbar Marg will take thangka commissions. **B.B. Thapa's Art Gallery** in Ekanta Kuna, Jawalakhel, sells what he calls "primitive-style" paintings, paubha-type landscapes. You can commission one with scenes from your trip, and have yourself included in the painting.

ARCHITECTURE

Superbly arranged and skillfully built, the cities, temples, and palaces of the Kathmandu Valley are the Newars' finest artistic achievement. From the ordinary house to the multitiered temple their buildings are masterpieces of design, decorated with exquisite detail. Grouped together in an urban setting, Newari architecture creates a pleasing environment which allows incredible population densities to live together in harmony.

Cities are organized by neighborhoods *(tol)* centered about the *layaku* or palace square. These Durbar squares inspired the very finest architecture, sponsored by wealthy kings who brought in only the best artists. Kings and gods dwelt together in sprawling palaces adorned with woodcarvings and crowned with multi-roofed temples. More shrines sprang up in the public squares in front of the palaces, creating a virtual forest of pagodas, pillars, and temples. Many of these creations have since crumbled, falling victim to fire, earthquake, or simply time. Most of the existing great architecture is less than 300 years old, the legacy of the Three Kingdoms era and the result of fierce artistic competition between rival kings.

These large-scale artworks were a collaboration between craftsmen and kings. Only royalty could afford to finance such magnificent buildings, roofed and ornamented with tremendous quantities of gilded copper. They were maintained by endowments established by wealthy donors and administered by the Valley's guthi system. A Newar social group organized by neighborhood or caste, and an integral, but now disappearing, part of Newari society, the *guthi* were responsible for carrying out religious rituals and maintaining temples, water tanks, resthouses, and other public buildings. They also administered income from endowment lands, using it for festivals, celebrations, and upkeep of buildings. The system acted as a sort of social cement, preserving cultural traditions and social connections as well as physical buildings.

Palaces

Royal palace compounds are designed like ordinary houses, with thick mud walls, massive carved pillars, and shaded porticoes embracing central courtyards. The resemblence ends there, however; the decoration of palaces has more in common with elaborate temples than ordinary houses. Kings employed the finest craftsmen to raise their magnificent palaces, which together with temples represent the pinnacle of Newari architectural achievement.

The former palaces of the Three Kingdoms were huge, sprawling affairs of linked courtyards. The Bhaktapur palace is supposed to have encompassed 99 courtyards, the Kathmandu palace 55, though only a few remain today. These were used as staging grounds for rituals and entertainment, as halls for public receptions, as dwellings for the royal harem, or as the elephant stables. What remains today is only a fragment of the glories of the past, preserved through painstaking restoration projects and in remarkably good condition.

TEMPLES

The dwelling places of the gods, temples inspired the very finest talents Newari artists had to give. They were built with a special type of "oiled" brick burnished with a glaze of red clay, inset with lavish carvings, and decorated with "jewelry" of finely wrought metal ornaments. The classic Hindu temple or *mandir* is a miniature encapsulation of the universal order built on the geometric design of a mandala, with the four directions symmetrically balanced and the deity residing in the exact center. The equivalent Buddhist shrine is the *stupa,* a solid hemispherical dome which is not a place of worship but a symbol of perfection and enlightenment. Worshippers walk around temples and stupa clockwise, in an ancient act that replicates the sun's journey across the sky.

Like Newari art, temple architecture is infused with symbolic meaning and crammed with detail.

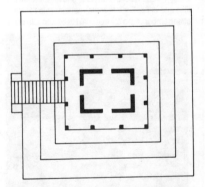

BOB RACE

side view and mandala floor plan of a Nepalese pagoda

One visit to a temple is seldom enough, and the greatest are inexhaustible treasuries you can never see too many times. Each return visit reveals more unnoticed details hidden away in corners, fine touches that you just can't appreciate the first or second time.

Pagoda Temples

Classic Newari temples are masterpieces of majesty and balance, reaching up to the heavens like mountain peaks connecting earth and sky. There is much dispute over the origins of the pagoda-type temple now found across Asia, but at least one school of thought believes the Newars first developed the design, which then spread from Nepal into China and beyond. Whether or not they originated the idea they undeniably perfected its execution, using harmonious local materials of rich red clay bricks and dark sal wood, accented with shining gilded ornaments.

Symbolically the pagoda is a mandala in three-dimensional form, its square base sheltering the *garbha griha* or "womb house" of the deity inside. Every inch is a vehicle for the gods, with art, myth, and religion lavished in an all-out display of talent.

Temples large and small dot streets and corners, are inset into rows of buildings, or centered in courtyards. They may have anywhere from two to nine roofs (most have three) topped by a gilded finial or *gajura,* symbolizing their sanctity. Most of the time the roofs are square, but temples dedicated to Bhairab are always rectangular; rare round and octagonal pagodas have also been built.

Builders ingeniously combined structural needs with visual art. The heavy slanted roofs are supported by massive struts locked into transverse beams above, which cunningly conceal the projecting roof beams and provide a surface for the gods to appear in the form of woodcarvings. The design of squares within squares evenly distributes the tremendous

WOODCARVING

Wood is abundant in Nepal, and Newar craftsmen early on perfected their skill at manipulating it with chisels, scrapers, shavers, hammers, files and drills. Their favorite medium was the dark, strong timber of the sal tree, said to be capable of enduring 1,000 years of immersion in water. On it they inscribed fantastic carvings, geometric designs, and graceful figures of deities. Set into the facades of temples, palaces and houses, wood was treated like the pages of a book, a blank surface on which to inscribe a story, usually the standard religious themes of the gods and mythical beings. Houses too were decorated with delicate traceries of "wooden lace" adorning door and window frames.

The Newari language has a technical term for each part of a carved pillar, window, or screen. Complex carvings were made from separate pieces of wood skillfully fitted together to create a single, nearly seamless, piece. Window grills are made with a special technique: precisely cut strips are fitted together in an interlocking pattern that is both structural and decorative, requiring no nails or adhesive. The slightest error can ruin the assembly of the finished piece. The technique produces an endless variety of patterns: squares, diamonds, circles, sunbursts, lotuses, geometric forms.

Door jambs, lintels, brackets, frames and entablatures were just as lavishly treated. A temple pillar might be carved with 14 different motifs: jewel, flower, lotus, leaf, skull, beading, dragons. Window frames and temple *torana* were carved in separate pieces, then skillfully fitted with nearly invisible joinings.

The most dramatic carvings are displayed on the slanted wooden struts supporting the sloping roofs of pagodas—tilted at just the right angle to convey a message to a viewer standing below. Carvers used

KERRY MORAN

erotic carving at the base of a temple strut

weight of the tiled roofs onto the body. Temples are set atop stepped pedestals to increase their imposing grandeur, the steps echoing the lines of the stacked roofs.

Craftsmen adorned the brick facade with intricate woodcarvings and delicate metalwork. Semicircular wooden tympanum or *torana* are mounted above doorways, windows, and sometimes even pillars, serving as message boards advertising the deity residing inside. Most important is the *dyo torana* mounted above the main entry, which identifies the god to worshippers. Usually the design is surmounted with the *kirtimukha,* the fearsome "Face of Glory," flanked by sea-serpent makara spouting strings of pearls and gems, another character from Indian mythology. On the richest temples the torana might be rendered in fine metalwork. But public temples are open to thieves as well as worshippers, and many shrines now bear gaping holes where an irreplaceable 15th-century image once stood. Other images have been secured with ugly metal bands to protect them from a similar fate, or hidden behind metal grills.

The Malla kings lavished so much gold on temples that small trenches were dug beneath to capture the particles washed off during monsoon downpours. Temple roofs were gilded as a symbol of purity, and delicate fringes of metalwork and bells decorated the edges of roofs, accenting them against the skyline. One peculiar feature is the *pataka,* a descending banner of hammered metal which runs from the pinnacle to the lowest story and is draped halfway to the ground. It serves as a sort of runway for the gods, a divine lightning rod through which a deity descends to listen to, and hopefully act upon, prayers made to him.

Shikara

Shikara means "mountain peak," and this soaring stone or brick temple is designed to replicate the towering peaks of the Himalaya. This form was introduced into Nepal from Northern India in the 14th century. The square base symbolizes the mountain cave used for religious retreat, topped by a cigar-shaped tower faceted into multiple planes and surmounted by a gilded finial. Symmetrical porticoes and arcades are

these strategically placed surfaces to tell more about the god enshrined inside. Temple struts might display dozens of different incarnations of the main deity, or other members of the pantheon and minor deities and spirits. The earliest date from the 14th century and include *yaksha,* ancient nature spirits converted to Buddhist demigoddesses. These graceful nymphs are depicted clinging to a cluster of foilage, their tall, slender bodies extended in curves beneath. A temple's corner struts, the largest, are always carved in the form of winged griffins *(vyala)* with horned heads, clawed feet, and giant phalluses. Originally the carvings were displayed in natural wood, but as time wore away their features they were brightly painted in an effort to disguise the wear. One of the most time-consuming tasks facing restoration projects is the patient chipping away of layers of gaudy paint.

Below the main figure are minor scenes where the artist's imagination could run free, unfettered by the rigid iconography of the main struts. Here he turned to depicting mythical beings like yaksha and naga, minor deities, dwarfs, ascetics, even scenes from daily life. Most notorious are the erotic carvings featured mainly on Hindu temples, displaying multiple participants—animals and servants included—contorted in impossible postures. Many theories have developed to explain these apparently "obscene" vignettes. Experts hypothosize they were meant to train the population in resisting temptation, or conversely to increase the reproductive rate; to attract people to temples, or to serve as a sort of tantric manual for ritual sex. The standard cliché delivered by tour guides maintains the explicit scenes are meant to frighten away the virginal goddess of lightning; it's an old standby, as Daniel Wright quotes it in 1870. Actually, all these attempted explanations are superfluous. Erotica needs little explanation in Nepal, where cults of fertility, the Mother Goddess, and tantra combine to make it seen perfectly natural.

Today woodworking is a dying art, vanishing as the demand dwindles. Tourists buy small and generally crude pieces, but wealthy Newars now build cement houses instead of traditional brick ones, and nobody sponsors the construction of new pagodas. Competent woodworkers exist and create carved wooden doors and windows for new upper-class homes, but the quality and delicacy of their work doesn't rival the originals, in part because patrons are less perfectionist than the Malla kings of old.

arrayed about the edges, supported by graceful columns. In the center is a small shrine housing the deity. Shikara may be of brick, stone (rare and expensive in Nepal, and thus sponsored only by royalty), or even entirely of terra-cotta, as in Patan's Mahaboudha temple. The finest example is without a doubt the delicately carved **Krishna Mandir** of Patan's Durbar Square.

> *The temple is as much a part of life in Nepal as the supermarket in American life, more. People sleep beneath the temple eaves, light fires on its porch, hang their clothes on its rafters, store their grain in its inner shrine, tie their goats to it, dry their onions on it . . .in short, they live with it.*
>
> —Ronald Bernier,
> *The Nepalese Pagoda*

Stupa And *Chaitya*

Exclusively Buddhist monuments, stupa are hemispherical half-domes, sanctified by sacred relics enshrined inside. The whitewashed dome of the stupa is topped with a 13-story gilded spire culminating in a filagreed pinnacle, symbolizing the stages to enlightenment. Painted upon the square base, the all-seeing eyes of the Buddha stare out over the four directions, a uniquely Nepalese addition to these originally Indian monuments.

Chaitya are small stupas, often elegantly detailed monuments of carved stone set up as memorials. Some date back to the 5th century. Historians believe they preceded the stupa and served as inspiration for the later, larger monument.

There are many distinct styles of stupa-chaitya, all derived from the original Indian model, which was based on burial mounds. Nepal's northern border regions have many Tibetan-influenced stupa called *chorten,* "supports for worship." Tibetans revere them as a tangible symbol of the Buddha's enlightened mind, enshrine sacred texts and images inside, and circumambulate them in worship. The different parts of the stupa are associated with the five elements: the square base represents earth,

the round dome water, the spire fire, the pinnacle air, and the surmounting ornament the invisible ether.

Bahal

These sprawling multistoried residential structures set around a central courtyard are scattered through the main cities of the Valley, lending their names to many neighborhoods, including Thamel (a contraction of Tham Bahal). The bahal (also called *vihara*) began in the 7th century as a monastery for Buddhist monks and a center of religious learning and art. As Newari Buddhism evolved, monks dropped their vows of celibacy to became householder priests, and bahal were transformed into housing for Buddhist lay communities. Families live in separate

a chaitya shrine, Kathmandu Valley

BOB RACE

THE VALLEY'S BEST ART AND ARCHITECTURE

Stonework

Ancient, classic stone sculptures litter the Valley, just waiting to be discovered. The hilltop shrine of **Changu Narayan** shelters some of the finest pieces: a breathtaking Vishnu revealing himself in his divine glory before an awed Arjuna (a scene from the *Bhagavad Gita*); another Vishnu in the act of taking three massive strides spanning the worlds; a curious, huge stone Garuda with the features of a long-dead king, and the Valley's first piece of recorded history, an inscribed stone victory column dating back to 464 A.D. The **Tulsi Hiti**, the royal bath in the courtyard of Patan's old palace, contains dozens of precisely executed stone sculptures set in a curved, sunken bath (as well as an exquisite metalwork spout). The **Reclining Vishnu** at Budhanilkantha is marvellous, though much of the charm has been destroyed by an ugly concrete fence. Finally, just look anywhere about the city and surrounding fields to find chaitya, linga, and the worn, shapeless ancient stones worshipped for millenia by the Newars.

Bronzes

Visit the **National Museum** for close-up views, and admire the bronze images of **Malla kings** mounted on pillars in the three Durbar Squares. Bhaktapur's famed **Golden Gate** needs no introduction, but the slightly lesser known **Golden Temple** of Patan outdoes it with an abundance of images and gilded sheathing. Nearby, in a courtyard of the old Patan palace, life-sized images of the goddesses **Ganga and Jamuna** guard a locked temple door. Pay your respects to the two **Tara** at Swayambunath, and the lush leafy trellis overrunning the torana of the **Seto Machhendranath Temple** in Kathmandu. As a sad sidelight you can note the many carefully wrought metal torana once inset with small images, now scarred by gaping holes where thieves have wrenched them out.

Paintings

This genre is more limited, but the **National Gallery** in Bhaktapur has some nice examples of thangka and paubha, plus rooms of restored frescoes from the former royal palace. In Bhaktapur's Woodcarving Museum, a room of painted frescoes is being painstakingly restored. The **Tibetan monasteries** of Boudhanath are overflowing with beautiful thangka and wall murals. Some of the finest Buddhist wall murals can be seen in the small **Sherpa monasteries** of Solu, especially Thubten Choling, Junbesi and Tragsindhu Gompas.

Woodcarvings

The finest temple struts are the oldest: the 14th-century struts at Kathmandu's **Chusya Bahal, Musya Bahal,** and **Itum Bahal,** and especially Panauti's **Indreshvara Mahadeva** temple. To marvel at lavish Newari woodwork and window screens you need go no farther than Kathmandu's Durbar Square to see the restored detail on the old palace (especially **Basantapur Tower**) and the **Kumari Bahal.** Bhaktapur's old **Pujari Math**, a former Hindu priest's house, has been transformed into a woodcarving museum. The building itself is the finest example with its intricate windows and decorations, including the famed **Peacock Window.**

Pagodas

The hilltop Vishnu temple of **Changu Narayan** is perhaps *the* classic pagoda temple, richly decorated and dating back to the 17th century (the site itself has housed a temple for over 1,500 years). Bhaktapur's five-story **Nyatapola** is the tallest, gracefully balanced on a stepped plinth. The mysterious, aloof **Taleju Temple** rising above Kathmandu's old palace is the most imposing, perfectly executed and richly adorned. You can only admire it from the outside, however: the temple is sacred to Taleju and is closed to all but the Royal Family, the Kumari, and its high priests.

---

apartments or houses in the compound, sharing the public space of the courtyard.

Every bahal has its own shrine set in the center, either free-standing or directly opposite the main entrance. The ground floor is for public worship, while the second story houses the bahal's *agama* or family deity. Sculptures and chaitya dot the courtyard, offerings from past generations that now provide local children with the ultimate playground.

The greatest concentration of bahal is in the thoroughly Buddhist city of Patan, where the linked courtyards form an invisible world behind the streets. From outside you see only the main entrance, often guarded by stone lions. Inside is a quiet sanctuary, punctuated by the cooing of pigeons and the shouts of children.

Resthouses

Today most of the *dharamsala* dotting country and city landscapes are crumbling, but once they provided shady resting places and overnight shelter for travelers and religious pilgrims. They range from the *pati*, a simple raised and covered platform used by wayfarers, to more substantial *sattal*, for longer-term shelter, and *mandapa*, large open pavilions used as a sort of community meeting hall. All these were built and maintained by wealthy patrons as an act of community service; naturally, sponsors expected to earn religious merit as well.

The wealthy also sponsored the construction of sunken fountains and water taps *(dhara)*, still used today for drinking water, laundry, and bathing. The only difference is now the rich have indoor taps, while the poor line up at the ancient outdoor ones. The old stone water tanks *(tutedhara)*, built to dispense drinking water to thirsty passersby, have long fallen out of use, but can still be found all over the Valley: look for a smooth stone slab set into a wall with a round spigot drilled in the middle.

CRAFTS

Less refined than classical art, but equally appealing and certainly cheaper, are Nepal's wide range of crafts. Their charm comes from their practical nature: brass plates polished from years of use, durable hand-knotted woolen carpets, whimsical clay elephant planters. Many of the goods on the market are modern innovations created solely for the tourists. Included in this category are filigree figurines, puppets, dolls, and most of the prayer wheels, jewelry, and doodads sold on the street.

Nepal is also the international "back door" for genuine Tibetan goods. China has slapped heavy restrictions on the export and sale of old Tibetan artifacts, but it's simple enough for dealers to visit Lhasa, buy up art at low prices, then have their purchases smuggled across unguarded mountain passes into Nepal.

A similar process happens in the restricted Himalayan kingdom of Bhutan. Buyers travel through the countryside searching for fine old embroidered dresses, offering new ones and extra cash in exchange. They bring their finds to Kathmandu, where international dealers make the yearly

wooden puppets of masked dancers, Kathmandu

rounds and take the best abroad to sell for ever-increasing prices.

Buying Crafts

Plan on making your purchases in the Valley, which has the widest range of goods. Similar knickknacks are sold along major trekking trails, passed off as a "real Tibetan prayer wheel" or "very old thangka." Actually most of this genre of souvenirs (prayer wheels and beads, small statues, wood-blocks engraved with gibberish and "Tibetan" bracelets inset with *Om Mani Padme Hum* written in Nepali script) is cranked out in Valley workshops for the tourist trade; prices and mystique simply increase with altitude. Occasionally you may find an old carpet, a brass-bound *tongba* pot or antique turquoise for sale, or your porter may offer his khukri.

Spend your first few weeks getting accustomed to the wide range of arts and crafts available in the Valley. Investigate different qualities and prices, then buy everything you want in the last few days, after you've had time to educate yourself and weed out what you don't want. Something that looked

MARK MORRIS

good the first week may well seem junky by the end of your stay, once you're able to compare.

Shops in luxury hotels have luxury prices, and even with bargaining you're starting with a disadvantage. Check out the many small crafts shops in touristed areas. Competition is heavy, especially in the off-season, but be sure to comparison-shop and visit several. Starting prices can vary by 300% from one shop to another. For the best price and selection, shop specific areas for each craft (Thimi for pottery and masks, Patan for metalwork) and explore smaller shops. The craftsman who makes goods for luxury shops will often sell his work directly, at a much lower price.

Several shops specializing in handicrafts produced by women and the handicapped sell quality goods at very reasonable prices: pillow covers, fabric and clothing, knitted goods (excellent sweaters), cotton carpets, pottery, toys and stationery. **Dhukuti** and **Hastakala** in Kopundol on the main road to Patan are two of the best (there's also a Dhukuti branch in Thamel). The **Mahaguthi Shop** in a courtyard of Patan's old royal palace stocks hand-loomed cotton fabric among other goods. **Himalayan Leathers,** just beyond Patan Hospital, sells batiks and leather goods made through the Nepal Leprosy Association.

You need to bargain practically everywhere (an exception are the above mentioned handicrafts stores). Be ruthless with the street vendors, who ask, and often get, ridiculous prices for their generally trashy trinkets. Keep in mind the real value of the rupee (see "Money") and don't feel like you have to leap on a purchase. Impulse buyers usually lose out in bargaining. It's better to take your time looking around, because 90% of things are available all over the place, and asking prices at four or five different locations will produce a wide range. A little patience and research will reveal vast differences, and ensure that you get the best for your money.

Exporting Arts And Crafts

The Department of Archaeology requires all thangka, metalwork (including jewelry), old carpets, statues, and antiques to be checked for historic value before they're taken out of the country. There is a ban on exporting any item over 100 years old, but generally speaking there's no problem with new goods, which seldom rival the quality of antiques. If you're shipping or mailing home items you need to show a certificate of approval to customs before sealing your package. Get it at the Department of Archaeology on Ram Shah Path in the National Archives Building (down from Singha Durbar), open Sun.-Fri. 1000-1500. If you're going through a shipping company they will obtain the certificate for you.

METALWARE

Plastic bowls and aluminum pots may be taking over the market, but metalworkers still hammer out traditional cooking vessels and utensils of brass and copper. The north-central quarter of Patan is a major center, and the villages of **Bhojpur** and **Chainpur** in eastern Nepal produce finely finished metalware famed for its detailed decoration.

Usually copper is mixed with zinc (brass) or tin (bronze); the more copper, the higher the quality. Brass water pots, *ghada,* are an important part of a bride's dowry. Nepali women carry them balanced on their hip, one arm wrapped about the narrow neck, in a perfect symmetry of form and balance. Smaller, more portable items include the *amkhora,* a simple waterpot, and the *karuwa,* a water pot with a stubby spout. *Anti* are tall decanters with long curved spouts topped with a metal lid adorned with a bird, used to pour raksi for festivals and celebrations.

An old-fashioned status symbol is a full set of hand-hammered, tempered brass dinner plates, used to feed crowds at festival and wedding feasts. They are said to last practically forever: some owners claim their plates are 200-300 years old, and the assembly of cooking utensils nailed up under the eaves of certain temples in offering certainly must include plates that old.

More finely worked are ritual articles like tall incense burners, metal baskets to hold puja offerings, and the beautiful little oil lamps or *sukunda,* used for puja. The image of elephant-headed Ganesh sits behind the shallow dish that holds the lampwick; behind him is the oil pot, guarded by five serpent deities rising up in a fan. A small spoon is used to ladle out mustard oil from the pot into the dish. Another style of hanging oil lamp, trimmed with a delicate fringe of hammered metal leaves, hangs in front of the carved wooden windows of older houses. Occasionally they turn up in shops but good ones are hard to find.

Khukri

The wicked, curved Nepali knife has long been famed as the Gurkha soldier's weapon of choice. With it he is said to be able to split open an enemy soldier with a single stroke, prompting a British officer to marvel at "these little men . . . with the terrible *khukri*." So famous did the Gurkhas make their weapon that Bram Stoker had his hero dispatch Dracula with a khukri, in combination with a bowie knife.

The khukri is an indispensible item for hillmen, who use it to chop through the undergrowth, sharpen a stick, or lop off a goat's head with a single stroke. There are all kinds of elaborate khukri on the market, in wooden and metal sheaths, with handles of filagree, inlaid bone, or carved wood. These are rich-man's knives, more for show than for use. The genuine item is unembellished and wicked, kept in a wooden sheath. It will have a notch at the base for the blood to run off of, and two smaller tools fitted into the sheath, used for smaller cutting jobs and starting fires. The best khukri come from eastern Nepal, particularly Bhojpur.

Shopping For Metalware

Explore Kathmandu's old bazaar if you're looking for modern brass. The detail work on new pieces is usually clumsy, so stick to simpler designs. Or look in antique shops and souvenir stalls for older pieces, expensive (Rs500-2,000 depending on size and work) but miniature masterpieces glowing with the patina of age. **Chainpur Brass** on Durbar Marg stocks old brass and also has a selection of good new work from eastern Nepal. Several shops in Bhaktapur's main bazaar sell old pieces. To distinguish old from new, run your finger around the bottom rim. It should be smooth and worn in an older piece, sharper in a new one. Time smooths down detail work and gives a distinctive patina. Usually the quality of detail reveals the age—modern craftsmen rarely match the skill of the old ones.

JEWELRY

Kathmandu has a wide selection of semiprecious gems at reasonable prices. Skilled Newar silver and goldsmiths will craft a setting, or an entire piece of jewelry, for little more than the price of the metal.

Gems

Some of the gems are mined in Nepal; many others come from various parts of Asia to Kathmandu's international bazaar. Local gem mines are centered near Chainpur in eastern Nepal (tourmaline, garnet, ruby, and citrine). Recently ruby and garnet mines have been opened in central Nepal's Ganesh Himal. Usually the stones are cut, drilled, and polished in India, then returned to Nepal for sale.

Tourmaline is the principal high-quality gem: it comes in pink, rose, green, and more rarely, lemon yellow. Some crystals display several colors along their length. The facet structure should be carefully assessed before buying, as tourmaline is tricky to cut. Yellow citrine (locally called golden topaz, but it's not) and purple amethyst are other good buys. Beware of citrine or smoky quartz passed off as topaz, a gem which is not found in Nepal.

ALISON WRIGHT

Chainpur metalworker surrounded by his wares

Nepali stones tend to lack the rich coloring of the finest grade of gems. Its pale-blue aquamarines, light-red rubies, and pink sapphires are medium value on the world market, but are still good buys. Garnets from the Chainpur mines are plentiful; look for deep dark red with high luster and transparency. Most are sold in rounded, polished beads, but a few are of facetable quality.

Good buys in imported semiprecious stones include lapis lazuli from Afghanistan (look for deep blue with gold inclusions rather than white) and turquoise and coral, the mainstay of Tibetan jewelry. Increasingly, artificial versions of both are appearing on the market as the supply of genuine top-quality stones is slowly depleted. Hong Kong imitation turquoise is made of powdered, dyed stone (complete with black veins) or even plastic. Look for sky-blue rather than blue-green turquoise. Dark, smooth antique turquoise can be found for about Rs200 for a medium-sized piece. Good coral is hard to find; it should be deep rather than light red. The coral included in ready-made necklaces is usually of inferior quality; some may even be plastic imitations.

Buying Gems
If you're serious about gem-buying, do it from a large reputable dealer. Visit several different dealers and ask them to explain the fine points of assessing quality. Most will be happy to show you varying grades of gemstones, and seeing the entire range will educate you for buying. Larger gem shops are clustered on New Road and Durbar Marg and inside hotels. **Himalayan Gems** has a factory at the Patan Industrial Estate in Lagankhel and an outlet on TriDevi Marg across from the Immigration Office.

The cut of a faceted stone can make a difference of several times in value. To judge it, hold the stone directly to the light so it reflects through the bottom towards you, and observe the percentage of internally returned light. The internal reflection should bounce off the facet angles and return an even brilliance, free of dark patches and flaws. A stone with a dark center of unreflected light or "window" is worth less.

Precious Metals
Gold and silver are sold by the tola (an old unit approximating 11 grams) at prices periodically set by the government. In 1990 gold was Rs6,180 per tola for hallmark (certified) gold, silver was Rs194 per tola. The workmanship comes in free or nearly so. Nepalis prefer soft, pliable 24-karat gold. Only those who can't afford gold will settle for silver, but it's is the most popular medium in the tourist market. Beware of "white gold," usually silver plated with rhodium.

You can choose a traditional design or pick something out of a Tiffany's catalog if you happened to bring one along with you. Good jewelers can copy from a sketch or photo. Goldsmithing is a caste occupation carried out in tiny, dark shops in the heart of the old cities. The Buddhist Shakyas preserve traditional arts and styles, working primarily in silver filagree and deep-carved traditional designs. The best workers are found in Patan. The Hindu Sunar caste specializes in etching, *jali*-cutting, and cutout work. Both castes work with simple home-made tools, hammering the metal on tiny anvils, heating their fire with blowpipes, and often anchoring the piece with their toes as they work.

Traditional Jewelry
From Newari silverwork to the golden earrings of Magar and Gurung hillwomen and the massive turquoise necklaces of Bhotias, peasant women display an amazing amount of wealth. Gold jewelry is almost always the real thing, representing a large portion of family wealth. Instead of putting money in the bank, savings go into jewelry, an investment passed on from generation to generation. Regardless of what happens to the rupee, gold is always valuable, and jewelry worn on special occasions is a bold statement of status and wealth. The finest pieces may contain US$5,000 in pure gold and are saved for weddings and big festivals. A bride from a wealthy family is decked from head to foot with gold: earrings, nosepin, headpiece, necklaces, bangles, anklets, finger and toe rings, and gold-embroidered sari.

Every ethnic group has its own distinctive jewelry designs, usually dramatic and heavy. Gurung women wear impressive large golden flowers pierced through the main body of the ear, so heavy a string is looped over the top of the ear to support the weight. Tamang women wear these or large flat golden discs hanging from their ear lobes. Bhotia women wear huge necklaces and hair ornaments of coral, turquoise, and amber, sacred *dzi* stones, and richly filagreed amulet boxes suspended about their necks. These pieces aren't bought in stores but commissioned from village smiths. It's surprisingly hard to find ready-made ethnic pieces unless you buy them directly off a woman.

Boudhanath is the center for Tibetan-style jewelry of all sorts. Gold and silver work can be found or ordered in one of the many small shops in the old cities. Visit Patan for the best work. Many jewelry shops in Thamel and on Freak Street sell silver jewelry in Nepali-inspired designs. **Sadle Traders** in Thamel has a variety of interesting pieces, designed by a Canadian jeweler who incorporates a variety of Asian motifs. Other shops sell ready-made and unstrung beads and stones. You can pick through their odds and ends to find a few unique pieces and have them strung into a necklace. Hollow silver beads, sold by weight, are popular. Indian beads come shaped like fish, butterflies, shells, or tiny hearts, but the silver content is low compared to Nepali-made beads, melon-shaped, round, or diamond-cut. You can commission a silversmith to make a set of die-cast beads, or buy ready-made ones.

The Bead Bazaar

At the *pote pasal* or the "Kashmiri Bazaar" behind the east side of Indra Chowk, it's Christmas year-round. Tiny stalls display shimmering, colorful strands of glass beads; it's worth walking through here just to enjoy the glittering hues. Most shops are owned by Muslim beadmakers whose ancestors were invited into Nepal in the 18th century to sell their wares. Their *potay pasal,* necklaces of many strands of tiny colored glass beads, are an essential possession for married Hindu women. Red and green are the preferred colors, often inset with a golden *tilhari,* a ridged cylindrical ornament.

Beads come from Eastern Europe and Asia, in a rainbow of colors and shapes. Prices depend on the quality of glass, color, and cutting. Czechoslovakian beads are generally high quality, especially the hexagonal ones, faceted or unfaceted, or round. Belgian beads are usually square. Japanese beads come in blunt cut, round, square, diamond or long bugle beads; most are opalescent. Taiwanese beads offer similar colors but lower-quality cutting and correspondingly lower prices. At the top of the line are beads of 18-karat gold, or centers of gold and an outside of faceted clear glass.

You can buy ready-made (expect a discount for several pieces) or custom-order special necklaces, bracelets, belts and earrings and choose color combinations and the type of closure and thread. The shopkeeper will arrange for a stringer to make your order.

TEXTILES

Handwoven Cloth

Weaving was once a widespread cottage industry in Nepal: a spinning wheel was an essential part of a Newari bride's dowry, and every household produced its own cloth—cotton, wool, or for the poor, the durable, warm *allo* fabric woven of fiber extracted from the stinging nettle plant. The introduction of cheap foreign cloth in the '20s practically destroyed the indigenous tradition; today, most cloth comes from India.

The clack of the handloom is still heard on the sidestreets of Bhaktapur and Kirtipur, where Newar peasant women weave cotton cloth for their black, red-bordered *patasi* skirts. Cotton hand-printed with wooden block patterns is popular among Rai and Newar peoples. Cotton *dhaka* cloth with colorful geometric patterns is used for topi and shawls, and now appears in placemats, neck scarves, and dress borders.

Weaving involves every family member. Old women sit spinning in the sun, children sort piles of yarn, men hang freshly dyed skeins up to dry, and women wind thread between bamboo poles, stretching it to reduce its bulk and prepare it for use as the warp of a loom. Though cotton is no longer grown on a large scale, Terai men still travel from village to village looking for work, twanging the string of the odd musical-looking instrument they use to clean and fluff the cotton filling of quilts and pillows.

Radi

These rough woolen carpets in natural colours are an ancient Nepalese craft, traded as far back as the 4th century B.C. Hill people make them with coarse, undyed wool, weaving it into simple patterns on a loom. The radi are soaked in water, then stamped upon to make them thick and smooth. A temple just north of Indra Chowk is nearly hidden beneath a permanent radi display; others are sold by hillmen who wander the streets with a load, looking for buyers.

CHRISTOPHER GAMM

woman weaving on backstrap loom, eastern Nepal

Buy the material in the Kathmandu Bazaar. The stretch from Asan down to New Road must have a hundred different cloth shops, with the more expensive imported varieties concentrated on Sukra Path and in the Supermarket (silks, wool and shimmering gold-embroidered sari material). Shops on the street leading from Chhetrapati to Durbar Square specialize in more exotic fabrics: raw silk from Assam, printed felt from Tibet and Ladakh, Chinese brocades and shiny silks, and Bhutanese wool woven in geometric patterns.

Ask a tailor how many meters you'll need for an item, and check the width before calculating the length. Some of the higher-priced boutiques have their own stock of special material and will sew to order. The best tailors are always busy and may need one to two weeks to finish a big order. Investigate tailors on the street down from the American Library (Puykha Tol), on New Road, or in Bagh Bazaar. Charges are quite reasonable: Rs60 for a man's shirt, a simple dress, or a pair of trousers.

Thamel has many small embroidery shops specializing in T-shirts with dozens of motifs, anything from the Grateful Dead logo to Annapurna Circuit souvenirs and shirts proclaiming: "No Rupees. No Change Money. No Hash. No Problem." They'll also custom-make designs.

Ready-made Clothing

Ready-made items range from handpainted crepe-de-chine ensembles, beaded evening blouses and Rs5,000 silk trousers from Durbar Marg designer boutiques, to cheap cotton garments sold by Indian peddlers in outdoor markets. Cotton drawstring trousers, shirts and skirts are sold all over, not very durable but cheap purchases for a trekking wardrobe. Some items are overruns from local or Indian factories, and among them you can find name-brand label garments at a fraction of what they'd sell for in the West. Among the custom boutiques, **Yashah's** in Thamel is among the best, with creative designs in nice Indian fabrics. More expensive are **Wheels** and **Mandala** on Durbar Marg.

Nepali-style ready-made clothing includes the two-piece Indian Punjabi, a comfortable and practical choice for women. The chic versions appear in ever-gaudier colors, but you can choose your own material and get one custom-

Pashmina

Pashmina is the cashmere of the Himalaya, an incredibly warm, soft wool fabric made from the silky long fleece that grows nearest the sheep or goat's skin. Shops near Indra Chowk and in major hotels sell shawls from Rs600-1600 depending on the percentage of pashmina. Or go straight to a factory, like **Everest Pashmina** in Gyaneshwar. The real thing is light and cloud-soft, easy to distinguish from acrylic. The natural-colored material is considered better quality than the synthetic mixed or artificially dyed fabric. Small pashmina neck scarves are soft and warm at a fraction of the cost of shawls.

Fabrics And Tailors

Kathmandu shops offer a wide variety of Nepali, Indian, Chinese, and Japanese fabrics, and tailors will stitch up a custom-made outfit in a few days for a reasonable fee. They do a reasonably good job with shirts, trousers, dresses and skirts, even jeans. Some have Western pattern books and catalogs, or you can bring in a favorite item to be copied.

made. Saris and simple cotton lungi are everywhere; a few shops sell Tibetan dresses in cotton, wool, polyester and raw silk. **Roof of The World Tibetan Boutique** on Kanti Path, and **Tsering's Boutique** in Thamel have ready-made chuba, or many tailors will make one.

"Tibetan" hand-knitted sweaters are a big item in Thamel, but don't be fooled by salesmen who tell you they're made of yak wool. Shop carefully, because the cheaper ones soon lose their shape and may develop huge moth holes within a year. **Dhukuti,** on the road to Patan, has excellent sweaters at very reasonable prices.

Bhutanese Embroideries

Because the tiny Himalayan kingdom of Bhutan admits only a few thousand tourists per year, Kathmandu is a major outlet for Bhutanese arts and crafts. Best known are the intricately embroidered textiles used for women's and men's robes, sashes and blankets. Men's robes *(gho)* are sewn into a chuba-like garment. Women's *(kira, thara)* are unsewn pieces of cloth, usually five by eight feet, meant to be folded and draped about the wearer and pinned at the shoulder. Unfolded, they make unique wall hangings, bedcovers, or even carpets.

It takes nine months to one year to complete a single large intricate piece, woven in panels on a simple backstrap loom. Old pieces (up to about 80 years old) are usually dark-blue or white cloth embroidered with hand-spun raw silk thread dyed in natural colors: black, blue, red, and sometimes green and yellow. They are more subtle than the new textiles embroidered with acrylic thread dyed in a rainbow of chemical hues. Modern weavers no longer spin and dye their own thread, and follow patterns with graph-paper charts. They work much more quickly than the weavers of the past, but the new pieces have lost some of the individuality that distinguishes antiques.

Prices vary with the age and condition of the piece, intricacy of the pattern, and fineness of detail; also size, type of thread and fabric, and whether the embroidery is on both sides or only one. Cheapest are the new embroideries of synthetic thread on cotton, about Rs3,000-4,000 for a kira. A traditional raw silk on cotton kira is Rs5,000-7,000, Rs10,000-12,000 for older pieces. The finest old pieces may bring US$5,000. But smaller pieces, like old sashes, can run as little as Rs300. Shops specializing in Bhutanese crafts (also bamboo butter boxes, arrow quivers, *chang* containers, and woven baskets) include **Zambala** and **Dragon Boutique Corner** in Thamel, plus many of the shops at Boudhanath.

TIBETAN CARPETS

Kathmandu is the international center for the Tibetan rug trade, both old and new. The modern carpet industry is big business, as weavers produce 500,000 square meters per year for export to Western countries, mainly Europe. Old rugs belong to a distinctly different tradition, now vanishing before the new techniques. The supply of old rugs is limited but is constantly replenished with carpets smuggled out of Tibet or brought by refugees and pilgrims to be sold for cash. Prices have skyrocketed in the last few years as dealers realized the value of these old pieces on the international market. Now it's nothing to pay Rs20,000-30,000 for an old rug. The only consolation is that these pieces are one-of-a-kind creations, and prices are bound to go even higher in the future.

Sizes

Tibetan carpets are practical art, meant to be sat on, slept on—but never walked upon. The most common size is the three by six-foot *khaden,* big enough to cover the benches lining the walls of a Tibetan home's main room. Smaller square mats *(khakama)* are placed atop these as seats for honored guests. In monasteries, long runner rugs of square subsections seat assemblies of monks. The finest carpets decorate the thrones of high lamas. Matched sets of saddle rugs are used for horses: the larger rug goes under the saddle, the smaller one over it. Smaller ornamental pieces are used for pack-animal trappings, window and door coverings, and nowadays motorcycle and car seat covers.

Designs

Tibetans borrowed Chinese and central Asian motifs to create their own distinctive designs, each with a particular meaning. Thunder is represented by an angular border, clouds by a rounded pattern, water by wavy lines. The an-

THE MODERN CARPET INDUSTRY

Nepal's Tibetan carpet industry is a stunning refugee success story. Starting 30 years ago with nothing but their skill, Tibetan refugees created a business which today is Nepal's largest earner of foreign currency, its major export, and probably its top industrial employer.

The tale begins in 1961, when a Swiss foreign-aid project began a carpet production center at the Tibetan refugee camp in Jawalakhel. With support from the Tibetan government-in-exile, additional centers developed over the next decade in Pokhara, Chialsa (in Solu), Boudhanath, and Swayambunath. In the '70s retail boutiques opened in Kathmandu; in the '80s, European exports rocketed. As demand has grown, private enterpreneurs, both Nepali and Tibetan, have opened their own factories. Tibetans have moved up into managerial and marketing positions, until today about 80% of the weavers are Nepali, many of them Tamangs from the hills surrounding the Kathmandu Valley.

The modern carpet industry has adapted traditional Tibetan designs and colors to suit Western tastes. Gone are the riotous colors of old rugs, replaced by muted natural hues of beige, gray, mauve, and blue. Simple borders surrounding plain fields are in vogue; dragons and tigers are among the few older patterns to remain popular, and even they have been adapted. Modern rugs come in larger sizes to meet the Western demand for floor coverings; in Tibet they were most often used to cover benches and beds.

The weaving process remains largely unchanged. Watch it from beginning to end at the Tibetan Refugee Handicraft Center at Jawalakhel (open Sun.-Fri. 0800-1200 and 1300-1700). The raw wool is sorted by color, carded, handspun, then dyed with chemical or natural colors in huge copper cauldrons heated over wood fires. In the cavernous weaving room, rows of women sit before large upright looms strung with cotton warp, swiftly knotting the patterns sketched out on the piece of graph paper before them. Up to five weavers work on a single carpet, each producing a portion of the pattern. As they work they talk, sing, or murmur prayers and mantras.

Tibetans are the only modern weavers to use the sophisticated "senna loop" method, which can be traced back to Egyptian carpets of 2000 B.C. The weaver loops each thread around a gauge rod, the size of which determines the height of the carpet pile. As soon as a row is finished, the knots are tamped down with a wooden mallet and slit to release the gauge rod, and a new row is begun. It all happens so swiftly the hands are nearly a blur. Weavers are paid by the square meter and can produce one simple three by six-foot carpet per month. Most prefer the simple large designs which hide mistakes. Few weavers are willing to tackle complicated patterns like checkerboards and tiger skins which require an exact knot count. As a final step a finished rug is clipped with loose-hinged shears to accentuate the design's contours; some get a chemical bath to enhance the sheen of the wool. The result is a completely handmade rug, born from the old Tibetan tradition but now gone far beyond it—for better or worse is up to you to decide.

cient swastika design symbolizing eternity came from Buddhist India, as did the Ashta Mangal or Eight Auspicious Symbols and the lotus, a symbol of purity. Pictorial elements like flowers, dragons and phoenixes, favored in modern carpets, are more Chinese in origin. Older designs are more geometric and abstract, like the medallion patterns adopted from Central Asian motifs. Tibetan carpets' unique "cut-loop" weaving technique restricts the use of curving lines and favors angular designs. Checkerboard patterns and tiger-pelt designs are more recent and popular inventions.

Color

"There are three things to consider when buying a Tibetan rug," the saying goes. "Color, color, and color." Brilliant-hued carpets brightened lives and homes in barren Tibet, similar to the vivid interiors of Tibetan temples. Lovers of intense color, Tibetans quickly adopted chemical dyes introduced in the late 19th century. Aniline dyes are more reliable than the old natural dyes distilled from roots, leaves, and insects, and produce a wide range of bright hues. The early and widespread use of chemical dyes means that an all-natural dye traditional piece is extremely rare. Most old carpets combine synthetic and vegetal dyes or are all synthetic. Judge color not by synthetic vs. natural origins, but by the trueness of individual hues and the harmoniousness of the overall pattern.

Weave

Tibetan rugs are not as delicately detailed as Persian carpets which can have up to 400 knots per square inch. The average ratio for both old and new rugs is 40-60 knots per square inch, going up to 100 in top-quality new carpets.

The quality of wool means as much to a carpet as the quality of wood does to a piece of furniture. Modern sheep are bred for fine, thin wool suitable for textiles, but the best carpet wool is from aboriginal sheep, whose coarser long wool gives greater durability and resilience and a smoother, more lustrous surface. Wool from Tibetan sheep is high in lanolin, and carpets made with it age exceptionally well, developing a special patina with decades of use. But the Tibetan wool supply is unreliable, so weavers now blend it with cheaper, cleaner New Zealand wool. Most new carpets are a 50/50 blend of the two wool types.

Buying Carpets

Unique, practical and durable, Tibetan carpets are probably Nepal's most popular product. Most likely, color and design will determine your purchase, but there are a few production standards to bear in mind. Take your time and shop around; there is a tremendous variety of design and quality, and prices vary wildly.

A carpet's value is determined by size, the quality of wool and dye, and the number of knots per square inch. Pure Tibetan wool carpets, if you can find them, are top quality. A few unscrupulous dealers may try to tempt you with exotic (and false) claims of yak-wool carpets.

Natural vegetal dyes have no advantage over quality chemical dyes other than their appeal to purists. The subtle hues in fashion nowadays are easy to reproduce with natural dyes or undyed wool, but properly fixed chemical dyes are equally durable. Vegetal dying is a complex art and modern production has lost some of the range of colors.

Most export carpets are in the range of 40-60 knots per square inch. Ask a salesperson to show you the knotting near an unbound corner to make the count. Highest quality and price is 100 knots. Older pieces are woven with coarser wool; a surprisingly low knot ratio is normal for this type of carpet.

The best carpet-shopping area is around the old Tibetan camp in Jawalakhel. Several dozen shops in a small area make it easy to compare and bargain. Quality is run-of-the-mill, with a few fine exceptions. **Master Weavers** has exceptional 100-knot carpets. Prices should be about Rs400-450 per square foot for top-quality carpets, cheaper for a lower knot ratio. You can also visit factory showrooms scattered about Kathmandu and commission a custom-made carpet to be shipped if your visit is brief. This lets you control all the variables: design, size, color, type of wool and dye, and knot ratio.

If you're looking for unique old rugs the collection is less predictable. Jawalakhel shops have a limited supply. Best bets are the shops on Durbar Marg (expensive: try **Ritual Art Gallery** and the Tibetan shops in the **Shakya Arcade**) and curio shops around Boudhanath. Explore, get a feel for prices and goods, then go back to review your favorites. Remember that the inexpensive, expert cleaning and repairs available in Kathmandu can repair tiny holes, hide unravelled edges and remove 50 years of dust, but little can be done with big holes or stains. A good cleaning works wonders for dusty, faded colors.

Export regulations allow one person to carry three carpets (any size) as personal baggage. Shop owners will wrap carpets in plastic and provide a rope handle for easy carrying. Carpets sent air or sea cargo are limited to 14 square meters per passport; to ship more you need an export license from the Department of Commerce.

MISCELLANEOUS CRAFTS

Terra-cotta Pottery

Unglazed red-clay pottery is one of the Valley's oldest and most practical products. Clay is transformed into bricks and tiles, kitchen vessels, flowerpots, firepots, ritual masks, and various smoking devices. The main production center is the village of Thimi, about three km west of Bhaktapur. In Kathmandu the biggest pottery selection is displayed on the steps of the temple

Mani Rimdu dancers, Thimi Gompa, Khumbu (Christopher Gamm)

(top left) Newari mother and daughter (Christopher Gamm);
(top right) Sherpa women viewing Mani Rimdu (Christopher Gamm);
(bottom) Newari women in Bhaktapur (Kerry Moran)

near Kel Tol. Go out the back door of the Seto Machhendranath temple compound into stacks of clay pots, urns, vases, jugs, ashtrays, candleholders and flowerpots. Look for the planters shaped like elephants, rhinos, and griffins. The smaller ones are transportable if carefully packed.

Potters do their work in odd corners of cities, on the street or in a courtyard. Slapping a lump of clay on the wheel, they deftly shape it while rotating the wheel. Larger, heavier items like the big water jugs are shaped by hand or beaten out with small hammers. The finished goods are spread out in courtyards, squares, and streets to dry in the sun, then baked in a makeshift kiln made of alternating layers of straw and clay stacked up to a man's height and heaped with straw and ash. Temperatures in these improvised ovens can reach 600-700° C.

The potter carefully watches the air flow, removing or adding more ashes to control the heat. Traditional pottery is always unglazed, though a few modern craft production centers now use simple glazes. The black pottery of Bhaktapur gets its glossy finish from carbon, left by the smoke trapped inside the kiln at the end of the firing process.

Papermaking

Durable handmade *lokta* paper, often mistakenly called "rice paper," is produced from the inner fibers of the bark of the daphne shrub, a relative of the birch. In the springtime villagers collect the fibers, which are repeatedly boiled, cleaned, pounded into pulp, then mixed with water and poured into rectangular frames and dried in the sun. The result is resilient, soft, pleasingly textured paper said to last for hundreds of years. Traditionally it was used for religious manuscripts and official documents. Now the market has turned to woodblock-printed greeting cards and cloth-bound volumes. The thick yellow *harital* paper for religious manuscripts and horoscopes is a special variety, made from several sheets of white paper glued together and coated with a mixture of rice-powder adhesive and powdered harital, a sulphide mineral ore. The dried paper is polished with a stone or conch shell to bring out the gloss and written on only with special *laha* ink, made in part from dried insects.

Incense

Along with light, food, red powder, and water, incense is one of the *panchopachar,* five essential articles which must be offered to the gods. Traditionally it was made by the women of a household, who rolled powdered herbs into long, thin strips of lokta paper, creating incense sticks up to three feet long for all-day temple puja. The most common incense includes juniper and jasmine root, but there are dozens of different types, each with a different function. There is incense to cure disease and cast out evil spirits, invoke the naga who bring rains, or invite Lakshmi, the goddess of riches and fortune. To cure spirit possession, jhankri burn special *boksi dhup,* "witch incense" made with chili, snakeskin, and the black seeds of the *lankashani* plant. Bhotia people burn dried juniper as a purifier and an offering to invisible spirits; the scent permeates Tibetan rituals.

Most of the ready-made incense sold in Kathmandu is Indian and sickly sweet. Tibetan stick incense, available in shops around Boudhanath, is a good buy. The best variety is Rs30 per bundle and worth the difference.

Antiques

Most interesting antiques are Tibetan: thangka, carpets, embroideries, ritual artifacts, jewelry, and household utensils like silver-lined wooden chang cups and copper teapots. Kathmandu shops are the first stop on the line for artifacts brought out of Tibet. The most exquisite rare antiques are soon whisked to galleries abroad, where they command even higher prices.

Fine antiques are seldom cheap in Kathmandu, but prices are a bargain compared to what would be charged in the West. The best season for shopping for these kind of artifacts is late winter and early spring. Highland people visit comparatively warm Kathmandu in the winter, selling off a few possessions to pay for their expenses. Shops and dealers replenish their stock at this time for the autumn tourist season.

The widest selection of Tibetan goods is found in the Tibetan curio shops on Durbar Marg and in the tiny shops ringing the Boudhanath Stupa. The former tend to be more expensive, since rent on Durbar Marg is among the highest in the city. Visit the **Ritual Art Gallery** on Durbar Marg to see a well-displayed collection of mainly Tibetan artifacts—old carpets, copper and brass and wood vessels, ritual implements and jewelry, and a few old thangka. Quality is high and so are prices. Carpets range from US$100-30,000 for a rare tiger-striped runner rug in excellent condition. **L'Hermitage,** tucked away on a side road in the suburban neighborhood of Maiti Devi, specializes in weavings and pottery.

MUSIC AND DANCE

Deeply influenced by religion, Nepali music and dance are also a folk art, a pure expression of the exuberance that infuses Nepali celebrations. Festivals are the best time to witness uninhibited singing and dancing in a variety of forms, especially the major autumn holidays. Ethnic diversity has created a rich store of traditional songs and dances, many of them vanishing as Radio Nepal music and Hindi films become more widespread.

MUSIC

Devotional Music
On auspicious evenings the men of a Newari neighborhood gather at a temple's porch-like resthouse to spend the night singing devotional hymns (bhajan). Eyes half closed in concentration, voices rising in emotion, their songs go on and on, accompanied by an old harmonium and cymbals and propelled by the subtle beat of the tabla (hand drum). For festivals like Krishna Jayanti or the Machhendranath processions the singing may go on all night. During Indra Jatra the Valley's best bhajan groups perform nightly at Indra Chowk.

Folk Music
Soldiers, Sherpas, and porters turn to song and dance for evening entertainment. Everyone gathers in a circle by the fire; a few drums (maadal) are first idly tapped, then pounded into a hypnotic rhythm, and a sweet-voiced singer strikes up a favorite song. Usually everyone knows it and joins in the repetitive chorus, then the singer launches into yet another stanza. Sometimes an improvisation contest evolves between two singers, each tossing out increasingly risqué verses until one or the other is left speechless, to the amused derision of the listeners.

A similar singing contest between boys and girls sometimes determined marriages. At big gatherings like festivals and mela, opponents would match themselves in front of a crowd, improvising question-and-answer verses

MIKE WELLINS

Newari musicians

set to a standard tune. The musical repartee might go on for hours until a contestant faltered. If the rivals were an unmarried boy and girl, the boy could claim the right to marry his opponent if he won.

Gaine

Gaine (GAI-ni) are a dwindling caste of wandering minstrels who claims descent from the celestial musicians of Hindu mythology, the *gandharva*. In pre-radio days gaine entertained villagers with their topical ballads accompanied by their droning one-stringed *sarangi,* a sort of tiny violin. Musically their songs are repetitious, lengthy and not very inspiring, but as a blend of narrative and news and a commentary on daily life, they're genuine folklore.

The gaine repertoire includes love songs and the laments of poor farmers, overworked new wives and young widows—all the bittersweet *sukkha-dukkha* (happiness-sadness) of Nepali life. Their ballads recount famous tales, like the great fire at Singha Durbar or Tenzin Norgay's conquest of Everest (with Hillary being dragged to the top by the valiant Sherpa). They provide political commentary as well. A song might detail the procedure of a coming election, criticize quarrelling political parties, or encourage the use of birth control. Development projects have sponsored gaine contests to find a catchy family planning song.

Gaine wander from place to place with their sarangi and cookpot, singing and begging, rewarded with a handful of uncooked rice or a few coins. A few still roam the suburbs of Kathmandu; the Pokhara Valley is one of their strongholds. Some have become tourist leeches, sawing out interminable verses of "Frere Jacques" until you're driven to pay them to stop; but others are proud of their tradition they represent and are pleased to deliver a traditional ballad for a few rupees.

DANCE

Festival Dancers

Spectacularly costumed masked dancers embodying Hindu deities perform at certain festivals, reenacting old myths with their gestures and steps. The old Newar festival of Pisaach Chautardasi features performances by en-

tranced masked dancers believed to embody the Ashta Matrika or eight Mother-Goddesses, culminating with performers drinking the blood of sacrificed animals. Kathmandu's great Indra Jatra festival in September includes eight nights of dance, returning the city to its medieval past. Wild-eyed red-masked *lakhe* dancers roam the darkened streets in torchlit processions, jingling bells strapped to their legs. Other dancers include the blue-masked, long-maned Bhairab and a two-man wickerwork elephant which careens about neighborhoods searching for its master, the kidnapped god Indra. In Kathmandu's Durbar Square various groups perform dance-drama pageants enacting religious themes like the ten *avatara* of Vishnu. The festival of Dasain, dedicated to the goddess Durga, features performances by Nava Durga dance troupes (see "Masked Dancers," p. 74) and reenactments of old pageants and plays dating back to Malla times.

Other festivals are marked by humorous or satirical non-religious dances, like the wild costumes of Bhaktapur's Gai Jatra and the folkdance performances of Indra Jatra. Dancers may rhythmically beat sticks or long poles, pantomime threshing grain or pouring water from a jug. Traditional costumes verge on the macabre, including furry *khyah,* who resemble yetis but are actually long-tongued companions to the mother-goddesses, *kowoncha* or grinning "little skeletons," and *betal,* minor demons. The steps, costumes, and masks have been passed down between generations of fathers and sons. Nepali women generally don't dance in public (the only permissable occasions are at the wedding of a son and during the Teej festival) so men or young boys impersonate female roles, sometimes with hilarious results. Gai Jatra processions include lipsticked young men dressed in their sisters' saris, tight choli stuffed to create a bosomy figure, mincing about pantomiming feminine gestures with great gusto.

During the harvest festival season villagers celebrate nightly with spontaneous song and dance. Someone taps a maadal and soon others pick up the beat, clapping and singing, while a young man moves to the center of the circle to dance, though the movements now owe more to Hindi movies than folk dance.

For Bhotias, song and dance are an integral part of weddings, village festivals, and New Year celebrations. Women line up on one side, the men on the other; linking arms, they sway back and forth in unison with a shuffling, stomping step, singing the long drawn-out melodies of Tibetan folk music. Celebrations may last until dawn, fueled by plentiful cups of chang.

Cham Dances And Mani Rimdu

Cham or religious Tibetan dance is said to have been started by Guru Rinpoche, the patron of the Nyingma sect, who once danced a blessing for Samye Monastery in Tibet. Monk-dancers impersonate the gods in these costumed pageants, bringing blessings to the watchers and the community at large. They are not possessed like the Kathmandu Valley's masked dancers, but similar to the Buddhist Vajracharyas, they strive to incorporate the gods through meditation. Cham dancing is profoundly religious, but it's also a gay social occasion, a chance for people to picnic in temple courtyards and meet seldom seen friends.

Tibetan gompa in Boudhanath often sponsor cham dances for Tibetan New Year (Losar) or immediately after; in Solu-Khumbu, festivals like Dumje are marked with cham dancing. Most famous are the Mani Rimdu dances, introduced in the 1940s from Rongbuk Monastery on the north side of Mt. Everest in Tibet. Since the destruction of Rongbuk it now survives only in the Solu-Khumbu region of Nepal. Tengboche Gompa's Mani Rimdu, held during the ninth Tibetan month (usually late October) is the best known because it coincides with the main trekking season. Equally vivid pageants less crowded with camera-wielding trekkers are Thami Gompa's performance during the fourth Tibetan month (usually May) and Chiwong Gompa's Mani Rimdu, held in Solu one month after the Tengboche dance.

Mani Rimdu involves a 19-day cycle of intense puja, community ceremonies invoking the protection and blessings of the compassionate bodhisattva Pawa Chenrezig (in Sanskrit, Avalokitesvara) upon the Sherpa community. The highlight is a day-long masked dance-drama retelling the story of the introduction of Buddhism to Tibet by Guru Rinpoche. Good and evil clash in the meetings of costumed demons and deities, and soon the demons are conquered and converted into protectors of Bud-

dhism. The storyline depicts actual history and Buddhism's victory over the old Bön religion. It's also a richly symbolic interpretation of the psychological and spiritual growth of the mind. The dense layers of meaning might be difficult to digest were it not delivered in the colorful, dramatic form of ritual dance. Laymen may not be able to explain the esoteric significance of Mani Rimdu, but everyone watches the familiar scenes with rapt attention, aware of their spiritual importance. Mani Rimdu is also a great social event, drawing Sherpas from surrounding villages and Kathmandu to celebrate their reunion with days of feasting and drinking.

The dance is preceded by the creation of a mandala delineating sacred space, and by the consecration of sacred rilbu, small "pills" distributed with blessings by Tengboche Rinpoche to the Sherpa community on full-moon day at the end of a day-long empowerment ceremony. The rilbu are supposed to bring spiritual blessings and wisdom as well as health and long life. The following morning the dances begin, a visual drama of 16 sequential acts, each illustrating a different chapter of the story. Dancers play the eight manifestations of Guru Rinpoche, and spiritual beings like dakini and protectors of the Dharma. Comic relief is provided by a skit of a yogi teaching a thick-headed novice. The dances conclude at the end of a long day with a final purification ceremony to disperse negative influences. The next day is the Fire Ceremony. A culminating offering of torma (sacrificial cakes) is burned on a juniper fire, the mandala is dissolved and its sand distributed as blessings, and people slowly drift back to their homes.

Buddhist Ritual Dance

The Newari caste of tantric Buddhist priests (Vajracharya) perform ritual dances (charya nritya) as a form of worship. Traditionally the dance is performed inside temple compounds, and is only seen by the initiated male members of the Vajracharya and Shakya castes. The tradition dates back to 7th century India and its intensely symbolic tantric rituals. A superficial version of charya nritya is often included in commerical dance shows, but without the deep symbolic meaning it's only a sequence of costumed movements. The real dance is at once worship, meditation, and performance, and is still performed for important occasions. One of the few public performances is held on the morning of Buddha Jayanti, when five Vajracharyas dressed as the Pancha Buddhas dance at the Swayambunath stupa.

Newari temple dance is meant to be a deeply religious experience for both the dancer and the audience. Backed by drums and cymbals, a singer chants out a *sadhana,* a ritual description of a deity recorded in tantric texts. Through gesture, costume and ornamentation, the dancer acts out the words, describing the deity to the audience. Feet follow the rhythm of cymbals and drums as hands trace out mudras, precise symbolic gestures which express emotions and concepts in a wordless language. The hands' movement from right to left symbolizes the energy pervading the universe; their separateness symbolizes the duality of mind and body. Each movement has a symbolic significance: the tilt of the head, the flick of a wrist serve to evoke the deity; even the eyes must be perfectly controlled. Far more than art or entertainment, temple dance is a spiritual exercise, a moving prayer. It's also a way for the dancer to attain higher consciousness. If the dance is precisely executed and the performer's mind is perfectly concentrated, the deity arises in his heart, and the dance becomes an act of worship and meditation.

Performances
The best performances are the genuine ones: the masked dances of the autumn festivals, cham dances performed in front of crowd of Tibetans and Sherpas, or secret Newari temple dances. Performances of these vary seasonally and are not advertised except by word of mouth. Organized dance troupes stage regular cultural performances for tourists. They include a variety of costumed ethnic dances but are generally stagey and inauthentic. Still, they're a rare evening's entertainment in Kathmandu. See "Entertainment" in "The Kathmandu Valley" for details.

The **Kala-Mandapa** (Institute of Classical Nepalese Performing Arts) based at the Hotel Vajra is in a category by itself. It performs classical Newari temple dance for largely Western audiences, a radical departure from tradition; but it's managed to retain the integrity of the medium. Look for advertisements or call the Hotel Vajra for performance dates and times, usually Friday evenings during the fall and spring seasons.

CONDUCT AND CUSTOMS

Plunged into a world as different as Nepal, travelers often react by clinging to their own behavior as a security blanket. Getting along in Nepal is mostly a matter of common sense, plus a little courtesy and patience and a large amount of observation. If you're unsure about where to put your plate or how to eat, take a cue from others. Nobody will mind if you make honest blunders; you're not expected to act like a native Nepali. But your dress, behavior and manners are all nonverbal expressions of your attitude toward Nepal, and are read accordingly. Nepalis rarely show their displeasure with insensitive or impatient tourists. They are gone soon enough, but they leave a chronic residue of mistrust.

COMMUNICATION

Meetings And Conversations

The traditional greeting is *Namaste* (Nah-mahstey, evenly accented), accompanied by folded hands raised in front of the face. The greeting persists but the gesture is slowly vanishing, though you'll find it used more frequently outside the Valley. Use the folded hands to show extra respect. *Namaskaar* is a more formal greeting, also used to indicate respect. A handshake is quite common among men but few Nepali women have adopted the custom.

When addressing people by name you can add the polite suffix "-ji" as a mark of respect. In general people are called by kinship terms: *daai* and *didi* are elder brother and elder sister; *bhaai* and *bahini*, younger brother and younger sister. Old couples are *baje* and *baji*, grandfather/grandmother. You can call shopkeepers *sahuji* (literally "wealthy one"), *sahuni* for women.

Out on the trail, the standard greeting is one of the multiple variations of *kahaa jaane?* and *kahaa bata aaeko?* ("Where are you going?" and "Where are you coming from?") These are so widespread that even if you don't catch the words, you can safely guess this is what people are asking you and call out the names of the towns in reply.

The Western compulsion to say "thank you" on every possible occasion has spread into Nepal. Originally there was no equivalent for the indiscriminate "thanks" used by English speakers. It's not that Nepali society isn't polite—formalities are highly structured—but the word *dhanyabaad* was reserved for great occasions, not for a shopkeeper returning change. Under the influence of the ubiquitous thank you, Nepalis are turning to dhanyabaad as an indigenous equivalent. Those accustomed to dealing with tourists may even dhanyabaad you first! It's better to skip the word altogether and do as local custom dictates, accepting change or your purchase, etc. with a nod of the head.

Many people will automatically assume a couple is married. No need to explain otherwise unless you're really uncomfortable with it. It's difficult to answer the next question—your lack of children—because birth control in Nepal is nearly synonymous with sterilization, and the concept of "waiting a while" is virtually unknown. Say "soon" or "working on it" rather than "never" —a truly incomprehensible reply.

Body Language

In a ritual sense the feet are the lowest part of the body, so shoes are likewise degrading. City people often leave their shoes at the door before entering their home, a sensible practice given the amount of filth on the ground. You should do the same when visiting someone's house or room. Leather shoes and handbags are forbidden in some Hindu temple compounds, while Buddhist gompa require that you leave your shoes at the door. Wear slip-on shoes or plastic sandals if you're going on an extensive temple tour.

The degraded status of the lower portion of the body results in a whole set of cultural taboos. It's insulting to step over people seated on the ground; they won't want to step over you either, so move your legs out of the way. When you sit make sure your feet are not pointed at anyone (including an image in a temple); sit crosslegged or tuck your legs beneath you. The head is the highest part of the body, so don't pat or touch people on it, children included. Pointing with the finger is impolite.

Trekkers coax a photo-opportunity from curious Hill children.

KERRY MORAN

Nepalis typically bob their head sideways to signal agreement, unsettling to Westerners who use the same gesture to signal no. Likewise, the hand signals for come and go are the opposite of what you would expect: "come" made with the hand turned out, "go" with it turned in. When a Nepali means "I," he points to his nose.

Because the left hand is used for cleaning after defecating, it's considered ritually impure; use only the right hand for eating or handing over an object. It's a sign of respect to give or receive an object with both hands. Extend your right hand out, and hold onto the right forearm with the left hand as you offer or accept an object.

Like much of Asia, physical contact between the sexes is frowned upon in public. Even holding hands is an overly intimate act; public clinging is in very bad taste. But physical contact between the *same* sex is perfectly all right: girls hold hands; boys hang on their friend's shoulder. Regardless of what it may look like to uptight Westerners, it's all perfectly innocent, though on a thoroughly unconscious level it may serve as an outlet for frustration. Homosexuality certainly exists in Nepal, but it's not indicated by public displays.

CONDUCT

Photography
There are few restrictions on photographing or filming activities beyond respect for people's privacy. The masked dancers who appear at certain festivals are an exception. The moment they don their masks they embody the gods and are treated as such by people, who will warn you against photographing them. In general, be sensitive with intrusive flashes and of people's privacy. Remember it's their celebration, their country, their life. Rituals and festivals are almost always sacred in some way or another, with a whole world of inner meaning beyond "getting a good shot."

It's polite to ask permission to take portraits, photos of people's homes or possessions, or their children, but Nepalis have gotten used to foreigners marching up and snapping away without even acknowledging them. If you ask for a portrait, many people will insist on getting dressed up and sit there stiffly without cracking a smile. It's the opposite of the spontaneous shot you had in mind, but to them photography is a serious business, a legacy to posterity. Don't be surprised if they expect an immediate photo—everyone has heard of Polaroids. Many will ask for a copy. Don't promise to send one unless you're sure you will. Mail in Nepal is unreliable.

Some people (particularly women) are too shy to pose. Respect their desire. Sometimes just hanging out with them for a while eases the awkwardness so that 15 minutes later it's all okay. Sometimes you can crack the ice and capture a completely spontaneous photo of them fooling around. Don't make it a big deal. Nepal has been over-photographed. Many people now realize their pictues may end up in a book or magazine, and they are not thrilled with the idea. Some believe all photographers sell their work and make lots of money.

Women Travelers

Hindu caste women tend to be more withdrawn and shy than Buddhist highlanders. The latter can be quite frank, with an amazingly ribald sense of humor they may exercise at the expense of a male guest.

Nepal is a relatively easy Asian country for female travelers, even women traveling alone. However, many Nepalis find anyone traveling alone, male or female, basically incomprehensible and rather pitiable. A solo woman traveler is *really* strange, since Nepali women rarely travel, and if they do they're accompanied by hordes of relatives. This doesn't mean a woman can't travel alone, just that she may encounter a certain amount of misunderstanding and suspicion and should be prepared to deal with it. You may want to create a fictitious husband and family to mention at appropriate moments. This applies especially to trekking. Fortunately the major routes are so crowded with foreign trekkers it's easy to find casual companions. When people ask you if you're *eklaai* (alone) in a tone of disbelief, you can cheerfully assure them "No, my friends are just behind," and be almost certain someone will turn up to fill the bill within an hour. Or you may want to hire a porter to provide a semblance of respectability. It's best to find an older man with some fatherly concern, or a woman porter (possible in Sherpa regions).

The situation in Kathmandu is degenerating, as stories circulate of what Western women do in blue movie videos, coupled with the easy conquests Nepali lads find in Thamel. You may be verbally hassled or very rarely groped, but offenders quickly melt if you confront them. Underneath it all they're easily intimidated, and their friends are happy to mock them as you put them in their place. Righteous indignation or an attitude of motherly amusement seem to work equally well.

Hustlers

Kathmandu's street hustlers work hard, selling trinkets, carpets, bags, Tiger Balm and drugs, and changing money. From their weary-obnoxious veneer, it appears that harassing tourists isn't a very nice way to make a living. The veneer is not yet too thick, though. Do something unexpected, like crack a joke or stop and actually talk to them, and the interaction might just progress to a human level.

Of course nobody has the time to do this with every hustler. There's a subtle art to handling them which is refined with practice. Don't lose your temper, and don't be excessively polite either. Be brief and minimally polite at first; act more interested in your companion's conversation or your destination than in the doodad being waved in your face. If they persist, just say clearly and calmly that you don't want it, and repeat it several times if necessary, moving away. These guys have a sixth sense for weakness and indecision, even if it comes from a misguided sense of politeness. If you're really not interested they'll go to someone else, but if you falter even a moment they'll be all over you, trying to pester you into buying something.

Begging

Begging is an ancient tradition that benefits both

a small hustler and a tourist

KERRY MORAN

parties, earning merit for the giver and a living for the beggar. Hindu saddhus roam temple precincts with a begging bowl, collecting handfuls of rice and a few coins from religious people. Gaine or wandering minstrels do the same thing, but they sing for their money. Tibetan Buddhist monks may sit at shrines reading scriptures, a cloth spread out in front to receive donations. These kinds of people are traditionally sponsored in modest ways by nearly everyone. So are the lepers, cripples, blind, and retarded people who can do little else but beg. Real beggars won't badger you for money; they sit and wait for whatever comes their way, and it's nice to drop them some extra change as you pass by.

The number of beggars is increasing as the big city draws desperate refugees from the countryside. Many are truly bad off, living outside and scrounging in the garbage; it's hard to turn away from them without giving a bit.

There's also a whole new breed of beggar, nurtured by the misguided generosity of tourists. Many of them are children. A few are genuine street kids, who live by begging and scrounging in the garbage, sleeping in the streets in burlap sacks. The cleverest (and wealthiest) stand outside Nirula's on Durbar Marg, pressing their noses wistfully against the glass in case you didn't quite get the point. But quite a few of them are well-dressed schoolchildren from middle-class families who like to shout out "one rupees" and await your response with interest. They do it out of curiosity, not need. Word has gotten out that Westerners give away "pen, rupee, chocolate, boom-boom (balloon)." Sometimes their mothers will even send them running after you, urging them to beg!

You can hardly blame them when you see the way some trekkers and tourists hand out pens, candy, or money, either out of guilt at the gap between rich and poor, or a simple desire to please. It can't be repeated enough: DON'T DON'T DON'T give to kids. Not even handing over a rupee to the raggedy little girl with the big eyes to see her smile, or the "iskul pen" to the boy who earnestly tells you he needs it for school. It may sound coldhearted, but the impact extends far beyond one little incident. Gifts out of nowhere teach kids that you and people like you are irrationally generous, unbelievably wealthy, and pretty dumb to boot. Giving something for nothing is totally out of any social and cultural context; it doesn't make any sense.

This doesn't apply to people with whom you've established a genuine bond. The best gifts of all are personal: a half-hour spent playing with a child, teaching them a new game or song, helping a student with his English. There are plenty of ways to develop rapport beyond the language barrier without giveaways: blow soap bubbles, draw funny pictures, play the harmonica; show people pictures of your family, home, country. Nepalis are always fascinated to see your mother, father, sister, brother (dog, car, and house too). Having a family makes you seem more real. A collection of postcards from your city or country makes a great picture show that can be replayed every evening in a different place. People also like to see pictures of their own country: the illustrations in this book, for example.

Then there are the people, kids and adults, who come up to you on the street with flowers and *tika* powder, and after you accept it demand money, ruining what appeared to be a charming gesture. Another questionable category are the young men standing by a trail, soliciting money from trekkers for a new soccer field/library/school building. Skepticism is usually justified, even if they have a stack of receipts—especially if their ledger book shows Rs1,000 donations.

Dress

Probably the single most frequent cultural conflict revolves around clothing. Nepalis are modest about dress, but they are also polite and tolerant. Frequently a tourist's casual wear will violate the norm, but seldom will he (or most often, she) realize it. A woman in running shorts and tank top who feels comfortable in Nepal is oblivious to the sidelong glances she's attracting, and fortunately can't understand what people are saying about her. It's only normal, since a woman in short shorts is exposing more female flesh than most men have ever seen in their entire lives. After you stay in Nepal a while, you'll get the same shocked jolt when you see short shorts, tight tights, and braless tank tops. The rate of hassling from Nepali men is directly proportional to the way a woman dresses.

Rules for men are more relaxed but still exist: men shouldn't go about the city bare-chested. Only lower-class men (porters, laborers, peasants) go bare-legged in shorts or loincloths. Hairy Western legs only make things stranger.

Getting a fix on the dress code may be complicated by the mixed signals sent out by Nepali mores. Women commonly wear tight-to-bursting choli, breast-feed their children in public, and bathe topless at the public tap (it's okay for a woman who's had a child to expose her breasts, but not before). But legs are as modestly guarded as in Victorian England. Nepali folk songs speak longingly of the brief glimpse of knee revealed by the bahini as she waded across the stream. Anything above the knee is really shocking.

Bathing at a village water tap is most easily done in baggy clothes or Nepali-style, with a lungi tied up underneath the arms. The same can be used for swimming. Men can get by with shorts for bathing and swimming. Nude bathing and sunbathing is shockng to Nepalis, but some trekkers like to do both these things along well-traveled trails (admittedly it's hard to find a secluded spot in overpopulated Nepal). A bathing suit is better than nothing for swimming, but it's pretty risqué out of the water. Once I saw a couple trekking through a village in quest of a good tan, she in a skimpy bikini, he in low-cut briefs. Everyone was nearly speechless at the sight, the equivalent of parading naked through the streets.

Eating

Caste restrictions affect the preparation and eating of food in orthodox Hindu homes, and in fact food and drink are among the most sensitive indicators of cross-caste relations. Because the kitchen is ritually sacred, lower-caste members are not permitted inside. Though technically Westerners are low-caste, ethnic people will generally treat them as equals. Brahmans and Chhetris tend to be a bit more orthodox. It's best not to enter inside a Hindu kitchen unless invited. Let your host direct you to a seat. Frequently the seat near the fire is reserved for the head of the family or honored guests, and the rest are distributed according to hierarchy.

Strict Brahmans will not eat with members of lower castes, nor accept food or water from them. You probably won't encounter this unless you visit Western Nepal, with a high population of orthodox Brahmans. If you ask for food from a Brahman house you may be served out-side; likewise you may be sheltered on the porch, but not inside. It's nothing personal; they do the same to everyone else who's not high caste.

Cooked food is a primary vehicle for ritual contamination; don't touch any cooked food unless it's been given to you to eat. Any food (or utensil) that touches the lips or tongue is *jutho,* ritually impure, and may not be eaten by anyone else (exceptions are made for children and for a wife, who can finish her husband's leftovers.) Food is dished out onto individual plates, avoiding the contamination that would result if people helped themselves Western-style from serving dishes. Whatever you take on your plate must be eaten by you or thrown out. Don't offer food from your plate to anyone once you start eating.

Your empty plate or glass is also contaminated and should be placed under the table or on the ground. Watch and imitate what others do if you're unsure. Jutho also applies to glasses, water bottles, etc. If you offer your porter a drink, he'll pour the water straight down his throat. It takes some practice to drink like this. People may watch aghast as you drink from a water bottle and pass it to your friend.

Most Nepalis eat with the right hand but spoons are becoming increasingly common in "modern" regions. If you choose Nepali style, wash your hands before and after with water provided in a jug. People usually eat quickly, the better to stuff down huge quantities. Leisurely mealtime conversation is unknown—eating time is for eating. A healthy belch at the end indicates pleasure with the meal.

THEFT

Until 20 years ago Nepal was virtually free of theft and violence. Though this is changing, Nepal remains one of the safest places in the world—far safer than most Western countries, especially regarding violent crime. A handful of foreigners have been attacked over the years, usually with robbery as a motive, but the odds of it happening to you are extremely low. Petty theft is increasing to the point where it's a problem, however.

There's no need to get paranoid about security in Nepal; just use common sense: keep valuables out of sight, money and passport safely on your person, and an eye on your possessions. Try first of all to keep valuables to a minimum. Watches, camera, and flashy jewelry are all statements, subtle or blatant, of wealth. As always, the lighter you travel, the less hassles there are.

Much of the theft in the Valley and Pokhara is blamed on junkies. Nepal's population of heroin addicts is estimated at 15,000-20,000, which may not seem like much but is significant in a country with a low urban population. The rest can be attributed to social dislocation, the crumbling of a once-cohesive social system which guaranteed a thief would be quickly noticed, and a gradual change in attitudes spurred by increasingly materialistic values.

Safeguards

Carry money, checks, passport etc. in a moneybelt or pouch close to your body, preferably under your clothes. Keep traveler's-check receipts and a photocopy of your passport's front page in a separate safe place. Be especially careful after changing money, when you've got a lot of cash on your person. Take as little as possible out with you on excursions. Unless you're planning on shopping you really don't need to carry much around the Valley.

Hotel rooms are usually safe as long as there's a sturdy lock on the door and the windows are barred, well-locked, or inaccessible. You might want to bring a combination lock from home (saves the hassle of sharing and losing keys) or buy a Chinese padlock in the bazaar if the hotel lock looks flimsy. In some hotels, theft by fellow travelers is probably as big a threat as theft by Nepalis.

The biggest danger is from pickpockets, often deft-fingered kids who dip into your bag or pocket in the middle of a festival crowd or bazaar, or on the packed public buses. Don't keep your valuables in the back or side pocket of a backpack, where they're ridiculously easy to steal. If someone bumps into you or starts an inane conversation, beware: one member of a team may be distracting you, while the other picks your pocket. If you find a hand rooting in your bag or pocket grab it and shout, loudly. The thief may already have cleaned out several other people nearby.

Traveling

On bus rides, keep an eye on your pack, which will be placed on top of the bus along with other luggage, bus riders, and possibly a few goats. Rarely will the entire pack disappear, but small articles may be pilfered from front and side pockets (the ride to Jiri is supposed to be especially bad). Bury valuables deep inside the pack and stuff the side pockets with undesirable items like old smelly socks. Locking zippers with a small padlock helps. Carry a smaller bag on the bus for travel necessities and fragile valuables like camera and Walkman, and never let it out of your sight, not even on short tea breaks.

Trekking Precautions

Leave nonessentials in Kathmandu with the hotel management (assuming the people seem trustworthy). When you turn it over, get an itemized list to avoid problems. Be discreet with the valuables you do take with you; the same goes for the considerable amount of cash required for a long trek. A very few lodges along main trails have a bad reputation for things disappearing; most likely you'll hear about them in advance, but it does pay to be consistently careful.

Group trekkers may want to lock their duffel bag with a small padlock every morning as insurance, though generally porters bundle the bag with other items to make it completely inaccessible (to you as well as everyone else). Try to keep track of your possessions so you know immediately when something turns up missing. Realizing your camera has been gone since last Thursday does little good.

Protecting your things in a tent is difficult. Keep your camera out of sight and way in the back. Items left by the door, even things like shampoo and combs, may be snatched up by children overcome by sudden temptation. Usually the large number of trekkers and staff around a campsite deters potential thieves. Don't leave your boots outside the tent (or a room)—they're very valuable items in Nepal. Bring laundry in at night too, especially nifty items like blue jeans.

A very few places in Nepal have problems with gangs of local thieves who creep up in the middle of the night to slash tents and steal things from inside. Sometimes they even make off with the toilet tent. Trekking staff will warn you about these places in advance, and will do their best to stand watch all night. Avoiding theft is one good reason to hire porters through a reputable trekking company rather than picking them up yourself, although local village porters are often

wonderful, completely honest men. Hiring staff through a company is a reasonable guarantee of their honesty, and provides at least some means of action if something does disappear.

ACCOMMODATIONS

Nepali accommodations span the extremes, from palatial hotels with marble floors to mud-walled, thatched-roofed huts. After a long day's trek you'll be just as happy in one of the latter as in the former, maybe even more so. Dozens of tourist-oriented lodges have sprung up in the last 20 years. Everything is Shangri-La this and Paradise that, with a whiff of Oriental exoticism, or named after a famous Himalayan peak.

The year-round occupancy rate for Kathmandu hotel rooms is only 45%, but the season peaks in autumn, with another minor surge in spring. You can always get a medium or low-priced room but the top hotels are booked solid in season, as are the most popular lodges. Summer is a popular season for Europeans on va-

cation and for Indian tourists, who come up to Kathmandu to escape the sweltering plains and shop for modern goods from Bangkok, Singapore, and Hong Kong.

URBAN ACCOMMODATIONS

The cheap lodge situation is in constant flux, so when searching for a place to stay rely on word of mouth. It's easy to meet and exchange info with other travelers in Kathmandu lodges and restaurants. When looking for a lodge check out the ventilation, and beware of potential nighttime noisemakers like dogs and radios. Only the most expensive hotels have heating, and rooms can get pretty chilly in the winter. Likewise, few places have air-conditioning or even a fan, so if you're visiting during the hot season look for a room with good ventilation, preferably not on the top floor. During mosquito season (worst is May-July) you may need to burn Chinese coils or buy a less pungent electric Japanese mosquito zapper, a gadget which heats up cardboard mats of repellent. The mosquito count fluctuates with the neighborhood and the amount of surrounding greenery.

Lodges And Guesthouses
Kathmandu's tourist lodges include tiny dark cubicles furnished with a single bed at Rs20 and large modern rooms for US$20. You can easily find a simple, clean double with shared bath for Rs60. The most pleasant places (not necessarily the most expensive) have big, quiet courtyard gardens where you can relax in the sun—especially nice in the chilly winter months. Next best are high-rise lodges with rooftop terraces, some with mini-gardens and mountain views. Kathmandu street life can be overwhelming at first, and it's worth it to spend slightly more on a pleasant place that will give refuge when you need it. After you're oriented and adjusted, you can look for cheaper accommodations.

hotel signboard tree, Pokhara

Most lodges are clustered in Thamel and around Freak Street (cheaper), with a few out in more remote and tranquil neighborhoods. Since Kathmandu is a relatively small city, location isn't that crucial. Accommodations are surprisingly scarce in the Valley's two other major cities (Patan and Bhaktapur). There are a few lodges and hotels scattered about the Valley rim at Himalayan viewpoints, and an overnight to one of these is a good way to see something beyond the city scene if you're not planning on leaving the Valley.

Pokhara's lodges are even more plentiful; you can find a pleasant place for Rs60. Few other towns in Nepal cater to Western tourists, and lodgings are of a different sort: if you're lucky, a cavernous cement-walled room with fluorescent lights, noisy neighbors, and cold-water tap and toilet down the hall. In southern border towns the clientele is Indian travelers and Nepali businessmen. Every major town along a road has a few "hotels," some of them marvelously seedy, as well as plenty of small, extremely basic accommodations, often without even a name.

Hotels

At the top end of the scale are Kathmandu's half-dozen or so luxury hotels, with wall-to-wall carpeting, magnificent high-pressured showers, air conditioning and heating, swimming pools, restaurants, and business services. Prices are slightly below international standard, a little over US$100 a day for a double. Kathmandu is the only place in Nepal with hotels of this standard. Service and cleanliness are up to par but the decor in these top-of-the-line places is usually less than imaginative. There are plenty of mid-range hotels for US$30-50; some of these offer a more creative atmosphere. Hotels may add a 10% service charge to the bill; all charge 10-14% government tax and expect the bill to be paid in hard currency.

Long-term Accommodations

If you're staying in the Valley a month or more you might prefer to rent a room from a Nepali family, or get an entire flat or house for yourself. Furnished flats or houses rented by foreigners are frequently up for sublet during the monsoon. Check the bulletin boards at the Kathmandu Guest House, Pumpernickel Bakery,

and the two Bluebird Supermarkets, or just start asking—most things happen by word of mouth. If you're looking for a long-term semi-deluxe place you might contact one of the real estate agents advertising in the *Rising Nepal.* Their fee is paid by the landlord, so you've got nothing to lose.

Available accommodations range from tiny low-ceilinged rooms in the old city, sans plumbing, for a few hundred rupees per month, to deluxe flats and houses with beautiful gardens and mountain views in Kathmandu's residential neighborhoods, up to Rs15,000 monthly for a real palace. Gairidhara, Lazimpat, Jawalakhel and Boudha are popular areas with foreigners. Prices vary according to what's offered, but it's easy to find a nice place big enough for two for Rs2000-4000 a month. Landlords will seldom ask for a deposit or advance except for the most expensive places. One thing to check beforehand is the noise level. Screeching radios and barking dogs are ubiquitous and can drive you mad faster than anything.

TREKKING ACCOMMODATIONS

All the major trekking routes have tourist lodges conveniently located along the entire length. There are some bare stretches but generally every few hours another village appears with an assortment of lodging, so that you need never stay in a tent. In fact, the utter lack of privacy makes a tent undesirable in populated areas. Wherever there are houses, you can count on finding shelter; even if there are no official lodges someone will put you up, generally in their house. Nepalis themselves have traveled in the hills for centuries without lodges; arriving in a village at nightfall, a few inquiries produces someone willing to feed and lodge a guest for the night for a small charge.

Lodges, Inns, And Houses

Lodges in the Annapurna and Everest regions reach unexpectedly deluxe levels, offering both dormitories and wood-partitioned private rooms with glass windows, thick foam mattresses, sometimes even balconies, gardens, or outdoor tables with stupendous mountain views. A lodge near Pokhara advertises "View of Himalaya from Bed." Some villages have hydropowered elec-

Sherpa lodgekeeper, Junbesi

tricity instead of the candles and oil lamps (or lanterns) that light most lodges at night. A few even have VCRs and show nightly movies—not that you walked two weeks into the Himalaya to watch a rerun of *Rambo*. Villages like Taatopani on the Annapurna trek or Junbesi and Namche on the way to Everest have become favorite stopping points for trekkers, and you can choose from a dozen different places. Ask passing trekkers to recommend good towns and lodges if you're interested in this type of accomodation.

These lodges are surprisingly comfortable and good, sociable places for meeting fellow trekkers who can describe next day's trail. Nepal's trekkers are in general a relaxed and friendly lot and it's easy to find social life along the trail and at night. After a while, though, the conversations may begin to sound like a rerun, and you realize these lodges are in a sense nothing more than tourist ghettos. The only Nepalis around are the family which owns it, and it's difficult to get to know them because they're frantically busy producing more lemon tea and pancakes.

When you reach this point, you can start to seek out alternatives—the smaller, less plush and less crowded lodges. Many of these are nothing more than a family's home opened to trekkers. Usually the family sleeps in the kitchen, the warmest room. After a day's walking you can join them by the fire, watching the woman deftly prepare the evening meal while the children play around her and a grandmother murmurs prayers in the corner. This kind of scene is a part of trekking life few get to experience.

In small settlements between big towns there may be only Nepali-style *bhatti* or inns catering to local travelers, consisting of a communal sleeping room with a few wooden beds. Usually the lodging is free as long as you eat your evening meal here. Water for drinking and washing comes from a stream or tap outside.

If no lodging seems forthcoming, simply ask if you can stay in a house (at this point it helps to speak a little Nepali, or have a porter). While they may not believe you actually want to stay in "an old house like this," once you've convinced them they'll be delighted and you'll get to observe real life. In orthodox Brahman and Chhetri villages, especially in western Nepal, people may not invite you inside their houses because of caste restrictions, though they'll feed you on the porch and let you unroll your bedroll there as well.

In many places the porch is a preferable sleeping place. The big disadvantage of staying in houses is the smoke from cooking fires, which often fills the main room, drifting up to the top floors as well. In lodges, avoid rooms directly over the kitchen. The fire may be banked when you arrive in late afternoon but soon enough it will be restarted, flooding your room with eye-stinging smoke.

Camping

Trekking in Nepal isn't like hiking through pristine wilderness. People *live* all over these mountains, in an intimate relationship with the land. Treating a trek like a wilderness adventure makes little sense, and camping in populated territory is an antisocial act. (The exception is trekking groups, which are basically self-contained). No matter where you pitch your tent you won't find privacy—the herders, grass-cutters, farmers, porters, and children will find you soon enough. Kids especially will stare at your mysterious habitat for hours, making you feel like a circus act just come into town. Tents are also a security problem since there's nowhere to store valuables, and valuables include your boots.

Uninhabited trekking areas exist, of course, but they're far off the beaten track and are best approached with some previous trekking experience, preferably a knowledge of Nepali, and a good guide. In a way it seems a shame to come to Nepal and miss its greatest asset, its people. **Lake Rara National Park** is probably the best-known camping-style trekking destination. A few other routes cross over high passes and require a night or two of camping. Sometimes you can find a herder's hut *(goth)* to shelter in at higher altitudes.

Trekking agencies have developed a remarkably well-organized system providing for nearly every need. Except for firewood and a small amount of fresh food, everything is brought from Kathmandu: mattresses, tents, cooking gear, lanterns, even tables and chairs for group members to dine upon. Usually trekkers double up in tents, unless you pay a singles supplement or there's an odd number of men or women in the party.

Toilets

Most toilets in Kathmandu are of the Asian squat variety, but all hotels and many lodges with upwardly mobile aspirations have commodes. Squat toilets usually have a tap or a bucket of water alongside them, with a cup for rinsing it down after you're finished. They tend to easily clog with large amounts of toilet paper, so use it sparingly or follow local custom and use your left hand and water. If you're revolted by the idea, you should realize that Nepalis think dry toilet paper is disgusting and unsanitary.

Finding a public toilet in the Valley can be a bit of a problem because there are hardly any (beyond the mobile toilet trailer parked smack in the middle of Durbar Square.) You can march boldly into the marble facilities of Durbar Marg hotels if you're in the vicinity. Otherwise, ask. Even tiny hole-in-the-wall restaurants have their own *chaarpi* hidden away where you'd least expect it.

Bus rides are a grueling experience, not least because of the scarcity of toilet facilities. When passengers agitate sufficiently, the driver will pull off the road and the passengers, usually 90% male, all pile out. Women will have a hard time finding a strategic roadside location unless they've thought to wear a skirt.

Most trekking lodges have their own outhouse-type chaarpi but frequently you'll have to resort to the great outdoors. Trekking etiquette requires defecating off the trail well away from any water source and burying the feces. Toilet paper, if used, should be burned or buried. On many trails it seems like every beautiful little off-trail grotto you find is marked with pink and white rosettes of discarded toilet paper.

Bathing

Most lodges in Kathmandu have hot showers, though you'll pay more for one in your room. On organized treks, kitchen staff bring basins of hot washing water to the tent door every morning for a quick scrub. Occasionally on a rest day you can get extra hot water for a thorough wash. Many trekking lodges offer hot showers ingeniously improvised from oil drums and piping. Some are heated by solar power or the ex-

toilet, Pasang Guesthouse, Solu

CHRISTOPHER GAMM

cess heat of the wood cooking fire; others have to be heated for you. Aside from the environmental price, showers cost Rs15-25. At lower altitudes you may prefer to bathe at the village tap (women can wrap a lungi about themselves) or in a nearby stream. At frigid high altitudes you'll find you bathe far less than usual. The dry air and intense sun dry out skin, leaving you in a freeze-dried state of preservation. You probably won't even feel your unkempt state until you descend to lower altitudes and begin to thaw out.

FOOD

Nepali food is practical rather than gourmet fare—which is not to say it isn't tasty. It grows on you the longer you stay. The national dish is *daal bhaat,* boiled rice *(bhaat)* with a thin lentil sauce *(daal),* accompanied by curried vegetables *(tarkaari)* and possibly a dab of pungent pickle *(achaar).* In rice-growing areas daal bhaat is eaten twice a day. The first meal is around 1000-1100, the second shortly after sunset. Sweet, milky tea and snacks like beaten or popped rice, flat bread, or curried potatoes tide the hungry over until mealtime. Beyond this there isn't a tremendous variety of dishes. Ethnic groups have their own specialties, but basically it's all subsistence food. Nepalis know the value of food as fuel. Walk a few days in the hills and you'll learn it too.

Nepali-style Dining

Meals are eaten twice a day, generally at home except for farmers in the field or porters on the trail. Restaurants are a recent phenomenon sparked by tourism. Before, the only restaurants were a few *bhatti,* trailside inns serving travelers.

Most Nepalis eat with the right hand, though urban diners are now adopting a spoon. Metal spoons are said to ruin the flavor of food and to make you thinner—not a good thing in Nepal. Food is sometimes served on a *thaali,* a metal plate divided into separate compartments. The method is to attack the mountain of steaming daal bhaat quickly while it's still hot. If the daal came in a separate bowl, pour it over the rice, breaking up chunks with your fingers as you do. Add a bit of tarkaari and/or achaar, squeeze it all together, and pop it into your mouth. Watch fellow diners to get an idea of the technique. The hand is in constant motion until the food vanishes.

Daal bhaat is an all-you-can-eat affair. Servers make the rounds with bowls of daal and veg-

etables and will ask, dubiously, if you want more rice. Westerners generally have a hard time consuming more than one plate in the beginning, but your stomach will stretch over time. A one-plate daal bhaat is rarely enough for a Nepali. The distance to a mountain pass can be measured by the amount of rice it takes a porter to reach the top, as in the famous "five-maanaa climb" into the Kathmandu Valley. On the trail, watch porters fill up on three plates before heading up a hill.

It's okay to refuse rice and load up on the daal and curry. When you're finished, wash your hand with the water from the washing pot set on the table, either pouring the water onto your finished plate or stepping outside the door.

The other ubiquitous feature of Nepali cuisine is milk tea, low-grade black "dust" tea boiled with milk and sugar into a sweet brew. *Chiyaa* warms up cold mornings, cheers up bored office workers, and envigorates tired porters; a round of it, fetched by small boys carrying the glasses in wire containers, accompanies every business and social interaction. Westerners tend to find it too sweet and prefer black or lemon tea, but trekkers should not underestimate the reviving power of this potion. Two glasses of tea and a packet of biscuits will get you several hours down the trail on sugar alone.

Rice And Grains

Grain, preferably rice where it's available, provides 90% of the calories in the national diet. Rice's fundamental role is underscored by the language: daal bhaat is *khaanaa,* simply food. A common greeting is *bhaat khaayo?*—literally, "Have you eaten rice?"

The finest rice is long-grained basmati, which exudes a special fragrance when cooking. The best can cost over Rs100 per kilo in the bazaar. Pokhareli is good quality and more affordable. Most people eat a mid-priced rice like Mansuli or

Marshi or the cheaper Tauli. After enough daal bhaat you become a rice expert, noticing the distinct differences in grain and aroma.

Though rice is everywhere in Kathmandu it's nearly impossible to find brown rice. A few shops off New Road stock it for health-food oriented Westerners. A hearty red rice grown around Jumla resembles brown rice in appearance and taste. Centuries ago it was carried down trade routes for the delectation of Malla kings.

There are dozens of ways to prepare and process rice, by soaking, drying, beating, toasting, popping. Newar farmers make *hakuwa* or "black rice" by heaping harvested stalks in haystacks for 10-12 days. On cold autumn mornings these mounds steam in new-mown Valley fields, as heat trapped inside slowly ferments the grain. The rice is threshed, boiled, and then sun-dried, resulting in a light, digestible grain that's a favorite with children and old people.

Rice is the favorite food in lower regions, a high-status dish. In the dry higher Hills it's often a luxury. Where it is available it must be portered in and is consequently more expensive. Roasted flour *(sattu* or *tsampa)* is the staple food here, made from local grains: maize, wheat, millet, barley, buckwheat. The main food of many, if not most, Hill families is *dhiro,* a cooked mush of maize or millet flour eaten alone, with fried vegetables, or a thin soup. Grinding the family's daily flour supply on a hand-operated stone mill is one of a housewife's time-consuming tasks.

Among the highland Bhotia the staple is the Tibetan food tsampa, ground roasted barley flour. Eminently portable, it requires no cooking—just mix with tea and perhaps a little dried cheese and eat. In highland mountain regions like the Sherpa homeland of Khumbu, potatoes are the staff of life. The main dish is simple boiled potatoes, peeled and eaten with salt and chili-garlic relish. High-altitude potatoes are marvellously tasty. Order up a kilo while you're waiting for the main meal, or make it the main course. Find a Sherpa woman to make you *rigi kur,* delicious crispy potato pancakes served with a big lump of yak butter.

Snacks *(Khaajaa)*

Chiura (flattened rice) is made by pounding soaked, uncooked rice with a heavy wooden mallet. Easy to carry and requiring no cooking, it's a popular snack with farmers and porters. Served with yoghurt, vegetable curry, achaar, and fried meat *(chuela),* it's an essential element of Newari ritual feasts. Try roasted chiura, crunchier and tastier than the plain type, mixed with yoghurt as a substitute for breakfast cereals. Roasted with butter and sugar, it rivals carmel corn. Popped chiura and popped rice *(khatte)* are the Nepali equivalents of Rice Krispies, popped in hot sand to distribute the heat evenly.

Other favorite snacks include *alu daam* (curried potatoes), *kerau* (dried peas in a sauce), *sukuti* (chewy dried meat) and *samosa* (deep-fried triangular dumplings). Breads vary from *sel roti* (fried rings of rice-flour) to Gurung corn cakes and Indian-inspired *chapati* (flat, thin wheat-flour disks) and the smaller fried *puri.* South Indian restaurants offer a variety of *dosa,* huge crispy thin pancakes of lentil flour filled with spiced vegetables and served with several sauces.

Momo, a Tibetan speciality of little steamed meat dumplings, are a big hit with Westerners and Nepalis alike. Try them dipped in tomato-chili achaar or Chinese-style with soy sauce and vinegar. *Thukpa* (noodle soup), is another popular Tibetan dish, but it's being replaced by instant noodles, introduced in the early '80s and now as popular as blue jeans. These chow-chow are quick, tasty, and easy to cook; kids like to crunch on them raw. The Thai-Nepal brand Wai-Wai is the most tolerable of the lot.

Sweets are eaten for special occasions or as snacks or breakfast. They are all of the intensely, tooth-achingly sweet Indian varieties. There's deep-fried orange *jelabi,* rich milk-based *barfi,* and all sorts of confections decorated with edible thin paper hammered from real silver. Recommended are the cardamom-flavored milky *rasmalaai* and warm *gulab jamun* soaked in a rose-water syrup.

Dairy Products

High-altitude herders turn extra milk into cheese, butter and curd, eating some and selling the rest for a cash profit. Fresh local milk from cows, yaks, yak-cattle crossbreeds or water buffalo is deliciously rich and makes wonderfully creamy yoghurt. Milk is hand-churned into butter. *Mahi,* the resulting buttermilk byproduct, is eaten with dhiro and said to be good for digestion. Highland herders sew the butter into skins and keep it until it's quite strong; farmers in lower regions boil it until the moisture vaporizes to make clarified butter or ghee (Nepalis call it *ghiu*), which they sell in Terai towns and India.

Chhurpi is dried cheese made from the solids of *mahi* or yoghurt, dried in the sun then cut into squares and strung on strings of yak hair, rather like an edible necklace. Rock-hard at first, chhurpi slowly softens when boiled in soup or stew. People gnaw on bits of it all day as a sort of Himalayan chewing gum.

In the '60s a Swiss development project set up a chain of cheese factories in eastern Nepal to buy surplus milk from farmers and turn it into Western-style cheese. The project has boosted local incomes and makes good cheese as well. Today the government-owned cheese factories produce yak and buffalo cheese; private companies make buffalo-milk mozzerella, camembert, parmesan, smoked, white and pepper cheeses, not all regularly available. Government Dairy Development Corporation outlets are in Jawalakhel, Dilli Bazaar, Basantpur and Lainchaur. A private company, Nepal Dairy Products, has outlets in Thamel and Mahaboudha.

Meat

For most Nepalis, meat *(maasu)* and eggs *(phul)* are infrequent luxuries eaten on festivals and special occasions. Only male animals are supposed to be slaughtered, but nowadays the taboo is ignored. Animal slaughter is legally prohibited on *aunsi*, the no-moon day, and the sale of meat is forbidden on *ekadasi*, the eleventh of the month and sacred to Shiva.

"Mutton" in Nepal usually refers to goat, not sheep; it's the one meat everyone will eat. Brahmans refuse chicken, buffalo and pork, and the strictest are completely vegetarian. Gurungs and higher-caste Chhetri shun buffalo meat, while the Newars refuse to eat pork. Meat is scarce out in the hills anyway. The best you can do many times is to buy a tough, stringy, expensive chicken.

Produce

The Kathmandu Valley is heaven for vegetables—immense cauliflowers, carrots, eggplants, cabbages, peppers, peas, beans, tomatoes, cucumbers, squash, spinach, lettuce, even fancy imports like broccoli and asparagus, plus local vegetables without English names. Out in the hills the supply is limited to the standard Nepali favorites: potatoes, onion, cauliflower, giant radishes (*mula*), and various greens. The latter are often fermented and dried into a strong-tasting mess called *gundruk*, rich in vitamins, iron and calcium.

The fruit picture is not so good. The Valley is too low for growing apples, too high for citrus. Excellent apples *(syaau)* grow in the northern Hills, but it's impossible to transport the crop. Nepalese oranges *(suntalaa)* are remarkably cheap and tasty in fall and winter. Most fruit is trucked in from India and suffers in the process. Bananas *(keraa)* are available year-round in several varieties, sold by the dozen. Citrus fruits arrive in the winter: suntalaa and grapefruit-like

fruit-sellers, Kathmandu

KERRY MORAN

pomelo, plus Indian apples. Spring is the best season for luscious tropical fruits. Mangoes (aap) have bright-orange juicy flesh surrounding large pits. Wash, dry well, cut in half or strips and dig into the sweet stickiness. The milder-flavored papaya (mewa) has fruit the color of orange sherbet, with hundreds of black seeds said to be a sovereign remedy for upset stomachs. During May-June the addictive litchi appear in grape-like bunches, corrugated red skin covering sweet white fruit. August-September bring the yellow-skinned ambaa (guava), with more Vitamin C than oranges. Peel it and eat in slices; the edible seeds provide a crunchy contrast to the soft flesh. The brown naspati or Chinese apple has the flavor and color of a pear and the texture and shape of an apple.

Seasonings

Women grind their spices fresh daily on a big stone mortar, using cumin, chili, turmeric, fennel, fenugreek, mustard seed, coriander and the mixed-spice masala. Bright orange besaar or turmeric, "poor man's saffron," gives curries their characteristic golden tint. Rubbed over the skin of butchered goats, it acts as a fly repellant and preservative.

Mustard is grown all over lower Nepal, carpeting fields with yellow flowers. Oil pressed from its seeds is used for cooking, as well as lamps, temple offerings, and massage. Food is fried in mustard oil and liberally seasoned with garlic, onions, and fresh ginger. More flavor comes from a spoonful of achaar, pungent pickled vegetables or relish which can be sweet, salty, sour, or hot. Try pungent mango pickle and sweet mango relish, and a simple and delicious achaar of chopped tomatoes, onion, garlic, lemon juice, and fresh cilantro.

Authentic Nepali food isn't burning hot but it does have a distinct bite of chili pepper (koorsani). Restaurants and tea shops catering to Westerners know by now to leave out the hot stuff, so you'll have to ask, or go off the beaten track, if you want the real thing.

Liquor

Home distillation is an ancient practice in Nepal, still managing to hold its own against modern distilleries. The Nepali brand-name hard liquors are best avoided. Often adulterated with chemicals, they can give a quick headache. Imported

---

HOMEMADE CHANG

You need four maanaa (1.65 kg) raw rice and one piece of marcha, white yeast sold in Valley shops. The better the quality of rice, the better the chang tastes. Boil the rice and let it cool slightly. When it's mildly warm but not hot, add the crumbled yeast and mix well with your hands. Place the mixture in a non-metallic container (a plastic bucket works well), wrap snugly in plastic, pile on some blankets to retain the heat, and let it ferment in a warm place for several days or a week, depending on the weather. You can judge when it's ready by the smell. When the mash is ripe, add three times the volume of water and mix well with your hands. Strain and drink.

---

brands are expensive. The Nepali beer market is booming, with at least four local brands and two local licensees on the market. Tuborg and San Miguel are the best; of the local brews, Iceberg is the best, but quality seems to vary monthly.

The finest alcohol is homemade stuff. Raksi is potent, exhilarating and smooth as velvet. To test for good raksi, toss a small amount on a fire and see if it burns. Women of a household pride themselves on their liquor, and will put the most effort and time into making raksi for a big celebration like a wedding. Different grains produce different flavors: rice raksi is rich and smooth, kodo (millet) is stronger and more fiery.

Less potent is home-brewed beer, jand (Nepali) or chang (Tibetan), a whitish, thin drink made from rice or millet with a refreshing sweet-sour taste. A variation served in mountain regions is tongba, fermented mash which is placed in a wooden container and mixed with hot water. You drink from a bamboo straw, sipping the liquid and avoiding the bits of millet; the hot water is refilled several times, and nursing a flask of tongba is a nice sport for a cold evening.

EATING OUT

Tourist Restaurants

Since the '60s Kathmandu has been a culinary paradise for Western overland travelers who, famished after the overland journey across Asia, stumbled into the Valley to find not only pagodas

restaurant menu,
Kathmandu

1. COLD DRINKS
2. HOT DRINKS
3. FRESH-FRUIT
        JUICE
4. TOAST
5. EGGS DISH
6. BRUNCH SET
7. SOUPS & MUSELI
8. CURD & MILK SHAKE
9. PANCAKE
10. CHOPUSY

10. MUSAKA
11. CHOWMEIN DISHES
12. CURRY RICE "
13. SPRING ROLLS
        & SALAD
14. BURGER WITH
        CHIPS
15. SPAGHITTIES
16. PIZZA
17. MACORANI SEIWE
18. LASSGANE SEIWE
19. CHILLY DISHES

KERRY MORAN

but pies. Trekkers spend the final days of their journey fantasizing about what to order in Kathmandu. The international smorgasbord of Thamel restaurants includes local versions of pizza, quiche, lasagne, enchiladas, crepes, steaks, tostadas, moussaka, soups, green salads, spaghetti, potato rosti, cheese sandwiches, and on and on. Dishes are tasty and well-laced with cheese but the appropriate spices are usually missing. Desserts can be fabulous, though Kathmandu's famed "Pie Alley" has practically vanished and the best ones are found in Thamel. It won't take long to find out where the best chocolate cake and apple pie are—it's a favorite subject among travelers. Prices are amazingly reasonable; Rs50 for a big meal.

Restaurants and coffee shops at the main hotels provide respectable conventional fare at reasonable prices. Two can dine moderately at Kathmandu's best restaurants for US$10 (excluding alcohol, which runs up the bill quite a bit). Another bargain are the many excellent Indian restaurants, often attached to hotels.

Nepali Restaurants And Teashops

Restaurants catering to Nepalis are usually modest cubbyholes in the old city. Usually there are no signs; you identify them by the roar of the kerosene stove or the display of food on the streetside countertop. The nationality or ethnicity of the proprietor determines the food: there are Newari restaurants serving specialities like fried blood, lungs, fermented bamboo shoots, and potent raksi; Tibetan momo stalls with thukpa and meat dumplings; pure Nepali *bhojnalaya* dishing out daal bhaat; Indian restaurants with all sorts of spicy, rich Indian food; even a few Chinese restaurants run by young enterpreneurs from the People's Republic of China, who make fiery *mapo dofu*.

Most pervasive is the local teashop or *chiyaa pasal*. It's the social center of a village, a place where men meet to argue and gossip over endless cups of sweet tea. Food is limited to daal bhaat, noodles, and snacks; maybe some fried bread and yoghurt. Again, signs seldom advertise its presence, but the amount of plates and glasses on the shelves is a sure giveaway. Sitting in teashops is a favorite way to pass the day, meet people, and chat; make it a point to visit them periodically if you want to stay in touch with Nepal.

PASSPORTS AND VISAS

Everyone except Indian nationals needs a valid passport and visa to enter Nepal. Once inside, you'll use it to change money, buy airline tickets, obtain trekking permits, ship air cargo, pick up packages, and dozens of other things. Losing your passport is a headache. Most embassies or consulates can issue a replacement within four working days *if* all your papers are in order; if not it takes longer. An amazing number of people lose their passports (and sometimes their money) immediately upon entering Nepal—possibly a result of jet lag. To replace a passport you first need a police report from the Interpol unit at Hanuman Dhoka Police Station. After a replacement is issued you have to get Immigration to reissue your Nepali visa. It really expedites matters if you've kept a photocopy of your passport's front page and your Nepali visa in a seperate safe place.

A one-month tourist visa can be obtained before arrival from any Royal Nepalese Embassy or Consulate. You need a valid passport and two passport-sized photos; the fee is US$10 or equivalent. If you didn't get a visa beforehand,

15-day transit visas are issued at entry points for the same fee. They can be extended for an additional two weeks free of charge at Kathmandu's Central Immigration Office; however, you'll need to show bank-rate foreign exchange receipts covering that period (US$140 or equivalent).

A tourist visa can be extended to a total of three months at the Immigration Office. Fees are Rs75 per week for the second month, Rs150 per week for the third. Late visas or permits are fined double the regular fee, in addition to the normal fee. Bring your passport, one passport-sized photo, and a filled-in visa application form which you can pick up at the information desk. In addition, you need an exchange receipt from a bank or hotel showing you've changed the equivalent of US$10 per day for the length of your proposed extension. Some budget travelers are hard-pressed to spend this much for food and lodging, but it's the government's way of ensuring it gets a minimum amount of hard currency from every tourist at the bank rather than the black-market rate. Keep your receipts—

ROYAL NEPALESE EMBASSIES

China
No. 1 Sanlitu Xilujie
Beijing
tel. 521-795

Norbulingka Road
Lhasa, Tibet
tel. 22880

France
7 Rue de Washington
Paris 75008
tel. (43) 592-861

Germany
15 Bad Godesberg im
Haag
Bonn 2, 84th Street
tel. 343097

India
Barakhamba Rd.
New Delhi 110001
tel. 332-9969

19 Woodlands
Sterndale Rd.
Calcutta 700027
tel. 452-024

Japan
14-9 Todoroki, 7-Chome
Setagaya-ku, Tokyo
tel. (03) 705-5558

Pakistan
Attaturk Ave.
House No. 506
Islamabad
tel. 823642

Thailand
189 Sukhumvit 7
Bangkok 10110
tel. 391-7240

U.K.
12A Kensington Palace
   Gardens
London W84QU
tel. (01) 229-1594

U.S.A.
2131 Leroy Pl. NW
Washington D.C.
tel. (202) 666-4550

upon departure you're allowed to convert 15% of remaining rupees back into dollars at the airport.

Longer Stays

If you want or need to stay longer, apply through Immigration for a fourth-month extension from the Home Ministry. They generally will grant extensions for reasonable cause like illness, but there's no guarantee. No tourist can stay more than four months over the course of a year. If you leave Nepal and reenter, say for a trip to India, you get a maximum one-month visa if you're reentering within three months of your departure date. If you've stayed three months already, you have to wait one month to reenter, and again you get a maximum of a month.

Tightening of visa restrictions in 1988 caused an exodus of Kathmandu's expatriate community. Non-tourist visas are available for students and researchers at Tribhuvan University, for enterpreneurs who have made a sizeable investment in a business with a Nepali partner, and for employees of a handful of organizations. Foreign women who marry Nepali men are allowed to live in Nepal, but foreign men married to Nepali women get only four months' visa per year.

Immigration Offices

The **Central Immigration Office** on TriDevi Marg, the main road into Thamel, is open 1000-1600 Sun.-Thurs., 1000-1500 Fri. During winter months closing time is 1600. A counter at the entrance issues application forms for visas and trekking permits. The reception counter inside accepts applications only until 1400.

There's another Immigration Office in Pokhara, near Damside. If you end up staying longer than expected in Pokhara (which has a way of happening in that seductive town), they can issue a two-week visa extension or a trekking permit for the Annapurna region.

Trekking Permits

You need a trekking permit to visit Nepal's interior, essentially any place more than a day's walk from a road. Central Immigration on TriDevi Marg in Kathmandu issues standard permits for the main trekking regions: pink for Everest, yellow for Annapurna, green for Langtang-Gosainkund-Helambu. Immigration will write special white permits for all sorts of lesser-known areas,

as long as they don't fall in the northern border restricted zone. Checkposts are rare in these areas, but you could be turned back without a permit. An expired permit is usually a *ke garne?* ("what to do?") affair, though sometimes you can find officials to extend it. If not, you'll be penalized when you renew your visa.

Procedure is similar to that for visa extensions; bring two passport-sized photos, patience, and bank exchange receipts equivalent to US$10 per day. (Going through a trekking agency eliminates the need for receipts, as you'll pay your agency bill in hard currency.) Fees are Rs90 per week for the first month, Rs112.50 per week for the second and third months. A trekking permit doubles as a visa extension—you get both a cardboard permit and a visa sticker in your passport.

Permits are available within a day or two in Kathmandu, same day from the Pokhara Immigration Office. Lines can be long in season, especially October, when the Dasain holiday coincides with peak trekking arrivals. Go early in the day, or do it through an agency—some trekking companies will arrange independent permits for a fee.

Foreign Embassies

Your country's embassy can possibly help you if you run into trouble by doing things like arranging a helicopter rescue or emergency medical care, delivering urgent messages from home, providing a limited amount of emergency cash, as well as more mundane things like receiving mail for its citizens (not all do this). But they can't work miracles; in fact the range of services is quite limited. Citizens of EEC countries not represented in Kathmandu can go to the embassy of the country of the current president of the EEC. Some embassies (like the U.S.) provide a registration service for citizens. Registering upon arrival in Kathmandu can help if you need a helicopter rescue, have your passport stolen, or receive an emergency message from home.

Customs

Checking at the Tibet and Indian border crossings is usually minimal; it's heavier at Tribhuvan International Airport. Usually officials concentrate on suspicious-looking characters coming from Bangkok and Hong Kong, prime gold-smuggling centers. Newspapers frequently report several kilos of gold discovered unclaimed in the toilet of a jet. The profit rate is high, but the runners who take the greatest risk get only a small part, and the risk of years in a Nepali prison is hardly worth it. The same goes for bringing drugs into or out of the country. Kathmandu jails have a rotating clientele of about 20 foreigners of every nationality who have been busted for gold or drugs, mainly hashish.

Legally speaking, duty-free allowance is 200 cigarettes or 50 cigars, one bottle of distilled liquor or 12 cans of beer. Bangkok's duty-free shop is a good place to stock up. Imported cigarettes and liquor are heavily taxed in Kathmandu, and duty-free items make good gifts if you don't consume them yourself. Johnnie Walker Red and 555 cigarettes are the preferred brands.

Vistors may import a camera, video camera, bicycle, tape recorder, etc. for personal use. It's usually no problem as long as you don't have a ridiculous amount of stuff. If you run into difficulties customs officials may write the item in your passport. If you can't produce it upon departure, you may have to pay duty.

Leaving Nepal, the only problem might be old art, since the export of any item over 100 years old is illegal. If you buy old-looking art you'll need a certificate, easily obtained, from

FOREIGN EMBASSIES AND CONSULATES

Australian Embassy	Bhat Bhateni	tel. 411-578
Austrian Consulate	Hattisar	tel. 410-891
Bangladesh Embassy	Naxal	tel. 414-943
Belgian Consulate	Lazimpat	tel. 414-760
British Embassy	Lainchaur	tel. 410-590
Burmese Embassy	Chakupat, Patan Dhoka	tel. 524-788
Chinese Embassy	Baluwatar	tel. 411-740
Danish Consulate	Kanti Path	tel. 227-044
Finnish Consulate	Khichapokhari	tel. 220-939
French Embassy	Lazimpat	tel. 412-332
German Embassy	Kanti Path	tel. 221-763
Indian Embassy	Lainchaur	tel. 410-900
Israeli Embassy	Lazimpat	tel. 411-811
Italian Embassy	Baluwatar	tel. 412-743
Japanese Embassy	Panipokhari	tel. 414-083
Netherlands Counsalate	Kumaripati	tel. 522-915
Pakistani Embassy	Panipokhari	tel. 411-421
South Korean Embassy	Tahachal	tel. 270-172
Sri Lankan Consulate	Kamalpokhari	tel. 414-192
Swedish Consulate	Khichapokhari	tel. 220-939
Swiss Consulate	Jawalakhel	tel. 523-468
Thai Embassy	Thapathali	tel. 213-910
U.S. Embassy	Panipokhari	tel. 411-179

the **Department of Archaeology** on Ram Shah Path (near Singha Durbar). Ask the shopkeeper for details. There's seldom a problem since 99% of souvenirs are obviously not old, even if they've been artifically aged. There's also a limit on the number of Tibetan carpets you can carry out with you. Three (any size) can go with your personal baggage, or 14 square meters may be shipped out per passport.

रूपयाँ एक शय

RUPEES ONE HUNDRED   100

MONEY

The Nepali *rupiyaa* or rupee is issued in notes of Rs1, Rs2, Rs5, Rs10, Rs20, Rs100, Rs500, and Rs1000. Different colors make them easy to distinguish, and amounts are written in English on the back side. Small change or *paisa,* which come in 5, 10, 25, and 50 paisa coins and larger one-rupee coins, is more confusing. The 25-paisa coin is called a *sukaa;* the 50-paisa coin is a *mohar.* Only Nepali numbers are written on them and many are so worn as to be indecipherable, so you need to learn them by size. If you get confused, you can always thrust a handful of change forward and have the shopkeeper pick out the change. Coins are worth very little, but they're handy for paying for the use of a bicycle pump, and as donations for beggars.

Nepalis have an aversion to old, worn bills. Shopkeepers are happy to give them as change but are loathe to accept them, though the note is still valid. You can smilingly insist, try slipping it in a large wad of bills, or turn it into the old-bill window on the ground floor of the Supermarket on New Road, a special bank branch set up just for this purpose.

Value

In spring 1991 the Nepali rupee was Rs32 per dollar, nearly double the rate of 1985. Inflation in the Kathmandu Valley averages 8-10% a year; the rupee is periodically devalued to keep it in line with the Indian rupee. Outside of Nepal rupees are a nonconvertible currency, so spend or convert all your money before departure (but remember the Rs450 airport tax). The airport bank will convert back 15% of the amount shown on your bank exchange receipts into foreign currency.

With one rupee roughly equal to three U.S. cents, it may not seem like a lot of money, but in Nepal, a rupee is a rupee—that is, it's the standard. Try not to think of it as "funny money." When judging prices, keep in mind that an average government worker supports his family on a salary of Rs1,000 a month and the average Nepali earns less than Rs4,800 per year. Even the Prime Minister earns Rs6,500 per month. Another way to get your financial bearings is to look at prices of vital necessities: a kilo of rice or sugar, a maanaa of cooking oil, a plate of daal bhaat, a glass of tea. These prices all vary with the isolation of an area and its distance from the road, imported goods becoming increasingly more expensive the farther one goes. Knowing local prices gives you the background knowledge necessary for bargaining, and puts the prices of luxury goods in glaring perspective.

Expenses

Nepal can be remarkably cheap even by Asian standards, but there's no limit on what you could spend if you put your mind to it. Out in the boondocks, it's sometimes hard to find *anything* to spend money on. At the high end of the scale, Kathmandu's luxury hotels charge up to US$120/ night, and there are many valuable high-priced antiques. Restaurants, though they may be excellent, are never really expensive. As long as you don't drink it's difficult to get a dinner bill much over Rs300 per person even in the most expensive restaurants.

At the other end is the budget traveler's circuit, where you can live for less than US$5 per day, though most people do spend more by upgrading their hotels. US$15-20 would be a more comfortable budget. Transportation costs are ridiculously low if you take buses, but domestic flights are usually at least US$60. It's only reasonable to add some extra funds for things you can't find anywhere else—a Tibetan carpet, a porter on a trek, a ticket for the mountain flight or an overnight in a resort.

Expenses for independent trekkers depend on the region. Things are cheaper in the lowlands, more expensive in the mountains where supplies must be carried in by porters. Count on a minimum of Rs150 per day (more for premium regions like Everest), then take twice as much as a cushion. Add more for a porter (Rs60-200 or more per day, depending on your bargaining skills) and luxuries like beer and soft drinks. Bottled water can eat a huge hole in your budget, and the plastic bottles are a big litter problem. It's far cheaper to treat it yourself.

Trekking companies vary wildly in price: local companies may charge as little as US$20 per person per day, while foreign-based operations running through them can charge US$60-100 for essentially the same thing. Group trekkers need less money on the trail, since food and lodging is taken care of and there's really not much to buy. Don't forget to bring enough to tip staff and porters at the end of the trek. Giving the money directly is better than handing it over to the sirdar to distribute.

Tipping

Not a Nepali tradition, but tourism is making it one. In more expensive Durbar Marg restaurants and hotels a small (5%) gratuity may be appropriate if you feel guilty. Some restaurants and hotels add a 10% service charge and 10% government tax; smaller establishments manage to avoid both of these. Other than tour guides and trekking employees, there's usually no reason to tip anyone unless they've given you exceptional service. Porters at the airport should get Rs2 per bag, although they like to harass you for US$5. Be wary of handing out lavish tips and accelerating the present trend. Money for nothing is disorienting, and that's what tips can seem like in a place where it's not customary.

The exception is trekking staff. Tipping has become institutionalized in the business, and because most are miserably paid, the end-of-trek bonus is a necessity. Some members hand out leftover goods, flashlights, frisbees, clothes, and boots at the end of a trip, but it's hard to distribute these equitably among the entire staff. The recommended method is for every member to pitch in US$1-2 per trekking day, to be divided up among the trekking staff, with the sirdar and cook at the top of the list. Trekking companies often provide guidelines on tipping etiquette. Hand the money over to a reliable person —the company manager or your trek leader—to distribute to the staff in Kathmandu. You can do it yourselves the last night of the trek, but inevitably some members are short of cash. Porters should be tipped the last day of the trek and might get two days extra salary for a two-week trek, less for those who joined up later.

CHANGING MONEY

The Nepali black market is the economy's way of leveling things out. The rupee can't be used outside the country, but hard currency can; thus it's worth more. The black market in Kathmandu is widespread and remarkably accommodating, accepting cash, traveler's checks, sometimes even personal checks; U.S. dollars are preferred. The rate is 15% higher than the bank rate, with better rates given for large denominations (easier for smugglers to carry out in bulk). Freak Street, New Road, and Thamel are full of disreputable characters hissing, "Change money? Good rate, better than bank." They are the small fish who bring clients to the big bosses, usually in tourist-oriented businesses (carpet and souvenir shops and travel agencies). You get a better rate dealing directly with these people, but needless to say, changing money on the black market is illegal. Periodically police sweep through and close down all the money-changers, arresting a few as examples.

Sorely in need of hard currency, the government attempts to control the situation by requiring bank exchange receipts for visa extensions and trekking permits. Some budget travelers find they can live on less, but there's no way to get around the restriction, beyond changing back 15% of your bank receipts upon departure. (If you're going on to India, it's easiest to change unofficially in Kathmandu.) If you've got money left over, put it towards a carpet or thanga or splurge at a fancy restaurant.

Banks

Modern banking and computers have arrived in Kathmandu, even if power outages frequently snarl the system. The government bank, **Nepal Bank Ltd.,** has several money changing outlets, including Thamel and Basantapur. A whole crop of new banks like **Grindley's, Nabil,** and **Indo-Suez** offer the same rate and more modern facilities, though they may charge a one percent commission. The rate is set daily and announced on the radio and in the paper; day-to-day variations generally are slight. The money-changing window at the Central Immigration Office offers the standard rate; the airport bank offers slightly less, but not enough to make a real difference. Major hotels will also change money for guests. Bank hours are Sun.-Thurs. 1000-1400 or 1430, Fri. 1000-1200 or 1230.

If you need money transferred from abroad and can't draw a personal check on a credit card, try one of the modern banks; each has a list of correspondent banks in various countries. Get the account number from them and have a relative, friend, or your bank telex transfer the money to their account, with your name and passport number on the order. If all goes well, the transfer can be completed in two working days. Money will be issued in U.S. dollar traveler's checks or Nepali rupees.

Outside major cities, money-changing facilities are scarce and sometimes uncooperative. If you're going trekking you should bring all the cash you think you'll need with you, and then some. Make sure a good portion is in small notes (Rs100 and less); it's hard to break larger bills on the trail. Always bring more than you calculate you'll need; 50% is a good cushion. If you're trekking in a region with regular STOL service (see "Getting Around") you might want to carry the one-way plane fare in dollars or traveler's checks in case you decide to fly out.

Cash, Traveler's Checks, And Cards

For safety's sake take the bulk of your money in travelers' checks (U.S. dollars are best), with a little cash for small deals and emergency changing. Only American Express offers replacement checks in Kathmandu. Credit cards can generally only be used at expensive hotels and travel agencies, though Thamel shops are rapidly expanding their capabilities. An AmEx card can also be used with a personal check to get up to US$1,000 in traveler's checks.

The **American Express office** just off Durbar Marg in the Hotel Mayalu (tel. 226-172/227-635) can replace lost cards and checks within three days, give emergency cash up to US$1000, and provide free mail service for clients. **Grindley's Bank** is the local MasterCard and Visa representative; **Nabil Bank** handles Visa.

Bargaining

Bargaining is not just a way to settle a price. It's a social interaction, a sport, and a favorite time-passer. Visitors from fixed-price societies take a while to appreciate the subtleties of bargaining, and even longer to hone their skills. Some people are naturals, others loathe it; it takes a certain personality to enter into the spirit. Whichever, it's essential to treat bargaining as a game rather than a deadly competition.

There's generally no need to bargain for general household items, medicines and food from shops, restaurant meals, bus tickets, and trekking gear rentals. Lodge rates are more or less firm in season, but if it's off-season or you're staying for a long period, ask for a discount of up to 50%. Some independent travelers insist on haggling for every item, ignoring the fact that they paid more for their air ticket to Nepal than most Nepalis earn in a lifetime. Paisa-squeezers like these aren't respected by Nepalis, and make life miserable for everyone. It's good to bargain, but don't take it too far.

Things to bargain for include fruit and vegetables from the bazaars (the fruit vendors especially mark up the going rate when they see you coming). Some vendors quote you the right price, others an inflated one. Ask several to get a feel for the range, and don't be surprised if they come down as you're walking away. The best way is to eavesdrop on a Nepali transaction, then insist on the same price.

The most stupendous markups are on items sold exclusively to tourists: souvenirs, jewelry, clothing, art. Bargaining is essential here, especially with street sellers who routinely ask for (and get) incredible prices from tourists. The best policy is to first go around looking and asking prices. Once you know what you're interested in, go back to the reasonable places and bargain. It's difficult to estimate the percentage the original price should be reduced, because sellers vary widely in their first quote. One shopkeeper might quote a price 300% higher than his neighbor for an identical product. It pays to shop around.

Some bargaining techniques: first off, ask for the seller's best price (thik bhannuhos). Armed with the research you've done, you'll be able to tell if it's a reasonable figure. Or just make a

reasonable offer to start out with and avoid inflated figures altogether. Often a merchant will ask you what you're willing to pay, hoping you'll state some ridiculously high sum.

Be patient and good-humored in bargaining; you can never bully a good deal out of anybody. Decide in advance the maximum you're willing to pay for something, than make an initial offer three or four increments below that. Inch your way up slowly; once you reach your last price stick to it. Sometimes if you've gotten stuck at a point close to agreement, it works if you pull out the money, saying "Look, it's all I've got right now."

Don't give away the fact you've got your heart set on something; act cool. Walking away with feigned disinterest has saved many a deal. If you've gotten close to agreement, 80% of the time the seller will call you back and take your last offer. If he doesn't—well, you can always come back the next day, but you've lost your leverage. Buying several items of anything should earn you an automatic discount on top of the bargaining you do for each piece.

HEALTH

Nepal's health situation is among the world's worst. Up to 50% of all children die before the age of five, victims of diarrhea, disease, malnutrition, or deadly combinations of the three. The high infant mortality rate pushes life expectancy down to 51 years—far better than in the early 1950s, when it was 28 years, but still among the lowest in the world.

Most Nepalis turn to traditional healers when they fall sick, usually a jhankri. These shamanistic healers have the ability to enter into a trance and contact the spirits believed to cause illnesses. A jhankri's treatment might include an exorcism ritual, animal sacrifice, herbal medicine or physical manipulation. As often as not the cure is successful, due more to the strength of their patient's faith than anything else. Jhankri may not be trained in modern medical techniques, but they make excellent psychotherapists.

The dire national health situation is less threatening to travelers, who are better nourished than Nepalis, are hopefully immunized, drink clean water, and in any case don't stay very

long. Most illnesses are gastrointestinal, transmitted through food or water contaminated by infected feces. You need to be careful about what you eat and drink, but constantly worrying about the purity of everything can spoil your trip. It's easy to get paranoid about potential contamination, but it doesn't help much. Do what you can by drinking only treated water and eating reasonably safe food; beyond that, don't worry about things beyond your control. Some kind of gastrointestinal illness seems to be inevitable the longer you stay.

The general feeling of siege makes health a favorite topic among travelers, and reports of last night's diarrhea are cheerfully given even to strangers. A favorite topic of speculation is where somebody got sick. It's pretty much impossible to tell since infections like giardia and amoebas take at least ten days to appear, and by the time you realize you're sick, you've long forgotten how you could have contracted it. Food poisoning is more immediate and does occur in Kathmandu restaurants.

Even worse than contracting an illness is to return home with some exotic bug unfamiliar to your doctor. The simple identification and treatment of giardia or amoebas can result in a spectacular bill. Try to clear up lingering illnesses in Kathmandu, where doctors are accustomed to these problems.

Immunizations
No immunizations are required to enter Nepal, but there's a long and intimidating list of recommended immunizations. Which ones you need depends on your plans and season. Someone going on a month-long monsoon trek needs more protection than a tourist visiting the Kathmandu Valley for five days in the dry autumn. Pick and choose from the list, get them all for the sake of peace of mind if nothing else, or skip them all—it's up to you.

Without insurance or a national health plan the pre-departure medical bill can run quite high. U.S. local public health departments often give vaccinations for a small fee. Or you can wait and get injections in Kathmandu (CIWEC Clinic charges $15-$25; the Infectious Disease Hospital in Teku also offers some vaccinations).

PREVENTION

Drinks
Regard *all* water as potentially contaminated. This includes the tap water in your hotel and crystal-clear mountain streams. Use treated or bottled water for drinking and brushing teeth. The drinking water and ice cubes provided in top hotels and restaurants can optimistically be assumed to be safe, but avoid it everywhere else, regardless of assurances. Bottled drinks, beer, and hard liquor are safe; locally brewed liquor is not. Club soda and bottled purified water are sometimes available, but often all you can find are soft drinks and beer—not much good for real thirst. Get in the habit of carrying a bottle of treated water when you go out for the day. The bottled water sold in Kathmandu turned out to be impure when it was tested in the 1990 monsoon.

Homemade liquor is usually dubious, and alcohol in general irritates gastrointesintal problems. Raksi is purified during distillation but it may be contaminated afterwards. The wonderful homemade beer called jand or chang is risky,

RECOMMENDED IMMUNIZATIONS

Tetanus-diptheria should have been updated within the last 10 years. A one-time polio booster is recommended for adults who received oral immunizations as children.

A **gamma gobulin injection** is 99% effective against hepatitis A, one of the three varieties of hepatitis prevalant in Nepal. For a one-month visit two cc. is sufficient; two months, three cc; three months four cc, four months, five cc.

Typhoid innoculations are recommended for trekkers and long-term visitors. They are usually given as a series of two injections, 30 days apart. Depending on the strain, these are 75-95% effective.

Meningitis is a potentially lethal disease only recently recognized in Nepal. A **meningococcal A and C vaccination** is highly recommended for trekkers. Effectiveness is 95%, beginning one to two weeks after the shot.

Japanese B encephalitis vaccination is recommended for those who will be traveling in India and/or the Nepali Terai for more than one month. Smallpox and cholera vaccinations are now unnecessary.

Rabies is endemic in Nepal, particularly Kathmandu. You might want to consider **pre-exposure rabies prophylaxis,** good for three years. This reduces the number (and expense) of required shots from five to two, plus eliminates the need for the initial injection. The post-exposure series of shots is not as painful as it once was, but it's quite expensive in Kathmandu.

Malaria, once rampant in the Terai and lower hills, is under control in touristed destinations, although serious outbreaks have occurred in far western Nepal. It rarely occurs above 1,200 meters, so the Kathmandu Valley is safe. **Malaria prophylaxis** is theoretically recommended for visitors to the Terai, though a few days in Chitwan doesn't present a serious threat, and the best treatment may be simply preventative—using mosquito repellant and sleeping under a net. If you choose to err on the safe side, take single 500-mg. doses of chloroquine phosphate once a week, starting two weeks before your arrival, and continuing four weeks after your departure.

since it's made with unboiled water squeezed through the mash with usually unwashed hands. Tongba, a hot toddy made from boiling water poured over fermented mash, is an in-between case—the water is probably okay, but the mash may not be. Sometimes you just have to live dangerously.

Treating Water
Boiling, the traditional method of purifying water, is guaranteed to kill all organisms if you do it long and hot enough, but it's impractical for travelers. Rarely are you in a position to boil your own water, and it's a drag to supervise someone else. At higher altitudes water must be boiled longer to compensate for the lower boiling point. Ten minutes of vigorous boiling is enough for altitudes up to 1,800 meters, which includes Kathmandu. Of course you can risk water boiled for a shorter time, and in fact you do whenever you order coffee or tea. But minimize the risk by treating drinking water in another fashion. On group treks you'll be provided with smoky-tasting boiled water; how long it's been boiled varies daily.

Iodine is the simplest, cheapest, most portable way to purify water, guaranteed to wipe out every organism. You can bring tincture of iodine or iodine crystals from home, or buy concentrated Lugol's Solution in Kathmandu pharmacies (but check that dosage for the particular concentration). Bring a small dropper bottle from home to make dispensing less messy. Since iodine eventually eats through plastic and rubber, look for a tough, tiny nalogene bottle with a dropper spout. Put four to five drops in a liter of water, shake and leave it for 10 minutes. If the water is cold the chemical reaction is slower and you should wait 20 minutes before drinking. Double the dosage if the water looks exceptionally polluted. The drawback to iodine is its strong taste, which some try to mask by adding powdered drink mix. The ascorbic acid in the mix reduces iodine's effectiveness; wait 10-20 minutes before adding flavoring.

Other purification methods are less than 100% effective against Nepal's wide range of bugs. Chlorine-based purifiers don't kill amoebic cysts; filtering removes bacteria and some cysts but doesn't destroy viruses like hepatitis. The same goes for the small portable pumps equipped with catadyne filters. These run over US$100 and take five minutes to process a litre of water—a hassle and expensive.

Food
Generally anything that's been thoroughly and recently cooked is safe, but avoid cooked food that's displayed unprotected on counters. Flies carry all sorts of diseases, and amoebic cysts are even found in dust. Raw vegetables and fruits should be soaked 20 minutes in iodized water, then peeled, then cooked. Okay, so you can risk a raw banana or orange, but be careful about how you handle the peel. Salad greens are especially risky.

Milk should be boiled before drinking to prevent tuberculosis, brucellosis, and typhoid transmitted by cows. The pasturized dairy milk sold in small plastic bags in Kathmandu should be boiled as well. Ice cream is risky if the scoop is rinsed off with tap water, as is usually the case. Yoghurt, made from boiled milk, is usually safe if you scrape off and discard the top layer. Raw cheese is okay too; wipe the piece off and cut off the rind.

GASTROINTESTINAL ILLNESSES

Sooner or later every visitor to Nepal gets some kind of gastrointestinal illness. The rate of infection among Nepalis has been estimated at 75-90% at any given time. The typical turista or "Delhi Belly" upsets due to unfamiliar *E. coli* organisms entering your system are as common here as anywhere else. Nepalis visiting Western countries complain of the same problem. Treatment for any diarrhea begins with a mild, reduced diet of food like plain rice, bananas, toast, soup, with plenty of fluids (no caffeine or alcohol). It's better to avoid heavy use of remedies like Lomotil which simply paralyze your bowels and may mask more serious symptoms. Pepto-Bismol is useful in treating temporary stomach upsets; bring some tablets from home.

A simple method highly recommended by some travelers is to take a single dose of tetracycline or co-trimoxazole at the onset of an attack. Often this dispels the problem. If it comes back in a day or two, you can bet you've got something more persistent requiring different medication.

Diarrhea And Dysentery

E. coli upsets end within five days without medication. Longer cases or different symptoms indicate a gastrointestinal illness (GI) caused by a variety of organisms: *giardia lamblia,* amoebas, bacteria, or worms. If you're in Kathmandu, get a stool test and advice on medication from a local clinic. Trekkers must be prepared to treat themselves. Most viral and bacterial upsets will eventually go away without medication, but parasites like giardia and some types of amoebas are persistent and require medication.

Giardia organisms inhabit the upper intestine, causing stomach pain and bloating, nausea, frequent diarrhea, and telltale sulphuric "rotten-egg" burps. Symptoms may come and go, and frequently the organism won't show up on stool tests. Recommended treatment is usually remarkably effective: two grams (four 500 mg tablets) of tinidazole (Tiniba) taken at one time. Take after dinner to minimize potential side effects, which include headache, a metallic taste in the mouth, and nausea, and avoid drinking alcohol.

Amoebic dysentery is caused by a protozoan living in the large intestine. Symptoms include abdominal pain, diarrhea, and possibly fever and bloody stools. A stool exam is useful in diagnosing amoebas. The treatment is again two grams of Tiniba as a single dose (again no alcohol), this time taken three days in a row. This should be followed up with 21 days of diodoquin (650 mg three times daily) to eliminate cysts.

Bacillary dysentery, less common than amoebic, has similar symptoms with the addition of fever and chills, severe stomach cramps, and stools with mucus or occasionally blood. Treatment is an antibiotic like ampicillin; for this kind of disease you should see a doctor.

Worms rarely cause symptoms beyond mild abdominal discomfort, but they're not something you want to bring home. Ask a pharmacist for worm medicine if you suspect you might have them.

OTHER DISEASES

Less frequent but still common illnesses include typhoid, hepatitis, tuberculosis, and cholera, the latter two rare among tourists. Typhoid fever is a severe, debilitating illness that can last for weeks. Since there are several varieties of typhoid and immunization provides only partial immunity against one, avoiding it is a good reason for being careful about what you eat and drink.

Hepatitis, a viral infection of the liver, is marked by lassitude, nausea at the sight of food, dark urine and whitish stools, possible fever, and mild liver pains (right side). By the time the skin and eyes turn the telltale yellow of jaundice, you know you've got hep. Western medicine offers no treatment beyond rest and a good diet. Victims should avoid anything that taxes the liver, like drugs, liquor and greasy food. Dr. Mana's Ayurvedic treatment for hepatitis (see "Medical Treatment" below) includes herbal pills and a special diet. Like most ayurvedic remedies it works slowly and is scientifically unproven, but many Westerners swear it speeded their recovery.

Animal Bites

Rabies is endemic in Nepal, and any bite by a dog, monkey, or whatever should be regarded as serious, especially if the attack was unprovoked or the animal was acting strangely. The bite should be immediately flooded with water for 15 minutes, followed by Betadine, which will hopefully reduce the amount of germs introduced. If possible, check up on the animal 10 days later; if no signs of rabies have appeared by then, you don't have to worry. If it's not possible to follow up, consult a doctor or clinic about obtaining the series of shots, which is very expensive. You might want to include pre-exposure rabies vaccination on your immunization list. While it doesn't give 100% protection it reduces the number of shots needed after a bite.

TREKKING AND HEALTH

Trekking places you in an unusual medical situation. Not only are you exposed to risks unique to the mountain environment, you're days or weeks away from medical care. Realizing this and going prepared is the single most important thing you can do. It's a good idea to take out a temporary insurance policy before you leave your country, one that will cover the costs of medical evacuation or helicopter rescue if necessary—an unlikely but expensive event.

Your responsibility extends to your porters and companions. Victims of hypothermia or altitude sickness may quickly become disoriented and unable to care for themselves. Don't send them back down alone if you suspect one of these conditions; they could easily wander off and die (and occasionally they do).

Treating Nepalis

Trekkers are often besieged with requests for *aushadi* by villagers with specific problems or long lists of general aches and pains. It's easy to feel trapped between a natural desire to help and an honest lack of knowledge. *If* you're certain of the problem and can somehow make sure your treatment is correctly understood, it's worthwhile to help. Cleaning and dressing wounds and explaining the need to do so is helpful because people can then do it themselves, but indiscriminately handing out antibiotics, Lomotil, or even aspirin does more harm than good. A failure can undermine belief in the system of Western medicine the government is trying to establish (not that much success has been achieved). A success will just encourage a villager to ask another uninformed trekker for treatment.

Foot Care

First rule: break in your boots before you start out on the trail. Tighten the laces going downhill to reduce sliding of the toes, and wear a double

ALTITUDE SICKNESS

Two percent of all trekkers to the Everest region once died from Acute Mountain Sickness (AMS) brought on by climbing too high too fast. Now, increased awareness has brought the rate down to one or two deaths a year across Nepal. Much of the credit goes to the Himalayan Rescue Association (HRA), a nonprofit private organization established in the early '70s to educate trekkers about altitude-related sickness. The **HRA** office in the courtyard of the Kathmandu Guest House (tel. 418-755) provides information on AMS prevention and treatment; in season, talks are held twice daily.

In fact, a counter-syndrome is now appearing: "AMS paranoia," in which healthy trekkers flinch at every cough and headache. Deaths from AMS occur when people ignore warning signals. Your symptoms will tell you how well your body is acclimatizing to altitude; all you need to do is pay attention to them and respect your personal limits.

The atmospheric composition at high altitude is the same as at sea level (20% oxygen), but a reduction in atmospheric pressure reduces the amount of oxygen taken in with each breath. At 5,500 meters, as high as any trekker will reach, you're breathing roughly half the amount of oxygen you're accustomed to. Not far above this height, the human body seems to hit a natural limit, slowly deteriorating no matter what is done. But up to this height and given time, the human body will adapt through a miraculous array of physiological changes (one trick is increasing the production of oxygen-bearing red blood cells). You're 80% acclimatized after 10 days, 95% after six weeks; you lose it just about as fast as you gain it.

AMS can strike as low as 2,500 meters, but most commonly it hits trekkers who fly into a high region then quickly ascend even higher—typically the Everest region, the highest popular trekking region in Nepal. The whys of altitude sickness are still being researched. Age, sex, physical condition, and prior experience at heights seem to have no effect on who gets it—some people are just naturally more susceptible, and there's no way to predict who. Well-trained young athletes have ignored the warning signs and died from AMS, while 70-year-olds breeze into Everest Base Camp.

At least 75% of trekkers experience mild symptoms after ascending to higher altitudes, but if the ascent is gradual these should decrease in severity after the third day. In two percent of cases AMS becomes serious, generally because the symptoms were ignored. If you feel worse after ascending, it's a sign to stay put or descend.

Symptoms include headache, fatigue, mild breathing irregularities, swelling of the hands, face and feet, loss of appetite, and drowsiness and yawning, paradoxically accompanied by restless sleep and vivid dreams. None of these are necessarily serious in themselves; they're simply warning signals telling you to slow your rate of ascent until you feel more comfortable. If you're experiencing mild discomfort, once you're above 3,000 meters limit your ascent to 300 meters in a day. Above 4,300 meters you should never go higher than 400 meters per day, no matter how good you feel. A rest day every third day is recommended above this altitude and seems to be particularly effective in reducing AMS.

continued on next page

The old adage "climb high, sleep low" appears to have some truth in it.

A severe headache is a clear signal to stop ascending. You should descend if it persists after a second night; usually 300-500 meters is sufficient. Ignoring mild symptoms and continuing higher can quickly lead to more serious complications: bubbly breathing signifying fluid in the lungs, severe headaches or lassitude, loss of coordination, delirium or confusion, and breathlessness even at rest. Any of these signs require immediate descent to a point where the symptoms ease. If things seem okay after a few days rest, you might cautiously reascend. Those who ignore AMS symptoms for several days can lapse into a coma and die within 12 hours.

There are a few other things you can do to aid acclimatization; mainly, drinking plenty of fluids to counter increased dehydration. Deeper, more rapid inhalation of cold dry air increases water loss through the lungs at a rate of up to four liters per day. Drinking more can also ease nausea, a common symptom of altitude sickness. Eating plenty of carbohydrates also seems to improve acclimatization. You'll probably need to make a conscious effort to eat because your appetite will be reduced. Greasy foods are especially difficult to digest up high; sweets are usually tolerated. Don't worry about vitamins—if you're in good nutritional shape, you have six months leeway before signs of a deficiency appear.

Avoid taking sedatives at altitude, even though difficulty sleeping is a common problem. They slow breathing and can lead to AMS. A certain medicine (Diamox/acetazolamide) reduces discomfort from minor symptoms of altitude sickness, but it doesn't speed up acclimatization or prevent AMS; it merely masks the warning signals. The best course—really the only course—is to plan a slow, steady ascent with rest days built in the schedule.

pair of dry socks (thin cotton or nylon under thick wool) to reduce friction between your foot and boot. Second rule: stop to treat hot spots the moment you sense them. If you wait until the end of a day a big blister will have developed that will take days to heal. Put moleskin or Second Skin on tender spots. Blisters need to be exposed to air, not bandaged. You can protect them with corn plasters or moleskin in which a hole has been cut out. Or, drain them with a sterilized needle, then bandage the site.

COLD AND HEAT

Temperatures shift quickly to extremes at high altitude. The sunny, hot morning vanishes when clouds, wind, rain, or snow roll in. When packing for a trek don't underestimate the warm clothing you need to cross a high pass, no matter how hot it seems in the lowlands.

Hypothermia
Hypothermia, a decrease in the body's core temperature, can occur rapidly even in temperatures above freezing. If you're underdressed, wet, underfed, dehydrated, and/or exhausted, your body's ability to retain heat may break down, and this condition will be aggravated by strong winds or wet clothing. Mild hypothermia begins with shivering and pale skin color. Poor coordination, apathy, and disorientation signal a further drop in the body's temperature. If not properly treated, hypothermia can end in coma and death within a few hours.

Hypothermia has killed quite a few underdressed, poorly equipped porters who have been abandoned by the trekkers who hired them. Whether you're with a group or on your own, porters are your responsibility. The victim should immediately be warmed up. Shelter plus fire or vigorous exercise works for milder cases; more serious ones may have to be stripped of wet clothing and put in a sleeping bag with another warm body, preferably naked. Severe cases are difficult to treat; the key is recognizing hypothermia before it becomes severe.

Frostbite
Frozen tissues caused by impaired circulation are often associated with hypothermia and can occur anywhere the temperature is below freezing. Odds are low as long as you're properly dressed, adequately fed, and moving reasonably quickly. Tight boots may cut off circulation to the toes and increase chances of frostbite, or you may risk it on high passes and summits if a snowstorm sweeps in and you're unprepared. Fingers, toes, ears, or nose are first painful and white, then become progressively number. A frostbitten area requires rapid rewarming in hot water, a medically delicate process. Like hypothermia, the best treatment is prevention.

(top left) cycle rickshaw, Freak Street (Christopher Gamm);
(top right) prayer flags at Boudhanath, Losar during the Tibetan New Year (Kerry Moran);
(bottom) Thamel street scene (Kerry Moran)

(top) family watching festival in Bhaktapur (Kerry Moran);
(bottom) merchant's stall at Pashupatinath, Shiva Ratri (Kerry Moran)

TREKKER'S MEDICAL KIT

The following is a list of bare-basics essentials to take on the trail. Most items are available in Kathmandu. Local drugs (generally manufactured in India) are inexpensive and available without prescription, but their purity and effectiveness is not 100% guaranteed.

✓ Band-Aids (assorted sizes)

✓ cotton gauze pads and adhesive tape

✓ antiseptic cream (Betadine): for cuts and scrapes.

✓ moleskin or Second Skin: for blisters.

✓ elastic bandage: for strained knees, sprained ankles.

✓ thermometer, scissors, tweezers, needle

✓ Tetracyclin or Bactrim: for bacterial dysentery, infections.

✓ Erythromycin: for strep throat, skin infections, bronchitis.

✓ Tiniba (500 mg): for giardia and amoebic dysentery.

✓ Pepto-Bismol tablets: for upset stomach and diarrhea.

✓ aspirin or paracetemol: for relief of pain and fever

✓ codeine (30 mg): for cough, pain, diarrhea.

✓ throat lozenges: for sore throat, common at altitude.

✓ Jeevan Jal: oral rehydration formula for diarrhea

Hyperthermia

Ascending a sweltering river valley can be even more debilitating than crossing a frozen pass. In hot weather drink more water than you consciously want—as much as possible. Wear light-colored, loose cotton clothing and protect your head from the sun with a brimmed hat, or, better yet, with a big black umbrella. This portable instant shade-maker can really cool down a sweaty walk.

Heat exhaustion occurs when too much blood is at the skin surface and too little reaches the brain, resulting in faintness, nausea, and a rapid heart rate. Rest in a cool, shady place and take in plenty of salt and liquids. Heat stroke is a genuine medical emergency in which the body's heat regulation process suddenly fails. Body temperature rises rapidly to 40.6° C (105° F) or higher, and the victim rapidly becomes disoriented and uncoordinated. Cool as quickly as possible by dunking in cold water or employing a combination of sponging and fanning.

Sun And Snow

Nepal's sun can be a real scorcher, for several reasons. The country's southerly latitude gives the sun's rays a tropical intensity. At higher altitudes, ultraviolet exposure is higher than normal because the thinner atmosphere filters out less of the sun's harmful wavelengths. In addition to this, snow and ice reflect 75% of incident radiation, giving a near-double dose. About two-thirds of a day's UV radiation occurs between 1000-1400 when the sun is directly overhead. Cloud cover doesn't reduce UV radiation; it merely scatters it. All this means that you should use a sunscreen with PABA, especially when traveling over snow. Don't forget lips and ears and the underside of the nose and chin. Even the inside of the nostrils can be painfully burned by reflected rays.

If you're traveling over snow, even on a cloudy day, wear good dark glasses to prevent snow-blindness, a temporary but extremely painful condition which is literally sunburn of the eye. There are no symptoms during the day but 8-12 hours later the eyes begin to itch, progressing to the point where they feel as though they're filled with sand. Snow blindness heals naturally in a few days, but a severe case can be excruciatingly painful.

Sunglasses should have side pieces to block reflected light: improvise temporary shields with cardboard and tape if you don't have glacier glasses. Your porter's eyes need to be protected too. The local method of smearing charcoal under the eyes to reduce reflection is not enough. Tibetans comb their long hair over the eyes, or you can fashion makeshift goggles by cutting slits in cardboard. Best to have an extra pair of cheap sunglasses to hand out if you encounter snow.

MEDICAL TREATMENT

Kathmandu has the country's best medical facilities, but for anything serious you'll want to fly to Bangkok or back home. Nepali hospitals are crowded and very basic. For most illnesses consult a Nepali doctor or visit a private clinic. **CIWEC Clinic** (tel. 410-983) in Baluwatar near the Russian Embassy is staffed by Western physicians and nurses and provides competent care, but a visit is expensive by Nepali standards, $25 plus lab fees. **Nepal International Clinic** (tel. 412-842) across from the Royal Palace is run by a Nepali doctor who studied in Canada. Both clinics have a doctor on-call after hours for emergencies. **Kalimati Clinic** near the Soaltee Oberoi Hotel (tel. 270-923) is open 1300-1430 Mon. and Fri., Wed. 1000-1130 and 1330-1430. It offers immunizations, including gamma globulin and post-exposure rabies vaccine, but doesn't generally diagnose illnesses.

For emergency treatment, hospitalization, and surgery the best facility is **Patan Hospital** in Lagankhel (tel. 522-278/522-295). Also known as Shanta Bhawan, it was founded and is still partially supported by the United Mission to Nepal. There's also an inexpensive dental clinic here. Next choice is the Tribhuvan University **Teaching Hospital** in Maharajganj (tel. 412-303/412-404). Avoid the government-run **Bir Hospital** near the Tundhikhel (tel. 221-988/221-119); it has expensive high-tech equipment like a Catscan but a chronic shortage of drugs and basic supplies.

Plenty of pharmacies are scattered about town, the biggest on New Road and near hospitals. If your problem is uncomplicated you may want to get an inexpensive stool test at one of Kathmandu's local labs and doctor yourself. No prescriptions are necessary and you can get a wide range of inexpensive medication, most of it made in India.

Ayurvedic medicines based on the ancient Indian system of herbal remedies are frequently used. An Ayurvedic practitioner popular with Westerners is Dr. Mana Bajracharya, whose office is behind the Mahaboudha stupa in a warren of buildings behind Bir Hospital. Tibetan medicine with its thousands of herbal-based remedies is also popular; the largest concentration of Tibetan doctors is in Boudhanath.

In Pokhara, ill travelers should visit the **Western Regional Hospital** (tel. 20066), which does stool tests and provides treatment. Larger Terai towns and district centers may have a government hospital, but out trekking, medical care is basically up to you—a good reason to carry medical essentials and be familiar with them. The Himalayan Rescue Association operates **Trekkers' Aid Posts** in Pheriche and Manang (Everest and Annapurna Circuit trails), staffed by volunteer doctors during the spring and fall trekking seasons. They can provide advice and care for altitude sickness, and doctors make the rounds of local lodges. Village health posts and centers offer minimal services and are frequently closed or out of medicine. Group treks usually carry a medical kit, but it may be poorly supplied and there's no guarantee the sirdar or trek leader will know how to use it.

Helicopter Rescue

For serious medical emergencies when a patient can't walk or be carried out, a helicopter rescue can be arranged through the Royal Nepalese Army. The service is expensive (nearly US$600 per hour, a typical rescue runs US$1200-2000) and must be paid for by the rescuee. Your embassy or trekking agency may vouch for you but they won't pick up the tab—a good reason to arrange for comprehensive trip insurance beforehand.

The Army must receive assurance of payment before it dispatches a flight. This will be provided by your trekking agency if you're with a group; embassies usually provide this for their citizens, but they may need to contact the family in advance. Registering at your embassy before a trek greatly expedites this process. Once the helicopter takes off, you're liable for the costs even if it doesn't find you.

Independent trekkers should have a radio message sent to their embassy (through police, national park, or local airport) including the injured person's name, passport number, location, medical condition, the need for a med team to accompany the helicopter, and identification of person supplying the information. Give accurate details of the person's medical condition so rescuers can assess the urgency, and make sure the location is described as specifically as possible—this last major detail is frequently forgotten in panicky messages, engendering an expensive search.

SERVICES

MAIL

Postal System

Nepal's postal system is slow and unreliable for both domestic and international mail. Airmail letters take 10 days to three weeks coming or going to the U.S., a little less for Europe. Sea mail takes four months, and airmail sometimes equals that, as a Christmas card arrives in May after some mysterious detour. The mail is also afflicted with a 10-20% disappearance rate; sometimes packages are pilfered and you receive only the empty wrapping. Avoid sending and receiving valuables and important documents by post. Either wait until you leave Nepal, or pass it over to a departing traveler to mail from another country. Registered mail provides some reassurance, but registered letters and packets still disappear and are impossible to trace.

Receiving Mail

As in all of Asia, letters should be addressed with the surname first, in capital letters and underlined. Many travelers use the poste restante at Kathmandu's **General Post Office** (located at Sundhara near Bhimsen's Tower). Letters are filed according to last name in open boxes which you sort through yourself. The scene is chaotic in tourist season, but it seems as reliable a place as any. Poste restante hours are Sun.-Fri. 1015-1700 (closing time during the winter months 1600, 1400 on Friday). If a package arrives you'll get a slip directing you to the **Foreign Post Section** just north of the GPO, which is open Sun.-Thurs. 1000-1300 and Fri. 1000-1200. Bring your passport and go early because there are multiple lines to wait in.

The American Express office located in Hotel Mayalu just off Durbar Marg provides an efficient free mail service for holders of an AmEx card, traveler's checks, or travel voucher. Nonclients must pay US$1 per enquiry. You need a passport, AmEx card or checks as identification to receive mail. Pick-up time is Sun.-Fri. 1000-1300 and 1400-1700. They hold mail for one month and will forward for a charge of US$3. The address is c/o American Express, P.O. Box 76, Kathmandu, Nepal.

Some embassies (including the U.S., French, and British) provide mail service for their citizens, usually only letters and printed matter. The West German and Indian embassies don't accept any mail. You can also have mail sent to you care of your hotel or trekking company.

Sending Mail

While there are post offices across Nepal, domestic mail is unreliable and slow and it's really best to send everything from Kathmandu. General Post Office hours are Sun.-Fri. 1015-1500; stamps are sold 0800-1900. Mailing a letter involves waiting in several lines. First a lesson in line etiquette. Formerly as in many Asian countries, mobs clustered about the windows thrusting money and letters at harried clerks. Now everyone is supposed to *linema basne,* and iron railings have been installed to channel the crowd. People in a hurry may shove in front of you because they think you won't protest, but you have every right to reassert your place.

The postage rates for different countries are displayed in the lobby. It saves time to buy a lot of stamps at once and use them over the course of your visit. There are different windows for stamp-selling, registration, insurance, and franking. This last is essential. If your stamps aren't cancelled in front of your eyes, there's a chance someone may tear them off and reuse or sell them, and your letters will go in the trash. For this reason, never use the post boxes around town. Trekking companies and big hotels send a worker down daily to get letters franked and mailed, so you can be reasonably confident about turning your mail over to them.

Small packets and bulky letters must be weighed at the franking counter before buying stamps. Postcards and envelopes are sold outside the gate, but it's cheaper to buy them in town. Nepalese envelopes are always short on glue; seal with extra glue or tape. Aerogrammes *(hawapatra)* are about half the price of regular letters; buy them at stamp-selling windows.

Shipping Goods

You can mail goods yourself from the Foreign Post Section just up the street from the GPO, but you'll have to spend several hours doing it. Bring your passport, packing materials, a bank exchange receipt covering the value of the goods purchased in Nepal, and a certificate from the Department of Archaeology if the goods appear in any way to be old. Don't seal the box until it's been inspected by customs.

Certain limitations apply to mailing packages. Maximum length is 30 inches; total diameter is 50 inches maximum. There's a 10-kilogram limit for air mail, and the postage rate is high. Air mail takes a maximum of two weeks; sea mail, which has a 20 kilogram limit and is more reasonably priced, takes up to three months. Anything over 20 kilos will have to be shipped air cargo.

It's easier and cheaper to use a shipping company. Try **Sharmasons** on Kanti Path, **Overseas Movers** in Thamel, or **Mobile Packers and Movers** or **Universal Packers and Movers** on Durbar Marg. A good one will provide packing materials for a reasonable fee, help you pack your goods and make a customs list, get clearance certificates from the Department of Archaeology and National Handicrafts Association if necessary, and clear your package through customs. You need to provide a bank exchange receipt covering the total value of the goods. Air cargo takes 7-10 days and is reliable; goods are automatically insured for US$20 per kilogram by the airline and you can purchase additional insurance. Cost per kilogram depends on total weight and destination. The 5-45 kilogram range costs US$4.60 per kilogram to Europe, US$6.70 per kilogram to the United States. Sea cargo is cheaper but slow (three to six months) and slightly less reliable as the goods must go through India.

TELEPHONE AND TELEGRAPH

Public phones are scattered about town in various shops; many others allow the use of their private phones for a slightly higher fee. Ask a shopkeeper for the location of the nearest telephone; sometimes they're impossible to spot. Fee is Rs1-2 for local calls. Finding a number can be difficult given the lack of a standard telephone book, though *Nepal Traveller* publishes an annual business directory. Local directory assistance is 197, or a hotel switchboard can assist you in finding the number.

International telephoning has improved markedly in recent years, and direct-dial facilities are all over the place. Nepal has direct dial service to 35 countries; dial 186 to place an international call to other destinations, 187 for calls to India. Only Japan, Canada, and the U.K. accept collect calls from Nepal. However, most places don't mind having your party call you back. Rates abroad to Nepal are more reasonable than rates from it, so this only makes sense.

Some hotels will place calls for non-guests, and "international communications centers" in Thamel and on New Road, offer telephone, fax, telex and mail services. These are efficient and reasonably priced, far more pleasant than the old **Central Telegraph Office** across from the National Stadium (which does however remain open 24 hours a day, and charges 15% less). Phone/fax fees are Rs105 or Rs120 per minute for most countries, with an extra Rs20 for the first minute. Private offices let you call for as little as one minute, whereas the telegraph office has a minimum of three minutes. Telex and fax services are also available at larger hotels and travel agents; try businesses on Durbar Marg.

HIGH-TECH SERVICES

Photocopy shops are all over the city; quality varies widely but the usual charge is Rs1 per page, and you can get double sides, enlargement and reduction, even binding. If you're going trekking, photocopying route descriptions from a trekking guidebook will save the weight of carrying the whole thing.

If you bring a computer to Nepal customs may write the equipment in your passport, but there's no problem as long as you can show it on departure. Kathmandu is not the place to get either computer supplies or repairs, but if you get stuck there are a few places in town. **Data Systems International** and **Mercantile Exchange,** both on Durbar Marg, provide computer service. **Natasha Shakya** in the shop just north of the Hotel de l'Annapurna repairs all sorts of electronics, including computer hardware and tape recorders. **Beltronix,** around the corner on Kanti Path, rents laptops by the week or month, has a helpful computer service division upstairs, and also sells locally made "spikes" or surge suppressors, essential for operating equipment on Kathmandu's erratic power.

TIME

Nepal is 15 minutes ahead of Indian standard time, more as a symbol of political independence rather than any actual time difference. Nepal time is two hours and fifteen minutes behind Chinese/Tibet time (three hours and fifteen minutes April-Sept.) and five hours and 45 minutes ahead of Greenwich Mean Time. When it's noon in Kathmandu it's 0615 in London; 0115 in New York; 2215 the preceding evening in Los Angeles.

As does much of Asia, Nepal has its own concept of time: "rubber time," some call it. Scheduled events invariably start 30 minutes or an hour late, bus rides are always longer than you expect, and *bholi-parsi* is the common phrase for when something will get done, i.e. "mañana." It's advisable to keep checking up on your travel agent or whomever, and also to keep a sense of humor about it all.

Business Hours

Government offices and many business offices operate 1000-1700, closing an hour earlier from Dec.-Feb and 1500 on Fridays. Most shops are open 1000-2000 or later. Bank hours are Sun.-Thurs. 1000-1430, Fri. 1000-1230. Government offices have no official lunch break (the late start is meant to let office workers eat their main meal before they go to work) but many business offices close for lunch around noon. Given the late opening hours, long lunches, and constant tea breaks, contacting someone can be a frustrating exercise. The best times seem to be 1100 and 1500; otherwise, people are in and out.

Saturday has been the weekly holiday since Chandra Shamsher Rana proclaimed it in the 1920s. Being an inauspicious day, it's considered better to stay at home and do puja than go to work. Most stores and businesses are closed on Saturdays, leaving little to do in town. Aside from this there are plenty of holidays, the biggest being Dasain. Offices close for the final three days, but restaurants and tourist shops stay open.

ELECTRICITY

Electricity is 220 volts/50 cycles, with occasional tremendous surges that can fry the insides of delicate equipment like computers. You need a surge surpressor ("spike") to cut out the high peaks during operation. Kathmandu just got 24-hour-a-day power in 1984, and neighborhood outages are still frequent. Less than 10% of Nepali households have electricity, and they tend to be concentrated in the Valley, the Hetauda-Birgunj area, and the Terai. A few mountain villages have hydropowered electricity, but most villagers rely on oil lamps and firelight and go to bed early. The lack of electricity is compensated in part by spectacular star shows and brilliant moonlight. Even on moonless nights in the mountains, you can see by starlight. A good flashlight (or two) is a must for travelers. A small Mini-Mag-type light easily slips into a pocket if you're going out at night. Good streetlighting is rare even in Kathmandu.

PHOTOGRAPHY

With the arrival of automatic developing machines, many shops offer same-day service. Try **Das Color Lab** on Kanti Path, **Photo Concern** on New Road (also good for camera repairs), **Lotus Studio** in Lazimpat (with branches in Thamel and on Durbar Marg), or **Nepal Color Lab** in Thamel. For black and white prints, try Photo Concern or **Ganesh Photo Lab** in Bhimsenthan. Don't get slides mounted in Kathmandu; inevitably they come back scratched. Ask for developing only (even these are sometimes scratched), or wait until you leave. Kodachrome can't be processed in Nepal; the nearest place is Australia, and mailing it from Nepal is a risky proposition.

A number of camera shops clustered around Photo Concern on New Road will rent cameras, lenses, lights and flashes, even video cameras (a popular item during wedding season). There are no instant do-it-yourself photo booths, but many photo shops offer inexpensive visa or passport photos, necessary for trekking permits and visa applications. It's a good idea to get a few dozen if you'll be traveling for a while.

INFORMATION

Tourist Offices
Nepal's Department of Tourism operates several Tourist Information Centers. The main one is on Ganga Path, next to Basantapur Tower, just down from Durbar Square; there are also offices by the Pokhara Airport, Birgunj, Bhairawa, Kakarbhitta, Janakpur and Jomosom. The Kathmandu office is open Sun.-Thurs. 0900-1700, Fri. 0900-1600 and is the best by far. The staff can answer questions and help you find locations on maps, but they seldom have much beyond a few brochures: currently one on trekking, one on Pokhara, and one outlining Nepal's attractions. The main Department of Tourism office (behind the National Stadium) hands out free scenic posters and stickers.

Newspapers And Magazines
Two daily newspapers, *Gorkhapatra* (Nepali) and the *Rising Nepal* (English) are published by the Gorkhapatra Corp., a semi-autonomous

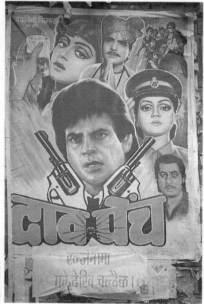

KERRY MORAN

Indian movie poster

government offshoot. There are at least 60 other small Nepali-language independent dailies published in various parts of the country, even more local fortnightlies and weeklies—pretty amazing for a country with a 35% literacy rate. Until the April 1990 revolution the *Rising Nepal's* front page was devoted to obsequious coverage of the royal family, but the current tumultous political scene has perked it up. Leafing through it, you find oddly edited wire service stories, vignettes of Nepali life (minor crime and bus accidents), ads from development organizations, and a daily saying from King Birendra on the editorial page.

The *International Herald Tribune, Time, Newsweek, Asiaweek,* and *The Far Eastern Economic Review* are available in larger bookstores and hotels. Other magazines are hard to come by, and are a good thing to pack if you've got some extra room—they become much more fascinating in Nepal, and Nepalis love to look at the pictures and ads. Plenty of magazines and newspapers are available in the reading room of the **American Library** on New Road, though officially it's only for Nepalis and U.S. residents of Nepal. The **British Library** on Kanti Path has a periodicals section and is open to all.

Locally published English-language magazines focus mainly on politics. The *Nepal Traveller* is a tourist magazine distributed free through hotels and airports. It contains useful information and informative articles, including a rundown of the season's festivals. *Kailash—A Journal of Himalayan Studies* is a sporadically published anthropological journal presenting a scholarly cross-section of Himalayan life, anything from the spatial implications of a Bhaktapur procession to the development of modern art in Nepal.

Most provocative and interesting of the lot is *Himal,* published every two months under the motto "For Development and Environment." Published in Kathmandu, it emphasizes Nepal but covers these issues across the Himalaya. Articles include critical looks at foreign aid and tourism, book reviews, and essays on things like "Dharma and the Environment" or "The Shangri-La Myth," plus photo essays on subjects like Nepali porters and restaurant workers. Readable and thought-provoking, it's essential reading for anyone interested in the region and provides a good background education on issues.

Radio And Television

Government-run Radio Nepal, the country's sole radio station, brings music and news to thousands of remote villages and is a major force in the creation of a common "Nepali" identity. The day starts at 0600 with the broadcasting of a religious song (a different one for every day of the week). Programming includes Nepali folk music, radio dramas, and development-oriented skits interspersed with commercial jingles for soft drinks and laundry soap. News in English is broadcast daily at 0800 and 2000.

The Nepal Television Corp. began broadcasting in Dec. 1985. Programs are from 0730-0830 and 1830-2200 daily; English news is aired at 2140. Many television owners put up aerials so they can pick up Indian broadcasts. A television set and a VCR have become the new status symbols in Kathmandu, not least because of the heavy import duties slapped on them. Now it's not uncommon to see an aerial sprouting from the tiled roof of a traditional house. Video rental shops around the city stock all sorts of films; most popular are Oriental kung-fu epics and "sexy" films shown in video dens.

Books And Bookstores

Kathmandu is an international center for books on Himalayan regions, especially Nepal and Tibet. There are probably 200 titles on Nepal and just as many on Tibet and Vajrayana Buddhism. Other regional specialties include mountaineering, the Himalaya, Tantrism, Hinduism, India and Asian travel accounts by Westerners, plus dozens of lavish photographic books on the Himalaya, surely one of the most photographed regions on earth.

Few travelers realize that Kathmandu's bookstores offer bargains on new as well as used books. Some are sold at Asian edition prices, 35-50% less than in the West. Locally published books are remarkably cheap, and Indian editions are reasonable. You can find specialty books long out of print or unavailable in the West. Best of all are the many discounted books sold on remainder, often of popular titles which are being pushed off the market by new arrivals. A new paperback listed at US$8.95 may sell

for Rs160, or half-price, and you can get especially good bargains on expensive photographic books.

Kathmandu's oldest booksellers, Ratna Pushtak Bhandar in Bhotahiti, operates **Ratna Book Distributors** in Bagh Bazaar near the French Cultural Center. They publish *Kailash* and the *Biblioteca Himalayica* series of inexpensive reprints of rare classics on the Himalaya. Another place to check is **Himalayan Booksellers** in Bagh Bazaar (also with a Thamel outlet). **Mandala Bookpoint** on Kanti Path has an excellent selection of regional books. **Pilgrim's Bookhouse** in Thamel has a vast selection with an emphasis on New Age topics and Eastern religions. A smaller branch up the street stocks rare books on all sorts of Asian subjects. **Educational Booksellers** on the Tundikhel has a good range of Penguins, modern fiction, and children's books, plus shelves of textbooks and business books, including Asian editions of computer software manuals retailing for half the Western price.

Kathmandu's used bookshops are famous for their eclectic selection provided by Western travelers. In essence they're like a perennially rotating library; you can sell books back for 50% of the original price and buy more. Shelves are stocked with a genuine cross-section of travelers' reading. Generally quantity predominates over quality; thick historical novels are popular buys for long treks.

Maps

Good maps of Nepal are hard to find. Apa Production's new Nepal map is probably the best available, with 1:500,000 overview of roads and trails and an inset city map. The general detail is too large to be useful in specific regions, however. Mandala puts out a 1:800,000 Nepal map that at least depicts roads and trails across the entire country. See "Trekking" for more on specific trail maps.

The Schneider maps of Kathmandu and Patan are exquisitely detailed, fascinating if you want to research the convoluted back streets of the old cities. For basic navigation pick up a copy of the big yellow Kathmandu map which you can tote around until it crumbles. For Valley walks or mountain bike trips, the Schneider map of the Kathmandu Valley is indispensable.

Trekking Maps And Information

Schneider maps are a series of 1:50,000 regional maps based on early '60s surveys of Eastern Nepal by Erwin Schneider, published by Research Scheme Nepal Himalaya, Vienna. These superbly detailed eight-color maps include topographic lines, natural features, and villages. The series covers areas of Eastern Nepal: Khumbu Himal (Everest), Likhu Khola, Tamba Kosi, Shorung/Hinku (Solu), the Dudh Kosi, Lapchi Kang, Rowaling Himal, and Gaurishankar, at Rs200 each. The National Geographic Society has come out with a beautiful map of the area immediately surrounding Mt. Everest—not very practical for trekkers, but a stunning souvenir. Another exceptional issue is a color topographic map of the Annapurna region published by ACAP (Rs150, with lots of regional information on the back).

Unless you're a map freak with a fondness for topographical lines the Schneider maps may be *too* detailed for an ordinary trek; at any rate they're only available for eastern Nepal. Locally published dyeline trekking maps by Mandala cover most of the country. They're barely adequate for rough navigation. Villages are often missing (either on the map or in reality) and at a scale of 1:250,000 the contour lines are a travesty. The descriptions and rough sketch maps in trekking guidebooks will serve just as well on main trails, where you'll mainly rely on villagers and other trekkers for directions. On remote trails you'll have or need a local porter-guide. In Nepal, maps are only supplements to finding your way.

Thamel and Lakeside in Pokhara are hotbeds of trekking information; just ask other trekkers. For information on remote regions, ask trekking agencies in Kathmandu or Pokhara, though you may have to hunt to find one knowledgeable with a particular trek.

The **Himalayan Rescue Association** in the courtyard of the Kathmandu Guesthouse keeps a log-book of comments from recently returned trekkers, a gold mine of information on trails and weather, if you can decipher the handwriting. Useful talks are held here twice daily in season on prevention of altitude sickness, what to take, etc. There's also a notice board for trekkers searching for partners, or check restaurants around Thamel.

WHAT TO TAKE

Clothing

Bring comfortable, casual clothes which are easy to wash and dry. What you pack is dictated by the season and where you're headed (see the Temperature Chart on p. 18). Medium-weight cottons are a good choice year-round. Short or long-sleeved shirts are good for spring and fall; add a pile jacket or sweater for chilly evenings. From Nov.-Feb. in the Valley you'll need a warm sweater, jacket or down vest for chilly mornings and evenings, plus warm sleepwear as only the expensive hotels have heating.

It's easy to expand your wardrobe in Kathmandu, either by buying ready-made cotton clothing, or by visiting a tailor for custom-made anything. Better to travel light and leave plenty of room for purchases than to haul over massive amounts of clothing you don't really need.

Unless you're in Kathmandu on official business you won't need dressy clothes, sport coats, or ties. A blouse or sport shirt and a pair of chinos will suffice for dining at the finest restaurants. More important is that clothes be comfortable and sufficiently modest. This last applies mainly to women. Though Thamel is full of Western women in skimpy shorts and tops, such dress is not acceptable. Long, baggy walking shorts are better, but best are loose trousers, a below-the-knee skirt, or a local outfit like a Punjabi or bhakkhu. Men shouldn't wear shorts or go bare-chested in the city; bare chests are also inappropriate while trekking. Bring comfortable walking shoes that can withstand the often muddy roads of Kathmandu, and another, lighter pair to wear around your hotel and possibly the shower (plastic sandals are good, available locally in smaller sizes).

The virtues of a full mid-calf length skirt for women can't be stressed enough. They're useful even in the Valley, but for women on a trek they're essential. A skirt minimizes the difficulty of finding an absolutely private place to pee. In cool weather you can wear tights or long underwear beneath it for extra warmth, then slip them off as the day warms up.

TREKKING

Some trekkers spend as much on the latest outdoor gear as they do on their plane ticket to Kathmandu. But high-tech isn't as important as comfort, and simplicity has its own virtues. Your pack is lighter, for one thing; for another, you don't appear quite as alien to local people. The price of a Goretex jacket exceeds the average annual income of a rural Nepali. Finally, remember the innate modesty of traditional Nepalis and dress accordingly.

The trend in trekkers is distinct: most group trekkers seem to bring far more than they need, while independent trekkers are often underprepared and underdressed for the surprisingly cold temperatures encountered up high. Make sure you'll be sufficiently warm and dry when you've got everything on. Two complete changes of clothes is a basic trekking minimum, with a few extra outfits for Kathmandu. If you forget anything, it can most likely be replaced in Kathmandu, but prices for foreign goods are higher than at home.

Clothing
Trekkers should boost their supply of clothing to deal with temperature extremes: aside from ignoring altitude sickness, the single biggest mistake people make is to underestimate how cold it gets up high. Start with a basic layer of T-shirt or cotton shirt/blouse, plus skirt or lightweight pants. Pack long underwear (polypropylene or silk). The bottoms make warm leggings beneath a skirt, and the set can be used as sleepwear. From here on, start thinking in layers: a heavier shirt, a non-bulky wool sweater, a pile jacket, maybe a down vest, and a warm cap. Remember that you'll usually be warm while walking (except for extremely cold places like the Thorung La on a windy day). The extra clothes are for evenings and chilly mornings, especially if you're staying in a tent rather than a lodge. Metabolisms vary wildly, so figure out in advance if you get cold easily and pack accordingly.

If you're going over 3,000-3,500 meters or are trekking in the winter you need a warm coat. The best choice is a good down jacket—it's as warm as you could possibly need, squeezes into a small stuff-sack, and doubles as a pillow. (Look for expedition weight if you're going high for long periods.) Coats are rented in Kathmandu's trekking equipment shops, but in season it can be hard to find a good one.

Raingear depends on the season. Spring is wetter than autumn, but occasional showers occur even in Oct.-Nov. The lightweight minimum is a good rubberized poncho with hood, which protects both you and your pack. (A poncho's virtue is that it can double as a groundcloth or a bedbug-proof undersheet in questionable lodges.) In anything more than a brief downpour, though, you'll soon be soaked. Often you can wait out the storm in a teashop, but on more remote trails these are few. In this case, high-tech expensive raingear comes into its own. In general, though, it's nice but certainly not necessary.

Pick up a big plastic bag or two from the bazaar to protect your load from rain. Split open, a bag provides emergency shelter (it will keep your porter dry as well). The crowning touch is an umbrella, which doubles as a sunshade. Small collapsible ones are easiest to carry but the big black local variety provides maximum protection—indispensable in the monsoon. Finally, don't forget a brimmed hat to keep the sun off your face.

Footgear
Boots, well-fitting and broken in, are a vital nonrentable trekking item. Trekking shops sell used boots, mostly the outdated, clunky leather variety. New Korean-made lightweight models are available, but larger sizes are scarce.

Running shoes are okay, but most trekkers favor lightweight, ankle-high, lug-soled hiking boots. Stiff leather alpine boots give extra support if you're carrying an exceptionally heavy pack over rugged terrain, but generally they just add an extra half-kilo to each step. Even brand-new lightweight boots may start to dissolve after 200 km or so of Nepal's rugged trails, so bring a shoe repair kit (heavy glue and thread) or an extra pair if you're planning heavy trekking. Village cobblers can work wonders with crumbling boots, but they're not always there when needed.

MISCELLANEOUS CHECKLIST

(* indicates items specifically meant for trekkers)

lightweight towel (save space with one smaller than full size)

good durable sunglasses with cord attached, or *glacier glasses with lenses and sidepieces for the high-UV light at altitude. Spare eyeglasses if you wear them, plus a copy of your prescription.

sunscreen and lip balm, *dry skin lotion for high altitudes

Swiss Army knife

lightweight nylon cord (available in trekking shops) and clothespins (bring from home)

*medical kit (see p. 129)

flashlight and *extra batteries and bulbs, useful in Kathmandu at night, vital outside of it

*extra plastic bags for litter, wet clothes, dirty shoes

small pack or shoulder bag for day-trips

iodine for purifying water (See "Water" under "Health")

toiletries, including tampons and razor blades (available only in Kathmandu and Pokhara). Good toothpaste, shampoo, and dental floss are available but expensive. Pack them in a big durable Zip-Loc bag so you can see what's inside.

sewing kit: at minimum light and dark thread, *plus some strong enough to repair packs and boots. Throw in a few big safety pins in case a zipper breaks.

*sleeping bag (easily rented in Kathmandu)

*sleeping pad, if not provided by trekking company or you plan on going off the beaten track.

*a few candles thick enough to stand alone, or headlamp/reading light

*butane lighters or good (non-Nepali) matches

an inexpensive, inconspicuous, waterproof watch—or quit wearing one altogether

money belt or pouch

*khatak (prayer scarves) if you plan on visiting lamas of Buddhist monasteries (available in Kathmandu)

leakproof, durable plastic water bottle, one per person (hard to find in Kathmandu)

a few feet of ripstop duct tape for repairs of all sorts of things

*waterproofing protector for leather boots

journal or small pocket notebook for recording immediate impressions

entertainment: novels, cards, small portable backgammon or chess set; crossword puzzles, soap bubbles to blow for kids, harmonica or small flute. A Walkman, maybe with a microphone and a blank tape for recording Nepali sounds (a great accompaniment to a slide show).

photos of your home and family, postcards of your country

*trekking permit

*maps and/or a photocopy of the trekking route description from a guidebook

*a few rounds of emergency snack food for long days on the trail. Peanut butter is an excellent source of energy and is locally available in plastic jars. Also nuts, dried fruit, biscuits, hard candies—heavy on the sugar for quick energy when you need it.

Also bring an extra pair of lightweight shoes (sneakers, thongs, Chinese slippers) to change into at the end of the day and to serve as emergency backups. Use the double-sock system to avoid blisters. Thin, slick nylon or silk socks under thick woolen socks reduces friction and cushion the feet. Bring at least four sets, since clean dry socks are essential to avoid blisters.

Packs And Sleeping Bags

If you're only visiting the Valley, any kind of luggage will do. If you'll be riding buses a backpack or duffel bag is easiest to load on and off yourself. Internal frame packs minimize potential damage. Be sure to bring vital spare parts like extra screws, bolts, and nuts to hold the frame together. You'll need a day-pack or comfortable shoulder bag for brief excursions.

Group trekkers are requested to use duffel bags, which are easy for porters to carry. If you're hiring a porter on your own, he may carry your pack on his back or simply put it in his *dokko*. You'll probably have to show him all the adjustments.

When renting or buying, watch out for faulty zippers on packs and sleeping bags. Cold, dust, and frequent use create brittle, snagged or broken zippers. Look for wide-toothed plastic zippers or get a top-loading pack. Rubbing softened candle wax on a zipper temporarily cures a sticky one; sometimes broken zippers can be repaired by straightening bent teeth with a pair of pliers, but you're not likely to find pliers outside Kathmandu.

Every trekker needs a sleeping bag; weight again depends on season and destination. If you're doing a long trek from low to high altitudes, you'll probably find the weight you need is *too* warm in the lower valleys. Sleeping with the bag unzipped and spread over you greatly reduces heat retention. There are seldom pillows in lodges, so bring an inflatable one, or stuff a sweater or coat into your sleeping bag stuff sack.

Sleeping pads are unnecessary for lodges on the Everest and Annapurna trails—many have foam mattresses! On other trails they're good just in case, and double as a lounging pad for rest breaks. Black polyurethane pads are cheap and durable; Therma-Rest air mattresses (seldom available in Kathmandu) are lightweight and make sleeping on the ground a pleasure. Some trekking companies provide mattresses; others ask clients to bring their own.

Renting Trekking Equipment

Everything from boots and bags to crampons and climbing ropes is sold or rented in Kathmandu's trekking shops, some of it brand new, some extremely used. The ability to rent a down jacket or sleeping bag saves travelers on the Asian circuit from hauling cold-weather gear around various tropical countries. But in Oct.-Nov. it may be difficult to find a good warm bag or coat. Check beforehand for small holes or sticky zippers; you're responsible for returning equipment in the same condition. The shopkeeper will want a significant deposit for valuable gear: a passport, your plane ticket, or traveler's checks. The last is preferable in case you need your passport or ticket in an emergency.

Rental prices are pretty much standardized: Rs15 per day for a down coat; Rs10 for a sleeping bag in 1991. Shops used to sell good used equipment at bargain prices, but no more—with the latest catalogues on hand, proprietors are now well aware of the market value. Still you can sometimes find barely used expedition goods for 20-30% off the new price.

You can also rent sleeping pads, raingear, crampons, and ice axes, though the latter two items are rarely needed. If you're heading up to Everest, heavy boots, crampons, and ice axes are available for rent in Namche Bazaar, not that you'll necessarily need these items.

Photography

Unless you're a serious photographer leave your clunky single-lens reflex and multiple lenses at home and take one of the light, portable new generation of auto-focusing subcompacts. Condensing your equipment down to one small piece lessens the worry of theft and the amount of stuff you need to lug about. A thousand dollars of camera equipment about your neck is more than many Nepalis earn in their entire lifetime.

Bring all the film you think you'll need, and then some. Several brands of slide, print, and black-and-white film are available in Kathmandu and Pokhara, but they're more expensive and occasionally have been damaged by heat or age. Check the expiration date on the flap before purchasing. Bring several sets of extra camera batteries (available in Kathmandu) if you're going trekking. Cold drastically reduces battery life, but you can preserve them by keeping them warm in your pocket or sleeping bag at night. At cold high altitudes, you might want to put your camera in your sleeping bag as well, to have it operating for early morning shots.

A telephoto lens or zoom is great for unobtrusively capturing candid close-ups of people, while a wide-angle lens packs in architectural details. Avoid intrusive flashes in temples where people are doing puja, and ask permission before shooting the interior of any shrine. Usually it's okay to photograph the exterior. It may sound stupid, but don't move about while looking through the viewfinder. Several trekkers have died from nasty falls taken while trying to frame the perfect shot.

The different light at high altitude combines with snow to really bring out the blue tint in Ektachrome; Fujichrome or Kodachrome give better, warmer results. Automatic metering systems may fail in exceptional situations like metering bright white, snowy mountains. You may want to manually set the exposure, compensating for the glare by deliberately overexposing one or two stops. Definitely bracket your shots up high. You can also set the meter by reading a gray rock, a friend's sweatshirt, or a nearby wall; anything that's medium-toned and in similar light. Also take lens-cleaning paper, fluid, and an air brush. Nepali children love to touch exposed lenses.

GETTING THERE

Reaching Nepal is no longer the adventurous ordeal of forty years back, when you had to be exceptionally lucky just to have permission to visit. The journey started in India, as you traveled by train to Raxaul and switched to the tiny meter-gauge train which crept across the Nepal border and deposited you at Amlekhganj, the meeting point of the plains and hills. From there you went on foot, horseback, or sedan-chair, up the steep, narrow footpaths leading across two mountain passes. From the rim of the Chandragiri pass, the Kathmandu Valley spread below, its red-roofed buildings and gilded pagodas huddled amid fields. From here it was a steep descent to the village of Thankot, where the Maharaja's personal car would be waiting to meet honored guests. Altogether the journey took 3½ days of steady travel.

Today 80% of visitors arrive by air, a far easier alternative. The remainder come overland through India, via one of the nine border crossings opened to foreign tourists. A tiny fraction trickle across the northern Tibet border along the Chinese-built highway, but the percentage is nothing compared to the mid-80s, when Tibet was opened to independent travelers and the Lhasa-Kathmandu route was in full swing. Political unrest in Tibet has caused China to close it to all but group tours, but there's always the possibility it may reopen sometime in the future.

AIR CARRIERS/FARES

Kathmandu's **Tribhuvan International Airport** is the country's single international air entry point. Ten international airlines serve Kathmandu directly, and at least 20 others have offices in Kathmandu. Direct flights arrive from Delhi, Varanasi, Calcutta, and Patna in India;

Dhaka in Bangladesh; Paro in Bhutan, plus Bangkok and Singapore. Other routes include London-Frankfurt-Dubai (or Karachi)-Kathmandu and Hong Kong-Dhaka-Kathmandu.

Generally, travelers from the U.S. West Coast, Australia, and the Pacific Rim side arrive in Kathmandu after overnighting in Bangkok. Travelers from Europe, the Middle East, and the U.S. East Coast come via Delhi (or another Indian city with direct flight service to Kathmandu). The Bangkok route is easier: you get a two-week Thai visa on arrival and can catch a flight the following morning to Kathmandu. Ask the efficient hotel reservation desk at the Bangkok Airport for a list of inexpensive hotels; they'll call in advance and even give the taxi driver directions.

The national air carrier is **Royal Nepal Airlines** (RNAC). International service includes flights to Calcutta, Delhi, Dhaka, Dubai (US$225), Hong Kong (US$275), Bangkok, Singapore (via Dhaka), plus Frankfurt-London (via Dubai), Colombo, Karachi, and Lhasa. Prices are comparable to other airlines listed below. It also operates regular charters to Tokyo.

Two top-class Asian airlines provide the extensive international coverage that RNAC is lacking. Experienced travelers rave about the impeccable service on **Thai Airways International,** which flies to 60 destinations in 17 Asian countries and Australia, and operates a Bangkok-Kathmandu flight several times a week (US$190). **Singapore Airlines** is also famous for good service: its network covers 54 cities, including a direct weekly Singapore-Kathmandu flight (US$259).

From Europe, **Lufthansa German Airlines** and RNAC fly between Frankfurt and Kathmandu (US$450) with a connection to London. Other routes include **Pakistan International**

TRIBHUVAN AIRPORT

Tribhuvan International Airport, four km east of Kathmandu, was once a grazing ground for the sacred cows of Pashupatinath temple; its early name, Gauchar Field, comes from *gauchar,* "grazing pasture." The new international terminal opened in 1989 can handle over 1,000 passengers per hour, a far cry from the old terminal with lines snaking out the doorway and an open-air waiting lounge.

Arrivals

The entry area includes a bank; there's another one in the main lobby. Rates are the same as in town. There's also a duty-free shop for last-minute purchases of imported liquor and cigarettes, highly valued in Kathmandu. There are separate immigration counters for those with visas and those applying for visas on arrival. Luggage and customs are downstairs: free luggage carts are available for use inside the building. There are no luggage storage facilities. Outside customs, the lobby has several assistance booths. The **Hotel Association of Nepal** (HAN) will make reservations at 70 middle- and upper-priced hotels; some will pick you up at the airport. There's also a **Tourist Information Center** with some very basic brochures, and a booth for limo, minibus, and bus service.

Departures

Departing passengers are processed through the terminal's north end. Anyone without an air ticket needs an Rs5 entry ticket. Check-in and customs are on the ground floor; immigration, departure lounge, and restaurant on the second floor; another air-conditioned restaurant and an observation deck are on the third floor. Airport tax for international passengers is a whopping Rs450. If you have any rupees left over, you can convert them at the ground-floor bank. You need to show your bank exchange receipts to change 15% of the total.

The domestic terminal is in a more modest building about one km north; the restaurant on its second floor is good and more moderately priced.

Airport Transportation

Trekking companies and major hotels meet arriving guests at the airport, with representatives waiting just outside the door. Taxis are available, though most insist on Rs80 or more to go to Kathmandu—double the metered fare. A few medium-priced hotels pick up guests; it's worthwhile to call if you've picked out one in advance, though some will only pick up guests with reservations.

The easiest cheap way to reach Thamel is via the **Sajha** transport company's regularly scheduled bus service between the airport and downtown Kathmandu (0800-2200 daily). The route from the airport goes past the Everest Hotel, Hotel Blue Star in Tripureshwar, north to New Road and "Freak Street," then up Kanti Path to Thamel and Durbar Marg, and back to the New Road Gate. Fare is Rs15. If you're going *to* the airport, you can call 521-064 or 522-146 for details on bus times and pick-up places. An ordinary (read: crowded) city bus shuttles between Shahid Gate-Ratna Park in central Kathmandu and the airport; the stop is behind the tourist bus service on the main road. Fare is Rs1.50; service is supposed to be every 30 minutes.

Airlines's Karachi-Kathmandu flight (US$160), a possible hookup from Europe and the Middle East. **Biman Bangladesh** flies from Europe, Singapore, or Bangkok to Dhaka, then Dhaka-Kathmandu (US$75). Finally, **Air India's** worldwide network originates from Delhi. Its domestic division, **Indian Airlines,** operates daily Kathmandu-Delhi flights (US$142) plus frequent service from Calcutta (US$96), Patna (US$41), and Varanasi (US$ 71) to Kathmandu. However, IA is notorious for bumping passengers, and it's better to fly another airline if you have a choice. Both Indian Airlines and RNAC offer a 25% discount in certain sectors to passengers under 30 years old, no student card needed.

Weekly flights from the Tibetan capital of Lhasa (US$190) operate during tourist season (summer), whenever the political situation is calm. Currently RNAC and a Chinese carrier, **Southwest China Airlines,** fly Lhasa-Kathmandu once a week. **Burma Airways Corp.** (BAC) has an office in Kathmandu and used to fly twice weekly to Rangoon (US$160), but the political situation in Myanmar has reduced tourism to near zero and flights are sporadic if at all. Bhutan's national carrier, **Druk Airways,** flies once a week from Kathmandu to Paro (US$150) but reservations can only be made with an approved visa through the Bhutan Tourist Corporation. Only groups of four or more tourists are admitted to the country on expensive guided tours.

OVERLAND FROM INDIA

Coming by road from India is slow but cheap, and those who have been traveling through India a while usually enter Nepal by a combination of train and bus. The main crossings are Sunauli (from northern India, Delhi, or Varanasi) and Birgunj-Raxaul (for those coming from Calcutta and the only crossing for motor vehicles). An entry point at Kakarbhitta in far eastern Nepal provides access from Darjeeling and the Indian town of Silaguri, but the 610-km journey takes two solid days of bussing to reach Kathmandu, and is seldom used by Western travelers.

From major Indian towns like Gorakhpur, Muzaffarpur, and Patna railway lines switch over to slower meter-gauge track. It's best to switch to buses at these points to reach the border. Nepal's minimal railway system (a total of 51 km of track) carries mainly freight and doesn't go anywhere of interest. Traveling by bus (see "Getting Around") has its own hazards and delights. From border crossings, multiple buses depart for Kathmandu twice daily, generally between 0600-0900 and 1900-2100 or later. Night buses are slightly more expensive and also slightly faster (less stops during the night). They're worth it if you're able to sleep on them, but the seats can be painfully cramped. If you want to avoid grueling bus rides altogether, take a train to the Indian town of Patna and fly direct to Kathmandu for US$41.

The most popular overland crossing is the Delhi-Kathmandu route via Sunauli; en route you could visit Lumbini, the birthplace of the Buddha, and Pokhara. Take the Delhi-Lucknow-Gorakhpur train (16 hours) and a one-hour bus ride to the border at Sunauli. (The Varanasi-Sunauli bus takes nine hours.) Border formalities are usually minimal. Buses are waiting morning and evening to take you to Kathmandu, a 12-hour journey at best. The route crosses the Terai and passes the town of Narayanghat on the Trisuli River to reach the roadside stop of Mugling (nicknamed "Daal Bhaat Baazar" for its many eateries). Mugling is located midway between Pokhara and Kathmandu. Visitors to Pokhara can go direct from Sunauli on a morning bus up the 188-km Siddhartha Rajmarg, which also passes by the hill town of Tansen.

The Raxaul route up the Tribhuvan Rajpath, the original India-Kathmandu Highway, is more direct (200 km), heading straight north, but it's also a slower journey as the road heads straight over the mountains. Mountain bikers come this way because the road is less traveled and more spectacular. The logical point of departure is Calcutta. Take the 12-hour train ride to Muzaffarpur, then a three-hour bus ride to Raxaul. From Raxaul you cross into Birganj. Buses run through Amlekhganj and the industrial town of Hetauda, crosses the Rapti Valley (with Chitwan National Park), then crests the rim of the Valley and joins the highway through Thankot. There's also a twice-daily flight from Birganj-Kathmandu for Rs390, cheaper than flights from other border towns like Bhairawa (US$72) and Biratnagar (US$77).

OVERLAND FROM TIBET

The three-day overland journey from Lhasa to Kathmandu is a rugged but spectacular trip, taking you through an incredible range of terrain, from high-altitude frozen plateau down to lush Nepali farmland. It's dusty, bumpy, cold, and nearly devoid of accommodations, but it's an unforgettable way to enter Nepal. From Lhasa, the road passes through Tibet's second city of Shigatse, crossing several 5,000-meter-plus passes along the way. Near the village of Tingri the north side of Mount Everest is briefly visible. The road crests once more with the 5,050-meter Lalung La pass, then suddenly drops down in a seemingly endless descent. Within a few hours you've left the frigid Tibetan plateau and entered the pine forests surrounding the dramatic gorge of the river called the Sun Kosi, "River of Gold." Nepal lies just beyond and below the border outpost of Zhangmu or Khasa. The latter name is Tibetan for "Mouth-Place," accurately describing its role as Himalayan gateway.

Down the hill and across the "Friendship Bridge" is the small Nepali village of Kodari; seven km further is the larger town of Taatopani, with natural hot springs. From Kodari it's 114 km to Kathmandu along the Chinese-built Arniko Rajmarg. The distance is relatively short but the road between Zhangmu and Barabise is frequently blocked by landslides during monsoon, and you may have to traverse destroyed sections along narrow foot trails. Porters can be hired to carry luggage, and vehicles of some sort (buses, jeeps, trucks) are always waiting on the other side to ferry you to Kathmandu.

LEAVING NEPAL

By Air

Don't forget to save enough rupees for the Rs450 **airport tax**. Outgoing flights from Kathmandu are generally cheaper than one-way fares from the West. Kathmandu-Seattle flights run about US$600 with occasional discounted fares. To Frankfurt it's US$450; to London, US$800. The last two cities are known for their "bucket shops" selling reduced-fare tickets. Kathmandu-Bangkok one way is US$190, Singapore and Hong Kong are each US$275; again, you can easily pick up reduced-fare air tickets in these cities for onward journeys.

Those planning on visiting several destinations in the U.S. might want to check out the "Visit America" packages through **Northwest Airlines** (flying its Pacific route to the West Coast) and **TWA** (or any international carrier). These low fare-coupons, offered only outside the U.S., are worthwhile if you plan on a lot of internal travel.

There are no "bucket shops" in Kathmandu; check out prices among travel agents to find the most competitive offer. Frequently one will know of a deal his neighbor knows nothing about, so it's worthwhile to shop around. Most offices are on Durbar Marg. A word of warning: flights are usually fully booked Oct.-Nov., around Christmas, and in April. Make reservations as far ahead of time as possible and periodically reconfirm them to avoid losing your seat.

Overland To India

Many small travel companies offer special bus/train packages to India via Sunauli and Gorakhpur, presumably saving you the hassles of buying so many different tickets. But beware: many travelers complain of rip-offs; with such complex arrangements it's almost certain something will go wrong. Most commonly, you don't get the sleeper reservations from Gorakhpur you were promised and paid for. A visit to the stationmaster may help turn up a sleeper, but you'll have to pay extra. Even recommended companies can turn out to be shady; the biggest problem is their clients never return to confront them. When dealing with these companies double-check everything, don't leave without your tickets, and hang onto all receipts. **Student Travels and Tours** in Thamel (tel. 221-348) is perhaps the most reliable of the lot. You can also buy Indian bus tickets in advance to reach

a tourist office, Pokhara

Darjeeling or Delhi, but it's generally no problem to get a seat on the spot. Remember if you're exiting via Kakarbhitta in eastern Nepal you need a special permit from the Indian embassy for Darjeeling.

In season it's also possible to sign up on a returning overland bus to Europe. Trips take six to eight weeks, passing through India, Pakistan, Iran and Turkey to Istanbul. A typical fare is US$700.

To Tibet And Bhutan

Currently the only way to visit these countries is with a tour group, though the definition is flexible and a group could be one person. While expensive and restrictive, it's better than not going at all.

Several companies run regularly scheduled departures for Tibet; it's easy to sign up on the spot. Prices run around US$900-1000 for ten days. Probably the best is **Arniko Travels and Tours** in Nagpokhari (tel. 414-594); **Tibet Travels & Tours** (tel. 410-303) on TriDevi Marg is another alternative. For the wealthy, custom trips can also be arranged.

Traveling overland one way is rigorous but worth it for the sights along the road; otherwise

you just see Lhasa, and the Kathmandu-Lhasa airfare is steep, US$190 one way. Experiences vary according to the tour guide, who is assigned through China International Travel Service and is strictly luck of the draw. There are horror stories about Chinese guides, but some prove quite nice, and occasionally there are Tibetan guides. Generally you're free to wander about Lhasa on your own, but further travel is difficult (although some people have told their guide they're flying onto Chengdu and managed to stay a few extra days on their own). Talk to recently returned travelers in Thamel to get the latest story.

For trips to Bhutan, contact **Shambhala Travels & Tours** behind Mike's Breakfast (tel. 227-229). Packages run from 4-12 days, and you can fly direct from Paro to Delhi or return to Kathmandu. Price depends on season, with April and October considerably more expensive than the low season (Jan.-Feb., June, and December). Figure roughly US$150 per day for individuals; group rates (over five people) can drop as low as US$85 per person per day. Bhutanese tours are even more structured than Tibet; basically a guide escorts you around the country according to a strict itinerary.

KERRY MORAN

GETTING AROUND

For years Nepal held the title for the country with the least amount of roads per area. Though a thin network of roads now covers the southern Terai, the mountainous interior north of the Kathmandu-Pokhara Road is reachable only on foot. The steep, narrow trails are often too rugged even for pack animals, making manpower, rather than petrol, the force that keeps the economy spinning.

15,000-20,000 km of footpaths web the country; distances here are measured not in kilometers but in the time it takes to walk them—more relevant than a simple measurement, since steep ascents and descents, rapid streams, rough trails, and a dozen other things combine to slow progress. Distances can also be measured in cigarettes (the number it takes to get a man from one town to the next), in rice (the quantity needed to get a loaded porter to the top of a pass) or *kos,* a vague measurement roughly equal to two miles. All these measurements are maddeningly flexible, like Nepali time. Ask how far away the next village is, and one man will tell you *pugihaalcha,* "you've already arrived." The next passerby might well say *aaja pugdaina,* "You won't reach it today."

Highways

In 1952 Nepal's transport network consisted of less than 100 km of railway track connecting Nepal to India, and a few short roads in the Kathmandu Valley and Terai totaling 376 km. The fastest way to cross Nepal was to go to India, ride the railway to a point vaguely south of one's destination, then walk back up north. Even the wheel was largely unknown except for the temple carts of the Kathmandu Valley. The first bullock cart in Pokhara was delivered in 1953—by air.

Most of Nepal's roads have been built with foreign assistance; India and China in particular have competed in this politically sensitive area. The network now totals roughly 6,300 km, concentrated in the flatter Terai region and in central Nepal.

Constructed with Indian aid in the '50s, the **Tribhuvan Rajpath** linking Kathmandu to India was the Valley's main supply route until new roads made its twisting, winding curves obsolete. Today little traffic comes down the mountainous 200-km highway, making it an ideal route for bike riders and motorcyclists.

The construction of the 114-km **Arniko Rajmarg** by the People's Republic of China in the '60s caused a big commotion, inspiring King

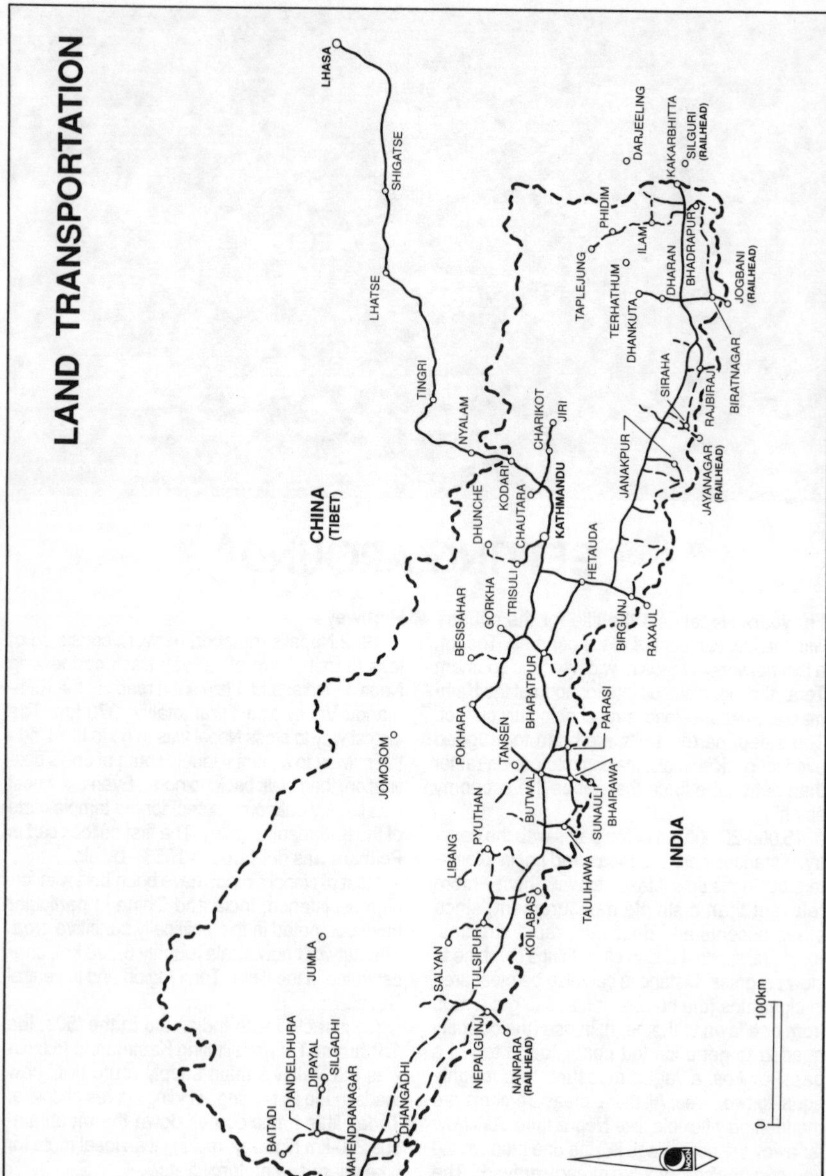

LAND TRANSPORTATION

CHINA (TIBET)

INDIA

LHASA
SHIGATSE
LHATSE
TINGRI
NYALAM
KODARI
DHUNCHE
CHARIKOT
JIRI
CHAUTARA
KATHMANDU
GORKHA
BESISAHAR
TRISULI
HETAUDA
JOMOSOM
POKHARA
TANSEN
BHARATPUR
BIRGUNJ
RAXAUL
JANAKPUR
SIRAHA
DARJEELING
KAKARBHITTA
SILGURI (RAILHEAD)
BHADRAPUR
JOGBANI (RAILHEAD)
BIRATNAGAR
RAJBIRAJ
JAYANAGAR (RAILHEAD)
PHIDIM
ILAM
DHARAN
DHANKUTA
TERHATHUM
TAPLEJUNG
PARASI
BUTWAL
SUNAULI
BHAIRAWA
PYUTHAN
LIBANG
TAULIHAWA
KOILABAS
SALYAN
TULSIPUR
NEPALGUNJ
NANPARA (RAILHEAD)
JUMLA
DHANGADHI
BAITADI
DANDELDHURA
DIPAYAL
SILGADHI
MAHENDRANAGAR

0   100km

© MOON PUBLICATIONS, INC.

Mahendra's famous remark: "I pity those who believe Communism arrives in a taxi-cab." This road connects Kathmandu with the Tibetan border. China also built the **Prithvi Rajpath,** the 200-km highway between Kathmandu and Pokhara. The first half of this road (presently in miserable condition, with repairs scheduled for completion by mid-1993) connects with the Siddhartha Rajmarg leading to Bhairawa, Sunauli and the Indian border. This route is now the main highway for goods and travelers to and from Kathmandu.

The most ambitious project is the 1,000-km East-West Highway (the **Mahendra Rajpath**) crossing the length of southern Nepal. Started under the reign of King Mahendra, the project is finallly finishing up over 30 years later; the final stretch west of Nepalgunj is expected to be completed around 1992.

LONG-DISTANCE BUS TRAVEL

Bus rides in Nepal can be as adventurous and punishing as the hardest trek. Fellow passengers may include chickens, goats, and 100 passengers squashed into a space designed for 60, with more riding on the top. Buying a ticket in advance guarantees you a seat (or a portion thereof), but the aisles crammed with short-term riders and the painfully slow progress make bus rides a test of endurance. They can also be perversely enjoyable if you can get in the right frame of mind to totally stop thinking about time and just be where you are.

The distances seem short on paper, but the rickety vehicles plying the treacherous curved mountain roads travel no faster than 25 km per hour, and a simple 200-km journey that would take 1½ hours on a modern freeway ends up taking all day. Journeys are further slowed by frequent police checks, various checkpoints, and tolls, plus regular breakdowns. Rarely will a bus complete a journey without at least one puncture; often two or three tires blow out in rapid succession. There's nothing to do in these situations but resign yourself to the inevitable wait. Drink another glass of tea, smoke another cigarette (the hassles of Asian travel seem to demand it), and make sure you've got a good book to read.

DESTINATION / TIME / FARE (Day/Night)		
Barabise	5 hours	Rs15.50
Bhairawa/Butwal	13 hours	Rs57/62
Bharatpur, Narayanghat	4 hours express	Rs31/36
Biratnagar	8 hours	Rs116
Birganj	10 hours	Rs53/59
Daman	4 hours	Rs15
Dharan	13 hours	Rs91 (night)
Gorkha	5-7 hours	Rs26
Hetauda (Chitwan)	7 hours	Rs44/49
Janakpur	12 hours	Rs82
Jiri	6 hours	Rs65
Kakarbhitta	13 hours	Rs134
Lamosanghu	5 hours	Rs14
Pokhara	8 hours	Rs100/44
Trisuli	6 hours	Rs15

The main long-distance bus terminal is the **Central Bus Park** on the east side of the Tundikhel, where most private bus companies have their ticket booths. At Sundhara, near the post office, the government-affiliated **Sajha Yatayat** sells tickets to most destinations. These two stations cover all major destinations except Trisuli and Dhunche, the starting point for the Langtang trek. For here, go to the small office in Sorakhuttepati, north of Thamel near the Lainchaur Dairy.

Night buses, some of them deluxe coaches with roomier seating, go to many destinations. These are a good choice, especially if the weather is hot or you want to reduce travel time. They're less crowded than the day buses, and short-legged passengers can even sleep on them. Most routes have "regular" and "express" buses, the former being even slower than the latter, making more stops.

There's a growing trend towards "tourist buses," better maintained vehicles which charge double the going price and supposedly don't stop to pick up passengers. They're less crowded, more comfortable, and at least slightly faster than regular buses. Travel companies advertise them all over Thamel; at least five go to Pokhara, and a new service has started from Kathmandu to Narayanghat (near Chitwan National Park) and on to Lumbini.

Buying Tickets

Get your tickets several days in advance. Buses are especially crowded during the autumn festival season, when many Nepalis visit their villages. Ticket booths are in the Central Bus Park, grouped together under prominently displayed destinations, or you can purchase your ticket through a travel agent (which often requires too much follow-up and prodding to be worthwhile). Prices and service tend to be the same; rates are fixed by the government and are quite cheap. Consult the accompanying chart for sample OW fares and times from Kathmandu.

Your ticket includes a seat number (written in Nepali) guaranteeing you a seat. Some ticket-sellers will let you pick out a seat on a chart. To maximize leg room, minimize jolting, and

Depending on fellow travelers, sitting atop a long-distance bus is often more comfortable than inside.

make the best of frequent stops, get a seat in front as close to the door as possible. Seats over the rear wheels and in the back are the absolute worst. Ticket-sellers from Pokhara like to place all the foreigners in back, so beware. Buses are scaled to Nepali size and can be torture for anyone over 1.6 meters tall. Sometimes if you're a special case (like a woman), you can sit up front in the glassed-in cab with the driver, a bit roomier but crowded with his friends.

Nepalis smoke voraciously on buses, and when one lights up everyone else does too. Many (especially women) are notoriously poor travelers, losing their lunch at the slightest provocation. Hard to say whether you should sit near the window, or let your sick neighbor have the seat.

Big pieces of luggage go on top—you haul it up there yourself or pay a rupee or so to have someone else do it. There's usually a tarp to protect against rain and possible pilferage, but theft of trekkers' luggage is increasing, especially on the Jiri bus. Bring a small day-pack or bag for vital travel goods (water, valuables, maybe some food, and a good thick book) to be carried on your lap, or possibly wedged in an overhead shelf, but never let out of your sight. Occasionally passengers are allowed to ride on the roof of the bus once it's pulled out of town, though this is illegal and you'll be asked to climb back inside for police checkposts. Riding on top is a lot more fun and more comfortable than the inside (as long as it's not too cold) and might even offer great mountain views. A comfortable, sunny spot on the roof can make a bus ride downright idyllic. As for safety, well, one school of thought says you're better placed to jump should the bus roll down an embankment.

Bus drivers are usually admirably dedicated and stop only for a few short tea breaks and a quick meal break. If you're traveling to Pokhara or Bhairawa the food stop will be at Mugling, "Daal Bhaat Bazaar." The driver will usually shout out the length of the break. You'll have 20 minutes or so to stuff down a plate of ready-made daal bhaat, wash up, and be back. Imminent departure is signaled by tremendous honking and revving of engines; try not to be late and make people wait, or worse yet, lose your bus.

KERRY MORAN

RENTALS

Cars

Private vehicles give the maximum freedom to visit remote places at your own pace with a minimum of time and hassle. The main drawback is cost, aggravated by the high price of petrol (Rs19 per liter in 1991). There are two rental car offices on Durbar Marg: Hertz, represented by **Gorkha Travels** (tel. 224-895) and Avis, represented by AmEx representative **Yeti Travels** (tel. 224-895). Major hotels and travel agencies can also arrange car rentals. Cost is US$40-50 per day for a Mazda, Nissan, or similar vehicle. That charge covers petrol, driver (mandatory; you can't drive yourself) and 50 km of travel within the Valley. Longer distances cost US50 cents-$2 per kilometer, depending on the model of car.

Hiring a taxi for the day is much cheaper and seldom difficult to arrange. You'll need to discuss your itinerary and determine the price in advance. Rs500 should cover a full day if you don't go too far out of the way. You can arrange for the driver to drop you off and pick you up several hours later at the end of a day hike. Hotel staff may be able to help you arrange a taxi, or just start asking taxis on the street. Private cars with drivers looking for work are usually waiting on the narrow street behind Mike's Breakfast, but they tend to be more expensive than taxis.

A taxi can also be hired to take you to long-distance destinations like Pokhara, Jiri, Tansen, Lumbini, or Chitwan, though this may require a bit of a search for a willing driver. Sharing the cost with several others makes this kind of travel reasonable; trekkers might consider taking a taxi to the trailhead rather than spending an exhausting day (or night) on the bus. Renting a taxi is definitely cheaper than a rental car; bargain hard and ask Nepalis to help you calculate the price. Figure Rs1700 for a full day of travel. Often drivers will wait several days at Chitwan or Pokhara and take you back too

Motorcycles

Motorcycles are available for rent at about Rs350 per day. Several shops are located on Dharma Path south of New Road, near the Fresh House, and there are a few in Thamel. Motorbikes range from 100-125 cc to 250 cc, the largest available. You'll need the extra power if you're planning trips uphill with a passenger. You're responsible for returning the bike in the same condition you received it, so check it out carefully before taking it. Some shops will ask for your passport as a security deposit. A Nepali or International Driver's License is required for motorcycle rental. If you have a valid foreign license you can get a Nepali license within a few days from the police station at Hanuman Dhoka. Motorcycles can be fun, but you need to be extra cautious in the hectic traffic of the city, and equally careful of ducks, chickens, dogs, and children in villages. Don't be overly optimistic in planning how much territory you can cover. Nepal's roads are rough, and long journeys are more tiring than you might expect. It's best to go slowly and stop for lots of tea breaks.

DOMESTIC FLIGHTS

RNAC's domestic division flies to 41 locations inside Nepal, many of them remote grassy landing strips perched high in the mountains, served by 19-seat Twin Otter and even smaller Pilatus Porter aircraft. Flights to these STOL (Short Take Off and Landing) strips are exciting and sometimes hair-raising, though RNAC's pilots have an excellent safety record. On-board service is limited to a few pieces of hard candy and some cotton-wool to stick in your ears, but flights are usually brief. Sit directly behind the pilot for the expansive view from the cockpit. There's a baggage limit of 15 kilograms per passenger on these small aircraft, which may be strictly enforced.

Few STOL strips have radio communications, and the propeller-driven planes have no electronic navigational equipment on board, so pilots must resort to unorthodox methods like judging windspeed and direction from treetops and the smoke from chimneys below, and memorizing the shapes of mountain peaks as navigational aids. These small, light planes need

> *We don't fly into clouds, because in Nepal, the clouds have rocks in them.*
> —RNAC pilots' maxim

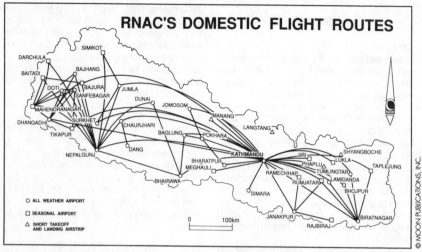

RNAC'S DOMESTIC FLIGHT ROUTES

○ ALL WEATHER AIRPORT
□ SEASONAL AIRPORT
△ SHORT TAKEOFF AND LANDING AIRSTRIP

0   100km

© MOON PUBLICATIONS, INC.

good weather to land, and flights are frequently canceled due to clouds or high winds, sometimes several days in a row. If this happens, you basically start all over again. Passengers on the next scheduled flight retain their seats, and you go onto a waiting list for vacant seats, whenever they may appear. In Kathmandu canceled flights are not a big problem, though you may spend several successive mornings waiting at the airport, but out in the mountains a flight cancellation can leave you stranded for days. The scene is especially chaotic in Lukla, the bottleneck for the Everest region. There's really nothing you can do but wait however long it takes, or walk out—in the case of Lukla a hard five-day journey to the nearest road, and a long bus ride back to Kathmandu. Your ticket is refundable in Kathmandu (in rupees) if you choose the latter.

Mountain Flights

RNAC's regular mountain flight is the easy (nontrekking) way to glimpse the eastern Himalaya and Mt. Everest. The plane flies within 20 km of the Khumbu Himal, at an altitude of about 6,000 meters. At least 18 peaks in that group rise above that height, so the views are pretty spectacular. Tickets are US$94; flights operate three times daily except Sat. from late Sept.-May, depending of course on the weather. The earliest flight offers the best chances of clear views and crisp light. You can photograph from the windows and visit the pilot's cockpit as well. Seats can be booked through an agent or from the RNAC office on New Road; in season, reservations need to be made several days in advance.

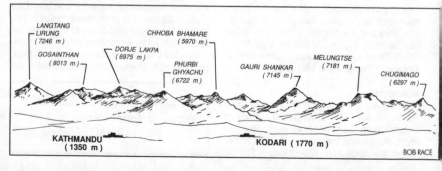

BOB RACE

ONE-WAY FARES FROM KATHMANDU

DESTINATION	LOCALE	FARE
Bhairawa	Lumbini, Indian border	US$72
Bharatpur	Chitwan National Park	US$50
Biratnagar	E. Nepal, Koshi Tappu WR	US$77
Janakpur	Terai	US$55
Jomosom	Annapurna region	US$50
Jumla	Shey-Phoksumdo and Rara NPs	US$127
Lukla	Sagarmatha NP, Everest region	US$83
Meghauli	Chitwan NP	US$72
Mahendranagar	Suklaphanta WR, Khaptad NP	US$160
Nepalgunj	Bardia NP, Rara NP	US$99
Phaplu	Solu-Khumbu region	US$77
Pokhara	resort town, Annapurna region	US$61
Pokhara-Jomosom	Annapurna region	US$50
Simara	Chitwan NP	US$44
Taplejung	East Nepal, Kangchenjunga trek	US$110
Tumlingtar	East Nepal, Makalu region	US$44

Popular destinations have two price lists: one for Nepalis and Indians, and another, more expensive fee for tourists, the latter payable only in foreign currency. More obscure destinations will sell you a ticket in rupees. Consult the chart for sample OW fares in early 1991.

Flights are frequently booked in season. In fall and spring it's advisable to make reservations at least one week in advance. Return reservations to Kathmandu are especially problematic, as remote airstrips don't have phones and the reservation list is sent off from Kathmandu by plane several days before. Book far in advance, or do it immediately upon arrival at the airstrip, but don't count on getting a seat.

Buying Tickets

RNAC's Domestic Service Office is in Thapathali (tel. 223-453, 224-497) but reservations for Lukla and Pokhara are made at the main RNAC office on New Road, which is now computerized and relatively efficient. It may be simpler make reservations through a travel agent, who gets his commission from the airline, not from you. It's often possible to get a seat on a crowded flight, but this requires constant checking and return visits—another good reason to go through an agent. RNAC has regular service to 16 of Nepal's airports and STOL strips; the rest are on a charter basis only.

If you cancel more than 24 hours in advance there's a 20% cancellation fee; 33% for less than 24 hours. No-shows lose the entire price of the ticket. If you cancel, be sure to have it marked on your ticket. Flight cancellations due to bad weather or breakdowns mean you can get your fare back, but only in Nepali rupees, and only in Kathmandu.

MOUNTAIN FLIGHT SKYLINE

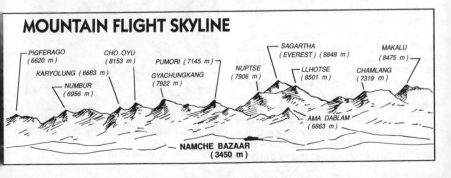

PIGFERAGO (6620 m) — KARYOLUNG (6683 m) — NUMBUR (6956 m) — CHO OYU (8153 m) — PUMORI (7145 m) — GYACHUNGKANG (7922 m) — NUPTSE (7906 m) — SAGARTHA (EVEREST) (8848 m) — LLHOTSE (8501 m) — AMA DABLAM (6863 m) — CHAMLANG (7319 m) — MAKALU (8475 m) — NAMCHE BAZAAR (3450 m)

BIKING AND WALKING

This is an ideal means of transport in the Valley and in Pokhara, both of which are relatively small and relatively flat. Both mountain bikes and regular cycles are easily rented in both locations, though you should thoroughly check the condition of the machine in advance.

Bicycles

Renting a cycle is the ideal way to get around if you're slightly adventurous and reasonably in shape. It's also a good way to train for a trek. Cycling's advantages are unequaled by any other means of transport: it takes you out in open air through the countryside, at a pace faster than walking but still slow enough to enjoy. A clunky old rented cycle may not be sleek, but it frees you from worrying about theft or damage when you lock it up to go exploring on foot.

For a basic bike look for cycles lined up on the pavement in Thamel, around Freak Street, and in Bhotahiti. Rental fees are around Rs15 per day if the market is tight, but during the off-season you can easily bargain it down. If you're renting for a full week you should get a substantial discount. No deposit is necessary—just give your hotel name and room number.

These bikes are Indian or Chinese models, sturdy clunkers of the type you haven't ridden since you were a kid. Get a Chinese-made bike (Flying Pigeon and Phoenix brands) if you can; they're better made and more comfortable than Indian models, and worth the higher rate. In tourist season good bikes are hard to find, so you might want to rent one the preceding eveninig if you're planning a trip. Check them over carefully before renting, looking for bald or leaky tires, wobbly wheels, bad brakes, loose or uncomfortable seats, loose chains. Good brakes and a bell are essential; a light is nice if you'll be riding at night. Getting a reasonable machine will save the trouble of having repairs done out on the road.

If you do get a breakdown look for a streetside repair shop—sometimes no more than an orange crate, a strip of rubber, and a pump. Mechanics working on motorcycles may also take the time to help you out and fix your bike. Shops may have an air pump leaning against the doorway. You can pump your own tires for a minimal charge of one *sukaa* (25 paisa) per tire.

Cycles come equipped with built-in locks on the back wheel. Only for a mountain bike will you need more than this. At places like Swayambunath, children swarm around new arrivals in a sort of blackmail, fighting for the privilege of "watching" the bike. If you decline, you may find your tires mysteriously deflated upon your return.

Kathmandu and Patan are encircled by the **Chakra Path** or Ring Road, a 32-km wonder of even pavement built by China in 1976 as part of a grand plan to divert traffic from the crowded city center. Few vehicles use it besides huge roaring brick trucks, but it makes a great cycling route, surrounded on both sides by the Valley's lush fields and offering mountain views on the southern portion.

Walking

On foot, the way most Nepalis travel, is the best way to explore Nepal, in conjunction with judicious amount of motorized travel or bicycling to speed up the process. Walking is really the only way to pleasurably get through the crowd-

a porter

MOUNTAIN BIKING

Short, fat-tired, and frisky, mountain bikes are made for Nepal. They're a bit much for the city, but on the rugged dirt backroads of the Valley they come into their own, and they're a great option for highway travel. A mountain bike is half as fast as a bus, and about ten times more pleasant. With one you can travel at your own speed, stopping to explore interesting places without worrying about bus connections.

Serious bikers will want to bring their own cycles, since the quality and reliability of Kathmandu's rental cycles are pretty low. Most airlines will take a bike as part of the baggage allowance. Some cyclists pedal up from India on the old **Tribhuvan Rajpath**, overnighting at the small village of Daman with its spectacular Himalayan views. When Tibet was open to independent travelers, many bikers pedaled down from Lhasa to Kathmandu; a few even made the 800-km journey up. If you're planning lengthy touring you should bring a good selection of tools and spare parts. Both are in short supply in Kathmandu and completely nonexistent on the road.

If you do bring your own bike, be extremely careful about theft in Kathmandu. Keep it in your room at night if possible, or ask your innkeeper to lock it inside a downstairs room. On the street, be sure to lock it securely, and don't leave it for too long. Even Kryptonite locks can be cut. (This is one good reason to rent an old clunker for in-city touring.) You can sell a bike for a good profit at the end of your trip, but beware of a potential buyer pedaling it off for a test ride, never to return.

Mountain bike rental shops in Thamel charge Rs50-160 per day, depending on the bike, the seasonal demand, and your bargaining skills. Most bikes are Taiwanese; sturdier American-made ones are more expensive. Five gears is adequate for most Valley tours, but for ascents to mountain viewpoints or out of the Valley you really need 18 gears. For a long trip, search hard for a durable, well-maintained bike. Renting by the week should get you a discount.

A handful of companies run organized mountain bike excursions, ranging from one-half day to several weeks. The original is **Himalayan Mountain Bikes** in the courtyard of the Kathmandu Guest House (tel. 413-632). Long trips run around US$100 per day, including bike, helmet, gear, accommodations and food, and a guide trained in Nepali culture, first-aid, and mechanics. The group is followed by a backup vehicle for gear and tired riders. The company's short day-trips are less expensive, and a good way to break into mountain biking if you've never done it before. Destinations include Swayambhunath-Kakani-Budhanilkantha, Nagarkot, and various backroads tours of the Kathmandu Valley and surrounding Hills. Write to HMB, c/o Marco Polo Travels, P.O. Box 2769, Kathmandu for more information.

For solo cyclists, the Schneider map of the Kathmandu Valley provides great inspiration. You might want to start off with a fairly level day-trip to Godavari, Dashinkali, Sundarijaal, or Sankhu. The next step might be an overnighter to Nagarkot. The 24-km ride takes only two to three hours from Kathmandu via Bhaktapur, but the road is steep. There are plenty of lodges at the top where you can catch views of the Himalaya, descending on the rough dirt road to Sankhu the next day. A slightly longer trip would be to Dhulikhel, 35 km east of Kathmandu. Take the back road out of Bhaktapur through Nala to Banepa, then continue on to Dhulikhel for an overnight stay. Combined with visits to Namobuddha and Panauti, this makes an ideal two- to three-day tour.

For longer destinations, consider the tough day's ride to Daman (classic), the four-day round trip to the Tibetan border, or the Pokhara-Butwal road via Tansen. Biking to Chitwan via Daman is possible, but the Kathmandu-Pokhara isn't recommended—too busy, and in bad shape. Beyond these standard routes are plenty of virtually untested possibilities; in particular, mountain biking across eastern Nepal's network of roads.

A few gung-ho bikers are pushing the limits of the possible by bringing their cycles onto trekking trails. This involves a considerable amount of carrying (a trail that's 50% cyclable is considered good) and is frequently dangerous to those on foot. Local people have not been pleased with bikers zooming around corners, and bikes have been banned from Sagarmatha and Langtang national parks.

ed old bazaars; even pushing a bicycle is a hassle in the densely packed crowds. Only on foot can you journey slowly enough to appreciate the wealth of detail packed into Newari cities and villages, and travel through the surrounding countryside on narrow paths through fields of green rice or yellow mustard. The outlying Hills and mountains, virtually untouched by roads, can only be explored on foot—a pursuit which is for some reason described by the old Dutch term "trekking."

BOB RACE

THE KATHMANDU VALLEY

The largest piece of flat ground in a mountainous country, the Kathmandu Valley dominates Nepal's political, economic, spiritual, and cultural life. The Valley *is* Nepal, in name as well as fact. Traditionally it's known as Nepal Khalto ("Nepal Valley") or simply Nepal, and many Nepalis still call it that today.

With its superb mix of manmade treasures and natural beauty, the Valley is often called an "open-air museum." Actually it's far better than a dry, stuffy exhibition—it's a living, breathing entity, a vital culture that has, miraculously, survived to the end of the 20th century.

Forty years ago a visit to the Kathmandu Valley was unthinkable for all but a handful of Western travelers lucky enough to receive official permission. They then faced an even more formidable obstacle than red tape: the encircling mountains created a natural barrier which the suspicious Ranas had done nothing to improve.

British art historian Percy Brown, who visited in 1912, described the journey from Raxaul to Kathmandu as "a materialized nightmare. . . . Before the end is reached, most known methods of locomotion and several unknown ones will

have been called into requisition. Usually an elephant, two horses, several kinds of palanquin, and one's own feet, are all utilized," he wrote, going on to describe the "restful" experience of being carried in a palanquin by a team of barefoot porters, the usual means of travel for those who could afford it.

THE LAND

Today 80% of Nepal's visitors arrive by air. Flying into the Valley is the perfect way to appreciate its unique geographical position, a miraculously flat oasis set amid the rugged Himalayan foothills. The Valley is a roughly oval bowl measuring 24 km east-west and 19 km north-south, its flat bottomland patterned with textures of plowed, planted, and ripening fields. Cities appear at intervals, compact clusters of red-brick buildings crowned by the golden spires of temples and the stacked roofs of pagodas. Tiered terraces rise up the hillsides. Beyond, mountains recede into the hazy distance, culminating in the stark frozen peaks of the Himalaya, the closest less than 50 km north.

THE KATHMANDU VALLEY

TO LAMOSANGHU, KODARI, & TIBET

BANEPA

PANAUTI

NAGARKOT (ELEV. 1985 m.)

MANICHAUR LEKH (ELEV. 2030 m.)

SHIVAPURI FOREST

SHIVAPURI (ELEV. 2732 m.)

SANKHU

VAJRA YOGINI

CHANGU NARAYAN

SANGA

SANGA PASS

BUDHANILKANTHA

SUNDARIJAL

GOKARNA

BAGMATI RIVER

NAKDESH

BODE

THIMI

BHAKTAPUR

SURYA BINAYAK

BISANKHU NARAYAN

GODAVARI

PHULCHOWKI (ELEV. 2782 m.)

DHOBI KHOLA

BOUDHANATH (STUPA)

GUHYESWARI

TRIBHUVAN AIRPORT

HANUMANTE RIVER

LUBHU

NARASIDDHI

VAJRA VARAHI

KOXHU KHOLA

LELE PASS

LELE

TOKHA

VISHNUMATI RIVER

RING RD.

SANAGAON

CHABAHIL (STUPA)

PASHUPATINATH

NAKHU KHOLA

BUNGAMATI

THECHO

CHAPAGAON

BAGMATI RIVER

DHARMASTHALI

BALAJU

ICHANGU NARAYAN

SWAYAMBHUNATH

KATHMANDU

PATAN

TRIBHUVAN UNIVERSITY

CHOBHAR

KOKANA

KOTWAL GORGE

PANCHMANE PASS

JAMACHO (ELEV. 2096 m.)

NAGARJUN BAN FOREST

MANIMATI KHOLA

BALKHU KHOLA

KIRTIPUR

TAUDAHA

PHARPING

SHIKHAR NARAYAN

DAKSHINKALI

KAKANI

TO TRISULI

RAD PASS

BALAMBU

MACHHEGAON

THANKOT

CHANDRAGIRI DANDA (ELEV. 2242 m.)

TO POKHARA & INDIA

5 km

0

= ENCIRCLING RANGE

© MOON PUBLICATIONS INC.

> *Cresting a low range of hills, which runs along the valley, we at length came in sight of Kathmandoo. This is another most remarkable view, and a very beautiful one. A picturesque and quaint-looking temple and a cluster of red wide-eaved houses, profusely adorned with carved woodwork, form a pretty foreground. In the plain below is a broad river, on the opposite bank of which stands the town, with its numberless Chinese-looking temples, the brasswork with which they are ornamented glittering in the sun . . .*
>
> —Francis Egerton, *Journal of a Winter's Tour in India, with a Visit to Nepal*

After you've been in the Valley a while, head up to a hillside viewpoint to repeat the aerial overview at a more leisurely pace. It's easy to pick out the three main cities; Kathmandu, Patan, and Bhaktapur, each once a kingdom in its own right. Smaller settlements dot the countryside, their houses huddled together to maximize precious farmland. The Newars, the original inhabitants, tend to live in the fertile bottomland near the Valley's center, while later arrivals such as Tamangs, Brahmans, and Chhetris settled on surrounding slopes.

The luxuriant forests of oak, bamboo, and rhododendron which once covered these hillsides are vanishing fast as the demand for fuel wood and farmland grows. A century ago the woods swept all the way down to the Valley floor; now most hillsides have been carved into terraced fields.

The flat alluvial plain is ribboned by the shimmering tracks of sacred rivers: the Vishnumati, the Manohara, the Hanumante—a total of six, all flowing into the most sacred of all streams, the Bagmati. From its source high on the slopes of Shivapuri the Bagmati bisects the Valley and exits to the south, eventually joining India's sacred Ganges.

The Climate

The Valley's combination of subtropical latitude and 3,500-meter altitude creates a near-perfect climate: sunny days, cool nights, abundant monsoon rain, and snow only once in a generation (the last snowfall was in 1944). Average daily temperatures range between 10-30° C, with seasons marked by the changing colors of crops rather than distinct shifts in weather. In monsoon season the rice paddies begin as floating mirrors, soon turning to vivid green, then gold. The autumn harvest gives way to the textured browns of fallow fields, followed by the green of spring wheat and the gold of flowering mustard.

Farmers coax two or even three crops per year from the fertile earth, enriched by the sedimentary soil of its long-ago lake. The traditional fertilizer is *ko,* phosphatic black clay mined from riverside deposits and mixed with the soil to condition it. In fallow times the earth itself is harvested: farmers lease their fields to brickmakers, who carve the earth into blocks which they bake in kilns to feed the modern building boom.

HISTORY

Ancient past and modern present blend in the Valley, which faces an increasingly uncertain future. On one hand are the political and economic realities of Kathmandu city, the only real urban metropolis in a rapidly growing country of 19 million. On the other are the Valley's rural roots (two-thirds of it is still farmland) and its ancient status as a sacred space. The Valley itself is considered a mandala, its outlines delineated by pilgrimage routes linking temples and shrines. Groups of gods and goddesses guard the four directions in sacred quartets fervently worshipped to this day.

Now the old traditions are being eroded by new social, economic, and cultural mores. Change is inevitable; what's amazing is that traditions 1,500 years or older have survived to the end of the 20th century. The Valley's culture preserves customs and beliefs long vanished from the rest of the world—Indian Buddhism, medieval Hinduism, and folk traditions. How much longer these can endure is questionable, probably a few decades at the most. The culture's extreme vulnerability makes the situation all the more poignant. The Valley's rich heritage represents an irreplaceable treasure, not just for Nepal, but for the entire world.

Early Times

Legend says the Valley was once covered by a lake until the Bodhisattva Manjushri raised his sword of wisdom and sliced a passage through the mountain walls, draining the water and creating the first settlements. Certainly the Valley has been inhabited since prehistoric times. By the 4th century A.D. it was a flourishing center of trade; by the 7th century it was a highly advanced civilization, producing exquisite stone sculptures under the Licchavi Dynasty.

Valley culture reached its peak under the Malla Dynasty (1220-1768). Its splendid art and architecture was funded by wealth amassed from its rich soil and from its strategic location on the main trade route between India and Tibet. Described as "the turntable of Asian culture," the Valley acted as a cultural bridge between India and Central Asia. Here Gangetic and Himalayan cultures meet: the cross-cultural interplay has resulted in a rich tapestry of diverse strands.

The Newars

The Valley embraces most of Nepal's diverse ethnic groups, but the warp and woof of this tapestry are the Newars, its indigenous inhabitants and the creators of its splendid civilization. Less than five percent of Nepal's total population, they are a steadily decreasing minority even in their homeland, forming perhaps 35% of the Valley's population.

Their influence, however, remains disproportionately high. Although the Newars were conquered over two centuries ago with the Gorkha unification of Nepal, they have managed to retain their identity and traditions. Their rich culture is distinctly nonmilitary, which perhaps explains their conquest by those consummate soldiers, the Gorkhas. The Newars turned their energy and talents to trade, farming, religion, and above all, art.

The Valley's magnificent heritage is all the more astounding for its relatively small size. Nearly 3,000 monuments are packed into 570 square km. Seven of them (the three Durbar squares, Swayambhunath, Boudhanath, Pashupatinath, and Changu Narayan) have been placed on UNESCO's World Heritage List, the densest concentration of such sites anywhere, and the entire Valley has been proclaimed a UNESCO World Heritage Site, "a refuge of beauty and spiritual repose."

> *... This comparatively small area [is] a veritable art museum of a particularly interesting character, with all the drawbacks to such an institution removed but with many an added charm.*
>
> —Percy Brown, *Picturesque Nepal*

Living Art

Far more than a well-preserved art collection, the Valley is a living, breathing creation, imbued with life by its people, who follow ancient customs and beliefs. Its temples, villages, and cities blend harmoniously with nature—miraculous when you consider that Valley villages have an average population density exceeding 567 persons per hectare, greater than most modern skyscraping capitals. In urban neighborhoods this figure can exceed 74,000 per square km, making places like Asan Tol among the most densely populated regions on earth. City-dwellers live in a vertical dimension, people piled atop people, crammed into tiny rooms. The crowded bazaar lanes are only a half-hour away —but a world apart—from the open fields and sleepy peace of village life. The contrast between the two creates the Valley's inexhaustible charm.

THE OLD CITIES

The old cities are warrens of narrow streets lined by densely packed buildings, regularly punctuated by courtyards, water taps, plazas, and of course, temples, hundreds in each city. The masterful distribution of public space controls any feeling of crowdedness, though Kathmandu's back streets are jammed by the influx of motor vehicles into an area not designed for them. Patan and especially Bhaktapur better preserve the original atmosphere of Newari cities, where courtyards, squares, and temples serve as stage sets for the constant spectacle of daily life.

Newari cities and villages are harmonic masterpieces of manmade and natural environments. The red brick and dark wood blend into the landscape, complementing rather than dominating it. The Newars excelled at urban design, and their generous use of public space makes the cities a joy, for wanderers as well as residents. Houses may be cramped and chilly, but courtyards and plazas are at everyone's disposal, and especially in the winter months people are outside all day, working, chatting and sleeping in the warm sunlight. Life penetrates every space—there's no separation between life and work, or work and religion; all intermingle in a single setting, exemplified by women threshing wheat and children playing in a temple courtyard.

The Valley's city-states were once medieval fortresses surrounded by thick walls and pierced by multiple gates. After the Gorkha conquest the walls lost their protective function and gradually crumbled or were cleared away. The cities were designed in the form of a mandala, with the royal palace and its facing Durbar Square of temples in the center. From here neighborhoods fanned out, arranged by caste into *tol*, groups of 100 or so houses clustered around smaller temple-studded squares. The caste organization created a tightly woven net of social relationships. Occupations tended to cluster together, with potters living in one quarter, silversmiths in another, and so on. Low-caste and untouchable communities dwelt outside city walls; here also were the fearsome cremation grounds, haunted by terrible ghosts. Cities were protected against evil influences by strategically placed shrines, often oriented to the four directions.

Social Structure

Though the Valley's cities may seem dirty and dilapidated today, they were once maintained by a well-organized social system. Royalty and the wealthy classes built monuments, water taps, and temples, and donated land and funds to maintain them in perpetuity. Even simple farming villages boasted bricked gutters, sewers, and water systems. *Guthi* organizations maintained temples and public places, carrying out necessary rituals and repairs. And low-ranking Newar castes cleaned the streets, hauling away garbage and waste to be used as fertilizer in nearby fields. The old cities were hardly spotless

THE GUTHI SYSTEM

The survival of ancient traditions and temples has for centuries been ensured by *guthi*, associations bound by caste, kinship, or neighborhood links. These informal but very important Newari institutions fulfill social and religious obligations, acting as an unofficial but highly effective social regulator.

The guthi system goes back to Licchavi times; its present form dates to the Malla era, when it was a vital part of the social fabric. A guthi's authority was backed by the temple endowments it administered. Wealthy patrons would donate plots of farmland for the support of temples, water taps, or resthouses. These were rented to tenant farmers, and revenues were used to maintain buildings or to sponsor the performance of an important ritual or festival.

As an integral part of an intensely communal society, guthi were extremely effective in supporting traditions and behavior codes. Their duties were taken seriously, as shown by old inscriptions invoking curses on those who tamper with temple endowments. At Changu Narayan, the miscreant is threatened with rebirth as an insect in human excrement, or with being cooked in a pot, while the giver of land is promised 60,000 years of bliss. Another inscription threatens "he who defaces this wall" with sin equivalent to the crime of slaughtering 10 million cows, 10 million Brahmans, 10 million women, and 10 million children. Too bad the vandals who deface temples with graffiti can't read the old Newari inscriptions.

Beyond preserving temples, guthi served as a sort of social glue, preserving shared values and beliefs and transmitting them through the centuries. But the institution has declined in recent years. Land reforms in the early '60s nationalized guthi endowments, stripping local institutions of revenues and prestige. Guthi remain active, but fewer young men are joining them, and with their authority diminishing, they're slowly turning into social clubs. So far, no other agency has stepped in to replace the guthi in its vital role.

—a 19th-century Englishman wrote, "From a sanitary point of view, Kathmandu may be said to be built on a dunghill in the middle of latrines"—but the breakdown of the old social system and the rapid increase in population has not improved the situation.

Houses

Newari houses are closely clustered to conserve valuable space, piled up vertically like the encircling mountains. Long rectangular buildings set end-to-end turn narrow city streets into canyons where the sun seldom penetrates. Other houses are joined behind to form courtyards, peaceful refuges from city streets. Thick walls of clay brick make the buildings cool and dark. Doors and window frames are decorated with lavish carvings, and the varied patterns make each home different.

Because of the high level of water in Valley subsoil, the damp ground floor is seldom used for living quarters. In rural areas it's a stable, while in the cities it's used as a shop or workshop. In some houses the ground floor is sealed off and used as a trash dump, cleaned out perhaps once in a generation, only when it becomes absolutely necessary.

On the upper stories are living quarters: sleeping rooms on the middle floors, and a general work/sitting room on the top floor where family members spend much of their time seated on straw mats, weaving, preparing food, chatting, or gazing through the latticed windows onto the street below. A large projecting bay of three or five beautifully carved windows admits light into the main living area. The kitchen and the family shrine are always on the topmost story, for both are ritually sacred and walking over them would be disrespectful.

By Western standards living quarters are unenviable: unheated, often without running water and toilet facilities, and maddeningly low-ceilinged for anyone over 5 feet 5 inches. Garbage and wastewater are flung out the window onto the street, and woe to whoever happens to be below In the winter the thick-walled buildings retain the cold, and life moves outside into sunny squares and courtyards.

Though houses are well-built, clay and wood cannot stand forever, especially in the earthquake-prone Valley. Cities are filled with crooked, leaning, and downright tottering houses, some propped up by wooden beams, looking as though they might collapse at any moment (some do). Most are still inhabited despite their precarious state. In 1975 an entire Kathmandu neighborhood dropped down 10 meters overnight, its hardened base of garbage having softened in the monsoon rains, and over two dozen houses crumbled into rubble.

CHANGING TIMES

It's easy to romanticize the Valley's cultural and artistic treasures. It's also easy to be shocked by one's first sight of life in a third world country. Reality lies somewhere between the extremes of a fairy-tale kingdom and a miserable hole. The Valley is a traditional society in decline, threatened by forces at work over the globe: development, concrete, pop culture, even tourism. In this sense the Valley is a fragile microcosm, a cultural laboratory in which to observe the effects of "modernization."

Part of the problem is the population boom. The Valley's population has grown from 400,000 in 1951 to over one million today and is expected to triple in the next decade. Add 200,000 tourists per year (that's two for every three Kathmandu residents), and you start to strain both

a Newar village   BOB RACE

(top left) Image of Ganesh, Bhaktapur (Kerry Moran);
(top right) gilt repoussé images of bodhisattvas, Swayambhunath (Kerry Moran);
(bottom) masks for sale, Kathmandu (Kerry Moran)

(top) fresco of Bhairab painted on wall of Chandesvari Mandir (Kerry Moran);
(bottom left) Newari boy next to Buddha displayed during Gunla, Golden Temple, Patan (Kerry Moran);
(bottom right) brightly painted facade of Minnath Mandir, Patan (Kerry Moran)

KERRY MORAN

*sacred cows on
Kathmandu city streets*

society and infrastructure. Taxis, cars, and trucks clog narrow streets that were built centuries before the invention of the combustion engine. Gridlock has become a daily event on the city's main roads. Smog veils the Himalayan views, and the sacred rivers carry raw sewage and chemical wastes.

Urban Sprawl

Meanwhile, the traditional landscape of the Valley is radically and rapidly transforming. The lovely old red-brick buildings are obsolete, replaced by modern concrete boxes. The general rule seems to be the bigger and uglier the better. Some houses exceed even the bad taste of the Ranas, which at least was confined to walled compounds. The very concept of private housing is a break with the past. Previously several generations of a family shared a building; now the trend is towards single-family dwellings isolated from the web of caste and kin, set out in neighborhoods which until recently were farmland.

Urban sprawl is gobbling up the Valley's rich fields at a frightening rate. About two-thirds of the Valley is still agricultural land, but a recent report predicts that 60% will be covered by buildings within 30 years. The cementing over of some of the country's richest farmland is accompanied by the destruction of farming villages and their traditional way of life.

Within Kathmandu, the old skyline is also disappearing. The skyrocketing value of city land drives landowners to erect highrise con-

crete boxes, maximizing the rental value of their tiny plots. One *ropani* (a standard 74- by 74-foot plot) on Durbar Marg costs an incredible Rs150,000,000, about US$5 million. The city skyline is changing from a sea of red-tile roofs to a jumble of concrete boxes festooned with power lines. The old neighborhoods remain, but they're vanishing fast.

Though urban planning has existed for decades, it often works in the city's worst interests, as in the case of the official "concretization" drive accompanying Queen Elizabeth's 1961 visit. Similar efforts to modernize the city occur before major events or state visits, as officials frantically renovate monuments, plant flowers, widen roads (and frequently demolish all the houses in the way, with no compensation to the owners). Countless teams of advisors have devised countless urban development "master plans," but little has been implemented. As things stand now, Kathmandu seems doomed to lose its remaining charm. One can only hope the plague will not spread to the rest of the Valley.

Vanishing Art

Accompanying this is the demise of the Valley's religious art and architecure. Ancient temples crumble from neglect and art treasures disappear in the hands of thieves. Local people care, but have few resources; international aid is already spread thin, and the government, besieged with its own problems, hasn't much to offer. How can it justify the tremendous expense of preserving ancient monuments when water, sewers, and paved roads are desperately needed? Traditionally, restoring temples was the duty of the wealthy, who increasingly are abandoning the old gods for VCRs and shiny new Land Rovers. Organizations like UNESCO and aid missions from various European governments have stepped in to restore masterpieces like Hanuman Dhoka, Swayambhunath, and many important buildings in Bhaktapur, but these constitute less than one percent of the Valley's priceless heritage.

In this sense, development (or whatever you want to call it) threatens not only artifacts but the fabric of society itself. One side effect is the increasing alienation and frustration of Kathmandu's youth, evident in rising drug abuse and suicide rates. The social network which preserved traditions for centuries is unravelling—and as in societies around the globe, there doesn't seem to be much anyone can do about it.

Having said all that, it's necessary to state that the problems are relative. The capital is by far the most pressured part of the Valley. Much of Patan remains virtually untouched, and Bhaktapur is still a world apart. Travelers tend to base themselves in Kathmandu, which has facilities to suit every taste and wallet. But spending all of your time here can prove disappointing, not to mention exhausting. To glimpse what the city was like even 20 years ago you need to venture beyond, to Patan, Bhaktapur, and further out into the surrounding countryside, where village life continues much as it has for centuries. Exploring the Valley reveals treasures beyond those outlined in guidebooks, even more rewarding for their element of surprise.

Jyapu women pounding rice

KATHMANDU

INTRODUCTION

The city still awakens with prayer, the tinkle of morning puja bells and chanting, followed by the first taxi horn, raucous throat-clearing spitting, and the 6 a.m. Radio Nepal reveille.

Dawn and dusk are the best times to explore the back streets of Kathmandu. The slanting light gives a magical, timeless quality to the narrow lanes. They are also the preferred hours for puja, especially early morning, when women head out to take care of the day's religious obligations. Again after office hours, the streets fill with shoppers who automatically reverence the shrines they pass.

By late morning, the bazaar is in full swing, and the stream of shoppers picks you up and sweeps you along. Small shops brimming with goods line the street, their colorful contents most intriguing when quickly glimpsed rather than closely examined: stacks of brass pots, bolts of cloth, mountains of nails, gold and red saris, porcelain cups, a dozen kinds of dried lentils, sacks of saffron-colored turmeric, freshly severed goat heads, flower garlands, brown cannonballs of soap. Taxi horns merge with the solemn clang of temple bells; the scent of fresh oranges and flowers mingles with the blood of butcher shops and the filth of an open sewer. Crowds eddy and swirl around the little golden island of a temple, where people pause to fold hands and recite a brief prayer, or simply touch their forehead in respect as they pass by.

A little farther along the ambience changes in the tourist neighborhoods of Freak Street or Thamel. Signs shout "Good News! Inquire here for trekking, bus to Pokhara, river rafting, jungle safari" . . . "We have Set Breakfast" . . . "Mousaka, French Onion Soup, Crassant" (sic). Rock music blares out of restaurants, and hustlers whisper incantations: "Change money . . . good rate, better than bank"; "Buy hashish, cocaine, marijuana"; "Massage, madam?" even the all-purpose "Anything?" Salesmen fling themselves in front of you to point at "Caaarpet," "Baaag," "Cheap price"—anything to get your attention.

Contrast is Kathmandu's single common denominator, and centuries are compressed into a few blocks. Herds of sheep are driven past Durbar Marg's luxury hotels, and cows amble amid traffic jams. Around the corner from a group of blue-jeaned punks (that's the Nepali word, too) is a threshing scene straight out of a Breughel painting. Traffic roars around ancient temples, sweating porters compete for the right-of-way with sleek black Hyundais, TV antennas sprout from thatched roofs; everywhere the ancient past and busy present rub elbows.

GETTING ORIENTED

Legend has it the Valley's three cities were laid out in the form of sacred symbols: Patan in the shape of a wheel, Bhaktapur as a conch shell, and Kathmandu as Manjushri's sword, with the handle at the confluence of the Bagmati and Vishnumati rivers and the apex in the outlying village of Timmale. Today "Timmale" is Thamel, no longer a village but a busy tourist district, and Patan and Kathmandu have more or less merged into a single sprawling mass. The legend of a deliberate design is certainly a legend: cities were not planned but evolved over time as separate villages grew together.

Upper And Lower Kathmandu

The old city is located on a bluff at the confluence of the Bagmati and the Vishnumati rivers, an easily defended site with rich soil and plentiful water. This core is traditionally divided into two sections: "lower" (southern) Kathmandu and "upper" (northern) Kathmandu. The traditional rivalry between the two was vividly demonstrated in the annual stone fight between inhabitants of each side, held on the festival of the warrior god, Kumara Sasti. This was serious stuff—wounded participants were dragged away by members of the opposing side and sacrificed in temples. Prime Minister Jung Bahadur Rana

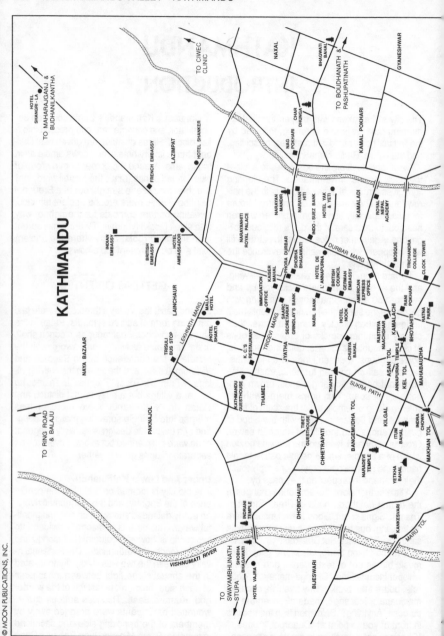

KATHMANDU

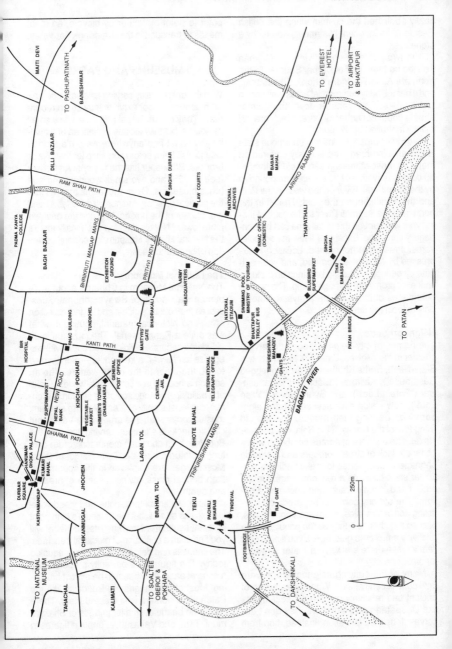

finally abolished the custom when the British Resident, an innocent bystander, was hit by a stone.

The two portions were divided at Makhan Tol, the northern end of Durbar Square. To the north are Asan Tol, Indra Chowk, Chhetrapati, and Thamel, busy commercial areas well known to travelers. Few venture down the quieter streets south of Durbar Square, which are still mainly inhabited by Jyapu.

Even in its present relatively enormous state Kathmandu's urban area is easily covered on foot. The most interesting part of old Kathmandu covers only about five square km, bounded by the Vishnumati River on the west, Kanti Path and the Tundikhel on the east, Thahiti in the north, and the Bagmati River to the south. Finding your way around this small area can be wonderfully confusing. Except for a few major boulevards, streets are not named. Location is expressed by *tol* or neighborhood, and you navigate by periodically taking bearings on a stupa, shrine, or prominent garbage dump. The precise boundaries of these tol are a mystery known only to local residents.

Neighborhoods

The names of city neighborhoods deserve a chapter in themselves: Battis Putali ("Thirty-two Butterflies"), Sorha Khuttapati ("Sixteen-legged Resthouse"), Kalimati ("Black Dirt"). Baneshwar ("Forest Lord"), and Gyaneshwar ("Wise Lord"), now watch over new suburban neighborhoods bearing their names, and the old "Kingdom of the Nagas," Nag Sala, has become Naxal. The plethora of names combines with a complete lack of street numbers and a chronic shortage of telephones to make finding a particular shop or home a real challenge. On the other hand, simply wandering becomes a delight. The old city contains hundreds of interesting nooks, crannies, courtyards, and shrines, packed together as tightly as the populace. The relatively small area guarantees you'll never get *really* lost—there's always a major street or landmark nearby.

Many of the outlying neighborhoods were until quite recently fields. With the exception of ancient and relatively unchanged settlements like Deopatan and Hadigaon, they don't deserve intensive exploration. Instead, hop from point to point by taxi or by bicycle, an ideal means of transport in the surprisingly flat Valley.

MUSEUMS AND PARKS

With the entire Valley serving as a vast open-air art museum, indoor exhibits may seem redundant. They're not. Nepal has only a few small museums, but they include ancient art of a quality you won't find anywhere else. It's a good idea to visit them before you shop for thangka or bronzes. Bhaktapur has the National Art Gallery (see p. 226) and two small woodcarving and brass museums. Other museums that fall into the political category memorialize the father and grandfather of the present king and are oriented more toward Nepalis than tourists. Finally there's the Natural History Museum, an oddball collection of birds and beasts.

The National Museum

The National Museum in Chhauni, about a 10-minute walk south of Swayambhunath, possesses the country's oldest and largest collection of art and historical material, housed in what was once a Rana arsenal. The museum is divided into separate buildings you could well categorize as "Newar" and "Gorkha"—one devoted to art, the other to the art of warfare. The art section is housed in a tiered white wedding cake of a building. Its stone sculpture section is probably the least significant, as there are so many masterpieces scattered around the Valley, but classics include a famous carving depicting the Buddha's birth and three monumental 13th-century sculptures from the Terai district of Bara. Most images are displayed in the open rather than behind glass, giving a sense of breadth and depth.

There are small terra-cotta and woodworking exhibits as well, but the museum's high point is metal sculpture. Nowhere else in Nepal will you find such a collection of medieval treasures. The fineness and delicacy of detail is unequaled today. The figures are perfectly proportioned; resting at ease, they seem to be almost breathing. Most of the images are Buddhist, like the Patan metalworkers who created them. There are some beautiful smaller images of Shakyamuni, Tara, and Vajrasattva, popular figures in shops today, which you can study for pointers. Most spectacular is the massive 14th-century Sukhavarna Samvara, a tantric deity with five heads, 16 legs, and 32 arms, each hand holding a different implement, each fingernail perfectly proportioned. His consort wraps her legs around his massive body, head lolling back with tongue touching nose, representing power and sex combined. Equally elaborate is a man-sized mandala of Lokesvara, its filagreed metal inset with crystal, ivory, turquoise, and garnets.

The painting section has some beautiful old thangka and sequences of small meditation paintings. Upstairs is a random assortment of artifacts, jewelry, and inlay work, a few illuminated manuscripts, and some Tibetan ritual objects made by Newaris.

The ornately decorated red building resembling a temple is a memorial/museum dedicated to the life of King Mahendra; his favorite hunting jeep is enshrined in a small pavilion beside it. Opposite the art museum is the **Historical Museum,** actually a multi-purpose blend of politics, history, and miscellanea. The ground floor features a rather motley natural history display, including the mandibular bones of a blue whale, a stuffed baby rhino, and a Nepali rock taken to the moon aboard Apollo XI. The second floor holds a vast collection of weapons, medals, and uniforms. Displays include the personal arms of Jung Bahadur and other Ranas (an average of six swords per person), a leather cannon captured during the Nepal-Tibet War, and full-length oil paintings of Nepal's rulers. Museum hours are 1000-1430, closed Tues. and holidays; admission is Rs5. You can picnic in the overgrown gardens, and there's a teashop outside the gate.

Natural History Museum
Located off the road leading up to Swayambhunath, this museum resembles a giant science classroom, with specimens of animals, birds, reptiles, fish, insects, plants, and minerals crammed inside one large room. Exhibits include jars of pickled marijuana, a large collection of birds, and an impressive family of Kathmandu's native rats, the largest nearly 1½ feet long. Amid the stuffed cats, goats, and guinea pigs are more exotic creatures typical of Nepal: the *danphe* pheasant, the *gharial,* the Himalayan black

bear, and the barking deer. Open 1000-1600 daily except Sat.; admission Rs5.

Tribhuvan Memorial Museum
Set in a wing of the old palace, this museum is devoted to the life of King Tribhuvan, grandfather of the current king, who reestablished the Shah Dynasty's leadership in 1951. Drowsing guards and reverent exhibits make for a weird experience. Exhibits begin with "The Royal Babyhood" (tiny royal baby clothes, even then encrusted with gold braid) and progress through the king's coronation at five years old in 1911, and his marriage to a pair of Rana sisters at the age of 13. Newspaper accounts document his break to the Indian Embassy and his historic return as Nepal's ruling monarch on 15 Feb. 1951. Don't miss the display of personal effects, including the royal gun, the royal punching bag, the royal monogrammed bicycle, the royal aquarium (drained), and the royal parakeet (stuffed). Museum admission is included in the Rs10 ticket to the palace complex; open 1030-1615 (1515 in winter, 1415 on Fri.), daily except Tuesday.

Parks
If museums are redundant, parks are even more so: in a Valley which is still 60% agricultural land, little attention is paid to urban green space. Public squares and courtyards serve much the same function for city-dwellers, while temples and mountain viewpoints scattered about the Valley are far more interesting than conventional parks. Attempts at establishing Western-style gardens have not been very successful: they tend to be overrun with litter and street vendors and portions serve as open-air toilets (Ratna Park at the north end of the Tundikhel is a good example).

The **Tundikhel** itself is the largest green space in the city, a vast grassy sward serving as the *maidan* or parade ground. The **Exhibition Ground** (Bhrikruti Mandap) a little to the east occasionally hosts month-long exhibitions and fairs, including kiddie rides. There is a little-visited **Peace Park** northeast of the city on the Ring Road, a grassy expanse fenced off from surrounding fields. The best proper park is at **Balaju,** three km north of Thamel, a combination picnic ground and pilgrimage site popular with Kathmanduites (see p. 237).

DURBAR SQUARE

Kathmandu's old Durbar Square (Hanuman Dhoka) is perhaps the Valley's number-one tourist attraction. Patan's Durbar Square is lovelier, and Bhaktapur's is more peaceful, but Kathmandu's sprawling complex seethes with life. On warm summer nights people linger on temple steps, and vegetable-sellers by the Kasthamandap display their wares by candlelight. The square is even more evocative early on a winter morning, with the pagoda roofs barely visible through the fog. Temple bells clang in the mist, and women hurry past wrapped in shawls, bearing trays of puja offerings.

Durbar Square has more than 50 monuments, the oldest dating back to the 12th century, when the area was already an important center at the junction of two major trade routes. Most of the temples you see today are a mere three or four centuries old, the bequest of Malla kings. Greatest of all of them was Pratapa Malla (1641-1674), the self-described "Pearl in the Diadem of Kings." Amorous (he had over 3,000 concubines) and quarrelsome, he was also a talented artist, poet, and performer. Most importantly he was a generous patron, endowing the palace and the facing square with some of their finest gifts. The Shah kings moved into the palace after their 1786 conquest, but more interested in warfare than art, they continued to patronize Newari artists, ensuring a continuity of style.

A WALKING TOUR

Start at the west end of New Road, where a statue of former Prime Minister Juddha Shamsher Rana stands majestically amid swirling traffic. He presided over the rebuilding of Kathmandu after the 1934 earthquake, pushing through New Road atop the ruins. Continue straight ahead until the pavement ends and ancient flagstones begin.

Basantapur
On the right the red brick and dark wood of the old Royal Palace appears. This wing is dominated by the nine-storied, four-roofed **Basantapur Tower,** which lends the neighborhood its name. Tradition says Malla kings were born on the first floor of the tower, held audiences on the second, viewed their dancing girls on the third, and climbed to the fourth floor every evening to survey the smoke from the city's cooking fires and make sure none of their subjects were going hungry—a dubious story, as the tower was much shorter in Malla times. The structure's variegated brick reveals many different eras. It's inset with superb woodcarvings, some of the best in the Valley. The struts depict tranquil gods with frantic erotic scenes beneath.

flute-sellers in Basantapur Square

CHRISTOPHER GAMM

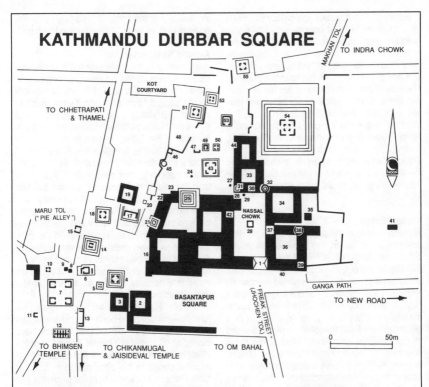

KATHMANDU DURBAR SQUARE

1. Basantapur Tower
2. Kumari Ghar
3. Sikhamu Bahal
4. Trailokya Mohan (Vishnu Temple)
5. Garuda statue
6. Lakshmi-Narayan sattal
7. Kasthamandap
8. Ashok Binayak (Maru Ganesh)
9. Bhagavati Temple
10. Shiva Temple
11. Shiva Temple
12. Singha Sattal
13. Kavindrapur Temple
14. Maju Deval (Shiva Temple)
15. agam chen (temple of a family deity)
16. Gaddi Baithak
17. "Shiva-Parvati Temple" (Navadurga)
18. Narayan Temple
19. Laykhu Bahal
20. Taleju Bell
21. Bhagavati Temple
22. gilt and ivory windows
23. Seto Bhairab
24. King Pratapa Malla's pillar
25. Degu Taleju Temple
26. Hanuman Dhoka
27. Hanuman figure
28. coronation platform
29. Narasingha statue
30. audience hall and portrait gallery
31. Malla agam chen
32. Panch Mukhi Hanuman
33. Mohan Chowk
34. Mul Chowk
35. Durga Temple
36. Lohan Chowk
37. Kirtipur Tower
38. Bhaktapur Tower
39. Lalitpur (Patan) Tower
40. Vilas Mandir
41. Sleeping Vishnu
42. Tribhuvan Memorial Museum
43. Jagannath Temple
44. stone inscription
45. Krishna Temple
46. Taleju drums
47. Kaalo Bhairab
48. Hanuman Dhoka Police Station
49. Indrapur Temple
50. Narayana Temple
51. Kotelingesvara Temple
52. Vishnu Temple
53. Kagesvara Temple
54. Taleju Temple
55. Mahendresvara Temple

Before the earthquake, the palace sprawled far beyond its present boundaries. The tower looks down on red-bricked **Basantapur Square,** which once held stables for royal elephants. Now it's a display ground for souvenir vendors, and acres of their wares glitter in the sunlight. The area is also home base for hordes of roving vendors selling everything from flutes and jewelry to hashish and black-market rupees. The street running south alongside it is the notorious **Freak Street** (the local name is Jhochen Tol), once a hippie haven in the anything-goes '60s. Traces of its exotic past remain in shops selling Indian brocades and silver jewelry, but the hash houses are gone, as are most of the flower children.

Kumari Bahal

At the west end of the square is the richly decorated Kumari Bahal, the home of the young girl chosen to serve as Royal Kumari (see p. 67). Inside and out, it's decorated with beautiful woodcarvings; check out the gilded window directly over the entrance. The building was raised in the mid-18th century by Jaya Prakash, Kathmandu's last Malla king. Its style is that of a Buddhist bahal, but the iconography is a weird mix of Buddhist and Hindu. Most of the doorway torana depict Durga slaying the buffalo demon; Kumari, though a Buddhist herself, is considered an emanation of this fierce Hindu goddess. The lower temple enshrines the Five Tathagatas behind a wooden screen. The main shrine is upstairs in the Kumari's living quarters, where she grants worshippers a daily audience; non-Hindus are not admitted. If you want to glimpse the Kumari, for a few rupees donation she'll make a brief appearance in the upper window across from the entrance. You'll see a little girl dressed in red, her eyes lined with black kohl and her hair pulled up in a topknot. No photographs allowed; for this you'll have to wait for one of her official appearances at festivals.

Leaving Kumari Bahal, there is a large and impressive **Vishnu temple** to your left. On the opposite (west) side, a massive and finely sculpted stone **Garuda** kneels, waiting to serve its divine master. The main portion of Durbar Square lies to your right, but continue further west for a moment, past a row of money-changers and flower-sellers operating out of an ancient building which over the centuries has been converted from resthouse to Vishnu temple to shops.

Around Kasthamandap

Just beyond is the broad-roofed Kasthamandap, a large multi-storied open hall ringed by a picket fence, with a new shrine to Goraknath on the ground floor. Although it's not much to look at, historically it's quite important, one of the oldest buildings in Kathmandu. It once lay at the start of the Tibet trade route, serving as a resthouse *(sattal)* for travelers and pilgrims. Later a king donated it to saddhus of the Kanphatta sect, and their descendents lived here until the mid-'60s. Records trace the building back to the 12th century and the site may easily be twice as old, but the current structure dates back no more than 500 years and has been restored many times, most recently in the mid-'80s. Legend says the structure was built from the wood of a single magical tree, thus its name, Kasthamandap or "Pavilion of Wood," which eventually became the source for the Gorkha name "Kathmandu."

The old **"Pie Alley"** (Maru Tol) of hippie days runs downhill along the north side of Kasthamandap; nearly all its renowned pastry shops have closed or relocated in Thamel. At the top of the street is **Ashok Binayak,** a small but extremely popular shrine to the elephantine god of fortune, Ganesh. Decked with metal pennants and a gilded roof, the tiny temple would be easy to miss were it not for the steady stream of people circumambulating it. Travelers come here before their journey (some even maneuver their motorcycles about it) and the number of worshippers doubles on the unlucky days of Tuesdays and Saturdays, sacred to Ganesh. Inside a stone image of the elephant-headed god rests beneath a gilt replica of the *ashoka* tree said to have once shaded this shrine. Across the road is a wonderful gilded image of Ganesh's mount, the faithful rat Musa. The square to the south, surrounded by minor temples, is filled with farmers selling produce, illuminated at night by small oil lamps.

The Main Square

Head back to the main square and climb the steps of the tall triple-roofed **Maju Deval Mandir** consecrated to Shiva to survey the scene below. Tour groups are tailed by souvenir vendors and sellers brandishing flutes; porters and rickshaws jostle for space, and a few brightly dressed pseudo-saddhus wander about, earning a living posing for photos.

Across the way, brightly painted doll-like mannequins of **Shiva and Parvati** lean from a top window of a large rectangular temple. Actually the Navadurga goddesses are enshrined below, but the whimsical figures above dominate the shrine, looking more like a pair of happy householders than the great Lord of Yogis and his consort. The temple is set atop a low raised platform where costumed dances were performed in Malla times. Just behind it is a massive **bell** dedicated to Taleju, cast in 1786.

Directly ahead is a rather startling intrusion: the neoclassical white facade of **Gaddi Baitak,** a Rana addition to the royal palace which served as an official hall of state in the early part of the century. Modeled on the National Gallery in London, it once included tiers of grandly sweeping steps, now removed to make room for traffic.

Continue northeast up a flagstoned lane between the Shiva-Parvati temple and a beautifully decorated wing of the old palace, crowned with a small pagoda and housing souvenir thankga shops on the ground floor. The second-story windows are classical masterpieces; monkeys occasionally scramble over the tiled roof. Glance at the last set of windows on the corner, where kings once sat and watched their subjects. Their insets of carved ivory and gilded metal were hidden under layers of dirt until the palace underwent a thorough cleaning in 1975.

Around Hanuman Dhoka

Here the street opens onto a second forest of temples, more peaceful than the first and a favorite haunt of pigeons. This area is called Hanuman Dhoka, after the entrance to the old Royal Palace. On the right is a large latticed screen of painted wood: peer between the slats to see the fierce, painted metal mask of **Seto** (White) **Bhairab,** one of the 64 terrifying manifestations of Shiva, erected to drive evil spirits away from the palace. The gilded image, four meters tall, is unveiled only once a year during the week-long festival of Indra Jatra, when crowds garland it with flowers and paper streamers. In the evenings, rice beer flows from a spout projecting from Bhairab's mouth, and crowds of young men jostle beneath to catch a mouthful.

Across the way, seated atop a lotus-capped column, is a beautiful memorial statue of **King Pratapa Malla,** who financed many of Durbar Square's monuments. Surrounded by smaller images of four sons and two favorite wives, his statue kneels facing his former private prayer room on the third floor of the **Degu Taleju Mandir.** The Malla kings of all three cities chose to immortalize themselves kneeling in prayer, gaining eternal blessings—the opposite of the martial poses of monuments to Shah and Rana rulers.

Continuing past an open arcade, you arrive at the actual **Hanuman Dhoka.** The doorway's namesake and guardian stands nearby, robed in red and shaded by a royal umbrella. This is Hanuman, the Monkey King of the *Ramayana,* his features completely obscured by layers of sindhur mixed with mustard oil, three centuries worth of offerings. Hanuman was a favorite patron of the Mallas, protecting them and bringing victory on the battlefield. It's said the image is endowed with the evil eye to keep smallpox, witches, and demons away from the palace; the thick coating of sindhur prevents innocent worshippers from getting zapped.

The golden *dhoka* is brightly painted, flanked by lions bearing images of Shiva and Shakti. Above the lintel are more painted figures, including Pratapa Malla and his queen on the right. Admission tickets are sold here (Rs10 for foreigners) for the palace complex; hours are 1030-1615 (till 1515 in winter, 1415 on Fri.), daily except Tuesday.

THE OLD ROYAL PALACE AND ENVIRONS

This complex was once far more extensive, with 40 to 50 courtyards reported in 1880. Today perhaps a dozen remain; much has fallen into ruin or been destroyed by the 1934 earthquake, while other portions have been demolished. The remainder still covers more than five acres. Though none of the buildings predate the Malla era (the Hanuman Dhoka area is a mere 300 years old), there may have been a palace here as far back as 500 A.D. Sections from many different rulers and eras are cobbled together in a maze of buildings, temples, towers, courtyards, and passages. This is really a Malla Dynasty dwelling. The Shah kings occupied it for little more than a century before moving out in 1896 to the more modern Narayanhiti Palace, the site of the present palace. They left the old Durbar to be used for ceremonies, storage purposes, and offices. The ancient palace still retains great ceremonial importance, perhaps explaining why so much of it is closed to the public.

Nassal Chowk

The first courtyard is Nassal Chowk, named after the dancing form of Shiva. During Malla times, dance dramas were performed on the low raised platform in the center. The Shah kings have turned this into the coronation courtyard; all have been crowned from atop the platform.

Immediately after the entrance to the left is a spectacular silver-edged black sculpture of the man/lion **Narasingha** disembowelling a demon with his bare hands. Narasingha is one of the ten incarnations of Vishnu, who took this form in order to kill the demon, who could not be killed by man, beast, or weapon, on earth, water, or land. Taking the demon on his lap and rending it with his bare hands, Vishnu broke the charm. The installation of the statue involves another interesting story: Pratapa Malla once impersonated Narasingha in a masked dance, and was afflicted with the deity's restless spirit afterwards. On the advice of his priests, he commissioned this image to absorb the troublesome god.

In the open gallery on the left are portraits of the complete Shah Dynasty, each king wearing the fantastic plumed Sri Pech which serves as the royal crown. Once this was the audience hall of Malla kings. The courtyard's northeast corner is crowned by the unique five-storied round pagoda of **Panch Mukhi Hanuman,** "Five-Faced Hanuman," the five-times powerful protector. Atop the northwest corner (also visible from the outside) is a small pagoda marking the site of the **Agam Chen,** which houses the family deity of Malla kings. Both these temples are still kept secret, though their ruling dynasty is long gone.

Mul Chowk

Beyond the northeast corner lies Mul Chowk, the palace's oldest remaining portion, built in 1564 and used by the Mallas for coronations and weddings. Much of it is dedicated to Taleju: the southern wing shelters a shrine to her, roof struts depict her destroying demons, and animals are still sacrificed to the goddess here during Dasain. It's closed to all but the Royal Family, though Hindus are admitted during the ninth day of Dasain to watch the animal sacrifices. You can, however, stand in the doorway and admire the splendid carvings.

Woodcarvings

In terms of pure lavishness, Nassal Chowk has some of the finest woodcarvings you'll ever see. Windows are framed by a riot of complex patterns; protective naga run the length of the brick walls, their heads emerging at doorways; the doorjamb to Lohan Chowk is ribboned by 22 different designs. The tall rectangular **Basantapur Tower** in the southeast corner has more magnificent carvings, including struts with vigorous erotic scenes at the bases which require a telephoto lens to decipher the tangle of limbs. Prithvi Narayan Shah added additional stories onto an existing tower, building it up to its present height of 30 meters. His goal was to create a pleasure pavilion; thus its name, "Pavilion of Spring." Ascend the tower's series of narrow, steep staircases to get a dizzying overview of Basantapur Square and the palace's many roofs, especially the dramatic pagoda of Taleju Mandir to the north, built in the form of Taleju's yantra (magical diagram) atop a 12-story plinth.

At the southeast corner of Nassal Chowk an elegantly carved doorway surmounted by Ganesh leads into **Lohan Chowk,** the living quarters of Malla and early Shah kings. Later it housed the government loan office. The four corners of the courtyard support different towers, said to have been donated by the former city-states of the Valley after their unification by Prithvi Narayan Shah: the copper-domed **Kirtipur Tower,** the octagonal **Bhaktapur Tower,** the square **Lalitpur (Patan) Tower,** and the tall rectangular **Basantapur Tower,** Kathmandu's own. Between the latter two is the finely carved facade of the three-storied **Vilas Mandir,** "Temple of Luxury," with a riot of patterns on the grillwork of its windows.

The beauty of this portion of the palace owes as much to the skill of its renovators as to the original artists. By the early '70s, between rotten timbers and structural damage from the 1934 quake, the palace was on the verge of collapse. UNESCO and UNDP funded an extensive four-

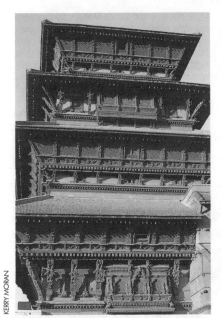
Detailed woodwork adorns the Basantapur Tower inside the old Royal Palace.

year restoration project, combining the skills of local craftsmen with modern techniques. Entire buildings, like the copper-roofed Kirtipur Tower, were dismantled and reconstructed with new timbers. All the elaborate woodwork, totalling over 20,000 pieces, was dismantled, carefully numbered, cleaned of layers of paint and grime, and replaced in its original unpainted condition, letting the beauty of the carving speak for itself.

Sleeping Vishnu

Beyond Lohan Chowk's eastern wall, in the royal gardens or **Bhandarkhal,** is the Valley's third great Sleeping Vishnu sculpture. The gardens are closed to visitors, but you can get a bird's-eye view from the roof garden of the Hotel Crystal behind. Pratapa Malla discovered the statue in a pond in Gyaneshwar and ordered a tank built for it, to be filled with water from the "original" Sleeping Vishnu in Budhanilkantha. Workmen labored for a year to build an embankment, in the process unearthing the Kaalo Bhairab which now stands outside the Durbar.

The day the water arrived, Pratapa Malla worshipped Vishnu. That night he had a dream warning him if he or his successors visited Budhanilkantha, they would surely die. From that time on no king has gone to the site.

On the way out, you can duck briefly into the **Tribhuvan Memorial Museum** near the exit; admission price is included in your ticket. Exhibits are devoted to the life of King Tribhuvan (see p. 167).

Back In Durbar Square

Exiting the palace, admire the erotic carvings on the base of the struts of the 14th-century **Jagannath Mandir,** the oldest temple in this area. The steps are carved with inscriptions in many languages. A duplicate of this strange conglomaration lies across the way, where a low picket fence protects a *tutedhara,* a stone drinking tank inset into the palace wall. In a fit of grandeur, Pratap Malla had the slab inscribed with a potpourri of verses praising the goddess Kali, written in 15 different languages and alphabets. Supposedly great pandits who decipher the entire inscription will receive milk, not just water, from the tutedhara—and the inscription proclaims those dummies who fail are "worthless." Some say the inscription contains coded directions to a treasure Pratapa Malla buried beneath Mohan Chowk. The words *l'hiver, l'otomne,* and *winter* can be distinguished, possibly obtained from Capuchin missionaries who visited the Valley in the 17th century.

Retrace your steps past the Seto Bhairab and head north. On the left is the unusual octagonal **Krishna Mandir** which Pratapa Malla built in memory of two of his favorite queens; the images inside are said to resemble the king and his wives. Just after is a pair of **giant drums,** consecrated to the goddess Taleju and installed in 1800. They are reputed to have great power: according to one account, a goat and a buffalo must be sacrificed before they can be beaten. Like the giant bell to ring away evil spirits, the drums were once used in daily worship, but today remain silent.

On the right is the luridly painted **Kaalo** (Black) **Bhairab,** a huge bas-relief adorned with six arms and a garland of human heads. The sculpture is said to have been discovered several centuries ago in a field by workmen digging a water pipe from Budhanilkantha to Kathmandu. The image was installed in Durbar Square and quickly gained a reputation as an infallible lie detector. It was said that anyone telling a lie in its presence would vomit blood and instantly die. Civil servants were sworn into office in front of it, and criminals were dragged before the image and forced to swear their innocence while touching its feet. Perhaps not coincidentally, the city's main police station is right across the street.

Taleju Mandir

Finally, one of the largest and finest temples in the Valley rises behind a locked gate on the

Taleju Mandir, Durbar Square

right: the splendid Taleju Mandir, dedicated to the royal family's patron deity Taleju Bhawani. The main entrance is from the old palace compound. Access to the temple is restricted to its high priests, the Royal Family, and the Kumari, who is invested here in a secret ceremony. Once a year, on the ninth day of the Dasain festival, Hindus are admitted.

Even from the outside this potent, powerful temple projects a remarkable presence. On a moonlit night it towers against the sky, aloof, remote, and somehow forbidding. Taleju is a bloodthirsty form of Durga, and well-founded legend says human sacrifices were once performed here. The temple towers 40 meters above the street, surrounded by sixteen smaller symmetric pagodas. The embossed golden gates and woodwork are masterpieces, though they're difficult to examine without a telephoto lens or binoculars.

The building was erected in the mid-16th century by King Mahendra Malla, who poured an incredible amount of effort and money into outdoing the Taleju temples of Bhaktapur and Patan. To make it the highest of all he had it set atop a 12-tiered plinth, and issued a royal edict banning the construction of any building taller than it. For centuries this served as an effective housing code, preserving the skyline of Kathmandu. The Taleju temple also saw the fall of the Malla Dynasty. King Jayaprakash Malla hid here as the invading Gorkhas breached the city walls, and made a desperate last-ditch attempt to blow up the shrine and its attackers with gunpowder. Fortunately his efforts fizzled, and the temple remains today. Another bit of history is on the left as the road turns: green metal gates mark the entry to the old courtyard called the **Kot,** scene of the bloody massacre which swept Jung Bahadur Rana to power in 1846.

THE NEW TOWN

The central portion of the city is mainly busy roads and concrete buildings. It lacks the character of the old town but contains most of the modern offices and shops, and encompasses quite a bit of history which is not readily apparent. Knowing the landmarks makes getting around easier and a bit more interesting. This is one tour you probably won't walk all at once, but you're bound to do bits and pieces over the course of your visit.

ALONG DURBAR MARG

Narayanhiti Palace
Start at the north end of Durbar Marg. At the head of the street is Narayanhiti Royal Palace, the official residence of Shri Panch Maharajdhiraj Birendra Bir Bikram Shah Dev, otherwise known as King Birendra. The Shah kings moved to this compound from the old palace in the late 18th century. The new edifice was inaugurated in 1970 on the occasion of the wedding of then Crown Prince Birendra. The compound is immense, surrounded by high walls and guarded by grim-looking soldiers. Obviously, casual visitors are not welcome. The palace is open to the public once a year on the tenth day of Dasain, when the king and queen distribute tika to their subjects. Check out the western entrance's gateposts topped with "snow" resembling whipped cream rendered in cement.

The palace takes its name from the **Narayanhiti,** a recently restored water tap opposite and a little east of the main entrance. Most makara spouts have downward curving snouts, but this pair curves upwards—in disgust, it's said, from a royal parricide they once witnessed. Across the road hidden behind high whitewashed walls is the shikara-style **Narayan Mandir** built in 1793, its shady courtyard a peaceful park-like haven.

Durbar Marg is the elite street of Kathmandu, with top airline offices, travel agencies, restaurants, shops, and hotels. Property here is the most expensive in the country, and prices of goods and services are correspondingly high.

A statue of the late King Mahendra, the father of the present king, presides over a traffic roundabout. A block further is the city's main **Muslim mosque** (three percent of Nepalis are Muslim); past it is the campus and distinctive white clock tower of **TriChandra College,** built in the Rana era. Turn left at the next intersection to tour **Bagh Bazaar** and **Dilli Bazaar,** major shopping areas for household goods and furniture.

The Tundikhel
On the right is **Ratna Park,** one of the city's few, overcrowded and unmaintained. Along the pathway behind it a crowded open-air bazaar sells Indian-made goods and clothes.

Behind it stretches the huge grassy swath of the Tundikhel, Kathmandu's *maidan* or parade grounds for official functions and displays of military might. The king occasionally observes these from the reviewing stand on the north end. This is the city's largest open space, and is a favorite practice ground for soccer and cricket. During the monsoon, the grass is maintained by peasant women, who cut huge mounds of grass and haul them away to feed their goats and buffaloes. On the corners are massive **bronze statues** of Ranas majestically mounted on horseback, cast in Europe and carried in over the mountains by porters—at 4,000 pounds the heaviest objects ever hauled into the Valley.

Midway down, the long-distance **Bus Park** is on the left. At the lower end of the Tundikhel the large **Bhadrakali Mandir** provides a convenient roundabout for one-way traffic. Branching off to the left is **Prithvi Path,** among the widest, smoothest, and best-paved roads in Kathmandu, leading (naturally) to the government offices of **Singha Durbar.**

The road curves round the Bhadrakali Mandir and swings west, bisecting the Tundikhel. Midway down is the marble arch of **Martyrs' Gate** (Shahid Gate), commemorating a group of revolutionaries who plotted to overthrow the Ranas and restore King Tribhuvan to power. Five ringleaders caught in 1940 were tried and convicted of attempting to contact the king. Four were promptly executed; the fifth was thrown

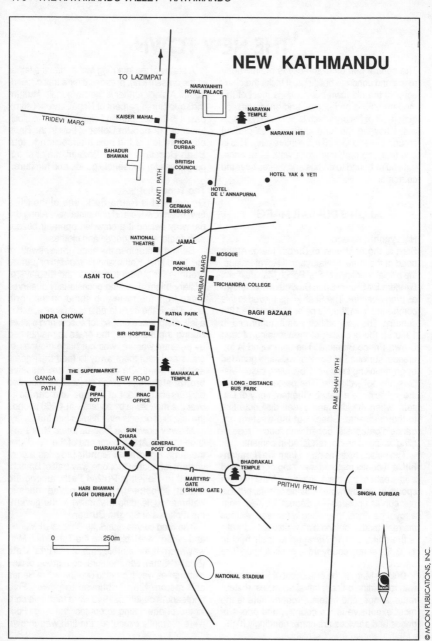

NEW KATHMANDU

TO LAZIMPAT

NARAYANHITI
ROYAL PALACE

NARAYAN
TEMPLE

TRIDEVI MARG

KAISER MAHAL

NARAYAN HITI

PHORA
DURBAR

BAHADUR
BHAWAN

BRITISH
COUNCIL

HOTEL YAK & YETI

KANTI PATH

HOTEL
DE L'ANNAPURNA

GERMAN
EMBASSY

NATIONAL
THEATRE

JAMAL

MOSQUE

RANI
POKHARI

DURBAR MARG

ASAN TOL

TRICHANDRA COLLEGE

RATNA PARK

BAGH BAZAAR

INDRA CHOWK

BIR HOSPITAL

RAM SHAH PATH

THE SUPERMARKET

MAHAKALA
TEMPLE

GANGA
PATH

NEW ROAD

LONG - DISTANCE
BUS PARK

PIPAL
BOT

RNAC
OFFICE

SUN
DHARA

DHARAHARA

GENERAL
POST OFFICE

BHADRAKALI
TEMPLE

HARI BHAWAN
(BAGH DURBAR)

MARTYRS'
GATE
(SHAHID GATE)

PRITHVI PATH

SINGHA DURBAR

0   250m

NATIONAL STADIUM

© MOON PUBLICATIONS, INC.

SINGHA DURBAR

This immense building is (or rather was) the most magnificent of all Rana palaces and the largest private residence in Asia, with 17 courtyards and up to 1,700 rooms. It was built in 1901 by the order of Prime Minister Chandra Shamsher Rana. Teams of laborers worked round the clock for nearly a year to complete it in record time for a cost of Rs2.5 million. The exterior facade, with its acres of colonnaded white stucco porticoes, was the last word in Rana Baroque. The interior was equally magnificent, overflowing with mirrors in gilded frames, Carrera marble, and Belgian crystal chandeliers. Every bit of this splendor was imported from Europe and carried over the mountains by porters.

Chandra made the building large enough to accommodate his extensive family, but soon his sons were agitating for palaces of their own. So he sold Singha Durbar to the state to be used as the Prime Minister's official residence (in those days the Prime Minister *was* the state) and with the proceeds built palaces for all his sons.

The giant palace must have been something of a white elephant: the last Rana Prime Minister is said to have employed 1,500 servants to maintain it. After 1951 Singha Durbar became headquarters of the new government, its rooms filled with hundreds of crosslegged scribes wielding writing brushes. The great reception halls were maintained for official functions. They were adorned with "as many stuffed animals as a natural history museum" (according to one visitor), and include a famous side audience hall with distorting mirrors brought back by Jung Bahadur Rana from London.

Singha Durbar endured until July 1974, when a disastrous two-day fire fanned by monsoon winds consumed overstuffed furniture and official government documents alike. The center section was finally dynamited in order to save the palace's majestic front facade and the reception halls; much of the remainder burned to the ground. A lengthy inquiry never determined the cause, but popular suspicion was arson. The staterooms are sometimes opened to the public; inquire at the gate. You can usually walk up the main drive to admire the facade and reflecting pools.

BOB RACE

in prison, his life spared only because he was a Brahman and thus not subject to capital punishment. Bronze busts of the quintet flank an image of King Tribhuvan in the monument.

ALONG KANTI PATH

Dharahara
The road soon meets Kanti Path, the main northbound street. The **General Post Office** is at this intersection. A little behind is the white watch tower of the Dharahara, frequently mistaken for a Muslim minaret. Actually it's the bequest of

Prime Minister Bhimsen Thapa, who built it in 1830 to "amaze the populace." Originally it had eleven sections, but the two topmost ones toppled in earthquakes. Popular belief has it that the Jung Bahadur, founder of the Rana Dynasty, once leapt from the tower astride his horse, holding an unfurled umbrella as a parachute. The horse died, but he survived.

The plaza around the Dharahara is another open-air market for cheap Indian clothes, mostly factory overruns. Nearby is the giant **Sundhara** or "Golden Water Tap," a popular bathing place for those without indoor water. Opposite and hidden from the road are the crumbling remains of **Bagh Durbar,** the Tiger Palace, its gates once guarded by two live (albeit caged) tigers. It was built by Bhimsen in 1805; he eventually met a bloody end here.

New Road

Heading north up Kanti Path, the **RNAC Office** is at the next intersection, identified by a strange sculpture of a carafe-bearing yeti. This is New Road, straddled by a painted white plaster gate. The road's official name is Juddha Saddak, but everyone calls it New Road, the "New" referring to 1934, when Prime Minister Juddha Shamsher Rana pushed the wide boulevard through the earthquake's rubble. Wealthy Nepalis shop here for electronic goods, watches, modern clothes and shoes, jewelry, cameras, toys, perfume, all brought in from Hong Kong and Bangkok on the "gray market," and expensive compared to the West. Indian tourists flock here in the sultry pre-monsoon for the fresh air and liberal shopping.

Midway down on the left is the **Pipal Bot,** a very old and sacred tree presiding over a few small idols and numerous news and shoeshine stands. This is one of the best places for political gossip in the city; if you can't track down a rumor here, it hasn't even started yet. At the end of New Road is the **"Supermarket"** (Bishal Bazaar), a shopping center with more New Road-type stores, boasting the country's first escalator.

Mahakala Mandir

Back on Kanti Path and heading north, the small Mahakala temple on the right is one of the city's most popular shrines. The black stone image with silver eyes is laden with jewelry offered by devotees. To Hindus, Mahakala is "The Great Black One," a form of Shiva/Bhairab. To Buddhists, Mahakala is a protective deity, created by the great Indian sage Nagarjuna as the protector of the Swayambhunath Stupa. A tantric Buddhist priest is said to have once glimpsed Mahakala flying over the Valley, and impressed with his size and power, decided to lure him to Kathmandu. Fashioning an image, he forced Mahakala to enter it by the power of mantra. Unhappy, the god offered to visit voluntarily on

Saturday evenings if he would be released, and the priest agreed. You'll notice larger crowds here on Saturdays. The image is said to be exceptionally powerful and is worshipped to relieve pain and injury; conveniently, it's located close to **Bir Hospital.**

Rani Pokhari

Further up on the same side is Rani Pokhari, the "Queen's Pond," an artifical tank created in 1670 by King Pratapa Malla to console one of his wives after the death of their son. Water from 51 sacred pilgrimage sites was poured in to sanctify the pond. Despite this, Rani Pokhari quickly acquired an unsavory reputation. First it was ghosts (Pratapa Malla met his *kichkinni* lover here); later it became a popular suicide spot for non-swimmers, necessitating the high fence now surrounding it.

At the north end is **Jamal,** which links Kanti Path to Durbar Marg; from here public tempo ply regular routes to northern Kathmandu. Continue up the street, past the **German Embassy** and the **British Council Library.** Opposite the latter is the Election Commission, housed in the big old renovated palace of **Bahadur Bhawan,** once the site of Boris Lissanevitch's Royal Hotel.

Palaces

This neighborhood, now filled with offices, is honeycombed with fragments of old Rana palaces. On the right is the American Recreational Center compound (for official residents only), housed on the grounds of the old Phora Durbar palace. Before fire and the demands of modern life fragmented it, this palace stretched all the way to the Yak and Yeti's Lal Durbar, over one kilometer away. You can still glimpse bits of the facade behind the buildings of Durbar Marg.

Yet another palace is across the street on the opposite corner: **Kaiser Mahal,** now housing the Ministry of Education and Culture. A portion is occupied by the **Kaiser Library,** a fabulous collection of 35,000 old volumes open to the public on a non-borrowing basis (see p. 209). On the opposite side is the southwest corner of the Royal Palace; Durbar Marg lies one block east.

THE OLD CITY

THE OLD BAZAAR

The old trade route to Tibet began at the Kasthamandap resthouse and ran through Durbar Square to Indra Chowk and through the heart of what's now Kathmandu's main bazaar. Perennially crowded and fascinating, this area always has something to watch, and sometimes even something to buy. Most of the goods on sale are necessities of daily life.

Indra Chowk

Start at Indra Chowk, one block north of the New Road Supermarket in the heart of the old town. Six streets feed into this busy square, each one of them interesting. The crossroads is dominated by the rectangular shrine to **Akash Bhairab,** guarded by four leaping, gilded griffons and inset with whimsical ceramic tiles. The temple's ground floor houses small shops; their steps are a good refuge from the crowd. The second story (open only to Hindus) enshrines the blue mask of this particular Bhairab, miraculously fallen from the sky *(akash)*. Old men

gather in the evening here to sing bhajan, accompanied by drums and the gentle wheeze of a harmonium. The chowk itself is crammed with fruit- and flute-sellers, and porters and laborers from the Hills looking for work.

Tucked behind buildings in a narrow passageway opposite the temple is the **Bead Bazaar,** especially lovely at night with its strands of glittering glass beads. Nepali women shop here for red or green *pote,* multi-strand necklaces which married women set with a golden *tilhari.* There are beaded earrings, belts, and a wide variety of necklaces (see p. 92). Most of the traders are Muslims, descendants of 18th-century merchants invited to the city to sell their wares.

The **Shiva Mandir** on the north side of the square is overflowing with displays of carpets and shawls which hide the ancient sculptures set in the base. This is a big neighborhood for pashmina shawls made from goat's wool, but make sure you get the real thing instead of acrylic. Real pashmina is silky-soft and most often undyed.

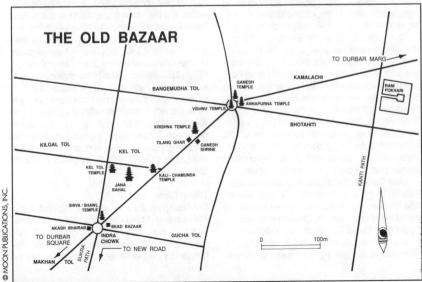

shop set up under the eaves of the Kel Tol temple

KERRY MORAN

Jana Bahal

This classic Newar temple honors Seto Machhendrenath, a form of the compassionate Bodhisattva Padmapani Lokeswara. This "White" *(seto)* Machhendranath is the patron deity of Kathmandu's Buddhist Newars; his red counterpart Raato Machhendranath looks after Patan. The temple is set in a courtyard on the left. Look for a tall flower-carved stone pillar topped by back-to-back Buddhas standing by a white plaster archway. The front of the big courtyard is filled with chaitya and a diverse array of offerings, among them a Greek nymph used as an oil lamp, and adopted by Nepalis as an *apsara.*

The magnificently proportioned main temple is caged in lotus-patterned iron grillwork to protect its fine metal images from theft; too many have already disappeared. Over the main door is a richly worked leafy trellis of bronze, set with a triple torana and images of Buddhas and bodhisattvas. In the sanctum is the doll-like image of Seto Machhendranath, bejeweled and robed in royal garments, tended to by lay priests. The lower struts depict the bodhisattva Avalokitesvara, and the first story is ringed by framed paintings of the deity's 108 manifestations.

Jana Bahal's charm lies in its fantastic metalwork, its great importance with local people, and its huge courtyard which offers a different scene every time you visit. Children play, women bathe near the well, pigeons coo, shopkeepers tend small stores selling nails, cloth, grain. Sometimes at night there's bhajan-singing in the entrance portico. Elaborate puja is often performed in the courtyard, with offerings of red powder, incense, flowers, and rice presided over by a Newar Buddhist priest.

Go through the low passageway in the courtyard's rear wall to **Kel Tol** and a temple stacked with with all sizes and shapes of red clay pottery. More spills out the doorways of surrounding shops: ashtrays, *chillum,* hookah bowls, clay molds for festival cakes, flowerpots embossed with Vishnu or shaped like rhinos and griffons. The largest urns are used to store grain and water. On the corner, streetside barbers give haircuts and shaves to squatting clients.

This area specializes in printed Indian cottons. Terai men loiter on the street with strange stringed instruments they use to fluff the cotton filling of pillows and quilts. Head back east down Kel Tol to the main road. At the crossroads is a small temple to the terrible **Chamunda** or Kali, its twin doors embossed with the symbol of the Ajima or Mother Goddess—an eye over a full water pot. Disarmingly, it's been turned into an outdoor shop selling makeup, mirrors, and the red cotton strands used to lengthen women's braids.

Tilang Ghar

Continuing up the main street, on the left is the 19th century Tilang Ghar, with green shutters and a stucco frieze of marching soldiers. Beside it is an old octagonal-roofed pavilion. Inhabited by ginger-sellers, it looks like a resthouse but is actually a **Krishna temple,** its back side long vanished into surrounding buildings. It has lovely carved pillars and windows, worth examining if you can find a firm foothold against the crowds.

The bazaar is a living river of people endlessly flowing past tiny shops, each with its own specialty: dried fruits and nuts, toys and tinseled holiday decorations, plastic housewares, brass pots. The oldest are so tiny the shopkeeper can reach every item without shifting from his cross-legged position. Merchants sit thus from morning to night, watching the changing street scene. Friends stop by to share a glass of milk tea, play a round of chess, or puff meditatively on an old waterpipe.

Asan Tol

This crossroads is the heart of Kathmandu. Six streets meet in a crowded bazaar filled with vegetable-sellers, turmeric, ginger, garlic, fruit, oil, spices, and wandering cows on the prowl for a mouthful. You can buy anything in Asan, but most of all it has the best and cheapest produce in the city, carried in before dawn by local farmers who rise at 3 a.m. to guarantee they get a good selling point. The center is packed with regulars, who pass their official space down through their family for generations. Many buy their produce from wholesalers before dawn and have it portered to Asan. Along the side lanes fruit-sellers from the Terai operate from basket-laden bicycles.

Asan is a nonstop uproar of bicycle bells, vendors advertising their wares, porters shouting to clear the way for rattling pushcarts, and the occasional blare of an auto horn trying to get through the dense crowd. Don't even *try* to bring a motor vehicle through Asan except late at night; even a bicycle is difficult. The rush of activity is overwhelming, so find an out-of-the-way corner to watch from. The second-story Annapurna Seed House is a good place for photographs.

ODDITIES

Some of the mysteries seen in the Kathmandu bazaar:

Animals: Kathmandu's sacred cows generally have owners who milk them daily and set them loose to feed for free off the streets. Bulls are usually ownerless. According to Hindu custom, 11 days after a man's death his son chooses a bull calf, brands it with the trident of Shiva, and sets it free as a living memorial. Other members of the streetside menagerie are the huge and stinking male goats dedicated to temples and set free. A pendant tied around the neck identifies it as a sacred animal.

Sticky brown cakes: This is *gur*, unrefined molasses, fed to recently calved cows and nursing mothers to build up their strength. It's sometimes mixed with tobacco and smoked in a hookah.

Large matte brown "cannonballs": Actually cheap laundry soap made from the oil of the *neem* tree, mixed with a special kind of clay and sold by weight.

Flower garlands: Used for worship or to honor a person—leaving for or returning from a journey, for example.

Sacks of golden powder: Turmeric, a spice produced from a rhizome similar to ginger, is a vital element in Nepali and Indian cooking. Called "poor man's saffron," it's also used as an antiseptic and skin softener.

Stacks of green leaves: Stitched together with bamboo fiber, the glossy leaves of the sal tree are used as plates for ceremonial feasts and offerings—100% biodegradable! Great quantities are imported from outside the Valley to fill the demand for a ritually pure material for use in religious rites.

Bins of dried fish: These are used as a salty flavoring for *achaar*.

Brown bricks: These are pressed blocks of Tibetan tea made from poorest quality leaves and preferred by Tibetans. Shaped like a brick, and about as tasty as one.

Orange-tinted goat heads: Seen nailed to posts at butcher shops, which also sell bright orange goat meat (the color comes from turmeric). After slaughtering, the skin is rubbed with a mixture of mustard oil, lemon juice, ashes, and turmeric, said to keep the meat fresh and repel flies. Newari cooking utilizes every bit of the animal: head, eyes, lungs, even the blood, cooked into a coagulated jelly.

Three small temples are nearly hidden in the blur of activity. The beautiful little **Annapurna Mandir** is dedicated to a form of Lakshmi, the goddess of wealth. Annapurna means "Full of Grain," and she's represented by a silver *purna kalasha* or overflowing vessel, a symbol of abundance. People visit here all day long to toss in a coin and whisper a brief prayer with folded hands, for this is the Valley's most popular Lakshmi shrine—and Lakshmi, the giver of wealth, is a very popular goddess. The old grain market, now moved southeast to Mahabudhha, used to stand in front of the temple, and a few vendors remain nearby, their scales hanging from a tripod.

Nearby, barely visible behind mountains of fruit and a maze of electrical wires, is small **Ganesh Mandir,** its steps a good vantage point on the surrounding bustle. The third and smallest shrine is the **Vishnu Mandir,** with some ancient stone sculptures. To reach it you must wade over brimming baskets of eggplants, potatoes and cauliflowers.

From here streets radiate out in every direction. The one heading northwest leads to Thamel, while two to the east connect Asan Tol with Rani Pokhari. The lower one goes via Bhothahiti, a name which means "Tibetan watertap." In the old days Tibetan traders congregated here at the site of a spring-fed public bath. The tap was eventually buried and forgotten, and the name became just another one of Kathmandu's mysteries until it was recently unearthed, its water still running, during excavations for a pedestrian subway.

KATHMANDU BACKSTREETS

This route traverses old Newari neighborhoods full of little-known temples and bahal to join Durbar Square with Kanti Path.

Yetkha Bahal

Head west from the **Shiva-Parvati Mandir** on Durbar Square and turn right on the first street. This nameless road leads to Chhetrapati and is a good, less trafficked route to Thamel. The southern portion has several shops selling Indian musical instruments like sitars and tablas. A little ways down on the right a green metal gate marks an entrance to the infamous **Kot,** the scene of the 1846 massacre which brought the Ranas to power. The original buildings have been demolished, but the courtyard once ran red with the blood of Nepal's ruling class.

About 100 meters down on the right is a **Kankeshwari temple** to a bloodthirsty Mother Goddess, set into a larger building and marked by two doors. The first is of gilded metal embossed with eyes and a dancing skeleton, and the second is of carved wood with a six-pointed star carved in the window above—a very old Hindu symbol, used among other things to represent the goddess Kali.

Just past the second door is a crumbling **16th-century resthouse** with beautiful nymphs carved on the wooden struts. Next is a small street inhabited by sign painters (license plates dry in front of their shops), and some of the few **stonecarvers** still working in Kathmandu.

Opposite, a narrow doorway leads to the spacious open courtyard of **Yetkha Bahal,** built around a stupa with slightly startled-looking painted eyes. The 14th-century wooden struts on the temple behind were taken down for safekeeping a few years ago, but may be reinstalled.

Continuing north, on the right is a crumbling but beautiful three-roofed pagoda with a big electrical tranformer right next to it. Beside it, inset into an ordinary building, is the **Deshu Maru Jhya,** "The Window Without Equal in the Country." Bordered by a a series of narrow receding bands carved in a dozen different patterns, this masterpiece is held together without a single nail.

Naradevi Mandir

At the next intersection is the richly decorated Naradevi Mandir, dedicated to a fierce tantric goddess who is a form of Kali. Painted struts show the Ashta Matrika, while the goddess herself, skeletal and terrifying, appears as the central figure in the golden torana. Naradevi is said to have appeared to a king in a dream to request the temple and a platform for dances. The masked Naradevi dance troupe performs in the small open square opposite the temple during the spring festival of Pisaach Chautardasi. The fact that the temple survived the 1934 earthquake unscathed was considered proof of the goddess's power, but the quake's high death toll was attributed to her appetite for human flesh.

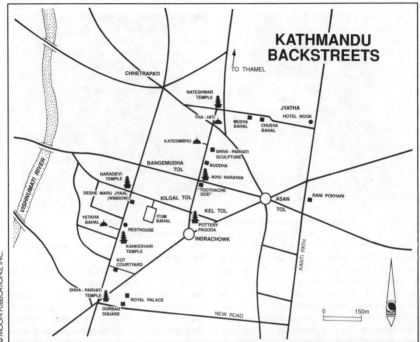

KATHMANDU BACKSTREETS

CHHETRAPATI

TO THAMEL

NATESHWAR TEMPLE

JYATHA
HOTEL NOOK

THA - HITI

MUSYA BAHAL   CHUSYA BAHAL

KATESIMBHU

SHIVA - PARVATI SCULPTURE

BANGEMUDHA TOL

BUDDHA

NARADEVI TEMPLE

IKHU NARAYAN

DESHE MARU JYAAL (WINDOW)

"TOOTHACHE GOD"

KILGAL TOL

ASAN

RANI POKHARI

YETKHA BAHAL

KEL TOL

TOL

RESTHOUSE

ITUM BAHAL

POTTERY PAGODA

KANKESVARI TEMPLE

INDRACHOWK

KOT COURTYARD

KANTI PATH

SHIVA - PARVATI TEMPLE

ROYAL PALACE

DURBAR SQUARE

NEW ROAD

0   150m

VISHNUMATI RIVER

© MOON PUBLICATIONS, INC.

Itum Bahal

Turn right here onto **Kilgal Tol.** About 75 meters down on the right a sign for Krishna Printers points into a vast open courtyard dotted with chaitya and shrines. This is Itum Bahal, one of the city's oldest. The main temple is in another courtyard midway down on the right. Over the entrance is a 16th-century wooden torana depicting the temptation of Buddha, a superb if dusty example of the storytelling function in Nepalese art. Demons and the tempting daughters of Mara surround the main figure of the Buddha, seeking to distract him from his meditation, and in response he simply touches his right hand to the earth, calling it to witness.

The inner courtyard is said to have once housed Guru Mapa, an ogre with a taste for young children. When his appetite became too excessive and local children began disappearing in great numbers, residents coaxed him to move to the Tundikhel and leave their offspring alone in exchange for the yearly sacrifice of a buffalo. The deal is kept to this day, as courtyard residents deliver the feast to the Tundikhel. Two embossed copper plaques on the north wall depict Guru Mapa: in one he's devouring a child; in the second he's munching on his buffalo-meat substitute. Aside from this diversion into folk religion, the shrine is properly Buddhist, with Licchavi-era chaitya and an unusual 9th-century chaitya composed of a quartet of standing Buddhas. Itum Bahal has some very ancient (14th century) and beautiful wooden struts—not the painted ones over the main temple, but the slender yaksha on the rear wall over the entrance, both inside and out. They are exquisite, but so worn they seem to be vanishing before your eyes. A few have already vanished and been replaced by plain wooden planks.

Bangemudha Tol

Returning to the road, continue east through a busy and interesting Newari neighborhood to the next intersection, where the **Kel Tol Mandir** sits with its stacks of pottery. Turn left here and proceed to the next corner, where **Washya Deo,**

KERRY MORAN

metal plaques depicting Guru Mapa devouring a child (left), and munching on his buffalo-meat provided by residents of Itum Bahal

the Newari "toothache god," dwells in a chunk of wood mounted on the side of a building. Toothache sufferers seeking a cure have driven hundreds of nails into the slab. If this folk remedy doesn't work, there's plenty of dentists' offices up the street with great shop windows and advertisements. This neighborhood is called Bangemudha or "Crooked Stick" after an immense and legendary piece of wood of which the toothache god's abode is only a fragment. It's a busy corner, as yet untouched by many modernities. Porters frequent the small tea stalls here, some no more than a kerosene stove and a few glasses set in a niche on the street.

Continue north past a square ringed with many shrines, including the small **Ikhu Narayan Mandir** with recently restored struts and a 10th-century Vishnu image. On the north side of the square, set into the wall, is a small standing Buddha image which is perhaps 1,500 years old. Next come the aforementioned dentists' offices, and a little farther up on the right, a beautiful 9th-century **Uma-Mahesvara sculpture** set in a cemented niche. Shops here specialize in exotic cloth—Bhutanese striped cotton, Chinese brocade and silk, and bolts of gauze prayer flags. On the left, its doorway flanked by two tubas, is a shop renting uniforms and musical instruments for raucous Nepali wedding bands.

Kathesimbhu

A little further on the left is a courtyard housing the gilt-topped stupa of Kathesimbhu, literally the "Swayambhu of Kathmandu." For the aged and infirm a pilgrimage to this stupa is said to earn as much merit as the 365-step ascent to Swayambhu. Every detail of the original is replicated, down to the five "mansions" of the elements and the pagoda temple to the smallpox goddess Sitala in the rear right-hand corner. Supposedly this stupa was constructed with earth and stones remaining from Swayambhu. According to another legend, it was built in 5th-century Buddhist India. A Nepalese sage happened to pass by, and the builders challenged him to breathe life into the monument. The sage muttered a mantra and strolled over the hills back to Kathmandu, with the stupa following obediently behind. While the stupa itself is probably not nearly as old as these tales imply (the present one was built in the 17th century), the site is very ancient, as proven by some magnificent Licchavi stone sculptures, including a Padmapani Lokeswara embedded in a wall near the Sitala Mandir.

Thahiti And Beyond

The next intersection is Thahiti, the site of a miraculous fountain which once spouted forth gold, until it was covered over in the 15th century by a Tibetan-style stupa ringed with prayer wheels. Behind it is a small shrine to Nateshwar, the dancing form of Shiva, decorated with embossed metal images of divine musicians. Go east down the narrow street beyond, passing a well-known Tibetan sweater shop. About 200 meters down on the left a pair of stone lions mark the entrance to the ancient and beautiful **Musya Bahal.** A little further down on the same side is the larger **Chusya Bahal,** which dates back to 1649. It has superb carved struts and a beautiful entrance torana depicting the Buddhist goddess Prajnaparamita. Continue east on this road past the neighborhood of Jyatha, and you'll soon reach Kanti Path.

TRIPURESHWAR AND TEKU

Most travelers know this busy neighborhood near the Patan Bridge as the home of the Bluebird Supermarket. Behind the streetside shops many old temples line the ghats on the banks of the sacred Bagmati River. Exploring this little-known neighborhood takes an interesting few hours, during which you'll see hardly any other foreigners but plenty of Nepali life. Be forewarned that this trip is not for the fainthearted. Sacred as it is, the Bagmati also serves as the sewer of Kathmandu, and its tributary streams are pungent. This tour is best done on foot (you can easily catch a taxi at the end) but if you've got a bicycle you can manage by pushing it along.

Kalmochan
Start by descending the staircase beside the Patan Bridge on the east side of the Bagmati. In winter pilgrims pitch their ragged tents on the grassy riverbanks. In a nearby courtyard on the right is Kalmochan, an unusual Moghul-inspired temple. Its bulbous white dome topped by a cupola of gilded serpents is visible from the road, but the entrance is from the ghat. Construction was started under Prime Minister Bhimsen Thapa in the early 19th century and completed by Jung Bahadur, who is said to have hidden the ashes of the victims of the Kot Massacre in the foundations. Giant gilded griffons leap from the four corners, salvaged from a long-ago temple on the Tundikhel. The gilded figure in court dress atop a pillar facing the eastern door is of King Surendra Bahadur Shah, also transferred from the Tundikhel. Though his hands are folded in prayer, he's armed with a rifle and a wicked-looking sword.

Tripureshwar Mahadeva
The next shrine is an impressive large pagoda set a little back from the river in another courtyard. This is Tripureshwar Mahadeva, built in 1818 by a wife of the ill-fated King Rana Bahadur Shah (assassinated in 1806) for the rest of his soul. A gilded image of the queen kneels atop a naga-carved stone pillar, while a gilded bull and a giant trident identify this as a Shiva temple. The temple is mainly impressive because of its size, but the crumbling courtyard

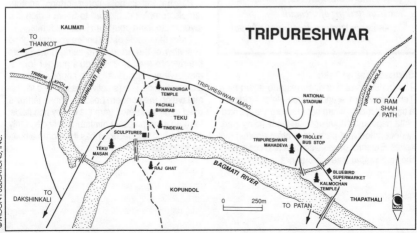

TRIPURESHWAR

has a charm which has been lost in the impeccably restored and varnished temples of Durbar Square. Squatter families who have taken over the surrounding buildings give this entire area a rural feeling.

Back out on the riverbank, it's a ten-minute stroll to the next cluster of temples, across an open field and past bathers, herds of goats, and women doing laundry. In the winter, vegetables are planted right up to the river, making use of every available scrap of land. Round cremation platforms *(masan)* appear at intervals along the bank. Nowadays most cremations take place in Teku, near the big old suspension footbridge visible downstream. This is a very old holy site located at the confluence of the Vishnumati and Bagmati rivers, like all river junctions an auspicious and sacred place. On this spot they're said to be joined in spirit by the Ganga, Jamuna and Sarasvati, the three most sacred rivers of Hinduism.

> *For here and there, through carved and corrugated old archways, are glimpses of courtyards and shrines, containing idols smeared with vermilion and ghee, festooned with flowers, and framed with burnished brass ornament. . . . delightful conglomerations of bright colour, rich shadows, flickering sunlight, religious devotion and unmitigated dirt, the last not the least striking of them all.*
>
> —Percy Brown, *Picturesque Nepal*

Shrines Around Teku

The buildings and shrines resume again near Teku. Look for the unusual temple of **Tindeval,** a triple-domed shikara set in a courtyard. Terracotta naga and nagini encircle the building, partly decoration and partly to protect against evil spirits. Exit through the side door and continue to the huge pipal tree visible in a nearby courtyard. Multicolored thread wrapped around the trunk is part of a ritual advised by astrologers for unlucky people whose horoscopes are mis-aspected by Saturn.

With its twisted roots, the huge pipal tree provides an appropriately mysterious setting for the elemental shrine of **Pachali Bhairab,** a fearsome manifestation of Shiva. This simple open-air shrine is among the Valley's most important for Newars. The deity is actually embodied in a small boulder set along the edge of the pit, but a small gilded figure in front has become the focus of worship, honored with flower garlands and red powder. Nearby is a brass image of Betal, a goblin-like being depicted as a supine, naked corpse with a ghastly grin. As Bhairab's companion and vehicle, he receives blood sacrifices on the god's behalf. Tuesdays and Saturdays are the most popular days for worship here, but local people are constantly passing by.

From here two roads lead to the main **Tripureshwar Marg,** less than ten minutes' walk north. At the junction is a small **Navadurga temple,** its ancient woodwork set into a recently constructed replacement. Goat tails are stuck on the wall as tokens of sacrifices.

Before you leave, though, return to the ghats to see the interesting and unusual collection of sculptures of various deities, not particularly old but very well-executed. There are also stone bulls and linga of varying sizes, plus more old temples, including a pagoda near the bridge with some mildly erotic struts. Across the bridge is **Rajghat** with its hot sulphur springs, another temple complex dedicated to Shiva which is a favorite stopping point for Hindu saddhus.

From the middle of the bridge you get a good overview of the area: sand being mined from the river to feed Kathmandu's hunger for cement, water buffalo wallowing happily, perhaps a cremation on Teku's active masan, and the Himalaya on the northern horizon. These temples used to be separated from the city by rich fields, forming an impressive miniature holy city. Only over the last few decades has it become a built-up extension of Kathmandu.

SWAYAMBHUNATH

OVERVIEW

The most ancient and enigmatic of all the Valley's holy shrines lies two km west of Kathmandu, across the Vishnumati River. The golden spire of Swayambhunath Stupa crowns a wooded hillock which has been a holy site since ancient times. Historical records of its existence date back to the 5th century but the stupa's origins may go back even further. Trying to avoid its tongue-twisting name, visitors often call it the "Monkey Temple" after the bands roaming the surrounding forest.

Swayambhunath's roots go back to the legendary beginnings of the Kathmandu Valley (see p. 30). The *Swayambhu Purana* tells of a miraculous lotus which blossomed from the lake that once covered the Kathmandu Valley, radiating a dazzling light called "Swayambhu," the

SWAYAMBHUNATH

1. Anantapur shikara
2. gilded vajra
3. Pratapur shikara
4. observation platform
5. Vasupur
6. Akshobya
7. Vairocana
8. Ratnasambhava
9. Amitabha
10. Amoghasiddhi
11. Nagapur
12. Harati-Sitala-Ajima temple
13. metal images of Tara
14. Vayupur
15. sculpture museum
16. Tibetan gompa on top floor, resthouse on ground floor
17. International Buddhist Library (good views from the roof)
18. standing Buddha (9th C.)
19. Agnipur
20. seated Buddha sculpture
21. Shantipur
22. Tibetan gompa
23. pilgrim's resthouse

KERRY MORAN

Swayambhunath

Self-Created or Self-Existent. Gods and men both came to worship this miracle, until a wise monk named Shantikar Acharya, sensing the coming of the present dark age, buried the magic light underneath a stone slab and atop it built the stupa. In another version, after the bodhisattva Manjushri drained the waters of the lake to reveal the Kathmandu Valley, the lotus was transformed into the hillock, and the blazing light became the stupa. Either version is a fitting explanation for the origins of the Valley's most sacred Buddhist shrine, the equivalent of the Hindus' Pashupatinath. Swayambhunath's worshippers include the Vajrayana Buddhists of northern Nepal and Tibet, but Newari Buddhists are its most fervent devotees, crowding here for festivals and rituals. During the sacred summer month of Gunla, hundreds come daily to worship, assembling before dawn in Kathmandu to make the journey together.

Getting There

Swayambhu is a short taxi ride west of Kathmandu, but it's nice to bike or walk, leaving the

city's hustle for the quieter neighborhoods on the banks of the Vishnumati River. The old pilgrim path from the city passes a number of interesting temples. Beside the bridge is an **Indreni temple** dedicated to a fierce goddess the Newars call Luti Ajima, who once demanded human sacrifices. Across the river is the shrine of **Shobha Bhagwati** ("Beautiful Goddess"), the most famous of Kathmandu's many temples to the great goddess Durga, as well as a reported haunt of witches.

Curve past the Hotel Vajra to reach Swayambhu's **main entrance gate,** a brightly painted plaster confection in Tibetan style. Your bicycle may prove troublesome here, as gangs of kids extort protection money to "watch" it ("Or else the Tibetans will break it," they'll tell you). Confronting them directly risks a flat tire on your return. Either leave your bike before the entrance, or promise them anything and then suddenly discover you have no change. If you give in, a couple of rupees is sufficient baksheesh.

You can also take a taxi around the south side of the hill to a small parking lot just below the stupa. Tour buses use this route to avoid the steep stairs on the west side, but the ancient stairway is the traditional pilgrim route and is guaranteed to earn you more religious merit.

The Climb Up

Just past the main gate sit three giant orange-and-yellow Buddhas constructed of carved and fitted stone blocks. The oldest dates back to 1750. This is **Buddha Akshobhya,** the Buddha of the Mirror-Like Wisdom, seated in the earth-touching gesture. Further up is a more recent trio of Buddhas donated by the great-grandfather of King Birendra.

Worn stone steps, 365 in all, lead straight to the top, where Swayambunath's painted eyes peer down at all comers. There are plenty of shady places along the way to pause and watch the monkeys sliding down the railing. Some Tibetan refugees have set up shop here carving mani stones for sale.

THE STUPA PLATFORM

At the very top is a gigantic **gilded *vajra*** resting on an embossed mandala, set on a stone base carved with the 12 animals of the Tibetan calendar. King Pratapa Malla donated this, and raised the imposing white **shikara** on either side. These temples are dedicated to secret tantric deities and christened Anantapur and Pratapur in honor of the king and a favorite wife.

The Five Buddhas

The stupa behind has grown in layers over the centuries, as it has been repaired from earthquake damage and from destruction in the brief Muslim invasion of 1349. Centuries of royal gifts make it the most magnificently decorated of all Nepal's stupas. Records show a typical 17th-century repair session at Swayambhu required 39 kilograms of gold. Much of the wealth has gone into the shrines for the five directional Buddhas (Pancha Buddha or Dhyani Buddha) attached to the stupa's dome. Directly across from the stairway is the shrine of **Buddha Akshobya,** the Buddha of the East; close beside it is that of **Vairochana,** usually envisioned in the center. Look for the animal vehicles of each Buddha set in niches below the shrines. The Buddhas' consorts appear in smaller shrines beside them.

Above the stupa's painted eyes, gilded *torana* depicting the Pancha Buddha continue the theme. The quintet are symbolic expressions of the five elements: earth, air, water, fire, and ether. More tangible than the formless light of Swayambhu, they serve as intermediaries in worship, receiving the stupa's offerings. Their wisdom is said to be embodied in the stupa's dome, and their infinite compassion is represented by a diamond set atop the spire.

The Swayambhu hilltop offers a commanding view of Kathmandu city; at one time the site was also used as a military fort. To the left of the Anantapur shikara is a **bricked observation platform,** created in 1979 as a byproduct of reinforcement work after a landslip threatened the entire hill. From here you can see the red brick of the old city rapidly being swallowed by cement buildings, and on clear days, a line of Himalayan peaks. The view is splendid at dusk, as city lights flicker on one by one, and even better when a full moon hangs in the sky.

Vasupur And Amitabha

Like all stupas, visitors should move around Swayambhu clockwise, keeping it on their right. Just behind and a little beyond Anantapur is the small copper-roofed shrine of Vasupur, sacred to the Buddhist earth goddess Vasundhara. Her graceful seated figure appears on the left of a row of sculptures inside. This is the first of Swayambhu's five ancient shrines or "mansions" *(pura)* dedicated to the five elements—a relic of ancient folk beliefs which combines with the worship of the Five Buddhas. A little further west is the marble-faced shrine of **Vayapur,** the Sanctuary of the Wind, worshipped in the form of a boulder. Behind this is a small **museum** with a good collection of stone sculptures discovered around Swayambhu—perhaps the only museum in the world where the exhibits are still actively worshipped.

The stupa's western side is the major focus of activity. It houses the shrine of **Amitabha,** Buddha of Boundless Light and the favorite among the Pancha Buddha. Facing him are two lovely statues of **Tara,** now encased in a metal cage to protect them from theft. Between them Amitabha's mount, the peacock, is perched on a pillar. Behind it is an open **resthouse** crowded with families preparing offerings and feasts.

Harati/Sitala Mandir

The small heavily gilded temple just beyond the resthouse is among the busiest shrines in the Valley. A nearby chalkboard outlines the day's worship schedule, and families reserve space in front of the temple for their priests to perform puja. It's dedicated to the terrible goddess of smallpox, who well into this century plagued the Valley with fearsome epidemics. Hindus call her Sitala; to Buddhists she's Harati or simply Ajima, one of the ancient Newari grandmother-goddesses. The story goes that Harati was in the habit of kidnapping and eating one child a day, until finally the Buddha appointed her the protector of Valley children, promising that she could dine on the first of his offerings. Harati is still placated before any other deity at Swayambhunath. Devotees bring duck eggs, grain, yoghurt, and incense, lighting the lamps around the temple and carrying their children inside for a blessing. Inside the temple is a black stone image of the goddess surrounded by a half-dozen children, a silver skullcup around her neck to hold offerings. This replacement is a mere two centuries old; the original was smashed by the order of King Rana Bahadur Shah in a fit of fury after his beloved queen died of smallpox.

To the left of this shrine is a building housing an **International Buddhist Library;** climb up to the roof for a good overview of the temple compound. Past here and to the left a cluster of whitewashed memorial chaitya honor the dead. In the southwest corner is a three-meter-tall **standing Buddha,** a fine 9th-century sculpture. The northwest corner holds **Agnipur,** the Mansion of Fire, embodied in an elliptical white-painted stone guarded by a pair of lions.

Shantipur

Descend the flight of steps in the courtyard's northeast corner. Just beyond a large seated **Buddha,** inside a beige rectangular building, is an ancient locked door guarded by two fierce Tantric deities and a pair of strange painted eyes. Seldom visited, the place has a strongly mysterious air. This is Shantipur, the "Mansion of Peace," representing the mystic element of ether. Inside, in a secret underground chamber, the 8th-century tantric master Shantikar Acharya is said to live still, seated in a meditative trance which has preserved his life for centuries. Shantikar Acharya was a great magician, so skilled in mantra he could control even the gods. It's said he once drew a magical mandala to invoke the monsoon, using the heartblood of the Eight Great Naga as ink and snakeskin as parchment. Sealing the scroll in a copper tube, he placed it by his side in the underground chamber. When the Valley is threatened by drought, the King of Nepal is to retrieve the mandala and rain will fall.

Pratapa Malla did just that in 1658. Purified by rituals and prayer, he braved guardian ghosts and serpents to enter the sealed room and take the copper tube. The moment the mandala was unrolled in the light of day, rain began to fall. All this is detailed in an account written by the king, inscribed on a stone slab beside Shantipur's locked door. Frescoes painted on the walls depict the story, complete with slithering naga; unfortunately this shrine is largely neglected except by a few devout worshippers, and the walls have been defaced by graffiti.

Nagapur

Head back to the north side of the stupa and the shrine of **Buddha Amoghasiddhi.** In front of it is a simple open pit set with an oblong stone. This is **Nagapur,** the Mansion of Water, ruled by the serpent kings; worshippers light lamps and burn incense here in supplication for rain. Nearby is a **Tibetan temple** housing a huge image of Shakyamuni, where monks perform puja early in the morning and again in late afternoon. A little further and you're back to the western stairway.

Other Sites

You can explore the quiet wooded hill, a popular picnic site for Newari families, or visit Swayambhu's second, lower summit to the west. The main attraction is a small stupa dedicated to Manjushri, the bodhisattva who drained the lake to found Kathmandu. Hindus worship Saraswati here, and images of the pair guard the top of the stairway. Dozens more chaitya and stupa are scattered about the quiet forested ridge, each with their own legend. Watch out for the monkeys, though, who can be very aggressive.

PASHUPATINATH

OVERVIEW

The temple of Pashupatinath is Nepal's most sacred Hindu shrine and one of the subcontinent's great Shiva sites, a sprawling collection of temples, ashrams, images, and inscriptions raised over the centuries along the banks of the sacred Bagmati River. The essence of Hinduism is condensed into a rich brew, as pilgrims, yogis, priests, and devotees worship Shiva in his form of Pashupati, "Lord of the Beasts" and divine protector of Nepal.

Despite the "For the Hindus Only" signs posted at the entrance to its major temple (or perhaps because of them), Pashupatinath is a magical place. The largest temple complex in Nepal, it retains its integrity as a living place of worship. There is *so much*. Where most temples have a few pieces, Pashupatinath's grounds are set with rows of linga, long lines of stone Nandi, and Licchavi-era sculpture fragments jumbled in careless heaps. Even without access to the main temple the grounds deserve several hours of exploration. Early morning or evening, the prime puja hours, are the best times to visit.

Pashupatinath's supreme holiness stems from two things: the Shiva linga enshrined in its main temple, and its location on the banks of the Bagmati. Little more than a stream in the dry winter months, it flows past ghats where worshippers and mourners mingle with pilgrims intent on mundane tasks like laundry and dishwashing. Daily, devout Hindus plunge into the holy (if polluted) waters, immersing themselves three times and reciting verses from the ancient Vedas. The spiritual equivalent of bathing in India's sacred Ganges, a dip in the Bagmati assures release from the cycle of rebirth.

The same promise applies to the dead, and Pashupatinath is Nepal's most renowned Hindu cremation site. Wrapped in cloth and placed on a bamboo litter, bodies are delivered by barefoot pallbearers accompanied by male relatives and mourners (women stay at home to weep). At the cremation ghat, the eldest son performs rites to assure the soul a smooth transition into the next world. The body is placed on a log pyre, and the white-clad mourners retreat to a nearby porch to observe its slow destruction. A few hours later the ashes are swept into the river, where they are carried south to join the Ganges. Such open-air ceremonies are entirely public and are conducted with apparent disregard to tourists on the banks filming the scene with video cameras. A sense of propriety still applies, vultures with 1,000-mm lenses notwithstanding.

The temple grounds are littered with hun-

woman doing laundry next to 6th-century Buddha image, Rajarajesvari Ghat, Pashupati

KERRY MORAN

dreds of stone linga, the ancient symbol which is Shiva's self-proclaimed "double self." The cylindrical stone shaft generally stands in a *jalhari*, an oval, spouted base which represents the feminine counterpart of the phallic linga and serves to drain off the liquid poured in offering.

Pashupatinath is also a mecca for wandering yogis or saddhus, ascetics who have renounced family and caste to follow Shiva. Both Indian and Nepali, their proud bearded faces are marked on the forehead with bright designs representing their particular sect. They may be naked and dusted with ashes or wrapped in splendid robes. Some spend their lives performing austerities, refusing to lie down for years on end or surviving on a diet of milk. Others are skilled musicians, while still other red-eyed saddhus smoke tremendous quantities of Shiva's favorite herb, ganja, consecrating each hit with the invocation "Bom Shankar." Like any slice of humanity, the saddhu population encompasses saints, sinners, and rogues. A conversation with one is guaranteed to be interesting.

History
Of all the gods in the Hindu pantheon, it's Shiva with his 1,008 names and forms who dominates the Kathmandu Valley. As Pashupati (the name means "Lord of the Animals"), he watches over the souls of men and is worshipped as the pa-

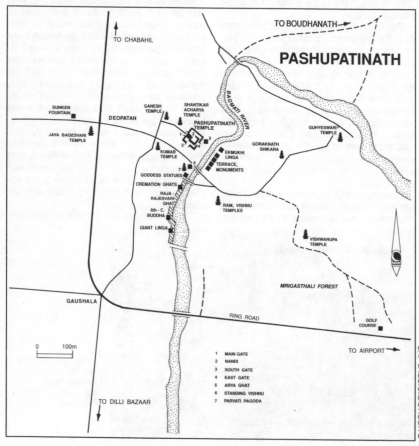

1   MAIN GATE
2   NANDI
3   SOUTH GATE
4   EAST GATE
5   ARYA GHAT
6   STANDING VISHNU
7   PARVATI PAGODA

© MOON PUBLICATIONS, INC.

Newari girl and temple guardian, Bhaktapur (Kerry Moran)

Worshippers circumambulate the Golden Temple during a festival. (Kerry Moran)

tron deity of Nepal. The cult of Pashupati began in 2nd-century B.C. India but soon became closely associated with Nepal. Lord Pashupati is invoked in official treaties, pledges, and political speeches, and appears on coins and the royal coat of arms. Visits to Pashupatinath begin and end a pilgrim's circuit of the Valley's holy places. Thousands of Indians flock here as well: Pashupatinath is one of the great holy Shiva places of the Indian subcontinent, and no pilgrimage is complete without a visit to it.

The temple's origins are obscure: the oldest inscription is dated 477 A.D., but a shrine may have stood here nearly 1,000 years before that. Legend says that Shiva, weary of throngs of worshipping demigods, once took the form of an antelope and sported unknown in the Mrigasthali Forest on the river's east bank. The gods caught up with him and, grabbing him by the horn, forced him to resume his divine form. The broken horn was worshipped as a linga, and over time was buried and lost. Centuries later an astonished herdsman found one of his cows showering the earth with milk. Digging deep at the site, he uncovered the divine linga of Pashupati.

The temple complex has been ceaselessly renovated and improved over the centuries, one result being it little resembles typical Newari architecture. Most of the present temple, a two-roofed gilded pagoda, dates from the reign of King Pratapa Malla, but every king and prime minister since has added to it, sheathing the temple doors in embossed gold and silver and contributing to the temple's treasury. Rumors of Pashupatinath's fabulous wealth have inspired many thieves, among them Kathmandu's last Malla king, Jaya Prakash, who ransacked the treasury to pay his troops in the doomed war against Prithvi Narayan Shah.

The Sacred Linga

The temple's famous linga is a meter-high cylinder of black stone carved with four faces, each depicting a different aspect of Shiva. On top is the featureless and omnipotent fifth face, said to be infused with the power of the sun, hot enough to instantly evaporate water. Only the priests of Pashupatinath are allowed to touch the sacred linga. They serve as intermediaries for worshippers, delivering offerings and dispensing *prasad* (blessings) like tika and flower petals.

These priests, Brahmans from Karnatak in Southern India, are chosen on the basis of their scholarly and ritual knowledge. Clad in red robes and rosaries of rudraksha seeds, they conduct an elaborate round of ritual worship beginning at 0400.

Daily, the linga is undressed and bathed in the "five nectars," a mixture of yoghurt, ghee, honey, sugar, and milk, then bathed again in sacred water collected from holy pilgrimage sites. In the winter months, it even gets a hot bath. Wrapped again in brocade robes, it's adorned with tika; a Shri Yantra is drawn on its topmost face with sandalwood paste, and it's shown its reflection in a mirror. Later in the afternoon it's offered a selection of food: sweetmeats, fruit, and daal bhaat.

Entrance to the shrine is restricted to "Hindus only," a definition which stretches to encompass Buddhists, Sikhs, and Jains, but not Western converts to Hinduism. Ancient Vedic regulations mean the shrine would have to undergo extensive purification if the ritually impure were to enter. You can get a good view of the eastern facade from vantage points across the river. If you're really curious, a replica of the temple and the famous linga stands in Bhaktapur's Durbar Square. King Yaksha Malla built it in the 15th century so that he could perform his daily devotions closer to home.

The Way There

Taxi, bike, or take the bus to Gaushala (the airport bus passes by here also). If you bike out, stop briefly at the superbly carved linga of **Bhandareswara,** the guardian of Pashupatinath's treasury. Its placement indicates how far west temple grounds once extended; priests of the temple still swear an oath here before assuming their duties.

At the top of the hill, go straight instead of to the left as most traffic does. At the intersection with the main road is a large temple to **Jaya Bagesvari,** one side painted with a colorful mural. The image of the goddess is bedecked with ornaments, the final offerings of widows going to Pashupati's ghats to be burned on their husband's funeral pyre, a custom only outlawed in 1920.

The sunken fountain across the way dates back to Licchavi times; from here on as you head east is one of the most ancient settlements in the Valley. Known as **Deopatan,** "City of the Gods," it's now a minor suburb of Kathmandu, but it's still riddled with sculptures, chaitya, inscriptions, and fragments from ancient temples incorporated into the structure of slightly less ancient ones. Just about every piece of stonework you see here is likely to be 1,500 years old.

BOB RACE

TEMPLE SIGHTS

The Main Gate

Cross the main road and head east through this mass of ancient relics towards the westernmost side of Pashupatinath. The neighborhood around the temple is crowded with shops selling sweetmeats and vegetarian Indian food, rosaries of rudraksha seeds, and tika powder in a rainbow of colors. The temple's **main gate** is on this side, topped by a giant plaster image of Shiva as Yogeshwara, Lord of Yogis. Though you're not allowed to enter, you can't miss viewing the backside of the massive kneeling **bull** (Nandi), the vehicle of Shiva, with hoofs of silver and tail and horns of gold. Jagat Jung Rana had the ancient figure regilded to atone for the sin of having accidently shot a cow on a Terai hunt.

The South Side

Continue around the temple's south side, past more shops, until the path meets the Bagmati. A pair of **small bridges** spanning the river are

the perfect vantage point to observe Pashupatinath's constant round of bathing and cremation, death and laundry. Upstream, marked by another "For Hindus Only" sign, is **Aryaghat,** reserved for cremations of the Royal Family and important persons. Between the cremation platforms are slanted stone slabs, upon which the dying are placed, feet in the water, and given a last drink from the sacred Bagmati—a ritual which brings great blessings. Downriver are four square platforms for general public cremations.

On the shore between the two bridges is a small **pagoda** with beautiful woodwork, including some vivid erotic struts and torana depicting Durga slaying the buffalo demon. Next to it, sheltered in a brick shrine, is a massive terracotta image of **Vishnu,** and near the lower bridge are two ancient but robust images of goddesses (eight-armed mother goddess **Bachhlesvari,** and **Lakshmi** standing on a tortoise), both embodiments of the word "statuesque."

Raja-rajesvari Ghat

Before crossing the bridge, walk down Raja-rajesvari Ghat on the right, with a museum's worth of ancient sculptures scattered along its length. Finds include a serene 6th-century **Buddha;** just beyond is a flight of steps, and immediately to the left, enclosed in a circular wall, is the biggest **linga** ever, over 1,500 years old, nearly forgotten and listing to one side. Many doorways on this side enter into courtyards housing cows, dogs, and every imaginable variety of temple and shrine, plus a large population of pilgrims and squatters. Daily life gives the scene a rural flavor: women cook, spin wool, and comb their hair; men wash clothes and chat; children play and old people doze in the sun.

Across the River

Across the bridge and a little upstream is a row of identical, elaborately decorated monuments, each housing a polished Shiva linga. At the end of the line is a classic 6th-century *ekmukhi* or **"one-faced" linga.** A steep flight of steps leads past courtyards built about three temples dedicated to Rama and Vishnu: to the right is the forest of **Mrigasthali,** where Shiva once roamed as an antelope. Now it shelters several hundred scowling, red-bottomed rhesus monkeys; guard your camera!

At the top is a shady, quiet wooded glen dotted with shrines, inscriptions, and statues. Shiva appears everywhere, embodied in the abstract linga or as a four-armed deity displaying a yogi's possessions: rosary, water pot, trident, and shaman's drum. The large shikara temple is dedicated to the yogi **Gorakhnath,** a favorite patron of saddhus.

Follow the steps down to **Guhyeshwari Mandir,** sacred to Shiva's consort Durga or Sati, who is said to have immolated herself over an insult her father had offered her husband. Mad with grief, Shiva wandered the skies with her corpse; as pieces of the goddesses' body drop-

ped off and fell to earth, they created sacred sites or *pitha,* 51 in all. Sati's "secret" parts *(guhya)* fell near Pashupati, thus the name Guhyeshwari, "Secret" or "Hidden" Goddess. An extremely holy site, it's closed to non-Hindus as well.

The shrine's painted front gate is the departure point for a shortcut to the Boudhanath Stupa, 20 minutes' walk north. Cross the Bagmati over the footbridge from the Guhyeshwari temple (if the bridge is washed away there's a more permanent one to the west), and follow a dirt road past fields and huts to the main road in front of the Boudha Gate. The road gets pretty disgustingly filthy towards the end.

BOUDHANATH

OVERVIEW

The Great Stupa of Boudhanath, seven km east of downtown Kathmandu, is one of Nepal's most distinctive monuments. Simple, massive, and powerful, it rises above a huddle of buildings, its painted eyes gazing solemnly over the countryside. Among the most important Buddhist sites in Nepal, Boudha draws pilgrims from across the Himalaya: eastern Tibetan men with red tassels woven in their hair and women wearing huge lumps of turquoise; Ladakhi women with seed pearl earrings and winged hats; Bhutanese with cropped hair, knee-length robes, and argyle socks; Nepalis from remote regions like Dolpo and Mugu, wrapped in striped woolen blankets.

Stupas are as essential to Buddhism as the cross is to Christianity, a tangible symbol of the Buddha's enlightened mind. Like a giant onion, Boudha has been formed by layers of additions and improvements over centuries. Like a time capsule, its core shelters ancient relics: Boudha is said to hold the remains of Kasyapa, the Buddha of a previous age. A cross-section bore of the great stupa would be most instructive for archaeologists, but will never be allowed as long as there are people to worship it.

With a diameter exceeding 100 meters and a wall-to-wall length roughly equaling a football field, Boudha is among the largest stupa in the world—certainly the biggest in Nepal. Set atop a triple-terraced plinth, it rises 36 meters above the

street. Its form, alternated squares and circles, replicates a mandala; in fact, it *is* a three-dimensional mandala, a perfectly proportioned embodiment of abstract religious concepts. Every portion has symbolic significance: the

Tibetan woman giving a donation to a monk, Boudhanath

CHRISTOPHER GAMM

base, dome, square *harmika,* spire, and pinnacle represent the five elements; the 13 tiers of the spire stand for the stages to enlightenment, while the umbrella atop is the symbol of royalty. Most striking are the painted, bow-shaped eyes, variously described as mysterious, indifferent, compassionate, and knowing. The addition of eyes to the square *harmika* is a stroke of genius unique to Nepali stupas. They are said to represent the eyes of the primordial Adi Buddha, or the guardians of the four directions; or perhaps they symbolize the omniscience of enlightenment. Whichever, they add an uncanny presence to the stupa, endowing it with a curious intelligence.

History
Some historians believe King Manadeva I built the original stupa in the 5th century, but its origins remain obscured. A Tibetan version of its creation centers around Jadzimo, a poultry keeper (or alternatively, a prostitute) with four sons who somehow managed to amass a fortune. Wishing to build a stupa she asked the king for a piece of land—nothing much, just big enough to be covered by a buffalo skin. He granted this seemingly modest request, and the shrewd woman then cut the hide into thin strips and girdled off a considerable plot. The king was forced to concede this was all according to their agreement, but his rueful words *"Jarung kashor"* gave the stupa its Tibetan name. Translated from the telegraphic original, it means something like "Saying it was okay to do this was a slip of the tongue."

Another legend tells of a terrible drought at the time of construction, forcing builders to spread out sheets to catch the morning dew for brickmaking—thus another name, the "Dewdrop Stupa." A Tibetan religious text says at Boudha's consecration, the essence of 100 million Buddhas dissolved into the stupa's dome, imbuing it with immense spiritual power. Tales of the miraculous materialization of relics (tiny white pellets called *ringsel*) are common even today.

The old Tibetan trade route passed near Boudha, and Tibetans early on adopted the stupa as their own, taking responsibility for its upkeep. Local families still scrupulously maintain it. Several times a month painters touch up the eyes, whitewash the dome, and top off their work by flinging buckets of saffron-tinted water to create a golden lotus pattern.

Boudha is a magnet for the Tibetan community in Kathmandu, and also for native Tibetans who flock here on pilgrimage in winter. Their faith transforms Boudha into a miniature Lhasa, a showcase of Buddhist practices—prayer beads, mantras, prayer wheels, prostrations, plus the inevitable vendors selling Tibetan/Chinese goods, both old and new. All day long people walk clockwise about the stupa doing *kora,* an act of worship that combines religious merit and motion. Crowds are greatest during mornings and evenings and on full and new moon days when religious acts are said to earn extra merit— and beggars line up to profit from the maxim.

THE STUPA AND ENVIRONS

Besides being an object of devotion, the stupa is a playground for children and frisky goats, a roost for pigeons, and the hub of the surrounding community. The shops ringing it once housed Newari gold and silversmiths who made Tibetan jewelry and ritual objects. Now they're given over to Tibetan-oriented souvenirs of varying quality. Best buys are Tibetan carpets and artifacts, incense, jewelry, and small brightly painted wooden tables. A few metalworkers hammer out ritual implements, and carpet weaving is a rapidly growing business.

The Main Circuit
The elaborate plaster gate on the main road is, technically speaking, only a side entrance; the proper entry is on the north side. There, inset in the wall girdling the stupa, is a small shrine with a silver image of Ajima, one of the terrible Newari mother-goddesses who must be placated to prevent disaster. Puja is held here on auspicious days, with chanting, music, and offerings—mountains of puffed rice decorated with oranges, packets of biscuits and white bread, all soon snatched by children and beggars. Opposite, up a flight of steps, a shrine housed in an old white building has good but soot-covered frescoes and an image of Guru Rinpoche flanked by his consorts Mandarava and Yeshe Tsogyal. Behind the Ajima temple is a small courtyard set with Hindu and Buddhist images,

a giant prayer wheel alongside it. Steps lead up to the stupa's three terraces, the topmost one offering sweeping views.

Tibetan Monasteries

With six major gompa or monasteries and many smaller ones, Boudha is headquarters for a vigorous revival of Tibetan Buddhism, a hopeful indicator that this ancient religion may survive despite China's dogged attempts to eradicate it in its homeland. After the 1959 Chinese invasion about 10,000 Tibetans fled to Nepal, and the community has since grown to over 90,000. Many of them settled around Boudha, where contributions from the local community and from Buddhists abroad financed the construction of monasteries, which continue their role as religious and cultural centers of the community. A monastery's temple serves as a public shrine; its monks conduct ceremonies; its lamas give spiritual advice. Finally, it's a treasurehouse of art, filled with statues, thankga, woodcarvings, embroidered banners, and murals, all in the vivid Tibetan color scheme.

Boudha's monasteries are all relatively new, but some rival their ancient predecessors in splendor. **Tarik Rinpoche's** large maroon-painted gompa to the northeast has three elaborately painted chapels. The big white **gompa** (Ka-Nying Shedrup Ling) has a beautiful lhakhang. Inside **Jamchen Yiggha Choling,** the first (yellow) monastery on the left after the Boudha gate, is a 35-foot tall figure of Maitreya, the Buddha of the Coming Age, inset with turquoise and coral. In the **Nyingma Gompa** on the main road before the gate, a jewelled reliquary stupa contains the remains of Dudjom Rinpoche, the head of the Nyingmapa sect.

Most exquisite is **Shechen Tennyi Targye Ling,** constructed in the early '80s with support from the King of Bhutan, who sent the best of everything, including 200 master craftsmen. This monastery's head lama, H. H. Dilgo Khyentse Rinpoche, is tutor to the Bhutanese royal family and one of the greatest living masters of the Nyingmapa sect. The main shrine houses three Buddha images; panels on either side depict the sixteen Arhats, and the wall frescoes illustrate masters of the four major Tibetan Buddhist sects.

BOUDHANATH

Gompa Etiquette

Don't let the maroon-robed monks racing about on motorcycles fool you—monasteries are traditional and conservative communities, and female visitors especially should dress modestly. Take off your shoes in the sheltered porch before you enter the main temple, and ask permission first if a ceremony is being held inside (it's usually okay to pull aside the door curtain and take a peek). If the door is locked, the key can often be found nearby—ask. You may even find a younger, English-speaking monk to show you around. Inside the *lhakhang* (literally "god's house"), walk around the room clockwise. Photos are usually okay but again, ask first. A small donation to the altar or offering box goes to maintain the temple and support the monks.

The terms *monk* and *lama* are not synonymous: most monks aren't lamas, and a lama does not have to be a monk. A lama's role is that of a spiritual teacher, one able to transmit realization and guide others on the path to enlightenment. If you have questions about Buddhism, it's possible to meet the lamas of some monasteries (see p. 209). A white *khatak* or prayer scarf is a formal gesture of respect symbolizing pure intention; you can buy them in Boudha shops. Fold it in seven folds (a monk can show you how) and present it fully extended in both hands. The lama will return it, draping it around your neck as a symbol of acceptance.

Inside The *Lhakhang*

Tibetan temples are rich in both color and symbolism. There are butter lamps, from tiny cups to huge standing chalices, their flames symbolically dispelling the darkness of ignorance. In Tibet these would be fueled with pungent yak butter, but Nepali monasteries substitute vegetable ghee. Offerings like incense, food, and flowers symbolize the dedication of sensory pleasures to enlightenment. Simplest of all are the small silver or copper bowls of water lined up on every altar, representing one's essential pure nature.

Torma, conical offering cakes molded of barley flour mixed with water, are an essential part of many ceremonies. In historical terms they're substitutes for the animal sacrifices of the ancient Bön religion. Decorated with red-dyed dough and knobs of butter, they are made in different shapes and sizes, according to the rite and deity—at least 108 different kinds, ranging in height from 30 cm to three meters.

Usually monks perform two pujas per day, one in the early morning and again at dusk. Periodically longer ceremonies are held, some lasting several weeks. The endless chanting is accompanied by music, driven by the clash of cymbals and the slow beat of the hanging drum. Tibetan musicians don't seek to produce a melody like a Western orchestra; instead they accompany and enhance the chanting of texts and prayers. *Bugcham,* large cymbals, set the beat for the rest. The *gyaling,* an oboe-like horn decorated with silver or gold and precious stones, is among the most difficult instruments to master. *Radung* are three-meter-long telescopic trumpets with deep, booming tones, requiring tremendous lung power. Other instruments include small cymbals, *kangling* (a small trumpet

made from a human thigh bone) and the booming conch shell. All join at the end of a recitation in a clashing crescendo which dies to sudden silence before the chanting resumes again.

PRACTICALITIES

There are plenty of Tibetan-run restaurants serving tasty and cheap momo, thukpa, fried rice, and fried noodles. The perennial standby is the **Bir Restaurant,** a few hundred meters before the gate. The Austrian-cum-vegetarian **Stupa View Restaurant** on the main circuit has nice decor, safe if bland food, and stunning views.

For lodging there's the **Lotus Guesthouse** behind Tarik Rinpoche's gompa and the **Tashi Delek** across from the main gate. More elaborate, expensive and distant are the **Taragaon Hotel** and the **Stupa Hotel.** The Bir Restaurant has inexpensive rooms. It's easy to find a room to rent from a Tibetan or Sherpa family if you plan a longer stay; just ask around. The big drawback of staying in Boudha is transportation: taxis don't like going there after dark, and buses are slow and crowded.

SIGHTS AROUND BOUDHANATH

En Route

About one km before Boudha on the main road is the **Chabahil stupa,** said to have been built with the bricks and earth remaining from the construction of Boudha. The Chabahil stupa is smaller and more dilapidated than its cousin—probably much closer in appearance to its Licchavi-era original, except for the lightbulb dangling above the stupa's third eye. Not so long ago Chabahil lay on the very outskirts of Kathmandu. Families of Newari traders bound for Tibet once traveled this far to send them off, thus its name, "Monastery of the Overnight Stop." The Chabahil community is one of about a dozen in the Valley that chooses a young girl as Kumari.

Chabahil was an early Licchavi settlement, and the stupa's grounds are littered with ancient chaitya, sculptures and architectural fragments, many now badly worn. The dome is adorned with unusual relief plaques from about

BUDDHIST WALL PAINTINGS

The Tibetan Buddhist pantheon embraces a bewildering array of beings: Buddhas, bodhisattvas, *yidam, dharmapala* protectors, *daka*, and *dakini*. All these beings are not deities in the conventional sense but expressions of different aspects of the enlightened mind, symbols which reach beyond words. They appear in painted form on the interior walls of temples, protecting the shrine against evil influences and reminding all who see them of the existence of the supernatural.

Buddhas are fully enlightened beings, while bodhisattvas are compassionate emanations on the way to full enlightenment. The *dharmapala* are ferocious protectors of the faith, often local deities converted over to Buddhism who devote their energies to preserving the doctrine. Their terrifying forms usually appear on the back walls nearest the entrance, guarding the temple. *Yidam* are tutelary deities visualized in meditation, appearing in both peaceful and wrathful forms. The fiercer versions, multiheaded, many-armed, and wreathed in flames, may be hard to reconcile with peaceful Buddhas, but they embody the energy necessary to banish anger, desire, and ignorance from the mind, leaving the clear Buddha nature behind. Appearing amid these fantastic beings are actual historical figures of great lamas, teachers, and founders of different lineages, often shown surrounded by disciples or scenes from their life.

The outside entrance porch of a gompa is dominated by the guardians of the four directions. These gigantic figures, colored yellow, white, green, and red, each display a different symbol—Kubera, the Southern God of Wealth, clutches a mongoose spewing jewels from its mouth, and so on. On one side is a cosmological diagram of Mount Meru, the center of the universe according to traditional Tibetan cosmology, surrounded by the various continents and worlds.

On the other side is the Wheel of Life, a complex figure depicting the manifold but ultimately limited possibilities of samsaric existence. The fanged and clawed monster is Mahakala, Great Time. Within his grasp the Wheel of Life *(Sipe Khorlo)* revolves in an endless circle of suffering. It's driven by hatred, desire, and ignorance, symbolized by the snake, cock, and pig in the hub. Surrounding this is a narrow ring with a chain of human bodies ascending to enlightenment or descending into suffering, driven by their karma.

From here extend the six realms of samsaric existence, each with a Buddha standing inside symbolizing the possibility of release. At the bottom are the hells—eight varieties each of hot and cold hells, where demons torment sinners. On the lower right is is the world of hungry ghosts *(preta)*, strange-looking beings with needle-thin throats and huge bellies. Eternally tortured by hunger and thirst, everything they touch turns to filth or burning flames. Rebirth in this realm is the fate of stingy souls, but it also symbolizes a state of mind driven by greed. On the lower left is the animal realm, dominated by ignorance. Above it is the human world, showing scenes of daily life. This is considered the most fortunate of the six realms, as only humans have the opportunity to practice the Dharma and gain liberation. The upper two realms, divided by a miraculous tree, show the warlike *asura* or Titans battling for the magical fruit with the gods. Asura are celestial beings who lead long and blessed lives, but they too will die and be reborn according to their karma.

Set along the outer ring are the 12 interdependent links of origination, a complex series of allegorical scenes which symbolize the search for the ultimate cause of samsara—ignorance, rooted in the belief in the individual ego.

KERRY MORAN

the Wheel of Life

the 7th century but their details are nearly completely obscured by time and whitewash. In a small brick building in the rear left corner, marked by five faded Buddhas painted over the doorway, is a beautiful standing bodhisattva **Padmapani Lokeswara,** in black stone.

The old and remarkably unchanged Newari bazaar of **Chabahil** is 100 meters north of here; take a left at the main intersection. In the center is an interesting old temple to Ganesh **(Chandra Binayak),** one of the Valley's quartet of sacred Ganesh shrines, this one said to cure disease and grant fame and riches.

Walks
A network of dirt roads north of Boudha leads through fields and small villages; very scenic, if you can tolerate the kids shouting "Hello, monkey!" Most wanderers head to **Kopan Monastery,** where Tibetan and Western monks and nuns are happy to answer questions about Buddhism (see p. 209). It's about a 45-minute walk from the stupa—just head north towards a few small buildings set atop a hillock. Villagers will point the way, even if you're not planning on going there.

PRACTICALITIES

ACCOMMODATIONS

Things have evolved considerably since Kathmandu's first tourist-class hotel opened in 1954. Today hundreds of lodges, guesthouses and hotels cater almost exclusively to foreign tourists; Nepalis themselves generally stay with family or friends when traveling.

The current travelers' scene is **Thamel** ("Ta-MEL"), successor to the notorious Freak Street. Here dozens of lodges offer everything from dormitories to spacious carpeted rooms with attached bath and telephone, all reasonably priced. It's incredibly easy to find decent lodgings, since so many are clustered in a small area. The best plan is to simply hit the street and investigate places yourself. If jet lag is imminent, you might want to settle for something merely decent the first day. You can always move later after you've tracked down the perfect place. The drawback in this area is the intense concentration of tourists and hustlers: Thamel is a world unto itself, only marginally Nepali.

Freak Street has declined since its hippie heyday but it remains as a poor cousin to yuppie Thamel. Lodges and restaurants are cheaper and its street scene is seedier but perhaps preferable to high-intensity Thamel. Ringed by old Newari neighborhoods, it's slightly more conveniently located (just off Durbar Square). If either place gets to be too much, find a quiet lodge in **Chhauni** (south of Swayambhunath) or around **Boudhanath.** These neighborhoods are beyond walking distance of town, but may be worth it for peaceful surroundings. Mid-range and expensive hotels scattered throughout town are another way to avoid the tourist trap syndrome.

Prices cited here are standard rates as of early 1991 and are bound to rise with inflation, perhaps 10% a year. However, they are bargainable by as much as 50% in all but the busiest seasons, so request a discount if you're staying more than a few days.

All except the cheapest lodges require payment in foreign currency and state their prices in U.S. dollars—meaning you have to show a bank exchange receipt to pay your hotel bill. Medium and upper-range establishments add 10-12% government tax to the bill, depending on the number of stars in their ratings.

Inexpensive
Cheaper lodges quote their prices in rupees. Starting in Thamel, **Yeti Cottage** (tel. 417-089), a favorite with overland buses, is Rs60 s, Rs120 d, with a nice garden and restaurant. **Cosy Corner** (tel. 417-799) next to Le Bistro charges Rs44 s, Rs77 d. Around the corner and behind it is **Lodge Pheasant** (tel. 417-416), quieter, partly housed in an old Rana palace, Rs60 s, Rs80 d, with more ambience than most. **Om Guesthouse** is a good deal, charging Rs100 s, Rs120 d with attached bath. Other decent cheap lodges in and near Thamel include **Holy Lodge, Himal Cottage, Earth House,** and **Stupa Guest House. Sita Home,** a little west of

Thamel in Chhetrapati on the road to Swayambhu, is set away from the tourist scene, with rates US$3 s, US$5 d.

Freak Street offers rock-bottom prices: **Century Lodge** (tel. 215-769), in the same courtyard as the Kumari Restaurant, has rooms for Rs35 s, Rs50/65 d, and dorm beds for Rs25. The **Sayami Lodge** (tel. 212-264), run by a friendly Newari family, is very good, as is its **Lunchbox Restaurant.** They charge Rs60 for a clean two-bed room. **Friendly Home** (tel. 220-171), down a sidestreet near Om Bahal, lives up to its name, with a pleasant proprietor and clean rooms, rates are Rs24-30 s, Rs42-58 d, triples for Rs70-80. Other cheap lodges in the neighborhood include **Mustang Cottage, Royal Guest House,** and **Monumental Lodge.**

Kathmandu Lodge (tel. 214-893) is an old and popular standby, just off Durbar Square (behind the Big Bell Cafe). It charges Rs60 s, Rs 80 d for common bath, Rs130/160 for attached bath. **Kumari Lodge,** also on the square, is another scenic if basic possibility.

If you're looking for peace away from the street scenes of Thamel and Freak Street, try Chhauni, across the Vishnumati River and south of Swamyabhu. The popular **Hotel Cat-nap** (tel. 272-393) charges Rs100-150 s, slightly more for doubles. **Peace Lodge** in Tahachal on the road to the National Museum has budget rooms, as low as Rs50 d. **Hotel Shrestha** (tel. 270-528) near the Soaltee Oberoi has rooms for Rs100 s with shared bath, Rs150/200 d with private bath.

Low To Moderately Priced

Most hotels in this category have three price ranges: rooms with common bath, rooms with attached bath, and "deluxe" rooms with extras like wall-to-wall carpeting, telephone, and balcony. They're bargains considering the comforts you get for the low price.

Hotel Shakti (tel. 410-121), behind the Hotel Malla just north of Thamel, is quiet, with character and a nice garden, US$3-8 s, US$4.50-11 d. Nearby **Hotel Thamel** (tel. 412-744) has good rooms, a rooftop terrace with views, and is conveniently located yet still reasonably quiet. Rooms are US$16 s, US$20 d; a few dollars more for a private balcony.

Jyatha Tol, a street in southeast Thamel, has a whole string of new hotels, many run by Ti-

betans. **Lhasa Guest House** (tel. 213-019) charges US$6 s with common bath; US$7 s with attached bath; doubles are US$9-11. They also have single economy rooms for US$5. Down the street, **Hotel New Gajur** charges US$8.80 s, US$11 d. The **Blue Diamond** and **Hotel Pumori** are similarly priced. Mustang Holiday Inn is clean and well-kept with a friendly staff and good garden; US$3-4.50 s, US$5-9 d.

Southwest of Thamel is Chhetrapati, a busy neighborhood which retains its Nepali character. **Shambala Guest House** (tel. 225-986) has carpeted rooms with telephones, a quiet courtyard, balcony garden, and rooftop views; US$5.50-10.50 s, US$7.50-12 d. The street between Chhetrapati and Thamel is lined with lodges: **Potala Guest House** (tel. 220-467), near Narayan's Restaurant, has rooms for US$7.70 s, US$11 d. **Tibet Guest House** (tel. 215-893) is favored by mountaineers and for good reason: friendly staff, nice rooms, and a rooftop garden with views; rates are US$9-15 s; US$9-16 d. **Trans-Himalayan Guest House** next door offers similar prices and accommodations if Tibet Guest House is full.

In north Thamel **Hotel Garuda** (tel. 416-776), with a very friendly and helpful staff, takes the prize: US$8-11 s, US$10-13 d. Just down the street **Hotel Mandap** offers rooms for US$17 s, US$21 d, with discounts for long stays. Across the street, **Hotel Iceland** has singles for US$6-10, doubles for US$8-16. Slightly further north is **Hotel Marshyangdi** (tel. 213-084), one of the most upscale of Thamel's establishments, charging US$30-50 s, US$40-60 d (deluxe rooms are air-conditioned). Back and around the corner into Paknajol is the popular **International Guesthouse** (tel. 410-533), with rooms for US$10/16 s, US$16/19 d.

Beyond these main areas, the government-operated **Taragaon Hotel** in Boudhanath charges US$13 s, US$18 d. Call there (tel. 410-409/410-634) for information and reservations for the other Taragaon hotels at Nagarkot, Kakani, and Pokhara. Other accommodations in Boudha include the new **Lotus Guesthouse** behind Tarik Rinpoche's gompa, and the **Hotel Stupa** (tel. 470-385) on the main road, with rates US$9 s, US$13 d. It's seven km from downtown Kathmandu, but the Tibetan community of Boudha is interesting in itself.

Mid-range Hotels

This category includes three of the nicest hotels for the price in the city, with ambience exceeding the usual quota. They tend to be booked in season, so reserve in advance, preferably via phone, fax or telex (faster and more reliable than the mail).

The **Kathmandu Guest House** (tel. 413-632) was Thamel's first hotel, and it continues to be popular though plenty of competition has appeared, and it's no longer inexpensive—US$14 s, US$17 d for rooms in the new wing. The smaller old wing is a remnant of a Rana palace and has a few rooms without bath, as low as US$3-8. This establishment has all sorts of extras: art gallery, laundry service, money-changing counter, airport service, bike rentals. Nice rooms and garden, friendly staff, interesting clientele, located in the heart of Thamel but set off the main road. A favorite with groups and overlanders. Usually full in season; reserve in advance by writing to P.O. Box 2769, Kathmandu, or telex: 2321 BASS NP.

umbrella repair shop set up in the porch of a resthouse

Also good is the **Hotel Vajra** in Bijeswari (tel. 271-545/272-719), across the Vishnumati River, a 20-minute walk from both Thamel and the Swayambhunath Stupa. Quiet surroundings and imaginative design (using traditional materials) more than compensate for the slightly out-of-the-way location. Nice rooftop terrace with city views, gardens, and a full schedule of cultural programs. The Vajra hosts a Newari dance troupe, theater productions, and art gallery, plus an excellent library. This is a favorite place with scholars, filmmakers, and artists. Rates are US$9-23 s, US$11-25 d; with a new wing offering deluxe suites for around US$50. Reserve in advance in season by writing to P.O. Box 1084 or telexing 2309 HVGHPL NP.

The Dutch-managed **Summit Hotel** (tel. 522-694) is set atop a hill in Kopundol (Patan) with stunning views of the city. Its Holland House wing for budget travelers has nine rooms at US$10 s, US$16 d. Rooms in the garden wing are US$55 s, US$65 d. Despite its out-of-the-way location it's quite popular, and many clients are return visitors. Write to P.O. Box 1406 or telex 2324 SUMMIT NP.

Expensive

These luxury hotels are international standard, with restaurants, shopping arcades, business and communications services. For location and ambience, the best choice is the **Hotel Yak & Yeti** (tel. 222-635/413-999) on Durbar Marg, built around a wing of an old Rana palace. On the top floor are two $200-a-night "Presidential Suites," one with Tibetan decor, the other Newari style. Extensive garden and fishponds (rowboats too), swimming pool, lighted tennis courts, sauna; US$95 s, US$105 d, P.O. Box 1016 or telex 2237 YKNYTI NP.

Hotel de l'Annapurna (tel. 221-711/221-411) across the street is less exotic but boasts the best swimming pool in town; US$80 s, US$90 d, P.O. Box 140 or telex 2205 AAPU NP. The **Hotel Soaltee Oberoi** (tel. 272-550) in Tahachhal is inconveniently located with a rather bland atmosphere, but it's got the subcontinent's only casino; US$95 s, US$110 d. The **Everest Hotel** in Baneshwar (tel. 220-567/220-476), formerly the Everest Sheraton, is also remote but high-class: US$100 s; US$110 d.

Many hotels in the US$60-$90 range offer facilities and services just about equal to the

THE LEGENDARY BORIS

His name was Boris Lissanevitch, but everyone knew him simply as Boris, a larger-than-life character possessed of superhuman charm. He seemed to have lived ten lives in the space of one: White Russian émigré, ballet dancer, raconteur, master chef, big-game hunter. It was only natural that he would end up running Kathmandu's first hotel.

The Royal Hotel, opened in 1954, was not just the first; it was the *only* hotel for 450 miles, all the way to Calcutta. One guest characterized it as "a sort of stranded Ritz." It was situated in a wing of the 700-room Bahadur Bhawan, a huge white-colonnaded Rana palace (a remodeled fragment now houses the Election Commission).

The Royal was decorated in "Kathmandu Baroque," all tigerskin rugs and overstuffed furniture. Its Yak and Yeti Bar was the social center of Kathmandu's foreign community, a meeting place for mountaineers, diplomats, journalists, tourists, and Boris's international coterie of friends. The liquor supply was equally eclectic—it generally had either Scotch or soda, but never both at the same time.

Boris is often portrayed as the father of tourism in Nepal. The first official tourists entered the country in 1955, and naturally stayed at the Royal Hotel. Boris arranged a reception, which was attended by the king and his ministers. The king is said to have been visibly surprised at the sight of tourists fighting one another to buy out a display of handicrafts. From the very next day, visas were issued to all who requested them.

Kathmandu in the '50s had many things to offer tourists, but facilities were not among them. Linen, soap, silverware, toilet fixtures, glassware—all the little things that make a hotel had to be imported from Europe and hauled into the Valley by porters. Cooking was done over wood fires, and water was heated in small boilers attached to the fireplaces that were an essential part of every room in the Royal.

Food was another problem, as the only items available in abundance were rice and buffalo meat. Boris arranged for fish and fruit to be flown in from Calcutta; everything else was ordered from Europe and arrived via India. Constant battles with Indian customs meant that many crates of food arrived past their prime. Boris planted vegetables on the grounds of his palatial hotel, introducing many to the Valley for the first time. He raised ducks and pigs to supplement the menu, adding to the hotel's bizarre atmosphere. It already housed a zoo with Himalayan black bears, deer, mountain goats, panthers, and an anteater.

Boris served as master chef for Kathmandu's official banquets, serving crepes à la Boris, sole à la Boris, wild boar à la Boris. He catered the banquet for King Mahendra's coronation, and the state visit of Queen Elizabeth II in 1961. For this the largest hunt in history was organized in the Terai. A tented camp was erected, with an eleven-room tent for the royal couple. Boris had 48 tons of goods shipped in and requisitioned elephants to serve as "bar elephants," with waitresses and drinks on their backs. The Queen was said to have been delighted.

The Royal Hotel closed in 1970; Boris died in 1985. The Hotel Yak & Yeti preserves vestiges of his reign over Kathmandu's social scene, like the original copper-chimneyed fireplace from Boris's Yak and Yeti Bar which is now installed in the Chimney Room Restaurant. The biggest memorial is perhaps the tourist trade which Boris helped start, now approaching 200,000 visitors per year.

most expensive lodgings. The **Hotel Himalaya** (tel. 523-900) on the road to Patan has sweeping Himalayan views and is under Japanese management. **Hotel Kathmandu** (tel. 413-082) in Maharajgunj; **Hotel Malla** (tel. 410-320) in Lainchaur, conveniently close to Thamel; and **Hotel Sherpa** (tel. 228-021), a deluxe establishment on Durbar Marg, are all good. **Hotel Shanker** (tel. 410-151) in Lazimpat is housed in an old Rana palace with extensive gardens. The best and most reasonably priced hotel in this range is the **Hotel Shangri-La** (tel. 410-051), featuring beautiful decor and gardens with a small swimming pool and some better-than-average restaurants. It's located in Lazimpat, a 20-minute walk from Thamel, with rates US$55 s, US$70 d.

FOOD

Kathmandu is a paradise for hungry trekkers and overland travelers, offering everything from borscht to brownies, quiche to kebabs. Travelers usually assume that Western-style restaurants are more sanitary than local ones (perhaps because the dining rooms look better) but there's no guarantee as to what goes on in the kitchen. If you're worried take a look yourself in the back, or go to a Japanese restaurant where chefs prepare meals in open kitchens.

The Western food is a deal: you can get a huge plate of quiche, assorted vegies, and salad for less than US$2, a reasonable breakfast or monster slabs of cake or pie for less than half that. Set breakfasts are even cheaper. Don't stick solely to steaks and lasagne, though. Kathmandu is a great place to try Indian food, one of world's richest and most varied cuisines, and something must be said for Tibetan and Nepali food as well.

More expensive restaurants add 10-15% government tax to the bill; a few places add a service charge as well. Tipping is not mandatory, but in the better restaurants it's come to be expected, and if you're patronizing a place often the staff will appreciate it. The traditional 10-15% is perhaps excessive; try 5%. Only the most expensive restaurants in the height of the tourist season require reservations.

Thamel-area Eateries

Dozens of restaurants serve a kaleidoscopic variety of foreign dishes, from spaghetti to tacos to apple pie. **Le Bistro,** near the Kathmandu Guest House, is an old standby with a wide range of vegetarian and meat dishes and a courtyard and rooftop for outdoor dining. People start lining up at 10 a.m. for the incredible chocolate cake; good lemon cheese pie too. **K.C.'s Restaurant** is famed for its sizzling steaks, cheese-laden pizza, and excellent desserts; prices are slightly higher than other places but worth it. The **Pumpernickel Bakery** across from K.C.'s serves inexpensive sandwiches, bread, bagels, and croissants in its back garden. Other recommended Thamel eateries include **Helena's Restaurant,** the Kathmandu Guest House's **Ashta Mangala, Sanghimitra,** and the **Rum Doodle.** The Hotel Garuda's coffeshop does a nice breakfast.

The **Him-Thai Restaurant** is something different, with an outdoor garden and dining room in an old Rana palace redecorated Thai style. Some dishes are authentically spicy, while others resemble good Chinese food. They also have continental food and an extensive drinks list.

Down towards Chhetrapati **Pizza Maya** is popular for vegetarian food. **Narayan's Res-taurant** is an old standby, with an extensive menu and famous cakes, but the stuffy atmosphere is typical of too many Thamel eateries.

Coppers Restaurant serves rather bland British-inspired dishes in a nicer setting than most Thamel restaurants. They have a good drinks list and sandwiches for lunch. **The Old Vienna Inn** serves Austrian food: bratwurst, sauerkraut, wiener schnitzel, goulash, and apple strudel. **Utse Restaurant** is the oldest eatery in Thamel, serving Chinese-Tibetan standards like chow mein and momo, good for the very cheap price. **Namkha Ding** has a similar menu, while **Gombu's Restaurant,** hidden down a side alley, has good momo.

The **Nepalese Kitchen** has come up with the innovative idea of serving Nepali food to curious Westerners and is doing quite well; it does get beyond the standard daal bhaat. Some tourist restaurants offer "Special Nepali Meal" at inflated prices—not a good deal. Try the fare in a *bhojnalaya* (several good ones around Chhetrapati); or get invited to someone's house, where you'll get the daal bhaat of your life.

For dessert, try the **Hungry Eye, Le Bistro, Helena's,** or anywhere with a mouthwatering window display. Give Thamel's Italian restaurants a skip, though; none yet manage to produce convincing versions, though the coffee at **La Cimbale** is good. The **Rainbow Restaurant** in the garden of Yeti Cottage serves good pizzas.

Freak Street And New Road

Freak Street fare tends to be cheaper and less memorable than Thamel's offerings. An exception is **The Lunchbox,** with unbeatable breakfast specials, cappuccino and good desserts. **Kumari Restaurant** has a simple menu; **The Oasis,** with a small garden courtyard, is pleasant. **Jasmine's** serves Chinese food. **The Cosmopolitan** overlooking busy Basantapur Square is good for tea and views. The dessert shops on Pie Alley (Maru Tol) have nearly all vanished, but **The Snowman** near the Lunch Box may still produce magic brownies.

Right in Durbar Square, **Big Bell Cafe** has a peaceful rooftop terrace with nice views. The rooftop garden of the **Hotel New Crystal** (covered with turf!) serves Western and Indian dishes. Better than the food are the fabulous views of the city skyline and the adjoining old Royal

street vendor selling
pineapple, Kathmandu

Palace; climb up for tea even if you don't eat.

There are a number of good Indian restaurants on New Road: **Ghoomti** in the Supermarket, **Shiva's Sky,** and lots of inexpensive diners around the movie theatre, including the old standby **Tripti Restaurant,** serving southern Indian food.

Durbar Marg And Central Kathmandu
Mike's Breakfast is a hidden gem, set off the road to the Yak & Yeti in a house and garden created for a Rana concubine. Breakfast includes homemade bread, muffins and preserves, and limitless brewed coffee. There are daily lunch specials, and both meals are accompanied by good music—classical for breakfast, jazz for lunch. More expensive than most places (up to Rs100 for breakfast) but worth it; their huevos rancheros is the closest approximation of Mexican food in town. Open 0700-1600; Mondays are pizza night. Special buffet dinners for Western holidays.

Nearby **San Francisco Pizza** (tel. 225-159) specializes in pizzas cooked over a wood fire, plus pasta dishes. Reasonably priced, and they pack takeout orders in a wicker *nanglo* or winnowing tray. **Nanglo's Pub** has Western food and good daal bhaat, served around a fireplace in the winter, in their rooftop garden in the summer, a good place to bring a Nepali friend. You can also order from the menu of Nanglo's **Chinese Room** downstairs. **Mero Pub** down the street is more of a bar, with nonstop videos and a burger/chips menu. The **Aroma Restaurant**

near Rani Pokhari has a rooftop garden with nice views and the usual Western/Chinese/Indian menu.

More expensive, hotel coffeeshops offer conventional Western food in a mercifully quiet, air-conditioned setting; try the **Yak & Yeti, Hotel de l'Annapurna,** or **Hotel Sherpa.** Hotel Shangri-La's **Shambala Garden Cafe** is the city's only 24-hour restaurant, serving Asian and Western food indoors or out in the big lovely garden.

Kathmandu has several Chinese restaurants, but the hard part is finding food that hasn't been Westernized into chop suey. The **Xue Shan** on the east side of Kanti Path is popular with Westerners and Nepalis and reasonably priced. The same goes for the **Mei Hua** across the street, run by a Chinese emigrant who serves good hot-and-sour soup and steamed *baozi.* For more of the real thing try the small Chinese restaurants around the Thahiti stupa, serving *jiaotze* (the original momo) and noodles. Wang at the **Beijing Restaurant** will cook *hot* Szechuan food on request.

Kathmandu has perhaps the world's cheapest Japanese food. **Kushifuji** and **Koto's** are both on Durbar Marg and both good; Kushifuji has the nicer dining room. The set-menu *bento,* a lacquered lunchbox with an array of goodies, is the best deal, including pickle, salad, miso soup, rice, tempura, and several meat and fish dishes. Around the corner on Kanti Path is the **Fuji Restaurant,** slightly more expensive and with a nice outdoor terrace overlooking fishponds; try it for lunch. Few tourists hear about **Tamura Res-**

taurant in Jhamsikhel, just past the North Korean Embassy in Patan. It serves excellent Japanese lunches and dinners, including sushi and *bento.* Best to make dinner reservations (tel. 526-732).

The **Bangalore Coffee House** near Mero Pub is a very basic place popular with Nepalis, serving cheap, good southern Indian food (try the special *masala dosa*) and a Rs20 special *thali.* **New Kebab Corner** in the Hotel Gautam isn't the bargain it once was, but they still have a wide menu of Mughlai food, tandoori, and powerful air-conditioning for the hot months. The **Amber Restaurant** and the **Moti Mahal** on the southern end of Durbar Marg are similar, serving good Indian food in a semi-deluxe setting. There are also a growing number of "fast-food" takeout places around town serving tandoori chicken, *naan,* and spicy vegetables, if you're looking for picnic fare or an in-room feast.

For ice cream it's **Nirula's,** an Indian chain serving 24 flavors, plus a coffeeshop-style menu. The original shop on Durbar Marg is a popular hangout for teenagers, and there's a smaller branch on New Road. **Kwality** is the second choice (limited flavors), with branches scattered around the city.

Top-class Restaurants

Kathmandu's best restaurants are mainly found in its best hotels. Prices are a bargain by international standards as long as you don't indulge in the high-priced imported liquor. Figure on less than US$10 per person for a multi-course splurge without drinks.

The **Gurkha Grill** at the Soaltee Oberoi, and the **Kokonor Room** at the Hotel Shangri-La both serve continental food. The Soaltee also has the city's best Italian restaurant, **Al Fresco,** expensive but more imaginative than most.

The Yak & Yeti's **Naachghar** offers classical Indian dishes in the rococo setting of an old Rana theater—mirrors, crystal chandeliers, stuccoed pillars, and dancing and music nightly. Next door, the **Chimney Restaurant** continues the late Boris Lissanevitch's culinary traditions with a European/Russian menu that includes his famous borscht and Chicken Kiev, plus baked Alaska for dessert. It's all rich and a bit bland, but nice atmosphere, including the original copper fireplace from the bar of Boris's Royal Hotel.

For Chinese food in an elegant setting try the Szechuan restaurant at the Hotel Malla or the Shangri-La's **Tian Shan. Ras Rung** in front of Hotel Shanker is less expensive. For Nepali food there's **SunKosi** on Durbar Marg or the **Bhanchha Ghar** (tel. 225-172) in Kamaladi. Seasonings tend to be toned down while settings (and prices) are jazzed up. The SunKosi is favored by tour groups and has set menus to facilitate ordering. The Bhanchha Ghar, located in a beautifully converted old Newari house, is a little more special, with Nepali musicians serenading diners.

Indian food is a true bargain in Kathmandu. Most restaurants specialize in Mughlai food, a Persian-influenced cuisine from Northern India which gets its complex flavors from dozens of spices enriched with cream. It's as sophisticated as French cooking, and as taxing on the digestive system. Order plenty of *naan* (oven-roasted breads) to balance the rich vegetable and meat dishes, plus spiced yoghurt *(raita)* for cooling relief. The tandoori dishes roasted in a special clay oven are flavorful and juicy without the extra spices.

The city's best restaurant is generally considered the **Ghar-e-Kebab** at the Hotel de l'Annapurna, featuring nightly performances of classical Indian music, plus the opportunity to watch chefs skewering tandoori and stretching naan in the glassed-in kitchen. Reservations suggested in season (tel. 221-711). The Soaltee Oberoi's **Himalchuli Room** is a close rival, while **Far Pavilions** at the Everest Hotel has the added bonus of night views of city lights. Both have excellent Mughlai food and nightly entertainment.

Buffets

A buffet makes a nice splurge if you're returning from a trek with an amplified appetite. The Yak & Yeti's **Sunrise Coffeeshop** has an Rs170 breakfast buffet daily from 0700-1000; for lunch there's an Indian buffet and a salad bar. The **Soaltee Oberoi's** breakfast buffet takes second place. The Everest Hotel has a Saturday buffet from 1200-1430; the price includes swimming in season. The **Summit Hotel** holds an outdoor barbecue Friday evenings, with a great view of city lights.

During tourist season many hotels offer weekly buffets with performances of Nepali music and dance—inauthentic, but still entertaining. The Hotel Shangri-La's **Bhaktapur Night,** held most Fridays in the garden, combines a barbecue buffet with traditional masked dances by torchlight. Other dinner/show combinations are held Sunday evening at the Everest Hotel; Wednesdays and Saturdays at the Hotel Himalaya; Sunday and Wednesday at the Hotel Kathmandu. Call in advance to confirm dates and times.

Grocery Shopping

The **Subji Bazaar** behind New Road, and the big **Asan Tol market** have the widest variety and lowest prices for fresh produce. Both these markets sell mushrooms, tofu, lettuce, and other delicacies favored by foreigners, even asparagus and strawberries in season. In the spring, papayas and many varieties of mangoes are cheap and delicious. Make sure you're getting the right price, though—shop around.

Small mom-and-pop stores scattered throughout town sell butter, cold beer, and other perishable items. They're nicknamed "cold stores" or "fresh houses" because they possess refrigerators. If they're in areas where foreigners live, they will stock imported chocolate (only slightly more expensive than Indian chocolate and far better), ice cream, even beef.

Easiest one-stop shopping is done at new supermarkets like **Nanglo Bazaar** on Ram Shah Path and the old, original **Fresh House** near the Subji Bazaar. Largest are the two **Bluebird Supermarkets,** one in Tripureshwar on the way to Patan, one in Lazimpat. Prices are higher but it's convenient to find everything in one place. These stores also sell imported and expensive tinned goods and liquor you won't find anywhere else.

The **Pumpernickel Bakery** and others of its ilk sell whole-wheat bread, rolls, croissants and other picnic fare. Get cheese at cold stores or **Nepal Dairy,** which has a well-stocked small outlet in Thamel near Les Yeux Restaurant.

ENTERTAINMENT

Beyond restaurants and hotel bars, there's not much nightlife in Kathmandu—perhaps a relic of Rana times, when a nightly curfew kept people inside from 2300. Even the city's five movie theaters show exclusively in the daytime. They specialize in Hindi movies (occasionally Nepali), bursting with exaggerated action, song, and dance. These are musical comedies in the true sense of the word, and you don't need to understand what's being said to figure out the plot. Many rental shops offer a full range of Western and Hindi videos; some rent TVs and VCRs as well. A few tourist lodges offer nightly video shows. Small, dark video dens around town show Western movies, with the emphasis on sex and violence. The French, German, and British cultural centers often screen films (see "Libraries" below).

Dance Performances

Many of the larger hotels offer entertainment and dining packages, usually a Nepali-style buffet with music and/or a dance show. See the "Food" section for listings, or check *The Nepal Traveller.* Nightly entertainment is featured at the **Naachghar Restaurant** in the Yak & Yeti as well as Soaltee Oberoi's **Himalchuli Room.** The **Ghar-e-Kebab** and the Everest Hotel's **Far Pavilions** feature classical Indian music and *ghazal* singing. Dance performances without the dining are put on by the **New Himalchuli Culture Group** (tel. 410-151) at the Hotel Shanker, and the **Everest Cultural Society** (tel. 220-676) at the Hotel de l'Annapurna.

These shows are entertaining but hardly authentic, with heavily made-up performers in hokey costumes. All the more reason not to miss the classical Newari dance performances of the **Kala Mandapa Troupe.** On a good night these sacred temple dances can be a powerful experience (see p. 100). Usually held on Friday nights at the Hotel Vajra, call the hotel for dates and times of performances.

Bars And Discos

Cocktail lounges in expensive hotels are plush, quiet, and more or less the same. **Spam's Spot** in Thamel has draught beer, darts, and British pub food (say it the Nepali way: "EEspam's EEspot"). **Pub Maya** in Thamel is small and crowded and plays obnoxiously loud music. **Mero Pub** on Durbar Marg offers food, drink, and videos in a genuine bar-like environment. The **Rum Doodle Bar** in Thamel is where expedition members hang out, if you want to hear tall tales. And of course you can drink with the locals in the many small raksi and chang shops, which serve brew of dubious purity but proven potency.

Discos appear and disappear regularly in Kathmandu. They suffer from a chronic shortage of women, and are usually shut down after a brawl generated by some innocent asking the wrong girl to dance. Currently there's only the **Damaru Disco** at the Hotel Woodlands on Durbar Marg, open nightly except Tues., 2100-0100. Admission is Rs350 per couple; single men not admitted. The U.S. Marines (stationed as guards at the U.S. Embassy) sometimes host Friday night parties—cash bar, loud music, and dancing at their residence near the Pakistani Embassy in Lazimpat. Bring your passport, as they check IDs closely at the gate.

Casino

Casino Nepal at the Soaltee Oberoi Hotel is the only casino on the Indian subcontinent and relies heavily on Indian tourists (Nepalis not allowed). It's an odd scene, interesting for a while, but the stuffy atmosphere of the basement building soon becomes suffocating. If you bring your passport and used airline ticket in within a week of arrival, you'll get 100 Indian rupees worth of free game coupons good for poker, roulette, blackjack or slot machines. Open 24 hours a day, every day of the year. Complimentary buses will pick you up from major hotels from 2000-2300, and make hourly returns from 2300 on.

Fortune-telling

Palm readers in Durbar Square will entertain you for a small fee. **Babu Singh,** who's been in the palm-reading business 40 years, serves customers from his stand on the driveway of the Kathmandu Guest House. **Lalji** treats palm-reading as psychological analysis, and is supposed to be uncannily accurate. His office is in Hathi Durbar, near Narayan Hiti; no telephone, so show up between 0900-1200 to make an appointment. **M.R. Joshi** of Patan (tel. 521-159) is reportedly a good astrologer.

RECREATION

Olympic-sized public **swimming pools** at Balaju and behind the National Stadium at Tripuresh-war are permanently crowded—better to visit a hotel pool. All are open to guests of hotel guests for a fee, and most sell day passes and monthly memberships to non-guests. Largest is the Hotel de L'Annapurna's, 35 meters long. Hotel Shangri-La, the Everest Hotel, the Summit Hotel, the Soaltee Oberoi, and the Yak & Yeti are other possibilities, more for paddlers than serious swimmers. Pools are usually crowded on weekends and hot afternoons, so go in the morning for laps.

The four top hotels (Hotel De l'Annapurna, Everest Hotel, Soaltee Oberoi, and the Yak & Yeti) all have **tennis courts,** exercise facilities, and good beauty/massage parlors. Kathmandu has bargain-priced luxuries like pedicures, massages, and facials. A sauna at the Annapurna, the Yak & Yeti, or the Hotel Vajra is nice after a trek. **Kathmandu Physical Fitness Centre** in Lazimpat (in front of the Hotel Shankar) has Universal weight-training equipment, exercycles, sauna and a daily aerobics class; a day pass for the weight room is Rs60.

Runners should avoid the daytime traffic and pollution, which does more harm than good. Either get up very early to jog about the Tundikhel as Nepalis do, or head out to the Ring Road or a similar remote location—and watch out for dogs.

WORK AND STUDY OPPORTUNITIES

It's illegal to work on a tourist visa, and obtaining a non-tourist visa has become extraordinarily difficult. Local language institutes often need foreign teachers for language classes (especially English), but they can't provide visas and don't pay much. Foreign-aid missions hire professionals from their home countries, and volunteer organization like the Peace Corps and VSO (U.K.) also select applicants in their home countries.

Several programs offer college students the chance to spend a semester or a year in Nepal for college credit. Students may study Nepali or Tibetan, research special projects, go trekking or live with Nepali families. The **Experiment in International Living** has its school in Naxal (tel. 414-516); write to them at Kipling Road, Brattleboro, VT 05301 U.S.A. The University of Wisconsin-Madison's **School of South Asian**

Studies offers a College Year in Nepal program.

Tribhuvan University's **Campus of International Languages** (tel. 226-713, near the Exhibition Grounds) offers courses in Nepali, Sanskrit, Newari, and Tibetan, beginning every August. A student visa is provided but you must attend class (two hours daily) and pass your exams. The quality of instruction depends largely on the teacher; you may end up doing rote work instead of learning to speak. For information on private language lessons, see "Language" in the general Introduction.

Libraries

The **Goethe Institute** (tel. 220-528) in Ganabahal near the Post Office has a small German library, open late afternoons. The **British Cultural Center** on Kanti Path (tel. 221-305) has a large library with periodicals and a good reference section on Nepal and Tibet. The **French Cultural Center** (tel. 224-326) in Bagh Bazaar also has a library. All three of these institutions periodically sponsor concerts and film shows; call for the schedule. The reading room at the **USIS Library** on New Road is open only to Nepalis and foreign residents, but occasionally art and photographic exhibits and concerts are open to the public.

For information on Nepal, the **Tribhuvan University Library** in Kirtipur has a huge room filled with books on Nepal, India, and Tibet. Finally, the **Kaiser Library** in the Ministry of Education and Culture, on the corner of Kanti Path and TriDevi Marg, is worth a visit for the decor alone. Along with its 35,000 volumes are a stuffed Bengal tiger, European suits of armor, mounted buffalo heads, and marble nymphs, plus oil paintings of Shiva, King George V, and the library's founder, Kaiser Jung Bahadur Rana. A sweeping formal staircase leads to the second floor, where you'll find more books and old photos of Ranas wearing their spectacular plumed helmets. Window seats overlooking the overgrown garden make the perfect hideaway for a rainy or too-hot afternoon spent browsing through volumes like *Topee and Turban* and *We Ended in Bali*. The collection is particularly strong on British travel epics, the best kind.

Buddhism

Ironically, Buddhism is the most popular religion for foreigners to study in the world's only Hindu kingdom. The scene focuses around Vajrayana Buddhism, fueled by the great number of Tibetan refugees who have settled in the Valley.

The **Himalayan Yogic Institute** near Maharajganj has for years introduced Westerners to Tibetan Buddhism through workshops, seminars, and short meditation sessions. Look for posters around Thamel or call them at tel. 413-094; the house is down the road opposite the Police Training Center (the first right past the Kathmandu Hotel). It's operated by Western Buddhists who are happy to answer questions; they also have a small library and bookstore.

The institute is also linked with **Kopan Monastery,** about a one-hour walk or a bumpy taxi ride south of Boudhanath. Set atop a hill in the middle of fields, it houses about 100 Nepali and Tibetan monks and nuns and sponsors residential courses of varying lengths for Westerners interested in Buddhism. A ten-day course is Rs1300, including dorm accommodations and food; private rooms are also available. The month-long seminar in the fall is particularly popular, and there's another in the spring. They also welcome casual visitors with questions. Write or call Himalayan Yogic Institute, P.O. Box 817, Kathmandu (tel. 413-094) for information. The **Kathmandu Western Buddhist Center,** located in the Hotel Asia in Thamel, holds similar courses in the main season; look for signs around Thamel.

Several lamas in Boudhanath give teaching sessions translated into English, generally in the fall and winter months. Tulku Chokyi Nyima's two-week October seminar is popular; write to the **Rangjung Yeshe Institute** at P. O. Box 1200 for details. In a Hinayana mode **Dharma Shringa Nepal Vipassana Centre** north of Budhanilkantha offers frequent and serious ten-day meditation retreats (tel. 225-230). A small office is located behind Nabil Bank on Kanti Path.

Volunteer Opportunities

The Sisters of Charity in Chabahil sometimes take volunteers. The SOS Children's Home in Jorpati and Kopan Monastery will take medicine and clothing you don't need. Doctors can sign up to staff the Himalayan Rescue Association's Trekkers' Aid Posts in spring and fall seasons, though the waiting list is already several years' long.

Lonely and bored foreign prisoners in Kathmandu's jails appreciate visitors, especially those bringing food and reading material. There's a rotating supply of 15-20 prisoners of various nationalities, arrested for trying to smuggle gold into the country, or hashish out of it. Notices posted in popular restaurants generally list their names, nationalities, and which jail they're in.

GETTING AROUND

The vast majority of Nepal's vehicles are crammed into the Kathmandu Valley, onto narrow roads that not long ago served as footpaths. The amount of traffic in the Valley is rapidly swelling. Venturing out in rush hour is already a harrowing experience for drivers, cyclists, and pedestrians alike. Right-of-way is better termed might-of-way, claimed by the largest vehicle. Trucks and buses thunder past at a terrifying rate, air horns blasting. Taxis screech to a halt so the drivers can chat with one another in the middle of the road; buses park anywhere to deposit their passengers; motorcylists pass on blind curves going uphill. Sometimes a vehicle will try to pull around another vehicle that's *already* passing, in a mad race to see who can get ahead before being obliterated by a head-on collision.

Motorized traffic is a fairly recent addition to Kathmandu's urban environment. Roadways are still considered public domain, the proper place to dry grain and stand and chat. People do look before they cross the street, but usually just one way—in the opposite direction as they step into a lane of speeding traffic. Some villagers are so intimidated by traffic they simply bolt across the street, head down, in sheer panic. Drivers and cyclists must make allowances for all these things, plus dogs, chickens, sheep and goats, kids racing along rolling wobbly hoops, and sacred cows sleeping in the middle of the road. The constant repair of water and sewage pipes means roads are frequently dug up, but the open manholes and trenches are never marked with more than a sprig of bamboo. For this reason if no other, you should never go fast, especially at night. Cows slumbering in the middle of the Ring Road have occasioned more than one nasty after-dark accident, as a biker barreling downhill crashes into their bulk and goes head-over-heels onto the pavement.

Taxis And *Tempo*

Taxis are an easy, reasonably priced way to get around the city. Flagfall is presently Rs2.40, with a charge of Rs2 for each kilometer after that. Trips within the city are usually under Rs30. Metered taxis have black license plates with white letters; private vehicles have red. Just look for the meter in front—and expect the driver to use it for all daytime, in-town fares. If you're going to a remote corner of the Valley you'll have to bargain in advance.

After dark taxis become scarce, though you can usually find one up to 2300 in Thamel, on Durbar Marg, and on New Road. Drivers are reluctant to go just about anywhere at night, and you'll have to pay extra. The going rate after dark is supposed to be *dedhi,* one and one-half times the metered fare, but if your destination is a remote neighborhood you may have to pay double. A **Night Taxi Service** eases the after-dark transport shortage. After 2000, call 224-374 and they'll send a taxi to your location. The meter starts from their office at Bhugol Park (New Road).

Occasionally metered fares are raised due to rising petrol costs. If the driver hasn't had his meter adjusted he may ask for an extra 10-20% of the fare, but generally you should only pay what the meter reads. If the driver doesn't seem inclined to use it, find another taxi. Taxi drivers are usually Newari or Tamang, and they can provide some of the most interesting conversations you'll have in Nepal. A taxi ride is a great opportunity to catch up on the latest political news or get filled in on the current petrol situation.

Tempo are roaring little black three-wheeled scooters that can seat three passengers in a pinch. They're noiser, bumpier, and slower than taxis, but their drivers seldom argue about destinations, and they're about 25% cheaper. They are also less refined vehicles. Drivers grasp the handlebars of the contraption like cowboys mounting a bucking bull, and wrestling with the steering leaves their heads ringing and shoulders aching. You may have the same feeling after a ride.

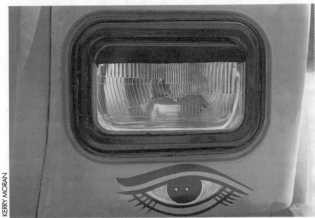

KERRY MORAN

*a protective eye painted
below a truck headlight*

For short in-city hops down narrow streets, cycle rickshaws are convenient for getting around crowded bazaars and can be found in Thamel, Durbar Square, Durbar Marg, and other tourist areas. They're supposed to be cheaper than motorized transportation, and they are, for Nepalis, but they won't be for you unless you bargain hard. Negotiate the fare before you climb in. A few blocks should be Rs5; a journey of several kilometers should cost less than Rs20.

City Buses

The Valley is covered by buses, minibuses and public tempo running regular routes, but these are not recommended means of transportation. Service ends early in the evening, there are no route maps, and destination signs are written only in Nepali, so you'll have to ask to find the correct bus. Buses are always crowded, and jammed solid during rush hour, 0900-1030 and 1600-1800. And they are slow, making frequent stops to disgorge and admit more passengers. Finally, they're hotbeds of pickpocketing. However, they're cheap—Rs1.50 or so for fares inside town, up to Rs8 for fares to the edges of the Valley.

A modern fleet of blue buses donated by the Japanese government plies regular city routes between 0530-1930 daily. Main bus stops are at Ratna Park and Shahid Gate, across from the post office. Main routes include Jorpati (passing Pashupatinath, Chabahil, and Boudhanath), the Tribhuvan University campus near Kirtipur, Thankot on the Valley's western rim, Tribhuvan International Airport, Patan Dhoka, and Lagenkhel in Patan (near Jawalakhel). From this last stop, mini-buses run to Dashinkali and Godavari, but these can take two hours to travel 15 km; better to bike or hire a taxi. Buses to north Kathmandu (Lazimpat, Maharajgunj, Balaju, Budhanilkantha) operate from Jamal, across from Rani Pokhari.

Private minibuses cover the same routes, the driver roaring at death-defying speed as riders cling to the rear door, more stuffed inside the windowless van. These are more uncomfortable than public buses and more expensive, but faster. From Jamal (near Rani Pokhari) six-seater tempo operate regular routes up through Lazimpat and Maharajgunj to Balaju and back.

The 10-km Chinese-built trolley bus line from Tripureshwar to Bhaktapur is an exception among city buses. Efficient and seldom crowded, it's a convenient, cheap way to reach or return from that city. The route ends south of Bhaktapur, about a 15-minute walk from the Durbar Square.

Rentals

Rental car companies are overpriced at US$50 and up per day, but it's easy to arrange for a taxi driver to take you about for a flat fee, say Rs500 for a full day of touring in the Valley. See "Getting Around" in the general Introduction for more details.

Bicycling

With its flat terrain, gentle climate and spectacular views the Valley was made for cycling. Downtown traffic can be intimidating at first, but it diminishes outside the city center. Both mountain bikes and regular cycles can be rented in Kathmandu; see "Getting Around" in the general "Introduction" for details.

Walking

On foot is really the best way to explore the Valley. Within the old cities, it's practical because of the dense crowds; beyond them, walking through fields and villages provides an intimate look at the countryside. The Schneider map suggests endless possibilities for day hikes. Especially if you're not going trekking, you should get out into the countryside to get a feel for the rural life which characterizes 92% of Nepal.

Organized Tours

Travelers with limited time may want to try packaged tours to Valley sites, either privately or with a group. This is an easy way to visit several places in a single morning or afternoon. Dozens of travel agencies, most clustered on Durbar Marg, offer both customized and regularly scheduled guided tours for Rs150-250.

Popular itineraries include Pashupatinath and Boudhanath stupa; Patan and Kathmandu Durbar squares; Patan and Swayambunath; Bhaktapur, and excursions to Himalayan viewpoints (Nagarkot, Dhulikhel, Kakani) for sunrise and sunset mountain views. This type of sightseeing can be a convenient way to reach out-of-the-way places, though you won't have much time or freedom to explore on your own.

PATAN AND BHAKTAPUR
PATAN

OVERVIEW

This ancient city, once a kingdom in itself, is set atop a high plateau across the Bagmati River from Kathmandu. Until recently the two cities were separated by an expanse of fields; now buildings have gobbled up the open space, merging them into a single urban mass. Despite its proximity (the old city gate is only four km from downtown Kathmandu), Patan preserves the tranquillity and charm which Kathmandu has nearly lost. The heart of the city around Mangal Bazaar and Durbar Square is definitely urban, but busy in a peaceful way. Ten minutes' walk in any direction and you're in the blend of urban and rural so typical of old Newari cities—ducks and pigs wander the streets, and grain is threshed in the open squares which break up the long lines of densely packed houses.

A 20-minute bike ride from Kathmandu, Patan ("PA-tan") is a world away in terms of ambience. Frequent visits are prescribed for anyone disappointed by Kathmandu's modernity or stressed out by its noise and traffic. Walking down the quiet, narrow streets still lined mainly by traditional buildings, it's hard to believe this is Nepal's third largest city (Biratnagar is second). About 80% of its 100,000 inhabitants are Newars, who resolutely retain their identity. During the democracy movement of 1989, the people of Patan "liberated" their city by digging trenches to block the entrance of police vehicles. For over a week the city was essentially a free zone, with the then banned Congress Party flag flying from the city gate.

About a third of Patan's residents are farmers, most living on the edges of the city near their fields. Many of the inner city residents are craftsmen who work in tiny shops, clustered in different quarters by occupational caste—stonecutter, metalworker, etc. Patan's metalworkers are es-pecially renowned: for 1,000 years they've produced fine images and jewelry, and they continue to dominate the market today. The city's special atmosphere makes shopping for metalwork here a far more interesting experience than in the tourist shops of Kathmandu. Patan's classical name, Lalitpur ("The Beautiful City"), refers to the masterpieces of its artists as well its exquisite temples and buildings. The finest artists have always come from Patan's Newar community, which even today remains largely Buddhist, a holdout in 90% Hindu Nepal.

History

Patan retains the most ancient air of all the Valley's three main cities, beginning with its unproven reputation as the capital of the near-mythic Kiranti Dynasty. Another mystery is the "Ashoka" stupas, four primitive-looking grassy mounds set around the outskirts of Patan, said to have been built by the Indian Buddhist Emperor Ashoka. This story is almost certainly untrue—Ashoka never visited the Valley—but the strange mounds might even predate the 2nd century B.C. emperor.

During the Licchavi era Patan was more important than Kathmandu, with settlements concentrated around the Mangal Bazaar/Durbar Square area. By the 7th century it was one of the major Buddhist cities of Asia. Pilgrims, scholars, and monks from India, Tibet, and China traveled here, often staying in the city's countless monasteries or bahal. At one point half of Patan's population was said to be monks—the other half were artists.

As Nepalese Buddhism gradually declined under Hindu influence, its priesthood became hereditary, and Patan's bahal changed from monasteries to trade guilds, comprised of families sharing the same caste and profession. The bahal sent out offshoots as their population swelled, until today they number over 150. Along with Patan's more than 50 major pagoda

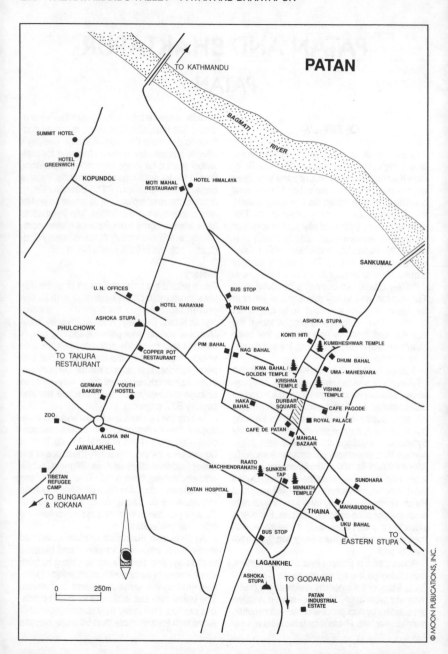

PATAN

TO KATHMANDU

BAGMATI RIVER

SUMMIT HOTEL

HOTEL GREENWICH

KOPUNDOL

MOTI MAHAL RESTAURANT

HOTEL HIMALAYA

SANKUMAL

U. N. OFFICES

BUS STOP

ASHOKA STUPA

HOTEL NARAYANI

PATAN DHOKA

ASHOKA STUPA

PHULCHOWK

KONTI HITI

KUMBHESHWAR TEMPLE

PIM BAHAL

NAG BAHAL

DHUM BAHAL

COPPER POT RESTAURANT

KWA BAHAL / GOLDEN TEMPLE

UMA - MAHESVARA

TO TAKURA RESTAURANT

KRISHNA TEMPLE

VISHNU TEMPLE

GERMAN BAKERY

YOUTH HOSTEL

HAKA BAHAL

DURBAR SQUARE

CAFE PAGODE

ZOO

ROYAL PALACE

ALOHA INN

CAFE DE PATAN

JAWALAKHEL

MANGAL BAZAAR

RAATO MACHHENDRANATH

SUNKEN TAP

SUNDHARA

TIBETAN REFUGEE CAMP

PATAN HOSPITAL

MINNATH TEMPLE

TO BUNGAMATI & KOKANA

MAHABUDDHA

THAINA

UKU BAHAL

TO EASTERN STUPA

BUS STOP

LAGANKHEL

ASHOKA STUPA

TO GODAVARI

PATAN INDUSTRIAL ESTATE

0   250m

© MOON PUBLICATIONS, INC.

temples and countless smaller monuments and shrines, they give the city the title "Town of a Thousand Golden Roofs."

Medieval Patan was the largest of the Three Kingdoms, encompassing all of the prosperous south Valley and beyond. Most of its architectural glory dates to the late Malla era (16th-18th century). Until it was annexed to Kathmandu in the late 16th century the city was ruled by powerful feudal lords. In 1619 a wise and talented Malla king, Siddhi Narsingh, ascended the throne. He, his son, and grandson remade the city, contributing much to its present splendor.

Following the Gurkha conquest of the Valley, Patan stagnated, ignored in favor of the capital Kathmandu. Foreign visitors noted its forlorn and gloomy air: "Ruined buildings and deserted shrines, broken archways, and mutilated sculptures meet the eye at every turn . . . the city looks much too large for its inhabitants," wrote Ambrose Oldfield in the late 19th century. The city became a quiet provincial backwater, a hidden stroke of fortune which has helped preserve its medieval air to the present day.

DURBAR SQUARE

Patan's Durbar Square is the finest collection of Newari urban architecture in all Nepal. Kathmandu's may have a more impressive palace, and Bhaktapur's Durbar Square may have rivaled it before the 1934 earthquake, but Patan takes the prize for loveliest ensemble. An extraordinary variety of monuments built over the course of centuries blends into a magical whole, each perfectly placed and balanced. Frenchman Sylvain Levi described its dreamlike beauty in 1901: ". . . a world of almost luminous white stone, of pillars crowned by bronze statues, of light-filtering colonnades, and of fragile dream temples—guarded all by a company of fantastic beasts, chimeras, and griffins."

Set in the heart of the city at the junction of two ancient trade routes (the same as Kathmandu's), the area is the best integrated of all the three city squares. It began as the site of a pre-Licchavi palace, later becoming the favorite neighborhood of the rich nobles who ruled Patan. After a Malla king ascended the throne in 1619, Durbar Square and the palace emerged in its full glory. Much of its splendor is due to a fa-

Patan Durbar Square with statue of King Yoganendra Malla

KERRY MORAN

ther-and-son succession of kings: Siddhi Narsingh Malla and Shrinivasa Malla, whose combined rules spanned 1619-1684. They renovated and rebuilt the small existing palace and added a number of the great monuments in the facing square, for the glory of themselves and their gods.

There are two ways to reach Durbar Square: the main road leading directly to Mangal Bazaar abutting the south side, or an interesting 15-minute walk from Patan Dhoka (the public bus stop) along a winding street leading to the square's northern end.

A Walking Tour

At the north end of the square is **Bhimsen Mandir,** a richly decorated three-story pagoda with an assortment of household goods—pots, pans and brooms—nailed up under the eaves, customary offerings to assure comfort for the dead in the afterworld. Bhimsen, a legendary strongman from the Mahabharata, is the patron of merchants, and wealthy traders seeking his

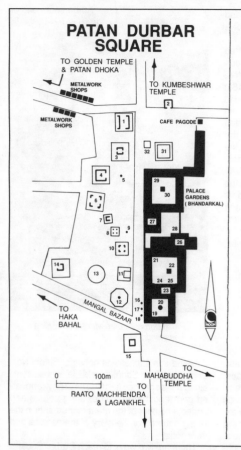

PATAN DURBAR SQUARE

TO GOLDEN TEMPLE & PATAN DHOKA

METALWORK SHOPS

METALWORK SHOPS

TO KUMBESHWAR TEMPLE

CAFE PAGODE

PALACE GARDENS (BHANDARKAL)

MANGAL BAZAAR

TO HAKA BAHAL

MOON

0   100m

TO RAATO MACHHENDRA & LAGANKHEL

TO MAHABUDDHA TEMPLE

LEGEND

1. Bhimsen Mandir
2. Ganesh temple
3. Vishwanath Mandir
4. Krishna Mandir
5. Garuda pillar
6. Chaar Narayan Mandir
7. Narayan Temple
8. Narasingha Temple
9. King Yoganendra Malla's pillar
10. Hari Shankara Mandir
11. Taleju bell
12. Chyasin Dega
13. fountain
14. Bhai Devala Temple
15. Shiva temple (good views)
16. Narasingha statue
17. Ganesh statue
18. Hanuman statue
19. Sundari Chowk
20. Tulsi Hiti
21. Mul Chowk
22. Yantaju shrine
23. Taleju Mandir
24. Ganga statue
25. Jamuna statue
26. Taleju Temple
27. Degutale (main Taleju shrine)
28. Nassal Chowk
29. Lumjhyal Chowk
30. Narayan shrine
31. Manga Hiti
32. Mani Mandapa

© MOON PUBLICATIONS, INC.

favor have endowed his temple with offerings like the fake-marble facade and the silvered wooden struts of the first story. Above are older, classic gilded struts of deities with their consorts. From the rooftop a long golden *pataka* streams down, a pathway for the gods to descend.

Beside it is **Vishwanath Mandir,** a classic Newari-style pagoda dedicated to Shiva and built in 1627. Until recently it was one of the square's finest buildings. It collapsed without warning in the 1990 monsoon, killing several people. It's now being reconstructed, using as much of the beautiful old carved sal wood as possible.

The following temple, the **Krishna Mandir,** is Nepal's finest piece of stone architecture, a delicate, airy creation which defies its heavy material. It was built at the command of Siddhi Narsingh, a passionate devotee of Krishna, who dreamed he saw Krishna and Radha in union on this spot. A black stone image of Krishna with consorts Radha and Rukmini is installed on the second floor, which is closed to non-Hindus. Unlike most Durbar Square temples, which tend to be monumental showpieces only, this is a very active shrine and the sound of singing and bells often drifts down from the open gallery.

The temple's inspired architecture surrounds a solid Indian shikara with airy Moghul-influenced colonnades, an improbable combination which succeeds brilliantly in this massive yet delicate structure. Scenes from the *Mahabharata* with explanations etched in Newari encircle the entire first story; the second-story pavilions are banded by friezes from the *Ramayana*. Atop a stone pillar in front, a brilliantly executed large metal **Garuda** kneels in homage.

As an ensemble, the Durbar Square in Patan probably remains the most picturesque collection of buildings that has been set up in so small a place by the piety and pride of Oriental man.

—Percival Landon, 1928

Next is **Chaar Narayan Mandir,** a rather stodgy pagoda and the oldest surviving temple in the entire ensemble, completed in 1566. The main image, scarcely worshipped today, is a four-faced Vishnu, each side depicting one of his main emanations. The bases of the struts are carved with imaginative couplings of women, men, and mythic beasts.

Beside it is a small fenced-in **park** with laundry drying atop its clipped hedges and two small cement shrines built in 1972. The first encloses a black stone image of **Radha** with a flute-playing **Krishna,** unearthed by workmen digging the foundations for the second shrine, which holds a large bronze **Buddha.**

Fronting this is a stone pillar supporting a gilded image of **King Yoganendra Malla,** shaded by the spread hood of a royal cobra. Hands folded in prayer, he faces the impressive triple roofs of the palace's main **Taleju temple.** This 17th-century king is said to have renounced his throne in grief after the death of his son and wandered off as an ascetic holy man. Before he left he told his people that as long as the face of the statue was bright and untarnished and the small bird atop the cobra's head remained, they would know the king was still alive. The bird is still there, and for more than a century a mattress was laid out nightly in a palace room, with the window left open for the king's return.

The next large three-story pagoda is **Hari Shankara Mandir,** jointly dedicated to Vishnu and Shiva, and very similar to the collapsed Vishwanath Mandir. Next is a large cast bronze **bell** dedicated to Taleju and erected in 1737, for worship and also "in order to terrify the king's enemies."

At the south end of the square is **Chyasin Dega,** an unusual eight-sided stone shikara built in 1723 by the daughter of Yoganendra Malla in memory of the eight wives who followed her father's body onto the funeral pyre. Shikara generally have an odd number of facets, but this one is dedicated to Krishna, who is said to favor eight-sided temples. The temple steps are a favorite resting spot for porters waiting for work.

Beyond here is **Mangal Bazaar,** an important and ancient trading center forming the heart of Patan's commerce. Across the road, the rooftop of the corner building, crowned with a small stone shrine, gives an impressive overview of the square: stacked temple roofs fringed with delicate bells, all set against the white massif of Langtang Himal.

The Old Royal Palace

From here you can double back to explore the former **Royal Palace** along the eastern side of the square. It's much smaller than its Kathmandu counterpart, a simple row of quadrangles laid out side by side, but unlike the Kathmandu Durbar all of the courtyards are open to the public. After the fall of the Mallas, the Patan palace was largely ignored by the Shah Dynasty, and thus retains much of the exquisite detail of the 17th-century original.

The southernmost compound is called **Sundari Chowk,** the "Beautiful Courtyard." Its entrance is flanked by some uninspired stone guardians: **Ganesh, Narasingha** disemboweling the helpless demon, and a red-smeared effigy representing **Hanuman** the Monkey King. Over the entrance, which once held golden doors, is a dilapidated **gilded window** flanked by two of carved ivory. The courtyard is the palace's finest, lined with columned arcades, ornamented windows, and screened galleries. In the middle is the fantastic **Tulsi Hiti,** the royal bath, built in 1646. The walls of the sunken oval basin are inset with a double row of finely sculpted deities and topped with more—over 70 in all, a miniature museum. Most are of stone, a few of gilt metal; all are multi-armed and tantric in their complexity, including the eight Ashta Matrika, the eight fierce Bhairab, and the eight Great Naga. The delicacy of the carving is nicely set off by the moss and greenery growing in crevices, creating a grotto-like setting. A pair of sinuous stone naga embrace the rim, an unusual example of the *nag bandh* which keep away evil influences.

Though the water has long stopped flowing, the gilded conch-shaped waterspout is another work of art, topped with gilt repoussé figures of Vishnu and Laxmi atop Garuda. Directly above is a small stone replica of the Krishna Mandir standing in Durbar Square. Another image of Hanuman kneels humbly between the bath and a huge stone slab said to have been the bed of the ascetic King Siddhi Narsingh, who spent his nights in meditation and worship.

The next and central courtyard, **Mul Chowk,** is the palace's oldest section, dedicated almost entirely to the Malla patron goddess Taleju. In the center is a small gilded **shrine** to Yantaju, a sister-goddess of Taleju, once also an important Malla deity, now almost forgotten. On the southern side is the **Taleju Mandir,** marked by a small and rather clumsy triple-roofed pagoda perched atop the main roof. The temple's lovely repoussé door is topped with a 1715 torana, now bearing nothing but gaping holes—the images were stolen in 1970. The door is flanked by two life-sized metal images of **Jamuna** atop a crocodile and **Ganga** on a tortoise. The graceful goddesses are deified representations of India's two holiest rivers; similar pairs guard the Taleju shrines of the palaces of Kathmandu and Bhaktapur, but those courtyards are closed to the public.

From Mul Chowk you can see two other Taleju shrines: in the northeast corner a triple octagonal **pagoda** with a gilded shikara as its spire, and a bit further back in the northwest, the **main temple,** built in 1736 and reconstructed after collapsing in 1934. As in the main Taleju temple of Kathmandu, the shrine is open to Hindus one day a year during Dasain. Behind this courtyard are the palace gardens, generally closed to the public but set with interesting stone sculptures you may be able to see on request.

The northernmost courtyard is known as **Lumjyal Chowk,** after the golden window crowning the entrance. Inside is a small white plaster shrine to Narayan. This courtyard was extensively renovated in the 19th century and underwent more work in 1991. Its major feature is the entrance, the local equivalent of Bhaktapur's famed Golden Gate. According to its inscription, this 19th-century addition was financed by the sale of old gilded images from the palace treasury. The glittering door is framed by a braided band of naga fanning out into a royal crown at the top; just about every deity in the popular pantheon is depicted in the golden windows above.

On the north side of the palace is the ancient sunken water tap of **Manga Hiti,** recently restored. Water spouts from three carved stone makara while real little girls struggle with water jugs as big as themselves, proof that neighborhood residents still use the tap as they have for at least 1,500 years.

EXPLORING PATAN'S BACKSTREETS

Old Patan is even smaller than old Kathmandu—about three square km, a 20-minute walk from end to end. Taking Durbar Square as your center and starting point, you can explore in every direction, wandering through neighborhoods dedicated to metalworking or stonecarving, past ancient bahal and temples. A few of the highlights are described below, but there are many more routes to take on your own. Visit at different times of the day to capture the city's varied moods—the elusive mist of a winter morning, or sunset gilding the temple roofs.

Kumbheshwar Mahadev

Walk straight north past Bhimsen Mandir. Shortly after on the left is a crumbling old **pagoda** dedicated to Krishna, with grass growing on its roof, beautiful wooden struts, and a big electrical transformer right beside it. Just beyond on the right is a small **Vishnu temple** with a caged Garuda in front. After these look for a small shrine set back from the road on the right, containing a classic 10th-century sculpture of **Uma-Mahesvara.**

Soon the road branches: take the red-brick lane to the left and look for the slender five-storied pagoda of **Khumbeshwar,** Patan's oldest

to worship the embossed silver sheath worn by the temple's sacred *linga* the preceding month, which is placed in a special pavilion in the middle of the tank. Boys frolic in the suddenly sacred waters, splashing worshippers, and the temple attendents wear rain slickers.

On the opposite side is a much visited rectangular shrine with green-painted woodwork. Inside the goddess **Bagalamukhi** is embodied in a tiny image beneath an elaborate silver torana and canopy of snakes. A manifestation of the Great Goddess Durga, Bagalamukhi is considered the sender of cholera, which still plagues the Valley in the rainy season.

Outside the temple's main entrance is the old **Konti Hiti,** a busy neighborhood water tap set with lovely sculptures. The city's northern **Ashoka stupa** lies a few minutes down the road behind the temple compound: go out the back gate by the ancient pipal tree and follow the road for a few hundred meters. The hemispherical stupa is on the left, completely plastered over and shining white. Set on the edge of a bluff, the stupa's compound provides good views of the rich fields surrounding Patan and the mountains behind.

Return to Durbar Square via the road leading south from Kumbeshwar's main gate, and you'll pass the Golden Temple in a few minutes.

Kwa Bahal
If you spend any more than two minutes in Durbar Square, an eight-year-old tour guide is certain to volunteer to lead you to "Golden Temple." With or without him, you should visit this lavish bahal, called Hiranyavarna Mahavihara in Sanskrit or Kwa Bahal in Newari. Starting from Bhimsen Mandir, it's a five-minute walk west and then north down the main street, on the left-hand side through a lion-guarded stone archway. The courtyard is a glittering example of Newari metalwork. A gilt-roofed freestanding shrine in the middle stands in front of the gilt and silver-covered facade of the main temple, the whole surrounded by images of strange animals, donors, and mythic beasts. The detail work deserves several visits; there's simply too much to take in at one glance. Take off leather shoes to enter the courtyard and examine the facade close up. In particular look for a tiny three-cm-high frieze at eye level, showing scenes from the Buddha's life, beginning with his moth-

Janal Purnima being celebrated at Kumbheshwar Mahadev Mandir, Patan

KERRY MORAN

temple. It houses the Lord of the Water Pot (Kumbha), one of the many names of Shiva, who is said to dwell here during the six winter months; in the summer he migrates to Mt. Kailas in western Tibet. This is one of the Valley's two five-storied temples (the other is Bhaktapur's Nyatapola). Tall and slender, its graceful proportions are all the more remarkable when you consider it was originally constructed in 1392 as a two-storied shrine; the upper three tiers were added by Srinivasa Malla in the 17th century. The many sculptures and linga scattered about the compound, some dating back to Licchavi times, mark this as an exceedingly ancient holy site.

On the north side of the compound is an open **tank** fed by a nearby spring, said to be mystically linked by an underground channel with the sacred lake of Gosainkund, four days' walk north of Kathmandu. Kumbeshwar serves as a convenient substitute for the difficult pilgrimage to the Himalayan lake. On the festival of Janai Purnima (usually the August full moon) thousands come

er's auspicious dream of a white elephant to his birth, his four fateful excursions in the chariot, and so on.

Unlike many crumbling bahal, Kwa Bahal is still actively supported and is a good place to visit during Buddhist festivals. The wealth has been accumulating since the temple's founding in 1409, but much has been donated relatively recently by wealthy devotees. The tradition extends back to the days of Tibetan trade, when Newari merchants donated a portion of their earnings to temples. The courtyard is ringed by balconies and shrines, including one to **Tara** on the left and a **Tibetan-style shrine** on the second floor with nice frescoes, rafters painted with sacred mantras, and a big prayer wheel.

Mahabuddha

From the southern end of Durbar Square walk east five minutes to a sunken water tap on the right with four gilded spouts, the locally renowned **Sundhara** or "Golden Tap."

Take the broad road leading right, passing many shops specializing in bronze images. Just before the end of the street a plaster archway and narrow passage leads to a small courtyard, nearly completely filled with the shikara-style temple of Mahabuddha. It's said to have been built by a 17th-century Nepali pilgrim who visited the great temple of Bodhgaya in India and returned home determined to reproduce it. His memory perhaps failed over the ensuing 36 years it took to complete, because the resemblance is vague at best, but it's pleasing in its own right. The facade is decorated with terracotta relief plaques of tiny Buddhas, floral designs, and images, creating an ornate monument whose dense detail can hardly be absorbed at such close range. Climb to the second floor of a courtyard building to get a better view of the soaring tower, crowned by a small gilded stupa. The structure completely crumbled in the '34 quake and was reconstructed. The leftover pieces were used to make a smaller shrine nearby, dedicated to Maya Devi, the mother of the Buddha.

This courtyard and the surrounding neighborhood are fertile hunting grounds for **statues** of Buddhist deities. Tibetans as well as tourists prowl the streets, looking for the perfect image. Ratna Jyoti Shakya's shop in the courtyard's

southeast corner has nice statues and samples of the different casting stages which he's happy to explain. The passageway leading into the temple also has a few superior shops.

A few steps past the Mahabuddha entrance at the end of the road is **Uku Bahal,** an ancient and rich *vihara* dating perhaps back to Licchavi times. The courtyard houses a bizarre menagerie of mythic beasts wrought in metal. The sight of them leering from the evening gloom caused caused a British historian to call the temple "one of the weirdest sights in the whole of Nepal." There's also a bronze image of a Rana general reading a proclamation and several Licchavi-era chaitya. The wooden struts on the courtyard's rear wall are very fine early examples, with graceful nymphs standing atop crouched dwarves.

Return towards Durbar Square by heading west down the street in front of Uku Bahal, through the old and busy metalworkers' quarter of **Thaina.** The constant pounding of hammers on metal tells you you're on the right street. In less than 10 minutes you'll reach the main road and bazaar. Turn left and continue to the first large clearing on the right, where the Minnath temple stands behind a large sunken water tap.

Minnath Mandir

From Durbar Square go straight south down an interesting, crowded bazaar lane selling everything from fresh ginger to brass pots. Look for an old white house on the right with second-story windows flanked by plaster maidens modestly draped in Grecian style—one of those unexpected bits of Victoriana introduced by the Ranas. (In a Newari-style house the maidens would be uninhibitedly nude, and very beautiful.) About five minutes down is a large sunken water tap on the left, with a temple compound set behind it. This shrine is dedicated to Minnath, an ancient local deity associated with the bodhisattva Padmapani Lokeswara. He resides in a richly decorated small pagoda, its woodwork painted in shockingly bright candy-colored hues. The old buildings of the compound are unfortunately being replaced by modern cement boxes. Behind the temple are two gigantic timber shafts once used for Machhendra's chariot.

In appearance the red-faced image is nearly identical with the famous Machhendranath image across the street. Minnath is usually described as Machhendranath's "son" or "daughter," or sometimes as "little" (saano) Machhendranath; actually his cult is even older. Around the 7th century he and many other local deities were honored with yearly chariot processions. After the arrival of Machhendranath these celebrations were all terminated in favor of the new god. But various omens indicated that Minnath was displeased at losing his annual outing, and his smaller chariot now accompanies that of Machhendranath's every spring.

Raato Machhendranath Mandir

Take the small path across the street from the Minnath temple to a large grassy compound surrounding a 17th-century pagoda, the home of Patan's most beloved deity. Nepalis call him Raato or Red Machhendranath; to Newaris he's Bunga Dyo, "God of Bungamati." A menagerie of bronze animals stands on pillars in front of the temple, while the carved struts depict different forms of Padmapani Lokesvara, the bodhisattva closely associated with Machhendranath. On the bottom portion are miniature scenes of sinners being tortured in hell—boiled in oil, beaten in a pestle, all rather appalling for a temple dedicated to the Bodhisattva of Compassion.

Inside is enshrined the strange flat-faced idol of Machhendranath, painted red, with staring eyes and large gilded ears, draped with jewels, gold, and flower garlands. Some say the image is made of wood, others of clay-covered gold or even ground bone mixed with clay. For half the year (Dec.-June) the deity dwells here; the other six months he's enshrined in his temple in Bungamati, a Newar village six km south of Patan.

The god's history is lengthy and convoluted, blending elements of Buddhism and folk beliefs. As a local deity, Bunga Dyo existed by the early 7th century. He soon became associated with the bodhisattva Padmapani Lokesvara, whom legend says was the creator of the world and the guru of Brahma and all the other Hindu gods. By the 18th century he had assumed another title: Machhendranath, "Lord of the Fishes," or "Master of the Senses," according to the mystic terminology of tantra.

He has long been Patan's favorite deity: coins were struck in his name, and a royal edict proclaimed no building could top the towering spire of his chariot. His annual chariot procession, dating back at least to the 13th century, is the city's biggest festival. It begins with a public bathing ceremony, usually in late April. The spirit of the god then retires to a sacred water pot as members of a special caste refurbish and paint the image. Then the deity is loaded into his great wooden chariot and slowly pulled through the city, spending a night in each neighborhood, according to ancient schedule, so that residents can worship him.

The chariot is laden with other deities as well: five Bhairavs are said to inhabit it, one in each wheel and one in the gilded image at the prow. Naga occupy the ropes and streamers hanging from the mast, and the King of the Nagas resides in the shaft. Usually the parts are reassembled yearly for the festival, but every 12 years the entire chariot is built anew. The great curved wooden shaft is carted off by a guthi to serve as a bench, and many can be seen scattered around Patan in various bahal and resthouses.

By late May the chariot reaches Jawalakhel, where it may wait several days for the astrologically perfect moment for the Bhoto Jatra, the climax of the whole celebration. The Patan Kumari and the King of Nepal attend this ceremony, usually held around the first week of June. Machhendra's magical jeweled vest (bhoto), a doll-sized black shirt, is held up to the adoring crowd, and if all goes well rain begins to fall at this exact moment, signaling the beginning of the rice-planting season. As a sort of Newari rain god, Machhendra is closely associated with the arrival of the monsoon, which explains his importance with Newari farmers. After this grand finale, the deity is hauled off to Bungamati on a palanquin for a six-month stay at his "family home."

Haka Bahal

A short walk west through Mangal Bazaar leads to Haka Bahal, home of Patan's main and once royal Kumari. She is chosen from the daughters of the Vajracharya or priestly caste who inhabit the complex. Some of these families still follow the old and peculiar profession of retrieving precious metal from the sweepings of metalworking shops. Haka Bahal once stood on Durbar Square, where Sundari Chowk and the royal bath is now located. When the palace expanded southward in the 17th century the entire building was dismantled and relocated at its present location. Bright ceramic tiles and gilded images of ten Buddhas decorate the facade.

PRACTICALITIES

Accommodations
There are no lodges in Patan's old town, which pretty much defeats the purpose of staying there at all. The following are on or near the main road. The only inexpensive facility is the **Mahendra Youth Hostel** just before Jawalakhel, with dorm beds for Rs25. Mid-priced lodging includes the **Aloha Inn** (tel. 522-796) near Jawalakhel; and **Hotel Narayani, Summit Hotel** (tel. 521-894) and **Hotel Greenwich** (tel. 521-780), all in Kopundol. Top of the line is the Japanese-run **Hotel Himalaya** (tel. 523-900).

Food
With Kathmandu so close by, Patan has developed few restaurants of its own—rather inconvenient when, after a few hours of walking, hunger forces you to retreat to Kathmandu. There are however some good places—you just have to know where they're hiding. The Hotel Himalaya's **coffee shop** is very *pukka,* not terribly expensive, and has wonderful mountain views. For the ravenous, the **Mini Mahal** across the street has a plush dining room and serves huge Rs100 *thali* and good reasonably priced Mughlai food. There's *ghazal* music at night, too. **Takura Restaurant** in Jhamsikhel (past the North Korean Embassy) is out of the way but has excellent Japanese food in a pleasant setting, open for lunch and dinner.

For more modest fare, southwest of Durbar Square is the small **Cafe de Patan** with a tiny garden courtyard. The **Cafe Pagode** on the opposite end, behind Manga Hiti, has a rooftop terrace with nice views. Many inexpensive restaurants along the main road leading to Jawalakhel serve Chinese and Indian dishes.

The **Copper Pot** has a wider variety of Western cuisine. Near the zoo is the **German Bakery,** with brewed coffee, sandwiches, and cakes.

Shopping
Patan is *the* place to look for metalwork. There's still a lot of schlok, and the best Kathmandu shops buy direct from Patan artists and thus rival or even exceed the quality you may find here, but a hunt down Patan's narrow streets has its own brand of charm. Some of the best shops are on the street north of Durbar Square; also try the area around Mahabuddha.

The old Tibetan Camp in Jawalakhel has the city's largest and most reasonably priced selection of new Tibetan carpets and is also a good place to hunt for rare old ones. It's worth a visit just to see how they're made in the large factory here (see p. 95).

For naive paintings of the Valley, visit the **B. B. Thapa Gallery** at Ekantakuna, Jawalakhel, past Master Weaver's. The **Arjun Art Gallery** just north of Bhimsen Mandir does similar paintings. There are several good woodcarving shops at **Patan Industrial Estate,** which also has metalworkers and thangka painters. **Nepal Traditional Crafts** in a big yellow building on the west side of the street in Pulchowk has all sorts of metal objects and various handicrafts.

The main road after the bridge has many shops specializing in household goods for foreigners, catering to the large community of foreign-aid workers in west Patan neighborhoods. Most interesting are the shops marketing handicrafts made by low-income women and handicapped people. **Dhukuti** and **Hastakala** have large selections of reasonably priced handmade paper, block-printed and handwoven material, quilted cushion covers, women's clothing, pottery, wooden toys, and the best sweaters in the Valley. The **Mahaguthi Shop** in a courtyard of Patan's old royal palace is also worth a visit; there's also a branch on Durbar Marg in Kathmandu. **Himalayan Leathers** south of Patan Hospital has inexpensive leather goods and batiks marketed by the Leprosy Association.

BHAKTAPUR

OVERVIEW

Once the capital of the entire Valley, Bhakta-pur is now the most isolated and unchanged of the three former kingdoms. Its peaceful yet busy streets preserve nearly intact the medieval atmosphere of bygone days. Bhaktapur is one of Nepal's greatest treasures, but few tourists will spend more than an afternoon touring its main squares. This is a pity, because more than any other place it embodies the essence of the Newari city. A few days here will reassure you of the possibility of a sane urban life, and provide a better picture of how most of Nepal—the rural 92%—lives.

Stretched along a ridge above the sacred Hanumante River 14 km east of Kathmandu, the city grew from a collection of villages strung along the old trade route to Tibet. The view from the Chinese highway below is worth seeking out: huddled red-tiled roofs punctuated by the soaring spire of the five-story Nyatapola Mandir, set against the movie-set backdrop of the Himalaya and surrounded by lush fields.

Bhaktapur is virtually 100% Newari and adamantly rural at heart. About 60% of its 160,000 people are farmers, among the country's best. From the rich black soil they coax forth giant cauliflowers and rice yields which are the highest in Nepal. Bhaktapur's deep roots in the land are apparent in the people on its streets: Jyapu women in their characteristic red-bordered black saris pleated in front and raised high in back to reveal blue tatooes above their ankles; farmers with double baskets of giant radishes suspended from their shoulder poles; work crews of laughing girls heading out to the fields with hoes for a day of backbreaking labor.

Until 1966, when a Chinese-built road finally linked Bhaktapur to Kathmandu, it was a dusty 14-km walk to the capital. Bhaktapur has remained a world apart, economically self-sufficient and strongly independent. A village in many ways, it maintains a rich cultural and religious life rooted in Newari traditions. A 1974 survey found only 50 non-Newars in the entire town. Bhaktapurians speak a dialect of Newari

distinct from Kathmandu's, and even today many older people don't understand Nepali—living in a pure Newar society, they don't need to. Bhaktapur has always been a more purely Hindu city than mixed Kathmandu or Buddhist Patan; its name translates as "City of Devotees," and its resolutely Hindu character reinforces its conservatism.

History

Bhaktapur began as a collection of farming villages, perhaps as early as the 3rd century, when irrigation was first brought to the Valley's fields. In the 12th century King Ananda Deva of Banepa, a powerful mini-kingdom just outside the Valley rim, shifted his capital to Bhaktapur and built a royal palace in the city's western quarter. For the next three centuries, until the fragmentation of the Three Kingdoms era, Bhaktapur ruled as the capital of a unified Valley. It

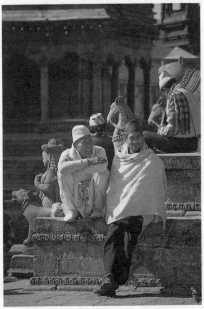

men chatting on the steps of a Bhaktapur temple

KERRY MORAN

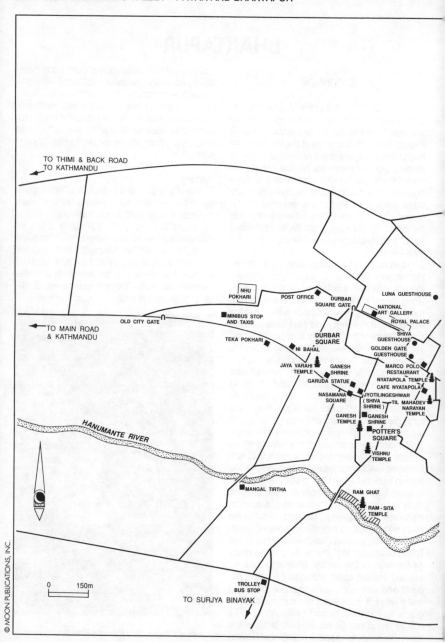

BHAKTAPUR

TO THIMI & BACK ROAD
TO KATHMANDU

TO MAIN ROAD
& KATHMANDU

OLD CITY GATE

NHU
POKHARI

POST OFFICE

DURBAR
SQUARE GATE

LUNA GUESTHOUSE

NATIONAL
ART GALLERY

ROYAL PALACE

MINIBUS STOP
AND TAXIS

DURBAR
SQUARE

SHIVA
GUESTHOUSE

TEKA POKHARI

GOLDEN GATE
GUESTHOUSE

NI BAHAL

MARCO POLO
RESTAURANT

JAYA VARAHI
TEMPLE

GANESH
SHRINE

NYATAPOLA TEMPLE

GARUDA STATUE

CAFE NYATAPOLA

NASAMANA
SQUARE

JYOTILINGESHWAR
(SHIVA
SHRINE)

TIL MAHADEV
NARAYAN
TEMPLE

GANESH
TEMPLE

GANESH
SHRINE

POTTER'S
SQUARE

VISHNU
TEMPLE

HANUMANTE RIVER

MANGAL TIRTHA

RAM GHAT

RAM - SITA
TEMPLE

0   150m

TROLLEY
BUS STOP

TO SURJYA BINAYAK

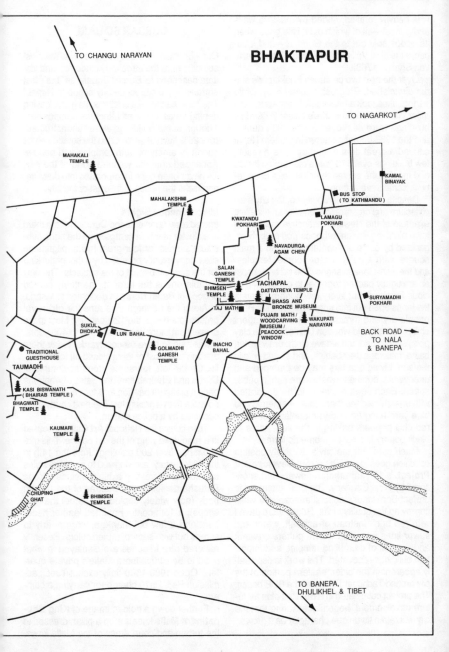

TO CHANGU NARAYAN

BHAKTAPUR

TO NAGARKOT

MAHAKALI
TEMPLE

MAHALAKSHMI
TEMPLE

KWATANDU
POKHARI

KAMAL
BINAYAK

BUS STOP
(TO KATHMANDU)

LAMAGU
POKHARI

NAVADURGA
AGAM CHEN

SALAN
GANESH
TEMPLE

TACHAPAL

BHIMSEN
TEMPLE

DATTATREYA TEMPLE

SURYAMADHI
POKHARI

BRASS AND
BRONZE MUSEUM

TAJ MATH

PUJARI MATH /
WOODCARVING
MUSEUM /
PEACOCK
WINDOW

WAKUPATI
NARAYAN

SUKUL
DHOKA

LUN BAHAL

BACK ROAD
TO NALA
& BANEPA

GOLMADHI
GANESH
TEMPLE

INACHO
BAHAL

TRADITIONAL
GUESTHOUSE

TAUMADHI

KASI BISWANATH
(BHAIRAB TEMPLE)

BHAGWATI
TEMPLE

KAUMARI
TEMPLE

CHUPING
GHAT

BHIMSEN
TEMPLE

TO BANEPA,
DHULIKHEL & TIBET

was heavily fortified, ringed by massive walls and a moat—all of which did it little good when its troops sold out to the Gorkhas—and it became the final Valley city to fall to Prithvi Narayan Shah in 1768.

Over the next two centuries Bhaktapur's status diminished. Progress passed it by, while earthquakes took a heavy toll. Bhaktapur is the most vulnerable of the three cities: 70% of its buildings were destroyed in the 1934 quake, and the 1988 tremor centered in eastern Nepal caused a great deal of damage. As a result, few buildings over 170 years old remain intact, and most of the sacred temples have been rebuilt, some several times.

Despite the frequent rebuilding, the city's architecture and organization remains an excellent example of the Newars' instinctive mastery of town planning. Neighborhoods (tol) roughly organized by caste are centered around a main square, with a public water source, temples, and the local Ganesh shrine. The tall brick houses are tightly packed together to conserve precious farmland, but every few hundred meters the lanes open out into spacious squares. Here people dry and thresh grain, pound pungent chili peppers in old wooden pestles, shape clay pots, spin thread and weave cloth, draw water, bathe, massage their babies, and sit and chat in the sun. Living quarters may be cramped and unenviable, but the townsfolk are rich in public space. Each square seems to be decorated with unexpected touches: coils of emerald and blue yarn hung up to dry; mountains of shiny red chili peppers baking in the sun, acres of black pottery laid out in geometric forms.

Much credit for the city's relatively pristine condition goes to the **Bhaktapur Development Project,** a 15-year urban renewal effort sponsored by West Germany. The BDP attempted to protect Bhaktapur's special atmosphere while improving the quality of life. Roads were paved with red brick instead of asphalt; water and sewer lines were laid; storm gutters created; and dozens of crumbling temples and important buildings renovated. The work is especially apparent in the older, eastern portion of the city around Tachupal Tol where the BDP began. The project culminated in a detailed plan for future development, hopefully ensuring that the city will retain its unique character as it grows.

DURBAR SQUARE

Once Bhaktapur's old royal palace was the most splendid of all the three old kingdoms', and visitors described its Durbar Square as "the most entrancingly picturesque city scene in Nepal." The 1934 earthquake shattered its glory, leaving gaping holes in the architectural composition. Though some buildings were reconstructed, over 25% have been lost, and the square seems curiously empty of both temples and people. Appended onto the western edge of the city, it's never been quite incorporated into daily life, and lacks the bustle of the rest of the city.

Miscellaneous Sights

Immediately upon entering Durbar Square there is a cluster of **minor temples** on the right, substitute shrines for four great Indian pilgrimage sites, conveniently provided by a thoughtful king for the spiritual benefit of his subjects. The only notable one is the largest, the finely carved pagoda of **Bansi Narayan** dedicated to Vishnu.

Along the northern side runs the **old royal palace** founded in the 12th century. Most of the present structure dates back 300 to 400 years. It was said to have 99 courtyards; today there are only six, most of them closed off to the public. On the left, fearsome stone sculptures of **Durga** and **Bhairab** flank the gates of what was once a pleasure pavilion for Malla queens, now no more than a grassy lot. The next courtyard is occupied by a police station.

Then comes the **National Art Gallery,** housed in a renovated wing of the old palace. This museum has over 200 paintings from the 14th to the 20th century, allowing you to compare styles and colors. Interesting exhibits include a Yoga Purusha depicting the chakras of the human body (now widely copied in Thamel thangka shops), a 15th-century painted leather handbag, and a few old thangka, worn nearly to shreds but with superb, muted colors. Recently restored rare frescoes are displayed in what used to be Bhupatindra Malla's private quarters. Open 1000-1600 daily except Tues.; admission Rs5, Rs10 charge for carrying a camera.

Further down a golden image of **King Bhupatindra Malla** kneels atop a pillar, dressed in the turban and court dress of the Malla kings,

Bhaktapur Durbar Square

sword and shield by his side. Dignified and grave, his is perhaps the most beautiful of the Valley's three royal portraits. Bhupatindra's statue was made in imitation of the others, and he was forced to ask the Kathmandu ruler for help in raising the pillar. The king obligingly sent a team of workmen along, with secret instructions to break the pillar. They obeyed, but then quickly repaired their mistake, pleasing both kings and earning a handsome reward from each.

Golden Gate And Mul Chowk

The statue faces the Golden Gate of Bhaktapur, perhaps the most famous piece of art in all Nepal. Much of the credit for this goes to Percy Brown, who in his 1912 book raved on for pages about it. Percival Landon called it "perhaps the most exquisitely designed and finished piece of gilded metalwork in all of Asia." It is an incredibly extravagant monument, set up in 1753 by Jaya Ranjit Malla to honor the goddess Taleju, whose richly decorated temple lies in the palace's central courtyard. Repoussé sculptures of deities are set in the doorjambs, and sea serpents swirl about an image of Taleju set in the middle of the torana. The workmanship is superb, but what astounds is the sheer quantity of gold lavished on the gate—just one example of the wealth of the Valley's kings.

Go through the Golden Gate and around the corner to the entrance of Mul Chowk, the palace's central, oldest courtyard, dedicated to Taleju. Here the three last Malla rulers huddled together during the siege of Bhaktapur, until

Gorkha soldiers broke down the golden doors and found them, finally joined in defeat. Mul Chowk and the smaller **Kumari Chowk** behind are said to be the most beautiful structures in the Valley, but both are closed to non-Hindus. From the doorway you can see golden lizards, elephants, dragons, and snakes swarming over a temple roof ahead. The main temple to the left is hidden from view, but if you stretch you can glimpse one of the statues of Ganga and Jamuna, even finer than those in the Patan Durbar. Beside the outer door are two huge copper drums dedicated to the goddess, formerly beaten daily for her worship.

In the northeast corner of the outer yard a small wooden door leads to an overgrown and nearly forgotten courtyard with the **bathing pool** of Malla kings. Once it was surrounded by elegant buildings. Statues filled the empty niches, and oil lamps illuminated the gilded metalwork. The surrounding buildings have crumbled and the fine statues have disappeared; about all that remains is the beautifully worked spout, bursting with sea serpents and nagas. A golden naga is coiled above the tap, and another rises from a column in the middle of the pool. The water is said to be piped in from the hills 15 km away.

Palace Of Fifty-five Windows

Back out in the square, the famed Palace of Fifty-five Windows stretches off to the east, built in 1697 by Bhupatindra Malla. In one window he enshrined a single pane of glass brought from

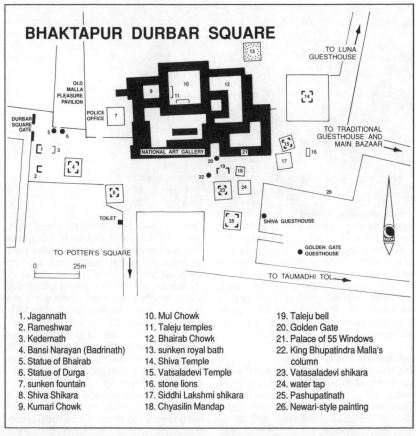

BHAKTAPUR DURBAR SQUARE

1. Jagannath
2. Rameshwar
3. Kedernath
4. Bansi Narayan (Badrinath)
5. Statue of Bhairab
6. Statue of Durga
7. sunken fountain
8. Shiva Shikara
9. Kumari Chowk
10. Mul Chowk
11. Taleju temples
12. Bhairab Chowk
13. sunken royal bath
14. Shiva Temple
15. Vatsaladevi Temple
16. stone lions
17. Siddhi Lakshmi shikara
18. Chyasilin Mandap
19. Taleju bell
20. Golden Gate
21. Palace of 55 Windows
22. King Bhupatindra Malla's column
23. Vatsaladevi shikara
24. water tap
25. Pashupatinath
26. Newari-style painting

© MOON PUBLICATIONS, INC.

India, "an object of wonder for the people." The wing was completely rebuilt after the 1934 earthquake, and only 53 windows remain today. Nothing is left of the extensive palace or the great square to the east except a vast open plaza marked by a few sad reminders—a pair of stone lions standing guard over nothing, and the massive platform of a once-great Shiva temple, now crowned by a dumpy white plaster shrine.

One recent success story in the restoration of Bhaktapur Durbar Square is the octagonal pavilion in front of the palace, rebuilt by local craftsmen with support from Germany. **Chyasilin Mandap** or "Eight-Sided Pagoda" was first raised in the mid-18th century; from it, nobles may have watched festivals and rituals in the

square. Its collapse left a gaping hole in the harmony of the square, and its resurrection, completed in 1990, adds an important piece to the jigsaw puzzle. Restoring it was no easy feat. The original carved columns had to be retrieved from resthouses where they'd been installed. Everything else, including the entire upper story, was reconstructed from scratch, using a set of old etchings as guidelines. Some carvings are a startling match of old and new, but if close up the building jars (the steel reinforcements used to make it earthquake-proof were deliberately left exposed), from a distance it adds a vital element to the square. The top floor is a great people-watching viewpoint, just as it was for 18th-century nobles.

Pashupati Mandir

Behind is the imposing, heavy-roofed pagoda known as the Pashupati Mandir. It was built by King Yaksha Malla in the 15th century as a convenient substitute for the original Pashupatinath he was in the habit of visiting daily—a 12-km roundtrip. The struts depict forms of Shiva and characters from the *Ramayana,* with erotic scenes below. Inside is a large black stone linga carved with four faces of Shiva, a replica of the sacred linga of Pashupati.

Behind here a narrow street funnels tourists down to the next great square, Taumadhi. Predictably, it's crammed solid with souvenir shops. A more interesting detour would be to head down the narrow street behind the prominently labeled "Tourist Toilet" on the south side of the square. Each house has a carved stone lotus set in the ground in front of its entrance, a symbol of the god Kumar, worshipped every morning with puja. Five minutes down the lane brings you to Potters' Square.

POTTERS' SQUARE

This is the neighborhood of the potter caste, called Talako or simply "Potters' Square," after the hundreds of vessels of all shapes and sizes set out to dry in the sun. Entire families work in the open, producing tiny oil lamps for puja, disposable clay teacups and yoghurt bowls, flowerpots, water jugs, plus more whimsical items for tourists—small animals, candlesticks, ashtrays and the like. Men and boys sit amid a sea of pots feverishly spinning more, sculpting the cones of wet black clay into vessels of all sizes. In the last few years many have abandoned their heavy wooden wheels for old truck tires fitted with a crossbar, lighter and easier to spin. The products are set out to dry, and other family members thump the bottoms of vessels flat with blunt sticks, polish dried pots with a smooth stone, etch them with designs and dip them in liquid clay to give a red finish to the finished product. The final step is firing, in ingenious temporary kilns of heaped straw which slowly burn down into huge heaps of ashes.

The square has its own assortment of deities, including a little 17th-century temple to **Ganesh** donated by a long-ago potter, its small main image brightly polished from constant worship. Five minutes to the south on the riverbank is an interesting temple to **Rama** and **Sita** set in a compound. Returning, take the same road all the way back up to join a main lane which soon enters Taumadhi.

TAUMADHI TOL

This second great square is more important than Durbar Square to local people, more closely woven into daily life and festivals. It marks the center of the "new" town, the western portion of Bhaktapur which has developed since the 12th century.

Bhairab's chariot after smashing into a building during Bisket Jatra, Bhaktapur

KERRY MORAN

Nyatapola Mandir

Taumadhi is dominated by the five-roofed Nyatapola temple, at 30 meters the tallest temple in Nepal, so perfectly balanced it has survived numerous quakes since its construction in 1702. Set atop a stepped five-story plinth mirroring its receding roofs, it's decorated with beautiful carvings berfeath layers of bright paint. The 108 struts depict Durga in her different forms, as well as other gods. The main stairway is guarded by protective images: first the beefy wrestlers Jai and Patta Malla, said to possess the strength of ten men; then pairs of elephants, lions, griffons, and minor goddesses, each ten times stronger than the preceding pair. These guardians protect a hidden tantric goddess—which one is open to dispute, as the temple is closed to all but its high priests, who worship there at night. Some call her Siddhi Lakshmi, others Bhairabi or Durga, while some say there is no image at all inside, only the goddess in spirit form.

Kasi Biswanath

This powerful goddess has an intimate relationship with the ferocious Bhairab inhabiting the large temple to the east. The Kasi Biswanath is a finely proportioned rectangular pagoda, with three roofs (the topmost one gilded), elaborately carved struts, and a rich gilt-inlaid facade. Bhupatindra Malla had this deity brought from Benares and installed for the protection of the kingdom. The Bhairab proved so troublesome that priests suggested placing the tantric goddess of the Nyatapola nearby to counterbalance him—and indeed the unruly deity was said to calm down after the secret goddess arrived on the scene.

The Bhairab mask inside is worshipped unseen; offerings are shoved through a small niche cut in the temple facade. Every spring his gilded mask is set in a massive chariot and pulled about town in a rowdy, joyous procession called Bisket Jatra. The front facade of the temple is actually the rear wall: the proper entrance is behind, via a small shrine to **Betal**, Bhairab's companion and *vahana* or vehicle. This minor and malignant godling accompanies Bhairab on his yearly jaunt, mounted on the prow of the great chariot. Betal is worshipped for a brief half-hour period during the festival, and afterwards is strapped face-down to the rafters of his temple for the rest of the year, for he's said to be a troublesome and pesky spirit.

Cafe Nyatapola

The Cafe Nyatapola in the middle of the square was renovated from a crumbling old pagoda in 1978 by the Bhaktapur Development Project. Food is rather expensive and the menu's limited, but the chance to eat French fries in a pagoda is too good to pass up, and the views from the upper story are fascinating. Periodically a tour group sweeps in with video cameras whirring, surrounded by vendors thrusting forth necklaces, peacock feather fans, and souvenirs. Bhaktapur's salespeople are the most tenacious of all the three cities, but they concentrate on tour groups—one good reason to visit the town on your own.

Til Madhava Narayan Mandir

The western side of the square is flanked by lovely old houses, their ground floors occupied by souvenir shops. A small doorway in the middle of the square's south side leads to the Til Madhava Narayan Mandir, a very important Vishnu temple founded in 1080. The metal torana depicts a dancing Shiva atop his bull, but inside the temple is enshrined a very ancient and worn standing Vishnu, adorned with a silver necklace. The temple's name refers to the story that this image was discovered buried in a merchant's heap of sesame seeds *(til)*, which despite brisk sales miraculously remained undiminished. Once a year the god is massaged with ghee and worshipped with offerings of sesame sweets in memory of this event. On certain auspicious dates the quiet courtyard is the center of great pageantry, as groups of local girls dressed in dazzling finery undergo the *ihi* ceremony wedding them to the god Narayan.

THE MAIN BAZAAR

Take the broad road winding east through the city's main bazaar, following the path of the old trade route. The 15-minute walk to the next main square showcases Bhaktapur's thriving local economy, with shops selling daily necessities, tea, and sweets, interspersed with temples and water taps. About halfway down on the right is the small **Golmadhi Ganesh Mandir** with struts depicting Bhairab and Ganesh. It's a typical example of Bhaktapur's many tiny Ganesh shrines, one in each tol, worshipped daily for good fortune.

This brick-paved winding street and the interesting side lanes and courtyards branching off it reveal the heart of Bhaktapur. Life spills out onto the street in a public display, as women pound laundry, children play, and old men share a hookah in a shop doorway, squatting in the sunlight for a morning chat. The only traffic is an occasional tractor, and deities still reside in the middle of the road in the form of sacred rocks embedded in the ground and worshipped daily. Even a short walk gives the sense of Bhaktapur's continued vitality. Society here is still strongly integrated, resisting the dislocative forces of change that are ripping apart Kathmandu.

TACHAPAL TOL

The street debouches into Tachapal Square, the old, old, original center of town, dating back perhaps to the 8th century when Bhaktapur was no more than a village. Tachapal is still the heart of "upper" or eastern Bhaktapur (as opposed to "lower" Bhaktapur centered around Taumadhi), and its day begins at dawn as farmers come to sell fresh vegetables and milk straight from the water buffalo. The square is lined with ornate Hindu *matha,* nine in all, the densest concentration of these Hindu monasteries anywhere in the Valley. These houses once sheltered communities of male ascetics gathered around a religious leader. Like the Buddhist bahal, the matha have long since been taken over by secular families and turned into private dwellings. Many of Tachapal's old matha now house craft shops, like the splendid **Tajmath** on the right, with a five-paneled window edged with delicate carvings and woodcarvers working in its courtyard.

Dattatreya Mandir
These matha and the **Bhimsen Mandir** on the square's western end once fed and housed pilgrims and wandering Hindu saddhus. They came to worship at the Dattatreya temple at the eastern side of the square. This ancient building began itself as a resthouse for pilgrims and yogis. In the 14th century it was expanded into a full-fledged temple. Saddhus occasionally stay in the temple's screened gallery, and on the day after the great festival of Shivaratri hundreds come here to worship.

Dattatreya is a three-headed combination of Brahma, Vishnu, and Shiva, with Vishnu predominating in the trinity; thus his symbols the conch, the wheel, and the Garuda, mounted on stone pillars in front. The painted doll-like image peering out of an upper window is not Dattatreya but Indra, hoisted up decades ago by tipsy revelers during Indra Jatra. Guarding the temple's door are images of the two legendary strongmen, Jai and Patta Malla, who also guard the Nyatapola. Malla rulers adopted them as protectors because of their names, but actually they were historical figures, Indian warriors who died defending a Rajput fort. Their images still stand guard at Rajasthani palaces.

Pujari Math
Just behind the temple on the right is the famed Pujari Math, its intricate woodwork restored with German assistance as a wedding present to Crown Prince Birendra in the early '70s. Appropriately, it now houses the National Art Gallery's **Woodcarving Museum,** a small but fine collection of freestanding statues and old temple struts. In one room 400-year-old murals are being painstakingly restored, and the uncovered portions glow in warm jewel-like colors. Open 1000-1600 daily except Tues., admission Rs5, Rs10 additional for a camera.

The building itself, especially the interior courtyard, is decorated with fantastic carvings of cavorting wild boars, monkeys and sea serpents. The famous **Peacock Window** is down a small alley on the northern side. While its design is undeniably brilliant, it's been overrated, and too many copies rob one of the surprise of seeing it unexpectedly. There's a **Brass and Bronze Museum** (hours same as the Woodcarving Museum) housed in another old matha across the street, but its collection of ritual and household vessels can be skipped unless you have a particular interest.

Navadurga *Agam*
Beyond this square the main road leads past more temples and houses and abruptly ends in full countryside, with sweeping views of fields backed by the ridge of Nagarkot, and behind it, the Himalaya. This neighborhood turns to pottery-making in full force during the dry winter months. Just before the paved crossroads, turn left up a narrow street and head uphill. Almost at

the top is the long rectangular building dedicated to the famed Navadurga, the fierce Nine Durgas, depicted on the shrine's many carved torana. The painted masks used in the goddesses' dances (see p. 74) are kept on the first floor and worshipped with blood sacrifices. From here you can make a short loop back to Tachapal or continue north of the main road to explore an interesting section of back streets.

AROUND BHAKTAPUR

Bhaktapur offers many possibilities besides the city itself, best explored in a visit of several days. Stroll in the surrounding fields, where peasants may laughingly try to recruit you to help with planting or harvesting. Go down to the highway past the trolley bus stop to photograph the unbelievable view of the city backed by gigantic peaks. On the way back explore the ghats and sacred shrines lining the banks of the Hanumante River. Many are crumbling, and the river is filthy, a wallow for bristly haired black pigs.

Further afield, the ancient temple of **Changu Narayan** is an easy two-hour walk north, while the mountaintop viewpoint of **Nagarkot** is a longer hike (very slow buses run daily from Bhaktapur). The main road past the Dattatreya temple continues through countryside and villages to the Newari village of **Nala** and from there to **Banepa** on the Chinese highway—a wonderful mountain bike ride or a longish hike.

Kamal Binayak
Northeast of town on the Nagarkot road, just beyond the city, is Kamal Binayak, a large pond which is as close as the city gets to a park. This is a favorite site for picnics and feasts as well as buffalo baths and laundry. There's a small **Ganesh shrine** in the northeast corner.

Surjya Binayak
One of the four most sacred Ganesh temples in the Valley, this "Sun Ganesh" is a 20-minute walk up the paved road south of the last trolley bus stop. People come here to pray for a happy marriage, strong and clever children, success in business, and just about anything involving luck. The temple is set amid a cluster of shops and houses; just below are good views of Bhaktapur, ringed by fields. A steep flight of steps leads to

the shrine, set in a shady forest on the eastern side of a wooded hill. Ganesh dwells beneath a golden torana and a big white shikara. Mounted on a pillar in front is a large and very realistic rendition of his vehicle, the rat. At the top of the hill there's a shrine to Ganesh's mother and good mountain views. The peaceful surrounding forest is a popular picnic ground for Nepali families. You'll see the most worshippers on Tuesdays, many bringing Ganesh's favorite offerings: radishes, *ladoo* (a sweetmeat), and sesame seed balls.

Thimi And Vicinity
This old Newari village is three km west of Bhaktapur, set in the exact center of the Valley. Thimi is surprisingly large—in fact it's the fourth largest town in the Valley—but its form is long and narrow, strung out along a raised plateau, a typically crowded Newari village surrounded by a sea of fields.

A paved and little traveled back road links Thimi and Bhaktapur to the main highway, a good alternative route for bikers endangered

a Thimi family

by thundering trucks. Intersecting with this is the town's main road, which runs north from the highway bus stop. It leads up a very steep hill and through the heart of town, linking a series of temple-studded squares.

The first is the town's main shrine, a pagoda with three gilded roofs dedicated to **Balkumari,** "Child Kumari." This is the most important of the Valley's many shrines dedicated to this tantric mother-goddess, whose mount, a gilded peacock, perches atop a pillar in front of the temple. She's worshipped by farmers for rain, by women hoping for children, and by parents for the cure of ill offspring. A peculiar offering sacred only to her is the coconut, a fertility symbol. Dozens are nailed up on the temple facade. Every April for Nepali New Year, the goddess is paraded about in a palanquin in Thimi's major festival.

In the next square is a temple to the bodhisattva **Karunamaya** (Avalokitesvara), ringed by paintings of his 108 manifestations. The walk continues thus, alternating Buddhist and Hindu shrines strung along the constant thread of Newari village life. The road eventually joins the paved backroad to Bhaktapur, then continues on to the village of **Bode** and the riverside shrine and picnic site of **Nilvarahi.** Few travelers visit here; the same goes for the village of **Nagdesh,** "Country of the Nagas," which lies slightly northeast of Thimi.

Thimi's famous pottery and papier-mâché masks are sold in shops clustered on the eastern side of town. It seems Bhaktapur has taken the lead in producing portable pottery for tourists, but Thimi's intricately painted masks are still good buys.

Bode

This small village is a 20-minute walk north of Thimi and centers around a famous temple to the tantric goddess Mahalakshmi. On Nepali New Year's a bizarre tongue-boring festival is held here. A village man prepared by days of purification and fasting has a thin metal spike thrust through his tongue by the temple's priest. The penitent parades around town bearing a bamboo rack of lit oil lamps. Returning to the temple, the needle is removed and the wound packed with mud scraped from the temple floor. If no bleeding occurs, it's a sign that he's earned great religious merit with this offering of his body.

PRACTICALITIES

Accommodations

It's a good idea to overnight in Bhaktapur if you wish to capture the flavor of the city, or simply enjoy the Nepalese countryside without embarking on a trek. It's a quiet getaway, a good contrast to urban Kathmandu. So far, accommodations are very basic and limited to a few inexpensive tourist lodges. **Golden Gate Guesthouse** off Durbar Square is perhaps the best, with a friendly staff and a good restaurant serving momo; Rs50 s, Rs80 d. They have one beautifully decorated upstairs suite with extensive views, which sleeps two for Rs350. Next door is **Shiva Guesthouse,** with rooms for Rs100 and meagre servings of daal bhaat. **Traditional Guesthouse,** run by Ganesh Vajracharya, is in Sakotha, slightly east of Durbar Square; Rs70-90 for rooms, with a rooftop terrace with views and a restaurant for guests only. **Luna Guesthouse,** the oldest and cheapest of the lot (no hot water) is a few minutes north of Durbar Square.

Food

Food is another one of Bhaktapur's pitfalls, more expensive and less varied than Kathmandu's. Each guesthouse has its own restaurant, the best probably being the Golden Gate's. The **Marco Polo** on the corner of Taumadhi Square is also good. The **Nyatapola Cafe** doesn't serve much more than light meals, and closes early. There are plenty of tea and sweet shops in the bazaar for a sugar-ridden breakfast. Bring munchies, bread, and cheese if you plan on staying a few days, as Western-style picnic fare is not available.

Shopping

Best buys in Bhaktapur include **handwoven cloth,** still made in many households but hard to find in the bazaar. A shop in Tachupal Square near the Dattatreya temple has a reasonably priced selection, including the red-banded black cloth *(haka patasi)* worn by Jyapu women.

Bhaktapur is also a good place to look for **brass** household goods: polished plates, vessels, hanging oil lamps, *sukunda,* and embossed puja baskets. Several shops specializing in old and new brass are at the beginning of the

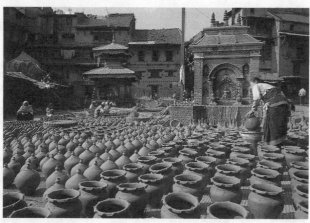

Potters' Square

KERRY MORAN

bazaar just outside of Taumadhi Square. The first one on the right, **Chandra Metals,** often has interesting pieces.

There is plenty of simple **pottery** sold around Potter's Square; wall planters, flowerpots, ashtrays, little animal figurines. Bargain hard. Visit nearby Thimi for **papier-mâché masks** of deities and wickedly funny salt-and-pepper shakers of the king and queen. Kanchha Chitrakar's shop, the last one on the right as you're heading to Bhaktapur, is particularly good.

Bhaktapur has become quite a souvenir capital, overflowing with the same items you'll find in Kathmandu—brass masks, tacky jewelry, wooden puppets, and the like. There are a few reasonable **thangka** shops around Durbar Square. Gyankar Vajracharya's shop in the easternmost section specializes in Newari-style animal paintings, different from the usual run-of-the-mill. Bhaktapur has some of the best **woodcarvings** in the Valley, especially the miniature windows and big painted rocking horses, elephants, and lions. Check the shop immediately before the entrance to Durbar Square, **Bhaktapur Handicrafts** in Taj Math (Tachupal Square), and the shop across from the Peacock Window.

Getting There

The city lies 14 km down the Chinese-built highway to Tibet, about a one-hour bike ride from Thamel. The road cuts through rich farmland and is lined by poplar trees. It's a recommended cycle for the energetic, especially at planting or harvest times when the fields are full of people and lovely in green or gold. There are an increasing number of factories along the road, and especially in winter you'll see a lot of brickmaking—some farmers lease their land for a period to harvest this profitable crop.

Crowded, slow public **buses** leave from Bagh Bazaar and stop at Nhu Pokhari, a five-minute walk from Durbar Square. A better choice is the electric **trolley bus** from Tripureshwar, less crowded and relatively efficient. It drops you south of town below Ram Ghat. From there it's an interesting 15-minute walk across the river, past the Rama-Sita temple and through Potter's Square into Taumadhi.

Coming by cycle, the Bhaktapur turnoff is just after the Hanumante Bridge. At the crossroads, take the right-hand fork up a pine-forested hill, passing army barracks where you just might hear a Gurkha soldier practicing the bagpipes. Near the big open field of the Tundikhel is **Siddhi Pokhari,** a huge walled-in pond dug in the 16th century, now filthy and neglected. A legend that a giant serpent dwells in its depths explains local people's reluctance to clean it. Don't confuse this with the equally large pond of **Nhu Pokhari** ahead, where the minibuses stop.

At Siddhi Pokhari the road forks. If you're in a hurry the left-hand side will bring you straight to Durbar Square, but the right-hand lane, only slightly longer, leads through interesting old neighborhoods, past Potter's Square, to Tamaudhi Tol.

EXPLORING THE VALLEY
INTRODUCTION

Beyond the bounds of the three old kingdoms lies an inexhaustible storehouse of fascinating destinations, limited only by your time, energy and imagination. The Valley's small size and relative accessibility makes it ideal for explorers. A day-trip is far simpler to arrange than a trek, yet it can be equally satisfying. You can combine temples, forests, villages, fields and mountain views all in one day, and be back in your hotel by evening. It's surprising what many people find most eye-opening: not the classic architecture or picturesque landscape, but the opportunity to see a traditional way of life that has vanished from the West, and is in the process of disappearing around the world.

Every shrine and temple in the Valley has its own special days when people flock to it for worship. A bit of planning can pay off in this respect. Time your exploration right and you can catch temple fairs, elaborate festivals, or full-moon pujas. Above all, don't hesitate to get off roads and into fields and villages, striking out more or less at random—you can't go wrong. In many ways these are best part of the Valley: crops and colors change with each season, and the rhythms of harvest and planting still control the pace of life.

The countryside also displays the ethnic diversity so typical of Nepal. Newari villages are clustered in the central and south Valley, with settlements of Hill people (mainly Brahman-Chhetri and Tamang) scattered about the fringes. It's easy to identify the different types of villages: Hill people generally live in thatched-roof, mud-walled houses painted two-tone ochre and white. Their homes are separated by fields and gardens, in contrast to the densely packed Newari farming villages, with their tall brick buildings set in rows.

PRACTICALITIES

Getting around the outer reaches of the Valley is best accomplished on a bicycle (mountain or regular) or a taxi hired for the day. With a little searching, day hikers can find a driver willing to drop them off at their starting point and meet them at their destination. Drivers generally enjoy the break from routine (as long as they make as much as they'd earn in a day of city driving), and you're spared the hassle of looking for transportation at the end of the day.

What to Bring
Water is scarce along Valley ridgetops, so bring plenty, plus sunscreen, sunhat, and possibly a little food. It's nice but not absolutely necessary to have a good map (the Schneider map of the Valley is a must for serious walkers), and a few direction-finding phrases in Nepali. Don't worry about getting lost for long in the Valley. There are people everywhere you look, and many will go out of their way to guide you to the major local attraction—even if it's *not* your destination.

Mountain Views
Many of the mountains ringing the Valley offer superb views of the Himalaya. Choosing the "best" among them depends more on the type of trip you'd like than the views, which don't vary that much. It's hard to be disappointed with Nagarkot, Phulchowki, or Dhulikhel on a clear day. Perspective differs slightly, but all are more or less spectacular.

Some of these sites can be driven to, while others require a day walk, no more than four hours. All can be combined with visits to nearby temples and villages. For walkers they provide a perfect warmup for a trek, while for non-trekkers they encapsulate the experience in a single day, with the comforts of Kathmandu close by. Shivapuri, Nagarjun, and Phulchowki are among the best hikes because of their comparatively lush forests.

Timing is crucial for views. Sunrise and sunset are the most stunning, as the mountains reflect the golden light. Even on foggy winter mornings you soon rise above the mist to marvel at the sight of mountains ringing the cloud-covered bowl of the Valley. Midday, even if clear, is often hazy. Wait for a windy day to magically blow away the dust, leaving hillsides 20 km distant distinctly visible.

Overnighting or camping at a viewpoint makes it easy to catch sunset and sunrise, and offers the chance of a moonlight Himalayan panorama or a spectacular star show on moonless nights. Nagarkot and Dhulikhel are the best-known resort areas; there are other resorts at Kakani and in the south Valley on Champa Devi; for still more adventure, pitch a tent atop a remote summit.

Most visitors to Nepal desperately want to see Everest, but the tiny nub glimpsed from Nagarkot and other viewpoints is not a very satisfying experience. RNAC's daily mountain flight brings you as close to the mountains as you can get without trekking—closer, in a way, since the plane flies at eye level along a stretch of the range and back. See p. 150 for details.

Another luxurious way to view the mountains is by driving out to Nagarkot or Dhulikhel for a meal in a resort restaurant (the food is better at Dhulikhel). Sunset views of the Himalaya, followed by fine cuisine (even a bottle of wine if you're prepared to splurge) is an unbeatable combination. Finally, practically the entire Valley south of the Ring Road offers surprisingly good Himalayan views without having to climb a bit.

> *The identification of very distant peaks is a harmless and fascinating amusement so long as the results are not taken seriously.*
>
> —H.W. Tilman,
> *Nepal Himalaya*

Mini-treks

The Valley's countless overnight hikes and mini-treks are largely ignored in favor of more remote and exotic regions, but they are definitely worth exploring. One interesting possibility would be to trace the old pilgrimage routes linking shrines. The 44-mile circuit of the four main Narayan temples is traditionally made in one day, but you could take several. It would be possible to do this entirely on your own, finding lodging in people's homes, although it would be necessary to speak Nepali and/or have a guide. Or you could arrange a fully equipped mini-trek through a local agency.

A partial or complete circuit along the Valley rim is a favorite for trekkers short on time; it can take anywhere from two to ten days and blends fields, forests, occasional mountain views, and small villages. Most popular is the two- to three-day walk from Nagarkot to Shivapuri via Sundarijaal. You can bunk in local teahouses, or trek through a local company, which will provide tents and food, guide and perhaps porters.

NORTH OF KATHMANDU

ICHANGU NARAYAN

One of the quartet of sacred Vishnu shrines in the Valley, this "Vishnu of the East" is set in a small pagoda hidden in the hills behind Swayambhunath. Follow the dirt road across the Ring Road from the Swayambhu bus stop, soon passing a limestone quarry. Beyond the scar of the quarry the road crests and turns into a trail, leading through beautiful scattered villages dotted with Narayan shrines. This is an old pilgrimage route: Ichangu was supposedly founded around the 5th century, though the present shrine and image are much more recent, and are rather unimpressive compared to its cousin Changu Narayan. Still, the trip is a pleasant, easy one-hour walk, relatively close to Kathmandu.

Another option would be to take the right fork at the village, which in a little over an hour leads uphill to the **Rani Ban Forest Preserve.** From here you can continue up to the summit of Nagarjun. Another trail, less strenuous, links Ichangu with Balaju, about an hour's walk away.

BALAJU

Once a pleasure garden for Malla queens, Balaju has been opened to the public as a combination pilgrimage site/picnic ground. The former small village of Balaju has been absorbed into Kathmandu's urban sprawl, and the willow-lined avenue leading here has become a dusty road lined with small industrial enterprises and wicker furniture factories. Balaju Industrial Estate, the country's largest, is immediately be-

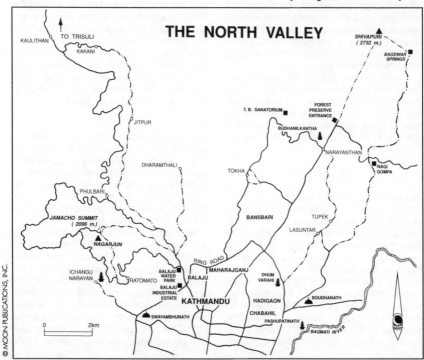

THE NORTH VALLEY

KAULITHAN — TO TRISULI — KAKANI — SHIVAPURI (2732 m.) — BAGDWAR SPRINGS — JITPUR — T. B. SANATORIUM — FOREST PRESERVE ENTRANCE — BUDHANILKANTHA — NARAYANTHAN — DHARAMTHALI — TOKHA — NAGI GOMPA — PHULBARI — JAMACHO SUMMIT (2096 m.) — BANSBARI — TUPEK — LASUNTAR — NAGARJUN — RING ROAD — MAHARAJGANJ — DHUM VARAHI — BOUDHANATH — ICHANGU NARAYAN — RATOMATO — BALAJU WATER PARK — BALAJU — BALAJU INDUSTRIAL ESTATE — KATHMANDU — HADIGAON — CHABAHIL — SWAYAMBHUNATH — PASHUPATINATH — BAGMATI RIVER

0 — 2km

© MOON PUBLICATIONS, INC.

fore the park, which is about three km north-west of Thamel.

Balaju's most famous attraction is its **Baais Dhara,** 22 stone spouts carved in the form of makara. The taps are used for daily bathing and laundry as well for ritual bathing by pilgrims who flock here for certain festivals. The largest crowds congregate for Balaju Jatra, usually the full moon in April, when it's believed the water magically flows from the Trisuli River.

The dhara are set in a well-maintained park with bamboo, flowers, trees, and fountains. There is also an Olympic-sized swimming pool on the grounds, perennially crowded. The main focus of worship is a Sleeping Vishnu set in a pond, a smaller replica of the image of Bud-hanilkantha. This is **Bala Nilkantha,** "Young Blue Throat," as opposed to Budha Nilkantha, "Old Blue Throat." For a long time it was thought to be a 17th-century reproduction of the famed Budhanilkantha sculpture; historians have now determined it's a contemporary, installed in the 7th century. There's also a 14th-century image of the smallpox goddess Sitala enshrined in a small pagoda, and various Hindu and Buddhist images. Most interesting is a 16th-century sculp-ture of Harihara, a rare composite of Vishnu and Shiva, holding the former's wheel and conch shell and the latter's trident.

For city dwellers, Balaju is the nearest place for picnics, and on Saturdays the grounds are crowded with families, friends, and merry-mak-ers. Go here to see Nepalis at play: feasting, playing cards, sleeping in the sun, bathing at the taps, strolling about admiring the flowers.

NAGARJUN

Not to be confused with Nagarkot, this hump-backed mountain is northwest of Swayambhu, closer to Kathmandu than any other of the Val-ley's surrounding peaks. The two-hour hike up to the grassy, open summit is fairly easy, following a wide ridge trail. There's also a steep, wind-ing motor road, unpaved.

The peak is named after the Indian Buddhist sage Nagarjuna, who is said to have meditated, taught, and died in a cave on the slopes of the mountain. His image is enshrined in a limestone cave high on the eastern side. Supposedly the Buddha entrusted his most profound esoteric teachings to the naga, instructing the serpents to guard them until mankind would be ready to re-ceive them. Centuries later the naga transmitted these teachings to Nagarjuna, in the form of 16 massive volumes of scriptures written in golden ink on paper of lapis lazuli. These texts, encap-sulating the *Prajnaparamita* or "Perfection of Wisdom," are enshrined today in Tham Bahal in Thamel. From them, Nagarjuna is said to have developed and spread the Mahayana doctrine of Buddhism.

The Newars call the mountaintop Jamacho, after the wooded ridges which cascade down its flanks like the pleated folds of the *jamma* (long skirt) worn by ritual dancers. The mountain is in-cluded in the **Rani Ban** or Queen's Forest, an old hunting preserve of Jung Bahadur's which is now administered by the government as a pro-tected forest. Its grounds shelter dense stands of rhododendron, bamboo, oak, and pine, plus pheasants, deer, wild boar, and a few small leopards.

The park's entrance is about a 30-minute bike ride from Thamel. Continue north on the Trisuli Road past the Balaju gardens to the en-trance gate on the left at Phulbhari, about nine km from the city. Here you can leave your bike and pay a small admission fee (25 paisa, or Rs10 if you happen to be riding an elephant). If you're camping in the preserve, register here and obtain a permit for a small fee, but remem-ber, there's no water on the summit.

The Trail

The trail begins just past the gate on the right, starting off steeply but leveling out on a ridgeline after 30 minutes. From here it's a relatively easy walk along the forested ridge up to the summit (2,096 meters), which is topped by a white stupa and a view tower strung with colorful Tibetan prayer flags. There are several slightly higher summits to the west but views are no better.

Nagarjun is a popular Buddhist pilgrimage spot. Some believe the Buddha once preached here; others say this is the summit from where the bodhisattva tossed the lotus seed that was to blossom into Swayambhunath. The summit is lit-tered with tiny colored slips of paper printed with Tibetan prayers. Tossed from the view tower, they flutter slowly down to earth, a pretty sight. There's a cooking shelter nearby and small picnic shelters on subsidiary hillocks. Many

view tower strung with prayer flags, Nagarjun

families combine worship with a picnic and spend all day up here, cooking an elaborate feast and whiling hours away with card games and tea.

Mountain views stretch from Annapurna to Sikkim on a clear day, though they are somewhat obscured by Shivapuri to the east. To the left is the ice pyramid of Manaslu, and beside it Peak 29 and Himalchuli. Directly north is Ganesh Himal, vaguely resembling an elephant's head. To the east are Langtang Lirung, Dorje Lhakpa, and the serrated peaks of the Jugal Himal. Nagarjun offers an excellent panorama of the Kathmandu Valley, especially Kathmandu.

Alternate Descents

The 37-km motor road leading up the mountain loops around the backside to exit at another gate further north, if you happened to drive up. Don't make the mistake of walking back down the road to the gate; with its many switchbacks it takes three times as long as the trail. An al-

ternative trail, difficult to find, starts southeast of the observation tower, descending south down a spur running to Balaju. About 45 minutes from the summit is a big limestone cave with an image of **Nagarjun** and **Buddha Akshobhya.** Further down, the trail joins the road which you can follow for three km to the gate, or else exit the preserve and cut across fields to Swayambhunath or Balaju.

KAKANI

Perched on the Valley rim about 29 km northwest of Kathmandu on the Trisuli Road, Kakani offers views of Langtang, Hiuchuli, the Annapurnas, and a superb closeup of Ganesh Himal. You can catch the Trisuli bus to here, mountain-bike the road, or look for group taxis leaving in late afternoon from the Trisuli bus stop at Sorha Khuttepati. The well-maintained road passes Balaju and Nagarjun, heading uphill to the small settlement of **Kaulithan,** or "Cauliflower Place." Leave the bus here and walk four km uphill to the small resort/village of Kakani (2,073 meters). The government-run **Taragaon Resort** here offers rooms and meals for overnighters who want to catch morning views. A trail from here leads to Balaju, an easy four-hour descent through oak and rhodie forests with good Valley views. Part of the way is on dirt roads. Stay near the ridgetop and avoid the trails descending to the highway. The trail passes through the villages of **Jitpur** and **Dharamthali,** where you can get directions and tea.

BUDHANILKANTHA

Hinduism's great creation myth centers around Vishnu in the form of Jalasayana Narayana, "Narayana Lying-on-the-Waters." For aeons the god slumbers in the primordial ocean, floating on the endless coils of the serpent Ananta. Finally, the creative force issues from his navel in the form of Brahma, bringing forth the universe and all its beings. A trio of unknown Licchavi-era sculptors masterfully interpreted this timeless theme in three huge statues of the "Sleeping Vishnu," as Jalasayana Narayana is commonly called. One is set in the Balaju Gardens; another is hidden in the old gardens of the Hanuman Dhoka palace of Kathmandu; the third, reputedly the original, lies in Budhanilkantha, a temple set in the small village of **Narayanthan,** nine km north of Kathmandu.

Consecrated in 641, the Budhanilkantha image is the largest (six meters long), most important, and the finest of the trio. Carved from a single block of black stone of a type not found in the Valley, the statue was most likely dragged here from afar by forced labor. Despite its massive bulk it seems to float in the placid waters. Vishnu slumbers with a half-smile, relaxing in the coils of the nine-headed serpent, whose hoods form a crown. The temple's founders chose one of the most beautiful sites in the Valley for this masterpiece, but much of its harmony was recently destroyed when a monstrous concrete fence was raised around the pool.

A small pier leads out to the sculpture, which is ministered to by Brahman priests, the only ones allowed to walk upon Vishnu's body. Devotees come all day long, bringing offerings which they hand over to the priests to deliver. Morning and evening there's an elaborate daily worship routine, as priests fan, bathe, annoint, and adorn the deity as carefully as if it were a human being. If you can figure out when they fall, the eleventh days *(ekadasi)* of both the light and dark fortnight are a good time to visit, as these dates are sacred to Vishnu. Three times a year a big temple mela held at Budhanilkantha fills the village with pilgrims and celebrators.

Buddhists come as well, for they've adopted the image as a form of Buddha. The temple's name, however, has nothing to do with Buddha; "Budha" (or "Burha"—the Nepali letter is exactly in between "r" and "d") means "Old," and "Nilkantha" is "Blue Throat." The name refers to the legend of Shiva, who drank down the poison produced from the Churning of the Ocean and had his throat burned blue as a result. What this has to do with a Vishnu temple is unclear, but the waters of the tank are believed to be mystically connected with the Himalayan pilgrimage lake of Gosainkund, where Shiva went to cool off.

A prophetic dream of King Pratapa Malla generated the belief that the King of Nepal should never visit this site on threat of death. But the explanation that the king, as an emenation of Vishnu, should not meet his own form doesn't hold water—he's allowed to visit hundreds of other Vishnu shrines, including the Sleeping Vishnu of

Balaju. Pratapa Malla even installed a Sleeping Vishnu in his palace grounds, where it remains today, hidden away in back.

Getting There

To reach Budhanilkantha you can hike, bike, take a taxi to Narayanthan, or catch a tempo or public bus from Jamal (near Rani Pokhari). Early morning is a good time to visit; priests perform daily puja around 0900.

Afterwards you can follow the motor road which branches off to the northwest from the temple. Past the old tuberculosis sanatorium a road curves south to the village of **Tokha,** an ancient Newar town with its own Kumari and good views of the Valley. The paved road north of Narayanthan is another nice walk, leading through rural territory with a real village feeling, plus a few roadside tea shops to nourish you on your "trek."

Finally, you could hike back several hours across fields to the Ring Road or beyond, over uncommonly (some would say mercifully) flat territory. Head southeast to the village of Tupek and cross the Dhobi Khola to **Lasuntar.** From this village follow the southwest footpath, crossing the Dhobi Khola again to reach the Ring Road. On the other side is the shrine of **Dhum Varahi,** with a 6th-century sculpture of Vishnu's incarnation as a boar. From here you can continue on back roads through ancient **Hadigaon** into Kathmandu. Alternatively, if you take the left fork at Lasuntar and veer slightly to the east, you'll soon meet a dirt road leading to Boudhanath, another easy place to catch a taxi.

SHIVAPURI

Shivapuri's views are not as complete as, say, Nagarkot's (Langtang is blocked), but the walk up passes through magnificent, protected virgin oak forests. There are no settlements on the higher reaches of the slope, and the multiple branching trails can make things confusing unless you have a good sense of direction. Take a guide if you have doubts, or consult a detailed trail description.

The Forest Preserve

Walk or taxi north from Budhanilkantha up a well-paved road to the gate of the forest preserve, which is guarded by soldiers. From here you can hike up a steep trail starting behind the white house, the most direct and steepest route to the summit. Or ride or walk up the gravel road (it's about a one-hour walk) to a point just below **Nagi Gompa,** a Buddhist nunnery. The small, peaceful *ani*-gompa is a 10-minute scramble above the road. Behind the main temple the trail continues up. After a steep half-hour climb along a ridge set with flapping prayer flags, the trail levels out through dense forest, passing through several clearings with mountain views—good campsites, but check to make sure there's water nearby.

Here the woods become superb: Shivapuri is protected from woodcutters and clearers and harbors an abundance of birds, langur monkeys, and game—leopards and even a tiger which has been repeatedly sighted near the gompa. About one hour below the summit you pass **Bagdwar,** literally "Bagmati's Door," a quiet, shady hideaway seldom visited by anyone but pilgrims. Look for a flight of stone steps leading down to a shady clearing marked by a few chaitya and fragments of old stone waterspouts and sculptures. Prayer flags and white prayer scarves mark the spot where water pours from a tiger-headed spout, the fabled source of the Valley's sacred river.

Legend says that aeons ago a buddha came to the Valley to worship Swayambhunath. Later he preached on Shivapuri, which was then waterless. To obtain the water needed to initiate his hundreds of disciples, he created a stream with the power of his voice—thus the name Vakmati, "Stream of Mantra"—endowing the water with the power to purify sins. From here the river flows east to Sundarijaal, then drops into the Valley, lined its entire length by sacred bathing sites and shrines.

The Summit
Shivapuri's summit, at 2,732 meters the second highest of the Valley's peaks, is a large flat open area. It's a good campsite if you want to catch early morning views; water is available nearby, but the army has recently set up camp here so you may have company. Descending via Nagi Gompa, you can walk all the way to Boudhanath along the prominent ridge which descends south towards the stupa. Alternatively, from the road below the gompa a steep, small trail drops south, leading to Budhanilkantha and buses or taxis in about 45 minutes.

SOUTH OF KATHMANDU

This prosperous region is thickly dotted with ancient villages, some well over a thousand years old, and full of fine old houses, temples, and sculptures. More than any other area the south Valley is a Newar stronghold; virtually all its villages are dominated by this ethnic group. The road to Dakshinkali is particularly interesting as it passes through Chobhar and Pharping, but the green tranquillity of Godavari and the perfect little villages of **Bungamati** and **Kokana,** only an hour's walk from Patan, are hard to pass up. The south Valley is slightly elevated and many areas offer stunning Himalayan views without climbing at all, or you could day-hike up flower-carpeted **Phulchowki** or, slightly easier, Champadevi.

GODAVARI

Well-paved and not too steep, the 20-km road to the Royal Botanical Gardens at Godavari makes a good cycling trip from Kathmandu. The first sight is the **National Potato Improvement Center** just past the Ring Road. Next is **Harasiddhi** or **Jala,** a compact Newar village with one of the most notorious temples in the Valley. The **Bhavani Trishakti** pagoda honoring Durga is said to have been the site of human sacrifices until this century. It's still served by tantric priests who dress in the old fashion, with long white pleated skirts and long hair in buns. Harasiddhi is also the home of a famous dance troupe which occasionally performs in the village.

Godavari is not a village as much as a collection of oddly diverse sights scattered at the foot of the massive mountain called Phulchowki. Minibuses from Lagankhel stop in front of **St. Xavier's,** a Jesuit-run boys' school partly housed in an old Rana summerhouse. The area receives the highest rainfall in the Valley with a correspondingly high leech count in monsoon.

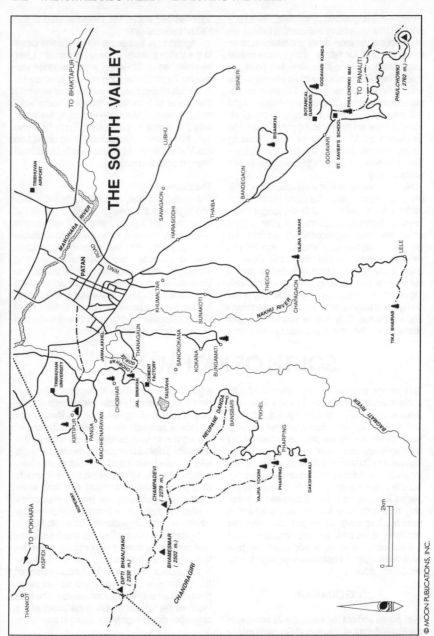

THE SOUTH VALLEY

© MOON PUBLICATIONS, INC.

BOB RACE

Royal Botanical Gardens

Slightly east of the school are the 24-hectare Royal Botanical Gardens, a peaceful green sanctuary far removed from city dust and noise. The well-maintained grounds include collections of orchids, cacti, ferns, succulents, a lotus pond and even a small Japanese garden. Technically picnicking is not allowed here (too much litter), but Nepali families crowd in on Saturdays with hampers of food, so you could certainly risk sneaking a sandwich. On clear days you can catch Himalayan views, including Manaslu and Annapurna to the west.

Godavari Kunda

Down the dirt road past the Botanical Gardens is a government-run fish farm, and before it, the sacred spring of Godavari Kunda. The water emerges from a natural cave and flows through nine carved stone taps into a stepped pool. This spring is the mythical source of the the sacred Godavari River in Madras. This legend began with the tale that an Indian saddhu once lost his ritual gear—rosary, club, bag, gourd, and tiger's skin—while bathing in Madras, and miraculously discovered them in Godavari Kunda. Once every 12 years, when Jupiter is in Leo, a mela held here attracts thousands of Hindu pilgrims.

Phulchowki Mai

Behind St. Xavier's school a controversial marble quarry has gouged a considerable hole in the hillside and is chewing away at the lush forests carpeting Phulchowki's flanks. Across from it is a triple-roofed pagoda dedicated to Phulchowki Mai, the ancient mother goddess of the forest. The deserted, tranquil temple has carved struts depicting the Ashta Matrika; nearby is a 17th-century sunken water tap.

PHULCHOWKI

This massive triple-peaked mountain is, at 2,762 meters, the highest of the summits ringing the Valley; on winter mornings snow dusts the top. Woodcutters and the marble quarry have depleted its once-virgin forest, but the subtropical climate, high rainfall, and varied altitude still supports a rich variety of butterflies, birds, and vegetation. In the spring its slopes are covered with pink, white and red rhododendrons and dozens of kinds of orchids, giving it the name Phulchowki, "Place of Flowers."

Summit Road

The winding, bumpy jeep road leading from St. Xavier's to the summit is barely manageable on a mountain bike or makes a leisurely walk. Taxi drivers may grumble about the rough ride, though it's generally possible to take a car up. The road is long but with lots of switchbacks so it's not very steep. For hikers, a steeper, faster foot trail starting behind St. Xavier's School cuts across the road's many switchbacks and takes about three hours to the top.

Atop the summit is the main shrine to the mother goddess of the forest, Phulchowki Mai, a simple open altar quite unlike her elaborate pagoda below. There's a telecommunications tower here too. Phulchowki offers spectacular views of the Valley, the ranges leading down to the Terai, and a 320-km panorama of the Himalaya from Annapurna to beyond Everest.

KIRTIPUR

Spread along the top of a long ridge in the southwest Valley, the old Newar village of Kirtipur is a natural fortress. Prithvi Narayan Shah and his Gorkha troops targeted the town for conquest early in their 18th-century campaign for the Valley. They besieged Kirtipur three times, finally succeeding in 1766. In revenge for the death of his brother, killed in an earlier siege, the conquerer ordered the noses cut off every Kirtipur male over 12 years, exempting only the players of wind instruments. According to the Chronicles, 865 people were mutilated, and their detached noses weighed 80 pounds. Another record noted the conqueror ordered the town's name be changed to Naskatipur, "City of Cut Noses."

After this bloody episode Kirtipur drifted into decline. Though its ridgetop location affords protection from earthquakes, many of its buildings are crumbling, and there's a general atmosphere of seediness about the town. In the early '70s the Tribhuvan University Campus was built on land belonging to Kirtipur's farmers; many have since turned to day work in the city or crafts like weaving. Both handloomed cloth and Tibetan-style carpets are made in Kirtipur homes.

Perhaps because of its proximity—only 10 km southwest of Kathmandu—Kirtpur is frequently visited by tourists. It's not among the Valley's best Newari villages, though; the streets are filthy and the people could stand to be a little more friendly. A pity, because there are interesting sculptures and shrines everywhere. The hilltop is dumbbell-shaped, with higher summits at either end, each marked by a distinctive shrine. The western portion of town is clustered around a stupa and is Buddhist; the upper town near the hilltop pagoda is Hindu. In between, set in a lower saddle, is the famous temple to Bagh Bhairab.

New Bazaar

The road to Kirtipur leads through the **Tribhuvan University** campus and curves left. It reaches the western side of Kirtipur's hill at the "New Bazaar," a wide shop-lined street. There's a number of good tea shops along here (look for anise-flavored fried bread, *malpuwa,* made from rice flour and served with spicy chickpeas). At the end of the road on the left is a strange intrusion: a **Thai-style temple** with pointed roof. This Theravadin temple complex was built in 1990 with contributions from Thai and Nepalese Buddhists. Gaudy plaster images set in an arcade depict scenes from the Buddha's life: his birth at Lumbini, his enlightenment at Bodhgaya, his first teaching at Sarnath, and his death at Kushinagar.

Chilamchu Stupa

Vehicles can be driven up to the Bagh Bhairab temple but it's more interesting to walk, taking one of several stone staircases set into the hill. At the top is the old town: close-packed houses lining flagstoned streets, and people everywhere. Look for the Chilamchu Stupa, in the middle of the ridge on the western end. It's set on a stepped pedestal and surrounded by four smaller stupas, all built in the early 16th century. A few beautifully decorated facades of old bahal remain in the surrounding square. Near the entrance an old pipal tree has nearly burst apart an ancient shrine, leaving fragments of carved stone entangled in the roots.

Bagh Bhairab

Continue east to the saddle in between the two hillocks. A large fenced-in pond is lined by houses; the one on the western side has a beautifully carved facade. At the north end of the square is

KIRTIPUR

the important and impressive temple of Bagh Bhairab, a large rectangular pagoda with Bhairab in the form of a tiger *(bagh)*. It's said that one day a group of Kirtipur children out tending their sheep fashioned a toy tiger out of clay, and carelessly left it for a moment. Returning, they discovered Bhairab had possessed their toy and devoured their flock.

The temple is imposingly large and well-proportioned, capped with a row of gilt pinnacles and decorated all around with unusual frescoes which are on the verge of completely fading away. Under the third-story eaves are nailed old weapons—daggers and wicked-looking curved swords—said to have been surrendered by the town's defeated Newar defenders. There are also a number of cooking pots and utensils given as offerings.

The compound contains a collection of interesting and ancient stone sculptures set in small shrines. Immediately to the right at the entrance a series of five buxom **mother goddesses** from around the fourth century are embedded in con-

crete, the boar-headed goddess Varahi on the right. The standing **Shiva-Parvati** set in a niche is equally ancient. To the rear a graphic image of a naked **Kirtimata**, "Mother of Kirtipur," lies on her back giving birth to an unidentifiable object. Behind the temple are fine views of fields, a large brick factory, and the temple of Swayambhunath backed by the green hill of Nagarjun. On the left-hand side is a gallery papered with posters of Hindu deities, where village men gather to sing bhajan.

Leave the compound and continue west, past a nearby house decorated with painted stucco plaques, including one of the tiger-god Bhairab. The upper portion of town is better maintained, with many resthouses sheltering images of Ganesh. Kirtipur's old palace was located around here, but there's nothing left to see. Five minutes from Bagh Bhairab is a tall but plain pagoda dedicated to Shiva and Parvati, recently rebuilt and not very notable. The stone elephants guarding the steps are perhaps the most interesting thing: they wear spiked saddles and one crushes the image of a helpless man underfoot. The shrine is set atop a hillock on the edge of town, with good views of Phulchowki to the south, Kirtipur stretching out below to the east, and to the southeast the smaller villages of **Panga** and **Nagaon**.

On Foot To Chobhar

The nearby village of **Chobhar** is set on another ridge to the southeast. To reach it from Kirtipur, return to the Chilamchu stupa and continue along the ridge to the next hill, passing a small **Vishnu temple** with many sculptures. Chobhar's Adinath Mandir is visible from afar, easily reached by a combination of roads and trails. From Chobhar it's an easy walk across the river to Jawalakhel in Patan. Reaching Kirtipur by bus is no problem since many go to the university from Ratna Park.

CHOBHAR

Adinath Lokeswar Mandir

About one km past the Tribhuvan University entrance, a flight of stone steps leads up a pine-forested hill and through an archway into the old Newar village of Chobhar. Tourists seldom come here, and motor vehicles never. Set on a ridgetop, Chobhar is accessible only on foot. The path leads directly to the temple of Adinath Lokeswar, dating back to 1640. Inside the pagoda is the image of Adinath Avalokitesvara, a replica of Patan's beloved Raato Machhendranath. To Buddhists, the deity is the embodiment of compassion; Hindus worship him as Surya, the Sun God.

Most amazing are the hundreds of pots, pans, and kitchen utensils nailed onto the exquisitely carved roof struts and under the eaves of surrounding buildings. These appear frequently on Valley temples, but nowhere in such profusion. There are many different explanations for the practice. Sometimes they're offered in gratitude to the deity for a granted wish or as a sign of devotion; newlyweds may offer them for a happy married life, or children offer them after the death of a parent, placing them in the keeping of the gods so that the gods will then provide these things in the next life. Every ten years or so the temple keepers take down the old contributions and bury them in a pit, in order to make room for

new ones. Facing the shrine is an old stone shikara, said to be built over a tunnel leading directly to the semi-legendary cave of Chobhar below the hill (see below). Inside it a Shiva linga is enshrined, a most unusual choice for a Buddhist temple compound.

Chobhar Gorge And Jal Vinayak

Below the village and a little further down the road the Bagmati flows through a narrow gash in the hills. Chobhar Gorge is firmly associated with the fabled sword cut of Manjushri, but actually that's the Kotwal Gorge further south at the rim of the Valley. This gorge is spanned by a beautiful old iron suspension bridge made to order for the Ranas by a Scottish foundry and erected in 1907. All the parts were manufactured in Glasgow, shipped to India, and carried in over the Hills by lines of porters. The trail beyond it leads back to the Ring Road and Jawalakhel.

On the west side of the gorge are several meditation caves cut into the rock. Tunnels behind them are said to lead to an underground lake; one, now bricked up, is said to emerge at the Adinath Lokeswar temple. Supposedly this passage was dug by Ganesh after he was left out of a gathering of the gods at the temple. Furious, he tunneled straight up from his riverside shrine to demand an explanation.

From the bridge you can see Ganesh's home just below the gorge, the 17th-century temple of Jal Vinayak set in a courtyard. On the riverbank behind are old cremation ghats and stone steps where women do laundry. The temple is one of the Valley's four most important Ganesh sites, and is a favorite pilgrimage site for worshippers seeking the boon of wisdom. The brightly painted struts depict the Ashta Matrikas, with clever erotic scenes at the base; on the front facade is a plaster portrait of the happy divine family: Shiva, Parvati, and young Ganesh seated on his daddy's lap.

The main image is a huge rock, vaguely resembling an elephant's head, ringed by a collar of gold. Besides granting wisdom, this Ganesh bestows fertility and is visited by women hoping to bear a son. Supposedly if they come 21 Tuesdays in succession, bringing a total of 1,000 red *mula* (a kind of radish) and 1,000 *ladoo* (Ganesh's favorite sweet), their wish will be granted. Ganesh's mount, a meter-long rat, is ensconced in front, offering a *ladoo* in his right paw. He's flanked by two bells; an inscription on their supports announces that these were made from the very first bag of cement produced from the nearby Himal Cement Factory. This dust-belching factory slightly down the road is labeled by environmentalists as the Valley's main polluter.

Taudaha

a naga

One km further is Taudaha, "Great Lake" (actually little more than a pond), the fabled residence of the King of the Naga. The legend of the Valley's creation says the naga all fled after their lake home was drained. Manjushri asked their king to remain as guardian of the Valley's fertility and prosperity, and provided an elegant underwater home in Taudaha, a golden palace with diamond windows and jewelled pillars. The naga are said to dispel the underwater gloom with the light of large jewels set in their foreheads. Though small, the lake is said to be immeasurably deep. In the last century, the Valley's rulers attempted to drag it for the fabled treasure but were defeated by the depth.

CHAMPADEVI

This relatively short hike offers good views with a minimum of walking, plus the chance to visit interesting sites along the way (it's just off the road to Dakshinkali). It's about a two-hour walk to the first summit.

Champadevi is a minor hilltop pilgrimage site, part of the larger Chandragiri Ridge. Several trails lead from small villages between Chobhar and Pharping; you can begin at **Bansbari** or at **Pikhel.** The trail ascends steeply to the ridgeline through a pine plantation. In about 45 minutes it begins to level out and the Himalaya appears. It's a moderate walk to the base of the summit, then another stiff climb to the top (2,278 meters), where there's a small Buddhist stupa and a Hindu shrine honoring the goddess Champadevi Mai. You can go back down to the saddle below and follow a wide trail for 30 minutes to the small lake of Taudaha, near the Himal Cement Factory. Or continue 45 minutes west to **Bhamesmar,** another higher summit along the ridge (2,502 meters), then drop down to meet a trail which eventually becomes a dirt road leading to Kirtipur. The most energetic can continue northwest to another saddle (**Dipti Bhanjyang,** 2,330 meters), where a cable ropeway used to haul freight over the hills intersects the trail. Follow a trail descending to **Kispidi** on the Kathmandu-Pokhara Road.

Haatiban Resort

This resort complex, opened in 1991, is set atop a ridge overlooking the Valley and the Himalaya. The turnoff is a dirt road on the right, nine km from Kathmandu; the resort is three km further down. The resort has 17 double rooms in four cottages, restaurant, bar, and gardens.

PHARPING

Eighteen km south of Kathmandu is the small fortress town of Pharping, once an independent kingdom, perched atop a hill for defense. The site draws both Hindus and Buddhists with its sacred shrines to Vishnu, Vajra Yogini, Gorakhanath, and Guru Rinpoche. The entire hill is loaded with shrines, temples, and monasteries, skillfully set into the beautiful natural setting. It's also the site of the Valley's first hydroelectric plant, built in 1911 to illuminate the government headquarters of Singha Durbar.

Shikar Narayan Mandir

For Hindus the main attraction is the Shikar Narayan temple (also called Sekha Narayan or Shesha Narayan), one of the Valley's four main Vishnu shrines. At the roadside one km before Pharping village is a series of pools filled with clear water from a sacred spring. Women do laundry here and hang the clothes up to dry on ancient sculptures, and there are still the slanted stone slabs upon which dying people are laid so their feet can touch the sacred water.

A stone stairway leads up past the **monastery** of the Tibetan lama Chatrul Rinpoche to the small Vishnu temple, set beneath a weird overhanging cliff naturally colored in orange, white and black stripes, in a cunning combination of cave and temple. The main Vishnu image, carved in the 15th century, was stolen several years ago and has been replaced by a glossy black stone sculpture. To the left is a natural stone representing Chamunda or Kali, here the *shakti* or source of Vishnu's energy. Bhajan singers come here to worship her with offerings of songs. To the right is another Vishnu sculpture, then a series of Buddhist deities set behind a metal grill. Monkey-faced Hanumans kneel in front of Vishnu's shrine, and a marble plaque of his sacred cow, Khamdhenu, is set in the pavement in front.

On the Buddhist side of things, the cave to the right is a Guru Rinpoche meditation spot, its roof marked with indentations said to be his hand and head prints. As he meditated here a jealous naga sent poisonous snakes to disturb him, but the great master froze them into stone with a blow from his *phurbu* (ritual dagger), transforming them into the stalactites hanging from from the crag overhanging the temple.

Vajra Yogini

Work your way around the east side of the hill, passing above a former royal summerhouse now turned into a boarding school, to the gilded pagoda temple of Vajra Yogini enclosed in a walled compound. The tantric goddess appears as the central figure in the 17th-century torana above the gate, her left hand bearing a skull cup, her right wielding a chopper to cut away delusion. Instead of being horrifying as ancient texts describe, here she's rather pretty. The temple's side courtyards or the open hillside make a nice place for a picnic lunch.

Asura Cave

A stone pathway leads from the pagoda to the village of Pharping, passing by a cluster of Tibetan monasteries on the south side of the hill. Above the buildings, marked by strings of faded prayer flags, is a natural and very sacred cave, actually little more than a cleft in the rock. Hindus worship it as a Gorakhnath shrine; his footprints, carved in 1390, are set in a platform in front. To Tibetans, this is the main meditation cave of Guru Rinpoche, where he did a *mahamudra* retreat and achieved the level of knowledge-holder. It's called the Asura Cave, because those blessed with inner vision can find here an entrance to the realm of the asuras. This area was once a favorite stopover point for pil-grims on the walk from India to Kathmandu. Tibetans will point out to you the head and hand-prints of Guru Rinpoche left in the rock. After Boudha, this is the holiest site in the Valley for Tibetan Buddhists, and many come here on pil-grimage.

Most of the recently built Tibetan **monasteries** clustered below belong to the Nyingmapa sect, and their temples display images of Guru Rinpoche. The lowest shrine is built about a miraculous Tara said to be appear from the rock. In 1978 a Tibetan lama built the "Sara-swati-Ganesh Temple" here, a good example of Nepalese religious diversity. The village's Newari Hindus come here to worship Saraswati, while Tibetans revere the beautiful golden image as Tara.

From here a flagstoned path leads to and through the old village of **Pharping,** a minia-ture replica of what Kathmandu was like a gen-eration or two ago. You can spend a pleasant 20 minutes winding through town, then follow the path to Dakshinkali two km further south.

DAKSHINKALI

Set in a shaded grotto beside the confluence of two streams, this is the Valley's most famous and popular shrine to Kali, "The Black One." Scowling and emaciated, with protruding tongue and red eyes, decked with a necklace of skulls, Kali is just another aspect of the great goddess Durga, Shiva's consort, appearing in fearsome form to battle with evil. Kali is said to be extremely powerful and accomplished *(siddhi).* Valley people hold she is the easiest to please of all Hindu deities, and once placated with a sac-rificial offering, will readily bestow gifts and bless-ings and absolve sins and even crimes.

Kali serves as family lineage deity *(kuldevata)* or personal deity *(ishtadevata)* for thousands of high-caste Hindus. Those with a family linkage must worship at her temple at least once a year, while *ishtadevata* devotees come as often as they like to beseech a boon. Before the road was built, Dakshinkali was a four-hour walk from Kathmandu, and the site was still popular. Today it draws 400,000 pilgrims a year, most visiting on Tuesdays or Saturdays, which are the preferred days for sacrifices.

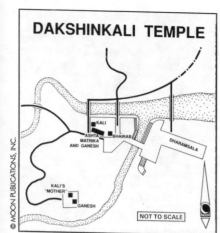

DAKSHINKALI TEMPLE

KALI

ASHTA MATRIKA AND GANESH — BHAIRAB

DHARAMSALA

KALI'S "MOTHER"

GANESH

NOT TO SCALE

© MOON PUBLICATIONS, INC.

Entering by road, you pass through a parking lot which is the site of a major traffic jam on Saturday mornings. The route leads down a shaded stone pathway lined by local people selling flower garlands and offerings for the goddess; buffalo-milk yoghurt dished out of black wooden pots; fresh vegetables, *khoya* (a condensed milk sweet); and in the springtime rhododendron blossoms, considered a sovereign antidote for bones stuck in the throat. Saturdays here are like a cheerful temple fair, with crowds of worshippers dressed in their best clothes, tea stalls doing a brisk business, and protesting goats and chickens dragged to the altar for sacrifice.

Down a flight of steps and across a bridge is the temple, open to the sky as Kali is said to prefer, decorated with a canopy of gilded snakes. The black stone image of Kali shows her squatting on a corpse, symbolizing victory over time. Grinning and hideous, she holds among other terrifying emblems a skull cup, a severed head, and a sword. Along the sides are enshrined images of Ganesh, the Ashta Matrika, and a plain stone Bhairab. You can photograph these but you're not allowed inside the sanctum.

The surprising dearth of legends about this place indicates it was probably a natural power spot to the mother goddesses taken over by Kali relatively recently (say, 500 years ago). This is the greatest site in the Valley for animal sacrifices, and Saturdays here are exceeded only by the Dasain festival. Only uncastrated male animals are offered, first sprinkled with water to make them shrug and signify their "assent." Caste butchers perform the sacrifice for a small fee or the animal's head. The carcasses are hauled off, eviscerated and cleaned in a nearby stream, and picked up by the donor, often to be immediately cooked and served at a family picnic on a nearby hillside.

At the top of the steep hill behind Dakshinkali a shrine said to belong to Kali's mother offers a nice view of the precincts. On the opposite side restaurants line the road, offering various types of snacks—fried breads, *pakora, chana* and other spicy Indian treats. There's been talk of developing a resort for tourists and pilgrims on the nearby hillside called Phema Danda.

Getting There

The road is in relatively good condition but it's uphill all the way; easiest on a mountain bike; coming back fast is the fun part. Dakshinkali is about a 45-minute taxi ride from Kathmandu. Roundtrip is Rs250-300 for a full taxi, but that includes only a brief stop. Pay more if you want the driver to wait while you explore other sites. Public transportation includes incredibly crowded public buses and minibuses leaving from near Martyr's Gate (extra ones run on Sundays). Finally, you can take a sightseeing tour with a local company for about Rs200; trips may include Chobhar, Shikaranarayan, and Kirtipur.

KOKANA AND BUNGAMATI

These two beautiful little Newar villages are on the opposite side of the Bagmati from the Dakshinkali road, about an hour's walk from Jawalakhel. To reach them head straight south from Jawalakhel, crossing the Ring Road and descending to the village of **Nakhu** at the river of the same name. The ominous-looking building on the right is a prison, housed in the remains of an old Rana arsenal. A Scottish-made iron suspension bridge spans the shallow river, and there's a motor bridge as well. Continue straight south about three km until the rooftops of Bungamati appear, clustered around a shikara in the center of town, looking like a medieval European village. Kokana is the smaller village to the right; both are nearly 100% Newar villages.

Bungamati village

KERRY MORAN

Turn around for a moment to appreciate sweeping Himalayan views fronted by fields and villages.

Bungamati

Bungamati is the winter residence of Raato Machhendranath, the beloved red-faced patron of Buddhist Newars, who divides his time between Patan and here. His association with the town goes back to the 7th century; he's also called Bunga Dyo, "God of Bunga." An 18th-century Capuchin missionary described the shrine's marble-tiled courtyard set with blue flowers as "magnificent . . . I do not believe there is another equal to it in Europe." The marble tiles and much of the magnificence has disappeared; today it's a big open square with a 30-ft. shikara set in the middle. All around are smaller crumbling shrines, mingled with scenes from village life. As in Bhaktapur, life is a public affair spilling out onto the streets, and it seems you meet most of Bungamati's 3,000 residents in the course of walking through the town.

Kokana

This equally interesting smaller village is a 10-minute walk northwest of Bungamati. Its exceptionally wide main street was built after the 1934 earthquake, which wiped out much of the old town. People line both sides of the lane, sitting in the sun to spin wool and massage their babies. At the end of the square is a temple to **Shekali Mai,** a local mother-goddess. Kokana is famous as an oil-pressing center; after the mustard harvest, the seed is pressed with heavy wooden beams and the resulting oil is used for cooking.

CHAPAGAON

The next road south from the Ring Road goes to Chapagaon, an old Newar village with a big temple to Vajravarahi set in a sacred grove. En route you pass through the smaller village of **Sunakothi,** with an old temple to Nasya Dyo, or Shiva as the patron of dancers. Niches in the compound once held a collection of beautiful ancient stone sculptures, recently stolen.

The next village is **Thecho,** and shortly after, Chapagaon. This town has many of the amenities typical of well-designed Newar villages, all now crumbling: stone water tanks *(tutedhara)* for thirsty passersby; ponds for bathing, laundry, and protection from fire; brick-lined gutters to channel waste water. Plus the classical art—old carved wood windows and a small pagoda in the center of town with elegant erotic carvings and an old torana. The turnoff to Vajravarahi Mandir is on the left, the narrow dirt road just past a Krishna sculpture. Ten minutes down is an eerily quiet forest of large, evenly spaced trees, harboring birds and an occasional leopard, and a favorite picnic ground for Nepalis. Tradition says it's ringed by eight cremation grounds. Parents with children slow to talk bring them here and leave them in the forest—guaranteed to make the kid talk, if not scream.

Vajravarahi Mandir

In the center is the compound of Vajravarahi, the boar-headed goddess who is the protector of livestock. People from all over the Valley come here to offer the first milk from their cows, pouring it over the large stone bull kneeling in front of the temple. The same ritual is used to seek a cure for sick cattle.

Built in 1665, the temple still lacks a pinnacle—supposedly the goddess herself insisted she didn't want one and kept disrupting its construction until builders gave up. On Saturdays people from all over the Valley bring offerings: Vajravarahi takes animal sacrifices, and the floor in front of her image is a sea of blood and flower petals. It's an undeniably powerful place, and the impression is reinforced if you happen to hear bhajan singing in a corner room, wilder and more macabre than the usual lilting melodies.

LELE VALLEY

About seven km further down the Chapagaon Road, up and over the Valley rim, is the small and isolated Lele Valley, a world apart from Kathmandu. Very few visitors make it this far. The main attraction, aside from its peaceful atmosphere, is a huge multicolored fresco of **Tika Bhairab** painted on a brick wall—no temple, just a simple altar in front. Bhairab's mouth is sunken into the ground; the composition focuses on his staring eyes, a striking representation that's unusually abstract for Nepali art.

EAST OF KATHMANDU

GOKARNA

This pilgrimage spot is located near the confluence of three rivers, at a point where the Bagmati River passes through a wooded gorge. On the western bank is the Shiva temple of **Gokarna MahaDev,** founded in the 14th century. An old cremation site, the temple retains its association with funeral rites. Here Newar Buddhists and Hindus of all ethnic groups celebrate special festivals in honor of their dead.

To reach here go to **Jorpati,** about one km east of Boudhanath, and turn left onto a wide dirt road. A few kilometers north the temple appears on the right. The compound was originally much larger but has diminished over time. What remains is beautifully preserved, thanks to a UNESCO-sponsored restoration project in the early '80s which repaired the crumbling buildings and left the pagoda and its surrounding buildings among the best maintained in the Valley. Aside from fine woodcarvings there's a remarkable collection of sculptures of various gods on the temple grounds, most not particularly old, but impressive *en masse*. The 8th-century **Parvati** placed in a small shrine in the northwest corner is exceptionally old and beautiful. Past the temple is the small Newari village of **Gokarna,** and further down, the waterfall of Sundarijaal. Across the river is a walled-in old game preserve of Jung Bahadur's, now operated as Gokarna Jungle Resort (see below).

SUNDARIJAAL

Five km past Gokarna Mahadev the road ends at a tiny village set at the edge of the Valley. Climb up a stone stairway alongside the stream about 20 minutes to Sundarijaal, literally "Beautiful Water," a waterfall set in the foothills ringing the Valley. Don't bother looking for the waterfall in the dry season; by April it slows to a trickle. The stream is one of the main sources of the sacred Bagmati. There are good picnic sites around here, or you can continue past the reservoir to the small village of **Mulkharkha.** If you *like* steep uphill hikes, you can even go up to the 2,400-meter pass of **Burang Banjyang.** Sundarijaal is one possible starting point for the Helambu and Gosainkund treks (see p. 340).

The best way to get here is to bike or take a one-way taxi and walk back to Boudhanath. The quiet road passes by fields and villages, a nice country stroll. Local buses leaving from Bagh Bazaar are cheap but very slow, and minibuses from Jorpati are crowded.

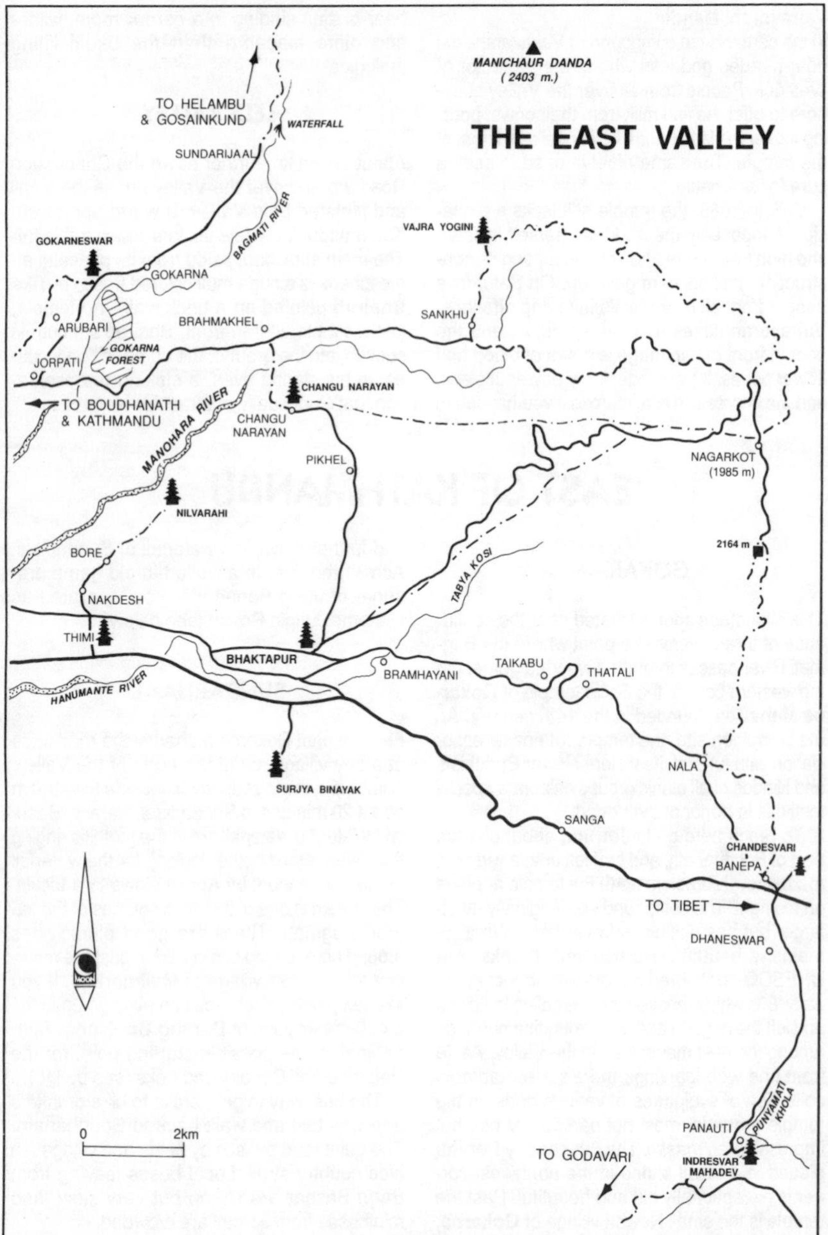

THE EAST VALLEY

MANICHAUR DANDA
(2403 m.)

TO HELAMBU
& GOSAINKUND

WATERFALL

SUNDARIJAAL

BAGMATI RIVER

GOKARNESWAR

GOKARNA

VAJRA YOGINI

ARUBARI

GOKARNA
FOREST

BRAHMAKHEL

SANKHU

JORPATI

TO BOUDHANATH
& KATHMANDU

MANOHARA RIVER

CHANGU NARAYAN

CHANGU
NARAYAN

PIKHEL

NAGARKOT
(1985 m)

NILVARAHI

2164 m

BORE

TABYA KOSI

NAKDESH

THIMI

HANUMANTE RIVER

BHAKTAPUR

BRAMHAYANI

TAIKABU

THATALI

SURJYA BINAYAK

NALA

SANGA

CHANDESVARI

BANEPA

TO TIBET →

DHANESWAR

TO GODAVARI

PANAUTI

PUNYAMATI KHOLA

INDRESVAR
MAHADEV

0   2km

MOON

© MOON PUBLICATIONS, INC.

GOKARNA JUNGLE RESORT

Three km east of Boudha is the Gokarna Jungle Resort, located in another one of Jung Bahadur's old hunting preserves. Walled-in and protected from local woodcutters, the lush vegetation shelters spotted and barking deer, wild boars, monkeys, and an occasional leopard. There is a variety of birds (267 have been counted), not to mention leeches in the rainy season. The biggest attraction is the Bengal tiger kept in a special enclosure, the subject of many impressive closeup photos.

For entertainment, Gokarna offers a nine-hole **golf course,** the only **elephant rides** in the Kathmandu Valley (US$7), plus the chance for four-wheel-drive game-viewing excursions in the evenings. The resort's pride and joy is "Tiger for Dinner," the chance to watch the tiger killing and eating a goat, followed by a barbeque dinner (presumably not goat). This requires a minimum of seven people, at US$25 per person. There's a restaurant (overpriced), bar, and double rooms for US$30 per night. It's a decent place to stroll about in the daytime and enjoy the woods; the day admission rate is Rs35. The resort's city office is on Kanti Path, tel. 223-008.

CHANGU NARAYAN

This superb pagoda temple has been called "a building that could stand alone to represent the very best in Nepalese art and architecture." The Valley's oldest proven existing temple and its holiest Vishnu shrine, Changu Narayan is endowed with glorious woodcarvings, metalwork, stone sculpture, and architecture. Despite its beauty few tourists make it here; in fact, most never hear of it.

The temple's setting makes an ideal holy site. Thirteen km east of Kathmandu and four km north of Bhaktapur, it's set atop a hillock at the end of a ridge descending from Nagarkot. On winter mornings the temple floats like an island atop a sea of mist.

Getting There
Coming from Kathmandu, about six km past Boudhanath you'll sight the hilltop temple on the right. Strike out across the fields, wading across the shallow Manohara River if there's no footbridge, and ascend the hill on a trail which later becomes an ancient stone staircase. (Push your bike up if you must, or entrust it to a family in the roadside village). Young boys will offer to "guide" you, but really you can't get lost—the temple is easily visible atop the top of the hill. A wide foot trail and a well-maintained road link Changu Narayan and Bhaktapur.

Temple Architecture
Changu Narayan's main image was installed at about the same time as the Shiva linga of Pashupatinath, in approximately the 4th century. Though the temple has been destroyed many times since by fire and earthquake, most recently in 1702, it's always reappeared, richer and more elaborate.

The classically proportioned triple-roofed pagoda is a masterpiece of form and decoration. The lower struts depict Vishnu's ten incarnations. Sometime during this century the woodwork was brightly painted, masking the fine detail but making the temple a riot of color. The main entrance is a stunning amassment of gilded repoussé copper, topped with a torana depicting Narayan. Inside is enshrined the sacred image, hidden to nonbelievers. A century ago Westerners were not allowed to set foot in the temple compound. French historian Sylvain Levi conducted his 1901 investigation by standing in the doorway and listening to a Nepalese assistant describe interesting objects.

The spacious temple compound contains smaller shrines dedicated to Krishna, Shiva, and the Ashta Matrika, and scattered all about are images of Buddhas, folk gods, linga, inscriptions, and above all, images of Vishnu in his many forms, many of them priceless masterpieces. There are several renditions of Vishnu astride Garuda (one on the north side appears on the Nepalese ten-rupee note), and a gruesome Narasingha disemboweling a demon with his bare hands. **Vishnu Vikranta** strides across the universe with mighty steps, a rendition of the old legend of Vishnu the Wide-strider. Finest of all is the 8th-century **Vishnu Vishvarupa** sculpture on the southern side, now set in brick. It's inspired by the chapter of the *Mahabharata* in which Vishnu displays his Universal Form to Arjuna. With ten heads and and multiple arms displaying different emblems, the god stands

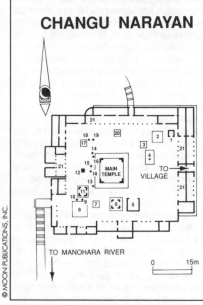

CHANGU NARAYAN

1. Shiva *linga*
2. Lakshmi-Narayan image
3. Vishnu image
4. Vishnu and Avalokitesvara images
5. Dashamahvidya (Durga) shrine
6. Shiva linga shrine
7. Vishnu Visvarupa ("Universal Form") sculpture
8. Lakshmi-Narayan temple
9. Vishnu Vikranta sculpture
10. Narasingha sculpture
11. substitute shrine for Pashupatinath
12. Malla king and queen
13. pillar with conch shell
14. Manadeva's pillar inscription
15. Garuda statue
16. pillar with wheel
17. Krishna shrine
18. Vishnu atop Garuda
19. Vishnu
20. Uma-Mahesvara (Shiva-Parvati)
21. *dharamsala* (resthouse)

MAIN TEMPLE

TO VILLAGE

TO MANOHARA RIVER

0   15m

© MOON PUBLICATIONS, INC.

atop Garuda, surrounded by multitudes of adoring deities. A Sleeping Vishnu appears below, resting on the cosmic ocean in the coils of a serpent. The detail and expressions of the figures are hauntingly beautiful.

There's more: the Valley's earliest **inscription,** dated the Nepalese equivalent of A.D. 464, is engraved on a stone column behind the Garuda image on the east side. It records the victory of King Manadeva over "barbarians" from the north and east. Nearby and encased in a wrought-iron cage are gilded images of Kathmandu's King Bhupalendra Malla and his mother the queen regent, players in Kathmandu's bloody 17th-century politics who, between plots and intrigues, found time to make generous donations to the gods. The rice grains and flower petals littering their enclosure indicate the elegantly wrought statues have become objects of worship in themselves.

The massive kneeling **Garuda** image beside them once crowned King Manadeva's inscribed victory column, until an earthquake toppled it off its perch. Some historians believe the figure is a portrait of Manadeva himself. Mustachioed, with pudgy cheeks and curly locks, it resem-

bles a well-fed archangel.

Inside the shrine is an even more sacred gilt image of Garuda, said to be self-manifested from a gigantic ruby. Once a year, on the festival of Nag Panchami, this image is said to sweat, commemorating the anniversary of Garuda's wrestling match with the great serpent Taksaka. Temple priests and local people collect the miraculous moisture as a remedy against naga-caused diseases like leprosy and ulcers.

Nearby Hikes
Changu Narayan offers many possibilities for outdoor exploring. The path out the western door leads to a hillside with sweeping views of fields, mountains, and the Manohara River, and the chance (if local children don't discover you) of a quiet picnic overlooking the Valley. Behind the temple to the east is a small village (also the **Changu Narayan Hill Resort,** a lodge and restaurant combo). To the south a path leads in two hours to Bhaktapur, an easy countryside ramble. More adventurous is the five-hour walk up the ridge to Nagarkot, as easy a trek as one could hope for in Nepal.

SANKHU

Sixteen km east of Kathmandu, the Boudhanath road ends at the large old Newari village of Sankhu, once an important stop on the old Tibetan trade route. Today it's been nearly forgotten. Peaceful and timeless, Sankhu seems almost untouched by the modern world except for a few radios and the plaster pillars ornamenting the facades of some old houses, a byproduct of the Rana-era fascination with European opulence.

Vajra Yogini Mandir

Besides the town itself, the major attraction is an ancient shrine to Vajra Yogini, who began as a nature goddess, was adopted by Buddhists, and is now revered by Hindus as a form of Durga. A new motor road leads to just below the temple, but driving up spoils the approach. Take the old flagstoned pilgrim path leading north of Sankhu and ascending the hillside. Small resthouses are scattered along the way, appropriated by local farmers as shelters for harvested grain. Midway up the staircase is a blood-spattered triangular stone emobodying Bhairab. The god symbolically receives blood sacrifices intended for Vajra Yogini, a neat way of getting around the Buddhist aversion to sacrifices.

A bit further up is the 17th-century temple, set in a pine forest. Its gilded repoussé torana depicts the unusually lovely goddess. Vajra Yogini is the wisdom deity Ugratara, defined in texts as a ferocious protector of the Buddhist doctrine, but here she's been tamed into a beauty. Inside the shrine she appears as a large clothed and ornamented statue, flanked by the *dakini* Baghini and Simhini (they also appear on the torana). The main image is usually kept hidden from sightseers. She's said to be the eldest sister of the Valley's four main Vajra Yoginis.

Next to the temple is another pagoda enclosing a replica of the Swayambhunath stupa. Vajra Yogini is said to have persuaded Manjushri to cut the Valley and release the waters of the lake, making possible the founding of Swayambhu and indeed the Valley's civilization. There's no doubt this is one of the most ancient sites in the Valley. During the Licchavi era it was a Buddhist holy site, later taken over by the tantric goddess Vajra Yogini—and even she is an ancient presence.

Behind her temple, a path leads up to her *dyochhen,* an unremarkable stuccoed building which conceals ancient sculptures like a 7th-century head of the Buddha, seldom revealed. Nearby is a well-carved sunken tap from the 10th century.

Manichaur

The temple is set midway up the forested hill of Manichaur ("Heap of Jewels"), said to be dotted with the meditation caves of Tibetan and Indian *siddha.* Further up is a government-run medicinal herb farm, and at the summit a grassy meadow with an image of Ganesh. A mela is held every August at the nearby spring. From the temple you can walk to Nagarkot along an old trading route, an uphill journey of about six hours.

NAGARKOT

This small hilltop resort on the Valley's eastern rim offers views of a big chunk of Nepal's Himalaya, including five of the world's ten highest peaks (Everest, Lhotse, Cho Oyu, Makalu, and Manaslu). As well, it has sweeping panoramas of terraced hillsides so typical of Nepal. Perched on a 2,300-meter-high ridge 32 km east of Kathmandu and 20 km north of Bhaktapur, Nagarkot is a popular destination for overnighters who stay to catch sunrise or sunset on the distant mountains. A point against it is that it's a resort rather than an indigenous village, little more than a few huts, a bus stop, and a few clusters of simple lodges. The surrounding hillsides are heavily farmed and denuded of forests, unlike Phulchowki or Shivapuri.

The lodges scattered along the ridgeline all offer more or less equally spectacular views, stretching from Manaslu and Ganesh Himal in the west through Langtang and Gauri Shanker, to the Solu peaks of Numbur and Karyolung in the east. Everest appears, but just barely, as an unimpressive nub amid much larger and closer summits. Nagarkot's true summit (2,164 meters), topped with a view tower, is a 40-minute walk up the road from the Taragaon Resort. The road has been blocked since the army took over the summit a few years ago, and sightseers are allowed to walk up only in the morning.

VIEW FROM NAGARKOT

ANNAPURNA SOUTH (7219 m)
MACHHAPUCHHARE (7050 m)
ANNAPURNA 3 (7556 m)
A - 1 (8096 m)
A - 2 (7937 m)
MANASLU (8156 m)
GANESH HIMAL (7406 m)
GOSAINKUND (5862 m)
LANGTANG (7246 m)
KIMSHUN (6745 m)
KATHMANDU (1350 m)

BOB RACE

If you arrive in the afternoon, take consolation in the fact the view isn't really that much better.

Accommodations

The road from Bhaktapur passes by a few inexpensive lodges and the **Hotel Flora Hill** (tel. 226-893/Kathmandu tel. 223-311), a resort with garden and (a rarity for Nagarkot) electricity. At US$38 d, it's the most expensive place here. The problem with this location is that you still

NAGARKOT

ROAD TO SANKHU (12 km)

TO THE FARMHOUSE

1   NEW PHEASANT LODGE
2   NIWA HOME
3   HOTEL VIEW POINT
4   PEACEFUL COTTAGE AND CAFE DU MONT
5   SUNRISE RESORT
6   GALAXY HOTEL

HILL (2200 m)

TEASHOPS

BUS STOP

LODGES

TO CHANGU NARAYAN

STAR HOTEL & RESTAURANT

BLUE HEAVEN GUESTHOUSE

TO BHAKTAPUR (20 km) & HOTEL FLORA HILL

ROADBLOCK

ARMY CAMP

TARAGON RESORT

TO SUMMIT (2164 m)

NOT TO SCALE

© MOON PUBLICATIONS, INC.

have a 10-minute climb up to the ridge with its mountain views, pretty much defeating the purpose of a visit.

The government-run **Taragaon Resort** (Kathmandu tel. 211-008) has a nice garden and relatively large rooms for US$18 d, but since the Nepalese Army has taken over the summit and blocked the road, it's become something of an anachronism—to reach it, you must walk 20 minutes along a foot trail. There are a few cheaper lodges near the Taragaon.

The main group is clustered atop a subsidiary hill (2,200 meters) a ten-minute walk north of the bus stop. This area has something to be said for it: the ridge towers straight up above a sea of terraces, overlooking the valley of the Indrawati Khola. Accommodations here are simple, as is food. Water is scarce along the ridgeline, and some of these places must haul it up by porter. **New Pheasant Lodge** and **Niwa Home** offer inexpensive accommodations. **Peaceful Cottage** has dorm beds for Rs20; simple rooms for Rs50 s, Rs100 d, plus the glassed-in **Cafe Du Mont.** Newest and nicest of the lot is **Hotel View Point,** with a spacious dining room and terrace and rooms ranging from US$5 for a basic single to US$15 for double with bath and balcony.

Probably the best place to stay is about four km further down the road to Sankhu. **The Farmhouse** is a massive mud-walled old Newari house run by the Hotel Vajra, which has been completely renovated: raised ceilings, tiled floors, fireplace, even a small library and a Monopoly game. Rates are US$15 s, US$30 d, which includes meals. The Hotel Vajra (tel. 271-545) will arrange a taxi (Rs600).

Lodge prices drop in the summer off-season by as much as 50%. Mountain views are scarce during the monsoon but they do occur, and Nagarkot is a good getaway from the heat, with

(top) trekkers setting up tent (Christopher Gamm);
(bottom left) chorten (stupa) at Tengboche Monastery, Khumbu (Kerry Moran);
(bottom right) trekkers in Khumbu (Christopher Gamm)

(top) valley scene near Bhaktapur (Kerry Moran);
(bottom left) Bhotia village of Thinigaon, with buckwheat fields, near Muktinath (Kerry Moran);
(bottom right) Junbesi village, Solu (Kerry Moran)

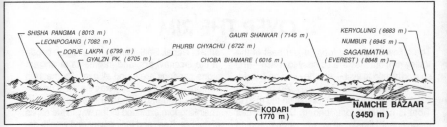

SHISHA PANGMA (8013 m)
LEONPOGANG (7082 m)
DORJE LAKPA (6799 m)
GYALZN PK. (6705 m)
PHURBI CHYACHU (6722 m)
GAURI SHANKAR (7145 m)
CHOBA BHAMARE (6016 m)
KERYOLUNG (6683 m)
NUMBUR (6945 m)
SAGARMATHA
(EVEREST) (8848 m)
KODARI
(1770 m)
NAMCHE BAZAAR
(3450 m)

green and flowers all around. There's not much to do besides eat mediocre food, admire the mountains, and walk; an overnight visit is plenty. It's also nice to head up very early—some tours leave well before dawn—to catch morning light on the mountains, have breakfast, and then walk downhill.

Getting There

Public buses run between Bhaktapur and Nagarkot three times a day, taking about two hours. A one-way taxi from Kathmandu would be about Rs250. You can walk up from Bhaktapur—there's a foot trail that's shorter than the winding road—cycle up the paved road and coast down, or arrange transportation through one of the Nagarkot lodges that have Kathmandu offices. In tourist season private minibuses (Rs125 roundtrip) depart daily from Thamel; check at Lodge Pheasant in Thamel and Niwa Homes' office on Kanti Path. Finally, many tour companies run sunrise or sunset trips to Nagarkot to catch the Himalayan views; some include overnight packages.

One of the best reasons to go to Nagarkot is the array of interesting options for downhill return walks. Sankhu is about four hours away, following the rutted road winding north, then west—a very rough ride for cyclists. Hikers can take the old trail that leaves the road about five minutes' walk past the lodges. Nearing Sankhu, you can circle around behind the town to the Vajra Yogini temple.

The hilltop temple of Changu Narayan is about two hours down a prominent ridge jutting into the Valley, as easy a trek as you could ask for in Nepal. The trail passes through fields and scattered Tamang and Chhetri settlements. The odds of finding a taxi in either village are small. Either arrange to have one waiting for you, or count on sporadic minibuses and walking to get you to Boudhanath and then Kathmandu. There's a decent-looking lodge and restaurant in Changu Narayan if you get down late. You can also walk southwards down through the old Newari village of **Nala** to Banepa, and from there catch a bus to Dhulikhel or Kathmandu.

OVER THE RIM

The following destinations lie just east of the Valley rim, but they are so easy to reach—and so worthwhile to visit—that they can be considered an extension of the Valley. An overnight visit to the old village of Dhulikhel on the road to Tibet is highly recommended. Dhulikhel has magnificent Himalayan views, lodges ranging from basic to deluxe, a pastoral setting, and plenty of good day walks. It combines villages, farmland, mountain views, and cultural sites, and is a wonderfully peaceful retreat from the bustle of Kathmandu. Especially if you're not planning on trekking, a visit here will provide a glimpse of rural Nepal, with the added bonus of Newari culture.

BANEPA

Beyond the Valley rim is the territory of the ancient kingdom of Banepa, once the most powerful in Nepal. Settlements in this region began in the Licchavi era, and fragments of ancient stone carvings are found all over. By the 14th century Banepa's nobility was the most powerful in all Nepal, dominating even Bhaktapur. Their kingdom extended all the way to the banks of the Sun Kosi, and their power and wealth derived from the constant trade passing through to Tibet. When China sent envoys to the Nepalese court in Bhaktapur, the shrewd Banepans, their first hosts, passed themselves off as the rightful rulers of the Valley, and for years intercepted and appropriated the rich gifts China intended for the Valley's rulers.

The town of Banepa, 26 km east of Kathmandu on the main road to Tibet, serves as a main bazaar for local hill people. Much of it was razed by fire in 1961, accounting for its modern look. The stretch along the main road is modern, dusty, and noisy, but if you turn left at the statue of a garlanded King Mahendra, you'll

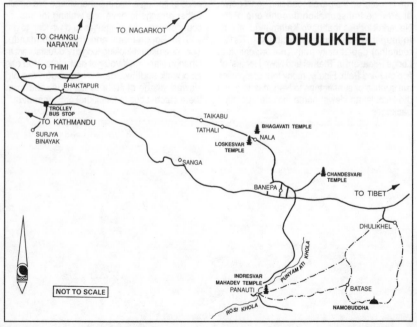

find the interesting old bazaar about one km north. Old houses and temples blend here and it's hard to believe this is the same town as the one on the main road.

Chandesvari Mandir

Take the right-hand fork at Banepa's first main intersection (marked by several shrines and a water tap) and head one km northeast to the ancient and impressive temple of Chandesvari. It's in a lovely natural setting in a wooded grove on the bank of a river gorge. Chandesvari is a beautiful, seductive, and angry young goddess, yet another manifestation of Durga, who appears in a modern plaster relief set over the compound's gate. Local people call her Chandesvari Mai, identifying her as one of the Newar mother goddesses. The temple's main image, laden with silver jewelry, is honored with an annual chariot procession. The fine temple struts, recently restored by local woodcarvers, depict the Ashta Matrikas and the eight Bhairabs. A stylized, colorful fresco painted on the western wall of the temple depicts a great blue-faced Bhairab, fangs bared and hands displaying tantric mudras. A gateway in the southern wall leads down the hillside to a local cremation site on the banks of the Punyamati River.

NALA

About four km northwest of Banepa is the Newar village of Nala, a medieval-feeling town seldom visited by foreigners. The children here have yet to learn to beg, though you can hear them giggling and whispering "give me one rupee" among themselves in practice. In the center of town, towering over the village, is a beautifully proportioned four-storied temple to **Bhagwati** built in 1647, one of two such four-storied temples in or near the Valley, and one of the sacred quartet of shrines to the great goddess. The image inside is so old (from the 12th century) it has weathered down to a nearly featureless stele.

To the west, at the very edge of town, is a shrine to **Lokeswar** or Karunamaya, a white-faced image dressed in robes and crown, framed by a gilt and silver torana. His appearance recalls the Seto Machhendranath of Kathmandu, and indeed this is another Buddhist

deity, this one said to be the guru of the nearby goddess Chandesvari. Nala is a rather odd setting for a Buddhist Karunamaya shrine, as it's a 100% Hindu village. The ancient shrine was abandoned long ago and recently revived by Kathmandu Buddhists, who funded the temple's restoration and have instituted an annual chariot procession.

To reach Nala travel west through Banepa's old bazaar. At the end a dirt road leads north three km through fields to the town. You can also walk down from Nagarkot, heading down a steep ridge to the east—probably a three-hour descent, since it's a four-to-six hour climb up.

DHULIKHEL

The town of Dhulikhel lies four km east of Banepa and 32 km beyond Kathmandu, set slightly southwest of the main road at an altitude of 1,440 meters. Once it was an important stop on the main trade route between Kathmandu and Tibet, and the wealth amassed through trade funded the construction of handsome buildings inlaid with intricate woodcarvings, many now alarmingly swaybacked and buckling. Dhulikhel is fertile ground for collectors of classic woodcarvings, though prices have skyrocketed as people realize the value of their old windows. With the money earned from their sale, they can build an entire modern house.

About 5,000 people live in this densely packed town; half Newar, the remainder Tamang and Brahman-Chhetri. Streets are lined with tiny shops selling vegetables, cloth, and metal pots hammered out on the spot. The main square includes a **Narayan shrine** and a rare temple to the deity **Harasiddhi**—depicted in the main torana as a goddess, but generally considered to be a god. Past it is a small hill topped with temples to Krishna and Bhagwati.

Official buildings like the high school, post office and jail are strung along the road to the southeast. Here also is the large grassy field of the Tundikhel, with views of the Himalaya and the valleys of the Indrawati and Sun Kosi rivers. The best mountain views are from the small **Kali shrine** topping the long ridge south of town, about a 30-minute walk. Get up early and walk up with a flashlight to catch sunrise; sunset is also good.

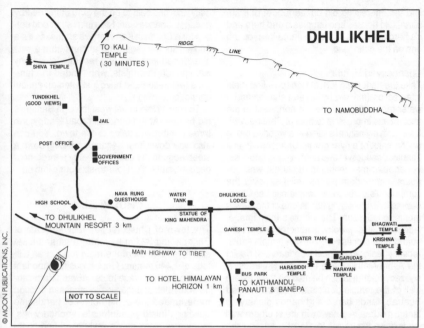

© MOON PUBLICATIONS, INC.

Practicalities

There are several inexpensive lodges located in the village. Best is the **Dhulikhel Lodge** (tel. 225-092 in Kathmandu), an old five-story Newar house in the midle of town with a courtyard, garden, and simple rooms (some with Himalayan views) for Rs40 s, Rs70 d (dorm beds are Rs20). This perennially popular place was started in 1969 by B.P. Shrestha; today his son Prem runs it. The restaurant offers good inexpensive food, including tasty daal bhaat. A good place to practice your Nepali with the friendly proprietors: the Peace Corps often holds training sessions here.

B.P. Shrestha now manages the more upscale **Hotel Himalayan Horizon,** set on a terraced hilltop one km west of town off the main road. Carved windows and woodwork salvaged from old Dhulikhel houses have been lovingly restored and set into new buildings designed in the old style, a total of 12 rooms, at US$30 s, US$40 d. A garden patio offers full-on mountain views; more secluded dining spots are set on terraces lower down. The restaurant serves Chinese, Indian, and continental food. The hotel's Kath-

mandu office on Kanti Path (tel. 225-092) can arrange reservations and transport for both Himalayan Horizon and the Dhulikhel Lodge.

At the top of the scale is the **Dhulikhel Mountain Resort** managed by Arun Shrestha, four km beyond town above the Tibet highway. The setting is rather isolated but striking: red-brick architecture harmonizes with landscaped hillside gardens, and the dining room and the thatched guest cottages offer spectacular views of the Himalaya and the Indrawati Valley below. The lack of electricity only adds to the ambience—candlelight and oil lamps provide light, and the star show is stunning at night. Prices are high: US$50 s, US$52 d, with meals adding another US$32 per day. Even if you don't stay, stop by for a meal in a spectacular setting—the cooking is good too. For reservations and assistance with transport, contact the Kathmandu office on Durbar Marg (tel. 220-031).

Outings

All these hotels arrange excursions in accordance with their means: the Dhulikhel Lodge hands out photocopied sketch maps of the area;

the other two can arrange guides for local hikes, vehicles for drives to nearby sites or up to the Chinese border, and rafting trips as well.

Possible excursions include hiking up the nearby "Red Mountain" to Gosainkund—not the famous pilgrimage spot to the north, but a smaller local *tirtha* where shamans gather for certain festivals (try Janai Purnima, the full moon of August). Walks to Namobuddha and Panauti (see below) are fairly easy and make good warmups before a trek, or good substitutes.

Getting There

Buses leave hourly from Kathmandu's main bus park and take about two hours to travel the 30 km; a taxi or motorcycle takes less than half that. If you contact one of Dhulikhel's major lodges in advance, they will help arrange transportation for a fee. Mountain biking is a good idea, as the main highway is not heavily trafficked. Even better is the back road from Bhaktapur to Nala and Banepa. Both lead past fields and terraces wearing the colors of the season.

NAMOBUDDHA

This Tibetan Buddhist pilgrimage spot is about a two-hour walk south of Dhulikhel, a nice mini-trek through fields, pine plantations, and small villages. There's also a dirt road but it's frequently undrivable. The route climbs up to the Kali shrine and continues along the ridge, dipping up and down. The **Dhulikhel Lodge** sells simple maps for Rs2, and there are plenty of people along the route to ask for directions if you have doubts.

Namobuddha means "Homage to the Buddha!" This site is one of the southernmost pilgrimage spots for Tibetan Buddhists, who flock here especially in springtime. To them it's one of the three main stupas in the Valley (after Boudha and Swayambhu). Somehow the Southeast Asian Jataka tale of the Buddha and the starving tiger has come to be associated with this place. In the Nepalese version, the son of the ruler of Panauti was hunting with companions when the group discovered a starving tigress about to devour a boy. Moved by compassion for them both, the prince offered the tigress his own body as food. Some say he went so far as to feed himself to her, piece by piece.

A carved stone slab at Namobuddha depicts the legend. The prince's remains are said to be enshrined in the main stupa, while a smaller one nearby marks the site where the sacrifice occurred. The teashops here are a good place to sit in the sun and watch pilgrims circling the whitewashed stupa, spinning prayer wheels and reciting mantras. Colorful prayer flags flutter in the breeze, and there's an inspiring 360-degree panorama of surrounding countryside. Atop the hill there's a small monastery and a retreat center nearby. For the return, descend from the corner of the first stupa to pass through forest and villages and wind back in a loop to Dhulikhel, or go on to Panauti if it's early enough in the day.

threshing wheat, near Dhulikhel

KERRY MORAN

PANAUTI

This ancient, nearly 100% Newar town is built near the auspicious confluence of two streams, the Rosi and Punyamati. A third, mystic, stream, the Lilamati, is said to be visible only to sages; it issues from the **Gorakhnatha shrine** on a hilltop above town. The confluence is a famous bathing and pilgrimage site; the first day of the month of Magh (usually mid-Jan.) is a big festival, and every 12 years a month-long mela is held here.

Panauti is a charming, as yet unspoiled village, larger and better maintained than most Newari towns. Its centerpiece is the **Indresvar Mahadev temple,** the oldest existing example of a Newari temple, dating back to 1294. The woodcarvings are not particularly elaborate, but the carved wooden struts are the best in Nepal, slender figures endowed with a grace and harmony that speaks across the centuries. Check out the lovely restrained figures carved on the base of struts—erotic in the best sense of the word. The 1988 earthquake left a gaping hole in the temple's south roof and smashed several of the struts; hopefully a restoration project will soon get underway to save this ancient treasure. The temple enshrines the linga of Indresvara, "Lord of Indra," a reference to Shiva. A chariot festival is held here in early autumn.

A little further north on the bank of the Punyamati River is a collection of more recent shrines and ghats, including an old Krishna temple and a big resthouse popular with the town's old men. With ducks paddling in the stream and temples all around, the place is incredibly charming. A suspension bridge leads across the river to the recently renovated 17th-century **Brahmayani Mandir,** dedicated to the patron goddess of Panauti.

Once a palace stood in the village's main square. Before the advent of the road Panauti was an important trading center, but Banepa has now replaced it. There are many tea and sweet shops, generally fly-ridden, but the only accommodations are at the very basic **Raj Lodge** near the bus stop. Better to stay in Kathmandu or Dhulikhel and day-trip here. Minibuses run down the seven-km paved road between Panauti and Banepa, or it's a two-hour stroll from Dhulikhel.

Start early and walk fast and you can visit Panauti in a single day from Namobuddha, following the trail descending from the northwest corner of the stupa. Catch a bus from Panauti to Banepa, and another to either Dhulikhel or Kathmandu. Other day-trips include the uphill hike from Dhulikhel to Nagarkot, and the moderately difficult walk from Panauti to Godavari, involving a four-hour ascent along a scenic ridgetop west up the valley of the Rosi Khola and an hour-long steep descent to St. Xavier's School.

PALANCHOWK

The small ridgetop village of Palanchowk is 15 km down the highway past Dhulikhel and up a dirt road. It shelters a famous and beautiful image of **Bhagwati**, one of the Valley's quartet of important Bhagwati images all supposedly carved by the same sculptor. The story goes that the Palanchowk Bhagwati was carved first, and was so fine the king who commissioned it ordered two of the sculptor's fingers chopped off to prevent him from making its equal. Undeterred, the sculptor produced the Bhagwati image of Nala, and promptly lost his right hand. He managed to carve the Shobha Bhagwati image with his left hand, and losing that too, produced Kathmandu's Naxal Bhagwati using only his feet. Carved of shining black stone and decked with silver jewelry, the Palanchowk image is indeed the most beautiful of the group, and it attracts devotees from a long way off.

BOB RACE

BEYOND THE VALLEY

As much as 80% of Nepal's visitors never get past the Kathmandu Valley. With its unequaled blend of luxuries and attractions, the Valley inspires inertia in its citizens as well. Nepalis seldom travel unless they have to, and rarely consider it pleasurable. Rugged terrain makes bus travel punishing even by Asian standards, and food and accommodations are generally very basic. Apart from a few pockets like Pokhara, Chitwan National Park, and the standard trekking regions, most of Nepal remains untouched.

Slowly this is changing. Nepalis are fond of pointing out that the Valley isn't Nepal any more than New York is the United States, or Paris is France—a standard cliché, but true. Over the last 20 years the realm of possibilities has widened to embrace Pokhara (now the number-two destination in Nepal) and Chitwan National Park, which has undergone a phenomenal increase in popularity over the last decade. The list is bound to expand further as adventurous travelers investigate new places, bringing them into the main circuit.

For now, non-trekking destinations outside the Valley are few and little-known, but exploring them brings great rewards—not least is the sat-

isfaction of being among the first. For mountain bikers, Nepal is one giant unexplored paradise, rugged and demanding but immensely satisfying. Renting a taxi and driver for several days is remarkably reasonable and an ideal way to get about. RNAC domestic flights are another option. Even the notorious bus rides are perversely enjoyable in their own way, especially if you break them into manageable chunks and plan plenty of time off the bus.

Nepal's expanding road network is centered in the Terai, which is largely ignored by travelers racing over the Indian border to Kathmandu. They're missing a lot: many parts have all the magic of India without the hassle, and the national parks and wildlife reserves here are among Southeast Asia's finest. If nothing else, the Terai deserves attention as home to nearly half of Nepal's population. The **East-West Highway** spanning the region is nearing completion, and soon it will be possible to drive the length of the country—a tremendous psychological shift for fragmented Nepal.

The balance of roads radiate from Kathmandu to penetrate the central Hills, with its rich and varied traditional cultures, steep terraced hillsides, and mountain views. Mini-treks from roadside Hill destinations provide a taste of rural Nepal without the exertion of a full-out trek, and are an easy way to reach seldom visited regions.

While these areas are bound to develop as time goes on, as of now they're virtually untouched: Lumbini, the peaceful birthplace of the Buddha; the hill station of Tansen; the vibrant Hindu city of Janakpur; the scenic roads to Tibet and India. This chapter demystifies a few of the most accessible and interesting of these.

THE ROAD TO TIBET

THE ARNIKO RAJMARG

The 115-km Arniko Rajmarg follows the ancient trade route linking Kathmandu to Lhasa. It perhaps sounds more exotic than it is, but as Nepali highways go this is quite a pretty one. The road was built by China in the mid-'60s, creating a big stir (rumors darkly hinted that it was "wide enough for one tank.") It was supposed to serve as a major trade link with Tibet-China, but its miserable condition, combined with the fact that Tibet itself is an awfully long way from China, have limited the economic benefits. Each monsoon the highway threatens to crumble, and each fall it's salvaged to last another year. Summer is not the time to drive down it—but this is the main season for travel to Tibet, and tour groups often end up walking across landslides to reach the border. Currently only groups are admitted into Tibet, but from 1985-87 this "back door" entry was popular with independent travelers, and there's always a chance China will relax controls.

Sights

For a drive out of Kathmandu the Arniko Rajmarg offers pretty scenery, following the gorge of the Bhote and Sun Kosi rivers. Motorcyclists can overnight at Taatopani; mountain bikers should allow four days total, with overnights at Dhulikhel or Barabise and Taatopani. From the road you see small factories producing handmade paper from the boiled bark of the daphne shrub. The truly spectacular part begins *across* the border, as the road climbs up to the Tibetan Plateau, all stones and sheep and open spaces compared to Nepal's lush greenery.

The highway winds past Bhaktapur and Dhulikhel, then drops into the red-tinted, severely deforested **Panchkhal Valley,** and crosses the braided strands of the **Indrawati Khola** at Dolalghat. Eighteen km beyond is **Lamosanghu** ("Long Bridge") and the turnoff to Jiri, the starting point for the Everest trek. Fifteen km further is **Barabise,** and from here it's pretty dicey. Each year engineers clear off monsoon landslides and cut a new road through the hillside, then the rains come again to send huge sections tumbling down again.

Regular bus service from Kathmandu may end at Barabise if the road is out; they've given up the border run after four successive monsoon wipeouts. Minibuses, jeeps, taxis, and trucks ply the drivable sections of the road— the situation changes annually. In the summer you may have to cross landslides on foot, but the road resumes after a few kilometers at most. As always in Nepal, porters are available to carry bags—bargain hard.

Taatopani And Kodari

As the road climbs, the river gorge deepens, strung with waterfalls and festooned with greenery. Twenty-three km further is Taatopani ("Hot Water"), a string of roadside buildings, basic lodges, and tea shops. The hot springs at the north end of town aren't exactly soaking tubs, just boiling hot water gushing out of five spouts— great if you've just made the dusty descent from Tibet. This is the last village of note in Nepal, and is certainly a better place to stay than the border town of Kodari, three km further on and little more than a collection of huts.

From Kodari you can gaze romantically across the river to Tibet. The landscape remains pure Nepal, a narrow river gorge cloaked in green forest and low-hanging clouds. At 1,640 meters Kodari is the lowest point along the entire Nepal-Tibet border; this, combined with easy access to the Kathmandu Valley, made it the preferred trade route to Lhasa.

Khasa

The town of Khasa appears high up on the opposite hillside. The name translates as "Mouthplace," referring to the yawning hole the Bhote Kosi has breached in the mountain wall (the Chinese call the town Zhangmu). This profitable trade entrepôt was snatched by Tibet after besting Nepal in a 1792 mini-war, explaining the border's unusual southward protrusion—generally it runs along the Himalayan crest. Since China runs its far-flung empire on Beijing time, Khasa is two hours and 45 minutes ahead of Nepal.

Those with Chinese visas can cross the self-proclaimed "Friendship Bridge," guarded at one end by Nepali soldiers, at the other by young, unsmiling Chinese in typically baggy green uniforms. Once there was a paved road to Khasa, but it will probably never be repaired. The 600-meter climb up to town takes about an hour. Again, porters are readily available; Nepalis can travel up to Khasa without a visa.

Khasa is a small new bazaar loaded with cheap Chinese goods. Its multinational mix is demonstrated by its tea shops, serving Tibetan butter tea, Nepali milk tea, and Chinese green tea. Lodgings include an expensive cement-block tourist hotel and several decent cheaper places, and there's a bank with inconvenient hours for changing money.

The road climbs through increasingly spectacular scenery up the sheer-walled Bhote Kosi gorge. It takes the better part of a day to ascend to a 5,050-meter pass and emerge onto the vast open plains of the Tibetan Plateau—surely one of the most spectacular transitions in the world.

DAMAN AND THE RAJPATH

ALONG THE TRIBHUVAN RAJPATH

The tiny ridgetop village of Daman, 75 km southwest of Kathmandu, offers some of the best Himalayan views in Nepal. The route there is one of the most exciting and hair-raising of the country's mountain roads. Completed in 1956, the **Tribhuvan Rajpath** was the first road to join the Kathmandu Valley with India and the outside world. It took India more than three years to build the stretch from Bhainse to Kathmandu. Drive down it and you'll see why—Nepal's Hills simply weren't made for roads, and this particularly rugged stretch was a major challenge.

Today most vehicles take the Sunauli-Mugling-Kathmandu route, longer but wider and less twisty and nerve-racking. This leaves the Tribhuvan Rajpath nearly empty, perfect for mountain bikers, motorcyclists, and private cars. Daman is about a two-hour drive one-way from Kathmandu or a tough all-day bike ride. The road is in decent condition throughout.

Daman's lodgings are pretty rough, if unique, but overnighters are almost assured clear morning views. Day-trippers from Kathmandu are taking a risk, though the weather is generally clear in fall and winter.

Mountain bikers proclaim the Daman route the best ride in Nepal. If you're biking up from India, this is a good way to reach Kathmandu. Only one bus a day (the government-run Sajha cooperative) runs between Kathmandu and Hetauda, reaching Daman around 1000. Another possibility would be to pass through Daman en route to Chitwan National Park—it's only an hour longer than the usual road, though you'd have to change buses in Hetauda.

The Road There

Past the Ring Road, the countryside gradually emerges from the recently built industrial overlay. Smells, sounds, and sights are thoroughly rural by the time you reach **Thankot,** an unattractive little town perched on the Valley rim 10 km from Kathmandu. Highlights include a police station and a **King Tribhuvan Memorial Park** enshrining an ill-proportioned statue.

Cross the prayer flag-strung pass behind Thankot and you're out of the Valley. The road abruptly drops—and drops and drops; hairpin curves twist far below, a taste of what's to come. Guard rails are practically nonexistent; this route is not for the squeamish. The road twists and turns a total of 52 times before arriving in the village of **Naubise,** 25 km from Kathmandu. Tea shops here are among the few places to eat before Daman.

Here the road forks: the main highway follows the Trisuli River to **Mugling,** while the Tribhuvan Rajpath branches off to the left. Narrow and twisting, the older road is far less trafficked than the road up to Naubise would suggest. There are few villages along the way, just a few homes of Buddhist Tamangs marked by prayer flags. The road climbs slowly to **Tistung Deorali** (2,030 meters, 34 km from the turnoff) and descends into the broad **Palung Valley,** an intensively farmed Newari settlement since Licchavi times. Cross the Palung Khola on a suspension bridge and pass through several nice bazaar villages. There's a telephone office and a few hotels (signs are in Nepali, so ask) in case you conk out before the final ascent.

The road climbs a final 10 km through pine forest. About three km below Daman is a strange clearing with gigantic concrete benches lined up facing the Himalaya—an abandoned campsite for giant tourists? Then comes Daman (2,322 meters), houses strung along a ridge and several dozen people carrying on their daily lives in front of one of the most incredible views in the world.

View Tower And Lodge
Daman's pride is the **Everest View Tower and Lodge,** an ugly squat cement tower topped by a round room, built and run by the government. The observation deck (admission Rs5) gives an expansive 386-km panorama from Dhaulagiri in the west, all the way east to Kangchenjunga, if you're lucky. The view is incredibly comprehensive: all the five Annapurna peaks, the impressive form of Himalchuli, Ganesh Himal, the Tibetan peak of Shishapangma (Gosainthan) rarely seen from Nepal, Langtang, the Jugal Himal, and the many peaks of Khumbu Himal,

including an excellent view of Everest.

The pivoting telescope is a marvelous idea (somebody should install one at Nagarkot) and lets you zoom in on peaks. The eastern Himalaya is partly obscured by a forested ridge, but a climb up past the schoolyard looks like it would give a completely unobstructed view.

You can actually stay in the view tower, in a glassed-in, circular room with four beds, Rs30 each. The setting is unique, but flaws include outdoor toilets, cramped quarters, and a number of shattered windowpanes. The battered guestbook makes good reading—evidently the windows have been broken since at least 1984. There's no electricity in the tower, but the stars and moonlight mountain views are incredible. And you can always turn the telescope upwards to get the "Whole Mountains and Space View from Bed" advertised by the billboard. A few restaurants near the view tower provide daal bhaat and can arrange lodging. That's it for Daman's facilities. The small hilltop **gompa** perched above the road, about a half-hour walk up, would make an interesting excursion.

Beyond Daman
Continuing south, the Rajpath crests at **Sim Bhanjyang** (2,487 meters), three km past Daman, then rolls down the gently sloping Lami Danda ("Long Hill") all the way to **Bhainse.** The transition between different altitudes is laid out as clearly as a botany textbook, as pines give way to rhododendron forests, jungle, and terraced fields.

The industrial town of **Hetauda,** 50 km from the pass, is the usual overnight stop for cyclists from India. **Motel Avocado** (tel. 20429) north of the bazaar is a pleasant surprise in this nondescript town, with rooms for around Rs200 and the only guacamole in Nepal. Bus riders bound for Chitwan National Park should catch a bus here to Narayanghat/Bharatpur and get off at Tadi Bazaar, about 60 km from Hetauda.

GORKHA

The ancestral home of Nepal's ruling family, this typical hill town is tucked away in the very heart of Nepal. Though Gorkha is easy to reach, only 18 km up a paved road off the Pokhara-Kathmandu Highway, few travelers stop here—and therein lies much of its charm. A brief visit on the way to or from Pokhara would provide more insights into Nepal than you're likely to get at Lakeside or Kathmandu.

Gorkha's small-town air belies its tremendous historical importance. From its hilltop fortress King Prithvi Narayan Shah launched his lifelong attempt to unify the independent states of Nepal, a wildly ambitious project which succeeded due to his brilliance, and to the effectiveness of his locally recruited troops. The British term "Gurkha" evolved from the name Gorkha, referring to the famed fighting men of the region.

Originally controlled by tribal chieftans, Gorkha was one of many petty hill states taken over in the mid-16th century by Hindu warriors from western Nepal. The Shah princes traced their lineage back to Rajasthani royalty displaced by the Muslim invasion. The claim was dubious, but they did replicate the Rajputs' concern with warfare and the purity of Hindu rituals.

The eighth in his line, Prithvi Narayan Shah was born following a dream of his mother's that she had swallowed the sun. He assumed the

throne at 20, and soon demonstrated he was more than the run-of-the-mill local ruler. His burning ambition to conquer the Kathmandu Valley inspired his people to support a long and costly war. He was shrewd enough to exploit the differences between the Valley's warring kingdoms, and preferred to persuade rather than fight whenever possible, a tactic which had increasing success as his power grew.

Prithvi Narayan and the Gorkhas devoted 26 years to the siege and conquest of the Valley, then turned to conquering new territory. By the beginning of the 19th century, Nepal had been welded into a nation, and Prithvi Narayan had earned a major place in its history.

GORKHA BAZAAR AND DURBAR

From the bus stop the road curves up to the local Tundikhel and an army camp. Near the small pond called Rani Pokhari is a cluster of temples. Facing the stone **Rameshwar Shiva temple** is a memorial statue of Prithvi Pati Shah, an ancestor of Prithvi Narayan who visited Kathmandu and brought back Newar traders and builders. He's credited with sponsoring most of Gorkha's monuments, all clearly Newari style. The Gorkhalis were happy to call in expert Newar architects and artists to improve their city, while they devoted themselves to warfare.

The cobbled road curves east from here to run through the bazaar. Gorkha is little more than a one-street town, but the lack of traffic makes it pleasant and moderately interesting. A typical hill bazaar, it's packed with small shops selling necessities of life alternating with tea stalls where men gather to argue politics. The women's meeting place is the public water tap (**Tin Dhara**) on the east end of town.

Roughly in the middle of town is **Tallo Durbar,** a mid-18th-century quadrangle probably used as administrative headquarters, in contrast to the royal abode up on the ridge. It's said to be built on the site of Gorkha's original, pre-Shah palace. Supposedly several attempts to shift the building higher ended with the stones returning by themselves at night, until people finally gave up. The

GORKHA

TO ALI BHANJYANG & TRISULI
TALLOKOT
KALIKA MANDIR
GORKHA DURBAR
UPALLOKOT
TO DARUNDI KHOLA & POKHARA
RANI POKHARI
RAMESHWAR
TUNDIKHEL
BUS PARK
TALLO DURBAR
POST OFFICE
BANK
HOTEL THAKALI
HOTEL GORKHA BISAUNI
TO PRITHVI HIGHWAY, KATHMANDU & POKHARA
0   300m

© MOON PUBLICATIONS, INC.

palace is currently undergoing renovation, and there's talk of establishing a museum here.

Upallo Durbar

The Shah palace, Upallo Durbar, looms over the town, perched atop a ridge like an eagle's eyrie. It was primarily built there for defensive reasons, but the intent was no doubt to impress as well. A stone staircase leads north off the main road up the hillside; the stiff half-hour climb will leave you breathless. There are a few pipal trees and water taps on the way up, but the open trail can be sizzling in spring. The ridgetop rewards with mountain views from Dhaulagiri to Ganesh Himal, with Manaslu (8,156 meters) rearing up straight ahead. To the south the buffer wall of the Mahabharat Range is visible, separating Hills from Terai.

Gorkha's palace is the holiest and most impressive of all central Nepal's hilltop forts or *kot*. First built by Ram Shah (1606-36), the palace was expanded and improved by succeeding kings who, even before they conquered Kathmandu, brought in Newar woodcarvers to decorate their abode. One of the most elaborate and best-maintained monuments outside the Kathmandu Valley, it's doubly impressive in tiny Gorkha.

The palace is in two sections, Kalika Durbar and the Raj Durbar, linked by the arcade-like Ranga Mahal. The westernmost portion enshrines a **Kali temple,** served by a special subcaste of Brahman priests. They and the king are the only ones allowed to proceed beyond the courtyard; it's said ordinary people would die if they gazed upon the goddess's image. Local people perform animal sacrifices at the entrance, reaching a bloody peak at the winter festival of Dasain and the smaller Chaitra Dasain in the spring.

The east block of the complex, **Dhuni Pati,** was once the royal living quarters. As the birthplace of the revered Prithvi Narayan Shah it's achieved the status of a shrine. Leather shoes, bags and belts are prohibited in this compound, as well as the temple side; so are photographs. There are plenty of unsmiling soldiers to enforce these rules.

Tourists aren't admitted inside the palace, which is semi-sanctified by its associations with Prithvi Narayan Shah. There's really not much to see in the courtyard beyond some fine recently renovated woodwork. A small **Pashupati temple** here was installed by Prithvi Narayan as a sacred substitute for Kathmandu's shrine.

The lower level of the palace includes a feast hall and pilgrims' resthouse built by Rudra Shah. The staircase ends at a shady *chautaara* on the palace's eastern side, where a trail links Gorkha with the surrounding hills. Twenty minutes up the ridge beyond is **Upallokot,** "Upper Fort," little more than an enclosed pen, now flanked by a microwave tower. Comprehensive mountain views include an impressive angle on the palace below.

On the opposite (western) side of the palace is the royal helipad, occasionally used by the king for ceremonial visits. A trail leads from here to **Tallokot,** another lookout point/fort with less impressive views than the higher viewpoint, but an easier walk. From here, a trail leads back down to Gorkha.

Gorakhnath Cave

Ten meters below the palace's southern side, the sacred cave temple of Gorakhnath is hewn out of the solid rock. Fraught with ritual significance, this is among the most important sites in Nepal for mainstream Brahman-Chhetris. Gorakhnath, an actual 12th-century yogi, has been semi-deified into a mysterious figure, sometimes revered as a creation or emanation of Shiva. As patron of the Gorkha kings, he's credited with assisting Prithvi Narayan Shah's stunning victories. It's said Gorakhnath made a promise to appear on battlefields wherever Gurkhas fight. From the palace interior, a flight of stone steps leads down to the shrine, which is crowded with images.

AROUND GORKHA

A few days in Gorkha would be enough time to explore the quintessentially Nepali countryside—Hindu villages, spreading pipal trees, and traditional tea shops. Seldom visited by foreigners, the rolling hills are laced with relatively easy trails, including the main Trisuli-Pokhara route. This lowland area is particularly nice to trek through in Dec.-Feb.; by April it's steaming hot.

From the *chautaara* beside the palace a trail leads to **Ali Bhanjyang,** climbs up an open ridge with good views to the Brahman village of **Tapli,** then drops down to **Khanchok Bhanjyang,** four hours from Gorkha. The trail continues to **Arughat Bazaar** on the banks of the Burhi Gandaki 20 km from Gorkha, and eventually joins the road at **Trisuli,** a three-day walk.

West of town, a trail drops to the **Darundi Khola,** 800 meters below, to meet the trail to Pokhara. The river is good for swimming, but remember that it's one hour going down, and nearly twice as long to get back up.

A good day's walk south is the renowned "wish-fulfilling" temple of **Manakamana,** reportedly one of the most effective shrines in the country. Supplicants sacrifice animals to the goddess Bhagwati here; a few tea shops put up overnight visitors. Several hours downhill the trail emerges at **Abu Khaireni,** at the intersection of the main highway and the Gorkha turnoff.

The three-day walk up the Darundi Khola to the big Gurung village of **Barpak** is best attempted with a guide, tents, food, and porters, unless you're prepared for very basic accommodations. That said, it's an interesting walk, and with a guide and tents you could loop back via the hilltop viewpoint of **Darche** (3,247 meters), returning via Khanchok Bhanjyang to Gorkha.

PRACTICALITIES

Accommodations And Food

Gorkha's facilities are the usual story, with most lodges clustered around the noisy bus station. **Hotel Thakali** is among the best of the lot, charging Rs35 for a room. The best place in town so far is **Hotel Gorkha Bisauni,** about one- half km back down the road from the bus park. Rooms are Rs80-100; dorm beds Rs20, and there's a decent restaurant, the only place in town that serves even pseudo-Western food, though daal bhaat diners are plentiful.

Getting There

Gorkha is a five-hour bus ride from Kathmandu (128 km), four hours from Pokhara (106 km); even closer (78 km) from Tadi Bazaar and Chitwan National Park. Direct buses are few, but you can get off at the small village of Abu Khaireni, eight km west of Mugling, and catch a local minibus or truck running up the paved 18-km road to Gorkha.

POKHARA

A country cousin to busy Kathmandu, the Pokhara Valley has gone in just a few decades from secluded Shangri-La to major tourist destination. Soon after Nepal opened to the outside world, rumors began to trickle out of a remote valley a week's walk (200 km) west of Kathmandu, where tropical flowers grew on the shore of a blue lake and Himalayan peaks filled the skyline. Its reputation was fueled by praise from veteran travelers like the Japanese monk Ekai Kawaguchi, who found Pokhara the most enchanting place of his five-year travels through the Himalaya. Toni Hagen, a Swiss geologist who has walked over 14,000 km in Nepal, called it "one of the most extraordinary and beautiful places in the whole world."

Pokhara's stunning natural beauty is enhanced by an air of decided relaxation. Soft-eyed water buffalo wander the lanes; women carrying loads of fodder are as common a sight as cars on the roads; rice fields surround guesthouses, and huge old pipal trees fill the air with the sound of their rustling leaves.

The tourist area of Lakeside, stretched out along the southeast shore of the valley's largest lake, is a little never-never land where life revolves around sun, fun, and the next meal. Restaurants playing old Simon and Garfunkel and Elton John tunes add to the feeling of a '60s time warp. In the height of tourist season the scene here borders on the absurd, as preening couples prowl the street in search of a new restaurant.

Despite its segregation and high-season claustrophobia, Lakeside has its own charm, especially in the evening, when darkness hides the clutter and the shops are lit up like Christmas trees. Shopkeepers sit in front of their stores along the strip, chatting and playing with their kids. It seems easier to meet people here than in Kathmandu, perhaps because both they and you have more time.

Trekkers know Pokhara as the starting point for classic routes like the Jomosom Trail, and as

water buffalo
swimming hole near
Pokhara

KERRY MORAN

the ideal site for lazy recuperation after the three-week Annapurna Circuit. For non-trekkers the valley offers mountain views and glimpses of rural Nepali life going far beyond those of the Kathmndu Valley. For everyone, Pokhara is a wonderfully relaxing place, the closest Nepal has to a resort.

THE LAND

The Pokhara Valley is a lusher, lowland version of the Kathmandu Valley, a blend of rich farmland and forests rimmed by hills. With an average altitude of 900 meters, the climate is mild, averaging between 15-26° C: steamy in the summer months, but downright balmy in the winter. Pokhara's average annual rainfall exceeds 4,100 mm, making it one of the wettest places in Nepal. Most falls during the monsoon, but afternoon thunderstorms occur even in dry winter months.

Greenery thrives in the gentle climate: orchids, bougainvillea, banana trees, poinsettias, big spiky cactuses, and of course rice—Pokhareli rice is famous for its flavor. The flower displays are magnificent year-round, and lush gardens turn even simple guesthouses into exotic hideaways.

Juxtaposed against this subtropical paradise are 7,000- and 8,000-meter-high Himalayan peaks, a few just 30 km north and separated only by low foothills. Pokhara's mountain views span a choice 140-km section of the central Himalaya: Dhaulagiri, the 56-km long Annapurna

Range (which has 16 summits over 6,000 meters), Manaslu, Himalchuli and most unforgettable, Machhapuchhare, a single soaring white spire.

The 124-square-km valley is dotted with a half-dozen lakes *(tal)*, the only ones of any note in the country beyond Rara Lake. The largest is Phewa Tal, three km long and the major tourist attraction—for many people, the *only* attraction. The valley is cut by the Seti Gandaki River, one of the famed Sapt Gandaki (Seven Gandakis) which bisect the central Hills and meet in the Terai. It's called Seti or "White" Gandaki because of the limestone which gives the water a milky tint. The river appears and disappears throughout its course, in some places carving dramatically deep and narrow canyons in the valley's soft subsoil.

HISTORY

Pokhara is the meeting point for two peoples: the Hindu caste groups now inhabiting the valley and its encircling low hills, and the Gurungs of the surrounding highlands. For centuries power ebbed and flowed between them, with the caste groups gaining the upper hand as they gradually moved eastwards across Nepal.

By the 17th century Pokhara was part of the kingdom of Kaski, one of the most powerful of central Nepal's Chaubise Rajaya ("24 Kingdoms"). Kaski was ruled by a sub-branch of the Shah royal family, who situated their court atop a windy, waterless ridge for reasons of defense.

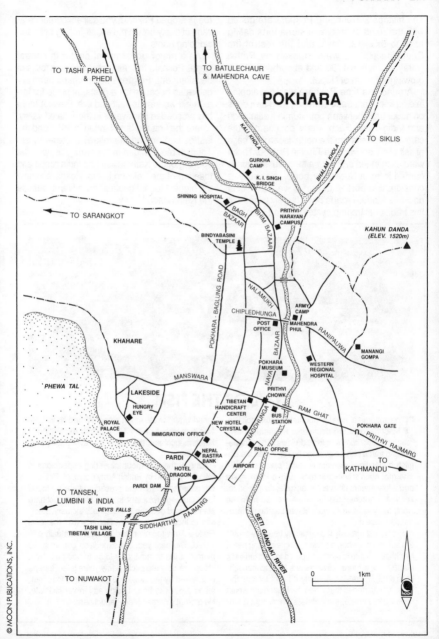

TO TASHI PAKHEL & PHEDI

TO BATULECHAUR & MAHENDRA CAVE

POKHARA

TO SIKLIS

KALI KHOLA

BHALAM KHOLA

GURKHA CAMP

K. I. SINGH BRIDGE

SHINING HOSPITAL

BAGH BAZAAR

BHIM BAZAAR

PRITHVI NARAYAN CAMPUS

TO SARANGKOT

BINDYABASINI TEMPLE

KAHUN DANDA (ELEV. 1520m)

POKHARA - BAGLUNG ROAD

NALAMUKH

CHIPLEDHUNGA

ARMY CAMP

POST OFFICE

MAHENDRA PHUL

RANIPAUWA

KHAHARE

NAYA BAZAAR

MANSWARA

POKHARA MUSEUM

MANANGI GOMPA

WESTERN REGIONAL HOSPITAL

PHEWA TAL

LAKESIDE

HUNGRY EYE

PRITHVI CHOWK

MAGDHUNGA

RAM GHAT

ROYAL PALACE

TIBETAN HANDICRAFT CENTER

IMMIGRATION OFFICE

NEW HOTEL CRYSTAL

BUS STATION

POKHARA GATE

PRITHVI RAJMARG

PARDI

NEPAL RASTRA BANK

RNAC OFFICE

HOTEL DRAGON

AIRPORT

TO KATHMANDU

PARDI DAM

TO TANSEN, LUMBINI & INDIA

DEVI'S FALLS

SIDDHARTHA RAJMARG

SETI GANDAKI RIVER

TASHI LING TIBETAN VILLAGE

TO NUWAKOT

0   1km

© MOON PUBLICATIONS, INC.

The hilltops surrounding Pokhara are dotted with the ruins of medieval stone forts dating back to this era. Kaski and the rest of the Chaubise Rajaya was annexed by Prithvi Narayan Shah in 1786 and absorbed into the growing kingdom of Nepal.

Around this time Pokhara was developing into an important trade entrepôt, lying as it does on major trails between both Jumla-Kathmandu and India-Tibet. Each winter dozens of mule caravans arrived from the north, laden with bags of salt and wool from the Tibetan Plateau. These were exchanged in Pokhara for grain and goods carried in from Butwal by porter. Naturally, a considerable portion of profits went into local pockets. Modern roads have largely wiped out this traditional trading system, but on trails and roads around Pokhara you still encounter caravans of dusty brown mules, all jingling bells and clopping hoofs.

As a major government center in central Nepal, Pokhara has naturally became a focus of development. Progress has perhaps been accelerated because it's a pleasant place for foreign-aid workers to visit and live. Development has proceeded backwards in the isolated valley, where the first airplane landed in 1952 and the first ox-cart arrived the following year—by air. Tourism really began in the early '70s, with the opening of the Kathmandu and India roads and the start of the trekking boom. Pokhara is now the biggest tourist destination in Nepal outside the Kathmandu Valley.

BOB RACE

TAIL OF THE FISH

The epitome of what a mountain should look like, Machhapuchhare dominates Pokhara, adding much to the Valley's splendid views. The tongue-twisting name can be avoided by relying on the English translation: *machha* is "fish," *puchhare* "tail." The mountain's twin summits, only one km apart and a few meters different in altitude, do indeed resemble a notched fishtail when viewed from the west, but you have to walk at least as far as Naudanda to see it.

From Pokhara only the austerely beautiful southern summit is visible, a perfect, single shining peak. Machhapuchhare is often compared to Switzerland's Matterhorn, a mere 4,572 meters to Machhapuchhare's 6,977 meters. Actually it far outshines the Alps. "Compared to that vision the Matterhorn would have looked crude, the peerless Weisshorn a flat-tened lump," wrote mountaineer Wilfred Noyce. He was a member of the 1957 British expedition to Machhapuchhare, the only one to ever attempt the mountain.

One of the first mountaineering expeditions in Nepal, it was led by British Army Col. J. M. Roberts. On reconnaissance the preceding year he found local Gurungs reluctant to help. Machhapuchhare stands guard over the Annapurna Sanctuary, a holy site to local Gurungs, but Roberts was the local Gurkha Army recruiter, and his clout eventually prevailed. The next year the expedition got within 60 meters of the summit, only to be turned back by a steep, ice-covered pitch. A few years later Roberts was asked by the Nepalese government to recommend a peak to be set aside as forever inviolate. He promptly named Machhapuchhare.

NEIGHBORHOODS

Little more than a village in many ways, Pokhara manages to sprawl in every direction, making getting about both time-consuming and confusing. The town is best described as three distinct areas, separated not just by distance but by character—it's hard to believe Lakeside and Bhimsen Tol belong to the same town.

Home base for travelers is **Lakeside,** on the eastern shore of Phewa Tal, and its sidekick, the Dam area or **Pardi,** one km further south. Lakeside's main road is a seemingly endless strip of lodges, restaurants, and shops. You have to scratch hard to find its Nepali roots, but the old Chhetri village called Baidam it once was lingers on Lakeside's back lanes, where rice fields, thatched-roof cottages and water buffalo remind you which country you're really in.

A good hour's walk northeast is Pokhara's new bazaar, another long strip taking its name from the nearby **Mahendra Phul** (Mahendra Bridge). It's like a dusty, flashy, noisy Terai town, crammed with new shops selling modern goods. The city's old, original bazaar, called **Bagar,** is a few kilometers northwest. Its small shops with a sleepy old-time feel form yet another world. Scattered between these three areas are offices, banks, hospitals, development agencies, a college campus, and the bus station and airport, which are not very close to anything at all. It's all chaotically unorganized, not to mention a very long haul between sections. Local bookstores sell yellow city maps, and there are plenty of You Are Here signs posted about town.

SIGHTS

Pokhara's sights are admittedly minor: there are no "must-sees" and most serve as excuses to wander about the lovely valley. Most visitors never make it past hypnotically seductive Lakeside—the rest of town seems impossibly distant. It's definitely worth rallying one's forces and getting out, though, if only for the pleasantly righteous glow you feel upon return.

Phewa Tal

Placid except for occasional spring windstorms, Phewa Tal is an idyllic playground. Brightly paint-ed wooden rowboats can be rented around Lakeside for Rs75 per day, Rs20 per hour. Hotel Fewa rents sailboats, but there's usually not enough wind.

A boat gives you access to the **Varahi temple** set on a small island near Lakeside. On Saturdays, colorful boatloads of Nepalis paddle here to perform puja and animal sacrifices. Secluded coves on the forested opposite shore make shady hideaways (they're not secluded enough to skinnydip, though). Lazing about in the sun is the best idea. Bring drinking water, sunscreen, a picnic lunch, and a good book. Mountain views are splendid, especially when the still waters reflect the peaks, creating a double range. The lake is neither deep (45 meters at most) nor particularly clean, but the water's warm and swimming is pleasant if you don't think about the probable pollution.

The lake's southern end is a vast flat expanse of rice fields (Phewa Faant), planted on recently reclaimed land. The Indian-built dam at the northern end supplies water for irrigation and electricity. It's actually enlarged Phewa Tal slightly, while the valley's other lakes are shrinking, due mainly to increased siltation from deforestation and farming. Siltation also threatens Phewa Tal. According to one gloomy estimate, the lake will be entirely silted in within 55 years if nothing's done to remedy the situation.

Pokhara Bazaar

Yes, there actually is a Nepali town called Pokhara, a world away and quite a distance from the tourist version. The old town lies between Sarangkot and Kanhu Danda ridges, at a point where the Seti River cuts a narrow gorge. The best way to get here is by bike, preferably with gears, as it's uphill all the way, although it looks deceptively level. The old bazaar beginning at Ganesh Tol is a good four km from Lakeside. With its ochre-tinted houses and broad quiet streets shaded by big pipal trees, it's retained its charm—you can almost imagine the mule caravans clopping through here.

Like many major trading areas in Nepal's Hills, Pokhara's old bazaar is essentially Newari. In 1752 the rulers of Kaski invited a group of Bhaktapur Newars to settle in their kingdom to improve local trade (Newars were even then renowned as astute traders with all the necessary connections). They've left their mark on the local architecture in a modest way. Minor temples stand in the middle of the road, each lending its name to the surrounding neighborhood, and there are a few magnificent old houses, including a huge pair on the western side of the road. Much of the old town was destroyed in a 1949 fire, which explains why the architecture is so bland. But even the rebuilt houses look old compared to Kathmandu, and a stroll through here reveals a typically busy traditional bazaar, with saris, soap, rice, and gold jewelry all jumbled together.

The town's only temple of note lies in the center of the bazaar. **Bindyabasini Mandir's** shady hilltop location is more interesting than its several shrines, none of notable design or antiquity. The original temple was destroyed in the 1949 fire, which started from a fire offering run amok. The main temple is of white plaster and is dedicated to a form of the goddess Bhagwati. Worshippers flock here to perform sacrifices, and especially on Saturdays the parklike grounds take on a festive air. A strange touch are the silvered, kneeling images of Nepal's rulers set atop a pillar facing the main shrine—not the usual 17th-century Malla kings, but the current king and queen.

Past the temple the bazaar becomes more densely packed and modern. If you're cycling, loop around to the east and return via a parallel road which passes **Prithvi Narayan campus** and heads through the new part of town. There's little of interest on this side apart from a view of the Seti Gorge, but it's a fast, swooping cycle downhill. A few kilometers south is the new bazaar area around **Mahendra Phul,** with modern shops and small Indian restaurants serving Sikh truck drivers. Veer off onto Mahendra Phul for a moment to peer down at the narrow slit of a gorge carved by the Seti River, barely two meters wide and 45 meters deep. Shortly after the road intersects with the Prithvi Highway, marked by a statue of Prithvi Narayan Shah. It continues past the airport to join the dam area around Pardi, three km past the intersection.

Museums
The **Annapurna Regional Museum** is located on the university campus east of the old bazaar. Its focus is natural history, primarily a butterfly collection. The only reason for a visit would be to pick up some of the informative literature of the Annapurna Conservation Area Project which might be available. Hours 1000-1600, closed Saturdays.

The **Pokhara Museum** is slightly more interesting, with exhibits of ethnic jewelry, musical instruments, costumes, photos, and brief descriptions of ethnic groups encountered in treks around Pokhara. Located between the bus station and Mahendra Phul, it's closed Tues., admission Rs5.

AROUND POKHARA

The sprawling valley is a great training ground for a trek and offers many options for those fleeing the fleshpots of Lakeside. Cycling is the best way to get around the roads, preferably by mountain bike; there are also many day walks, easily extended into mini-treks (or maxi-treks—you just keep going).

Sarangkot
The slightly lopsided summit topping the long ridge to the north of Phewa Tal makes an excellent day walk. Satisfyingly long but not too difficult, it rewards hikers with incredible views.

The shortest but steepest route starts south of Lakeside. Pass Khahare and round the bend into the next indentation; multiple trails run up a subsidiary ridge, past small farmhouses where you can get directions and tea.

A simpler route starts just before Bindyabasini Mandir, where a sign points the way up a dirt road which soon turns into a trail. It's a two-hour climb up, with progressively better mountain views as you ascend. Small tea shops sell simple food en route. The summit is a bald knob, crowned by the ruins of an old *kot,* a stone fortresses from the old Kaski kingdom. Junkies used to hang out up here, offering "ismack" to panting trekkers cresting the hill, but they seemed to have disappeared in recent cleanup drives.

To the north, the hillside drops straight down into the Suikhet Valley, with a breathtaking view of Dhaulagiri, the Annapurna range, and Machhapuchhare filling the horizon. You have to get up pretty early to be guaranteed a clear view, though. There are a few lodges and restaurants just below the summit if you want to overnight to catch clear morning views.

shepardesses near Pokhara

You can continue west along the ridge a half-hour to **Kaski,** once the capital of the surrounding country, now a minor touristy village with lodges advertising "View of Machhapuchhare from Bed." About 300 meters above the village are the ruins of the old Kaski Kot, reached by a stone staircase. The small Durga shrine, little more than a rock pen, is a favorite site for Dasain animal sacrifices. Many of the summits along this ridge have old temples to Durga or Kali, protectoress of the villages below.

Ninety minutes further along the ridge is the village of **Naudanda,** with good mountain views (including the first glimpse of Machhapuchhare's fishtail). Unfortunately it's been spoiled by several decades of day-trippers and is not particularly pleasant. There are lots of lodges and restaurants here; a police checkpost will prevent you from continuing further without a trekking permit, and the Baglung Road cutting across the ridge has pretty much ruined it for trekking—there's little joy to be had in plodding down a dusty road. A steep trail leads down north from Naudanda and reaches **Phedi** in

about 90 minutes. From here jeeps run back to the north end of Pokhara on a regular basis.

Kahun Danda

This ridge to the east of town is a bit lower than Sarangkot, with slightly less spectacular views. On the other hand it's closer, a shorter walk to the top, and far less traveled. Several trails lead to the 1,520-meter summit, including one from behind the university campus and another beginning just below the Manangi gompa a few kilometers east of Mahendra Phul. Either way it's about a 90-minute climb to the summit, which is crowned by the ruins of the inevitable kot and a view tower offering mountain views and a bird's-eye panorama of the Pokhara Valley, split by the gorge of the Seti Gandaki River.

Devi's Falls

The Pardi Khola flows from the south end of Phewa Tal for two km, then suddenly drops straight down into a dramatically deep sinkhole called Devi, David's, or Devin's Falls, scene of a dubious-sounding modern legend. Supposedly a foreigner named David (or alternately a "Miss Devins") was skinnydipping in the Pardi Khola when the floodgates of the dam were opened, sweeping him (or her) into the subterranean chasm, never to be seen again.

The falls are two km down the Siddhartha Highway, a 15-minute bike ride from Pardi or an easy walk along the river; cross the dam and head south. Moderately impressive in autumn, they dwindle to a disappointing trickle by January; the litter and the metal railings do little for the natural beauty. The entrance is lined by persuasive Tibetan trinket-sellers, many of them from the nearby Tashi Ling Tibetan setttlement across the street. A local high school has adopted the falls and collects Rs3 admission from sightseers, earning a hefty Rs100,000 per year.

Begnas And Rupa Tal

These smaller, unknown sisters of Phewa Tal are lovely and largely unvisited, all the better for the few who do make it out here. The lakes are about 15 km east of Pokhara, off the road to Kathmandu. Buses leave hourly from Chipledhunga in the New Bazaar but they're typically slow and crowded. Better to cycle 10 km down the Prithvi Rajmarg, then turn left onto a dirt road and proceed a few kilometers to the village of

Sisuwa. Begnas Tal is hidden just behind the village; boats are available for rent near the dam.

The lakes are divided by the forested **Panchbhaiya Danda** rising past the village. An hour-long hike up it to the viewpoint of **Sundari Danda** yields sweeping views of mountains and both lakes. There are a few tea stalls in Sisuwa, and very simple lodging is available should you stay late. A luxury hotel being built atop the ridge is expected to be completed in 1994. Two more lakes are nearby (Dipang Tal and Maidi Tal) but they're little more than ponds, swampy and choked with vegetation.

Batulechaur And Mahendra Gufa

A few kilometers north from the outskirts of Pokhara, Batulechaur is said to have once been the winter court of Kaski's kings. Royalty introduced the delicious oranges the village was famed for, but disease killed most of the trees in the '60s. Now the only remnant of the village's royal heyday is a community of *gaine* (see p. 99), the minstrel caste. They'll be more than happy to put on a show for you and your camera, tape recorder, or videocam, but will expect to be well-paid in return—say, the price of a goat for a community feast. Cross the K. I. Singh Bridge at the north end of Pokhara's old bazaar, and the village is less than an hour's walk north.

One km north is the Mahendra cave, locally called Chamero Odhaar ("House of Bats"). Shepherd boys are said to have discovered it around 1950. Supposedly it's immense and not yet fully explored—a Swiss team went in for two hours and still didn't penetrate to the end. (This is according to the man who sells tickets at the entrance, and must be taken with a grain of salt.) You can enter the first 150 yards, dimly lit by a fallible electrical generator. Best to bring a torch of your own—local boys vie to be your guide, but the candles they carry don't illuminate much. Most of the stalactites have been carted off by souvenir hunters and there's not really much to see unless you're a fan of caves and bats.

Tibetan Settlements

Between 1959-62, over 30,000 Tibetan refugees flooded into Nepal. As their numbers swelled, Swiss aid workers helped transplant several thousand from crowded northern border regions to refugee camps in the Pokhara Valley. In this subtropical land, so different from the high Tibetan plains, the Tibetans have built a miniature version of their old life, complete with white-washed houses, prayer flags, *chorten* and gompa.

Pokhara has three Tibetan settlements, their names all prefixed by *tashi*—"good luck." After years of hardship, life is gradually turning lucky for the refugees. Many have become moderately prosperous through tourism, mainly by weaving carpets or selling trinkets. Charmingly aggressive Tibetan saleswomen ("Just looking, looking only!" they tell you) are a Pokhara hallmark. A visit to a settlement involves a heavy dose of salesmanship, but it also provides insights into Tibetan life. People are more accessible than Kathmandu, and are eager to talk, especially if you express some awareness of the Tibetans' plight. As for shopping—it's an interesting venue, and prices are better than the street sellers', but don't expect any bargains.

The largest and most interesting settlement is **Tashi Pakhel**, also called Hyangja after a nearby Nepali village. It's a 90-minute walk northwest of Pokhara's old bazaar, set atop a low cliff overlooking the Seti Gandaki. Pass the old bazaar and the Shining Hospital and continue up the riverbank, along a course marked by prayer flags and chorten to the settlement of small whitewashed houses, marked by more prayer flags. Tashi Pakhel is home to nearly 1,000 Tibetans, many of whom work in the settlement's large carpet factory. Other handicrafts include jackets, boots, and jewelry. There are several small shops near the entrance to town, and nearly every resident sells goods from his home. There's also a simple **guesthouse** should you decide to stay overnight: it's a good base for exploring the surrounding countryside.

The smaller settlement of **Tashi Ling** can be combined with a trip to Devi's Falls. Tashi Ling is just across the road; look for the bright-yellow gompa. The settlement has a carpet-weaving factory and the usual persuasive salespeople. Nearby is a children's camp for Tibetan orphans.

Paljor Ling, better known as the Tibetan Handicrafts Center, is little more than a carpet-making compound with families in residence, but it's conveniently located just west of the bus station.

Manangi Gompa

This recently built Tibetan monastery was funded by Buddhists of Manang, apparently hoping to recycle some of their trading profits into religious merit. It's new and not particularly notable, but if you haven't seen a Tibetan monastery it might be worth a visit. Cross Mahendra Phul and continue two km east; up a dirt road to the left the gompa appears atop a small hill. There are good valley views from the steps, and monks perform their daily puja in the morning and afternoon. This is one possible starting point for a 90-minute hike up to the view tower at Kahun Danda. On the opposite side of the main road atop a wooded hill is a temple to the goddess Bhadrakali.

MINI-TREKS

Pokhara is the launching point for many interesting short trips as well. If your time is limited or you doubt your enthusiasm for a full-out trek,

consider spending just a few days exploring the nearby hills. One option would be to walk the first few days of one of the longer trips described in "Trekking"—for instance, the three-day walk to the lovely village of **Chomrong** at the entrance to the Annapurna Sanctuary, or the popular Ghorepani loop via Ghandruk, which could be squeezed into less than a week. Trekking permits are available from the Immigration Office in Pokhara, and bags, boots and jackets can be rented in local shops, though the selection isn't as good as Kathmandu's.

The ongoing construction of the Pokhara-Baglung Highway is swiftly changing the trekking situation north of Pokhara. At the time of writing the road had reached the lovely riverside town of **Birethanti;** in a year or two it will reach Baglung, currently two days' walk further west. Traffic is sporadic but buses and jeeps will be regular soon enough. The hilltop village of **Chandrakot** and Birethanti are both worth visiting; Ghandruk is a half-day's walk from Birethanti.

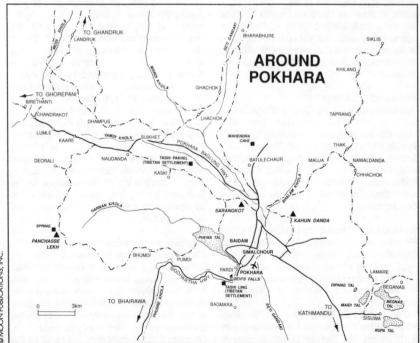

It remains to be seen how much the road will mar the charm of these places. As a general rule of thumb you need to walk two days past a roadhead before things start getting good, and they steadily improve the farther you get from the road. One illustration of this rule is the day-long hike to Naudanda (described above with Sarangkot). It's an easy overnighter from Pokhara and offers good mountain views, but the road's presence and Naudanda's proximity to Pokhara makes the town less than charming. Likewise the road has ruined the walk west to Chandrakot and Birethanti.

Ghachowk

A more promising and adventurous choice would be the five-hour walk to the Gurung village of Ghachowk north of Pokhara. Seldom visited by foreigners, it's one of the region's oldest settlements, an attractive mix of traditional houses and fields, with close-up views of Machhapuchhare. Start from Tashi Pakhel near Hyangja (it's possible to overnight here) or take a jeep to Suikhet on the Phedi Road. From here turn north to cross the Mardi Khola and continue through **Lhachowk** to Ghachowk. Farther upvalley, locally renowned **hot springs** bubble up at **Bharbhure.** You can return via an alternate route through the village of Batulechaur near Mahendra Cave.

Siklis And Ghandruk

Another seldom-visited Gurung village is Siklis, 24 km northeast up the Madi Khola. With over 500 neat slate-roofed houses huddled on a hillside, it's the biggest Gurung village in Nepal. Trekkers overnight in the village of **Thak,** then continue to Siklis. A more traveled route with better accommodations is the three-day walk via Dhampus to **Ghandruk,** another impressive Gurung town.

Nuwakot And Panchasse Lekh

Fifteen km south of Devi's Falls is the old fortress town of Nuwakot, formerly the headquarters for petty chieftans who once ruled the area. Since the construction of the road it's been neglected, but there are good views from the top of the summit.

Panchasse Lekh is the highest of the ridges encircling the the Pokhara Valley, cresting at 2,512 meters. This four-day trek offers interesting villages (Brahman-Chhetri and Gurung) at the beginning and end, and a two-day ridge walk in the middle with full-on mountain views of a 140-km stretch of peaks alternating with first-class jungle. The ridge is uninhabited except for a few woodcutters and shepherds, and you'll have to camp for at least half the trek—preferably with a guide and porters who know not only the route, but the location of water on the dry ridge. The first day takes you through the wonderfully named district of **Pumdi-Bhumdi;** reach it by boating across Phewa Tal or via the Siddhartha Rajmarg. The trek concludes at Naudanda, where you can drop down to Phedi and catch a jeep or walk into Pokhara via Sarangkot.

PRACTICALITIES

Finding a good cheap room is no problem. There are probably a hundred lodges, guesthouses, and hotels around Lakeside and Damside, and more are being built every month. Elaborate multi-storied brick buildings are gradually replacing the simple original lodges, raising the reasonable prices of the latter: Rs40-60 for a simple room without bath, Rs 150 with. Expect cleanliness and hot water, and look for a place with a nice garden and/or rooftop views—Pokhara's flowers are splendid year-round.

The vast majority of travelers stay on the east side of Phewa Tal, either in Lakeside or the Dam area (Pardi). Most "tourist-class" expensive hotels are inconveniently located across from the airport. Hotels in the bazaar areas and around the bus station cater mainly to Nepali and Indian businessmen. It's hard to imagine why you'd stay here unless you got stuck at night. There are lots of cheap lodges on the back road leading from the bus station. **Hotel Sayapatri** across the road is a little quieter and reasonably clean.

Lakeside Accommodations

For peaceful lodgings look down the many dirt roads leading east off the main strip. On these wide, quiet lanes tourist lodges alternate with fields and houses; often they're family-run operations. Lakeside's mountain views are spotty at best; the peaks are partly blocked by a ridge and progressively vanish as you head north. Disappointingly, there's only one lodge on the

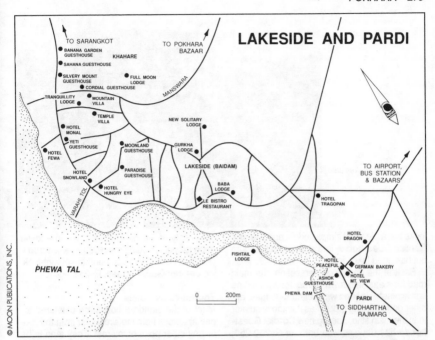

actual lakeside. The **Khahare** section at the far end is less developed, with good views of lakes and fields.

A few of Lakeside's many good lodges, beginning from the southern end, would include the **Gurkha Lodge,** down the road past the Baba Restaurant, with only three rooms set in a huge garden, Rs220 d, very tranquil. A bit further down, **New Solitary Lodge** has clean if small rooms and another nice garden, but it's a 10-minute walk from Lakeside. **Hotel Kantipur** on the main road has carpeted triples with bath for Rs300 and a good restaurant; one second-story room has lake and mountain views.

For a central location you can't beat the popular **Hotel Hungry Eye** behind the restaurant of the same name; a bit expensive at US$12 s, US$15 d. On the side road just beyond it are **Hotel Paradise** (nice garden and sunny rooms) and **Moonland Guest House** (quiet, with mountain views). **Hotel Monal** is one of the best places on the main road and more expensive than most: Rs175 s, Rs200 d without bath, Rs300 and up with. **The Snowland** is an old standby, right in the middle of the strip, charging

Rs75 d, Rs 200 with bath. For a cheap place on the main road try **Yeti Guesthouse** near the Monal.

Across the street the old **Hotel Fewa** is the only budget hotel fronting the water. A large garden and boathouse make it special; Rs75 d, Rs210 with bath. On the next side road down you'll find **Tranquillity Lodge** and the new **Temple Villa,** which looks more like a suburban house than a hotel.

Pokhara's official **campground** is at the next intersection. It's on the lake but treeless and guarded by police, altogether unpromising. With so many good lodges around one can only pity campers broiling in their cramped tents. North of here the pavement ends but lodges and restaurants continue in a less flashy vein into Khahare, the quietest and and most distant section of Lakeside. Remnants of Pokhara's hippie days congregate around here, and a more traditional Nepal begins to trickle back, as local tea shops alternate with tourist restaurants and children play in surrounding fields. The fanciest place is the new **Sahana Guesthouse,** with deluxe doubles for Rs300. **Silvery Mount Guesthouse**

"The Strip," Lakeside

KERRY MORAN

looks like a pleasant simple lodge, and **Banana Garden Guesthouse** further up is rock-bottom but has good lake views.

Back at the camping intersection, the main road runs east into town, a very long haul. The first kilometer is lined with yet more lodges, another good hunting ground as this too is quieter than the main strip. The big new **Cordial Guesthouse** has doubles with bath for Rs200-250; **Hotel Plaza** beside it is similar. **Himalayan Country Lodge** has nice individual bungalows for Rs100 s, Rs200 d; the nearby **Mountain Villa** also looks good. Further up the road, **Full Moon Lodge** is away from it all, perched atop a hill with good lake views, Rs35 s, Rs50 d.

Pardi

At the south end of the lake, midway between the airport and Lakeside, this up-and-coming area is a refuge for travelers fleeing Lakeside's scene. It's rapidly developing its own version, more subdued but still touristy. Pardi lacks the shady charm of Lakeside, which for all its faults is still honeycombed with fields and Nepali homes. Mountain views are better from the dam end, though, and there are some excellent new lodges, many owned by Thakalis.

Hotel Garden is scrupulously clean, with large, sunny rooms, a nice garden, and a decent restaurant. Prices range from US$2 s without bath to US$10-$15 for a carpeted double with bath. The nearby **Hotel Peaceful** and **Hotel Mountain View** are very similar; so is the large **Ashok Guest House,** one block behind. There

are plenty of smaller guesthouses in a lower price range, including the **Hotel Yak & Yuppie** (Rs75 d, Rs175 with bath) and the quaint-looking **Jeevan Guest House,** Rs25 s, Rs45 d.

Tourist-class Hotels

Most of the standard hotels are clustered together across from the airport, far from the lake or any other point of interest. They tend to be used by group treks and tours whose transport is prearranged. Independent travelers might feel stranded here, though the air-conditioning is an admitted plus anytime after April.

New Hotel Crystal (tel. 20035) is the largest and the leader of the lot, with a swimming pool and tennis court. Air-conditioned rooms go for US$34 s, US$50 d; larger, non-a/c rooms in the new annex are US$19 s, US$24 d. Next door is the nearly useless government **Tourist Office;** beside it the government-run **Hotel Taragaon** wears a similarly neglected air. Its rooms are clean and cheap for this location, though: US$13 s, US$ 15 d. Next is the big old **Hotel Himal,** an old standby popular with Sherpas and Tibetans. Rooms are cheap (Rs60 and up) but you may awaken with fleabites. The restaurant here serves good momo and thukpa. Last in the line is **Hotel Mount Annapurna,** run by Tibetans and decorated in Tibetan style. There's a big sunny garden with views, but the rooms are a bit cramped; US$19 s, US$27 d.

Two hotels in Pardi offer good value and a better location. **Hotel Dragon** has nicely decorated rooms with a/c for US$25 s, US$35 d, plus a big garden and good Thakali food in the restaurant. The new **Hotel Tragopan** on the main road is quite nice and reasonably priced at US$18 s, US$25 d; rooms have fans and the restaurant is good.

Lakeside has only one tourist-class hotel, unless you count **Base Camp Resort,** which bills itself as the "finest lodge in Pokhara" and charges US$33 s, US$45 d. It's a nice place, but the staff is a bit snooty. The **Fish Tail Lodge** is built on a promontory jutting into the lake and is across the outlet of the dam. You reach it by a rope-drawn raft, no doubt kept for drama; it would be simple enough to bridge the gap. The rooms are nothing special but the grounds are beautifully landscaped, the best in Pokhara, and offer superb views over the lake of the mountains. It's especially nice in the dry winter and spring, when other gardens look a bit scruffy. The round, glassed-in restaurant offers more good views, but indifferent food. The lodge is managed by the Hotel de l'Annapurna (Kathmandu tel. 221-711), which arranges reservations and transport. US$45 s, US$60, plus the 12% tax typical of this standard of hotel.

Food

Lazy Lakeside life revolves around the pursuit of food. Dining out is practically the only nightlife, and restaurants are a good place to meet other travelers, compare notes, and find trekking partners. You choose a restaurant by its clientele and music as much as by its food; the season's favorites are easy to pick out by the crowds. Most have outdoor dining, and the **Annapurna Restaurant** offers diners the use of a telescope.

Lakeside's Western food doesn't quite meet Kathmandu standards, but it tastes pretty good anyway after three weeks on the trail. Highlights include fresh fish from the lake and bamboo shacks selling fresh fruit juice. When you tire of the pasta and steak routine, there are lots of little momo shacks and tea stalls intermingled with the official restaurants.

Lakeside is one long string of restaurants, from the well-regarded **Baba Restaurant** on. **Le Bistro** is as popular as its Kathmandu counterpart. **Hotel Kantipur**'s restaurant is good if a little pricey; try it for pizza. **Hotel Snowland** has a rooftop dining area and serves five international varieties of breakfast. The two most popular restaurants in Pokhara are side-by-side: **The Hungry Eye** and **Don't Cross Me By.** Both do good entrees and exceptional desserts, but the Hungry Eye doesn't realize that egg is not an appropriate pizza topping.

There are several Tibetan restaurants, and while Tibetan food is not one of the world's great cuisines, it's worth a try, and you can sample chang and tongba. The **Little Tibetan Tea Garden** has a nice outdoor dining area.

In Damside there's **K.C.'s Restaurant** (no relation to Kathmandu's) with lake views and steaks, and an offshoot of the ubiquitous **German Bakery** for breakfast and snacks. **The Nest** at Hotel Tragopan serves good Indian food, including tandoori chicken, in a moderately elegant settling. One of the best places for an all-out splash, an Indian feast with several friends sharing dishes.

In terms of trekking provisions, Pokhara's supply is less varied but similar to Kathmandu's—chocolate, bicuits, cheese, whole-wheat bread, peanut butter, and granola are all available.

Entertainment

Nightlife focuses on dining; the other highlight is strolling up and down the strip, seeing and being seen. Beyond this there's not much—the bar at the Fishtail Lodge, playing *caroom* boards in local tea shops, drinking chang in momo shops. Stagey but enthusiastically delivered Nepali dance shows are put on nightly in the main tourist season at several hotels. Check the Hotel Dragon (tel. 20052), the Fishtail Lodge, and New Hotel Crystal (tel. 20035). Danphe Kala Mandir up in the old bazaar may also have shows, but it's a long way back to Lakeside.

Shopping

There's little in Pokhara that you can't find better selections of in Kathmandu. One exception are the batiks, perhaps because there are so many stores clustered together. There's a big huddle of **batik** shops past the airport in Nagdhunga. While it's not a native craft, some of the scenes of Nepali life come across surprisingly well.

A **dhaka topi** shop on the road into the old bazaar sells handwoven *dhaka* cloth and hats; a handicrafts store a little further north sells simple old brass pieces and the checked woolen blankets woven by Gurungs. Many shops are piled with *shaligram,* black stone fossils found in the Kali Gandaki Valley. Associated with Vishnu, they're regarded as sacred.

Persuasive, cheerful Tibetan hawkers are everywhere, presiding over the usual junky souvenirs imported from Kathmandu. Locally woven Tibetan **carpets** are sold in the Tibetan settlements and in Lakeside shops, but the best carpets are found in Kathmandu. The same goes for thankga. When it comes to authentic local goods, though, it's best to buy if you find something you like—things like wooden vessels, old Tibetan carpets, curios, and turquoise aren't necessarily rare, but each piece is unique.

Services And Information

The most convenient money-changing counter is the **Nepal Rastra Bank** at the intersection where the Lakeside road enters Pardi (across from Hotel Tragopan). There are more banks in the bazaar and a **Nepal Bank** office near the bus stop. The black market in Pokhara is subdued, and you'll have to hunt for someone to change at a better-than-bank rate.

The **Immigration Office** just north of the bank will issue **trekking permits** for the Annapurna region and extend visas for 15 days. Application hours are 1000-1600 Sun.-Thurs., 1000-1300 Fri.; usually you can pick up your permit on the same day.

The main **post office** is near Mahendra Phul, and the district **police** office is a little further north. Pokhara's telephone situation has improved markedly in the past few years—you can reach Kathmandu easily (Rs15 per minute), and international calls can be made from many lodges or from shops in Lakeside.

For medical emergencies, visit the **Western Regional Hospital** (tel. 20066); they do stool tests also. There are plenty of do-it-yourself pharmacies in Lakeside, Pardi, and in town.

Laundry is taken care of by local women who wallop the heck out of clothes, bringing them back clean, if a bit more worn. You'll probably be approached on the street by laundresses, or ask your lodgekeeper. A few places near the campground advertise laundry.

Pokhara's **Tourist Office** across from the airport languishes in a big building with a pathetically small amount of literature to hand out—at present, a brochure on the Annapurna Circuit, and that's it.

Lakeside **bookstores** sell maps and specialize in local publications about the region, with titles you might not find so easily in Kathmandu. They also have a great selection of fat novels to read while boating. Keep up with world events, if you must, with the *International Herald Tribune* and the usual U.S. news magazines, which arrive here a few days late.

GETTING THERE

By Air

RNAC runs several flights to Pokhara daily, and tickets are easily enough available in all but the busiest season. The US$61 might be worth it as long as the road remains in its present horrendous state. The half-hour flight passes by a 100-mile stretch of peaks, skimming over what used to be a seven-day trek. You're deposited at the **Nagdhunga Airfield,** with a spectacular view of the five Annapurnas and Machhapuchhare right in the center—among the best views anywhere in the valley. Unfortunately voracious taxi drivers and hotel touts don't give you any time to admire it. From the airport it's a half-hour walk to Lakeside. Taxis charge Nepalis Rs5 per head for the trip and cram five people inside, but they expect Rs50 from foreigners. If you can get one to Lakeside for Rs30 you're doing fine. There's a cycle rental stands outside the gate, and a few hotels, mostly expensive, along the way.

By Road

Public bus service is typically slow and crowded, taking eight to nine hours to make the 200-km journey from Kathmandu. Tourist buses charge over twice the price (Rs150) but are more comfortable and possibly faster. **Student Travels and Tours** and **Swiss Travels and Tours** in Thamel are among several companies running the service. With the road in its current dreadful condition, even tourist buses take eight hours to make the journey. They all drop passengers at the bus station at the end of the Prithvi Highway, leaving you at the mercy of hotel touts. This is one of the least pleasant places in town—take a taxi to Lakeside for Rs30 or plod the three km; Pardi is two km. Lakeside travel agents sell bus tickets onwards to other destinations for a Rs10 fee, sparing you a return visit to the bus station. If you're coming in from the

THE KATHMANDU-POKHARA ROAD

The 202-km Prithvi Rajmarg connecting Kathmandu to Pokhara was built in the early '70s by China and is already falling apart. The strech from Naubise to Mugling follows the course of the Trisuli River. Under reconstruction and widening for the past few years, it will probably remain torn up for several more, making the dusty, bumpy 81-km journey an average of three hours long.

Mugling, halfway between Kathmandu and Pokhara, is popularly known as "Daal Bhaat Bazaar" because everyone stops here for a meal. It's not really a village but a giant truck stop recently sprung up to cater to travelers. The wide main road is lined by dozens of wooden buildings purveying daal bhaat and tea; the bus driver pulls in, passengers pile out, and 20 minutes later—the time it takes to consume two plates of daal bhaat—it's time to go again. For a leg-stretcher, walk down to the suspension bridge over the Trisuli; the Marsyangdi River joins nearby. There should be no reason to stay overnight here, but there are plenty of small local hotels if necessary. **Motel du Mugling,** across the bridge, is an upperclass operation with a reasonable restaurant, managed by Hotel de l'Annapurna, US$23 s, US$33 d.

From Mugling, the road is in reasonable shape and the second half of the trip goes much faster, first following the course of the Marsyangdi Khola. Look for the sluiceways and turbines of the Marsyangdi Power Project, a recently-completed $200 million venture to fill Kathmandu's insatiable need for electricity. Shiny new metal towers line the road to Kathmandu, but the Valley's demand is increasing so fast that Marsyangdi was outdated even before it was completed.

Himalayan peaks appear on this stretch, mainly Annapurna, Himalchuli, and Manaslu. Eight km beyond Mugling is the small village of **Abu Khaireni,** and the turnoff to the hill town and fortress of **Gorkha** (see p. 267). It's a four-hour walk uphill is the wish-fulfilling temple of Manakamana. Ten km further is **Dumre,** a dusty, unlovely roadside stop which is the turnoff for the eastern part of the Annapurna Circuit —Manang and the Marsyangdi Valley. Local vehicles ply the dirt road up to **Besisahar.** If you come too late to catch one or prefer to walk, you can climb for two hours to the old Newar town of **Bandipur,** once a major trading village on the route to Manang.

The Pokhara Road continues through **Damauli,** a big bazaar town and district headquarters with good swimming in the Madi-Seti River if you happen to stop. Pokhara is 55 km further, following the course of the Seti Gandaki River. The main bus stop is at the end of the highway, marked by a statue of Prithvi Narayan Shah; it's midway between the airport and the bazaar, a long walk from Lakeside.

south on the Siddhartha Highway get off the bus at Pardi (Damside), only one km from Lakeside.

On Foot

The only way until recently—from Kathmandu, a gentle six- or seven-day trek through lowland hills, perfect in the winter. The trail starts at **Trisuli,** 44 miles north of Kathmandu. Three days away is the ancient city-kingdom of Gorkha, connected by road to the main highway should you decide to catch a ride. See "Trekking" for details.

GETTING AROUND

Pokhara on foot is out of the question unless you're a real fiend for walking: the vast distances between places will grind down even the most dedicated trekker. All taxis are unmetered; set the price before you start and look for people to share with. From Lakeside it should be about Rs40 up to the old bazaar, Rs30 to the bus station, Rs25 to the airport. You can usually find a taxi in Lakeside if you're patient, but if you're catching a flight or bus, have your lodgekeeper book one in advance.

It's surprisingly easy to find a car and driver for long-distance destinations like Tansen, Lumbini, or Kathmandu. If you can afford the price (Rs900 to be dropped off in Tansen, maybe Rs1700 to Lumbini, Rs2200 to Kathmandu) this is an ideal means of long-distance travel.

Local bus service is limited to a single slow loop around the bazaar, passing the bus station and airport en route. Catch it (but only if you must) across from the Hungry Eye. Service terminates at 1700.

The best way to get around the Valley is by bike. Roadside stands rent old clunkers for Rs3-4 per hour, Rs15-20 per day. A mountain bike is

Rs100 or more per day but worth it: roads are fairly smooth but the apparently level valley has a wicked slope from north to south, deceptively hidden until you're on top of it. Having gears transforms a northbound journey from a grind into a breeze.

TANSEN

Tansen is that great rarity: a Nepali town big enough to be interesting, yet so far utterly unspoiled. Set at 1,400 meters on the southern side of the Mahabharat Range in south-central Nepal, it's an ideal hill station, with a marvelously fresh climate.

A prosperous-looking collection of red-brick houses set on a steep hillside, Tansen is among the largest of the far-flung Newar trading posts scattered across the Hills. Sixty percent of its 16,000 people are Newar, but the surrounding region is Magar country, home to one of the most delightful of Nepal's ethnic groups.

Tansen once belonged to the Barha Magarat, a dozen small tribal states ruled by Magar chief-

tans. In the 15th century it became the capital of the powerful kingdom of Palpa, ruled by the Sen Dynasty, distant cousins of the Shah royal family. The semi-legendary king Mukunda Sen is said to have extended his rule all the way up to the Kosi River, launching an attack on the Kathmandu Valley and making off with a pair of gilded Bhairab masks he installed in two temples near Butwal. Tansen was finally brought into Nepal in 1806, the last of the independent kingdoms to be annexed. It became an important district headquarters and tax collection center, and an outpost for troublesome Ranas packed off to unofficial exile as regional governors.

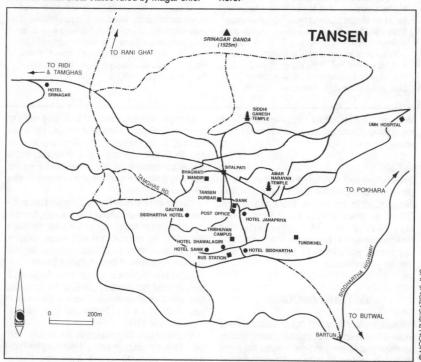

The town has a confusing multiplicity of names: Tansing is the original Magar name, Tansen the modern Nepali version. It's frequently called Palpa, the name of both the ancient kingdom and the surrounding district of which Tansen is the administrative capital.

SIGHTS

The Town

Tansen's greatest attraction is itself. Narrow cobbled streets, some set at impossibly steep angles, are lined with old brick buildings and filled with the cheerful bustle of city life, minus the racket of Kathmandu. Tansen is a friendly, unspoiled, completely natural place of a type seldom found without trekking into an unvisited part of the Hills. The kids haven't yet learned to beg, and people are remarkably blasé about the rare foreign traveler—a relief after the ogling sometimes encountered in the Terai and India. It's not that they're unfriendly; they just all seem to have something better to do. The main bazaar is full of Hill people in town to buy supplies—grain, jars of cooking oil, tiny dried fish from the nearby Barangdi Khola, all hauled back home in wicker *doko*. The people are handsome, and women in particular have glowing complexions, probably something to do with the exquisite climate.

Inside houses both men and women weave the city's famed *dhaka* cloth on upright looms. Woven with pashmina thread, Palpa *dhaka* is famous for its intricate patterns. Finished pieces, *topi* and shawls are sold in the main bazaar, or you could inquire of a weaver. The other speciality is metalwork (found in the Taksar area), but stick to simple metal vessels rather than sculpture.

Around Tansen Durbar

The center of town is dominated by the rambling pink Tansen Durbar, built in 1927. Once the Rana governor's residential palace, it now houses government offices. The north gate, Baggi Dhoka, is said to be the largest in Nepal, big enough for a carriage (*baggi* = "buggy") to pass through. Behind the Durbar is an ugly renovated temple to Bhagwati, built in 1815 to commemorate a Nepali victory over the British at Butwal. The glee was shortlived, as the British won the war the following year, forcing Nepal to cede most of its Terai holdings.

Further east is the **Amar Narayan Mandir,** one of the finest Newari pagodas outside the Kathmandu Valley. The erotic struts are clever and the small forest surrounding it is full of fruit bats. Twice a day, temple drums, bells, and horns are sounded in worship, adding to the town's timeless air.

There are plenty of other temples, most unnotable (the 1934 earthquake did a lot of damage), and a few Newari bahal and chaitya as well. The big open Tundikhel near the bus park gives views of the green Madi Valley below, on winter mornings filled with billowing silver fog.

Tansen is headquarters for a surprisingly large number of foreign-aid projects, including a United Mission to Nepal hospital. Most Nepalis will assume you're working there if you're headed to Tansen—the idea of tourism hasn't yet caught on, despite some feeble government efforts to develop the area.

Behind Tansen rises a 1,525-meter hill called **Srinagar Danda.** The crest is a half-hour climb from the **Siddhi Ganesh** temple on the hillside, or an easy ridge walk from the Srinagar Guesthouse. The ridge provides Himalayan views stretching all the way from Kanjiroba in the far west to Langtang. There's an incongruous helipad up here, the ruins of a few old Rana summer homes, and a **Panchayat Silver Jubilee Memorial Park.** The pine plantation here is a recent effort to combat the serious deforestation resulting from Tansen's population explosion. One effect of the tree-cutting has been the gradual drying-up of the town's water supply.

Sights Near Tansen

Practically untouched itself, Tansen is a launching point for day walks and treks into virgin country. With its unspoiled, friendly Magar villages, the surrounding region provides a taste of what popular trekking trails were like 30 years ago. Trekking possibilities include the 10-day walk between Pokhara-Dhorpatan-Tansen, or a four-day walk south along the Kali Gandaki from Beni.

For a brief stroll, there's the Magar village of **Chilangdi** an hour's walk from town. The potter's village of **Ghorbanda,** inhabited by Kumal people, is a few kilometers north off the Siddhartha Rajmarg.

Among the most intriguing day hikes is the 90-minute, seven-km walk downhill over Srinagar Danda and along the Kali Gandaki to **Ranighat,** a vast abandoned Rana palace on the riverside. Built in 1896 in memory of a Rana governor's wife, the huge edifice was designed by British engineers and constructed by Nepali soldiers. For a few years it served as a Rana guesthouse/summerhouse, then its builder fell into disgrace and the building was abandoned. It's on the verge of collapse, but the sight of the huge pillared edifice looming out of the forested riverbank is worth the trip. Returning, you could take an alternate trail along the Kali Gandaki to meet Ramdi Ghat on the highway and catch a bus back to town.

An unpaved road connects Tansen with the town of **Tamghas,** 40 km west. Buses run several times a day, but it's a slow journey. Ten km down the road is **Ridi Bazaar,** a mainly Newari town of about 2,000 at the confluence of the Kali Gandaki and the Ridi Khola. Its centerpiece is the **Rikheswar Narayan Mandir,** the local version of Kathmandu's Pashupatinath, with similarly auspicious cremation ghats. The image of Vishnu here is said to have begun no larger than an infant and gradually grown to the size and appearance of an adult. You can walk here via a 13-km route that manages to stay off the road most of the way, and return to Tansen by bus.

The **Palpa Bhairab Mandir** is eight km west of Tansen, just off the Tamghas road. Marked with a huge gilded trident, it enshrines a replica of Kathmandu's Kaalo Bhairab said to be so terrifying it's frightened several viewers to death, which explains why it's now hidden from view. The temple is heavily visited on Tuesdays and Saturdays by local people performing animal sacrifices.

PRACTICALITIES

Accommodations And Food
The rather squalid area around the bus station has many cheap hotels, marred by the racket beginning at 5 a.m. **Hotel Dhawalagiri** is slightly better than its front facade would suggest; most travelers pick **Hotel Siddhartha,** Rs35 d.

Sanik Lodge on the road behind is very basic, with bathrooms out back, but it's quiet; Rs25 s, Rs35 d.

Unless you're leaving very early in the morning it's best to stay in town, which is at least more attractive. **Hotel Janapriya** up the hill from the bus station is decent, Rs40 d, Rs 80 with bath. There's also **Hotel Rose** in the bazaar, and **Hotel Siddhartha Gautam** on the loop road into town. There are lots of small restaurants and snack shops around the bus station. Teashops scattered through town provide a more cheerful vantage point for people-watching, and there are a few Indo-Nepali restaurants around the bazaar.

The only *pukka* place to stay is **Hotel Srinagar** (tel. 20045), about two km northwest of the bus station, perched atop Bataase Danda ("Windy Ridge"). It's at least a 20-minute walk uphill, complicated by lack of directions. The motor road to **Gulmi** runs close by, if you have a vehicle at your command. Rooms are decent but nothing special (US$20 s, US$28 d, dorm beds US$8), but one wing faces the Himalaya while the other overlooks Tansen and the Madi Valley—splendid breakfast views either way. The bland "tourist standard" so painstakingly reproduced here is sadly typical of most places in Nepal, when actually something more exotic is called for, like the wonderful old Rana buildings now occupied by the university. For the ultimate in peace and views, the hotel operates two **guest cottages** on Srinagar Danda (US$30 d). They've been neglected but are supposed to be repaired soon.

Getting There
Midway down the Siddhartha Highway, Tansen is best reached from Pokhara or Bhairawa. By bus it's six hours from Pokhara; two hours from Bhairawa; six hours from Chitwan. Traveling directly from Kathmandu is more problematic, though there are a few direct buses. If not, you'll go via Butwal and catch a local bus for the one-hour ride to Tansen. From Pokhara, a taxi will drop you off in Tansen in four hours for about Rs900.

From Pokhara, the Siddhartha Highway twists through a winding gorge of the Anahi Khola, passing through small Magar villages with the usual supplies. Lunch stop is usually **Waling,** a miniature daal bhaat bazaar two hours out of

Pokhara. The most attractive place is small, shady Ramdi Ghat, where the road crosses the Kali Gandaki on a suspension bridge. Signs for "Gurkha Welfare Centers" indicate the strong hold soldiery has on local people—this is Magar country, and Magars constitute the highest percentage of British and Indian Gurkhas. Most families here are partly supported by remittances from soldiers.

Tansen lies three km up a spur road from the small town of **Bartun.** If your bus is not direct to Tansen you'll be deposited here. Take a minibus up the hill or walk via a steep footpath to Tansen's Tundikhel, near the bus park. Tansen itself is so steep vehicles rarely penetrate its roads—inconvenient, but a source of the town's great charm.

BHAIRAWA AND SUNAULI

The most convenient and popular border crossing between India and Nepal, Sunauli provides access to a big chunk of northern India, including Delhi, Varanasi, and Agra. There's not much to say about it besides the basics—Sunauli is so small it's barely a village, and the larger city of Bhairawa, four km north, is just another flat, dusty, charmless Terai town. In the winter months, the surrounding countryside has its redeeming features: mango trees, birds, oceans of rice fields, and villages with a feel very much like rural India. Few travelers visit nearby Lumbini, the birthplace of the Buddha, but a detour here is worth considering, if only because it's among the most important historical sites in Nepal.

Transport between Bhairawa and Sunauli is by cycle rickshaw (Rs10) or tempo (Rs2). Prearranged bus-train packages from Kathmandu to India often include an overnight in Sunauli, but if you have the choice Bhairawa is marginally more interesting and has better facilities. Sunauli

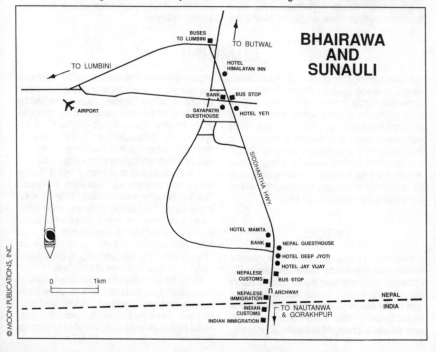

encompasses four or five basic hotels, a Nepal Rastra Bank (open 0730-1800 daily), and the generally mild Nepalese Customs. Just beyond is Indian Customs; formalities shouldn't take more than 30 minutes for both. Buses in either direction are plentiful; it takes 90 minutes to get to the railway station at Gorakhpur, and at least 12 hours to reach Kathmandu.

Accommodations And Food

Bhairawa's bus stop is the big traffic circle around the statue. This and the next street south constitute the main bazaar. There are lots of cheap, basic lodgings around here, averaging Rs40s, Rs60 d without bath. Generally the less said about them the better; Sayapatri Guesthouse near the bus stop and City Guest House are as good as any. The best place is Hotel Yeti (tel. 20551) right on the central circle: new, clean, and a refuge from the hot streets, Rs220 s, Rs275 d with bath. If it's full, you can walk ten minutes north down the Siddhartha Highway to the Hotel Himalayan Inn (tel. 20347), second choice but the only other upper-class place in town; Rs150 s, Rs200 d. Apart from the restaurants of these two hotels, food is lim-

ited to daal bhaat diners, tea stalls, and Indian food.

Getting There

Kathmandu-Bhairawa airfare is US$72; flights are five times weekly. From the airport take a rickshaw to the center of town. By bus it's a 13-hour journey from Kathmandu, nine hours from Pokhara, five from Tadi Bazaar and Chitwan National Park.

The Mahendra Rajmarg (Kathmandu and Chitwan) and the Siddhartha Rajmarg (Pokhara) both meet at Butwal, a nondescript Terai town huddled at the base of the hills. Through buses stop at the oddly named "Traphik Chowk" on the east side of town, a modern bazaar with plenty of cheap hotels. Butwal's redeeming feature is streetside cappuccino vendors who will serve you aboard the bus—okay, so it's Nescafé, but it's a change from the usual *chiyaa*. If for some reason you get stuck, there's the typical cluster of cheap hotels around the bus park and in the bazaar. The best place is Hotel Sindoor (tel. 21089) on the west end, charging US$18 s, US$26 d. Bhairawa is a half-hour south of Butwal.

LUMBINI

Travelers rushing through Sunauli and Bhairawa almost invariably bypass Lumbini, the birthplace of the Buddha 22 km west of Bhairawa. A Buddhist pilgrimage site marooned in the midst of Muslim-Hindu country, Lumbini is ignored by just about everyone except a few devout Japanese, Thai and Tibetan pilgrims. At 250 km from Kathmandu it would be a long journey in itself, but it fits nicely into a Pokhara-Tansen-Chitwan loop, and if you're heading to India an extra day is well spent at Lumbini.

HISTORY

Siddhartha Gautama, the man who became the Buddha (the title means The Awakened or Enlightened One), was born a prince of the Sakya clan ruling Kapilvastu, a small independent kingdom on the Indian plains. Lumbini only became part of Nepal in 1856, and it's unlikely Buddha ever set foot in present-day Nepal. After reach-

ing enlightenment at the age of 34, he spent the remainder of his life wandering the region around the middle Ganges, teaching the "Middle Way" to enlightenment. He died at the age of 80 in Kushinagar. Today the sites of his birth, enlightenment, first teaching and death—Lumbini, Bodh Gaya, Sarnath and Kushinagar—are visited by Buddhist pilgrims from across Asia.

The Buddha was born around 543 B.C. (the actual date is disputed). According to legend, Queen Mayadevi was traveling to her parent's home for the birth of her first child when labor pains started in the shady grove of Lumbini where her party had stopped to rest. The child was born painlessly from her right side as Mayadevi clung to the overhanging branch of a sal tree—a favorite scene of sculptors.

Upon his birth the infant Buddha is said to have taken seven steps to the north as lotus flowers sprang up beneath his feet, and proclaimed, "This is my final rebirth." Indra, Brahma, and a host of other gods descended to worship

(top) thatched hut by Pokhara's lakeside, Machhapuchhare in background (Kerry Moran);
(bottom left) boys on swing, eastern Nepal (Kerry Moran);
(bottom right) sunset over the Rapti River, Chitwan National Park (Kerry Moran)

Ghandruk, as seen on the Annapurna Sanctuary trek (Kerry Moran)

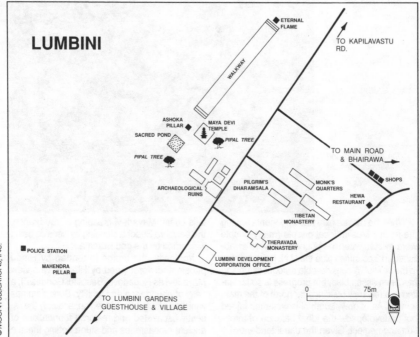

LUMBINI

ETERNAL FLAME

TO KAPILAVASTU RD.

WALKWAY

ASHOKA PILLAR

MAYA DEVI TEMPLE

SACRED POND

PIPAL TREE

PIPAL TREE

TO MAIN ROAD & BHAIRAWA

ARCHAEOLOGICAL RUINS

PILGRIM'S DHARAMSALA

MONK'S QUARTERS

SHOPS

HEWA RESTAURANT

TIBETAN MONASTERY

THERAVADA MONASTERY

POLICE STATION

LUMBINI DEVELOPMENT CORPORATION OFFICE

MAHENDRA PILLAR

0   75m

MOON

TO LUMBINI GARDENS GUESTHOUSE & VILLAGE

© MOON PUBLICATIONS, INC.

him, and family priests quickly realized this infant with the 32 marks of perfection on his body was destined for greatness—either a world monarch, they decided, or an Enlightened One.

Ashokan Pillar

Lumbini's earliest patron was the Indian emperor Ashoka, who came here on pilgrimage in 249 B.C. and commemorated his visit by erecting a stone column. A devout Buddhist, Ashoka had a habit of raising pillars, both as memorials and to demarcate the boundaries of his vast kingdom—there are two more at Niglihawa and Kotihawa, 33 km northwest and west of Lumbini. The Lumbini pillar handily proves the site's authenticity as the Buddha's birthplace.

Chinese pilgrims visiting Lumbini a thousand years after Ashoka found temples, monasteries, and stupas, but the site was already declining as Indian Buddhism waned. Already weakened by resurgent Hinduism, it received the final blow with the Muslim invasion. With Buddhism wiped out from the land of its birth, Lumbini slowly sank beneath the jungle. An an-

cient stone sculpture of the Buddha's nativity survived, worshipped by local women as a fertility symbol, but so completely forgotten was Lumbini that it took a German archaeologist to rediscover it in 1895 by uncovering the Ashokan Pillar from the jungle.

Little was done in the ensuing years to preserve or protect Lumbini. By 1967 it was in such disrepair that U Thant, Secretary General of the U.N. and a devout Burmese Buddhist, is said to have wept at the sight. An international development committee was formed shortly after, and the wheels of development began to creak.

The Master Plan

Ten years later came a master plan, designed by a Japanese architect, for a 45-square-km complex of gardens, monasteries, temples, monuments, and groves to be established at Lumbini. Up to 70% of the complex would be forested, welcome relief on the treeless plain, and appropriate in light of the Buddha's ecologically sound teachings.

the sacred pool and
Mayadevi temple

While the master plan has opponents among the mainly Muslim local people (many people were evicted when the boundaries were established), 13 countries plus the U.N. have enlisted in the project. A considerable amount of funding has been assembled, but progress is so far limited to a few new buildings far north of the main temple. As of now, Lumbini is well-maintained but undeveloped—the ideal balance of attention and neglect. Given the usual tendency for development to uglify, it's probably best to visit Lumbini now rather than later.

SIGHTS

There's little to see at Lumbini beyond the Mayadevi Mandir, the sacred pond, the Ashokan pillar, and a pair of rather ordinary monasteries. But the place radiates a feeling of peace, soothing the most restless souls. Somehow it's enough to sit in the shade of the big pipal trees and gaze out over the flat green plains. A few pilgrims circumambulate the temple, and local people drift across the parklike grounds, stopping to peer curiously inside the Tibetan gompa.

Tangible objects of interest are clustered near the **Mayadevi Mandir,** a boxy whitewashed structure sheltering an ancient stone relief of the Buddha's birth dating back to the second century. Worn almost smooth from centuries of worship, the features of the main figures were chiselled out by iconoclastic Muslim invaders. Beside it stands a modern marble copy, the de-

tails intact: Mayadevi grasping a tree branch, the newborn Buddha standing by her side being welcomed by the god Brahma.

Ironically, the image is tended by Hindu priests and worshipped by Hindus, who view Mayadevi as Rupadevi ("Beautiful Goddess"), a deity of abundance and fertility. Buddhism has vanished utterly from the region, and only the recently excavated and restored foundations of ancient monasteries and stupa dotting the site indicate this was once a stronghold, a sacred site at least from the second century B.C. to the ninth century A.D. The corrugated surface of the level plain around the temple complex indicates that many more ruins remain underground. Some archaeologists believe it's best this way, as excavated monuments are subject to vandalism and theft.

The **Ashokan Pillar** on the temple's western side is pretty unimpressive for the oldest historical monument in Nepal. The inscription reads: "The king, friend of the gods, he of the kindly countenance, came here in person twenty years after his coronation and rendered homage, because this was the birthplace of the Buddha, the saint of the Sakya." In an act of pure *chutzpah,* a marble Mahendra pillar has been erected nearby. The stepped square pool is said to be the one Mayadevi bathed in before labor. Here the infant Buddha was is said to have been washed after birth by two dragons, one spouting hot water, one cold.

Across the way are two modern monasteries, the first a typical **Tibetan gompa** constructed by Chopgye Trinzin Rinpoche, a Sakya lama who has a monastery at Boudhanath. It was built in 1968, but the frescoes at the entrance already look like they're a century old. The second monastery was built by the Nepalese government and forms an odd menage. Called the **Theravada Monastery** (Theravada is the Buddhism of Southeast Asia), it has a typically Vajrayana *dorje* over the gateway. Inside are Buddha images from Burma, Thailand, and Nepal, and wall murals including a Tibetan Wheel of Life and a scene of Hindu deities welcoming the Buddha. According to the Lumbini Development Plan, both these monasteries are to be demolished and relocated in new quarters.

A good distance to the north at the end of a long walkway (eventually it will be a reflecting pool) is the **Eternal Peace Flame,** brought from U.N. Headquarters in 1986 to mark the International Year of Peace. That also happened to be the 25th anniversary of the now discredited panchayat system, so the flame does double duty, according to the memorial plaque dedicating it. It sputtered out when the India-Nepal trade dispute deprived it of fuel, but has since been relit. Past here is a new, empty library and museum, and the sites of a number of planned but unmanifested buildings.

Less than 15 minutes walk south of the compound is the small village of **Lumbini,** relocated here when the park's boundaries were set over a decade ago. The open-air market held on Mondays involves lively trading under the mango trees, but local people traveling here make the buses even more crowded than normal.

The capital of Kapilvastu, the Buddha's ancestral home, has been uncovered near **Tilaurikot,** 27 km west of Lumbini and one km north of the village of Taulihawa. Ruins of King Suddhodhana's palace and several stupa are slowly being excavated here, but the site is not of great interest.

PRACTICALITIES

Accomodations And Food

Most people stay in Bhairawa and day-trip out to Lumbini, but there's a lot to be said for overnighting there. Bhairawa's hotels are pretty dismal, as is the town—better to stay in peaceful Lumbini and enjoy sunset, sunrise, and the birds. Minibuses run back to Bhairawa beginning at 0600; presumably they aren't so crowded early in the morning. If you book your ongoing bus ticket in Bhairawa before you head to Lumbini, you can board the bus directly on your return the next morning.

The pilgrim's **dharamsala** between the two monasteries offers simple rooms (the outdoor toilets are thoroughly disgusting) for the cost of a donation; food is available as well. **Lumbini Garden Guest House** is a 10-minute walk past the main compound, set in a shady grove just before the small village of Lumbini. It's nice enough but not cheap—US$14 s, US$20 d, dorm beds for US$10. Add three meals and it's another US$16 per day. If you're staying here, ride the minibus to the end of the line at the village, drop off your bags, then walk back to the garden area.

The only other eatery beyond village teashops is the **Hewa Restaurant,** an open-air tea shop which does noodles, daal bhaat and the like and closes at dusk. A few small shops across from here sell candy, cigarettes, bangles and (oddly enough) rosaries of *rudraksha* seeds, a Hindu device. At the top of the line is the new,

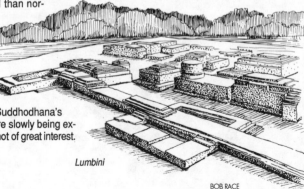

Lumbini

BOB RACE

super-deluxe **Lumbini Hokke Hotel,** a big Japanese-built edifice several kilometers north of the gardens. Rooms are US$60 and up; the hotel caters mainly to Japanese tour groups.

Getting There
See "Bhairawa And Sunauli" for details on transport to Bhairawa. One way to break up the bus rides into tolerable chunks would be to travel from Pokhara to the hilltop town of Tansen, visit Lumbini, and return to Kathmandu via Chitwan. A few tour groups do this loop, but due mainly to a lack of decent hotels and transport, it hasn't caught on with independent travelers.

In Bhairawa, jam-packed minibuses to Lumbini leave frequently from the highway intersection, about one km north of the main traffic circle. The ride is enjoyable if you sit on top, but bring a brimmed hat and sunglasses to avoid sun-scrambling your brains. It takes a little over an hour to cover the 22 km.

While minibuses are crowded, uncomfortable and slow, tempos (Rs45) are merely uncomfortable and slow. It would be worthwhile to hire a taxi, especially if you're with several people. All day at Lumbini costs Rs700, but two hours (Rs300) is sufficient for most people; being dropped off for an overnight would cost much less. Taxis can be hard to find on short notice, however.

Bicycling to Lumbini would be nice if it's not too hot; try early morning. Ask around town enough and a rental cycle will materialize—cycle repair shops are a good place to try. It certainly won't be a mountain bike, but the road is well-paved and level and the surrounding countryside is lovely—lush green fields with little roadside villages reminiscent of India, white bullocks pulling creaking oxcarts, and graceful sari-clad women balancing impossible loads atop their heads.

CHITWAN NATIONAL PARK

Nepal's Terai possesses a beauty that's totally unexpected in a country known mainly for soaring snow-covered mountains. Nowhere is this beauty better displayed than Royal Chitwan National Park, a majestic, powerful, downright primeval place teeming with wildlife. The noisy silence of the jungle is full of bird calls, and so lush you can almost hear the plants growing. A rhino looms out of the mist like the prehistoric prototype of the armored tank. Vast seas of elephant grass ripple beneath a blood-red sunset, and a pervasive sense of relaxation soaks in deeper the longer you stay.

Chitwan is among Asia's finest national parks, renowned for its dense concentration of wildlife and its top-class tourist lodges, which provide the opportunity to see animals in their natural environment without missing any creature comforts of one's own. Inexpensive lodges at the park's eastern entrance at Sauruha offer less luxurious but equally comprehensive budget safaris.

The park's fame rocketed in the mid-'80s, and the number of visitors has jumped from less than 1,000 in 1981 to over 35,000 in 1989. This has changed the experience, not all for the best—Sauruha in particular is becoming a Terai Thamel, and the piece of jungle directly across the river is definitely overused. Still, few visitors stay over two days, leaving the surrounding countryside, and the park interior, nearly untouched.

THE LAND

Chitwan is among the last surviving examples of the continuous band of forest and grassland which once extended from the Indus River in Pakistan to the Burmese border. Through the 1940s a huge swath of this prehistoric landscape was preserved in Nepal's Terai. Much has since succumbed to development, but remnants of the once vast forests and grasslands are preserved in Chitwan and a few other parks.

The Chitwan or Rapti Valley actually belongs to the inner Terai. It's the largest of the broad, flat valleys *(dun)* which lie between the two outermost Himalayan foothills—the Siwalik and Mahabharat ranges. The park's 932 square km (1,431 square km including the adjoining Parsa Wildlife Reserve) seems huge until you realize 40 years ago practically *all* the Terai was like this.

About 70% of the park is sal-forested hills, largely inaccessible to visitors but an important wildlife habitat. The best-known areas are the flat floodplains of the three rivers which bound the park—the Reu, the Rapti, and the Narayani. Carpeted with grasslands, this region is crisscrossed by ever-changing streams and dotted with marshes, swamps, and lakes.

MIKE WELLINS

elephants crossing Rapti River, Chitwan

CHITWAN NATIONAL PARK

© MOON PUBLICATIONS, INC.

Climate

Only 150 meters above sea level, Chitwan can get steamy from March-June, with peak temperatures reaching 43° C in the shade. Short grass makes Feb.-May the best game-viewing season, but the autumn months are gorgeous, with Himalayan views, and in winter Chitwan is pleasantly warm compared to Kathmandu. The monsoon season is intense, with pounding rain, swollen rivers, and luxuriant vegetation. While the rain isn't constant, the humidity is all pervasive, as are the leeches. Several lodges in and outside the park remain open through the monsoon.

Flora

About one-fifth of the park is savannah, carpeted with over 50 different species of grasses essential to the lives of local villagers. Every Jan. tens of thousands of villagers are admitted into the park to harvest grass, which is used as roof thatch, cane, mats, rope, animal fodder, or sold to paper mills. The cutting also has the side benefit of improving game viewing. Following the harvest villagers set the grasslands on fire, an old custom which ensures the growth of new grass and prevents the transition to forest which might otherwise occur.

Along the watercourses are riverine forests of quick-growing *shisham* and *khair,* valuable timber trees. Further inland are *kapok* trees, with their buttressed trunks, and "flame-of-the-forest" *(palash),* named for the bright red blossoms which emerge in early spring. The natural succession climaxes with forests of sal trees which grow up to 40 meters. Their excellent hardwood is used for railroad sleepers, bridges, and Kathmandu's famous woodcarvings, while the glossy green leaves are used as plates for feasts and offerings. Ridgetops are less densely forested, mainly with chir pines.

Fauna

Chitwan's inhabitants include over 40 species of mammals, including gaur *(gauri gai),* wild boar *(bandel),* sambar deer, the graceful little spotted deer *(chital),* the clunky hog deer *(laguna),* plus leopards *(chituwa),* various other jungle cats

CHITWAN NATIONAL PARK   295

TROUBLE IN PARADISE

At first glance Chitwan seems idyllic—neat villages and shining fields outside the park, thriving wildlife within. But the proximity of man and nature creates stresses seldom encountered in the West, where natural lands are neatly segregated from populated areas—and where population pressures haven't reached the rolling boil of Nepal.

Rapid population increases has centered on the Terai, now home to nearly 50% of Nepal's population. Within a few decades, the Terai's natural balance has shifted from coexistence to conflict. Parks are islands of virgin territory preserved by force: over 1,000 troops stationed at Chitwan protect it against poachers and woodcutters.

Thousands of villagers living in or near the park are prevented from tapping its resources, and for good reason. The area surrounding Chitwan has one of the highest livestock populations on the Indian subcontinent; unprotected, the park would soon become like the surrounding land, nearly bare of trees.

And yet . . . wildlife sanctuaries created to fulfill the needs of animals give short shrift to human needs. People who've always depended on the land find themselves barred from their ancestral heritage, unable to use the jungle for fodder, food, cultivation, and grazing lands. Increasing wildlife populations (especially deer and rhino) destroy up to 90% of villagers' crops. Unable to kill predators, farmers must sleep out in their fields and and scare them away with stones, shouts, and fire.

Understandably some local people feel cheated by the park, yet in the long term its existence is in their best interests. An example is the high-quality grass, now found only in the park. Every January 50,000 villagers harvest the grass, which plays an important role in traditional life and is used in dozens of different ways. Park tourism benefits hundreds of locals who are employed either by the park or by lodges or who sell goods to tourists. These kind of things demonstrate what planners are slowly discovering—national parks and wildlife preserves are not as isolated as their pristine ecology would suggest. Rather, they're tangled in a complex web of economic, political, and social forces. Ultimately the only sustainable method is to involve local people in the protection of their resources—for their own benefit, not just that of the animals.

---

and dogs, the dangerous sloth bear *(bhalu)*, and langur and rhesus monkeys *(bandar)*. Low-lying marshy areas and riverbanks support waterbirds and the aptly named marsh mugger *(magar-gohi)*, a sinister-looking crocodile which drowns its victims, then devours them. Rarer is the gharial, a slender-snouted crocodile. The Narayani River harbors the rare Gangetic dolphin, one of four species of freshwater dolphins.

Larger animals are the big attractions: the one-horned rhino *(gaida)* and the royal Bengal tiger *(bagh)*. Headed for extinction a few decades ago, rhinos are making a comeback at Chitwan; between 1975-86, the population increased by 26%. Rhino sightings are especially common around Sauruha, where they occasionally wander onto the grounds of lodges. Local farmers are dismayed by the increase—much of the year they must sleep out in their fields to protect crops from marauding rhinos. Twenty of the surplus animals have been transplanted to Royal Bardia Wildlife Reserve in western Nepal.

More elusive is the master predator, the royal Bengal tiger. Of the 3,000 or so left worldwide, about 60 live in or near Chitwan. A radio telemetry study conducted here in the '70s revealed that tigers require immense amounts of territory to roam, up to 60 square km for a male, which naturally limits the population in an area (one reason for adding on the adjoining Parsa Wildlife Reserve). The tiger's striped camouflage works so well that it's far more likely to see you than you it. Only the very lucky get daytime sightings of these mainly nocturnal beasts (Tiger Tops has stopped its nightly baiting for tigers). But finding a tiger's tracks or clawmarks on a tree or hearing a warning cough from the bush can be enough of a thrill.

HISTORY

Two factors conspired to preserve the Terai's virgin environment well into the 1940s. One was a high incidence of malaria, which frightened away everyone except the indigenous Tharus, who had developed a limited natural resistance. From the 19th century on, strategic Terai areas like Chitwan were deliberately protected by the Ranas, who banned poaching, woodcutting, and settlements. Part of their motivation was defense—no army could equal the deadly effect of malaria—and part was the fact they viewed portions of the Terai (especially Chitwan) as their private hunting reserve.

In spite of the periodic massive slaughter during the Ranas' wintertime hunts, the wildlife population remained relatively stable. It took development to destroy the Terai's virgin jungle. A malaria eradication drive launched in 1955 doused the region with DDT, virtually eliminating the disease in Chitwan by 1960. The Rapti Val-ley became the site of a model resettlement program sponsored by foreign aid, and hundreds of thousands of Hill people poured down to farm the flat, fertile fields of the Terai. By the early '60s two-thirds of the region's forest had been cut.

The ecological destruction and the accompanying threat to wildlife occurred so quickly it left officials gasping. Efforts had been made as early as 1962 to establish a rhino sanctuary in Chitwan, going so far as to relocate 22,000 Nepalis who had settled in prime rhino habitat. The World Wildlife Fund's Operation Tiger gave further impetus to the drive to preserve wildlife habitat. In 1973 Royal Chitwan National Park was created, the country's first. Other Terai

HUNTING IN CHITWAN

Chitwan's status as one of the finest wildlife habitats in the world owes much to a century of protection by the Ranas, who forbade settlement and poaching in the region. They were mainly interested in keeping the hunting for themselves. Chitwan was reserved for the exclusive use of the Ranas and their guests, who came each winter to shoot tremendous quantities of game.

Typical was the first Rana Prime Minister, Jung Bahadur, a tireless hunter who pursued his quarry day and night, impeccably clad in white gloves and patent leather boots. In a typical two-week hunt he shot enough animals to stock a Noah's Ark of endangered species: 31 tigers, 21 elephants, 20 deer, 11 wild buffalo, 10 boars, plus leopards, rhinos, a boa constrictor, and a crocodile. However, the record goes to Juddha Shamsher Rana, who over seven seasons shot 433 tigers, 53 rhinos and 93 leopards.

India's governor generals and viceroys and three generations of Britain's royal family took a similar toll on Chitwan wildlife. King George V and court shot 39 tigers in a 12-day spree. Their Rana hosts did their utmost to make their stay comfortable: for King George's visit in 1911, a special jungle camp was built that included electricity and hot and cold running water, while for the Prince of Wales's visit in 1921, 36 miles of motor road and telephone lines were laid. But they were careful to never invite the British into Kathmandu, lest India's rulers get any ideas about extending their domain.

Hunts were conducted on elephant back, both safe and comfortable for the shooter, or from game blinds (machan) camouflaged in treetops. The great-est shoots used the ring hunt, a spectacular event demanding an enormous number of trained shikar (hunting) elephants, expert drivers and beaters, and of course a plentiful supply of tigers. Preparations began months before, as roads were built in order to bring in vehicles and elephants. After the guests had gathered, several dozen buffalo calves were staked out overnight in different locations. As soon as one was killed the tiger's location was known. The elephants, up to 600 of them, were driven into a slowly converging circle. A white linen cloth stretched out at ground level helped close the circle further by frightening the tiger. The tiger might leap and charge in his attempt to escape, but he was an easy target for the hunters on elephant-back, for not even a tiger will charge an elephant. Given this method, success was practically guaranteed. Old photographs show hunters standing behind a row of tiger carcasses, lined up like so many rugs.

Rhino-hunting was a trickier matter, as elephants fear them more than tigers, and a rhino charge could break the ring. Usually they were stalked through tall grass, using only three or four elephants. The rhino's virtually impenetrable armor meant the hunter had to kill the rhino with an accurate shot between the eyes, or between an eye and an ear. A wounded rhino could charge even a fleeing elephant. Cleaned and cured, rhino hide made "capital water buckets," noted a British writer; "These are immensely strong, never break, and are impervious to water." The horns were turned into carved cups and khukri handles.

parks have followed, but apart from these small islands, the rich forests and jungles of the Terai have been virtually wiped out, either by farmers or by unscrupulous politicians and landowners logging large tracts for short-term profit.

The rapid destruction of the Terai's virgin lands must be balanced by what it's given Nepal: within a few decades the region has become the nation's major agricultural and industrial area. For several decades it's served as a sort of social pressure valve, absorbing excess population from the Hills. But even the seemingly endless Terai has its limit, and indications are it's reaching its maximum capacity.

EXPLORING CHITWAN

Park Practicalities
The tenor of your stay will be determined by your lodgings. Luxury lodges inside the park provide the works for their guests, filling the days with planned activities interspersed with relaxation. Independent travelers can replicate everything for far less cost, if slightly more hassle. The better lodges in Sauruha will help arrange activities if you outline a program, or you can hire guides, etc. through one of several services in town. The **government office** there books elephant rides (Rs200) and boat rides (Rs25), and sells admission tickets to the park (Rs250, valid for two days). The ticket office is across from the park **Visitor's Center,** which has some interesting exhibits on local wildlife and ecology; open 0800-1700 daily.

rhinoceros

BOB RACE

Things you'll want to bring include comfortable shoes that can stand getting wet, plus a pair of plastic flip-flops for showering and river-wading. A lungi is handy for bathing, swimming, and bathroom treks. Also consider mosquito repellent, sunscreen, sun hat, clothing in neutral colors for jungle walks (so as not to alarm wildlife), and malaria prophylaxis at your discretion. Park maps are available in restaurants; smaller ones are sold at the visitor's center, but it's not really necessary to carry one about.

Safety Concerns
A visit to Chitwan involves game-stalking by a variety of means—foot, dugout canoe, jeep, elephant-back. Don't let the term "safari" fool you into imagining broad savannahs teeming with game. Chitwan's wildlife is hidden in the dense jungle, forcing you to get out and actively look for it—which is most of the fun.

Chitwan is one of few wildlife parks in the world which allows visitors to enter on foot. For reasons of safety, it's advisable that you go with a guide. Tourists are occasionally injured or killed (usually by rhinos), because they foolishly assumed the animals are tame. If you're prudent there's usually not a problem; the big thing is to avoid hanging around mother animals with offspring, who are especially sensitive to intruders.

Some safety tips: if a rhino snuffles its signal to charge and lowers its head, climb a tree or run in big zig-zags, dropping a piece of clothing as a decoy—rhinos rely on scent rather than sight, and will stop to sniff it. Rhinos' eyesight is so bad they've been known to charge trees. Encountering a tiger is highly unlikely, but in case you do, back away slowly, and climb a tree (quickly). And make sure the tree is too small for the tiger to climb up after you. The most dangerous animal is the sloth bear, relatively small but with vicious claws and exceedingly poor eyesight. Again, climb a small tree.

Guides will sheperd you through these safety measures if necessary, but more than that, they'll enthusiastically share their intimate knowledge of the land, explaining different kinds of grasses and rare plants, pointing out animal tracks and sharing amusing anecdotes. Sans guide, you'll probably miss most of the wildlife: untrained eyes tend to look right past a rhino in the bush ten meters away. Most lodges provide guides for Rs50-75 per half-day, or ask around Sauruha.

Things to Do

Jungle walks give close-up opportunities to view animals as well as observe their tracks, signs, and sounds. Early morning and late afternoon are the best times to spot wildlife and avoid the midday heat. In the jungle across from Sauruha the most frequently spotted creature is another party of tourists. The luxury lodges inside the park put you in virtually untouched territory.

Two *machan* or treetop game blinds within 20 minutes' walk of Sauruha's visitor's center might be chanced alone. Ask beforehand to see if the blind is in operating condition. **Tal Machan** overlooks an oxbow lake that's a favorite rhino bathing spot; cross the river and go up the main Kasara road, and the *machan* is on the left. **Isle Machan,** a meadow wallow also favored by rhinos, is across the Dhungre River.

Dugout canoe trips down the Rapti River offer views of waterbirds: osprey, brilliant blue Eurasian kingfishers, egrets, ospreys, and ruddy sheldrakes, colored the ochre-white-black scheme of Nepali houses. There are also crocodiles in the winter, and views of local river-bank life—fishermen with nets, women digging a freshwater well. The standard routine is a 45-minute float downstream (ample time, in the cramped boat) followed by a two-hour jungle walk back. Tickets are sold near the visitor's center; the boats are moored just beyond.

Elephant rides are everyone's favorite thing about a visit to Chitwan. Luxury lodges maintain their own elephant stables and provide a wooden carrier with side railings, while beasts from the government stable in Sauruha are ridden more or less barebacked—quite a stretch for the second passenger straddling its girth. Rides are Rs200 per hour and competition in season is stiff; lines at the ticket office form long before opening. Most lodges will help book tickets, but give as much advance notice as possible.

A **jeep ride** through the jungle provides more game-spotting opportunities than might be ex-

ELEPHANTS

At least half the fun of an elephant ride is the chance to view one of these contradictory beasts close-up and in action. Bulky yet graceful, with a ridiculous appearance and a wise expression, the elephant shuffles along, its leathery skin a baggy gray suit two sizes too big for its body. Riding one is somewhat akin to being aboard a ship, rolling through a sea of grass instead of water. Elephants are remarkably surefooted, but from atop one the landscape pitches and heaves to a surprising degree.

The Asian elephant is slightly smaller than its African cousin, averaging five tons and 2.7 meters tall at the shoulder. A few odd facts: its ears act as heat regulators, with huge quantities of blood vessels on the posterior surface for cooling. Like rhinos, elephants need frequent baths (in water, dust, or mud) to cool their vast bulk. Elephants are simply too big to lay down—any more than an hour might damage their internal organs. They sleep only three hours a night, standing up. Elephants' lives closely parallel those of humans: work from age 15 to 55, followed by ten years or so of retirement. As they age, their heads turn paler, with mottled pink setting in, just like a human going gray.

Most amazing is the trunk, composed of over 40,000 muscles. It's used to eat, shower, drink, signal, and attack, and it has a very good sense of smell. As elephants grow up they learn more uses for it, scratching themselves with a stick or using it to shake dirt from grass clumps before stuffing it into their mouths. An elephant's trunk is so vital that paralysis of the trunk is invariably fatal.

Elephants in the wild must constantly forage for food in order to fill their minimum daily requirement of at least 200 kilos of food and 170 liters of water. Supplying food for each park elephant occupies the better part of a day for two men, though the bulk is reduced by feeding them concentrated grain instead of grass. Molasses, salt, and grain are wrapped into neat football-sized bundles of grass, just the right size for an elephantine mouth.

Each Chitwan elephant has three keepers to tend to its needs. Highest in status is the driver *(phanit)*, who sits behind its ears and provides encouragement by constantly drumming his knees on the beast's head, with occasional thwacks of a heavy goad. Due to the immensity of the elephant's skull, these mighty blows register as a dull thud. Why the huge beasts docilely submit to such treatment is a continuing mystery, rooted in an apparent fondness

pected and gets you beyond the overused strip of jungle across from Sauruha. The usual trip (Rs200) takes you to park headquarters at **Kasara Durbar,** 20 km southwest of Sauruha. Offices are in a former Rana hunting lodge from the '30s; nearby is a very small museum featuring mainly animal skulls. Nearby is the small jungle temple of **Bikram Babu,** a sort of local fertility shrine. Villagers might sacrifice a goat here after the long-awaited birth of a child.

The main attraction is the **Gharial Breeding Center** on the Rapti's banks near Kasara (admission Rs15). Here the slender-snouted crocodiles are hatched, raised, then released after two years. Operating since 1980, the project is showing signs of success—35% of the baby crocs are surviving, compared to two percent in the wild, and over 300 have been released. A jeep ride can be extended to **Lami Tal,** a birdwatcher's paradise teeming with crocs.

A **jungle trek** is worth considering, though most visitors don't stay long enough to do one. A standard two-day route runs from Sauruha

to Kasara, with a visit to Lami Tal, then crosses the river to Jagatpur, where you overnight in a village lodge. The next day you bus up to Gitanagar, walk along a canal to the many small lakes of Bis Hajaar Tal, and return to Sauruha. Guide cost is Rs300; lodges will provide packed lunches.

Rafting
An increasingly popular way to kill two adventure-travel birds with one stone is by rafting down the Trisuli River to Chitwan (actually only to Narayanghat). Trips start at Mugling or further up; it's a fairly gentle two- to three-day float down to Narayanghat, only eight km from Tadi Bazaar. Independent rafting companies in Kathmandu run trips for US$30-50 per day, or luxury lodges will arrange a raft trip for a supplement (see p. 304 for more information on rafting).

Nightlife
Sauruha is a quiet place after dark. Nightlife is limited to the bigger lodges, where thatched-

for man. Certainly no elephant can be forced into doing something it doesn't want to do.

As cousins of the god Ganesh, wild elephants were traditionally exempted from hunting in Nepal. The constant demand for hunting, parades, and ceremonial purposes was filled by annual roundups. Sometimes a lone male, excited by the sight and scent of tame females used as bait, would be lured into a pit and hauled up with ropes. An entire herd might be driven into a stockade, or a wild loner would be chased by phanit aboard tame elephants.

The captured elephant would then be subjected to a nonstop barrage of stimuli designed to break its resistence. Tied in a network of ropes, dozens of men working in shifts would climb about it day and night, pounding it with their bare feet and hands to keep it in a state of helpless panic. Later, to accustom it to noises, a brass band might play in front of it, while guns were fired from its back. This would continue with decreasing severity for several weeks, until the capitve was perfectly docile and ready to be trained in the fine points of *shikar*.

Elephants are a source of endless fascination. The biggest lodges give elephant briefings at their stables, or you can visit the government elephant stables **(Hattisar)** near Sauruha or the **Elephant Breeding Center** four km west of the village.

elephant and phanit, Chitwan National Park

roof bars concoct exotic-sounding drinks, and to the open-air **Jungle Pub** behind the Sunset Restaurant, a favorite for cold beer and popcorn. Groups of Tharu men go from lodge to lodge performing their famous **stick dance**, said to be inspired by the movements of farming (or alternately, hunting). If your lodge doesn't have a show, it's easy to find a performance put on for package tours. Shows are also performed on alternate nights at the Jungle Pub (Rs20). There's no electricity at Sauruha as of yet, and light comes from oil lamps, candles, or lanterns.

Outside The Park

Bikes, both mountain and regular versions, are rented in Sauruha and can considerably extend your range in the flat countryside. The government-run **Elephant Breeding Center** four km west of Sauruha has 22 elephants and two babies. The walk there leads through tidy Tharu villages of mud-walled huts, in the winter overflowing with stacks of freshly harvested grass.

A few kilometers north of Sauruha is **Bis Hajaar Tal** ("20,000 Lakes"), a forested sal grove scattered with small oxbow lakes which are a favorite habitat for birds and wildlife. You can walk here directly from Sauruha in two hours, but without a guide, it's best to cycle to the village of **Tikauli** three km west of Tadi Bazaar, then follow the path alongside a canal a few more kilometers to the lakes.

Thirty km east down the highway (two hours by bus or two by bike) is the small village of **Lothar** on the Lothar Khola. Just beside the bridge, a small path leads to a series of waterfalls, good for swimming as well as birdwatching.

PRACTICALITIES

The major decision is where to stay: luxury lodges inside the park or budget lodges at Sauruha. The vast price differential usually makes the decision for you. Those staying in Sauruha wouldn't dream of spending $150 a night, while guests inside the park wouldn't dream of staying at Sauruha. If you can pay the higher bill without flinching, you probably won't regret it. The fancy lodges sell not just accommodations but a complete experience, and the pampering and general relaxation is pure plea-

sure. On the other hand, you can replicate the whole experience at a more modest level for a fraction of the cost at Sauruha. Many of the small lodges will arrange activities at your request, though you'll be paying piecemeal for them.

Accommodations And Food

Deluxe lodges scattered through the park offer total immersion in the jungle, combined with solar-heated showers, Western food, and other unexpected luxuries. Unlike most "tourist-class" Nepali hotels, these are well-designed, built of natural materials, and blend into the natural setting. They offer a carefully planned balance of excursions, talks and relaxation—the elephants come to pick you up at the door, and you're off.

Booking offices are clustered on Durbar Marg, and prices include everything but the bar bill. While most people stay two nights, prices tend to drop for longer stays. Another option would be to move on to (or exclusively visit) the less expensive but still deluxe facilities available at some operations—camps with roomy safari tents, and/or Tharu-style longhouses with local decor.

The original, most famous and most expensive safari camp, **Tiger Tops** (tel. 222-706), has operated in Chitwan since 1965. It's in the western portion of the park about 40 km from Sauruha; most visitors fly into **Meghauli** (US$144 RT), where they're met by elephants for a two-hour ride back to camp. Prices are high: US$250 for the lodge, US$180 for the tented camp on an island in the Narayani River, US$110 for Tharu Village. Try to make lodge reservations 6-12 months in advance, especially for the fall season (P.O. Box 242, Telex 2216 Tiger Top NP).

Also in the western end of the park is **Temple Tiger** (tel. 221-585), which boasts safari tents with separate dressing rooms (US$160) and **Island Jungle Resort** (tel. 226-022), a tented camp on an island in the Narayani River (US$140).

Near Sauruha is **Gaida Wildlife** (tel. 220-940), one of the older deluxe lodges in the park (US$110). The lodge overlooks the Dungre River; the tented **Jungle Camp** (US$80) is 11 km east in an excellent birdwatching region.

On the more remote eastern side is **Chitwan Jungle Lodge** (tel. 228-918), charging US$125

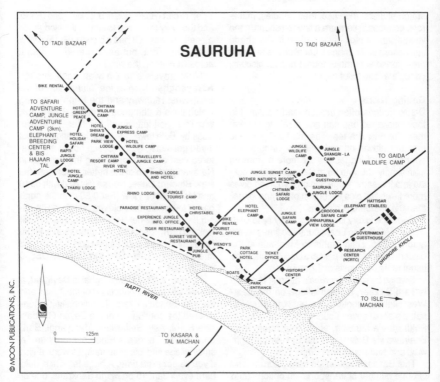

per night. **Machan Wildlife Resort** (tel. 225-001) is on the border with Parsa Wildlife Reserve; the lodge is US$154 per night; the tented camp charges US$70.

On the other hand, you don't *have* to spend a lot to visit Chitwan. The small Tharu village of Sauruha at the park entrance is a budget paradise, with dozens of inexpensive lodges that are among the nicest places to stay in Nepal. Prices are reasonable—Rs35 s, Rs60 d is the standard for a rustic, simply furnished small bungalow with mosquito nets and shared bathrooms. Some places have solar- or wood-heated hot water; most are clean, well-kept, and peaceful.

As in Pokhara, there's so many good accommodations in Sauruha it's difficult to recommend the best; names and owners change and new places spring up monthly. Look for some kind of shade or garden (some lots are as bare as football fields) and, ideally, a view. **Hotel**

Park Cottage is the best in this category, the only one with river and sunset views. Spacious grounds, nice bungalows, and a excellent staff; it's a bit more expensive than most at Rs150 d. **Hotel Shiva's Dream** and **River View Hotel and Lodge** (river view in name only) have nicer grounds than most; **Tharu Lodge** is set back from the main road near the river. If you want a private bath try **Rhino Lodge, Jungle Express Camp,** or **Jungle Tourist Camp,** and be prepared to pay Rs 120-200 d.

Semi-luxury lodges include **Jungle Shangri-La, Jungle Safari Camp** and **Hotel Elephant Camp.** Averaging US$90 per night, they're of dubious value, though Jungle Shangri-La does have nice grounds and bungalows. Hotel Elephant Camp's staff includes some of the slickest dudes in Sauruha ("Special guy[de], madam?").

Food is among Sauruha's low points. Most people eat in their lodges; to break the monotony there are several restaurants serving the usual starch-stuffers: fried rice, fried noodles, macaroni, potatoes. There are a few tea shops in the village, and snack carts parked in the shade sell *pakora* and bananas. Local shops are well-provisioned with major tourist needs: biscuits, chocolate, and toilet paper.

Getting There

Deluxe lodges often include land transport in their packages and can add a rafting supplement for an extra fee. The "budget" package trips to Chitwan offered by Kathmandu tourist agencies and lodges are far more expensive than simply showing up at Sauruha and checking into the same lodge. Doing it yourself gives more flexibility, plus the option of staying longer than the standard two nights.

Guests at luxury lodges frequently fly to Chitwan. RNAC flies to Bharatpur three times weekly for US$45. Daily flights to Meghauli in the eastern portion of the park are US$72; this is the usual route for guests at Tiger Tops.

Coming by road, Sauruha's nearest bus stop is **Tadi Bazaar,** a small village on the East-West Highway about 15 km east of Narayanghat. It's about seven hours from Kathmandu or Pokhara via Mugling, about four hours from Bhairawa via Butwal and the East-West Highway, and four hours from Birganj.

Tadi Bazaar is seven km from Sauruha and offers a number of transportation options (and plenty of aggressive hotel touts to help you decide): oxcart (Rs20, quaint but slow) jeep (Rs30, and they'll try to get you to stay at their lodge), or a one-hour walk. Or rent a bicycle (Rs15) if your luggage is light, but be prepared to push it across a river on the way in.

Most travelers to Chitwan pass through **Narayanghat,** lying at the intersection of the East-West Highway and the Prithvi Rajmarg which links Kathmandu to India. **Bharatpur,** with its airport leaping-off point for Chitwan, is close by. Both towns are busy, hot, and dirty, but if you get stuck, typical cheap hotels are clustered east of the bridge along the highway in Narayanghat. Two of the better options are the **New Bisauni Guest House** (Rs70 d with bath) and **Hotel River View** (Rs60-80 d) in the north part of town near the Pokhara bus park. Bharatpur has the semi-deluxe **Safari Narayani Hotel** (tel. 20130), a spinoff of Kathmandu's Hotel Narayani. It has a pool, tennis court, and a/c, and offers packaged safari tours to Chitwan; US$30 s, US$40 d.

Five km north of Narayanghat is **Devighat,** a sacred site at the confluence of the Trisuli and the Kali Gandaki rivers. Traditionally it's considered the confluence of the Seven Gandaki (the Burhi, Kali, Seti, Madi, Marsyangi, Bari, and Trisuli). There's a Hindu ashram here, a small village and lots of shrines; it's worth a visit if you've got extra time. A huge festival is held here every Jan. 15 on Magh Sankranti, one of the few celebrated on the solar calendar

BEYOND CHITWAN: MORE SAFARIS

If Chitwan's rocketing popularity makes it seem too crowded and commercial, more remote national parks and reserves beckon the adventurous traveler. Essentially they're like Chitwan was 30 years ago, nearly undeveloped, seldom visited, and pristine. Wildlife doesn't reach the incredible abundance of Chitwan, but there's plenty, including exotica like wild elephants. Another bonus: the Tharu villages of far western Nepal are fascinating, far more traditional than Chitwan's, which have nearly been absorbed into mainstream Nepali culture.

Luxury lodges in some of these parks provide the usual jeep drives, hikes with trained naturalists, canoe trips, river-rafting, elephant rides, etc. A visit here requires extra travel time compared to Chitwan, but the experience is unique. For budget travelers it's a different story: these places are hard to get to and even harder to get around in. There are practically *no* visitor facilities, though you can sometimes pitch a tent. Arranging for guides, elephants, jeeps and such would be trailblazing of a different sort. **Note:** For individual travelers, park admission is Rs250, usually good for one day.

Koshi Tappu Wildlife Reserve
Budget travelers will find the most accessible of these parks is the small Koshi Tappu Wildlife Reserve, set in the floodplain of the mighty Koshi River in the eastern Terai. A peninsula projecting into the Sapt Kosi River (it turns into an island or *tappu* in the monsoon), it's ringed by high embankments channeling water into the Kosi Barrage, a massive series of flood-control gates 12 km downstream.

The reserve lacks the glamor game of tigers and rhinos; it was formed to protect a herd of rare wild buffalo, currently thriving at 160. Huge quantities of birds stop here on their Asian migrations (there are 280 species of waterbirds alone), and there are spotted deer, *nilgai* (a type of antelope), wild boar, monkeys, and a semilegendary wild elephant known to locals as Ganesh Maharaj.

There's a very simple lodge at park headquarters in **Kusaha**, across the river from the reserve. Dugout canoes ferry passengers into the

reserve, which is small enough (155 square km) to explore on foot.

Koshi Tappu is easily reached by the East-West Highway, which runs along the edge of the reserve. Look for signs 12 km east of the barrage, or three km west of Laukhi, pointing to reserve headquarters at **Kusaha** three km north. A visit here is easiest if you're passing through Biratnagar or Dharan, perhaps en route to the Kangchenjunga region.

Royal Bardia National Park
Way out in far western Nepal, this is the country's largest remaining chunk of Terai wilderness. Similar to Chitwan but drier and more remote, it encompasses 1,000 square km of riverine grassland and sal forests. Bardia has the country's second largest tiger population, plus blackbuck antelopes, a few wild elephants, the usual crocs, birds, and mammals, and some rare Gangetic dolphins in the Karnali River on its western border. A small rhino herd was recently transferred here from Chitwan in an attempt to reestablish the population, wiped out by poachers in this century. Poachers found it ridiculously easy to trap rhinos, who deposit their cannonball-like dung in the same place, approached backwards. Hunters simply found an old mound, dug a pit and waited for the beast to back in.

You can camp near the **warden's office,** but bring all your supplies. Significantly, nobody's done it yet. The sole accommodations are **Tiger Tops Karnali Lodge** (tel. 222-706, US$150) and its **tented camp** (US$120) on the bank of the Churia River. Run by the same operation as Chitwan's Tiger Tops, these provide a similarly high standard but are less expensive and less crowded—for serious nature buffs rather than jungle socialites. It's advertised as offering a much better chance of sighting a tiger than Chitwan. Nightly tiger baiting is likely to bring one if nothing else (this is the only place in Nepal to practice baiting), but daytime sightings are surprisingly common, partly due to the fact the tigers haven't been hunted and are less wary than at Chitwan.

Guests fly to **Nepalganj** (US$100); the lodge is a three-hour drive from the airport, which will shorten when the road's finished. On your own, it's a four-hour bus ride from Nepalganj to Motipur, followed by a several-hour walk to park headquarters at **Thakudwara**. The office will move to Motipur when the highway's completed, perhaps by 1991.

Royal Suklaphanta Wildlife Reserve

This reserve was established in 1976 to protect swamp deer, which roam its grasslands by the thousands, as well as tigers and wild elephants. It's in far, *far* western Nepal on the plain of the Mahakali River. This region is dotted with *phanta* or open grasslands; the reserve encompasses a particularly huge phanta called *sukila* or "white" in the local Tharu dialect, because of the silvery blossoms which carpet the grasslands in October.

On your own, Suklaphanta is highly problematic, since pedestrians and cyclists aren't admitted—too dangerous. You need a jeep, unavailable locally. The only lodge is **Silent Safari Jungle Adventure Camp** (tel. 418-755), run by Col. Hikmat Bisht, among other things a former military attaché to the Nepalese Embassy in Washington D.C. Custom trips require a minimum of five days at US$65 per. The tented camp shifts around according to season and guests. Special features include overnights in a machan overlooking a bird-infested lake, and occasional glimpses of wild elephant herds. A gigantic lone bull nicknamed "Thulo Hatti" (Big Elephant) roams the region. From his two-foot-wide footprints, his height is estimated at over eleven feet at the shoulder, which would make him the biggest Asian elephant in the last 200 years.

To get there, catch the once-a-week flight to **Mahendranagar** (US$160) or a twice-weekly flight to **Dhangadi** (US$149), or travel overland from Nepalganj, an agonizing, bone-rattling journey as long as the East-West Highway remains under construction. Delhi is supposedly a nine-hour drive from the park, and the lodge can arrange travel into India.

RAFTING

Since the first launch in 1968, rafting has become Nepal's latest adventure industry, with over 50 companies and 10,000 permits issued in 1990. With the world's highest mountains and deepest river gorges, Nepal is virtually guaranteed good rafting. Its rivers drop 3,000 meters or more over a distance of 240 km—that's a lot of water rushing down at tremendous speed.

A river trip provides a different perspective than trekking. Mainly it's less strenuous; you simply float past the scenery. Apart from the popular Trisuli River, trips enter remote areas where Westerners never walk. There are plenty of chances to slip off and swim, and guides will alert you to "swimming rapids" that can be floated in a life jacket. Increasingly popular package deals combine a short trek with a few days of rafting, ending at Chitwan National Park for a mini-safari.

Rafting companies run their operations like a trek: five or six hours a day on the river, broken by a lunch stop. Camp is made on the riverbank, with time to swim, photograph, and explore. Many of the less expensive companies encourage "participation," which means clients help with cooking and setting up camp—fortunately, most people find this enjoyable. Food generally gets high ratings; companies provide all the gear, including sleeping bags and mattresses.

The best rafting season is fall; the rivers are excitingly high in October, a little milder and cooler in November. Winter trips are possible though a bit chilly. March and April is the second best season, with lower waters but warm weather and longer days. By May water levels have dropped and the rains are coming; rafting is slower and you may have to portage some stretches. A monsoon trip is limited to the tamest rivers.

A word of warning: as a new enterprise, rafting is open to exploitation of staff as well as ripoffs of customers—there are virtually no regulations, and many agencies haven't the faintest idea about safety concerns or professionalism. A rafting trip requires some serious shopping around.

The Rivers

About a half-dozen rivers have been explored enough to be raftable, but many are too remote. Companies generally run tamer, warmer stretches below 500 meters altitude. Most rapids are just wild enough to be fun, but nothing to be frightened of. A few companies can arrange remote trips for a higher cost, but you have to hunt for a knowledgeable guide.

The **Trisuli,** named after Shiva's trident, draws 90% of all rafters: it's easily accessible and trips are short, a maximum of three days. Put-in point is generally 20-30 km above Mugling; the best rapids are all in the first day. It's a three-day float down to Narayanghat, which is less than an hour's bus ride to Tadi Bazaar and Chitwan National Park.

Many companies offer rafting/jungle safari packages, booking clients at whichever lodge they have a connection with. If you prefer to choose a lodge on your own, avoid the bookings and arrange transport from Narayanghat yourself (see "Chitwan National Park"). **River View Guesthouse** in Narayanghat is good for overnighters, quiet and with an actual river view.

A more intense experience is the eight- to ten-day trip down the **Sun Kosi** ("River of Gold"). You put in at Dholalghat on the Chinese highway east of Kathmandu and float down to Chatara in the Terai; duration depends on the season and the water. Once you've started you're committed—no roads come near here. The Sun Kosi gets less than 1,000 rafters a year, and the area is remote and unspoiled. There are few villages on the riverbank, but local people materialize at stops to marvel at the big boats. The trip ends at Chatara, shortly after the Arun and Tamur rivers have joined the Sun Kosi to make the incredibly broad Sapta Koshi. Chatara is a one-hour jeep ride to **Dharan,** and a long, long ride back to Kathmandu. Break up the return trip with a visit to **Kosi Tappu Wildlife Reserve** or **Janakpur,** or explore eastern Nepal's excellent trekking regions.

Trips out of Pokhara are usually pretty tame, including a two-day float down the **Seti Gandaki** from Damauli to Narayanghat. Most other rivers are too remote to be popular. The **Upper Arun** is too challenging (the first expedition here lost everything in a total wipeout), while floating the **Lower Arun** from Tumlingtar to Chatara is interesting but logistically difficult. The same goes for the nearby **Tamur Kosi.** The **Kali Gandaki** is reportedly "boring," lacking fun rapids; the standard float is three days from Ramdi Ghat on the Siddhartha Highway to Narayanghat. In western Nepal, the **Bheri** is good for wildlife and unique vegetation, but it's remote and expensive. A trip here would combine well with a visit to **Bardia National Park.**

Arranging A Trip

Unlike trekking, you have to go through a company to raft in Nepal. The quantity of companies in Kathmandu, plus independent operators and trekking companies moonlighting in rafting, confuse the issue further. Everybody's jumped onto the latest outdoor adventure boomlet, but few do it well. The safety situation is often abysmal, though miraculously there's been only one death so far. Equipment may be in poor condition or missing altogether; guides may be untrained and inexperienced; and medical kits are rare (bring your own). The Nepal Association of Rafting Agents (NARA) hasn't done much to set standards yet except establish minimum prices.

It's the cheapest companies that cut the most corners; in rafting you get what you pay for. Shop around carefully. Asking hard questions is no guarantee, because some companies will promise you anything and still not deliver. The companies listed below are considered reliable; for cheapies, rely on recent word-of-mouth. A lot depends on your rafting guide, and they switch jobs frequently.

BOB RACE

White Magic, Jyatha (tel. 226-885). Best service ratings, good equipment. Owner Nima Sherpa is one of Nepal's best river guides, and one of the few Sherpas involved in the rafting business (the others are green with envy).

Karnali River Tour & Exploration, Kamaladi (tel. 226-130). Good service, and experience on lesser-known rivers.

Himalayan Encounter, in front of the Kathmandu Guest House (tel. 413-632). Less expensive, one of the "participation" companies that has clients help with camp work.

Himalayan River Exploration, Naksal (tel. 418-491). The old, staid, expensive standby, which arranges trips for Tiger Tops clients. Specializes in slower, less strenuous oar rafts, where only the guide paddles, mainly older clients looking for a quieter trip.

Trips need a minimum of four people, so get together with friends or sign up for scheduled trips. If you're hunting for a more unusual trip, it's easiest to let a travel agency do the calling. Their fee is paid by the company, not you, and companies often pool their individual clients if they can't make the minimum.

Prices range from US$15-75 per day, averaging US$30-40, and depending on the number of people. If you're with a few friends, try bargaining for a reduced rate. Services are more or less the same for middle- and upper-range companies. Cheaper ones may skimp on the food and cut corners on safety and reliability. Beware of the real cheapies; an offer of the Trisuli

for US$15 per day drew so many clients that the company ran out of basics like plates and tents—and simply sent people down the river without them.

Most important are life vests, helmets, and rafts in good condition. Guides should be experienced (ask, since there is a rating system for guides), speak decent English, and give a safety demo before you launch. Companies should provide tents, sleeping bags, mattresses, and all food. Ask about transport. Cheaper companies send trips off by local bus, but will arrange a minibus for an extra fee. It's worth it, unless you're a fan of Nepali buses. Companies are supposed to arrange rafting permits (US$5 per person), though some skip this formality and pocket the money themselves.

For your part, bring sunscreen, hat, and sunglasses; tie them on with a cord, or they're likely to fly off into the river. For daytime, a bathing suit is fine in hot weather; long shorts prevent the rash that sometimes results from sitting in the rubber boat. Wear cloth shoes, since plastic sandals get lost too easily, and bring warm clothes for the evenings. Daytime gear, like clothes and cameras, can be stowed in a plastic expedition barrel on the raft, but photographing on the river may be difficult unless you've got a waterproof camera. On the Trisuli, a vehicle loaded with gear may meet you at camp, but on other rivers everything goes in the boat, so pack light. Finally, if you've gotten good service it's a nice gesture to tip your staff.

JANAKPUR

Like India, only better, this Terai city is as intense and tasty as one of its Indian sweets. Steeped in brilliant colors and soaked in religious devotion, it's absolutely the best city in the Nepal Terai. Janakpur is an ancient pilgrimage site, and busloads still pour through here—more often than not making a shopping stop in Janakpur's new bazaar after their puja. Hundreds of pilgrim hostels *(kuti)* dot the city, as well as dozens of big water tanks, sacred ponds for laundry, swimming, water buffalo-bathing, and ritual ablutions. Supposedly over 1,000 tanks were constructed by King Janak to accommodate the gods who came to Janakpur

for Sita's wedding. It was a long and dusty journey from their Himalayan abode of Mt. Kailas, and King Janak couldn't expect the gods to *share*.

Rama And Sita

Janakpur is revered as the birthplace of Sita, daughter of King Janak and beloved heroine of the ancient Hindu epic the *Ramayana*. There actually was a King Janak, who reigned around 2500 B.C.—the legend is mostly fantasy, but there is a vague historical basis.

When Sita reached marriageable age, her father tested her suitors by asking them to shoot an arrow from the great bow of Shiva, which could be drawn only by the pure of heart. Hundreds failed, then Rama stepped up to pull the string easily, shattering the bow and winning Sita's hand. The pair went on to be idolized in the *Ramayana* as the ideal married couple. Rama is considered an incarnation of Vishnu, the epitome of masculine virtues, while Sita is associated with Lakshmi and immortalized as the model Hindu wife, chaste and devoted to the end. Janakpur's famous images of Rama and Sita are worshipped by Indian newlyweds hoping for a happy married life.

Janaki Mandir

This massive marble shrine in the center of town is less than a century old but looks timeless, with Mughal-style battlements and domes resembling a Rajasthani palace. A local queen built it in 1911 at a cost of nine lakh (900,000 rupees), thus the name "Naulakh Mandir." The 100-square-meter outer facade encloses the much smaller exquisitely decorated main temple, where images of Sita and Rama are worshipped morning and evening. The sanctum is open from 0500-0700 and again from 1800-2000; priests perform elaborate puja around 0800 and

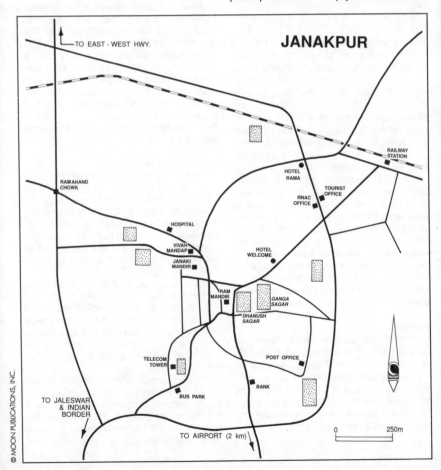

JANAKPUR

TO EAST - WEST HWY.

RAILWAY STATION

RAMANAND CHOWK

HOTEL RAMA

RNAC OFFICE

TOURIST OFFICE

HOSPITAL

VIVAH MANDAP

HOTEL WELCOME

JANAKI MANDIR

RAM MANDIR

GANGA SAGAR

DHANUSH SAGAR

TELECOM TOWER

POST OFFICE

BUS PARK

BANK

TO JALESWAR & INDIAN BORDER

TO AIRPORT (2 km)

0   250m

© MOON PUBLICATIONS, INC.

again around 1600. During the day the place is nearly deserted. Morning and evening are the time to visit, as devotees crowd inside to murmur prayers and hymns and make offerings to the images—a magical scene.

The huge plaza in front is the heart of town, where vendors sell sweets, flowers, and luridly colored religious pictures. Just north of the temple is the **Ram Janaki Vivek Mandap,** a new, squat edifice honoring the famous wedding. Inside are doe-eyed images of Sita and Rama in full makeup: red lips, blue eyelids, heavy tika, and golden robes, dressed as if for their wedding.

The City
To the south and east of the temple is the main bazaar, narrow streets of tiny shops. The southern portion houses more traditional goods, while the eastern part is the modern bazaar, catering to Indians looking for comparative bargains in modern goods. The major landmark is the pagoda-style **Ram Mandir,** and nearby the holiest of Janakpur's many ponds, **Dhanush Sagar** and **Ganga Sagar.** Here devotees perform religious ablutions in the early morning; during festivals they're the scene of much wet merriment.

The residential area to the north and west is surprisingly rural, with houses interspersed with wells, tea houses, and Janakpur's ubiquitous water tanks. Whitewashed mud houses are decorated with paintings of gods, peacocks, abstract designs and stick figures, protective devices painted by household women. Janakpur is the former capital of the ancient kingdom of Mithila, renowned for its literature and culture; Mithili women carry on the old traditions in their elaborate folk-art paintings (see p. 81).

Railway
Nepal's only operating railroad (a second was damaged in the 1988 earthquake) runs through Janakpur to the Indian railhead at Jayanagar, 28 km southeast. An equal distance to the northwest is the terminus of Bijalpur. A tiny steam locomotive pulls the old carriages along a narrow-gauge track, a scenic country ride past ricefields, villages and temples.

The easiest route would be towards India— you can get off along the way and wait for the return train, or continue to Jayanagar (but make sure to check in with the Nepalese customs office in Khajuri). The crowded southbound trains leave Janakpur at 0730 and 1530; come early to get a seat, or ride on the roof. A daily train to Bijalpur leaves at 1600, a little late for a day-trip.

PRACTICALITIES

Accommodations And Food
There isn't much in the way of tourist hotels. **Hotel Welcome** is the best, with rooms from Rs35 to Rs350 for an air-conditioned suite. Second choice is **Hotel Rama**, quieter and off the main street, with room and bath for Rs55 s, Rs110 d. Food is deliciously Indian influenced, with lots of sweets and vegetarian specialities for devout Hindus, though the lack of menus may reduce you to sign language or a point-and-eat system. Look around the bazaar or across from the Janaki Mandir for tea stalls, sweet shops and restaurants.

Getting There And Around
Janakpur is manageable on foot, and the lack of cars makes it an absolute pleasure to walk. Cycle rickshaws are plentiful and cheap (for once you don't have to bargain); good for visiting the semi-rural suburbs of Janakpur, with their village feel and many water tanks. Two km west of the bazaar is what's claimed to be "old" Janakpur, now more or less a village set with two ancient tanks, **Agni** and **Gyan Sagar.**

By "express" bus, Janakpur is 12 hours from Kathmandu and about seven hours from Kakarbhitta. From the East-West Highway, a 30-km spur road runs to the city. Take a cycle rickshaw from the bus station, only a few km from downtown. Flights from Kathmandu are three times weekly for US$55; the airport is two km south of town.

You could conceivably enter Nepal here from India via **Jaleshwar,** a border crossing about 20 km southwest. Frequent buses run from here to Janakpur; it's getting to Jaleshwar that's the problem. Lying at the end of a minor line in the Indian countryside, trains are exceedingly slow.

BOB RACE

TREKKING
INTRODUCTION

Nepal's unparalleled combination of natural beauty and cultural riches reveals itself only to those who walk. Practically the whole northern section of the country is untouched by roads: in order to explore it you *have* to trek. The greatest inducement is the Himalaya. With eight of the world's ten highest peaks, Nepal is loaded with spectacular mountain vistas. Rather than gazing at them from a distance, trekkers walk and live amid the mountains for weeks at a time. The leisurely pace creates a sense of intimacy with the land that goes far beyond that of a day hike or a wilderness weekend.

Mountains may be the main lure, but there are surprises along the way. For one thing, there are people amid this spectacular scenery—all sorts of people, living in a world nearly untouched by modern development. The realities of the Third World can be eye-opening; few Westerners have an opportunity to view how most of the world lives.

Reality Checks
As trekking makes the transition from cult to big business, trekkers' expectations become increasingly wilder. Herewith a few surprises many discover only on the trail. (For more trekking practicalities, see "Conduct and Customs," "Accommodations," "Passports and Visas," "Health," and "What To Take" in the general Introduction.)

Trekking is walking. Many organized trekkers are shocked at the effort required to trek, having been lured by seductive advertising into what they discover (too late) is a very physical enterprise. Some clients don't realize they'll be going to high altitudes, and join because "cruises are boring." Or they want to see Everest, but don't realize they have to walk three weeks to do so. If you've never hiked for a day up and down hills, try it before signing up.

On the other hand, trekking shouldn't frighten off anyone in reasonable health. It's demanding, but you can walk at your own pace, and there's an undeniable satisfaction in feeling your body do what it was made to do: walk.

> *As I stepped out on my first day's march in the Himalayas, a strange exhilaration thrilled me. I kept squeezing my fists together and saying emphatically to myself and the universe at large: "Oh yes! Oh yes! This is really splendid!"*
>
> —Sir Francis Younghusband

Trekking is a cultural rather than a wilderness experience. You *could* chose a remote trail avoiding populated areas, but it would be a shame to miss Nepal's people. The amount of personal interaction is dictated by the individual. Organized treks are commonly maligned for their limited cultural interaction, but many independent trekkers have even less contact with Nepalis. More than any other factor—age, physical fitness, type of trek, money spent, route —your trekking experience depends on you.

Finally, **trekking is a process rather than a destination.** As you get into shape it's easy to fall into walking-machine mode. You have to consciously remind yourself to stop at tea shops and shady chautaara, admire the views, splash in a stream, play with local kids. Walking and nothing but, day after day, provides illuminating insights into one's own mind and how seldom it's here in the moment. Even on the trail, thoughts race ahead to the next meal, the night's stop, the return to Kathmandu. Seldom do we delight in the pure present, but these sudden moments seem to come increasingly easily on the trail, as mind and body synchronize.

Largely for this reason, many people find their trek to be a personal watershed. Beyond the physical challenge, observing terrain and cultures completely unlike what you've ever experienced can be mind-blowing. Many trekkers find a new perspective on their own lives, and a high percentage of first-timers swear to return.

History

"Trekking" is an Afrikaaner term used by Dutch settlers to describe self-sufficient bush travel, usually with wagons packed with gear. The word was picked up by British mountaineering expeditions in Asia and spread to Nepal. Nepal officially opened its backcountry to tourists in 1964. The following year the first trekking company, Mountain Travel, was founded by Lt. Col Jimmy Roberts, a retired British Gurkha officer and an avid mountaineer. He believed people would pay much to see the Nepal Himalaya in style, and he was right.

Treks began in the classic sahib fashion, with long lines of porters bearing supplies, tents, even tables and chairs. This tradition remains in organized treks, but budget travelers soon discovered it was possible to go alone, staying in local tea shops and homes. Always eager to please, the accommodating Nepalis knew an opportunity when they saw it. They opened special tourist lodges, simple but modified to make Westerners feel comfortable, and business has been booming ever since. The number of trekking permits issued went from 13,000 in 1976 to 61,000 in 1988, and there are now over 100 trekking agencies in Kathmandu.

Seasons

Contrary to popular belief, it's possible to trek at any time of year: the trick is tailoring your route to the season. The main season, drawing nearly 40% of all trekkers, begins the second week of October and runs through the third week of

BOB RACE

November. The weather is indeed divine, with minimal rainfall and crystal-clear mountain views, but the main trails are packed. Autumn remains the best time to trek if you don't mind crowds; for remote trails it's unqualifiedly superb.

Dec.-Feb. are surprisingly undertrekked. Though it's admittedly freezing above 4,000 meters and high passes may be snowbound, winter is an ideal season for a lower trek (Solu, Helambu, Pokhara-Trisuli, the lower reaches of the Annapurna region). Late February marks the beginning of the spring trekking season, which peaks around mid-April. The weather grows progressively warmer, and while views are not as crisply inspiring as autumn's, days are longer and multicolored rhododendrons blossom at progressively higher elevations. By April lower elevations are steamy; by May they're practically unbearable.

Very few trekkers venture out from June-Aug., but a monsoon trek has its merits, especially for those who can't visit Nepal at any other time. Rainfall peaks in July and tapers off in Aug.-Sept. In late monsoon the entire country is green; herders are up in high pastures, and wildflowers and water are everywhere. Weather improves steadily from the last week in August, and there's still nobody on the trail. This is the time to visit high rainshadow areas: Manang, Khumbu, and the upper Kali Gandaki. Flying directly into these areas bypasses the slippery lower trails, but flights are particularly erratic in monsoon, so allow extra time.

The Walking

Anyone in reasonable shape can trek, but it helps to prepare in advance—weight-lifting emphasizing the leg muscles, running, stair-climbing, or simply some good hard walks (look for hills). Somehow, nothing completely prepares you for the real thing. Muscles are inevitably sore in the beginning; expect a definite slump the third day. By the end of the first week bodies loosen up. Most first-time trekkers are amazed at the energy and strength they discover, and by visible changes as weight drops and muscles firm. The pure physical pleasure of walking is reason enough to trek; finding out what your body can actually do may be the biggest thrill of all.

You learn on the trail how to gauge a hill, how to pace yourself on a long climb. Altitude fig-

Over the first few days of any march it is wise to draw a veil. The things that have been forgotten are gradually remembered, and the whole organization creaks and groans like your own joints. You wonder if man was really intended to walk, whether motoring after all is not his natural mode of progression, and whether the call of the open road is as insistent as you yourself thought or as the poets sing.
—H.W. Tilman

ures which at first seem arcane slowly begin to make sense, as your body learns what a 1,500-meter climb means, and how to adjust to it. At first the ups and downs seem endless, and you long for a level stretch. Downhill is harder on the knees, and long steep descents can be extremely tiring. After a while it doesn't matter which direction the trail is heading—you just walk it.

TREKKING STYLES

People tend to divide naturally into independent and group trekkers. Much is dictated by the time/money tradeoff: the more time/less money crowd goes alone, while reverse cases sign up for groups. Statistically the split is nearly even. The major trails are surprisingly easy to do alone. Group trekking's biggest advantage is its ability to open up remote regions which are practically inaccessible without porters, tents, and supplies.

Independent Trekking

Also called teahouse trekking, after the lodgings along main trails. Independent trekkers cluster on a few of Nepal's best-known trails, but you can teahouse trek wherever Nepalis live. Even if there's no sign saying "lodge," tea shops and local homes will put you up.

Independent trekking began in the tradition of mountaineers like Eric Shipton and H. W. Tilman, who pioneered the "living off the land" style. Over the past 20 years the main routes

A QUESTION OF IMPACT

A deep chasm divides group and individual trekkers. Trekking companies are suspicious of what they call "backpackers," and frequent articles denounce the money that's slipping away with independent trekkers. Individual trekkers, meanwhile, view group trekkers as packaged tourists missing out on the real thing; they pay a lot of money, rush through, and leave.

Often it seems trekkers of both styles leave nothing but trash and cultural havoc. Trekkers' support of local economies is supposed to make it all worthwhile for villagers. Actually, the impact on local economies is minimal. According to one study, only twenty cents of the average trekkers' daily expenditure of US$3 goes into the local economy (the figure is an average for group and individual trekkers).

This is more obvious in the case of organized treks, which haul everything in from Kathmandu. First off, a large chunk of money goes to the head office. The staff is from Kathmandu, and the porters are hired at the trailhead. Group trekkers are so well-drilled in the dangers of unclean food that they rarely even buy a glass of tea; at most the sirdar will buy

trekkers and porters carrying firewood, Pharak

firewood and a few vegetables. On the other hand, he can afford to pay any price for luxuries like chickens and eggs, driving them far above the reach of local people.

Individual trekkers contribute less than they might think. Most supplies—everything from beer and toilet paper to noodles and even rice in many areas—are imported from lower regions or Kathmandu. Prices are marked up to pay for porterage, and local profits are minimal. Local products are scarce, and few people have learned to raise or make goods to sell to trekkers. (In many areas there's little to sell but the scenery.) Finally, only a small percentage of the population does business with trekkers—less than one percent of Ghandruk's population operates shops or lodges.

Members of the trekking industry like to maintain their trips are environmentally correct, the main point being that teahouse trekkers stay in woodburning lodges and thus contribute to deforestation. They neglect to state that on many trails, group treks burn massive quantities of wood in preparing three elaborate meals a day—plus food for the staff and porters, who outnumber clients by at least three to one. Kerosene is supposed to be used for cooking in national parks, but cooks dodge this requirement whenever they can, and no matter what the staff does, porters still build fires.

The environmental impact of a group trek is much heavier than companies lead you to believe. Few bury their wastes sufficiently; often the toilet pits are left open, one at each campsite. Most Sherpas litter astoundingly. "Cleanup" means tossing tins and bottles into rivers or over a cliff—and there's a lot of such litter, since meals revolve around packaged food.

Individual trekkers are hardly much better. In season, woodstoves burn continually as lodges produce piecemeal orders from elaborate menus. (ACAP has sensibly moved to streamline local menus and standardize prices in the Annapurna Sanctuary.) But individuals are in a better position to control their impact. If you're traveling with friends, it helps to streamline food orders by requesting similar dishes at the same time. Cut down hot showers to absolutely necessary intervals, and realize that every bottle of beer, soda, or water you drink will remain there forever in some poorly located trash dump. And don't add to the pink toilet paper festooning trails—burn it, bury it, or live without it altogether.

have evolved a trekking subculture of their own, supported by Nepali entrepreneurs who are good at providing what people want: apple *pai*, pancakes, and cold beer. The Western food loses something in the translation, but trekking lodges suit most people. Fellow trekkers provide an international flavor to the conversation, while Nepal is the scenic backdrop. The result is a hybrid culture that's neither here nor there.

Most individual trekkers are in their twenties, often doing the Asian or world-travel circuit with a few months in Nepal along the way. The resulting far-flung conversations mean you can learn a lot about Kenyan safaris while sitting in a Sherpa lodge, but not much about Nepal beyond how difficult the trail is and what to eat where.

The daily schedule is dictated by yourself: you can stay a few extra days in a fascinating place, conk out early by the riverside, or sprint

---

In the big picture, the amount of firewood used to feed, warm, and wash 60,000 trekkers is negligible when compared to the eight million tons consumed annually by 19 million Nepalis. Environmental concern is fashionable nowadays, but far more serious is the cultural erosion caused by tourism. Trees can be replanted, but the loss of cultural identity is irreversible, and no amount of money can buy it back.

Annapurna Conservation Area Project (ACAP) director Chandra Gurung is more worried about tourism's impact on local culture than anything else. In the Gurung communities of the Annapurna region, he says, "Younger people aren't interested in learning about their culture; they don't wear the clothes, they hardly speak the language anymore; they don't want to work in the fields." ACAP is trying to emphasize the importance of cultural identity, improve local standards of living, and point out economic incentives, teaching people to use their experience in agriculture and handicrafts to sell products to trekkers. But intangibles like cultural changes are tough to pin down, and this is certainly ACAP's hardest battle.

So where's the solution? Increasing numbers of people, including many in the trekking industry, are warning of environmental dangers. Some go so far as to recommend closing overused regions for a few years' respite, or limiting the number of trekkers on major trails. So far the government has brushed these suggestions aside: as Nepal's largest source of foreign revenue, tourism is not lightly discouraged. It appears that new regions will be more strictly controlled, however. Part of the impetus in restricting Kangchenjunga and Dolpo to group treks was to control the environmental impact.

Better management will help, but ultimately the greatest responsibility lies with trekkers. Most people are well-meaning but unaware of the broad environmental and social consequences of their innocent vacation. The environmental dos and donts are relatively straightforward: coordinating and simplifying meals; minimizing hot water; burying waste or using local toilets as much as possible, carrying out garbage. Group trekkers can cheerfully prod and assist their staff into doing these things; a few companies are beginning to assume responsibility on their own.

Trickier are the more ephemeral issues of cultural contact: apparently innocuous things like dressing modestly (it applies to men as well as women), minimizing consumption (a good policy after the trek as well), discouraging begging, approaching people as human beings rather than photogenic objects, and realizing that every one of your actions is scrutinized and makes a far greater impression than you might think.

trekker with Langtang people

KERRY MORAN

ahead according to your mood. The routine is flexible compared to group trekking, but there's an equal danger of being isolated from Nepal. Most people expect trekking to be a remote and somewhat harrowing adventure, and are pleasantly surprised to find crowded trails. Social life is easy and there's almost always somebody to walk with with if you want—one reason to not worry too much about starting off alone.

It's certainly cheaper than group trekking, as little as Rs100-150 per day (compared to US$35-100 for a group). Double that for a porter, and add more if you're going to a remote high-altitude region like Khumbu. Prices increase steadily the farther you get from the road, since all goods must be carried in by porter.

Drawbacks include an increased risk of getting lost and a higher hassle factor—you have to

PORTERS AND GUIDES

Hiring someone to carry your pack is nothing to be ashamed of—portering is one of the few means of cash employment in the Hills, and carrying a pack is a holiday compared to the 100-kg bags of cement porters haul up trails. Aside from the distinct relief of getting the pack off your back, a porter can open up new avenues of communication with Nepal.

A guide, on the other hand, is really unnecessary for the major trails, which are virtual highways. A local porter will show the way if necessary, and carry your gear as well. On more remote trails a guide will serve you well, and it's all the better if he carries some of your gear.

Hiring a guide through a Kathmandu agency is the most expensive option, since you'll have to pay a higher salary (around US$12 per day, and the company takes a big cut), and his transportation. This is the only way to guarantee finding someone with good English, however. It's easy to find porters at roadheads and airstrips; ask your lodgekeeper to help if you don't come up with anyone yourself. Another option is to hire someone on the spot for a few rough days crossing a pass, though they may be hard to find when you need them. The current daily salary (set by the government) is Rs60 per day, higher in certain regions like eastern Nepal and during the autumn festival season when nobody wants to work. Most trekkers pay at least Rs100 per day; in Khumbu young Sherpas may get double that. When setting salary, make it clear that your porter will buy his own food. It's easier (and cheaper) to pay a higher daily rate than to fund his food bill. You may have to give a high altitude supplement as food prices rise, and it's always nice to throw in a few cups of tea and cigarettes along the trail.

Hiring a porter is a matter of instinct—search for the classic honest face. Older, more traditional men are preferable to cool young dudes who may be more interested in your sunglasses and Walkman. A drawback is that they seldom speak much English. A "professional" porter will go anywhere, while a farmer trying to earn some extra cash may get homesick a few days from his village and agitate to turn back. Try to determine beforehand just how far your porter will go, and don't be surprised if he doesn't. Women porters, usually Sherpas or Bhotia, can sometimes be hired but they're usually reluctant to travel far from home.

Don't expect your porter to cross a high pass without some help from you in terms of warm clothes, shoes, and equipment. Check in advance to see what he has, and loan, rent, or buy enough for him to make it over safely.

porter

arrange food and lodging yourself at every stop. Both of these are slight on well-trodden main trails. You do need a certain flexibility and an ability to deal with ambiguous situations which applies to all Asian travel.

For a first trek, it's advisable to stick to the main trails if you're going independently. Hiring a guide and/or porter expands the possibilities considerably. A good one will lead you down remote trails, interpret for you, and teach you a lot about Nepal in the process. Consider hiring a porter for main trails as well.

Organized Trekking

Trekking company clients tend to be slightly older than teahouse trekkers, generally late thirties and up. Usually they're professionals with steady jobs and limited vacations. Going through a company saves a lot of hassles and guarantees a trek will fit within a limited time.

Group trekkers live in comparative luxury. You still have to walk, of course, but in camp you've got chairs and tables in the dining tent, a toilet tent with paper, and staff to shepherd you down the trail if necessary. Food is Western-style and plentiful, and cooks work miracles, producing cakes, spring rolls, pizza—a different menu every evening. It's not all as good as it looks, but they try hard.

Accommodations are in two-person tents, cramped compared to some lodges but often cleaner, quieter, and free from smoky cooking fires. Pitched on snow, though, they're downright cold. The camping mentality of a group trek seems out of place on main trails where there are so many comfortable lodges, but it comes into its own in remote areas. For most people (especially first-time trekkers), off-the-beaten-track routes are best explored through a company.

The staff is led by a *sirdar,* an organizational wizard responsible for logistics, operations, and trekkers' general well-being. Almost all sirdars are Sherpa. In larger groups he's supplemented by a Western trek leader who acts as cultural interface. Other staff members include the cook, several "sherpas" who serve as trail scouts, guides, and go-fers, and a few kitchen boys, the hardest-working of the whole lot. Employees are usually charming, and a good staff can make a trek. Two to three weeks gives you time to get to know people; generally your greatest cul-

SOME RECOMMENDED TREKKING COMPANIES

Asian Trekking
TriDevi Marg
P.O. Box 3022
(tel. 412-821)

Nepal Himal Treks
next door to Asian Trekking
P.O. Box 3745
(tel. 411-949)

Guides for All Seasons
Gaidhidhara
P.O. Box 3776
(tel. 415-841)

Rover Treks & Expeditions
Naksal
P.O. Box 1081
(tel. 414-373)

Cho Oyu Trekking
Lazimpat
P.O. Box 4515
(tel. 418-890)

Yangrima Trekking
Kanti Path
P.O. Box 2951
(tel. 225-608)

tural interaction is with the staff.

Scheduling is strict. You're awakened with "bed tea," a vestigial custom of the Raj. Shortly after comes a basin of hot washing water. Pack your bags and stumble out to breakfast; while you dine, the staff is taking down tents, packing loads, and sending the porters along their way. The morning walk is a few hours to the lunch spot, which like the campsites is picked out in advance by the sirdar, who usually considers the availability of firewood and water more than the scenery. An awful lot of camps are in bare fields. Lunch is a two-hour break, followed by several more hours of walking to the evening's campsite. Dinner comes just after dark, and people are generally in bed by 2100—there's not much else to do in a cold tent. One or two rest days at scenic viewpoints vary this routine.

Drawbacks are price (booking through a company outside of Nepal, you pay US$50-100 per day) and the essential lack of freedom. Many people are willing to trade this for the reassurance of being taken care of every step of the way. Group dynamics are unpredictable, not surprising when you consider that basically a group of strangers is cast into the wilderness and expected to get along for several weeks. Some groups develop great camaraderie and organize regular reunions, while others can't wait to split up.

If organized trekking sounds attractive but prices seem high, consider going through a reputable local company. Foreign trekking agencies channel their clients through local companies, charging a higher price for the privilege of signing up abroad. Services are pretty much identical for local signups, but the cost can be half or less, depending on the size of your party. You can sign up in advance for scheduled group trips, but be prepared to make arrangements up to six months beforehand.

It's simpler just to go to Kathmandu: a week is enough to arrange most treks. Aside from the lower price, you can tailor a custom trek to your own specifications: go alone or with a few friends, bring your kids, indulge in birdwatching or photography, visit remote regions groups don't go to. At the lowest end of the scale, you could just hire a guide from a local company.

Choose a company belonging to **TAAN** (Trekking Agents Association of Nepal), which gives some recourse should something go wrong. The TAAN office on Kanti Path has a list of agency locations and numbers. Beware of rock-bottom cheap agencies, which cut too many corners and often don't know anything but the main trails. A recommendation from a satisfied recent client is the best way to choose a company.

TREKKING PEAKS

If trekking leaves you craving still more adventure, consider an ascent of a trekking peak. Eighteen peaks in this category were opened in 1978 through the **Nepal Mountaineering Association.** Unlike the 104 official expedition peaks, which require expensive permits and a liason officer and sirdar, trekking peaks are a simpler procedure.

The "trekking" part is a misnomer: actually these peaks are shorter, lower versions of full-on ascents. "Small peaks" might be a better term. They range from 5,687 meters to 6,654 meters. Anyone planning an ascent should know the basics of ice axe, crampons, and snow-climbing; winter mountaineering experience would be a plus.

Khumbu has the most trekking peaks (eight), and these in particular are prime viewpoints for the region's array of soaring mountains. The most popular include **Island Peak** (Imja Tse, 6,185 meters), **Mera Peak** (6,476 meters), and the more difficult **Kwangde** (6,187 meters) west of Namche Bazaar. In the Annapurna region **Fluted Peak** (Singhu Chuli, 6,501 meters) and **Chulu West and East** (6,419/6,584 meters) are popular.

Foreign trekking companies market these trips as mini-expeditions at premium prices. It's also possible to go with a few friends through local companies for a much lower fee. This way you have a choice of an expedition-style ascent with Sherpas, porters, and full camps, or a light alpine-style climb, carrying your own gear. Climbing permits must be obtained through a registered trekking company from the Nepal Mountaineering Association (office on Ram Shah Path). The fee is US$300 for the most popular peaks; a few minor ones are US$150. Bill O'Connor's *The Trekking Peaks of Nepal* provides detailed information on routes and planning for all 18 peaks.

BOB RACE

THE ANNAPURNA REGION

North of Pokhara, Nepal's spectacular diversity appears at its finest. The deep valleys and high mountains encircling the giant Annapurna Himal embrace a wide range of peoples and terrain, from subtropical jungle to a high, dry landscape resembling the Tibetan Plateau. This is the most popular trekking region, attracting over 75% of all trekkers (more than 30,000 annually). It's also among the tamest areas, with excellent lodges lining the main routes. Finding Nepal beneath the flood of trekkers can be difficult, but the scenery and culture are top-notch, and you can avoid the peak-season crush and still get fine weather and views.

Two main trails follow river valleys in relatively easy ascents: up the Kali Gandaki to Jomosom and Muktinath, and up the Marsyangdi to Manang. By crossing a high but straightforward pass, the Thorung La, these trails can be joined into the classic Annapurna Circuit. As the land climbs, thatch-roofed mud-walled huts are replaced by flat-roofed stone houses, and people change from farmers to herders, Hindus to Buddhists. The Annapurna region dramatically reveals the highland/lowland cultural and geographic frontier running across Nepal. Mountain views are frequent and good, and if they don't equal the heart-of-the-mountains feeling of Khumbu, there's the Annapurna Sanctuary, a secluded high-altitude hollow ringed by huge peaks.

POKHARA TO MUKTINATH

This major Himalayan highway follows the gorge of the Kali Gandaki River, crossing from subtropical jungle to high-altitude desert in less than one week. It's probably *the* most popular trek in Nepal, especially when you count short treks up the first portion to Poon Hill. Lodges are the highest standard anywhere, with private rooms, foam mattresses, enchiladas, and pizzas—even

> *It would be futile to describe the region, for in exclusively mountainous countries every beauty is too extreme to be conveyed by any words that I might choose. None of the books or photographs studied before leaving home had even slightly prepared me for such majesty. Truly this is something that does have to be seen to be believed, and that once seen must be continually yearned for when left behind, becoming as incurable a fever of the spirit as malaria is to the body.*
>
> —Dervla Murphy, *The Waiting Land*

a few VCRs en route. Mixed in the stream of international trekkers are Hindu saddhus walking to Muktinath and jingling mule trains heading down from Tibet loaded with bales of wool. Both are reminders of the trail's status as a major trade and pilgrimage route, an important cultural corridor across the Himalaya.

The endpoint is the ancient shrine of **Muktinath,** one of Nepal's holiest pilgrimage sites. Set in thoroughly Buddhist high country, Muktinath began thousands of years ago as a natural power place, later adopted by formal religions. The old animistic beliefs linger in influences on local Buddhism. The primordial guardian of the region was the sacred mountain **Dhaulagiri,** and its massive snowy white bulk dominates much of the trek.

The Kali Gandaki gorge is considered the deepest in the world. The river flows between Dhaulagiri (8,167 meters) and **Annapurna** (8,091 meters), which are less than 20 km apart and six km straight up from the riverbed. Walking through it, though, you don't even feel you're in a gorge—the peaks are so steep they're incredibly foreshortened.

The Basics
Figure at least two weeks to walk in and out, and allow a few extra days for exploration—the upper region in particular is lined with fascinating villages. Flying into Jomosom and walking back down is possible, but you'd have to acclimatize before climbing to Muktinath. You could fly from Jomosom to Kathmandu (US$75) or Pokhara (US$40), but flights are frequently cancelled due to high winds, creating a bottleneck during the main trekking season.

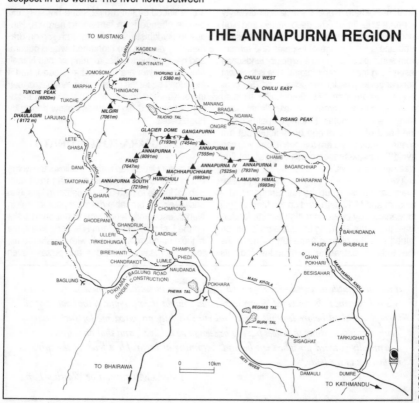

THE ANNAPURNA REGION

© MOON PUBLICATIONS, INC.

scene from lower portion of Muktinath trek

BOB RACE

The trail is in good shape, except for a few stretches in the middle which are plagued by landslides. Aside from the notorious "killer staircase" to Ghodepani (not as bad as everyone thinks), it's neither difficult nor high. The route follows the gentle uphill course of the Kali Gandaki River, with a final climb to Muktinath at 3,800 meters. Above Tukche, a strong south wind blows from late morning until sunset. It will literally propel you up the trail, but the return is like leaning into a wall.

The short trek up the first portion of the trail to Ghodepani and Poon Hill has achieved cult status among trekkers. Returning via Ghandruk makes a nice week-long trek, but heavy crowds in peak season make it difficult to recommend, and the route doesn't touch the fascinating high country of the upper portion.

For the adventurous, side trips up from the Thak Khola offer splendid mountain views—far better than the main trail—and a taste of wilder, more remote country. You'll need a local guide, plus shelter, food, and fuel for two to seven days. Or just day-hike up as far as possible. Possibilities include **Tukche** to **Dhampus Pass,** the **Dhaulagiri Icefall,** and the original **North Annapurna Base Camp** near the headwaters of the remote Mristi Khola.

To vary the return route, loop back to Pokhara through Ghandruk and Dhampus, or continue down the Kali Gandaki to Beni and Baglung. When the road from Pokhara becomes operational, this may become a standard route out. Three more days downriver is the seldom visited hill station of **Tansen.**

Phedi To Ulleri
The early stages of the route are currently in flux due to the construction of the Pokhara-Baglung Road. In early 1991 the starting point was Phedi, an hour-long jeep ride from Pokhara (Rs40). Alternatively, you could walk up the ridge via **Sarangkot,** a slower but less bumpy alternative. Either way you reach **Naudanda** and continue along the ridge through **Kaski,** the pretty little village of **Chandrakot,** and down through soggy **Lumle** to **Birethanti.** The road has already reached Birethanti, pretty much spoiling the walk. Soon a bus ride will chop off the trek's traditional first day.

Birethanti is a lovely village, complete with riverside cafes. As a roadside town its charm is likely to decrease. From here the road veers south and the foot trail begins, so steep no road will ever be built up it. The infamous 3,767-step stone staircase leads up from **Tirkhedhunga** to **Ulleri** (2,073 meters). From here the trail leads

> *In Nepal there are no roads and few bridges—and you really should make your will before setting foot on the ones there are. You climb and descend the whole time: from the depths of the valley to the summit, from the summit to the valley two or three times a day.*
>
> —Giuseppe Tucci,
> *Journey to Mustang*

through beautiful dense forest, nearly deserted apart from a few small lodges set in clearings.

Ghodepani

Ghodepani (2,850 meters) is perhaps the most extreme example of a trekking ghetto in Nepal. Until 1978, it was a lone cowherder's hut set in a dense forest, visited only by pack trains which watered here (thus its name, "Horse Water"). Now 18,000 trekkers tromp through here annually, and at last count 37 lodges were chopping down one hectare of rhododendron forest per year. The site is overused and littered, and sanitation is a serious problem.

Don't expect much from the village—there is none, just a collection of lodges ranging from shanty to chalet. What everyone comes for are views: **Poon Hill,** one hour's climb above, is renowned for having some of the finest mountain views in Nepal. More accurately, they're the finest views within a three-day trek. The Annapurnas and Dhaulagiri are pretty but distant, and the panorama doesn't compare with Everest or even Upper Manang on the Annapurna Circuit.

From Ghodepani the trail descends to a pass with mountain views nearly equaling Poon Hill's (Dhaulagiri looks even better) and drops to **Taatopani** (1,219 meters), famed for its excellent Thakali lodges and hot springs. The cement water tank is often crowded, but it's wonderful to bask in the hot water with the river rushing below and the stars glittering above. Local people use less-visited hot springs, 15 minutes' walk south on the Beni trail at **Raatopani.** The lodge here is a quiet alternative to touristy Taatopani.

From here on the trail follows the Kali Gandaki, climbing past the waterfall of **Rupse Chaharo** to cross the swirling river in a steep gorge. The next stretch can be a real cliff-hanger since frequent landslides wipe out the trail.

Ghasa, with its entrance chorten and small gompa, is the first Thakali village. Its flat roofs signal the diminishing rainfall. The Kali Gandaki soon becomes broad and tranquil, a meandering river instead of the rushing torrent a few kilometers downstream. Between Ghasa and the pretty Thakali villages of **Lete** and **Kaalopani** the land changes dramatically, as dense jungle is replaced by pine forests, then the dry vegetation of the Tibetan Plateau. The villages themselves are more Tibetan-influenced, a shift which becomes more distinct further on. Lete is directly below Dhaulagiri, and thus at the heart of the world's deepest river gorge.

The Thak Khola

The broad valley of the Kali Gandaki is called the Thak Khola, and its people, the Thakali, are distantly related to Tibetans. The men are famed as traders; the women once operated simple teahouses *(bhatti)* on the lower trails in winter months, known for their good cooking and cleanliness. When foreign trekkers arrived, the Thakali simply transferred their bhatti experience to running lodges, expanded their menus, and raked in the money.

the broad valley of the Kali Gandaki, near Ghasa

KERRY MORAN

Tukche (2,590 meters) is a major Thakali settlement, once a center of the Kali Gandaki trade route, as demonstrated by its name, "Flat Place for Grains." Here wool, salt, and turquoise from Tibet were swapped for rice, cloth, and cigarettes from lowland Nepal. Four powerful Thakali families with special dispensations from the government ran the trade. Since the Chinese takeover of Tibet, the enterprising Thakalis have shifted to other lucrative enterprises. Many have left their homeland for good, installing caretakers in their old houses.

Tukche's neglected old Buddhist shrines indicate the Thakalis' 19th-century switch to Hinduism in their climb to power. The oldest is the **Rani Gompa,** first built in 1621 and now on the verge of collapse. There's a small **Mahakali Gompa** in the center of town; at the north end is the **Gompa Sarpa,** once a big monastery.

Less than two hours up the trail is **Marpha** (2,665 meters), a fascinating collection of stone houses, prayer flags, and neat paved streets with an elegant system of covered sewers. Marphalis are related to Thakalis and own most of the mule trains seen on the trail. They're known for the apple and peach "brandy" (actually excellent raaksi) they produce from nearby orchards. Across the river the Tibetan settlement at **Chaira** is home to the souvenir vendors seen all along the trail; there's an 18th-century gompa here with an image of Padmasambhava.

The next town is **Jomosom** (2,713 meters), a drab government headquarters with dozens of offices, a bank, and a few fancy hotels near its STOL airstrip. The name is the Nepali corruption of Dzong Sarpa, Tibetan for "New Fort." The old section of town across the river is mildly more interesting and has several lodges. **Thinigaon,** two km east of Jomosom, is a large Tibetan-style village. If you're passing through in early fall you might catch its annual Yak Dance. The gompa above town is finely decorated and preserves all sorts of relics, including five terracotta images said to be brought from Samye Monastery in Tibet, also one of Guru Rinpoche's slippers, and the skull of a high lama imprinted with the Tibetan vowel 'A'.

En Route To Muktinath

The trail continues upriver through desolate barren landscape to **Eklai Bhatti** ("Alone Inn") and forks, with the right-hand trail going directly to Muktinath. It's worthwhile to take the half-hour detour down the other trail to **Kagbeni** (2,810 meters), an old medieval fortress town on the riverside. Kagbeni was once the center of an independent kingdom, as its ruined palace testifies. In the crumbling Sakya Monastery Giuseppe Tucci found 15th-century frescoes and mounds of ancient bronzes, both probably long gone. With its central wall of prayer wheels and close-packed mud-walled houses bristling with stacked firewood, it's hard to find a more Tibetan-feeling town in Nepal.

A checkpost here prevents one from crossing the river and continuing north into the legendary region of **Mustang.** All you can do is gaze over the strangely eroded and colored hills folding off into the distance—"fascinatingly ugly country, the more fascinating for being so little known," wrote H.W. Tilman. Geologically and culturally, Mustang is Tibetan. China conceded it to Nepal on the basis of a small annual tribute paid by its king, but it remained semiautonomous well into the '60s. Someday it may be opened to trekkers; for now the treasurehouse of Tsarang Gompa and the old walled city of Mustang remain off-limits.

Muktinath And Vicinity

From Kagbeni a trail leads up into a lovely high valley dominated by the ruined fortress of **Jharkot** (3,500 meters). Less than an hour further is the sacred pilgrimage site of Muktinath (3,170 meters). There's no real village, but lodges around the lower portion (**Ranipauwa**) put up pilgrims and trekkers.

This ancient holy site is a typically confusing blend of natural, Buddhist, and Hindu beliefs. The little Newari-style pagoda to Vishnu is a relatively recent addition. Muktinath has been sacred for over 2,000 years; the *Mahabharata* mentions it as Shaligrama, "Place of the Shaligram," the black fossil-stones sacred to Vishnu and found in abundance in the Kali Gandaki valley. Its holiness stems from flickering blue flames of natural methane gas burning on water, stone, and earth, and now enclosed in the shrine of Jwala Mai below the Vishnu temple.

Near the pagoda a sacred spring spurts out through 108 spouts shaped like bulls' heads. Devout pilgrims bathe in the freezing water to purify their sins and earn *mukti* or spiritual liberation. The place has ancient associations for

THE ANNAPURNA CIRCUIT

This classic 330-km walk joins the Manang and Muktinath treks by crossing the 5,380-meter Thorung La. It's an extraordinary trek, one of the world's best, requiring at least two weeks. It's also extraordinarily popular, and the Thorung La's limited season crams everyone into the fall and spring months. In Oct.-Nov. this trek becomes the "Annapurna Circus."

Nearly everyone follows standard trekking guidebook advice to do the circuit counterclockwise, crossing the pass from Manang. The main reason is that coming from the east you're higher and presumably better acclimatized, and the net ascent is 979 meters, compared to 1,578 meters from Muktinath. The rule isn't absolute, however; the pass *is* crossable from Muktinath if you're well-acclimatized and in good shape. Going reverse takes you out of the flow. Instead, you'll be passing trekkers the whole way—and saying "Bonjour, G'day, Namaste" all day long can be as tiring as traveling with the same batch of people for 23 days.

Whichever side you choose, the Thorung La deserves some respect as the highest commonly trekked pass in Nepal. Make sure you're well-briefed on altitude sickness, and be prepared for weather extremes. The guy who thought it was the "Thong La" and went over it in flip-flops is legendary, and fortunately not dead. You'll need good boots, warm clothing, and sunglasses. Take care of your porter as well. Lowland Nepalis are often woefully unprepared when it comes to highland trekking. Every year a few porters die from exposure or altitude sickness because their employers figured they knew what they were doing and ignored them. Most of these tragedies occur on the Thorung La.

The trail over the pass is steep but in good shape and not hard to follow. This is the one point of the entire circuit when you feel really *in* the mountains, which might compensate for the thin air. If altitude isn't a problem the day-long crossing is not difficult, but many people find themselves gasping for air and moving painfully slowly. Snow is a possibility, and you might find a stick or ski pole helpful.

The opening of teashops and lodges at Phedi and above Muktinath have made the crossing easier than in the past. Weather is the most se-

Buddhists as well: Guru Rinpoche is said to have passed through here en route to Tibet, leaving his footprints in a rock; the 84 Siddhas dropped their wooden staffs, which magically sprang up as the surrounding popular grove. There are many old Buddhist temples around here, including an eerie, abandoned shrine filled with life-sized terra-cotta images, crumbling yet serene.

The Muktinath Valley is well worth exploring. The magically clear light makes it absolutely radiant in clear weather. Blessed with fertile soil and plenty of water, the six small villages are prosperous and well-kept. Women weaving on rooftops may try to sell woolen blankets or Tibetan artifacts; most of the latter are the usual junk brought up from Kathmandu. In late summer the Pompo Yartöng festival (usually the August full moon) draws local people dressed in splendid finery for a day of chang-drinking, singing, dancing, and daring horse races.

The northwest side of the valley is guarded by twin peaks flanking the Thorung La Pass. Though it's usually crossed from Manang, this side is possible if you're well-acclimatized and in good shape. In the main season a few teashops are open higher up; overnighting here would give you a head start. Sometimes ponies are available to carry trekkers over the pass.

MIKE WELLINS

rious problem; snow can shut it down unexpectedly so keep an eye on conditions and be ready to turn back immediately in threatening circumstances. It's generally uncrossable from Jan.-March or mid-April, though local people will often plough a yak trail through the snow. Some years the snowfall is insignificant and it's crossable, though freezing, all winter long.

MANANG

This trek is invariably described as the first portion of the Annapurna Circuit, but it stands up as a destination on its own. Slightly shorter than the Muktinath trail, it offers the same combination of lowland Hindu and highland Buddhist villages, similar cultural and geographic diversity, and even more spectacular mountain views, the best closeups of the entire circuit. Upper Manang is more rugged and less populated than the upper Kali Gandaki, and even more evocative of highland Tibet. Finally, Buddhism here is much more active, and Manang's monasteries are among the best in Nepal.

Upper Manang has a pretty wild recent history. Early visitors like Tilman and Snellgrove commented on the rude reception they received, and a starving Maurice Herzog was sent back up to Tilicho Tal without a bit of food. The region above Chame was closed to trekkers until 1977, due to Khampa guerillas who controlled the valley for over a decade. Before that, an armed feud between Braga and Manang made it unsafe for visitors. Nowadays Manangis welcome trekkers with open arms, though it's not their innate sense of hospitality as much as their innate sense of trade.

Manangis began international trading in 1784, when a royal edict exempted them from customs and gave them unprecedented freedom to travel. They began by exporting herbs and musk to Southeast Asia; eventually they were bringing back gold, semiprecious stones, and Swiss watches. Visiting Manang in the early '50s, Toni Hagen was astonished to discover a remote valley full of Nepalis wearing gold Swiss watches, who, when he pulled out his camera, pulled out their own and took photos of him!

Though their privileges have been curtailed, Manangis remain Nepal's premier traders, specializing in Asian fashions, gold, and electronic goods. Rumor is that they built a special tunnel underneath the new airport to expedite customs. Not surprisingly, this is an exceptionally cosmopolitan mountain community, where young men in jean jackets mix with farmers and herders. Increasingly, Manangis are leaving their remote district to settle in more central locations, and Tibetans, Gurungs, and Bhotia take their place as tenant farmers and caretakers.

The Basics
Two weeks would give a little extra time to spend in Braga and Manang. There's an airstrip at **Ongre,** below Manang, but flights (US$88) are generally charters. Lodges are not as deluxe as on the Jomosom side, but are adequate and abundant. Do take warm clothing if you're crossing the Thorung La.

The trail adheres to the wall of a narrow gorge in places. Portions were once death-defyingly narrow, but blasting has expanded them into reasonably safe trails.

Above Chame snow piles up in winter, and local people start heading to lower settlements by mid-November A late monsoon trek in the rainshadow region of Upper Manang would avoid the crowds and much of the rain, if you're lucky.

The first step is to get to the dusty little roadside town of **Dumre,** a five-hour bus ride from Kathmandu or two hours from Pokhara. Local jeeps and trucks run from here up to Besisahar for Rs60-75—get together with a few others and bargain. The four-hour ride can be bone-rattling and obscenely crowded. It might be better to walk for a day and a half, taking a trail paralleling the road and perhaps veering off to visit the hilltop Gurung town of **Ghan Pokhari.** From Pokhara, you could walk to Besisahar in two to three days and avoid the jeep altogether. Starting from Begnas Tal, many trails weave east through the lowland hills; take a guide or be prepared to constantly ask directions.

Besisahar To Chame
Besisahar (823 meters) is a bustling little boomlet town, the usual roadhead mess. The trek's first two days lead through typical hill country inhabited by Gurungs and Hindu castes; this lowland portion is hot in springtime. The trail begins climbing around **Bhulbhule.** Past **Bahundanda** and **Syangje** the steep trail cuts

across a sheer-walled gorge. Once the route here went over wooden galleries lashed to the rock wall; it's been improved but is still steep and narrow.

The water buffalo and rice paddies continue up to **Chamje** (1,433 meters), then huge oak forests take over as the valley narrows. The village of **Tal** is set in the middle of a broad valley at the foot of a waterfall. The trail steadily rises through cooler zones, changing from pine forest to open meadows, and finally dry rainshadow. At **Dharapani** is the first of many entrance and exit chorten marking Manang's Buddhist villages. **Bagarchap** (2,164 meters) is an interesting village with a relatively new Nyingma gompa with nice frescoes. Houses here are both flat-roofed stone and sloped-roof wood, the latter soon vanishing in the higher, drier country ahead.

Tucked into a side valley up from **Kotoje** is the fascinating off-limits region of **Nar-Phu**, one of the three traditional regions of Manang. There's a guardpost here to make sure you don't visit it, as it falls within the government-decreed restricted zone. *Cloud Dwellers of the Himalayas* is an excellent survey of life in this secluded area (see Booklist).

Chame (2,685 meters) is the district headquarters, with the usual police posts, bank, government offices, lodges advertising 24-hour hot showers, and the biggest shops of the entire trail. Prices are reasonable here, but they rise as you go higher. There's a shallow but good set of hot springs near the trail before Chame, and another within reach of the town.

En Route To Manang

Beyond Chame are extensive apple orchards; spectacular views of the Annapurnas begin here, remaining all the way to Manang. Cross the river just before **Bratang**, which until 1975 was inhabited by Khampa rebels who virtually controlled the trail from this outpost. Ahead, the trail passes through a superb pine forest to **Pisang** (3,185 meters), the first village in Manang proper. The lower town has most of the lodges, but the upper portion, 100 meters higher and across the river, is the real village, with stone houses surrounding an old gompa. It's worth climbing up just for the views of the Annapurnas. Above the town towers the trekking peak of Pisang.

From here on you're in the rainshadow area of Nyeshang (Manang's traditional name), a dry 20-km-long strip of land with an average altitude of 3,500 meters. From upper Pisang, a trail climbs steeply through fields to **Gyaru** (3,700 meters), with more great views of Annapurna, and continues on through **Ngawal** to Braga. Practically everyone skips this wonderful high route in favor of a faster trail from lower Pisang, which leads past **Ongre** with its rarely used STOL airstrip. A half-hour further down the lower trail a **Trekker's Aid Post** operates out of a mountaineering school set up with Yugoslav assistance in 1980.

The trails join just before **Braga** (3,505 meters), a spectacular collection of flat-roofed houses stacked up against steep cliffs. Chulu East rises across the river; directly behind is Annapurna III. The town is dominated by a spectacularly located **Kargyü Gompa**, the largest in Manang and over 500 years old. In the main temple, 108 terra-cotta images surround statues of Tara, Samantabhadra, and Mahakala.

Few trekkers stay in this fascinating place; the lure of nearby Manang pulls them north.

CHRISTOPHER GAWM

Gurung girls in Bagarchhap, Annapurna Circuit

Braga village, Manang

There aren't many standard tourist lodges in Braga, but it's easy to find a house where you can sleep on the floor or (less smoky) on the roof. There are lots of day trips into the mountains behind crowned with prayer flags. On a ridgetop between Braga and Manang is **Bodzo Gompa,** the most active in the region, like Braga's, over five centuries old. The marvellous old frescoes admired by Snellgrove have been touched up by a heavy hand.

Manang
Manang (3,351 meters), the unofficial capital of the region, is a half-hour past Braga, about 500 houses huddled together and plenty of lodges and shops. Mountain views are again spectacular, with a foreshortened Annapurna and Gangapurna looming over town and Chulu East and West across the river. To the south is a full-on view of the north side of the Annapurnas, so big it's difficult to grasp their immense scale. Steep hanging glaciers cascade down between Annapurna IV and III. Manang's gompa is moderately interesting, but nothing like Braga's.

Trekkers crossing the Thorung La usually stay at least a day in Manang to acclimatize. There are lots of good day-trips: a small **glacial lake** across the river; the village of **Khangsar,** five km west; and the ridge north of town with views of Annapurna IV and II and Glacier Dome.

A day above Manang is **Phedi** (4,404 meters), a tiny little one-lodge stop at the foot of the Thorung La. Formerly a high-altitude dump, the place has been improved, but it's still windy

and crowded, and a good night's sleep is virtually impossible with trekkers rising at 0300 to get over the pass. Such efforts are usually unnecessary—the pass is a four-hour ascent and a three-hour descent, unless the altitude has really knocked the wind out of you.

THE ANNAPURNA SANCTUARY

In many ways this is the ideal trek: lovely, short, and intense, a direct route into the heart of the Himalaya. Some of the best of Nepal's diversity is compressed into less than two weeks of walking. Spectacular mountain vistas and easy access (only five days' walk from Pokhara) make it among the most popular treks, with over 10,000 visitors per year. Not surprisingly, the fragile alpine environment of the upper sanctuary is suffering from overuse. Up to forty trekkers arrive daily in season at the upper "base camps," and the crowding is compounded by the single narrow entry-exit trail.

The sanctuary is a hidden pocket of meadow, moraine, and glacier, ringed by magnificent sheer-walled 6,000-8,000-meter peaks: the Annapurnas, Gangapurna, Machhapuchhare, Hiuchuli. This is the sacred land of the native Gurung people, the abode of their gods. Traditionally, no women or low-caste men were allowed past here, impure food like meat, eggs, and garlic was forbidden, and hunting and butchering was prohibited. The sanctuary must have been an idyllic place, a haven for wildlife and wildflowers, visited only by a few shepherds who brought their flocks up to graze summer meadows. It's shocking to see the hordes passing through here nowadays (including plenty of women and garlic). Some Gurungs darkly attribute misfortunes—anything from trekking deaths to crop failures—to the sanctum's violation. Certainly the amount of trekker-supplied litter on the trail is enough to enrage even a god.

The Basics

A single trail enters the sanctuary between a high-walled mountain gorge, a portal cut between Machhapuchhare and Hiuchuli. The trail rises nearly 2,000 meters in the last eight km; obviously you need to plan for acclimatization. The trail is frequently slippery and there's danger of avalanches in a few places, so winter trekking

is unlikely. Accommodations in the lower portion (at least in Chomrong) are deluxe; the upper stretch is understandably simple—after all, nobody lives up here full time. Bring good boots and warm clothes for the upper portion: you may encounter snow.

You can gallop up the trail and back in 10 days from Pokhara only if you're already acclimatized from a previous trek; otherwise allot closer to two weeks. If you don't want to go high or are short on time, an idyllic lower circuit from Dhampus-Chomrong-Ghandruk-Birethanti can be done in less than a week. Add a few more days to visit Ghodepani and Poon Hill.

The Trail

From the Jomosom trail, trails lead off from Chandrakot, Birethanti, Tirkedhunga and Ghodepani, all within one-to three-days' walk north-

IN ACAP LAND

The 2,600-square-km area around the Annapurna Himal is the most highly impacted trekking region in Nepal. Over 40,000 people live off the land, and an additional 30,000 trekkers come through yearly, increasing the environmental pressure. Sensing the potential for ecological disaster, the **Annapurna Conservation Area Project** (ACAP) was launched in December 1986. The project is designed to improve local living standards, protect the environment, and educate trekkers on what they can do to help—or at least not harm—the region. On a 1990 trek, I discovered first-hand what ACAP is doing to promote these ideas.

Two days north of Pokhara we begin hearing talk of "Yeh-Kap." It takes some time for me to equate this with the Annapurna Conservation Area Project (ACAP). The first mention is in a Landruk lodge, as our young host agonizes over raising his modest prices. He asks us earnestly why foreigners who have traveled halfway around the world at tremendous expense will argue over one or two rupees, try to bargain down the cost of a bed, always seek the cheapest lodges, and sometimes walk out on the bill. "Don't they understand that this is how we make our living?" he asks in genuine bewilderment.

Then he tells us how a lodge owner's committee in Chomrong sponsored by ACAP has established standard prices to avoid the backbreaking competition common along main trails. Many lodgekeepers

provide services below cost, neglecting to charge for the wood they chop, the water they haul, the vegetables and milk they produce. "Since they didn't have to buy it, they think of it as free," he says.

The next day we reach **Chomrong**, an idyllic village with Swiss-chalet lodges and gorgeous flowers framing mountain views. One lodge here heats its water with solar power; most others have back-boiler water heaters installed behind the woodburning kitchen stove. This marvelously simple system uses convection to pull water through the pipes, heating it without burning extra wood. Needless to say, these innovations have been introduced by ACAP, which has also banned the use of firewood above Chomrong. Campers and group treks may burn only kerosene; even porters cook with it, and though they may furtively build a small fire at night for warmth, it's nothing like their usual bonfire.

Our Gurung lodgekeeper proudly shows off laminated certificates from an ACAP-sponsored lodge-owner training program and a month-long English course. In town we pick up a leaflet describing more about ACAP, which deals with trekkers as well as locals, distributing brochures and selling maps and a guide to regional wildlife. In addition, ACAP collects Rs200 from each trekker in the Annapurnas. The fee is paid with the permit, and unlike regular permit fees absorbed by the central government, the money goes back into the region.

west of Pokhara, and at the end of the Annapurna Circuit for most trekkers.

From Pokhara, take a jeep or taxi to **Phedi**
and climb up to the small ridgetop village of
Dhampus, a nice place to stay if you've gotten
a late start. The trail crests a pass and drops
to **Landruk,** pure Gurung hillbilly, then descends
to the Modi Khola.

Across and higher up is the interesting village of Ghandruk, but it's better to avoid the
steep climb and descent and visit it while returning. Take the trail leading upriver, crossing
and climbing *very* steeply for several hours up to
Chomrong (2,050 meters), a lovely Alpine-style
village with a few chalet-like lodges.

Chomrong is the last permanent settlement,
and a good place to wait if the upper trail is
blocked by snow or avalanches. Until recently

only shepherds went above here; now seasonal lodges line the trail (26 at last count). Facilities
are simple, and standardized rates set by ACAP
preclude competition. Unless you're coming off
a high trek you'll have to go slowly to acclimatize,
but the distance isn't that long—only two days'
walking.

The "entrance" to the sanctuary is past the
two lodges of **Dhovan,** where a small chorten
and prayer flags honor guardian spirit Pujinam
Barahar. Local men passing by leave a little
rice, some paisa, or strips of red cloth, offerings for safety and good luck.

A few hours further is **Machhapuchhare
Base Camp,** a rather pointless name, since
there's been only one expedition to Machhapuchhare (see p. 272). Two hours further is **Annapurna Base Camp** (4,130 meters). Moun-

---

Ghandruk is a tidy village of several hundred
slate-roofed houses perched on a hillside high above
the Modi Khola. A thin veneer of trekking culture is
laid atop traditional subsistence agriculture: women
thresh wheat in courtyards and boys drive water
buffalo up the muddy trails.

We ask our lodgekeeper about ACAP. "Up until
now, it's been good," he says, typically cautious
about anything perceived as government (actually
ACAP is a private, nonprofit organization). Then his
eyes light up as he lists what ACAP has done in
Ghandruk: built a water tap and installed a water
system, brought in furniture for the village school, improved trails, installed rubbish bins, planted trees;
and, he triumphantly concludes, a micro-hydropow-
er project is in the works to provide electricity to the
town.

While he credits ACAP, all this was actually accomplished by local people. ACAP provides support and encouragement, supplies matching funds for
projects, and accepts donated labor in place of cash.
Villagers thus have an incentive to use and maintain
what they've built themselves, and they generally
do.

The next day we visit ACAP's field office in Ghandruk. By a stroke of luck program director Chandra
Gurung happens to be in town for a few days and explains the beginning of ACAP. Dr. Gurung combines
a local perspective (he grew up in the village of Siklis) with a Ph.D. in human geography from the University of Hawaii. He says that project designers
spent four months in the field talking with people,
and soon concluded that the standard National Park

model would disrupt the lives of the region's 40,000
inhabitants. Instead, a multiple-use approach was
adopted to balance the diverse needs of local people,
trekkers, and the environment that accommodates
both.

Most important has been the emphasis on fulfilling
local needs, unusual for a conservation project, but
essential in Nepal. "Without addressing local needs,
we knew there would be no cooperation," Gurung
said—and without local participation, the project
would fail. By repairing schools and trails and con-
structing water taps and health centers, ACAP built
up local trust, creating a base for conservation efforts.
To deal with issues like woodcutting and forestry,
community groups have been formed with ACAP's
encouragement and support to make decisions on
their own—an effort to revive traditional systems of
regulating forest use, which virtually disappeared
after Nepal's forests were nationalized.

While ACAP is involved in a wide array of projects, its managers are careful not to spread efforts
too thin. The original pilot focused on the heavily
impacted 200 square km of the upper Annapurna
Sanctuary. ACAP will slowly expand to cover 800
square km over the next four years, establishing
more regional centers like Ghandruk's. Gurung is
eloquent regarding ACAP's ultimate goal: "To create
a small Utopia where all needs are available, an
area that is fully protected and conserved, where
people, forests and wildlife all live together in a harmonious manner." The vision *does* sound Utopian,
but ACAP's flexible, locally based approach holds
much promise.

tain views are supposed to be slightly better at the latter, but it's not likely you'll be dissatisfied with either. To get the best out of it (and to acclimatize well) spend a night at each. Sheer mountain walls ring the bowl of the sanctuary: Hiuchuli, Annapurna South, Fang, Annapurna I, Annapurna II, Machhapuchhare.

Returning, you'll have to backtrack beyond Chomrong. A nice alternate return would be via **Ghandruk** (2,012 meters), one of Nepal's largest Gurung villages, several hundred tidy slate-roofed houses perched on a hillside (most lodges are at the top). It's worth a day's exploration. From Ghandruk a relatively new route leads through lush, nearly virgin jungle and forest to Ghodepani, a long day's walk with only one stopping place en route, the lodges of **Tadapani.** Or you could continue south a few hours to **Birethanti** (soon to be connected to the Pokhara-Baglung Road), and join the main trail back to Phedi and Pokhara in a day.

SOLU-KHUMBU: THE EVEREST REGION

This classic walk through the Sherpa homeland of Solu-Khumbu is a tough trek with a clearcut goal—to see Everest. Much to their surprise, many people find the snout-like Everest outranked by peaks like Ama Dablam and the Lhotse-Nuptse wall. Khumbu is the best major region in Nepal for close-up mountain views. Enshrined in **Sagarmatha National Park,** it's visited by about 8,000 trekkers yearly—a mere handful compared to the Annapurna region.

Most Everest trekkers avoid the hardest walking by flying in and out of the crowded Lukla airstrip. If you've got the time and energy, the walk-in from Jiri through the Sherpa's traditional homeland is worth the extra effort. It passes through the lovely southern region called **Solu**

THE SHERPAS

This relatively tiny society of 8,000 people is the best known and most admired of all Nepal's ethnic groups. According to their oral history Sherpas migrated to the high valleys south of Mt. Everest from eastern Tibet about 450 years ago, hence the name Shar-pa, "People from the East." Their language, customs, and religion reflect their Tibetan origins. Sherpas follow the Nyingma school of Tibetan Buddhism devoted to Guru Rinpoche, and ancient beliefs linger as well. The Sherpa homeland is still dominated by the old mountain gods, the most sacred being Numbur in Solu and Khumbila in Khumbu.

Sherpas have long known how to maximize the potential of Khumbu's fragile mountain environment, farming on lower slopes and herding hardy yak and crossbred cattle up high. The shortfall was made up by skillful trading with nearby Tibet. This system collapsed with the Chinese occupation of Tibet, but in a stroke of fortune, foreign mountaineers were allowed to enter Khumbu at precisely the same time. Already famed for their work on British expeditions in the Indian Himalaya, Sherpas were quick to profit from new opportunities. The development of trekking has provided an added boon, a way to earn money without the danger of expedition work. Today up to

85% of households in some villages have members working in trekking and mountaineering.

Over 8,000 tourists visited Khumbu in 1989; that's five for every three Sherpas. Inevitably, Sherpa life is changing with increased exposure to outsiders—Nepalis as well as tourists. Milk tea is replacing salt tea; jeans and down coats are worn instead of chuba, and many Sherpas now prefer rice, imported at high prices, rather than the staple potato. Expedition sirdars have become the new upper class, nudging aside the old landed wealth, and plastic expedition barrels stand beside copper pots in many Sherpa homes.

These changes are cosmetic, however. Most observers agree that Sherpas are adjusting remarkably well to rapid change, adopting material benefits while retaining the essence of their identity. Religion remains a focal point of society. Unlike many traditional cultures, the Sherpa cultural renaissance was quite recent. It was fueled, oddly enough, by the 18th-century introduction of the potato in Khumbu, which supported a virtual population explosion.

The sudden surplus was channeled into the construction of Buddhist gompa: six have been built in Solu in the past 50 years, and many have active reincarnate lamas (tulku). In Khumbu, Tengboche

and the narrow gorge of the Dudh Kosi (**Pharak**) to reach the high mountain region of Khumbu in a little over a week. Khumbu is exceptionally high-altitude, with trekking routes going up to 5,400 meters: you don't just cross a high pass and descend; you *stay* high for a week or more.

While Solu can be trekked year-round, Khumbu's season is limited. Most trekkers pour in during Oct.-Nov. and March-May. Besides good weather, this period offers the five-day Dumje festival (usually April) and the masked Mani Rimdu dances held at major monasteries in spring and fall. Winters are cold, and you may not be able to go above Tengboche between mid-Dec. and mid-Feb., but in some dry years little or no snow falls and higher lodges stay open. Khumbu is a good region for a monsoon trek. High pastures are full of wildflowers and grazing yaks, and the people are relaxed, taking a well-deserved break from trekking and expedition work.

Solu-Khumbu's rugged landscape and high altitude are intimidating, and a higher propor-tion (slightly less than half) of Everest trekkers are on organized treks. The entire route is set up for teahouse trekking, with the usual range of lodges. Namche Bazaar's have electricity, hot showers, and fresh cinnamon rolls; above here simple stone huts predominate. Lodgekeepers are often expedition sirdars or Everest summiteers, though generally they're off working and their family runs the place. Independent trekkers may actually be better off in Khumbu, since tents aren't very enjoyable above 4,000 meters, and groups often end up crowding into lodges.

Namche Bazaar is the nerve center of Upper Khumbu: from here, trails branch out to explore at least four separate high valleys. It's a cosmopolitan little village, a good place to pick up tips on trails and conditions from descending trekkers. Food prices skyrocket above here, since all supplies must be carried in from a distance; budget extra for this trip.

Getting There
The approach to Everest is a classic case of

a Sherpa-run trekker's lodge, Junbesi

CHRISTOPHER GAMM

Rinpoche has led efforts to protect and revive important elements of Sherpa culture.

Anthropologist James Fisher feels that the rapid rate of change has actually intensified Sherpa identity, forcing them to consciously determine their values. It helps that Westerner have formed a fan club, admiring the Sherpas' legendary good humor, stamina, and common sense. For their part, Sherpas have a mixed view of Westerners. Many are mystified by the expense and effort tourists make to visit Khumbu. "Don't you have mountains in your own country?" they frequently ask. Certain sayings reveal a pragmatic attitude, like one related by Fisher: "Like cattle, tourists give good milk, but only if they are well-fed." Another Sherpa told a friend: "You people are like eggs—white on the outside, but you must be taken care of because you break easily."

Their open, casteless society has eased the adaptation; so has a Buddhist sense of equanimity. Citing their "gaiety and friendliness, their tolerance and kindness toward each other," anthropologist Christoph Von Fürer-Haimendorf called traditional Sherpa society "one of the most harmonious I had ever known." It appears to be stronger and more resilient than most traditional peoples. So far, Sherpas seem to be successfully walking the thin line between tradition and modernity.

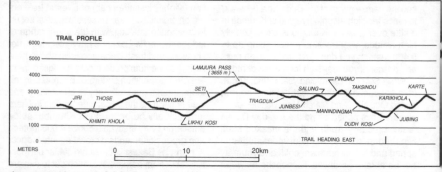

TRAIL PROFILE

the encroaching road. Originally the trail started in Bhaktapur; with the construction of the Tibet road it moved up to Lamosanghu. Now it's been pushed to the hill town of **Jiri,** and nobody seems to miss the week of hill walking that's been chopped off.

The bus to Jiri is the longest ride to a popular trailhead, ten hours of hell (modified if you sit on top). You generally arrive at dusk or later; there are plenty of lodges along the main street. Ask your lodgekeeper or enquire around the bazaar if you want a porter.

Flying into **Lukla** chops nearly a week off the trek, plummeting you within a long day of Namche Bazaar. Altitude problems seem to increase with fly-ins, and during peak season flights are booked solid by trekking companies. Inevitably flights are canceled and the place becomes a bottleneck in the fall and spring. Big agencies will do anything to get their clients out; individuals should enlist the aid of their lodgekeeper or some helpful local to deal with RNAC. Hassles like this are a big reason to fly into Lukla and walk out; it's far less nerve-wracking to be stuck in Kathmandu waiting for a flight.

Going against the flow is a good way to beat the system and miss the crowds. Most groups fly into Lukla in mid-October and in early April; thus there are plenty of flights going back empty to Kathmandu at these times, and you can often walk in and buy a ticket. Three weeks later the airport is crammed with returning groups; it's a good time to fly in, but don't count on getting out.

Another option is to fly in or out of **Phaplu**, which cuts off the first three hard days from Jiri and puts you in the best part of Solu. There's an excellent Sherpa-run lodge near the Phaplu airstrip. Heading north to join the main trail at

Ringmo, you pass interesting Chiwong Gompa. Backtracking a few hours to Junbesi is worth it if you've got the time.

Finally, increasing numbers of trekkers are taking the week-long back-door route out to eastern Nepal, and flying back from Tumlingtar or busing back from Hille (see p. 354). This varies the route if you've walked in from Jiri, but if you flew to Lukla the Solu route makes a more interesting return.

SOLU: JIRI TO NAMCHE BAZAAR

With its rolling hills and broad valleys covered with fields and forests, the Solu region (Sherpas call it Sho Rung) provides a gentler counterpoint to stark, spectacular Khumbu. Moderate altitude (2,600-3,200 meters) and climate make even a winter trek here feasible. Traditionally prosperous, Solu is as bountiful as Nepal's Hills get, and offers excellent insights into Sherpa life. Its impressive stone houses verge on mansions, some with private chapels as fine as any gompa. As an added plus, Solu is the center of a recent religious revival, with some of the finest **Buddhist monasteries** in Nepal.

The trail cuts across the grain of the land, heading east over north-south river valleys and ridges. Steep and seemingly endless, the ups and downs create incredible leg muscles by the time you reach Namche; it takes extra determination to walk this route. Lodges range from adequate to idyllic, with extras like apple pie and cheese factories to cheer up hedonists. Figure on at least a week to walk from Jiri to Namche, and try to add an extra day for exploring around Junbesi.

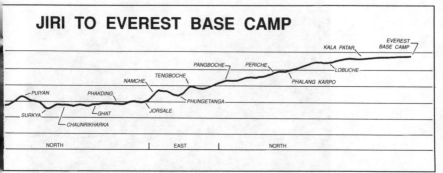

JIRI TO EVEREST BASE CAMP

Trekkers cluster on the main trail to Everest, but there are many other possibilities. Study the Schneider maps or talk to local Sherpas for ideas. An alternate and perhaps more interesting route to Junbesi drops down from Bhandar to cross the Likhu Khola to the south and climb through **Goli Gompa**. This ridge is parallel to, but south of, the one leading to the Lamjura Pass. The last settlement is the marvelously named **Ngowur** (as in "middle of"). If you have a tent, stove, and food you can linger on the next long day's walk, which ascends below the good

viewpoint of **Pike** (4,070 meters) to Pangbuk, then drops through pine and rhododendron forests to Junbesi. Either the Schneider Tamba Kosi-Likhu Khola sheet or a guide is essential.

Jiri To Junbesi
From Jiri (1,905 meters) the trail plunges straight into the hills, climbing to a 2,713-meter pass **(Deorali)** lined with new lodges. There's a cheese factory and small gompa about 45 minutes' walk above. Below the pleasant village of **Bhandar** sprawls out in a broad bowl-shaped

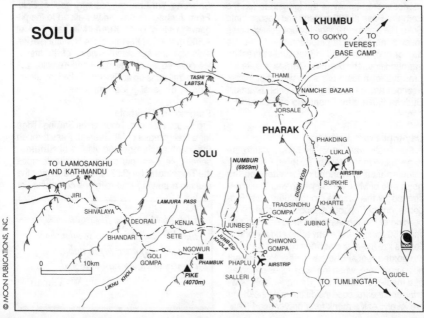

Junbesi village, Solu

CHRISTOPHER GAMM

tableland. Passing through the riverside town of **Kenja** (1,634 meters), the next event is a seemingly endless climb up a huge ridge, the first of many on this trek. The little village of **Sete** (2,575 meters) is the usual stopping place. It's worth a 15-minute detour to visit a nice gompa nearby. Continue climbing through rhododendron forests (and watch out for poison rhododendron honey in the lodges) to top the **Lamjura Pass** (3,530 meters) and descend into Solu. The charming village of **Junbesi** two hours away is an excellent place to spend an extra day or two, with good lodges and interesting surroundings. The **Junbesi Gompa** is quite impressive for a town this size, with imaginative frescoes and a two-story image of Shakyamuni Buddha flanked by Chenrezig and Guru Rinpoche.

Day-trips From Junbesi

A 90-minute walk up valley brings you to the large active monastery of **Thupten Choling,** a reincarnation of Rongbuk Monastery on the north side of Mt. Everest, which was totally destroyed by the Chinese in the '60s. Tulsi Rinpoche, one of Rongbuk's abbots, directed the rebuilding of the monastery in this secluded setting; 150 monks and many nuns and lay practitioners live in small dwellings clustered around the gompa. Local Sherpas gather for frequent pujas held here, when the place takes on the air of a medieval temple fair. It's undeniably powerful, and the frescoes inside the main lhakhang are lovely. Ask a monk for a prayer scarf (khatak) if you want to meet Tulsi Rinpoche.

Another day-walk is to **Chiwong Gompa,** about three hours southeast, set atop steep cliffs overlooking Phaplu. Masked Mani Rimdu dances are held here one month after the more famous Tengboche dance.

The Junbesi Valley is dominated by the white spire of **Numbur** (6,959 meters), also called **Shorung Yul Lha,** the "country god" of Solu. From Junbesi it's a two-day walk up to the pilgrimage site of **Dudh Kund** ("Milk Lake," about 4,500 meters) at the foot of the Numbur glacier. This site has spectacular views of the steep, ice-covered faces of Numbur and Karyolung. A return trail ends up at Ringmo. Take tent, stove, food, and a local guide from Junbesi.

Ringmo To Karikhola

From Junbesi the trail rounds the Sallung Ridge for a first glimpse of Mt. Everest. Pass through the small apple-oriented village of **Ringmo,** serving pie, juice, pancakes and cake, to cross the **Tragsindhu La** (3,071 meters). Just over the pass is a thriving little religious community of

> *I felt like I could go like this forever, that life had little better to offer than to march day after day in unknown country to an unattainable goal.*
>
> —H.W. Tilman

40-50 monks and nuns, and beautiful views. Exquisite murals (painted by the same artists who did Thupten Choling) decorate the lhakhang. You may have to ask around for the key. The slightly dilapidated lodge is run by a nun who grew up here before there was even a gompa.

Most trekkers stay in the **cheese factory** just before the pass and down a short side trail. It's run by a Jirel family who serve homemade bread, pie, yoghurt, and cheese (sometimes a bit underdone). Trail conversation all the way from Namche revolves around what to order here: raclette, grilled cheese, apple pie. . . .

From the pass the trail descends through an idyllic forest to **Nuntala** (also called **Maniding-ma**) and drops all the way down to 1,500 meters to cross the Dudh Kosi river draining Khumbu. (If you're coming the opposite way, this hill is a major climb; do it early before it gets hot.) Next are the pastoral little Rai village of **Jubing** and bazaar town of **Karikhola.**

From here the trail enters the region of

Pharak, an interim zone between Solu and Khumbu along the narrow gorge of the Dudh Kosi. This area seems gloomy and slightly poorer than Solu, partly because clouds tend to gather and the sun rises late and sets early. The trail continues its steep ups and downs past minor villages: **Poiyan** is a ghetto compared to most places on this trail. Try to make it to **Surke,** a nice riverside stop. Namche Bazaar is one long day's walk north of here; most people take longer. A side trail to Lukla joins this main trail at **Chaumrikarkha;** the remainder of the route to Namche is described below.

KHUMBU

Upper Khumbu is a land of dazzling light and immense spaces, of highland valleys ringed by soaring snow-covered peaks, including three of the world's seven highest mountains (Everest, Lhotse, and Cho Oyu). No other trek in Nepal equals the feeling of being in the mountains that

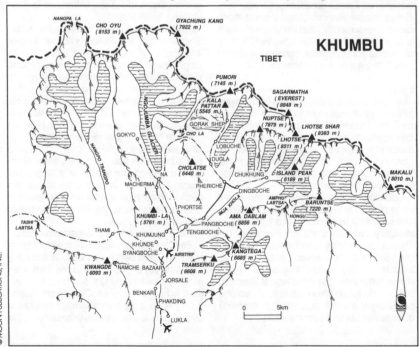

you get here. Instead of admiring them from a distance you walk amid them, and the shifting perspectives are endlessly fascinating.

The Sherpas say Khumbu was once a *beyul*, one of the sanctuaries set aside by Guru Rinpoche for Buddhists in times of trouble. The outer valley was opened and settled hundreds of years ago, but the inner, secret one is invisible; perhaps this accounts for the magical feeling permeating this high region.

Upper Khumbu region is spared the steep ups and downs of Solu, and the walking is not particularly rugged; but as the highest of the main trekking regions (over 5,000 meters), Khumbu's altitude knocks many people out. Those flying into Lukla seem particularly vulnerable. Go slowly, plan rest days at strategic altitudes, and monitor your adaptation.

Khumbu's unofficial headquarters is the relatively new village of **Namche Bazaar.** From here trails fan out into four different highland valleys, each offering stunning mountain scenery and glimpses of Sherpa culture. It takes about a week to visit Everest Base Camp, Chukhung, or Gokyo separately; combining them is much faster. The fourth valley and the village of Thami is only a day's walk from Namche. Visit as many of them as possible; these high regions are the payoff for the long walk in from Jiri.

Lukla

The flight to Lukla (2,850 meters) is an adventure in itself: the runway and the village are set on a small shelf halfway up a high mountain, and surrounding peaks rise up rapidly to meet descending aircraft. Passengers are plopped down in the highlands without the week's walk from Jiri, but spare a thought for those walking the tortuous switchbacks below.

Lukla life revolves around the airstrip, where up to nine flights land daily in peak season. Trekkers stuck here waiting for a flight may go stir-crazy, but there are a few diversions: the Thursday haat bazaar is as interesting as Namche's (in fact, it's the same one: porters move up to **Ghat** on Fridays and sell their goods in Namche on Saturdays). Day walks include the steep trail over the **Kaalo Himal** just east of town (the beginning of the trek to Hongu), or dropping down to visit **Surke** on the main trail.

Lukla has over a dozen lodges, with more going up yearly. **Hotel Lukla** alongside the airstrip offers privacy and surrounding meadows and forests. Private rooms are US$10 s; a dorm bed is Rs15. The **Sherpa Coffee Shop** beside the airfield serves cinnamon rolls to trekkers waiting anxiously for their morning flight. All in all, Lukla has come a long way from the *luk la* or "sheep place" it was a few decades ago. The airfield was built in 1964 by Sir Edmund Hillary to receive materials for a construction project involving a half-dozen of Solu-Khumbu's schools—his expression of gratitude to the Sherpa people who assisted his Everest ascent.

Namche Bazaar

From Lukla it's a long day to Namche Bazaar and you'd have to start early in the morning to make it; most groups overnight in **Phakding.** Rs250 entrance fee is payable at the national park entrance at **Jorsale.** Crossing the Dudh Kosi, the trail climbs steeply to Namche Bazaar, with a glimpse of Everest halfway up to cheer you on.

Namche Bazaar (3,446 meters) is the modern Sherpa capital, a collection of houses, lodges, and shops set in a horseshoe-shaped natural amphitheater facing splendid Lumding Himal, with Tramserku and Kangtega peeking over the rim behind. Namche is unique in the world of trekking villages, with shops stocked with paperback novels, eight kinds of chocolate, and fake Tibetan jewelry from Kathmandu. Here you can rent trekking gear for higher up—convenient for walk-ins from Jiri. Some find the town overly commercialized, and many Sherpas will tell you "all Namche people do is think about money." Still, most trekkers enjoy spending a near-obligatory acclimatization day here and revel in the deluxe lodges, cinnamon rolls, and shopping opportunities.

The **visitor's center** at Sagarmatha National Park headquarters (atop a hill east of town) has informative displays on local life and geology. Saturday's haat bazaar is the week's big event, as lowland porters and local Sherpas meet to haggle over grain, Chinese goods, and fresh yak meat. By early afternoon people are drifting away to chang shops to catch up on the week's gossip.

Khumjung, Khunde, And Everest View Hotel

If Namche's commercialism seems too gross, take refuge in Khumjung (3,780 meters), an hour's walk over the hill but a world away. Khumjung and its sister village Khunde are bastions of traditional Sherpa life, rows of stone houses nestled just below the sacred mountain Khumbi-la. The few small lodges in town are hard to find, but local families are happy to put you up if you can convince them you don't mind old houses like theirs. Try to persuade them to cook *riki kur,* crispy potato pancakes served with yak butter.

The trail to Khumjung passes the **Syangboche airstrip** above Namche. Perched above it on a ridge with stunning views is the "highest hotel in the world," the **Everest View Hotel** (3,870 meters). Reopened recently under Japanese management, the hotel boasts views of Everest, Lhotse, and Ama Dablam in every room and bathroom. Clients are generally flown in directly to Shyangboche (US$160) and walk, or rather stagger, up to the hotel. A number have nearly keeled over from the abrupt altitude change, but the hotel now has a pressurized Gamow bag to treat serious cases. Rooms are US$120 per person, and walk-ins must pay a fee to even look at the rooms, but the surrounding area has some great views for free.

Tengboche Gompa

Most trekkers continue up to Kala Pattar and Everest Base Camp. It's a beautiful one-day walk to Tengboche Gompa, through forest where you may spot nearly tame danphe pheasants. Founded in 1912 as a secluded meditation retreat, the monastery has become one of the premier tourist destinations in Nepal. Perched on a ridge and ringed by spectacular peaks, it's in an absolutely stunning natural setting, guarded by Khumbila and Kangtega, with Ama Dablam and the Everest massif rising in the northeast. The gompa's dual purpose creates some bemusing juxtapostions: prayer flags beside a solar-heated lodge; stupa along a helicopter landing pad; and a sign atop a wall of engraved prayer stones reading "Please do not stand on the mani wall."

Tengboche's recent history can be viewed as a lesson in the dangers of rapid modernization. A small hydroelectric station funded by the

Tengboche Gompa after the 1989 fire

American Himalayan Foundation was inaugurated here with much fanfare in April 1988. Nine months later the main temple burned to the ground, in a fire probably started by an unattended space heater. Aside from the structural damage about 80% of the gompa's artifacts were destroyed, including irreplacable treasures from Tibet like hand-lettered scriptures, dance costumes, images, and the magnificent frescoes adorning the interior walls.

Local and international contributions are funding the construction of a new and larger gompa, expected to cost US$800,000. Construction began in April 1990 and will take two to three years, and much longer to complete the interior. Tengboche remains the cultural and religious center of Khumbu, under the strong leadership of its abbot, Tengboche Rinpoche, who has sponsored efforts like a *shedra* or school for 25 young monks, and a **Sherpa Cultural Center** with exhibits for visitors. The gompa suffered a slump in the '70s when most of its monks left to work in trekking, but it's now back to over 40 monks. Every autumn the Mani Rimdu dances held here (see p. 74) retell the ancient story of Buddhism's conquest over the Bön religion, drawing hundreds of tourists and Sherpas. Surprisingly, the dances were only introduced here in 1942. The same dances, less crowded but equally interesting, are held at Solu's Chiwong Gompa a month later, and at Thami Gompa in May.

Tengboche's accommodations include a glassed-in **National Park Lodge** (built by New Zealand) and a slightly funkier monastery lodge where old monks cook up "yak steak" (generally buffalo meat) in the big kitchen-dining hall, and Ama Dablam and Everest peer through the windows of the dormitory.

En Route To Everest Base Camp

The trail continues by the small nunnery of **Deboche** to **Pangboche** village, with its old gompa built over the hermitage of Khumbu's saint, Lama Sanga Dorje. The juniper trees on either side are said to have sprung from hair he cut off his head, while a roof-like rock projection is a piece of the mountainside he pulled out for shelter one day. Yeti relics preserved here were sent to Europe for scientific examination and pronounced to be the 200-year-old skin of a Himalayan serow.

Pheriche (4,252 meters), the next stop, is nothing but a few stone herding huts-cum-lodges. In pre-trekking days it existed only as a summer yak-herding pasture; now it's the last permanently inhabited settlement. The **Trekkers' Aid Post** here gives talks on altitude sickness every afternoon in season. It's advisable to spend an extra day here to acclimatize, though the place is pretty dull. A day-trip up a side valley to Dingboche and **Chukhung** is good recreation (see below).

The main trail continues northwest and curves slightly to cross the terminal moraine of the Khumbu Glacier. A day from Pheriche is **Lobuche** (4,930 meters) with a few small and sometimes crowded lodges. These are still more comfortable than the last lodges up at the lakelet of **Gorak Shep**, where sanitation is poor. From Lobuche it's a day's walk to **Kala Pattar** (5,545 meters). This spur running from the peak of Pumori provides an incredible overview: the Khumbu glacier cascading down below, the broad snout of Everest, and Lhotse, a wedding-cake fantasy of swirling snow and ice. Sitting up here, watching distant avalanches dropping clouds of powdery snow, you feel on top of the world.

You can walk up the Khumbu Glacier to **Everest Base Camp,** a very long day-hike from Lobuche or four hours from Gorak Shep. However, the mountain is blocked from view and there's not much to see besides expedition camps, their accompanying litter, and across the way, the dangerous **Khumbu Icefall,** scene of most fatalities on Everest—generally Sherpa porters.

Gokyo

An alternate route heads up the Dudh Kosi Valley, crowned by the 8,153-meter peak of Cho Oyu and its companion peak Gyachung Kang. Gokyo vs. Kala Pattar is a favorite argument: those who have visited both seem to rate Gokyo slightly higher. Despite this it gets fewer trekkers; the lure of Everest Base Camp is too strong.

You can reach here directly from Kala Pattar by crossing the 5,420-meter **Cho La,** but you need a tent, four days of food, and a good map or guide; don't try if there's too much snow. Otherwise, backtrack down south and round the ridge through **Phortse** to enter the Dudh Kosi Valley. From Namche, head directly up via Khumjung, and pace yourself—it's easy to ascend too quickly.

By either route, it's a three- or four-day walk. Take the trail on the valley's west side, which has more lodges. Head through small summer herding settlements to skirt the giant **Ngozumba Glacier** and arrive at a series of small lakes. **Gokyo** (4,750 meters) is a tiny herding settlement by the third lake and has several lodges. Climb the 5,483-meter peak to the northwest (also dubbed Kala Pattar) for views of Cho Oyu, Everest, Lhotse, and Makalu, plus a host of smaller peaks. Several more lakes and **Cho Oyu Base Camp** lie north up the glacier.

Chukhung And The Imja Valley

This side valley branching off from the Everest Base Camp route is a good day walk from Pheriche. It's also a splendid and little-traveled destination in itself, with some unique mountain views. Cross the ridge east of Pheriche to **Dingboche** and continue up the steep-walled valley of the Imja Khola. Ama Dablam appears to the south with yet another bewitching perspective. A few hours later are the small lodges

EVEREST

The world's highest peak was discovered in 1852, when routine calculations of the Survey of India revealed a remote mountain on Nepal's northern frontier to be over 29,000 feet (8,848 meters). Peak XV, as it was labeled on the survey's map, was so isolated no local name could be found. Everest was nothing special to the Sherpas, who live surrounded by dozens of great peaks. (The Nepali—actually Sanskrit—name Sagarmatha, "Brow of the Oceans," was appended a few decades ago.) Tibetans living on the northern side had a number of names for the mountain, though efforts to translate them seem to have run aground. The list includes "The Cooking Pan of the Queen of the Five Sister Goddesses" and "Wind Goddess." Best-known is Jomolungma, poetically rendered as "Mother Goddess of the Earth," though "Valley Goddess" would be more accurate. (One Englishman insisted the name was Jomo Langma, "Lady Cow.") Survey officials took the most prudent course and named the mountain after their recently retired boss, Sir George Everest.

The first British reconnaissance expedition arrived on the mountain's north side in 1921, shivering genteely in the tweedy outdoor wear of the era. Looking at a photo of an early Everest expedition, George Bernard Shaw commented that it looked "like a picnic in Connemara surprised by a snowstorm." They returned the following year with a full-fledged expedition, carrying among other things five mule loads of copper coins and a store of 24 Homburg hats, considered the fastest way to the hearts of Tibetan government officials.

Early expeditions were more like war than sport, organized like a military campaign and relying on an arsenal of equipment and an army of porters. Parties laid siege against a mountain and attempted to batter it into submission. More often, they would beat themselves into exhaustion against the frozen immensity of Everest.

Eleven major unsuccessful expeditions were mounted over the next three decades. The Chinese takeover of Tibet sealed off access to the north side, but in a masterful coincidence, Nepal had begun admitting foreign climbers only a few years before. The southern side of Everest seemed doubtful at first, but a straightforward route was soon discovered and expeditions embarked on the race to the summit. New Zealand beekeeper Edmund Hillary and Sherpa Tenzin Norgay won the prize in 1953.

Six decades of Everest attempts make for good reading, beginning with George Mallory's eloquent accounts of the first British expeditions. Members of the 1963 American Expedition were overtaken by darkness after a successful ascent. They miraculously survived an open bivouac at 8,000 meters, though two members paid the price with their toes. The late '70s saw the first successful "climbing-style" attempt without oxygen or fixed camps by Reinholdt Messner and Peter Haebeler. In 1980 Messner returned to solo the mountain in four days without oxygen, part of his successful bid to solo all 14 of the world's 8,000-meter peaks.

The mountain continues to attract up to 30 expeditions per year. Climbers struggle to distinguish themselves from the 200-plus summiteers by using increasingly inventive methods. Everest has been done in winter, without oxygen, solo, and solo without oxygen, live on television, on skis, and by paraplane. If these attempts seem contrived, imagine the reaction of the locals, who were baffled by straightforward early expeditions. Hugh Ruttledge, the leader of an early British expedition, noted that every Tibetan they met asked what the party was doing in such a remote region. All were incredulous at the reply that they hoped to *climb* Everest. ("We must improve upon our story," Ruttledge concluded.) The Western view of mountains as a challenge, a test of the human spirit, is utterly foreign to people dwelling in their shadows, who respect and fear them too much to lay foot on them. Most Sherpas will privately admit they climb for the money rather than the thrill. The lama of Rongbuk met the first British expedition in 1924, and was astonished at their determination to accomplish such an odd goal. "I was filled with great compassion for their lot, who underwent such suffering for unnecessary work," he wrote in his journal, resolving to pray for their future conversion to Buddhism.

Just why humans continue to hurl themselves against Everest and other high peaks remains a mystery which has inspired countless eloquent answers, including Maurice Herzog's *Annapurna* and the quotes assembled in *Everest: The West Ridge*. It was George Mallory, who vanished high atop Everest in 1924, who gave the cryptic reply "Because it is there!" Whether it was a veiled metaphysical observation or an impatient brushoff is still a matter of contention, but it's as good an answer as any.

of **Chukhung** (4,734 meters), with views of Lhotse-Nuptse and Island Peak. Overnight here and climb **Chukhung Ri** (5,043 meters) to the north for breathtaking views of the Lhotse-Nuptse wall in total solitude. Further up the valley is **Island Peak** (Imja Tse, 6,189 meters), climbable if you've got gear and are comfortable using an ice axe, crampons, and rope. (Of course you need a trekking peak permit, too.) With a good map, you can hike past here along the edge of glaciers into a wilderness of peaks. Across from Island Peak is the high (5,780-meter) **Amphu Laptsa** leading into the remote **Hongu Valley.**

Thami

This is the easiest walk above Namche—warmer, lower, and with relatively few mountain views. It takes three to four hours to reach Thami, but not many trekkers go up here. The trail heads west around the ridge behind Namche and continues north up the Nangpo Tsangpo Valley through small villages. Above **Mende** is a gompa and retreat center associated with the Himalayan Yogic Institute in Kathmandu. Cross the river and climb steeply to **Thami** (3,780 meters), Tenzin Norgay's hometown. **Thami Gompa** is above the village, set in a rock wall facing several gigantic waterfalls cascading down Kongde Ri. It's a spectacular setting for the Mani Rimdu dances performed during the May full moon, an event as colorful as Tengboche's, and less crowded with tourists. To the west, the Thami River descends from the treacherous **Tashi Laptsa** (5,755 meters), an adventurous and currently restricted passage into the Rolwaling Valley. The valley north of Thami is also restricted, but two days' walk north is the broad **Nangpa La** pass leading into Tibet, a virtual highway through the Himalaya.

Mani Rindu mask

MARK MORRIS

TREKS NORTH OF KATHMANDU

Less than 30 km north and east of the capital are three relatively short yet interesting treks, ideal for trekkers with limited time. This region is generally bypassed in favor of Annapurna and Everest, which means trails are less crowded, yet there are plenty of simple lodges along the main routes. The easy access doesn't mean you lose out on quality. **Langtang** in particular is among the finest mountain treks anyone could hope for, a high mountain-ringed valley only four days'

walk from Kathmandu. **Helambu,** a Sherpa area northeast of Kathmandu, and the sacred lake of **Gosainkund** high atop an open ridge are admittedly more minor treks, shorter than Langtang, but worthwhile in themselves. Langtang, Gosainkund, and the northern reaches of Helambu are included in Langtang National Park.

The regions are usually visited separately but can be combined in as little as 16 days if

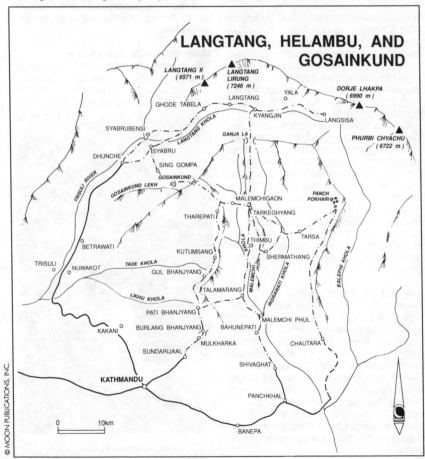

LANGTANG, HELAMBU, AND GOSAINKUND

high passes are open. Lower regions like Helambu are perfect for winter treks, and in springtime this region's rhododendrons are especially good. The people are a mixture of Tamang, Sherpa, and Bhotia, largely unaffected by the closeness of Kathmandu. Food and lodging are easily available along the main routes. A few high passes require carrying some food and possibly shelter, but usually herders' huts and rock overhangs can be found for an overnight on the trail.

HELAMBU

The most easily accessible of all trekking regions is the upper valley of the Malemchi Khola, called Yolmu, Helmu, or Helambu by its Sherpa residents. It's temptingly close to the Valley, just three days' walk northeast over the forested ridge. Helambu is below 3,000 meters and creates few altitude problems; it's short (less than a week) and so close you can take off on a whim. The monsoon is quite heavy here.

This is a ramble rather than a distinct trek. There's no real destination besides the higher ridges with their pleasant forests, occasional mountain views, and interesting Sherpa villages. The lower valley is comparatively dull and depressingly hot much of the year, so plan to spend most of your time up high. The trek provides a sudden, dramatic contrast betwen high and low regions and their characteristic cultures. The comparison isn't favorable for lowland villages, which seem hot, fly-ridden and unfriendly compared to the neat Sherpa villages above.

Sundarijaal To Kutumsang
The starting point is Sundarijaal on the northeast edge of the Valley. Taxi, bus, or walk two hours up the dirt road heading north from Jorpati, the next suburb beyond Boudha. Where the road ends at a row of teashops, a stone staircase ascends past the **Sundarijaal waterfall** and soon transforms into a footpath, heading steeply up through scattered Tamang villages to reach **Burlang Bhanjyang** (2,438 meters) on the Valley rim. The first night is usually at "Pub Pass" (**Pati Bhanjyang**, 1,768 meters), a slightly larger village named for its *pati* serving homemade rice beer.

The next day the trail runs along ridges to the small village of Kutumsang. From here to Malemchigaon, a longish day's walk, there are no permanent settlements. The trail traverses high pastures seldom visited except by shepherds and woodcutters; the solitude and semi-wilderness is rarely experienced on a main trail. Views are superb, and you may want to prolong the pleasure by overnighting in an empty herders' hut. About five hours from Kutumsang is a tiny tea shop run by Malemchigaon children, who will point out the steep trail descending through dense forests of rhodie and oak to their village, two hours' walk below. If you stay up on the ridge, **Gosainkund** is only one day's walk further, but you'll have to go more slowly to acclimatize.

Malemchigaon To Tarkeghyang
Malemchigaon (2,560 meters) is Helambu's finest Sherpa village, a collection of neat houses fronted by prayer flags and surrounded by orchards and fields. Lodges are pretty much peo-

boy with rhododendron, eastern Nepal

ALISON WRIGHT

ple's homes, a great opportunity to stay with a family. The Sherpas of Helambu are distant cousins of Khumbu Sherpas, speaking a related but distinct dialect; like Khumbu Sherpas, they emigrated from Tibet several centuries ago. According to legend Helambu was one of Guru Rinpoche's "hidden valleys" (belyul).

The trail drops down to cross the Malemchi Khola and climbs up the exact same distance to **Tarkeghyang** (2,560 meters), a larger and less secluded village than Malemchi. Poised on the main trekking route, it's more commercialized: every house sells souvenirs and instant "aged" thankga. There's a large restored gompa here dating back to the early 18th century. Ten minutes' walk downhill is an even finer old gompa called **Chure Gyang.**

Routes Out Of Helambu

With food, equipment and a guide, you could walk three days north to cross the difficult 5,123-meter **Ganja La** into the Langtang Valley. Exceptionally steep and icy, the pass is normally crossable from May-November. East of Tarkeghyang a ridge trail leads to **Panch Pokhari** (see "Jugal Himal"), a seldom-visited pilgrim's site. Again food, gear, and a guide are necessary; allow five or six days.

The main route out of Helambu continues south down the Indrawati Khola valley. From Tarkeghyang a pleasant high trail runs through the Sherpa village of **Shermathang,** then descends, while another drops directly to the river. The trail meanders through lowland Hindu villages, a distinct and rather depressing counterpoint to the highland Sherpa settlements. From **Mahankhal** the trail is incredibly wide and flat—once it was a jeep track. The last day can be miserable in hot weather, dragging on to the unpleasant town of **Shivaghat,** where minibuses run every few hours to Panchkal, Banepa, and Kathmandu. An alternate trail, steep and rather confusing, climbs back up from **Talamarang** to reconnect with the high trail and Pati Bhanjyang, allowing you to reenter the Valley on foot.

GOSAINKUND

In itself Gosainkund is really a mini-trek, only four days' walk from Kathmandu. However, high altitude means it's best done after a visit to Langtang or Helambu. It's easily joined with one of these regions, or can be used to link both, adding three or four extra days to a trek. If you come directly from Kathmandu (say for the big pilgrimage of Janai Purnima in August), figure on some extra acclimatization days en route.

This is the least-used of this group of trails, and until recently it was necessary to carry extra food and a tent. Simple lodges, open in the main trekking season, now line the entire route, and herders' huts and rock overhangs provide additional shelter. You might want to bring a little extra food to munch on while walking, though.

From the Langtang side, trails climb from Dhunche or Syabru past **Sing Gompa** (3,254 meters), where a cheese factory, monastery, and lodge are perched on the hillside. A clear trail climbs through rhododendron forests to reach **Laurebina** (3,901 meters), a collection of a few herders' huts and a lodge atop a ridge with good mountain views. Crossing over the ridge, the first of several lakes appears, each dedicated to a different deity. The third, **Gosain-**

Nepali shamans celebrating full moon, Syabrubensi (Langtang trek)

CHRISTOPHER GAMM

kund (4,298 meters), is sacred to Shiva, whom devotees claim they see floating in the bottom of the lake in the form of a large rock. According to a Hindu legend, the gods once churned the ocean to find treasure, and came up with a burning poison that threatened to destroy the entire world. They begged Shiva to drink and contain it and he did, burning his throat in the process. He fled to the high Himalaya, thrusting his trident into the rock to create the lake and taking refuge in its cold waters. The lake is said to be connected via subterranean channels to Patan's Khumbeshwar Mahadev Mandir, and thousands of pilgrims flock here for the Janai Purnima festival (usually the August full moon). A nearby summit to the north yields excellent mountain views.

The trail to Helambu and Kathmandu passes four more sacred lakes and reaches a pass (4,600 meters) in an hour. Dropping past scattered huts, it meets the trail junction to Malemchigaon five or six hours later (see "Helambu"). From here you can drop down to Helambu, or continue along the upper ridge to reach the Kathmandu Valley in a few days.

LANGTANG

This region extends north of Helambu all the way up to the Tibetan border. Langtang National Park protects a typical example of a high Himalayan valley. It's generally a ten-day trip, counting transportation time and a day above Kyangjin.

Getting There
Bus to Trisuli along a gut-wrenching, twisty road with one of the highest nausea rates in all Nepal (be careful of whom you sit near). Buses leave from Sorhakhuttepati just north of Thamel; leave early in the morning to reach Dhunche by night. **Trisuli** is an old trading town, and the backstreet bazaar behind the main road is worth a look if you have time. Most trekkers wolf down lunch and immediately catch a minibus to **Dhunche,** a nondescript little district headquarters and roadhead where you'll probably have to overnight. The park entry office here collects the Rs250 fee; keep your receipt as there are further checkposts along the trail.

Syabru To Langtang
The route begins with an uninspiring walk down the road, then starts to climb. The first day is through Tamang villages, "Tamang" being widely applied to a whole range of Bhotia people in this region. **Syabru** is a moderately interesting little ridgetop town with views of Langtang Lirung and Ganesh Himal. Its spring full-moon festival, with dancing jhankri and lots of chang, is not to be missed.

The trail drops through dense forests of oak, maple, and alder, then climbs surprisingly steeply alongside the Langtang Khola. A few hours later you cross and continue up the opposite side of the gorge. This part is similar to Colorado, with forest and mountain streams backed by peaks—some of the nicest forest to be found on a main trekking trail. One of the few clearings in the woods is the site of the **Lama Hotel,** run by a wonderful gravelly voiced Bhotia man.

The narrow valley begins to open out at **Ghode Tabela** (2,880 meters), a meadow with

above the Langtang River

CHRISTOPHER GAMM

a Tibetan-run lodge and an army checkpost. The land rapidly changes into a drier, colder, stonier realm inhabited by Bhotia—this time more or less pure Tibetans, including many refugees who fled south in 1959. Yak-herding is the main enterprise up here, since the surrounding country is superb pastureland. The Buddhist orientation is apparent from the many chorten and prayer flags, and some incredibly long mani walls.

Langtang (3,307 meters), though relatively small, is the region's largest village; it's good to overnight here to acclimatize. The upper valley is a grazing paradise, rich in flowers and grass and dotted with stone huts used in the summertime butter-making. Sewn in skins and exported to Tibet to flavor tea and fuel monastery lamps, butter was once the region's major industry.

Two hours above is **Kyangjin Gompa** (3,750 meters), the last permanent settlement with a small gompa, a cheese factory, and an excellent **National Park Lodge.** This is the base for day hikes exploring the upper valley, where you may sight *tahr,* a longhaired goat-antelope. Ringed by impressive high peaks, Langtang is a heart-of-the-mountains valley similar to the Annapurna Sanctuary. Traditionally it was a Buddhist sanctuary where hunting and butchering animals was forbidden.

From Kyangjin, climb up the small hill to the north for views of the graceful east face of Langtang Lirung, or head three hours upvalley to **Yala** (Tibetan for "up") and climb **Tsergo Ri** (4,984 meters) for stunning views, including Shisapangma across the Tibetan border. Not far from Kyangjin is the beautifully formed Fluted Peak christened by H. W. Tilman. The higher valley is dotted with summer yak-herding settlements; the last is **Langsisa** (4,804 meters). Above and across the river, the Langtang glacier rolls down from Tibet; a few kilometers further are two huge rock guardians called **Guru Rinpoche** and **Shakyamuni.** Five hours' walk up the glacier is a beautiful (if cold) camping spot.

Returning, you can vary the route by staying on the north side of the river all the way to **Syabrubesi.** There's a Tibetan settlement camp and hot springs nearby. With good weather, minimal snow, and some extra food, you could cross over to Gosainkund from Dhunche or Syabru, continuing down into Helambu or walking directly back to the Valley. Crossing the difficult Ganja La near Kyangjin into Helambu takes longer than coming from the south, and requires four to five days of food and good weather, plus equipment and a guide.

OFF THE BEATEN TRACK

Beyond the aforementioned "Big Three" trekking regions, Nepal is basically virgin territory for trekkers. Whenever trails start to seem too crowded it's reassuring to think of all those unknown ones. Trekking off the main paths is not only possible, but can be immensely rewarding, though you do need a sense of adventure and an increased ability to deal with the unexpected. First-time trekkers are probably best off choosing a main route, though some of the following are easy enough to qualify as a first trek. Unless you speak some Nepali or feel perfectly comfortable on your own, it's a good idea to take a guide. These treks range from teahouse to wilderness hikes. Frequently they combine both aspects by crossing over one or two uninhabited passes—a nice combination of company and solitude.

The main treks are popular for good reason, being the most spectacular scenery within easy reach of Kathmandu. Busing to and from trailheads in western and eastern Nepal will add three or four transport days onto your schedule unless you fly (and RNAC's domestic service is chronically unreliable). You need extra time to get beyond the standard routes, but rewards are great—not just mountain views, but increased contact with a wide range of Nepalis, and the chance to glimpse a completely different way of life.

WESTERN NEPAL

Overview

This is the most remote and least-known section of Nepal. When Toni Hagen came through in the '50s he met people who hadn't even heard of Kathmandu. It's safe to say many Kathmanduites still haven't heard of Jumla or Humla. Stretching all the way from Dhaulagiri to the Mahakali River on the nation's western border, western Nepal is half again as big as the central and eastern sections. To give an idea of distances, Jumla is a 500-km walk from Kathmandu.

The region is dryer and poorer than the rest of the country, and is characterized by lower, less spectacular Himalayan peaks with many long,

BOB RACE

forested ridges *(lekh)* extending southwards from them. Transport and supplies are often problematic, and few trekkers make it out here. Even organized treks are deterred by a shortage of supplies and reliable porters. If you're looking for something different Nepal's Wild West may be it—but it's not easy.

Historically part of the Khasa empire, western Nepal was the cradle of the Nepali language. Its hill people are predominantly Hindu castes: Brahman, Chhetri, Thakuri (a Chhetri subcaste which includes Nepal's king) and the low-caste occupational groups. Unlike the rest of Nepal, few ethnic groups live in the upper hills, but as usual there are highland Bhotia. Free from caste restrictions, these people are more hospitable to foreign trekkers, but many Bhotia regions fall behind the restricted line. You'll probably meet these people on the trail in their endless round of trade. Western Nepal's poor soil and low rainfall have forced them to keep up the Tibet trade even though the exchange has become less favorable. Herds of sheep or goats serve as pack animals, each carrying saddlebags loaded with 10 kilograms of salt, grain, or wool.

Both Buddhists and Hindus here worship Masta, an indigenous folk deity whose shrines are dotted across the countryside. Wooden *dok pa* figurines carved in the shape of humans guard bridges and trails, relics of a strong animistic tradition. Stone columns and stelae linger from the ancient Malla kingdom (no relation to Kathmandu's) which ruled the region between the 12th-14th centuries. Every village has its long-haired *dhami* or jhankri, entrusted with healing and religious rituals.

The hub of the region is the highland valley town of **Jumla,** but flights are often unreliable. The Terai town of Nepalganj can be used as a takeoff point for flights into the mountains, but again cancellations are frequent. One thing you need in western Nepal is plenty of time. If flights are delayed, the nearest road may be a week's walk or more away.

RESTRICTED AREAS

M any of Nepal's most interesting regions have been off-limits to foreigners since the early '60s, when the government drew a line blocking off a 25-mile-wide corridor along the northern border. Partly this was due to pressure from China, which feared unwanted visitors slipping into Tibet through the 18 major passes strung along the border. Both governments wanted to limit contact with Tibetan guerilla fighters who had established strongholds in Dolpo, Mustang, and Manang, which they maintained for over a decade until Nepal, at China's instigation, eventually rooted them out. Finally, there was an element of concern for trekkers' welfare—many of these regions were under Nepali control in name only, and were essentially lawless. Robberies occurred, as in the case of a Japanese expedition to Manaslu which was stripped of all its gear and most of its clothing.

For whatever reasons, the line remains today. You can approach the border only in areas like Everest and Makalu, where rugged terrain (or a high police presence) makes passage impossible. Fascinating regions like Dolpo, Mustang, and the upper Arun Valley are all off limits. These areas preserve some of the last untouched pockets of Tibetan culture; in a way it's just as well they're restricted. Things are changing, however. Hoping to reap economic benefit from tourism, the residents of several regions have petitioned the king to open their villages to trekkers. Lower Dolpo and Kangchenjunga were opened to organized treks in 1989 as a test case; odds are that other regions will gradually follow this pattern.

> *But if one professes and practices living on the country one must take the rough with the smooth, rancid yak fat and frogs along with buckwheat cakes and raksi.*
>
> —H.W. Tilman

Humla

A good late spring trek would be the highland route from Jumla to **Simikot,** the largest village in the remote Humla district. The trail turns off from **Sinja** near Rara Lake, drops down to the mighty Karnali River and crosses the Munla La into Humla to reach Simikot, at least a week's walk distant. The town is district headquarters of the remote Humla district; a seasonal airport here operates flights to Nepalganj.

For years now rumors have whispered of the official opening of a pass north of Simikot, allowing tourists to cross the Tibetan border to the fascinating tri-cultural trading town of Purang (Nepalis call it Taklakot). Lake Manasarovar and Mount Kailas, the sacred center of the Buddhist and Hindu universe, are only a day's drive north. If and when it opens, this route would be preferable to the long, tough overland journey across western Tibet, and would draw many trekkers to western Nepal.

Rara National Park

If you're looking for a wilderness experience, this is the trek. This small (106 square km) park in remote northwestern Nepal protects a high-altitude mountain lake ringed by snowy peaks and pine forests reminiscent of the Rocky Mountains. It might be cheaper and easier to simply camp in the Rockies, but Rara's solitude is rare in crowded Nepal. The trek itself is relatively easy and short; a loop is possible, and it can be done in less than two weeks if you manage to fly both ways.

RNAC's flights to Jumla are as unreliable as elsewhere. Going in is usually okay, but getting out is never guaranteed, and it's a rugged two-week walk back to Pokhara, or a one-week walk to the road at Surkhet. Flying via Nepalganj is a likely alternative, and there's an airstrip at Surkhet.

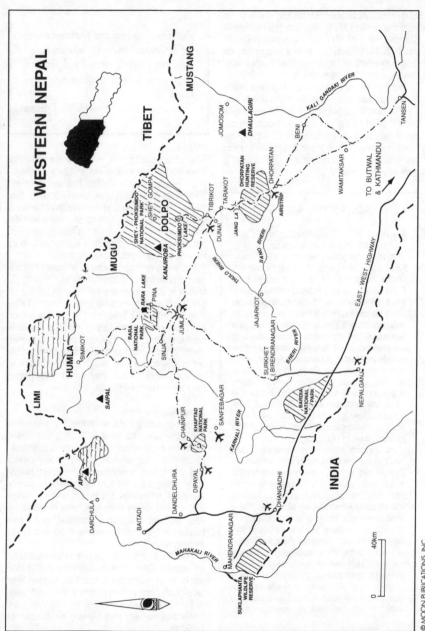

WESTERN NEPAL

Jumla is the district capital of a chronically poor and food-deficit region—bring most everything you need from Kathmandu, though you can pick up rice in the bazaar (the government flies in food from Nepalganj). The local health situation is terrible, and many foreign-aid agencies are stationed here. Short walks around town include a visit to nearby **Micha,** with a walled-in graveyard dating to the Malla Dynasty which ruled this region around the 14th century. To the east, just past the junction of the Chaudabise and the Tila rivers, a 4,000 meter-high ridge provides sweeping views of the western Himalaya from Saipal to Dhaulagiri.

From Jumla, two trails lead to Rara in three or four days; the easternmost is lower but has more ups and downs. It crosses the windy **Danphe Lagna** (3,688 meters) with spectacular mountain views (if there's snow, cross the lower Khali Lagna nearby), then tops the **Gurchi Lagna** (3,444 meters). Another trail passes through the ancient Malla winter capital of **Sinja;** it's usually taken as a return route. Both trails are relatively easy, cutting through rugged country inhabited mainly by Thakuri Chhetris. If you're very lucky you might glimpse the elusive Rauti tribal people who hunt and forage in the hills.

Rara Lake is perched on a high shelf, encircled by gray ridges and pine-forested hills inhabited by bears, jungle cats, and deer. Five by two km, it's the largest lake in Nepal. The best camping is on the grassy southern shore. A trail encircling the lake makes a pleasant eight-hour walk. It was built as a horse trail for King Mahendra's 1964 visit to Rara. The lake inspired him to verse:

O, did you collect all beauty's store
And pour it into Rara to make beauty more
Garland the wreath of snow ranges on the neck
In Himalaya, in Nepal, for pretty Rara's sake.

Local people say that once a foreigner tried to measure the depth by tying together the skins of seven buffalos and securing them to a rock. It was dropped into the lake, but never reached the bottom. Actually, a Japanese with an echo sounder found it to be 167 meters deep. Rara also has the typical legend of selfish villagers punished with a sudden flood for snubbing a

hungry beggar—a tale which seems to haunt every lake in Nepal.

The truth is actually much worse. Rara National Park was formed in 1975, and in a burst of zeal inspired by the Western national park model, two Thakuri villages were dispersed and relocated in 1978. Worst of all, they were sent to the Terai—a shocking change from nearly 3,000 meters to 500 meters altitude. Efforts to locate the transplanted villagers have been unsuccessful, and it's assumed many succumbed to the shock. Fortunately, Nepal's park policy has since been revised to accommodate rather than displace people.

Khaptad National Park

This tiny preserve in far western Nepal protects 225 square km of grassland and forested plateau, a small sample of the vegetation that once covered the entire region. Forests of conifer, oak, and rhododendron shelter wildlife, including barking and musk deer, and birds. Most exotic is the **Khaptad Baba,** a Hindu guru said to have lived here for over 40 years. The Baba is reportedly over 100 years old, a well-educated man who speaks fluent Hindi, Nepali, and English and commands great respect from local people and Kathmandu Hindus alike (supposedly even the king visits him). The park was created as a preserve for the Baba as much as for musk deer. A five-square-km core area in the park has been reserved for "meditation and tranquillity," with butchering, alcohol, and tobacco forbidden. Protected holy sites include the shrines of **Tribeni,** a confluence of streams believed to be the source of the Ganges. Ganga Deshara, a festival held here in summer (usually around the June full moon) attracts thousands of pilgrims. Two months later, Shiva is worshipped at the small lakelet of **Khaptad Daha.**

There have been few if any visitors so far, but Khaptad appears to be teahouse-able. Bring plenty of food, just in case. The park is a few days' walk from three airstrips: **Sanfebagar, Dipayal,** and **Chainpur** (the last seasonal but reportedly the easiest). Fares are US$60-70 from Nepalganj, about US$140 from Kathmandu. The entrance station and army guard post is at **Lokhada;** the Rs250 fee is payable here.

Trails climb through forest to emerge onto the rolling grassland of **Khaptad Lekh,** with views of Api and Saipal himal. From the single small teahouse-lodge at park headquarters you can day-trip to Tribeni and Khaptad Daha and visit Khaptad Baba's small hut. The park's main trail is an old trade route from **Dipayal,** an administrative town on the Seti River. You'll probably want to return via Dipayal as it has both an airstrip and a road (to Dhangadhi) in case flights get messed up.

Dolpo

The best known of the many isolated high Himalayan valleys across northern Nepal, Dolpo preserves one of the last remnants of traditional Tibetan culture. Legend says it's a *bayul,* one of the "hidden valleys" created by Guru Rinpoche as a refuge for devout Buddhists in troubled times. Surrounded by high mountains including the Dhaulagiri massif to the southeast and cut off by high passes closed by snow half the year, Dolpo's easiest access is from Tibet, where its people emigrated from perhaps 1,000 years ago.

Upper Dolpo shelters about 5,000 people, whose lives revolve around Buddhism, barley, and yaks; their villages (over 4,260 meters) are among the highest settlements on earth. A large portion of Dolpo has been set aside as **Shey-Phoksumdo National Park,** at 3,555 square km Nepal's largest. Meant to preserve a complete example of the trans-Himalayan ecosystem, the park shelters blue sheep, Himalayan black bear, leopards, wolves, and the elusive snow leopard, which provided the title for Peter Matthiessen's classic book on his 1973 journey through this region.

Largely thanks to *The Snow Leopard,* Dolpo is the best-known of Nepal's forbidden northern border regions. The 1989 announcement that the government was opening the region to group treks caused a flurry of excitement, but the result is disappointing. Only the low trail up to **Phoksumdo Lake** is currently open, leading through unexceptional forests and Hindu villages. The reedeeming feature is the lake itself, considered one of the most beautiful places in Nepal.

To reach here, you must trek through a registered company, which will obtain permits through a Byzantine procedure involving several ministries—no problem, but it takes a few working days. Groups generally fly from Nepalganj to the **Jufal** airstrip, then walk several hours

to the district headquarters of **Dunai** (2,100 meters). The trail follows the Suli Gad River, passing through thick conifer forests and a few Thakuri Hindu villages. The National Park checkpost is one day from Dunai; two steep days later, you reach Phoksumdo Lake.

Flying in and out, the trek takes less than two weeks. Longer but highly rewarding options would be to walk in from Dhorpatan over two high passes (about one week) or cross the 5,000-meter Kagmara Pass from Jumla. Kagmara means "Crow Death," either because it's so high the birds drop dead flying over, or because of a grisly rumor that they attack and kill victims of altitude sickness and snow blindness.

Phoksumdo Lake (3,627 meters) is the highlight of the whole trek, a basin of unearthly turquoise blue ringed by rocky crags and forest, framed by snowcapped peaks. Veteran traveler David Snellgrove raved over its beauty: "Here we set up camp, feeling that we had come at last to the paradise of the Buddha 'Boundless Light.' The water is edged with silver birch and the gleaming whiteness of the branches against the unearthly blue of the water is one of the most blissful things that I have known," he wrote in *Himalayan Pilgrimage.*

Legend says a demoness fled here during Guru Rinpoche's conversion of Tibet's resident spirits, offering local people a gigantic turquoise to keep her passage a secret. Guru Rinpoche transformed the turquoise into a lump of dung, and the disgruntled people revealed the demoness's hiding place. In revenge she called down a flood upon their village, submerging it beneath the lake. The legend is a concise mythic summary of the ancient struggle between Bönpo and Buddhists; the latter won, but the former remain, even here at Phoksumdo.

At the lake's eastern end is the village of **Ringmo,** also called Tso. The town's entrance chorten has nine complex Buddhist and Bönpo mandalas painted on its wooden ceiling, described in detail by Snellgrove. "These villagers dwell in one of the most glorious places on earth without being remotely aware of it," he noted of Ringmo's 100 or so residents. Perhaps they are too busy moving around between their various settlements. In late spring they plant crops in Ringmo and at a higher settlement; in winter they descend to another town to graze their herds. The people are Bhotia and only very distantly related to Tibetans. They are gradually becoming Hindu-ized, adding Chhetri surnames to their Tibetan names.

The Bönpo monastery, **Tso Gompa,** is two km from the village, set above the lake on forested cliffs with views across to Kanjiroba. Below the village, a gigantic waterfall cascades over a series of rock steps, draining into the Suli Gad far below. A visit to the Bönpo gompa at **Pungmo,** two hours up a side valley to the west, is a worthwhile expedition.

The best part of Dolpo lies beyond the lake, along a difficult trail that crosses a high pass into the real Dolpo. **Shey Gompa,** named after nearby Crystal Mountain, is several days' walk north of the lake. The closest you can come is to read *The Snow Leopard* or Eric Valli's magnificent photo book on Dolpo (see Booklist). Or perhaps you'll meet maroon-clad Dolpo-pa on the trail, as they drive their salt-laden yak caravans south in the fall and return to their high villages in the spring.

CENTRAL NEPAL

Pokhara To Trisuli

This lowland trek traverses classic hill country, with Newar and Hindu villages, huge spreading pipal trees, and good views of Himalchuli, Manaslu, Ganesh Himal, and the Annapurnas. It's a good introductory off-the-beaten-trek: altitude is low, the ups and downs are constant but not too steep, and the hill town of Gorkha with its motor road is midway in case you change your mind and want a *really* short walk.

It's short (a week at most), easily accessible, and one of those rare trails best done in the winter. There are plenty of local teahouses and travelers along the way, but few trekkers.

From Pokhara, start at **Begnas Tal** and pick one of many trails weaving east several days through Gurung country. Try to visit **Ghan Pokhari,** a lovely old trading town a few hours above the road to Besisahar. Cross the road near Tarkughat or Besisahar; the next day cross the Darondi Khola. The old fortress town of **Gorkha** is an hour's detour and well worth a visit.

From the old Gorkha Durbar the trail continues east through Khanchok Bhanjyang, dropping down to **Arughat** on the Burhi Gandaki and continuing two more days through bazaar towns to end at **Trisuli.** Swaying buses head down the winding 79-km road to Kathmandu. You can reach Kathmandu in two days or less on foot, avoiding the road most of the way and ending up at Balaju. If you've extra time in Trisuli, climb up to the old seven-story fort in nearby **Nuwakot.**

Dhorpatan

Few trekkers visit this broad, high valley less than a week's walk west of Pokhara. Even Nepalis from other regions are stared at by the locals; foreigners can expect to become minor celebrities. The region is manageable, with teahouses and decent trails throughout, but it's wild enough to be interesting, and it's definitely off the beaten track.

Tell people in Pokhara you're going to Dhorpatan, and they'll warn of freezing temperatures and rugged trails. They tend to exaggerate, but the pass *is* generally snowed over into late spring, and in winter many local people move to lower regions.

For now, count on ten walking days there and back, but when the Baglung Road is completed, it will chop off the first few days from Pokhara to **Beni**—a low stretch that's unpleasantly hot in the spring. From Beni the trail heads up along the Myagdi Khola to ascend the **Jaljala Pass** (3,414 meters). The last reliable food and lodging is at **Lumsum** or **Moreni,** about three hours below the pass; from here to the first settlements above Dhorpatan it's nothing but herder's huts and woods, so bring food for the day. The trail is obvious and frequently traveled by mule and pony trains. At the top are good

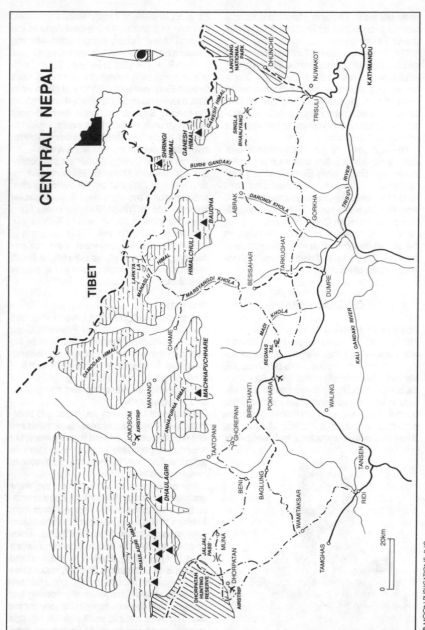

CENTRAL NEPAL

© MOON PUBLICATIONS, INC.

views of Dhaulagiri, the Annapurnas, Machha-puchhare, and the remote peaks of Nepal's western Himalaya. Haul up water from Moreni if you want to make a high camp and wait for mountain views—scramble up the ridge on the north side of the pass.

From here the broad Dhorpatan Valley opens out with vistas as wide as the American West. **Dhorpatan** is five hours beyond the pass, a mixture of Nepalis and Tibetans (many refugees settled here in the '60s). There's a small Bönpo monastery here. The surrounding ridges offer excellent views; the easiest is directly south of the airport, a two-hour climb. Side trips north into nearby **Dhorpatan Hunting Reserve** and blue sheep country require food and tents; you could continue on an even wilder trail via **Tara-kot** to **Jumla,** about two weeks away. Shorter loops to the west and northwest lead through country inhabited by the Kham Magar ethnic group. Return is about five days via the same trail or heading southeast to **Tansen** through interesting hill country, to emerge on the Sid-dhartha Highway south of Pokhara.

If the Jaljale Pass is snowed over, a lower unnamed pass (2,926 meters) to the south is generally open. The trail leads off from Baglung to emerge at **Wamitaksar,** a few days south of Dhorpatan on the Tansen trail.

Jugal Himal

This beautiful cluster of peaks northeast of Kath-mandu is dominated by Dorje Lhakpa (6,990 meters). It's relatively easy to reach, though the trail ascends steeply. Bring food, shelter, and a guide. Access is from **Chautara,** a trading vil-lage up a dirt road from Dolalghat. The trail runs up a long ridge, passing a sacred Shiva lake called **Bhairab Kund,** and continuing up to the five lakelets of **Panch Pokhari** (about 3,700 meters), a seldom-visited pilgrimage site. The ridge above the lakes offers spectacular moun-tain views. From here it's a long day's walk to the first settlement of **Helambu;** the trail eventually runs into Tarkeghyang.

Ganesh Himal

Rough and wild, this trek cuts through untraveled country south of the Ganesh Himal massif. Mountain views are good but the terrain is rough and the local people unaccustomed to trekkers.

Bring a tent and food for at least a few days; sometimes the only thing available locally is *dhiro.* A Nepali guide is a must. Even Sherpas get nervous in a few of these *jungli* Tamang vil-lages.

Several possible routes connect Gorkha and Trisuli; they all take about two weeks or more. One option heads up the Darondi Khola from Gorkha to the large Gurung town of **Barpak.** Dropping down through the nasty village of **Labrak,** you cross the Burhi Gandaki via a rude cable-car, and trek up into the mountains. Two days or so are through uninhabited high territo-ry with superb mountain views. Crossing **Singla Bhanjyang,** you drop down to reach Trisuli and the road two days later. A lower route avoids the high pass, which is frequently snowed over in spring.

Around Manaslu

Another little-known trek, this one a circuit around the eighth-highest mountain in the world (8,162 meters). A trail heads from Gorkha up the Burhi Gandaki through wild Gurung country, over the 5,105-meter **Larkya La** and down the Marsyangdi River valley into relatively civilized Manang. Figure on three weeks and bring a guide, and food and shelter for the northern por-tion. The trail is generally restricted, but there's always the chance. . . .

EASTERN NEPAL

Overview

Lower, greener and friendlier, eastern Nepal is altogether more welcoming than the west, yet it's virtually untouched by trekkers. It's lovely, as-of-yet unspoiled country where people greet you with wholehearted curiosity and the traditional palms-together "Namaste," a nicety that's dis-appeared on the main trekking trails.

The lower hills are the homeland of Rai and Limbu, while Sherpa, Tamang, and Bhotia herd yak and cattle crossbreeds up higher. There are plenty of uninhabited high ridges with sweep-ing Himalayan vistas, including Kangchenjunga, Makalu, and Everest. Culturally eastern Nepal is very interesting, with many local festivals and weekly haat bazaars, where different ethnic groups meet to exchange goods, gossip, and drink.

Eastern Nepal bears the brunt of the monsoon; vegetation is rich, with bamboo everywhere, and in springtime rhododendrons blaze across the hillsides. A less attractive consequence is frequent snow which can block high passes, especially in spring. The plentiful water supports intensive irrigation, and though the hill regions here are the most densely populated of all Nepal's Hills, the land doesn't seem overworked.

The region is relatively prosperous and comfortable: food, lodging, and porters are easier to find and transportation is at least marginally better than western Nepal, though it's still a long, long way to Kathmandu by bus (at least 22 hours from Basantapur). There are plenty of teahouses in lower regions, but don't expect the proprietors to speak English or to serve pancakes. As usual, it's best to hire a local porter-guide if you don't speak some Nepali.

The network of lower trails is delightful, especially in the winter months. **Phidim-Taplejung-Basantapur** and **Tumlingtar-Chainpur-Ilam** are easy one-week treks through unspoiled country. Much of the fascinating high country is off-limits, places like the old Bhotia trading town of **Walungchung Gola**, and the upper Arun Valley with its Bönpo villages. There's always the chance that restrictions will relax, and in any case adventurous trekkers can still find many interesting routes unhampered by checkposts.

Big changes are coming to eastern Nepal in the form of the Arun III project sponsored by

© MOON PUBLICATIONS, INC.

the World Bank. This dam has the potential to produce more electricity than the current installed capacity of the entire country. The entire project is expected to take ten years. First step will be an access road running up the valley from Basantapur to Num; construction may start by 1992. When completed, the dam will flood four km of the Arun Valley above Num; water will then be channeled through a 14-km tunnel to the powerhouse. The project will transform the lives of local people, though ironically, electricity for local villages is not part of the plan.

As a counterpoint to this massive development scheme, a national park has been proposed to protect the unique ecosystems of the upper Arun. The 1,500-square-km **Makalu-Barun National Park** will extend from the Tibetan border all the way south to the Salpa Bhanjyang Trail connecting Lukla and Tumlingtar. Adjoining Sagarmatha National Park and the Qomolungma Nature Preserve in Tibet, it will create one of the world's largest adjoining park systems. The combination of park and road will open up lots of new territory to trekkers. One sure bet is the Makalu Base Camp route up the Arun Valley, which will become far more accessible after the first three days of walking are replaced by the road.

Kangchenjunga

Eastern Nepal is dominated by Kangchenjunga, at 8,586 meters the third-highest mountain on earth. Its name is Tibetan, and means "Five Great Treasuries of the Snows." Straddling Nepal's eastern border, it towers over Sikkim, and the excellent views of it from Darjeeling made it the best-known peak in the Himalaya a century ago. For a time it was even believed to be the world's highest mountain. Mountaineers scaled the main summit in 1955, but severe weather and avalanches continue to challenge expeditions.

Like Dolpo, this formerly restricted area was opened in 1989 to organized treks. The restriction is intended to protect the region from environmental and cultural pressures (maximizing profits was another idea), but judging from the ribbons of toilet paper festooning the trail, the plan hasn't been too effective. Solo trekkers still manage to explore the region, but difficult logistics place it in the realm of an organized trek. There are no settlements along the upper por-

tion, so you'd have to bring food and shelter. Figure two to three weeks from Taplejung; walking to the road at Basantapur is an extra three days.

Groups generally fly to **Taplejung** (US$110). The bus ride from Kathmandu-Dhankuta and up to Basantapur is a grueling 22-plus hours; flying to Biratnagar would save a lot of time. There is a road to Taplejung, but bus service is erratic at best; ask around. The trail heads northeast through Rai and Limbu farm country; higher up Tibetans and Sherpas graze herds of yak, dzo and dzopkio. Cultural interaction on this trek is more limited than most; so, surprisingly, are the mountain views (until the end). The trail follows a high-walled valley, finally emerging onto one of the huge glaciers sweeping down from Kangchenjunga's flanks, to reveal a whole cluster of peaks above. One route goes up the Simbua Khola to **Yalung Glacier** (4,890 meters); another, slightly further west, goes through the Tibetan town of **Gunsa** to **Pangpema** (5,150 meters) on Kangchenjunga Glacier. Trails over the **Lapsang La** or the lower **Sinion La** connect these two in a long loop.

Jaljale Himal

This trip leads through pleasant low farm country up onto a remote, uninhabited ridge with fine mountain views of four of the world's five highest peaks. A guide is a must in the high country, to help find water as well as to show the way. (Above the Clouds Trekking in Kathmandu is one of the few companies to do this trek). The first few days out of Basantapur are easy, pleasant, and teahouse-able, leading up to **Gufa Pokhari**, where Makalu's reflection shimmers in the waters of a pond. A trail continues up the rhododendron-covered **Milke Danda** past herders' camps and onto **Jaljale Himal** (about 4,700 meters), a rocky ridge set with a few small lakes. The high portion is often snowed in, especially in spring. For the return, several trails run down side ridges to reach **Tumlingtar** in the west or **Taplejung** in the east. Figure at least two weeks walking, plus travel time.

Makalu Base Camp

This route is for the gung-ho only: you need to carry shelter and food for at least ten days. The difficult double pass is frequently snowbound. Count on two to three weeks trekking.

From the STOL strip of **Tumlingtar,** the trail leads through the bazaar town of **Khandbhari** up the increasingly deep gorge of the Arun River. Mountain views are spectacular in a few places, especially at **Munche.** The trail drops down to **Num** (a checkpost here prevents you from continuing upvalley) then descends to cross the Arun and reach **Tashigaon,** the last village along the way. Take a local guide for the rest of the journey; you may have to hire one lower to get a good English-speaking one. The route crosses the often foggy **Shipton La** and **Barun La** (4,110 meters), into the isolated upper Barun Valley. Snow here is often lighter than on the passes. The trail follows the Barun Glacier to **Makalu Base Camp** set beneath the massive 8,463-meter peak. For the return a possible loop heads down the western side of the river from Num, passing near the legendary **Khembalung Caves.**

Back Door To Everest

Trekkers usually do this as an escape route from overcrowded Lukla and Solu, but it could be an entrance as well. Simple food and lodging are available along the way, and the trail can go on as far as you like—less than a week to Tumlingtar's airstrip, or 12 days to Ilam, all the way across at the easternmost end of the country. You might want to hire a local guide if you don't speak Nepali.

The turnoff from the main Everest trail is less than a day south of Lukla at **Kharte,** above the Kari Khola.

MIKE WELLINS   *Tamang women, eastern Nepal*

The trail heads southeast over steep, forested hills, with Rai villages on the lower slopes and Sherpa villages above. H.W. Tilman passed through here en route to Khumbu in 1949. The discouraging descent and ascent between the towns of Bung and Gudel inspired this ditty:

> For dreadfulness nought can excel
> The prospect of Bung from Gudel;
> And words die away on the tongue
> When we look back at Gudel from Bung

Cross the **Salpa Bhanjyang** (3,350 meters) and descend into the steamy Arun Valley to reach **Tumlingtar,** about six days from Kharte. If you don't get a flight to Kathmandu (US$44) you can walk two days to Hille on the road. Or continue east to **Ilam,** either via Chainpur and Terhathum or Taplejung-Phidim. Ilam is a small hill town surrounded by tea gardens, a day-long jeep ride to the main East-West Highway. By now you're in the southeasternmost corner of Nepal, a two-day bus ride from Kathmandu, but very close to Darjeeling, which lies just beyond the border town of **Kakarbhitta.**

Hongu

This remote area southeast of the Everest massif is a tangle of high mountains, completely uninhabited and often snowbound. This trek is pure isolation, just ice, snow, and rock. The best season is April-May. You need full gear and a knowledgeable guide; an agency trek is almost a must. Flying in and out of Lukla, Hongu could be done in less than three weeks. The route heads over the steep ridge east of Lukla and continues for five or six days, crossing the 5,400-meter **Mera La,** with excellent mountain views. The same day you reach the Hongu Khola. Turning north, it's another few days up to **Panch Pokhari,** five small lakes that feed the river. From here you can retrace your steps to Lukla, or if conditions are good, possibly continue north, crossing over the 5,780-meter **Amphu Labtsa** into the Chukhung Valley.

NEPALI PHRASES AND VOCABULARY

(See "Language" in the general Introduction for more tips on learning Nepali.)

Pronunciation

Transliteration from Devanagri into English is fairly straightforward, but there are a few waffly points. 'B' and 'v' are interchangeable in Nepali; thus you'll find Bishnu and Vishnu. The same goes for 'f' and 'ph', leading to statements like "puck you!"

Things get more complicated when you get to 't' and 'd'. Different combinations of aspiration and retroflexion make four varieties of each. These are tricky points for English speakers to pick up or even note, but they can make a big difference in meaning.

Retroflex consonants ('t' and 'd') are pronounced with the tongue curled up and slightly back, touching the palate. To start, listen to the way a Nepali pronounces Kathmandu—the 'th' is almost a 'd'.

Aspirated consonants (kh, gh, jh, ph, bh, dh, th, and chh) have an extra 'h', signalling an extra puff of air. This point is fairly subtle, so don't worry too much, but remember 'th' is never pronounced as in "this"; the 'h' is simply aspirated.

The difference between 'aa' and 'a' is easily glossed over but shouldn't be. A single 'a' sounds almost like "uh," as in *ma*; *maa* (a suffix meaning "in"), is long and drawn out. Listen to someone say *chaamal* (uncooked rice) to get both.

BASIC GRAMMAR

Nepali grammar is relatively simple: the only plural is made by adding *-haru* onto the end of a noun; there's no gender, little future tense, and you can get by using one or two tenses for practically all subjects and times. The subtleties are endless, but picking up a basic operational framework is not too hard.

Order in a sentence is subject-object-verb: I'm studying Nepali—*Ma Nepali sikchhu.*

For **questions,** simply raise your voice at the end of the sentence: Are you going to Namche?—*Tapaai Namche-ma janne?*

Pronouns

I	ma
you (polite)	tapaai
(familiar, for kids)	timi
we	haami
he/she (polite)	wahaa
(familiar)	u

For **possessives,** add *-ko* to the pronoun, name, or noun:

Ram's daughter	Ramko chhori
wheat flour	gauko pitho
whose book?	kasko kitaab?

Exceptions are *mero, timro, usko* (mine, yours, his/hers).

The most important postposition is *-laai*, meaning "to" or "for":

Please give it to me. *Malaai dinuhos.*

Please tell that to him.
Wahaalaai bhannaidinuhos.

Nouns

Many modern words are adopted from English: *bas, tiket, motar, hotel, radio.* When in doubt, try the English word with a Nepali pronunciation.

book	kitaab
bottle	sisi
bridge	pul, saanghu
candle	mainbatti
chicken	khukhura
cow	gaai
cup	gilas, kap
dog	kukur
electricity	bijuli
fire	aago
firewood	daauraa
foot (and leg)	khutta
forest	ban
government	sarkaar
hill	lekh, pahaad, danda

house	ghar
inn, lodge	laj
kerosene	mattitel
knife	chakku, khukuri
light (lamp)	batti
load	bhaari
luggage	saamaan
matches	salaai
medicine	aushadi
pass	bhanjyang
pen	kalam, dat pen
place	thau
porter	kulli, bokne maanche
religion	dharma
river	khola, kosi, nadi
road	baato
room	kothaa
shop	pasal
snow	hiu
soap	saabun
sun	ghaam
toilet	chharpi
town	gaun
trail	baato
main trail	mul baato
tree	rukh
village	gaun
water	paani
(un)boiled water	(na-)umaaleko paani
drinking water	khaane paani
hot water	taato paani
washing water	dhune paani, nuhaaune paani

Verb Survival

Some of these suggestions are unorthodox pidgin Nepali, but they're readily understood, and handier than wrestling with formal verb conjugations your hosts may not use either.

1. Take the basic verb shown below and subtract -nu to get the root.

2. Add -nuhos to form a polite command:
Chiyaa dinuhos. (Please) give me tea.
To form a negative, add -na as a prefix:
Tyo nachunuhos. Please don't touch that.

3. Add -ne to form a simple, all-purpose form indicating the present and future:

Ma janne. I'm going
Janne? You're going?

4. Add -eko to form the past participle:
Khaanaa khaaeko? Have you eaten?

5. Add -yo to indicate completion:
sakyo finished
bhayo it's over with, accomplished, past
Wahaa hijo gaayo. He went yesterday.

As in Spanish, "to be" (hunu) has two forms: chha/chhaina used for location and quality, and ho/hoina, a more permanent definition. If you get confused, either is generally understandable.

arrive	pugnu
buy	kinnu
carry	boknu
come	aaunu
cook	pakaaunu
do	garnu
eat (also drink)	khaannu
(to be) enough	pugnu
forget	birsanu
give	dinu
go	jannu
help	madat dinu
look for	khojnu
meet	bhetnu
need	chaahinnu
put	raakhnu
read, study	padhnu
rest	aaram garnu
return	pharkanu, pheri aaunu
sell	bechnu
sit, stay	basnu
sleep	sutnu
take	linu
teach	sikaunu, padhaunu
throw out	phaalnu
try	kosis garnu (or "try" garnu)
understand	bujhnu
wait	parkhanu
walk	hidnu
wash	dhunu (face, clothes) nuhaaunu (body)
work	kaam garnu
write	lekhnu

Useful Dual Verbs

v. + *hunchha*: to be okay to
Haami yahaa basnu hunchha? Is it okay for us to stay here?

v. + *sakchha* to be possible to, able to
Tapaai bholi jaana sakchha? Can you go tomorrow?

v. + *parchha*: to must, have to do something
Bholi bihanaa saberai jaanu parchha.
Tomorrow we'll have to go very early in the morning.

v. + *man laagchha*: to like doing something
Ma Nepalma ghumna janne dherai man laagchha. I like wandering around in Nepal a lot.

Adjectives And Adverbs

a little bit	*ali ali, ali kati*
after	*pachhi*
again	*pheri*
all	*sab, sabaai*
alone	*eklai*
always	*sadhai*
angry	*risaayo*
another, the other	*arko*
bad	*kharaab, naraamro*
before	*aghi, agadi*
big	*thulo*
cheap	*saasto*
clean	*saphaa*
closed	*bhandaa*
cold	
(person, weather)	*jaado*
(liquid)	*chiso*
crazy	*bauluhaa*
difficult	*gaarho, muskil, aapt yaro*
dirty	*pohor*
easy	*saajilo*
everyone	*sabaai janna*
expensive	*mahango*
far	*tadaa*
fun	*ramaailo, maja*
good	*raamro*
heavy	*garungo*
hot	
(person, weather)	*garam*
(liquid)	*taato*
hungry	*bhok*

inside	*bhitra*
lazy	*alchhi*
less	*thorai*
(a) lot, many	*dherai, thupro*
more	*dherai, jyaada*
near	*najik(ai)*
new	*nayaa*
old	*purano*
only	*maatrai*
open	*kholeko, khulaa*
outside	*baahira*
quickly	*chitto*
scarce, lacking	*komti*
slowly	*bistaarai*
small	*saano*
strong	*baaliyo*
stupid	*murkaa*
sweet	*guliyo*
tasty	*mitho*
very	*dherai, ekdum*

How is it?	*Kaasto chha?*
How nice! Great!	*Kaasto raamro!*
What a person! (said disapprovingly)	*Kaasto manchhe!*

Feelings

afraid	*dar laagyo*
cold	*jaado laagyo*
drunk	*raksi laagyo*
happy	*kushi laagyo*
hot	*garmi laagyo*
hungry	*bhok laagyo*
lazy	*alchhi laagyo*
pleasant, nice	*ramaailo laagyo*
sleepy	*nidraa laagyo*
thirsty	*tirkhaa laagyo*
tired	*thakaai laagyo*

Question Words

who	*ko*
what	*ke*
when	*kahile*
where	*kahaa*
why	*kina*
how (in what way)	*kasari*

USEFUL PHRASES

Accommodations

Is there a place to stay (in that town?)

(Tyo gaun-ma) baas painchha?

Is it okay if we stay here?
Haami yahaa basnu hunchha?

Please show me a room.
Kotha dekhaunuhos na.

Is there anything better/cheaper/bigger than this?
Yo bhandaa raamro/saasto/thulo chha?

One person only.   *Ek janna matraai.*

Two people.   *Dui janna.*

My friend is coming.   *Mero ek janaa saathi aauncha.*

Food

(Where) Is there food available?
Khaanaa (kahaa) painchha?

What do you want to eat?   *Ke khaane?*

Is the rice cooked yet?   *Bhaat pakaeko chha?*

I have to cook it.   *Pakaunu parchha.*

What do you have for food/snacks?
Khaanaa/Khajaa ke ke chha?

How long will it take to cook food?
Pakaaunalaai kati time laagchha?

Give me a plate of daal bhaat, please.
Daal bhaat ek plaat dinuhos.

Don't add chili.   *Khursaani nahalnuhos.*

Please make it hot.   *Piro pakaaunuhos.*

Bring more food.   *Bhaat lyau/khaana lyau.*

Please give me a little bit.
Ali-ali (thorai) dinuhos.

That's enough/that's plenty.
Malaai pugyo. or *Bho, bho.*

I'm finished.   *Sakyo*

Please take it.   *Linuhos*

I don't eat meat.   *Ma maasu khaandina.*

Please give me a cup of tea.
Chiyaa ek gilas dinuhos.
    milk tea   *dudh chiyaa*
    black tea   *kaalo chiyaa*
    without sugar/with sugar
        Chini nahalnuhos/chini halnuhos

Another cup of tea, please.
Arko ek gilas chiyaa dinuhos.

The food is very tasty.
Khanna ekdum mitho chha.

Please give me a spoon
Chamchaa dinuhos.

It's okay; I'll eat with my hand.
Thik chha; ma haatle khaanchhu.

apple	*syaau*
banana	*keraa*
beer	*biyaar (jaar* or *chang* for local brew)
butter	*makhan*
cauliflower	*kauli*
candy	*mithaai*
chicken	*kukhurako maasu*
chili pepper	*khursaani*
coffee	*kaphi*
cookie	*biskoot*
corn	*makai*
egg	*phul*
fish	*maachhaa*
flour (wheat)	*gahuko pitho (maida* or *atta)*
fruit	*phalphul*
greens	*saag*
lentils	*daal*
liquor	*raaksi*
mango	*aap*
meat	*maasu*
buffalo	*raangako maasu*
chicken	*kukhurako maasu*
goat	*khasiko maasu*
pork	*sugurko maasu*
milk	*dudh*
noodles	*chow-chow*
oil	*tel*
orange	*suntalaa*
popcorn	*murali makaai*
potato	*aalu*
relish	*achaar*
rice (cooked)	*bhaat*
(uncooked)	*chaamal*
(in the field)	*dhaan*
salt(y)	*nun(ilo)*
snacks	*khaajaa*
spices	*masalaa*
sugar	*chini*

tea	*chiyaa*
vegetables	*tarkaari, subji*
water	*paani*
drinking	*khaane pani*
boiled	*umaaleko pani*
yoghurt	*dahi*

Meeting People

To address strangers, Nepali (like most Asian languages) uses kinship terms, a feature guaranteed to make you feel at home. To call a woman or man around your age or slightly older, say *Eh, didi/daai* (Oh, older sister/older brother).

Distinctly older than you:
  Eh, baabu/amaai (Oh mother/father)

Distinctly younger than you:
  Eh, bahini/bhaai (Oh younger sister/brother)

To call a shop- or lodgekeeper:
  Eh, sahuji (male)/*sahuni* (female)

-ji is a polite suffix that can also be added onto given names: "Ram-ji", "Bob-ji"

Hajur is a polite term for a man (like "sir") as well as a good way to say "Excuse me, I didn't quite catch that" when said in a questioning tone.

"Thank you" is seldom used in Nepali, though overeager Westerners have revived the Sanskrit term *dhanyabad*. For routine thanks, it's best to use the English (say "tenk you") or simply smile and nod.

When leaving, say "Namaste," or *Raamro sangha basnuhos* if the person is staying; *Raamro sangha jannuhos* if the person is departing.

See you tomorrow/again
  Bholi/pheri betaunlaa.

Go slowly, take it easy.
  Bistaari jaanuhos/aaunuhos.

baby	*bachha, nani* (girl), *babu* (boy)
children	*ketaa-keti* (lit. "boys and girls")
daughter	*chhori*
foreigner	*bideshi* (*ghuire* is an impolite epithet for Westerners)
friend	*saathi*

girlfriend	*keti saathi*
husband	*logne* (informal), *pati*, *srimaan* (most polite)
person	*manchhe*
inn- or shopkeeper	*sahuji* (m.)/*sahuni* (f.)
son	*chhora*
wife	*swasni* (informal), *patni, srimaati* (most polite)

Conversation

How are you?
  Tapaailaai kasto chha? (or simply *Aramai?*)

I'm fine, and you?
  Malaai sanchai chha, tapaai ni?

I'm/It's okay.   *Thik chha.*

Ke chha?   *What's up?*

Ke bhayo?
  What's the matter, what's happened?

What's your name?   *Tapaaiko naam ke ho?*

My name is _____.   *Mero naam_____ho.*

Where do you live?
  Tapaai kahaa basnu hunchha?

I'm from the U.S.   *Ma Amerikaan hu.*

How old are you?
  Tapaaiko umer kati bhayo?

I'm XX years old.   *Malaai XX barsha bhayo.*

Are you married?   *Tapaaiko bihaa bhayo?*

Yes I am/No I'm not.   *Bhayo/Bhaeko chaaina.*

Do you have children?
  Bachaa chha ki chaaina?

How many? Boy or girl?
  Kati janna chha? Chhora ki chhori?

What kind of work do you do?
  Tapaai ke kaam garnu hunchha?

Do you speak Nepali/English?
  Nepaali/English (kura) bolnu hunchha?

I speak a little   *Ma ali ali bolchhu.*

Please speak slowly.   *Bistaari bolnuhos.*

I understand/don't understand.
  Bujhyo/Bujhdaina.

I (don't) know.   *Malaai tahaa chha(ina).*

Pardon?   *Hajur?*

Excuse me.   *Maaph garnuhos*

Let's go.   *Jaau.* or *Jam.*

Don't worry.   *Chinta nagarnuhos.*

Don't be angry.   *Narisaaunuhos.*

Go away.   *Jau, jau.*

You shouldn't beg.   *Maagne hundaaina.*

I won't give anything.
Ma kehi pani dindaaina.

Don't give me trouble.   *Dukhaa nadiu.*

Health

I'm sick.   *Malaai biraami bhayo.*

Where does it hurt?   *Kahaa dukhchha?*

stomach ache   *pet dukhchha*

diarrhea   *disaa laagchhha*

fever   *jwaaro aayo*

headache   *tauko dukhchha*

Shopping And Bargaining

Do you have any . . . ?   *. . . chha ki chaaina?*

Where can I get . . . ?   *. . . kahaa paainchha?*

How much is this?   *Yesko kati?*

How much per kilo?   *Kiloko kati?*

How much is the food?   *Khaanaako kati?*

How much for one?   *Eutaako kati?*

How much total?
Jammaa kati bhayo/kati laagcha?

No, that's too expensive. Give it to me a little
cheaper, please.
*Hoina, tyo ta mahango bhayo. Ali sastoma
dinuhos na.*

Give me your best price.   *Thik bhannuhos.*

Please give it to me for Rs 90.
Nabbe rupiyaama dinuhos.

Here's the money.   *Paisaa linuhos.*

Please give me change; I don't have any.
*Chanchun dinuhos; mero chanchun
chaaina.*

Bill, please.   *Bil dinuhos/hisaab garnuhos.*

Transportation

Where is this bus going?
Yo bas kahaa jaanchha?

How much is a ticket to . . . ?
. . . jaane tikat ko kati?

What time will we reach . . . ?
. . . maa kati baaje pugchha?

What time do we go?   *Kati baaje jaanchha?*

Taxi! Are you empty?   *Tyaaksi! Khaali ho?*

Please go to Durbar Marg.
Darbar Margma jaanuhos.

Put on the meter.   *Mitaarma jaanuhos na.*

I'll give one-and-a-half times the meter.
Ma mitaarko dedhi dinchhu.

How much to go to Bhaktapur?
Bhaktapurma jaane kati paarchha?

Directions

Where is . . . ?   *. . . kahaa chha?*

Which is the trail to Namche?
*Namchema pugnalaai kun baatoma
jaanchha?*

Which trail is the best/fastest/easiest?
Kun baato raamro/chitto/saajilo chha?

How far is it?   *Kati tadaa chha?*

How many hours to reach (the next town)?
*(Pallo gaun) pugnalaai kati ghantaa
laagchha?*

Where are you going?
Kahaa jaanu hunchha?

Where are you coming from?
Kahaa bataa aaeko? or *Kaata pugera
aaunu bhayo?*

here/there	*yahaa/tyahaa*
right/left	*daayaa/baayaa*
straight	*sidha*
north	*uttar*
south	*dakshin*
east	*purbaa*
west	*paaschim*
up	*maathi, upallo*
down	*muni, tallo*
uphill	*ukaalo*
downhill	*oraalo*
level	*samma*

"Red mud, slippery trail." (proverb)
Raato maato, chiplo baato.

Porters

I'm going to Namche, and I need a porter for one week.
Ma Namchema jaanne, ma ek haptaa ko kulli chahinchha.

How much per day?
Ek dinko kati chahinchha?

I'll give you Rs80 per day.
Ma ek dinko aausi rupiyaa dinchhu.

without food   *khaanaa nakhaaera*

with food   *khaanaa khaaera*

For returning, how much do you need?
Pharkanako laagi dinko kati chahinchha?

Please come with me.
Ma sanghaa aaunuhos.

porter	*kulli, bokne maanche*
load	*bhaari*
heavy	*garungo*
light	*halungo, halaun*
salary	*talaab*
equipment, stuff	*saamaan*
let's go	*jam*
let's rest	*bhaari bisauu*
do you want some tea?	*chiyaa khaane?*

Time And Days

What time is it?	*Kati baajyo?*
It's three o'clock.	*Tin baajyo.*
It's 10:30.	*Saadhe das baajyo.*
today	*aaja*
tomorrow	*bholi*
yesterday	*hijo*
the day after tomorrow (vague future)	*bholi-paarsi*
a while ago (vague past)	*hijo-aasti*
one week	*ek haptaa*
one months	*ek mahinaa*
one year	*ek barsaa*
next week	*aaune haptaa*
last week	*gaaeko haptaa*
last year	*pohor saal*
morning	*bihanaa*
evening	*belukaa*
day	*din*
night	*raat*

eating time	*khaanaa khaane bela*
What day is today?	*Aaja ke baar ho?*
Sunday	*aaitabaar*
Monday	*sombaar*
Tuesday	*mangalbaar*
Wednesday	*budhabaar*
Thursday	*bihibaar*
Friday	*sukrabaar*
Saturday	*sanibaar*

Numbers

These are rendered difficult by the fact there's a different word for each; it's not as systematic as "twenty-five," "thirty-five," etc. Nepali numbers are frequently written in Roman, but the original system appears also. These are the same as Indian numbers, which were the original inspiration for Arabic numerals.

Another trick is adding counting particles onto numbers. Basically there are two particles: *wotaa* for things, *janna* for people. You can't say *tin kalam,* (three pens); you need to say *tin wotaa kalam.* Three people is *tin janna maanchhe.* Often you can drop the noun and just use the particle:

How many are in your party?
Tapaai kati janna hununhunchha?

We're only two.   *Dui janna matraai ho.*

Abbreviations are commonly used for lower numbers. One thing is *eutaa,* two *dui wotaa* or *duitaa,* three *tintaa.* After that add the full particle: *chaar wotaa,* etc.

½	*aada*	17	*satra*
1	*ek*	18	*athara*
2	*dui*	19	*unais*
3	*tin*	20	*bis*
4	*chaar*	25	*pachis*
5	*paanch*	30	*tis*
6	*chha*	40	*chaalis*
7	*saat*	50	*pachaas*
8	*aat*	60	*saathi*
9	*nau*	70	*sattari*
10	*das*	80	*aausi*
11	*eghara*	90	*nabbe*
12	*barha*	100	*(ek) sae*
13	*terha*	20	*dui sae*
14	*chaudra*	1,000	*(ek) hajaar*
15	*pandra*	100,000	*(ek) lakh*
16	*sorha*	10 million	*(ek) crore*

GLOSSARY OF NEPALI AND TIBETAN TERMS

agam—temple to the guardian deity of a family or lineage

ajima—one of the fierce Newar mother goddesses who must be placated with sacrifices to avoid sickness and misfortune

Ashta Mangal—the "Eight Auspicious Symbols," frequently used in Indian and Tibetan designs

Ashta Matrika— the "Eight Mothers," a collection of fierce goddesses representing different aspects of Durga

aushadi—medicine

bahal—former Newari Buddhist monastery complex, now inhabited by families

baksheesh—a tip given in advance to expedite service

bayul, belyul—"hidden valleys" created by Guru Rinpoche to provide refuge for Buddhists in troubled times

Bhagwati—the great goddess Durga

Bhairab—a fierce manifestation of Shiva

bhajan—religious hymns sung by Newar men

bhakku—see *chuba*

bhang—sticks and stems of marijuana, usually brewed into a potent tea

bhanjyang—pass

bhatti—trailside inn serving food and drink

bhoj—a ritual feast

Bhotia—general term for the Tibetan-influenced northern border peoples of Nepal

bodhisattva—a buddha-to-be who has renounced individual enlightenment to help other beings attain liberation

Bön—the old indigenous religion of Tibet, preceding Buddhism

Brahman—the highest Hindu caste

Buddha—a spiritually enlightened being

chaarpi—outdoor toilet

chaitya—a Buddhist monument, a smaller version of a stupa

chang—Tibetan barley beer

charas—hashish

chautaara—trailside resting place with stone supports for porters to rest their loads

Chhetri— the second-highest Hindu caste, like Brahmans considered "twice-born" or ritually pure

chillum—vertical clay pipe for smoking hashish

chorten—the Tibetan version of a stupa, appearing in slightly different styles

chowk—square or courtyard, road intersection

chuba—Tibetan coatlike garment, belted and with long sleeves. Women wear a sleeveless, wraparound variation, tying in the back.

crore—ten million

daal bhaat—the Nepali national dish, boiled rice with lentil sauce and curried vegetables

dakini—female spiritual beings who protect the Buddhist Dharma

danda—a hill or ridge

danphe—Nepal's national bird, the Impeyan pheasant

Dasain—Nepal's biggest holiday, a ten-day festival celebrating Durga's victory over the buffalo demon.

Das Avatara—the ten incarnations of Vishnu, a favorite subject for artists and storytellers

Devanagri—the script used to write Nepali, Hindi, and Sanskrit

dhaka—handmade cloth woven in colorful geometric patterns

dhami—see *jhankri*

dhara—a water tap, anything from a simple spigot to an elaborately carved series of spouts set in a sunken enclosure

dharamsala—a public shelter and resthouse used by travelers and pilgrims, usually an open-sided building

Dharma—the Buddhist faith

dhiro—cooked mush (generally corn), the staple of those who can't afford *daal bhaat*

dokko—a wicker basket used for carrying loads

Durbar Square—the temple-studded plazas opposite the old royal palaces of the Kathmandu Valley's three main cities

Durga—The Great Goddess who appears in many manifestations (Kali, Taleju, the Ashta Matrika, the Kumari), often fierce, to defend good and defeat evil

gaine—wandering minstrels who sing topical ballads and play the four-stringed fiddle (*sarangi*)

gandharva—celestial musicians, companions of Ganesh

Ganesh—the roly-poly elephant-headed god of luck, son of Shiva and Parvati

ganja—marijuana

Garuda—the winged man-bird who serves as Vishnu's mount

Gelug—one of the four main sects of Tibetan Buddhism, this one ruled by the Dalai Lama

gharial— a rare, long-snouted crocodile found in the Terai

ghat—steps lining the banks of sacred rivers, used for laundry, bathing, and cremation

ghee—clarified butter used in Indian cooking (Nepalis call it *ghiu*)

gompa—a Tibetan monastery-temple complex

guire—impolite word for Westerners

Gurkha—regiments of Nepali soldiers in the Indian and British armies, famed for their fighting ability

Guru Rinpoche—Padmasambhava, the 8th-century Indian tantric magician and teacher who established Buddhism in Tibet

gush—a bribe

guthi—informal Newar social organization which fulfills religious and social obligations

haat bazaar—weekly regional markets popular in eastern Nepal

Hanuman—the "Monkey King" appearing in the Hindu epic the *Ramayana*

himaal—snow mountains

hookah—water pipe generally used for smoking a mixture of tobacco and brown sugar

ihi—a Newari rite of passage. Young girls wed the fruit of the bel tree, symbolizing Vishnu, thus avoiding the stigma of widowhood if their human husband dies early

jatra—festival

jhankri—shamanistic healers widely consulted for both physical and mental diseases

jungli—wild, uncouth

jutho—ritually contaminated or impure

Jyapu—Newari peasant subcaste

Kali—the Dark Goddess, wild and terrifying, an emanation of Durga

Kargyö—a sect of Tibetan Buddhism

karma—the Hindu-Buddist principle that what goes around, comes around

ke garne?—"What to do?" Nepal's national saying, recited whenever reality overwhelms one's plans or intentions

khat—a palanquin carried on men's shoulders, used in festivals and celebrations

khatak—Tibetan prayer scarf, a length of white cloth presented at meetings and leave-takings as a token of respect and good intentions

khola—river

khukri—curved Nepali knife

kichkinni—a supernatural being, a beautiful young woman who seduces men and saps their strength

kot—hilltop fort

Krishna—Blue-skinned god of love, one of the ten incarnations of Vishnu

Kumari—a young virgin Buddhist girl worshipped as an embodiment of the Hindu goddess Durga. Of the Valley's 11 Kumari, the most famous is Kathmandu's Royal Kumari.

kund—small lake or pond

la—pass (Tibetan)

lakh—100,000

Lakshmi—the Hindu goddess of wealth and abundance, consort of Vishnu

laligurans—rhododendron, Nepal's national flower

lama—a Tibetan Buddhist spiritual teacher

lekh—a long ridge, generally a spur running off higher mountains

lhakhang—Tibetan Buddhist temple, literally "god's house"

Licchavi—Hindu dynasty which ruled the Valley from 300-879 A.D.

linga—ancient Hindu symbol associated with Shiva, among other things a phallic symbol of masculine generative power

lungi—long piece of printed cotton wrapped around the waist and worn as a skirt

maanaa—unit of volume used to measure grains, cooking oil, etc.—about two cups

machaan—treetop game blind

Machhendranath—"Lord of the Fishes," rainmaking patron deity of the Kathmandu Valley. Buddhist Newars worship him as an emanation of Avalokitesvara, Bodhisattva of Compassion.

Mahabharata—an ancient Hindu epic poem combining philosophy, ethics, and the myth of the great battle between the Pandava brothers and their cousins

mai—one of the "mothers" of Newari religion, generally bloodthirsty nature goddesses, remnants of ancient animistic beliefs

Mithila—belonging to the ancient kingdom of Mithila or Videha, centered around what is now the city of Janakpur in the eastern Terai

makara—a sea serpent of Indian mythology, often depicted spouting jewels and pearls

malla—Hindu prayer beads or rosary

Malla—the medieval dynasty which ruled the Kathmandu Valley from 1220-1768

mandir—temple

mani wall—"prayer" wall made of flat stones carved with mantras, a Tibetan Buddhist tradition

Manjushri—the sword-wielding bodhisattva of wisdom who drained the Valley's waters and opened it for settlement

mantra—mystic formula of Sanskrit syllables, chanted as prayer or to work magic

masan—cremation platform, usually round, found on the banks of sacred rivers

matha—an old Hindu monastery. Like Buddhist *bahal,* they are now inhabited by private individuals and families.

mela—temple fair, a religious celebration held at a temple or holy site

momo—a Tibetan dish, little steamed dumplings usually stuffed with minced meat (fried momo are called *kothe*)

Mughlai—a rich, spicy style of Northern Indian cooking, influenced by Persian cuisine

naan—disc-shaped Indian bread cooked in a tandoori oven, chewy and delicious

naga—serpent deities which dwell underground, guardians of wealth, bringers of water, and senders of illness. Particularly important in the mythology of the Kathmandu Valley.

Nandi—the name of the bull who serves as Shiva's vehicle

Newar—the indigenous people of the Kathmandu Valley

Nyingma—the "old sect" of Tibetan Buddhism, which especially reveres Guru Rinpoche

paisa—generally, money; more specifically, small change

panchayat—a system of "partyless democracy" used in Nepal from 1959 to 1989 and now discredited

Pancha Buddha—the Five Buddhas (also called Jina or Dhyani Buddha), especially important in Newari Buddhism. Each is assigned a particular direction, color, emotion, symbol, etc.; together they symbolize the varied aspects of enlightenment.

paubha—a Newari-style scroll painting (see *thangka*)

pipal—*Ficus religiosa,* a spreading tree with heart-shaped leaves often found shading *chautaara.* It's often called the "Bodhi tree," as it's said to be the tree beneath which the Buddha gained enlightenment.

puja—an act of worship, offerings presented to honor a deity

pujari—priest who tends to a specific deity or temple

Punjabi—woman's garment, a two-piece ensemble of drawstring pants and a long shirt slit up the sides

pukka—proper, real, genuine

raaksi—Nepali firewater, distilled from grain or potatoes

radi—handmade felt carpet

Ramayana—Indian epic tale of the adventures of Rama (an incarnation of Vishnu), whose wife Sita has been abducted by an evil king

Rana—the aristocratic Chhetri family which ruled Nepal for nearly a century, controlling the office of prime minister

rinpoche—literally "precious one," a title of respect used for lamas

rudraksha—the furrowed brown seed of the Eleocarpus tree, used in Hindu rosaries

saddhu—Hindu ascetic or holy man who's renounced family and caste to wander, beg, and pray

sahib—Term of respect used to address Westerners, despite its connotations of the Raj. Pronounced "saab," for women "memsaab."

Sakya—one of the four main sects of Tibetan Buddhism

sal—a hardwood tree found extensively in Nepal

Saraswati—Hindu goddess of speech, music, and learning, often depicted holding a lute and a book

sati—the custom, now banned, that a Hindu wife throw herself on her husband's funeral pyre

Shah—the ruling dynasty of Nepal, descendants of the 18th-century king Prithvi Narayan Shah

shaligram—ammonite fossils embedded in black stones found in the valley of the Kali Gandaki, considered an emblem of Vishnu

sherpa—an assistant trekking worker, called "sherpa" no matter what his ethnic group

shikara—a style of temple consisting of a tapered cigar-shaped tower set over a square shrine

Shiva—the Hindu god ruling over transformation and destruction, a powerful being with many names and forms, including Mahadev (the "Great God") and Pashupatinath, the protector of Nepal. His consort is the beautiful goddess Parvati, who is a pleasant variation of Durga.

shraddha—offerings made to satisfy the spirits of deceased ancestors

siddha—magical powers gained by intensive spiritual practices or asceticism

sindhur—vermilion powder used as a religious offering and to make *tika*

sirdar—leader of a trek or expedition, in charge of organization and logistics

stupa—Buddhist monument based on the form of ancient burial tumuli, a hemispherical mound topped by a conical spire

sukunda—small oil lamp used in worship

tal—lake

Taleju—patron goddess of the Malla Dynasty, a form of Durga

tantra—a mystic philosophy developed in ancient India which has influenced both Hinduism and Buddhism

Tara—benevolent female bodhisattva

tempo—a three-wheeled motor vehicle serving as an inexpensive taxi

Terai—the narrow, fertile strip of land along Nepal's southern border, an extension of India's Gangetic Plain

thaali—a metal plate with compartments for separate dishes

Thakuri—high Chhetri subcaste which includes the royal family and the Ranas

thangka—a Tibetan scroll painting of religious subjects; Newari thangka are called *paubha*

Tharu—aboriginal tribal people, among the original inhabitants of the Terai

thukpa—Tibetan noodle soup

tika—an auspicious mark made on the forehead as part of worship, usually with red powder or *sindhur*

tirtha—Hindu pilgrimage site

tol—neighborhood or quarter

tola—a unit of weight used for precious metals and hashish, approximately 11 grams.

tongba—hot Tibetan beer, made from boiling water poured over fermented mash (usually millet) and sipped through a bamboo straw

topi—hat worn by Nepali men, a brimless, slightly lopsided cloth cap

torana—semicircular tympanum mounted over the doorways and windows of temples, carved or embossed with images of the deity and mythological characters inside

tsampa—a Tibetan staple, roasted barley flour generally eaten mixed with tea

tso—lake

tulku—a reincarnate lama

Tundikhel—the central parade ground found in many Nepali towns

Uma-Mahesvara—Shiva with Parvati on his knee, a favorite theme of sculptors

vahana—the vehicle or mount of a deity

Vishnu—one of the main gods of the Hindu religion, Vishnu the Preserver is benevolent and beneficient, worshipped in ten main incarnations including Narayana, Rama, Krishna. His symbols are the conch, lotus, disc and mace; his consort is Lakshmi; his mount the winged man-bird Garuda.

yaksha—graceful nymph of Hindu mythology popular in Nepali art, especially woodcarving

yatra—pilgrimage

yeti—also known as the "Abominable Snowman," a hairy man-ape said to inhabit Nepal's remote highlands

BOOKLIST

DESCRIPTION AND TRAVEL

Forbes, Duncan. *The Heart of Nepal.* London: Robert Hale, 1962. Well-written account of a visit to Kathmandu and a trek through Helambu and Langtang, interesting for its glimpses of newly opened Nepal.

Gurung, Harka. *Vignettes of Nepal.* Kathmandu: Sajha Prakashan, 1980. A Nepali geographer's account of his travels across Nepal, incorporating history, geography, and culture in lucid English. Great for descriptions of remote regions.

Kasajoo, Vinaya Kumar. *Palpa As You Like It.* Tansen: Kumar Press, 1988. One of the few readable locally produced guides, full of information on obscure Tansen.

Matthiessen, Peter. *The Snow Leopard.* New York: Viking, 1978. Sensitively written account of a journey into Dolpo in pursuit of the elusive snow leopard. Vivid descriptions of the land interwoven with perceptive insights into the mind. A classic.

Murphy, Dervla. *The Waiting Land.* London: John Murray, 1967. Well-written as always, this is the adventurous Irishwoman's account of working in a Tibetan refugee camp (in Pokhara) in 1965. The descriptions and insights still apply.

Snellgrove, David. *Himalayan Pilgrimage: a Study of Tibetan Religion by a Traveller through Western Nepal.* Oxford, Bruno Cassirer, 1961. A Buddhist scholar's 1956 journey through Dolpo, the Kali Gandaki, and Manang, this book mixes anecdotes and observations, permeated with dry humor. In the process, it painlessly teaches a lot about technical Buddhism.

Tucci, Giuseppe. *Journey to Mustang.* Kathmandu: Ratna Pustak Bhandar, 1977. Local reprint of the Italian Tibetologist's account of his 1952 journey up the Kali Gandaki into Mustang, his practiced eye deciphering history and culture along the way. Fascinating reading for the trek to Muktinath.

van Gruisen, Lisa, ed. *Nepal Insight Guide.* Hong Kong: Apa Publications, 1991. A lavishly illustrated all-Nepal guidebook; Apa's *Kathmandu Insight City Guide* (1990) covers the Valley in more detail.

POP NEPAL

Greenwald, Jeff. *Shopping for Buddhas.* San Francisco: Harper & Row, 1990. Western consumers in hot pursuit of spirituality, a sometimes edifying, often funny look.

Iyer, Pico. *Video Night in Kathmandu: and Other Reports from the Not-so-far East.* New York: Alfred A. Knopf, 1988. A look at the East-meets-West clashes along the world travel circuit, with a single chapter (one of the more superficial) on Kathmandu. Weak on content, but slickly readable.

Robinson, Kim Stanley. *Escape From Kathmandu.* London: Unwin Hyman Ltd., 1990. An amusing romp through clichés, as the heroes rescue yetis, save a hidden valley, and climb Everest with a mountaineering lama.

COFFEE-TABLE BOOKS

Hagen, Toni. *Nepal—the Kingdom in the Himalayas.* Bern: Kummerley and Frey, 1980. The first photo book on Nepal, by a Swiss geologist who walked 14,000 km across the country in the 1950s. Especially interesting for the text, which has a unique perspective.

Kelly, Thomas L., and Patricia Roberts. *Kathmandu: City on the Edge of the World.* New York: Abbeville Press, 1988. An insider's look at the intricate patterns and cultures of the Valley.

Kelly, Thomas L., and V. Carroll Dunham. *The Hidden Himalaya.* New York: Abbeville Press, 1987. A loving, detailed examination of life in the remote Humla region.

Lloyd, Ian, and Wendy Moore. *Kathmandu: The Forbidden Valley.* New Delhi: Times Books International, 1990. One of the best-written and -photographed of the large-format books; among the lowest-priced, too.

Valli, Eric, and Diane Summers. *Dolpo: Hidden Land of the Himalayas.* New York: Aperture Foundation, 1987. An inside look at the Dolpo-pa, whose lives revolve around "Buddhism, barley, yaks, and barter."

ETHNIC GROUPS AND CULTURES

Bennett, Lynn. *Dangerous Wives and Sacred Sisters: Social and Symbolic Roles of High-caste Women in Nepal.* New York: Columbia University Press, 1983. An exploration of the lives of Brahman/Chhetri women in a central Nepal village, revealing the frequent conflicts of traditional family life.

Chorlton, Windsor. *Cloud-dwellers of the Himalayas: the Bhotia.* Amsterdam: Time-Life Books, 1982. Excellent photo essays and chapters documenting life in the remote region of Nar-Phu, north of Manang; applies to many Bhotia peoples.

Coburn, Broughton. *Nepali Aama: Portrait of a Nepalese Hill Woman.* Chico, CA: Moon Publications 1990. Black-and-white photos of the life of an old and very spunky Gurung woman, combined with quotes from Vishnu Maya herself, provide rare insights into a Nepali life.

Downs, Hugh R. *Rhythms of a Himalayan Village.* New York: Harper and Row, 1980. A sensitive evocation of Sherpa life in Junbesi, expressed through black-and-white photos, narrative, and masterfully selected quotes.

Fisher, James. *Sherpas: Reflections on Change in Himalayan Nepal.* New Delhi: Oxford University Press, 1990. Insightful observations on changing Sherpa society over the decades (the author's first visit to Khumbu was in 1964). Excellent, amusing section on how Sherpas and Westerners view one another.

Macfarlane, Alan, and Indra Bahadur Gurung. *Gurungs of Nepal.* Kathmandu: Ratna Pustak Bhandar, 1990. Slim but comprehensive volume detailing modern Gurung life; good reading for the Annapurna region.

Nepali, Gopal Singh. *The Newars.* Bombay: United Asia Publications, 1965. The standard account of Newar culture.

Peissel, Michel. *Mustang: a Lost Tibetan Kingdom.* London: Collins and Harvill Press, 1968. Well-written account by a Tibetan-speaking French adventurer who visited this restricted region in 1964.

Shepherd, Gary. *Life Among the Magars.* Kathmandu: Sahayogi Press, 1982. Personal account from a linguist who lived with his family in a northwestern Nepal village for 12 years.

Tucci, Giuseppe. *Tibet, Land of Snows.* London: Elek Books, 1967. Good survey of Tibetan traditions and religion, which also permeate northern Nepal.

von Fürer-Haimendorf, Christoph. *Himalayan Traders.* London: John Murray, 1975. Examination of Bhotia trading communities across Nepal and how their lives have changed.

LANGUAGE

Clark, T.W. *Introduction to Nepali.* Kathmandu: Ratna Pustak Bhandar, 1989. Comprehensive survey of the language, with lots of good sample sentences.

Karki, Tika B., and Chij Shrestha. *Basic Course in Spoken Nepali.* Kathmandu. Basic lessons on various aspects of Nepali using the situational approach (you really need someone to drill you).

Matthews, David L. *A Course In Nepali.* London: School of Oriental and African Studies, 1984. As comprehensive as Clark's book, but later lessons are in Devanagri.

Meerdonk, M. *Basic Gurkhali Dictionary.* Singapore: Straits Times Press, 1959. Over 16,000 English-Nepali and Nepali-English definitions crammed into a pocket-sized book.

HISTORY AND CULTURE

Anderson, Mary M. *The Festivals of Nepal.* Calcutta: Rupa & Co., 1988. The standard compendium of the Kathmandu Valley's multitude of festivals; highly readable.

Avedon, John. *In Exile From the Land of Snows.* New York: Alfred A. Knopf, 1984. An extremely moving story of Tibetan refugees in exile, dealing mostly with settlements in India, but providing essential background for anyone interested in Tibetans in Nepal.

Brown, Percy. *Picturesque Nepal.* New Delhi: Today & Tomorrow's Printers, 1984. Reprint of the 1912 work by an art historian; quaint by now, but some pertinent observations on Valley culture.

Farwell, Byron. *The Gurkhas.* London: Allen Lane, 1984. From the 1815 skirmish with the British to the Falkland Islands, the story of the Gurkhas, the "world's best infantrymen."

Landon, Percival. *Nepal.* London: Constable, 1928. Reprinted by Ratna Pustak Bhandar, these two volumes contain a thorough run-down of the Valley's history, marred only by obsequious praise of the Rana Maharaja who commissioned the work.

Oldfield, H. Ambrose. *Sketches from Nepal.* New Delhi: Cosmo Publications, 1974. Reprint of the 1874 observations of a British Residency surgeon: elephant hunting with Jung Bahadur and titbits on Valley customs and religion.

Slusser, Mary Sheperd. *Nepal Mandala: A Cultural Study of the Kathmandu Valley.* Princeton: Princeton University Press, 1982. At Rs4,000 for the two-volume set (plates and text), few will take this home, but it's an extremely detailed and readable study of the complex world of the Valley's Newars, interweaving art, architecture, religion, and history.

Smith, Warren W., ed., and Mana Bajra Bajracharaya, trans. *Swayambhu Purana: Mythological History of the Nepal Valley.* Kathmandu: 1978. Well-rendered version of the classic 16th-century text relating the Buddhist myth of the Valley's origin.

Stiller, Ludwig F. *The Rise of the House of Gorkha.* Kathmandu: Ratna Pustak Bhandar, 1973. One of many scholarly accounts produced by Jesuits in Nepal, this one is a readable story of Prithvi Narayan Shah's rise to power.

Whelpton, John. *Jang Bahadur in Europe.* Kathmandu: Sahayogi Press, 1983. An entertaining account of the Nepalese Prime Minister's 1850 visit to England and France, including a translation of a narrative written by one of his party.

Wright, Daniel, ed. *Vamsavali: History of Nepal, with an Introductory Sketch of the Country and People of Nepal.* Cambridge: University Press, 1877. Reprinted locally, this is a translation and commentary on the historical chronicles, the traditional history of the Kathmandu Valley.

DEVELOPMENT AND POLITICS

Bista, Dor Bahadur. *Fatalism and Development: Nepal's Struggle for Modernisation.* Madras: Longman, 1990. Astute examination of how caste hierarchy and a fatalistic attitude (among other factors) hamper development in Nepal, by a respected Chhetri anthropologist.

Blaikie, Piers; Blaikie, Piers, John Cameron, and David Seddon. *Nepal in Crisis.* New Delhi: Oxford University Press, 1980. Taking the construction of roads as a starting point, the authors examine the complex problems of "development" in Nepal. Heavy-duty but interesting.

Pye-Smith, Charlie. *Travels in Nepal.* London: Aurum Press, 1988. Combining travel writing with analyses of foreign-aid projects, this book is a palatable way to dive into development issues and myths. The author examines little-known subjects like outcastes, the poverty-stricken Chepangs, and the possibility that Nepal *isn't* sliding into the ocean (from erosion) after all.

Shah, Rishikesh. *Politics in Nepal: 1980-1990.* Kathmandu: Ratna Pustak Bhandar, 1990. Essays on the contemporary political scene, an updated edition of a formerly banned book. Good summary of the 1989 democracy movement.

Tutig, Ludmilla, and Kunda Dixit, eds. *Bikas/Binas: Development-Destruction.* Kathmandu: Ratna Book Distributors, 1986. A readable compendium of articles on environmental and cultural issues in the Himalaya, focusing mainly on Nepal. Examines the links betweeen ecology, development, and tourism, and deals with cultural as well as environmental pollution.

ART, CRAFTS, AND ARCHITECTURE

Aran, Lydia. *The Art of Nepal.* Kathmandu: Sayahogi Prakashan, 1978. Remarkably relevant study of Nepalese art focusing on the Kathmandu Valley and doubling as a study of religion.

Bernier, Ronald. *The Nepalese Pagoda—Origins and Style.* New Delhi: S. Chand, 1979. Scholarly yet readable unveiling of the complex symbolism of the pagoda; adds much depth to Valley sightseeing.

Gajurel, C.L., and K. K. Vaidya. *Traditional Arts and Crafts of Nepal.* New Delhi: S. Chand and Co. Ltd., 1984. Details the production techniques of arts and crafts: metalworking, brickmaking, weaving, and dyeing, paper—even food. Well-organized and written.

Kuloy, H. K. *Tibetan Rugs.* Bangkok: White Orchid Press, 1982. Over 260 color illustrations of antique rugs, with commentary.

Macdonald, Alexander W., and Anne Vergati Stahl. *Newar Art: Nepalese during the Malla Period.* New Delhi: Vikas, 1979. Architecture and paintings of the Kathmandu Valley examined in the context of classical Newari culture.

Oriental Rug Review. 9.4 (April/May 1989). An entire issue devoted to Tibetan carpets, essential in educating oneself in the business of collecting.

Pal, Pratapaditya. *Art of Nepal.* Los Angeles/Berkeley: Los Angeles County Museum of Art/University of California Press, 1985. A lovely collection of sculpture and paintings (with descriptions) from the Los Angeles County Museum.

RELIGION

Anderson, Walt. *Open Secrets: A Western Guide to Tibetan Buddhism.* New York: Viking, 1979. An accessible introductory book to Tibetan Buddhism, placing it in modern terms.

Bernbaum, Edward. *The Way to Shambhala.* Garden City: NY: Anchor Books/Doubleday, 1980. A fascinating account of the Tibetan tradition of "hidden valleys," and a good explanation of the many levels of Tibetan Buddhism.

Locke, John K. *Karunamaya.* Kathmandu: Sahayogi Prakshan, 1980. A scholarly yet readable study of the complex cult of Machhendranath, with many insights into Newari Buddhism.

O'Flaherty, Wendy Doniger, ed. *Hindu Myths.* New York: Viking Penguin, 1975. Introductions to the major gods in their many moods, a good way to soak up the riches of the Hindu pantheon.

Sen, K.M. *Hinduism.* London: Penguin, 1961. Standard overview of the social and historical development of Hinduism.

NATURAL HISTORY

Cameron, Ian. *Mountains of the Gods.* London: Century, 1984. An interesting illustrated survey of the entire Himalaya: history, geology, ecology, peoples.

Fleming, Robert L. Sr., Robert L. Fleming Jr., and Lain Singh Bangdel. *Birds of Nepal.* Kathmandu: Nature Himalayas, 1976. This masterpiece illustrates over 1,000 individuals of 753 species in color, with descriptions on facing pages for easy identification. Fun even if you aren't a birdwatcher.

Fleming, Robert L. Sr. *The General Ecology, Flora, and Fauna of Midland Nepal.* Kathmandu: Tribhuvan University Press, 1977. A thorough overview of the environment of Nepal's Hills, with an emphasis on the Kathmandu Valley.

Gurung, K. K. *Heart of the Jungle: The Wildlife of Chitwan Nepal.* London: Andre Deutsch, 1983. An extremely well-written account of the natural history of Chitwan National Park.

Hillard, Darla. *Vanishing Tracks: Four Years among the Snow Leopards of Nepal.* London: Elm Tree Books, 1989. How a San Francisco secretary spent four seasons in remote northern Nepal tracking the snow leopard. Enjoyable descriptions of the Himalayan mountain environment and the local Bhotia people, in their own way an endangered species as well.

MOUNTAINEERING

Herzog, Maurice. *Annapurna.* London: Jonathan Cape, 1952. The classic account of the conquest of the first 8,000-meter peak, told with enormous dignity (Herzog dictated the book from a hospital bed where he was recovering from frostbite that claimed most of his fingers and toes). A gripping story that captures the essence of mountaineering.

Hornbein, Thomas F. *Everest: The West Ridge.* Seattle: The Mountaineers, 1980. This account from the gigantic 1963 American Expedition rises far above the usual mountaineering saga, matching exquisite photos with meditative quotes.

Tilman, H.W. *The Seven Mountain-Travel Books.* Seattle: The Mountaineers, 1983. Only *Nepal Himalaya* deals directly with Nepal (the first reconnaissance of the Langtang, Annapurna, and Everest regions), but 886 pages of wry humor by the best expedition writer ever will have you rolling on the floor.

TREKKING GUIDES

Armington, Stan. *Trekking in the Nepal Himalaya.* Victoria, Australia: Lonely Planet, 1982. While it leans toward group trekking, there's a lot of practical information—the author has been in the business for 20 years.

Bezruchka, Stephen. *A Guide To Trekking in Nepal.* Seattle: The Mountaineers, 1985. The standard guide, a masterpiece of extremely detailed trail descriptions covering all major regions and a few minor ones. Thorough and sincere, with appendices on cultural and natural history.

Nakano, Toru. *Trekking in Nepal.* Union City, California: Heian International, 1985. Popular for its stunning photos, but text is marred by poor translation.

O'Connor, Bill. *The Trekking Peaks of Nepal.* Ramsbury, Marlborough: The Crowood Press, 1988. Descriptions of all 18 peaks, including trekking approaches and climbing routes.

Swift, Hugh. *Trekking in Nepal, West Tibet and Bhutan.* San Francisco: Sierra Club, 1990. The opposite of Bezruchka's hour-by-hour trail descriptions, Swift's enjoyable approach is to take a broad overview, leaving you to discover the details yourself. Great coverage of remote regions.

Wilkerson, James A. *Medicine for Mountaineering.* Seattle: The Mountaineers, 1985. The best medical book for trekking, detailed yet simple enough for laymen (but a bit bulky to carry around).

INDEX

Page numbers in **boldface** indicate the primary reference; numbers in *italics* indicate information in maps, charts, callouts, or illustrations.

A

accommodations: 108-112; camping 110-111; long-term 109-118; trekking 109-112; urban 108-109; *see also* practicalities, specific destination
Adinath Lokeswar Mandir (Chobhar): 246
Agni: 66
agriculture: 42-43
airlines: domestic 149, **150-151**; international 140-142, 143
airports/airstrips: Jufal 348; Nagdhunga 282; Sanfebagar 347; Tribhuvan International 140, *141;* Tumlingtar 354
altitude sickness: *127-128; see also* health
American Library: 134
Amitabha (Swayambhunath): 189
Anglo-Nepal War: 34
antiques: 97-98; *see also* art, crafts
architecture: 82-83, 160; *see also* art
Arniko Rajmarg: 264-265
art: 76-88, *87,* 161-162; architecture 82-83; Buddhist wall paintings *199;* galleries 82; painting 79-82; sculpture 77-79; shopping for 79, 80; temples 83-88; woodcarving 84-85
Aryaghat (Pashupatinath): 194
Asan Tol (Kathmandu): 181-182
Ashoka: 30
Ashok Binayak (Kathmandu): 170
Ashta Matrika: 67
Asura Cave (Pharping): 248

B

Bagh Bazaar (Kathmandu): 175
Bagh Bhairab: 244-246
Bagmati River : 163, 186
Bahadur Bhawan (Kathmandu): 178
bahal: 86; *see also* temples
Bahun: 49
Balaju (Kathmandu): 167, 237-

238
Banepa: 258
Bangemudha Tol (Kathmandu): 183-184
banks: 122; *see also* money
bargaining: 122
Barpak: 351
Basantapur (Kathmandu): 168-170; Tower 179
Bead Bazaar (Kathmandu): 92, 179; *see also* crafts
begging: 104-105
Bernier, Ronald: *86*
Bhadrakali Mandir (Kathmandu): 175
Bhagwati: 66
Bhairab: 66
Bhaktapur: 157, 158-159, 163 **223-234,** *224-225;* accommodations 233; Durbar Square 226-229; food 233; getting there 234; history 223-226; shopping 233-234; Tachapal Tol 231-232; Taumadhi Tol 229-230; vicinity of 232-233
Bhaktapur Tower (Kathmandu): 172
Bhatterai, K.P.: 39
Bhimsen: 66
Bhimsen Mandir (Bhaktapur): 231; Patan 215
bicycles/bicycling: 152, 212; mountain biking *153*
birds: *24 see also* fauna
Birendra, King: 37, 39, 41
Bisket Jatra: 71; *see also* festivals
Bode: 233
Bodhisattva Manjushri: 159
bodhisattvas: 69
bookstores: 135; *see also* communications
Boudhanath: 195-200, *197;* nearby sights 197-198; practicalities 198
Brahmans: *see* Bahun
Brahmayani Mandir (Panauti): 262
Brass and Bronze Museum (Bhaktapur): 231

British Council Library (Kathmandu): 143, 178
British Cultural Center (Kathmandu): 209
British Resident: 34, 186
Brown, Percy: *158, 186*
Buddha Akshobhya (Swayambhunath): 188
Buddha Jayanti: 72; *see also* festivals
Buddhism: 60-61, 68-69, 190, *199,* 209; ritual dance 100-101; wall paintings *199; see also* religion
Budhanilkantha: 239-240; getting there 240
buffalo, water: 21, *22; see also* fauna
Bungamati: 249-250
Burang Banjyang Pass: 251
Bus Park (Kathmandu): 175
bus travel: 147-148; *see also* transportation
Butwal: 288

C

calendar, Nepali: 70
Campus of International Language (Kathmandu): 209
carpets, Tibetan: 94-96, *95;* shopping for 96
car rentals: 149, 211-212; *see also* transportation
caste system: 48
Chaar Narayan Mandir (Patan): 217
Chabahil (Kathmandu): 198
chaitya: 86; *see also* temples
Cham dance: 100
Champadevi: 247
Chandesvari Mandir (Banepa): 259
chang: 115
Changu Narayan: 253-254, *254;* getting there 253; hikes 254
chantaara: 19
Chapagaon: 250-251
Chhetri caste: 49
Chilamchu Stupa: 244

Chitwan National Park: 23, 28
Chobhar: 246-247; gorge 246
Chusya Bahal (Kathmandu): 185
Chyasalin Mandap (Bhaktapur): 228
Chyasin Dega (Patan): 217
CIWEC clinic: 130; *see also* medical services
climate: 17-18; average monthly temperatures *18;* Kathmandu Valley 157; monsoons *16-17;* seasons 17-18
clothing: traditional Nepali 52-54; *see also* textiles
communications: 131-132, 134-135; bookstores 135; computers 132-133; mail 131-132; newspapers and magazines 134; radio and television 135; telecommunications 132
computers: 132-133
conduct: 46, **102-108;** customs 51-54; eating 106; family life 54-57; gompa etiquette 197-298
cows: *22,* 23; *see also* fauna
crafts: 88-98; antiques 97-98; carpets 94-96; exporting 89; jewelry 90-92; metalware 89-90; shopping for 88; textiles 92-94
credit cards: *see* money
customs: 118-119

D
Dakshinkali: 248-249; *249*
Damai caste: 50
dance: *74,* **99-101;** Cham 100; Mani Rimdu 100; masked dancers *74;* performances 101
Dasain: 73; *see also* festivals
Dattatreya Mandir (Bhaktapur): 231
deforestation: 26; *see also* environment
Degu Taleju Mandir (Kathmandu): 171
Deopatan (Kathmandu): 194
Department of Archaeology: 119
Deshu Maru Jhya (Kathmandu): 182
Dharma Shringa Nepal Vipassana Centre: 209
Dhorpatan Hunting Reserve: 29
Dhulikhel: 259-261, *258, 260;* getting there 261; outings 260-262; practicalities 260

Dilli Bazaar (Kathmandu): 175
Durbar Marg (Kathmandu): 175-177
Durbar Square (Bhaktapur): 226-229
Durbar Square (Kathmandu): 168-174; *169;* old royal palace 171-174; Taleju Mandir 174
Durbar Square (Patan): 215-218, *216*
Durga: 66

E
East-West Highway: 263
economy: 41-46; agriculture 42-43; tourism 45-46; trade 43-44
Egerton, Francis: *157*
electricity: 133
embassies: Nepalese *117;* foreign 118-119, *119*
energy: 44; *see also* environment
environment: 26-29, 161; deforestation 26; erosion 26-27; litter 27; national parks and preserves 27-29; pollution 27
Experiment in International Living: 60, 208

F
fauna: 21-25; birds 24; cows *22,* 23; leeches 24-25; livestock 21; monkeys 23; wildlife 23-25; yaks 21-23
fax: 132
festivals: 70-75; masked dancers *74; see also* specific festival
Five Buddhas (Swayambhunath): 189
flora: 19-21; flowers 20; forests 19-20; ganja 20-21; Phulchowki 243-244; pipal trees *19;* plants and flowers 20; sal trees 19
flowers: 20; *see also* flora
folk beliefs: 63
food: 112-116; *chang* (recipe) 115; eating out 115-116; etiquette 106; groceries 207; liquor 115; precautions 125; produce 114-115; snacks 113; *see also* practicalites, specific destination
foreign aid: 44; *see also* economy; Annapurna Conservation Area Project
forests: *see* trees
fortune-telling: 208
Freak Street (Kathmandu): 170

French Cultural Center: 209
frostbite: 128

G
Gai Jatra: 72; *see also* festivals
gaine: 99; *see also* music
galleries, art: 82
Ganesh: 66
Ganesh Himal: 351
Ganga Sagar (Janakpur): 308
ganja: 20-21; *see also* flora
Ganja La: 341
gems: *see* jewelry
General Post Office (Kathmandu): 131-132
geology: 16-17; *see also* land
Ghachowk: 278
Ghandruk: 278, 328
Ghan Pokhari: 323, 349
Gharial Breeding Center: 299
Ghat: 334
Ghodepani: 320
Ghode Tabela: 342-343
Ghorbanda: 286
Ghorkas: 33-34
ghosts: 63; *see also* folk beliefs, religion
Godavari: 241-243
Godavari Kunda: 243
Goethe Institute: 209
Gokarna: 251
Gokarna Jungle Resort: 253
Gokarna MahaDev: 251
Gokyo: 336
Golden Gate of Bhaktapur: 227
Goli Gompa: 330
Gorakhnath Cave (Gorkha): 268
Gorak Shep: 336
Gorkha: 33, **267-269,** *267,* 349; Bazaar 267; Durbar Square 267-268; getting there 269; history 267; practicalities 269; vicinity of 268-269
Gorkha Bazaar: 267
Gosainkund: 339, 340, *339;* 341-342
government: 39-41; constitution 40; foreign policy 41; political parties 40; royal family 41
Gufa Pokhari: 353
Gunla: 72; *see also* festivals
Gunsa (Tibet): 353
Gurchi Lagna: 347
Gurkhas: *38,* 48, 267
Gurung people: 50-51, 270
guthi system: 30, *159*
Gyaru: 324

H
Haatiban Resort (Champadevi): 247
Haka Bahal (Patan): 221-222
Hanuman Dhoka (Kathmandu): 168, 171
Hanumante River: 157
Hari Shankara Mandir (Patan): 217
health: 123-130; altitude sickness *127-128;* food 125; gastrointestinal illnesses 125-126; immunizations 124-125; jungle safety 297; medical treatment 129-130; prevention 124-125; treating water 125
Helambu *339,* 340-341, 351
Hetauda: 266
Hills, the: 14, ethnic groups 50-51; wildlife 23-24
Himalaya: 14-16, *15,* 19, 235-236, 270; mountain flight skyline *150-151;* wildlife 23-24
Himalayan Yogic Institute: 209
Hinduism: 60-61, 65-67, 192-193; caste groups 49-50
history: 29-39; Anglo-Nepal War 34; Bhaktapur 223-226; Chitwan National Park 295-297; Kathmandu Valley 157-160; Kirati 30; Land Act of 1964 43; Lumbini 288-289; Malla Dynasty 31-33; modern Nepal 37-39; Patan 213-214; Pokhara 270-272; prehistory 29; Rana Era 34-37; Transitional Period 31; unification 33-34
Holi: 75; *see also* festivals
Hongu: 354
Hongu Valley: 338
Hooker, Joseph: *14*
hospitals: 129-130; *see also* health
houses (Newari): 160
hunting: *296*
hyperthermia: 129
hypothermia: 128

I
Ichangu Narayan: 237
Ikhu Narayan Mandir (Kathmandu): 184
Ilam: 354
Imja Valley: 336-337
immigration offices: 118
immunizations: 124
incense: 97; *see also* crafts
India: 142, 143-144

Indigo Gallery: 82
Indra: 66
Indra Chowk (Kathmandu): 179
Indra Jatra: 73; *see also* festivals
Indresvar Mahadev (Panauti): 262
information: 134-136; books and bookstores 135; Department of Tourism 134; maps 135-136; news media 134-135
International Buddhist Library (Swayambhunath): 190
Island Peak: *316,* 338
Isle Machan: 298
Itum Bahal (Kathmandu): 183

J
Jagannath Mandir (Kathmandu): 173
Jaleshwar: 308
Jaljala Pass: 349
Jaljale Himal: 353
Jal Vinayak (Chobhar): 246-247
Jamchen Yiggha Choling (Boudhanath): 197
jana andolin (people's movement): 40
Jana Bahal (Kathmandu): 180
Janai Purnima: 72; *see also* festivals
Janaki Mandir (Janakpur): 307-308
Janakpur: 306-308, *307;* getting there 308; practicalities 308
Jaya Bagesvari (Kathmandu): 193
jewelry: 90-92; bead bazaar 92; buying gems 91; traditional 91-92
Jhankri: 64; *see also* folk beliefs
Jharkot: 321
Jiri: 331-332
Jomosom: 321
Jorpati: 251
Jorsale: 334
Jubing: 333
Jufal airstrip: 348
Jugal Himal: 351
Jumla: 345, 351
Junbesi: 331-332; Gompa 332
Jung Bahadur: 34-36

K
Kaalo Himal: 34
Kagbeni: 321
Kagmara Pass: 348
Kahun Danda: 275
Kaiser Library (Kathmandu): 178, 209
Kaiser Mahal (Kathmandu): 178

Kakani: 239
Kakarbhitta: 354
Kala-Mandapa: 101
Kala Pattar: 336
Kali: 66-67
Kali Gandaki River: 302, 317, 318
Kalimati Clinic: 130; *see also* medical services
Kalmochan (Kathmandu): 185
Kamal Binayak: 232
Kami caste: 50
Kangchenjunga: 353
Kanti Path (Kathmandu): 177-178
Kargyö Gompa: 324
Karikhola: 333
Kasara Durbar (Sauruha): 299
Kasi Biswanath (Bhaktapur): 230
Kaski: 275, 319
Kasthamandap (Kathmandu): 170
Kathesimbhu (Kathmandu): 184
Kathmandu: 157, 163-212, *164-165;* accommodations 200-203; backstreets 182-185; Boudhanath 195-200; Durbar Square 168-174; entertainment 207-208; food 203-207; getting around 21-212; New Town 175-178; Old City 179-186; recreation 208; Swayambhunath 187-190; tours 212; work and study opportunities 208-209
Kathmandu Physical Fitness Centre: 208
Kathmandu-Pokhara Road: *283*
Kathmandu Valley: 155-162, *156;* Bhaktapur 223-234; changing times 160-162; climate 157; east of Kathmandu 251-262, *252;* history 157-160; Kathmandu 163-212; land 155-157; northern treks 339-354; north of Kathmandu 237-241, *237;* old cities 158-160; Patan 213-222; south of Kathmandu 241-251
Kathmandu Western Buddhist Center: 209
Kenja: 332
Khanchok Bhanjyang: 269
Khandbhari: 354
Khangsar: 325
Khaptad Baba: 347
Khaptad Daha: 347
Khaptad Lekh: 347-348
Khaptad National Park: 28-29; 347-348
Kharte: 354

Khasa (Tibet): 265
Khembalung Caves: 354
Khumbeshwar (Patan): 218-219
Khumbu: 333-338, 333
Khumjung: 335
Khunde: 335
Kilgal Tol (Kathmandu): 183
King Tribhuvan Memorial Park: 265
Kirati: 30
Kirati Limbu people: 51
Kirati Rai people: 51
Kirtipur: 244-246, 245
Kirtipur Tower (Kathmandu): 172
Kodari: 264
Kokana: 249-250
Kopan Monastery: 200, 209
Koshi Tappu Wildlife Reserve: 29, 303
Kot Massacre: 34
Kotoje: 324
Krishna: 66
Krishna Jayanti: 72; see also festivals
Krishna Mandir: Kathmandu 173; Patan 216
Kumari: 67
Kumari Bahal (Kathmandu): 170
Kumari Jatra: 73; see also festivals
Kumbeshwar Mahadev Mandir: 61, 218
Kusaha: 303
Kwa Bahal (Patan): 219-220
Kwangde: 316
Kyangjin Gompa (Langtang): 343

L
Labrak: 351
Lake Rara National Park: 28, 111
Lakeside: 269, 273, 279; accommodations 278-280; food 281
Lakshmi: 66
Lalitpur Tower (Kathmandu): 172
Lami Tal: 299
Lamjura Pass: 332
Land Act of 1964: 43
land: 11, 12-18, 12, 14, 42; borders 13; Chitwan National Park 293; geology 16-17; Kathmandu Valley 155-157; Land Act of 1964 43; Pokhara 270; reform 42-43; rivers 16-17; three regions 13-16
Landon, Percival: 217 342, 343
Langtang National Park: 28

language: 58-60; books and courses 60, 363; phrases and vocabulary 355-359
Lapsang La: 353
Larkya La: 351
Laurebina: 341
leeches: 24-25; see also fauna
Lele Valley: 251
Lhachowk: 278
libraries (Kathmandu): 209
Licchavi Dynasty: 30, 48, 60, 158
Lissanevich, Boris: 203
livestock: 21; see also fauna
Lobuche: 336
Lohan Chowk (Kathmandu): 172
Lokhada: 347
Losar: 75; see also festivals
Lothar: 300
Lower Arun River: 305
Lukla: 330, 334
Lumbini: 288-292, 289; getting there 292; history 288-290; Master Plan 289-290; practicalities 291-292; sights 290-291;
Lumle: 319
Lumsum: 349

M
Machhapuchhare: 272; Base Camp: 327-328
Machhendranath: 60, 180, 221, 250
Magar people: 51
magazines: 134
Mahabuddha (Patan): 220
Mahakala Mandir (Kathmandu): 178
Mahankhal: 341
Mahendra Gufa: 276
Mahendra, King: 37
Mahendranagar: 304
Mahendra Phul (Pokhara): 273, 274
mail: 131-132; see also information; services
Main Bazaar (Bhaktapur): 230
Maithili people: 50
Maju Deval Mandir (Kathmandu): 170-171
Makalu-Barun National Park: 353
Makalu Base Camp: 353-354
malaria: 14, 19; see also health
Malemchigaon: 340-341
Malla Dynasty: 31-33, 158
Malla, Jayasthiti: 48
Malla, Jyoti: 32
Malla, Pratapa: 32, 168, 171

Malla, Yaksha: 32
Manakamana: 269
Manang: 323-325
Manangi Gompa: 277
Manaslu: 351
Manga Hiti (Patan): 218
Mangal Bazaar (Patan): 217
Manichaur (Sankhu): 255
Manidingma: see Nuntala
Mani Rimdu: 100; see also dance
Manohara River: 157
mantras: 64
maps: 135; see also communications
marijuana: see ganja
Marpha: 321
Martyrs' Gate (Kathmandu): 175-176
masked dancers: 74; see also dance
Mayadevi Mandir (Lumbini): 290
medical services: 129-130; see also health
Mera La: 316, 354
metalware 78-79, 89-90; see also art; crafts
Micha: 347
Milke Danda: 353
Minnath Mandir (Patan): 220-221
Mithila painting: 81-82
money: 120-123; banks 122; bargaining 122-123; changing 121-123; value 120
monkeys: 23,24; see also fauna
monsoons: 16-17; see also climate
Moreni: 349
motorcycles (rental): 149; see also transportation
mountain biking: 153; see also bicycles/bicycling
mountains: see Himalaya
Mrigasthali: 195
mudras: 65
Mugling: 266
Muktinath: 318, 321-322
Mul Chowk (Kathmandu): 172
Mulkharkha: 251
Munche: 354
Murphy, Dervla: 317
music: 98-99
Mustang: 321
Musya Bahal (Kathmandu): 185

N
Nagapur (Swayambhunath): 190
Nagarjun: 238

Nagarkot: 255-257, *256;*
accommodations 256-257;
getting there 257
Nagdesh: 233
Nagdhunga airstrip: 282
Nala: 259
Namche Bazaar: 329, 334
Namobuddha: 261
Nangpa La Pass: 338
Naradevi Mandir (Kathmandu):
182
Narayanghat: 302
Narayanhiti Palace (Kathmandu):
175
Narayani River: 293
Narayan Mandir (Kathmandu):
175
Nar-Phu: 324
Nassal Chowk (Kathmandu): 172
National Art Gallery (Bhaktapur):
226
National Museum (Kathmandu):
166-167
National Panchayat: 37, 39
national parks and preserves: **27-
29;** *see also* land; specific park
Natural History Museum
(Kathmandu): 167
Naubise: 266
Naudanda: 275, 319
Navadurga: 67
Navadurga Adam: 231-232
Nepalganj: 303-304
Nepali Congress Party: 40
Nepali language: 58-60; *see also*
language
Nepali National Congress Party:
37
Nepal International Clinic: 130
Nepal Mountaineering
Association: *316*
Newar people: 50, 158
New Road (Kathmandu): 178
newspapers: 134; *see also*
communications
New Town (Kathmandu): 175-
178, *176*
Ngawal: 324
Ngowur: 330
Ngozumba Glacier: 336
Nilvarahi: 233
Num: 354
Numbur: 332
Nuntala: 333
Nuwakot: 278, 349
Nyatapola Mandir (Bhaktapur):
230
Nyeshang: *see* Manang

O
October Gallery: 82
Old Bazaar (Kathmandu): 179-
182, *179*
Old City (Kathmandu): 179-186
Old Royal Palace (Patan): 217
Ongre: 323, 324

P
packing 136-140, *138;* for treks
137-140
pagodas: 83-84, *87; see also*
temples
painting: 79-82, *87;* see also art
Palace of Fifty-five Windows
(Bhaktapur): 227-228
palaces: 83, 178
Palanchowk: 262
Paljor Ling: 276
Palpa Bhairab Mandir: 286
Palung Valley: 266
Panauti: 262
Panchasse Lekh: 278
panchayat system: 37, 39
Panchbhaiya Danda: 276
Panch Pokhari: 341, 351, 354
Pangboche: 336
Pangpema: 353
Pardi: 273, *279;* accommodations
280
Parka Wildlife Reserve: 29
Parvati: 66
pashmina: 93
Pashupati: 60
Pashupati Mandir (Bhaktapur):
229
Pashupatinath: *61,* 191-195, *192;*
getting there 191-192
passports: 117-119
Patan: 157, 158-159, 163, 213-
222, *214;* accommodations
222; backstreets 218-222;
Durbar Square 215-218; food
222; history 213-215; shopping
222
Patan Hospital: 130
Patan Tower (Kathmandu): 172
Pati Bhanjyang: 340
Paubha: 81
Peacock Window (Bhaktapur):
231
Peace Park (Kathmandu): 167
people: 46-57; castes 48-50;
customs 51-54; dress 52-54;
ethnic groups 50-51; family life
54-57;
Phakding: 334
Phaplu: 330

Pharak: 333
Pharak River: 329
Pharping: 247-248
pheasant: *24*
Phedi: 319, 325
Pheriche: 336
Phewa Tal (Pokhara): 273
Phoksumdo Lake: 348
Phortse: 336
photocopies: 132; *see also*
services
photography: 103-104; camera
shops 133; photo labs 133; and
trekking 139-140
Phulchowki: 243-244
Phulchowki Mai (Godavari): 243
Phunsok Art: 82
Pie Alley (Kathmandu): 170
Pike: 331
Pipal Bot (Kathmandu): 178
pipal trees: *19; see also* flora
Pisang: 324
Poiyan: 333
Pokhara **269-284,** 349; getting
there and around 282-284;
history 270-272; land 270; mini-
treks 277-278; neighborhoods
273; practicalities 278-282;
services 282; sights 273-274;
vicinity of 274-278
Pokhara Bazaar: 273-274
Pokhara Museum: 274
politics: *see* government
pollution: 27; *see also*
environment
population: 52, 160; *see also*
people
porters: *43, 314*
Potters' Square (Bhaktapur): 229
pottery: 97; *see also* crafts
Prithvi Path (Kathmandu): 175
puja: 62
Pujari Math (Bhaktapur): 231

R
Raato Machhendranath Mandir
(Patan): 221
Raato Machhendranath Rath
Jatra: 72; *see also* festivals
Raatopani: 320
radi: 92-93
radio: 135
rafting: 299, 304-306; companies
305-306
Raja-rajesvari Ghat
(Pashupatinath): 194˙
Ram Mandir (Janakpur): 308
Rama: 66

Rameshwar Shiva temple (Gorkha): 267
Rana: 34
Rangjung Yeshe Institute: 209
Rani Ban: 238
Ranighat: 286
Rani Pokhari (Kathmandu): 178
Rapti River: 293
Rara Lake: 347
Rara National Park: 345-347
Ratna Park (Kathmandu): 175
religion: 60-69; Buddhism 68-69; folk beliefs 63-64; Hinduism 65-67; Kumari 67; offerings 62; tantra 64-65; worship 61-63
resthouses: 88; see also architecture
restricted areas: 345
Reu River: 293
rhinoceroses: 23
rhododendrons: 20; see also flora
Ridi Bazaar: 286
Rikheswar Narayan Mandir (Tamghas): 286
Ringmo: 332, 348-349
Rinpoche: 343
Rishi Panchami: 73; see also festivals
rivers: 16-17; see also land
RNAC (Royal Nepal Airlines): 140, 149-151; office 178; see also airlines
Roberts, Col. J.M.: 272
Royal Bardia National Park: 29, 303-304
Royal Botanical Gardens (Godavari): 243
royal family: 41
royal palace (Kathmandu): 171-174
Royal Suklaphanta Wildlife Reserve: 29, 304
Rupa Tal: 275-276
Rupse Chaharo: 320

S
sacrifices: 63; see also religion
Sagarmatha National Park: 28, 328; headquarters 334; visitor's center 334
Salpa Bhanjyang: 354
sal trees: 19 84; see also flora
Sanfebagar airstrip: 347
Sankhu: 255
Saraswati: 66
Sarki caste: 50
sati: 36, 57
Sauruha: 297, 298-302, 301

School of International Languages: 60
School of South Asian Studies: 208-209
sculpture: 77-79, 87; see also art
seasons: 17-18; see also climate
services: 131-136; information 134-136; mail 131-132; medical 129-130; telecommunications 132
Sete: 332
Seti Gandaki River: 305
Seto Machhendranath Rath Jatra: 75; see also festivals
Shah Dynasty: 33
Shah, Prithvi Narayan: 33, 36
Shakyamuni: 343
Shantipur (Swayambhunath): 190
Shechen Tennyi Targye Ling: 197
Shermathang: 341
Sherpa Cultural Center: 335-336
Sherpas: 43, 51, 328-329
Shey Gompa: 349
Shey-Phoksudmo National Park: 29, 348
shikara: 85; see also temples
Shikar Narayan Mandir (Pharping): 247-248
Shipton La: 354
Shiva: 66
Shivaghat: 341
Shiva Mandir (Kathmandu): 179
Shivapuri: 240-241
Shiva Ratri: 75; see also festivals
shopping: antiques 97; Bhaktapur 233; books 135; carpets 94; gems 91; jewelry 91-92; Kathmandu 179; metalware 78, 90; painting 80, 82; Patan 222; Pokhara 282-282; sculpture 79; textiles 93-94
Shorung Yul Lha: see Numbur
Siddhartha Gautama (Buddha): 288; see also Buddhism
Siddhi Narsingh: 215
Siklis: 278
Sim Bhanjyang: 266
Simikot: 345
Sing Gompa (Gosainkund): 341
Singha Durbar (Kathmandu): 36, 175, 177
Singh, Ganesh Man: 39
Singla Bhanjyang: 351
Sinion La: 353
Sinja: 345, 347
Sirjana Art Gallery: 82
Sisuwa: 275-276

Sitala Mandir (Swayambhunath): 189-190
Snellgrove, David: 48, 348
Solu: 328-333, 331
Srinagar Danda (Tansen): 285
Student Travels and Tours: 143, 282
stupa: 86; see also temples
Sunauli: 287-288, 287; getting there 289; practicalities 288;
Sundari Danda: 276
Sundarijaal: 251; waterfall 340
Sundhara (Kathmandu): 177
Sun Kosi River: 305
Supermarket, The (Kathmandu): 178
Surjya Binayak: 232
Surke: 333, 334
Surya: 66
Swayambhunath: 187-190, 187; getting there 188
Swayambhu Purana: 30
Swiss Travels and Tours: 282
Syabru: 342
Syabrubesi: 343
Syangboche airstrip: 335
Syangje: 323

T
TAAN: see Trekking Agents Association of Nepal
Taatopani: 264, 320
Tachapal Tol (Bhaktapur): 231
Tadapani: 328
Tadi Bazaar: 302
tailors: 93; see also textiles
Tal: 324
Talamarang: 341
Taleju: 67
Taleju Mandir (Kathmandu): 174
Tallo Durbar (Gorkha): 267-268
Tal Machan: 298
Tamang people: 50
Tamghas: 286
Tansen: 284-287, 284, 351; Durbar 285; getting there 286-287; practicalities 286; sights 285-286
tantra: 64-65
Tapil: 269
Taplejung: 353
Tarakot: 351
Tarkeghyang: 340-341
Tashigaon: 354
Tashi Laptsa: 338
Tashi Ling: 276
Tashi Pakhel: 276
Taudaha: 247

Taumadhi Tol (Bhaktapur): 229-230
taxis: 149; *see also* transportation
Teej Panchami: 73; *see also* festivals
Teku (Kathmandu): 185-186
telegraph: 132
telephone: 132
television: 135
temples: 83-87; *see also* art
Tengboche Gompa (Everest): 335
Terai, the: 13-14, 19; ethnic groups of 50; wildlife 23
textiles: 92-94, 179; embroideries 94; pashmina 93; ready-made clothing 93
Thahiti (Kathmandu): 184-185
Thakali people: 51
Thak Khola: 320-321
Thakudwara: 304
Thakuri caste: 49
Thamel: 163; food 204
Thami: 338
thangka: 80-81
Thankot: 265
Tharu people: 50
theft: 106-108
Theravada Monastery (Lumbini): 291
Thimi: 232
Thinigaon: 321
Thorung La Pass: 322-323
Three Kingdoms: 32
Thupten Choling: 332
Tibet: 142-143, 144; Arniko Rajmarg 264-265; Gunsa 353; Khasa 265
Tibetan monasteries: 197
Tibetans: *95*
Tibetan settlements: 276
tigers, royal Bengal: *28*
Tiger Tops: 300
Tihar: 75; *see also* festivals
Tilang Ghar (Kathmandu): 180-181
Tilaurikot: 291
Til Madhava Narayan Mandir (Bhaktapur): 230
Tilman, H.W.: *236, 311, 332, 345, 354*
time: 133
Tindeval (Kathmandu): 186
tipping: 121; *see also* money
Tirkhedhunga: 319
Tistung Deorali: 266

tourism: 11, 45-46; Dept. of 134
tours: Bhutan 144; Kathmandu Valley 212; Tibet 144
trade: 43-44; *see also* economy
Tragsindhu La: 332
transportation: 140-154; Bhaktapur 234; Kathmandu 210-212; Kathmandu Valley 235
traveler's checks: *see* money
Treaty of Segouli: 34
trees: 19-20; *see also* flora
Trekker's Aid Posts: 130; Ongre 324; Pheriche 336
trekking: 309-354; accommodations 109-112; companies *315;* environmental impacts of *312-313;* equipment rental 139; health 126-129; helicopter rescue 130; introduction 309-316; maps 136; permits 118, 282; precautions 107-108; seasons 310-311; types of 311-316; what to take 137-140; *see also* treks; specific area
Trekking Agents Association of Nepal (TAAN): 317
treks: Annapurna region 217-328; central Nepal 349-351; eastern Nepal 351-354; Everest region 328-338; Gosainkunbd 341-342; Helambu 340-341; jungle 299; Kathmandu Valley 236; Khumbu 333-338; Langtang 342-343; Manang 323; north of Kathmandu 339-343; Phidim-Taplejung-Basantapur 353; Pokhara and vicinity 277-278; Pokhara to Muktinath 317-322; remote areas 344-354; Solu 330-333; trekking peaks *316;* Tumlingtar-Chainpur-Ilam 353; western Nepal 344-349
Tribeni: 347
Tribhuvan International Airport: 140, *141;* airport tax 143; *see also* airports/airstrips
Tribhuvan, King: 37
Tribhuvan Memorial Museum (Kathmandu): 167
Tribhuvan Rajpath: 265-266
Tribhuvan University (Kirtipur): 245; Library 209
TriChandra College (Kathmandu):

175
Tripureshwar Mahadeva (Kathmandu): 185-186
Trisuli: 269, 349; River 302
Tse, Wang Hsuan: 30
Tso Gompa: 349
Tucci, Giuseppe: *11, 70, 73, 319*
Tukche: 319, 321
Tumlingtar: 353, 354; airstrip 354
Tundikhel (Kathmandu): 167, 175-176

U
Ulleri: 319
unification: 33
Upallo Durbar (Gorkha): 268
Upper Arun River: 305
USIS Library: 209

V
Vajravarahi Mandir (Chapagaon): 251
Vajra Yogini (Pharping): 248
Vajra Yogini Mandir (Sankhu): 255
Varahi temple (Pokhara): 273
Vasupur (Swayambhunath): 189
Vilas Mandir (Kathmandu): 172
visas: 117-119
Vishnu: 66
Vishnumati River: 157, 163, 186
Vishwanath Mandir (Patan): 216
volunteer opportunities: 209-210

W
walking: 152-154; *see also* trekking
Walungchung Gola: 352
Wamitaksar: 351
western Nepal: 344-349, *346*
Western Regional Hospital (Pokhara): 130, 282; *see also* medical services
what to take: *see* packing
women travelers: 104
woodcarving: *84, 87* 172
Woodcarving Museum (Bhaktapur): 231

XYZ
yaks: 21-22; *23;* see also fauna
Yalung Glacier: 353
yeti, the: 25
Yetkha Bahal (Kathmandu): 182
Younghusband, Sir Francis: *310*

THE METRIC SYSTEM

1 inch = 2.54 centimeters (cm)
1 foot = .304 meters (m)
1 mile = 1.6093 kilometers (km)
1 km = .6214 miles
1 fathom = 1.8288 m
1 chain = 20.1168 m
1 furlong = 201.168 m
1 acre = .4047 hectares (ha)
1 sq km = 100 ha
1 sq mile = 2.59 sq km
1 ounce = 28.35 grams
1 pound = .4536 kilograms (kg)
1 short ton = .90718 metric ton
1 short ton = 2000 pounds
1 long ton = 1.016 metric tons
1 long ton = 2240 pounds
1 metric ton = 1000 kg
1 quart = .94635 liters
1 US gallon = 3.7854 liters
1 Imperial gallon = 4.5459 liters
1 nautical mile = 1.852 km

To compute centigrade temperatures, subtract 32 from Fahrenheit and divide by 1.8. To go the other way, multiply centigrade by 1.8 and add 32.

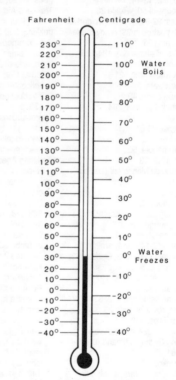

ABOUT THE AUTHOR

Kerry Moran received a Bachelor of Journalism degree from the University of Missouri-Columbia in 1981. Following a year in Paris and a stint as a newspaper editor in Northern California, she moved to China in 1984 with her husband Chris to teach English at Zhongshan University. From there she traveled overland through Tibet to Kathmandu, where she's lived since 1985, working as a freelance writer and trek leader. Her articles have appeared in *The Asian Wall Street Journal* and a number of inflight and travel magazines.

She speaks Nepali, Tibetan, and Chinese, and has traveled extensively in Nepal and Tibet, including 15 treks in Nepal and two journeys to Tibet's holy Mt. Kailas. With photographer Russell Johnson, she's the author of *Kailas: On Pilgrimage to the Sacred Mountain of Tibet,* published by Thames and Hudson Ltd. in the U.K. and Inner Traditions in the U.S. Her daughter Cassandra was born in Kathmandu in 1989, and has so far gone on three treks.

Moon Handbooks—The Ideal Traveling Companions

Open a Moon Handbook and you're opening your eyes and heart to the world. Thoughtful, sensitive, and provocative, Moon Handbooks encourage an intimate understanding of a region, from its culture and history to essential practicalities. Fun to read and packed with valuable information on accommodations, dining, recreation, plus indispensable travel tips, detailed maps, charts, illustrations, photos, glossaries, and indexes, Moon Handbooks are ideal traveling companions: informative, entertaining, and highly practical.

To locate the bookstore nearest you that carries Moon Travel Handbooks or to order directly from Moon Publications, call: (800) 345-5473, Monday-Friday, 9 a.m.-5 p.m. PST

The Pacific/Asia Series

BALI HANDBOOK by Bill Dalton
Detailed travel information on the most famous island in the world. 12 color pages, 29 b/w photos, 68 illustrations, 42 maps, 7 charts, glossary, booklist, index. 428 pages. **$12.95**

INDONESIA HANDBOOK by Bill Dalton
This one-volume encyclopedia explores island by island the many facets of this sprawling, kaleidoscopic island nation. 30 b/w photos, 143 illustrations, 250 maps, 17 charts, booklist, extensive Indonesian vocabulary, index. 1,000 pages. **$19.95**

SOUTH KOREA HANDBOOK by Robert Nilsen
Whether you're visiting on business or searching for adventure, *South Korea Handbook* is an invaluable companion. 8 color pages, 78 b/w photos, 93 illustrations, 109 maps, 10 charts, Korean glossary with useful notes on speaking and reading the language, booklist, index. 548 pages. **$14.95**

SOUTHEAST ASIA HANDBOOK by Carl Parkes
Helps the enlightened traveler discover the real Southeast Asia. 16 color pages, 75 b/w photos, 11 illustrations, 169 maps, 140 charts, vocabulary and suggested reading, index. 873 pages. **$16.95**

BANGKOK HANDBOOK by Michael Buckley
Your tour guide through this exotic and dynamic city reveals the affordable and accessible possibilities. Thai phrasebook, color and b/w photos, maps, illustrations, charts, booklist, index. 214 pages. **$10.95**

PHILIPPINES HANDBOOK by Peter Harper and Evelyn Peplow
Crammed with detailed information, *Philippines Handbook* equips the escapist, hedonist, or business traveler with thorough coverage of the Philippines's colorful history, landscapes, and culture. Color and b/w photos, illustrations, maps, charts, index. 587 pages. **$12.95**

HAWAII HANDBOOK by J.D. Bisignani
Winner of the 1989 Hawaii Visitors Bureau's Best Guide Book Award and the Grand Award for Excellence in Travel Journalism, this guide takes you beyond the glitz and high-priced hype and leads you to a genuine Hawaiian experience. 12 color pages, 86 b/w photos, 132 illustrations, 86 maps, 44 graphs and charts, Hawaiian and pidgin glossaries, appendix, booklist, index. 879 pages. **$15.95**

KAUAI HANDBOOK by J.D. Bisignani
Kauai Handbook is the perfect antidote to the workaday world. 8 color pages, 36 b/w photos, 48 illustrations, 19 maps, 10 tables and charts, Hawaiian and pidgin glossaries, booklist, index. 236 pages. **$9.95**

MAUI HANDBOOK: Including Molokai and Lanai by J.D. Bisignani
"No fool-'round" advice on accommodations, eateries, and recreation, plus a comprehensive introduction to island ways, geography, and history. 8 color pages, 60 b/w photos, 72 illustrations, 34 maps, 19 charts, booklist, glossary, index. 350 pages. **$11.95**

OAHU HANDBOOK by J.D. Bisignani
A handy guide to Honolulu, renowned surfing beaches, and Oahu's countless other diversions. Color and b/w photos, illustrations, 18 maps, charts, booklist, glossary, index. 354 pages. **$11.95**

BIG ISLAND OF HAWAII HANDBOOK by J.D. Bisignani
An entertaining yet informative text packed with insider tips on accommodations, dining, sports and outdoor activities, natural attractions, and must-see sights. Color and b/w photos, illustrations, 20 maps, charts, booklist, glossary, index. 347 pages. **$11.95**

SOUTH PACIFIC HANDBOOK by David Stanley
The original comprehensive guide to the 16 territories in the South Pacific. 20 color pages, 195 b/w photos, 121 illustrations, 35 charts, 138 maps, booklist, glossary, index. 740 pages. **$15.95**

MICRONESIA HANDBOOK:
Guide to the Caroline, Gilbert, Mariana, and Marshall Islands by David Stanley
Micronesia Handbook guides you on a real Pacific adventure all your own. 8 color pages, 77 b/w photos, 68 illustrations, 69 maps, 18 tables and charts, index. 287 pages. **$9.95**

FIJI ISLANDS HANDBOOK by David Stanley
The first and still the best source of information on travel around this 322-island archipelago. 8 color pages, 35 b/w photos, 78 illustrations, 26 maps, 3 charts, Fijian glossary, booklist, index. 198 pages. **$8.95**

TAHITI-POLYNESIA HANDBOOK by David Stanley
All five French-Polynesian archipelagoes are covered in this comprehensive guide by Oceania's best-known travel writer. 12 color pages, 45 b/w photos, 64 illustrations, 33 maps, 7 charts, booklist, glossary, index. 225 pages. **$9.95**

NEW ZEALAND HANDBOOK by Jane King
Introduces you to the people, places, history, and culture of this extraordinary land. 8 color pages, 99 b/w photos, 146 illustrations, 82 maps, booklist, index. 546 pages. **$14.95**

OUTBACK AUSTRALIA HANDBOOK by Marael Johnson
Australia is an endlessly fascinating, vast land, and *Outback Australia Handbook* explores the cities and towns, sheep stations and wilderness areas of the Northern Territory, Western, and South Australia. Full of travel tips and cultural information for adventuring, relaxing, or just getting away from it all. Color and b/w photos, illustrations, maps, charts, booklist, index. 355 pages. **$15.95**

BLUEPRINT FOR PARADISE: How to Live on a Tropic Island by Ross Norgrove
This one-of-a-kind guide has everything you need to know about moving to and living comfortably on a tropical island. 8 color pages, 40 b/w photos, 3 maps, 14 charts, appendices, index. 212 pages. **$14.95**

The Americas Series

NORTHERN CALIFORNIA HANDBOOK by Kim Weir
An outstanding companion for imaginative travel in the territory north of the Tehachapis. 12 color pages, b/w photos, 69 maps, illustrations, booklist, index. 759 pages. **$16.95**

NEVADA HANDBOOK by Deke Castleman
Nevada Handbook puts the Silver State into perspective and makes it manageable and affordable. 34 b/w photos, 43 illustrations, 37 maps, 17 charts, booklist, index. 400 pages. **$12.95**

NEW MEXICO HANDBOOK by Stephen Metzger
A close-up and complete look at every aspect of this wondrous state. 8 color pages, 85 b/w photos, 63 illustrations, 50 maps, 10 charts, booklist, index. 375 pages. **$13.95**

TEXAS HANDBOOK by Joe Cummings
Seasoned travel writer Joe Cummings brings an insider's perspective to his home state. 12 color pages, b/w photos, maps, illustrations, charts, booklist, index. 483 pages. **$11.95**

ARIZONA TRAVELER'S HANDBOOK by Bill Weir
This meticulously researched guide contains everything necessary to make Arizona accessible and enjoyable. 8 color pages, 194 b/w photos, 74 illustrations, 53 maps, 6 charts, booklist, index. 505 pages. **$13.95**

UTAH HANDBOOK by Bill Weir
Weir gives you all the carefully researched facts and background to make your visit a success. 8 color pages, 102 b/w photos, 61 illustrations, 30 maps, 9 charts, booklist, index. 452 pages.
$12.95

ALASKA-YUKON HANDBOOK by Deke Castleman and Don Pitcher
Get the inside story, with plenty of well-seasoned advice to help you cover more miles on less money. 8 color pages, 26 b/w photos, 95 illustrations, 92 maps, 10 charts, booklist, glossary, index. 384 pages. **$13.95**

WASHINGTON HANDBOOK by Dianne J. Boulerice Lyons and Archie Satterfield
Covers sights, shopping, services, transportation, and outdoor recreation, with complete listings for restaurants and accommodations. 8 color pages, 92 b/w photos, 24 illustrations, 81 maps, 8 charts, booklist, index. 400 pages. **$13.95**

OREGON HANDBOOK by Stuart Warren and Ted Long Ishikawa
Brimming with travel practicalities and insider views on Oregon's history, culture, arts, and activities. Color and b/w photos, illustrations, 28 maps, charts, booklist, index. 422 pages.
$12.95

IDAHO HANDBOOK by Bill Loftus
A year-round guide to everything in this outdoor wonderland, from whitewater adventures to rural hideaways. Color and b/w photos, illustrations, maps, charts, booklist, index. 275 pages.
$12.95

WYOMING HANDBOOK by Don Pitcher
All you need to know to open the doors to this wide and wild state. Color and b/w photos, illustrations, over 60 maps, charts, booklist, index. 427 pages. **$12.95**

MONTANA HANDBOOK by W.C. McRae and Judy Jewell
The wild West is yours with this extensive guide to the Treasure State, complete with travel practicalities, history, and lively essays on Montana life. Color and b/w photos, illustrations, maps, charts, booklist, index. 393 pages. **$13.95**

COLORADO HANDBOOK by Stephen Metzger
Essential details to the all-season possibilities in Colorado fill this guide. Practical travel tips combine with recreation—skiing, nightlife, and wilderness exploration—plus entertaining essays. Color and b/w photos, illustrations, maps, charts, booklist, index. 422 pages. **$15.95**

BRITISH COLUMBIA HANDBOOK by Jane King
With an emphasis on outdoor adventures, this guide covers mainland British Columbia, Vancouver Island, the Queen Charlotte Islands, and the Canadian Rockies. 8 color pages, 56 b/w photos, 45 illustrations, 66 maps, 4 charts, booklist, index. 381 pages. **$11.95**

CATALINA ISLAND HANDBOOK: A Guide to California's Channel Islands
by Chicki Mallan
A complete guide to these remarkable islands, from the windy solitude of the Channel Islands National Marine Sanctuary to bustling Avalon. 8 color pages, 105 b/w photos, 65 illustrations, 40 maps, 32 charts, booklist, index. 245 pages. **$10.95**

BAJA HANDBOOK by Joe Cummings
A comprehensive guide with all the travel information and background on the land, history, and culture of this untamed thousand-mile-long peninsula. Color and b/w photos, illustrations, maps, charts, booklist, index. 356 pages. **$13.95**

YUCATAN HANDBOOK by Chicki Mallan
All the information you'll need to guide you into every corner of this exotic land. 8 color pages, 154 b/w photos, 55 illustrations, 57 maps, 70 charts, appendix, booklist, Mayan and Spanish glossaries, index. 391 pages. **$12.95**

CANCUN HANDBOOK and Mexico's Caribbean Coast by Chicki Mallan
Covers the city's luxury scene as well as more modest attractions, plus many side trips to unspoiled beaches and Mayan ruins. Color and b/w photos, illustrations, over 30 maps, Spanish glossary, booklist, index. 257 pages. **$10.95**

BELIZE HANDBOOK by Chicki Mallan
Complete with detailed maps, practical information, and an overview of the area's flamboyant history, culture, and geographical features, *Belize Handbook* is the only comprehensive guide of its kind to this spectacular region. Color and b/w photos, illustrations, maps, booklist, index. 212 pages. **$11.95**

JAMAICA HANDBOOK by Karl Luntta
From the sun and surf of Montego Bay and Ocho Rios to the cool slopes of the Blue Mountains, author Karl Luntta offers island-seekers a perceptive, personal view of Jamaica. Color and b/w photos, illustrations, maps, charts, index. 213 pages. **$12.95**

The International Series

EGYPT HANDBOOK by Kathy Hansen
An invaluable resource for intelligent travel in Egypt. 8 color pages, 20 b/w photos, 150 illustrations, 80 detailed maps and plans to museums and archaeological sites, Arabic glossary, booklist, index. 510 pages. **$14.95**

PAKISTAN HANDBOOK by Isobel Shaw
For armchair travelers and trekkers alike, the most detailed and authoritative guide to Pakistan ever published. 28 color pages, 86 maps, appendices, Urdu glossary, booklist, index. 478 pages. **$15.95**

MOSCOW-LENINGRAD HANDBOOK by Masha Nordbye
Provides the visitor with an extensive introduction to the history, culture, and people of these two great cities, as well as practical information on where to stay, eat, and shop. 8 color pages, 36 b/w photos, 20 illustrations, 16 maps, 9 charts, booklist, index. 205 pages. **$12.95**

NEPAL HANDBOOK by Kerry Moran
Whether you're planning a week in Kathmandu or months out on the trail, *Nepal Handbook* will take you into the heart of this Himalayan jewel. Color and b/w pages, illustrations, 50 maps, 6 charts, glossary, index. 378 pages. **$12.95**

NEPALI AAMA by Broughton Coburn
A delightful photo-journey into the life of a Gurung tribeswoman of Central Nepal. Having lived with Aama (translated, "mother") for two years, first as an outsider and later as an adopted member of the family, Coburn presents an intimate glimpse into a culture alive with humor, folklore, religion, and ancient rituals. B/w photos. 165 pages. **$13.95**

Moonbelts

Made of heavy-duty Cordura nylon, the Moonbelt offers maximum protection for your money and important papers. This all-weather pouch slips under your shirt or waistband, rendering it virtually undetectable and inaccessible to pickpockets. One-inch-wide nylon webbing, heavy-duty zipper, one-inch quick release buckle. Accommodates traveler's checks, passport, cash, photos. Size 5 x 9 inches. Black. **$8.95**

New travel handbooks may be available that are not on this list.
To find out more about current or upcoming titles,
call us toll-free at (800) 345-5473.

IMPORTANT ORDERING INFORMATION

FOR FASTER SERVICE: Call to locate the bookstore nearest you that carries Moon Travel Handbooks or order directly from Moon Publications:

(800) 345-5473 · **Monday-Friday** · **9 a.m.-5 p.m. PST** · fax (916) 345-6751

PRICES: All prices are subject to change. We always ship the most current edition. We will let you know if there is a price increase on the book you ordered.

SHIPPING & HANDLING OPTIONS:
1) Domestic UPS or USPS first class (allow 10 working days for delivery):
   $3.50 for the first item, 50 cents for each additional item.

Exceptions:
· **Moonbelt** shipping is $1.50 for one, 50 cents for each additional belt.
· Add $2.00 for same-day handling.
2) UPS 2nd Day Air or Printed Airmail requires a special quote.
3) International Surface Bookrate (8-12 weeks delivery):
   $3.00 for the first item, $1.00 for each additional item. Note: Moon Publications cannot guarantee international surface bookrate shipping.

FOREIGN ORDERS: All orders which originate outside the U.S.A. must be paid for with either an International Money Order or a check in U.S. currency drawn on a major U.S. bank based in the U.S.A.

TELEPHONE ORDERS: We accept Visa or MasterCard payments. Minimum order is US $15.00. Call in your order: 1 (800) 345-5473. 9 a.m.-5 p.m. Pacific Standard Time.

ORDER FORM

Be sure to call (800) 345-5473 for current prices and editions or for the name of the
bookstore nearest you that carries Moon Travel Handbooks · 9 a.m.-5 p.m. PST
(See important ordering information on preceding page)

Name:_____Date:_____

Street:_____

City:_____Daytime Phone:_____

State or Country:_____Zip Code:_____

Quantity	Title	Price

Taxable Total	
Sales Tax (7.25%) for California Residents	
Shipping & Handling	
TOTAL	

Ship: ☐ 1st class   ☐ UPS (no P.O. Boxes)   ☐ International Surface

Ship to: ☐ address above ☐ other_____

_____

_____

Make checks payable to:
Moon Publications Inc., 722 Wall Street, Chico, California 95928 U.S.A.
We Accept Visa and MasterCard
To Order: Call in your Visa or MasterCard number, or send a written order with your Visa or
MasterCard number and expiration date clearly written.

Card Number: ☐ Visa   ☐ MasterCard

☐☐☐☐ ☐☐☐☐ ☐☐☐☐ ☐☐☐☐

Exact Name on Card: ☐ same as above   expiration date:_____

☐ other_____

signature_____

WHERE TO BUY THIS BOOK

Bookstores and Libraries:
Moon Publications Handbooks are sold worldwide. Please write our sales manager for a list of wholesalers and distributors in your area that stock our travel handbooks.

Travelers:
We would like to have Moon Publications Handbooks available throughout the world. Please ask your bookstore to write or call us for ordering information. If your bookstore will not order our guides for you, please write or call for a free catalog.

MOON PUBLICATIONS INC.
722 WALL STREET
CHICO, CA 95928 U.S.A.
tel: (800) 345-5473
fax: (916) 345-6751